M000265704

THE CLAIMS OF LITERATURE

The Claims of Literature

A Shoshana Felman Reader

EDITED BY EMILY SUN, EYAL PERETZ, & ULRICH BAER

Fordham University Press | New York | 2007

Copyright © 2007 Fordham University Press. All rights reserved.

No part of this publication may be reproduced, stored in a retrieval system, or transmitted in any form or by any means—electronic, mechanical, photocopy, recording, or any other—except for brief quotations in printed reviews, without the prior permission of the publisher.

Library of Congress Cataloging-in-Publication Data

Felman, Shoshana.
   The claims of literature : a Shoshana Felman reader / edited by Emily Sun, Eyal Peretz, and Ulrich Baer.—1st ed.
      p.   cm.
   Includes bibliographical references.
   ISBN-13: 978-0-8232-2712-9 (alk. paper)
   ISBN-13: 978-0-8232-2713-6 (alk. paper)
   1. Literature, Modern—History and criticism.   I. Sun, Emily.   II. Peretz, Eyal, 1968–
III. Baer, Ulrich.   IV. Title.
   PN710.F38   2007
   809—dc22

                                                                              2007018775

Printed in the United States of America
09 08 07   5 4 3 2 1
First edition

Contents

Editors' Acknowledgments

We wish to thank Irad Kimhi for valuable insights that inspired us in writing the introduction. The preparation of the manuscript was aided by the support of the Colgate University Research Council and the careful efforts of Jason Lusthaus and Kelly McGowan. Finally, we thank Shoshana Felman for sharing with us her personal photographs and for her assistance and encouragement at several stages of the project.

THE CLAIMS OF LITERATURE

EMILY SUN, EYAL PERETZ, AND ULRICH BAER

Introduction

It is a commonplace to think of literature as something that gives expression to the voiceless or to that which could not make itself heard before. But what does it mean to give voice to that which has not been heard yet? Does it mean, as many argue, to add those who have not been heard into the realm of those who have a voice? Is literature a means of expanding the canon — here meaning the equivalent, in the realm of art, of a representative majority — to include minoritized individuals and people? Is it merely a matter of adding a seat to parliament, of seeking representation, both political and symbolic, for those who were not represented, and who now have a chance, for the first time, to make claims for themselves? Or, rather, does literature give expression to the voiceless not in the sense of adding a voice or elevating the voiceless to meaningful expression, but instead in the sense of marking the voiceless as an interruption in the system of voices or, we may say, of representation? Paradoxically, literature gives voice to the voiceless *as* voiceless, and not by transforming it from voiceless to voice. This interruption does not mean that literature now expresses that which had been considered unrepresentable. It is not a matter of retrieving forgotten actual fragments of reality and adding them to our understanding of the world as if the point were to complete an ever-expanding puzzle. Literature alerts us to the essential incompleteness in any system of representation (language, the symbolic). Shoshana Felman traces this incompleteness through a series of figures: madness, woman, survivor, the body, the witness, the

1

child. For Felman, the critical activity of reading is not to identify these figures or find the madman, the feminine, or a representation of a survivor in a given text. Her objective is not to add another dimension or set of qualities to a given text that can then be attributed to child, woman, survivor. To read, after Felman, now means to activate in a text that (its childhood, its womanhood, its madness) which prevents it from closing in upon itself, for example, by providing us with a complete representation of something. Her critical activity is to show the infancy, or madness, or femininity of a text as witnessing an essential incompletion in any given system. In her reading of the trial of Eichmann in Jerusalem—for Felman's practice of reading extends to real events as well—she focuses on the collapse of the witness K-Zetnik while he is testifying on the stand as an allegory of the very activity of literature. K-Zetnik marks within the trial, and by extension within the law itself, a certain impossibility of the law to totalize itself, or to have everything within its jurisdiction, or to reach a verdict that accounts for everything that took place during the trial. Felman thus reads K-Zetnik's collapse as an allegory of the very activity of literature.

This view of literature as marking the place of incompleteness of a system is at the basis of Felman's main critical strategy, which we can call the strategy of the "and." Each of Felman's books and critical interventions always takes two discourses, one of which is literature and the other a discourse in which literature marks an incompleteness. As examples: psychoanalysis and literature (*Jacques Lacan and the Adventure of Insight*); writing and madness, history and literature, testimony, feminism, and literature (*What Does A Woman Want?*); law and literature (*The Juridical Unconscious*). How to read this "and" that is found in virtually all of Felman's books, and that has become one of her signature gestures. This "and" is no longer conjunctive but rather marks the tracing of an opening or an incompleteness within the discipline that is now paired with literature. Literature as witnessing marks the opening at the heart of history or at the heart of the law. Woman would now mark not another kind of substance or difference from man but the impossibility of man, as a discourse of mastery, from totalizing itself. The "and" is not additive and does not complete, continue, or distinguish. The "and" marks the blind spot within the other discourse. Literature has no other place and does not provide an alternative to the discourse to which Felman also pays attention. With the "and," Felman thus invents a new paradigm of interdisciplinarity that is not one of merging two fields or of demarcating the respective limits of knowledge in a given field.

The space of incompleteness marked by literature, or by the way madness interrupts reason, or woman interrupts man, or the figure of the child interrupts the authority of the parental figure in Felman's famous reading of Henry James's *Turn of the Screw,* can also be understood as marking a place of nonknowledge at the heart of knowledge. Felman teaches us to activate these interruptions, to make a place for nonknowledge. Nonknowledge is not something that we come to know but something out of which we create. It is not a lack of knowledge but the transformation from epistemological categories—of knowledge—into practical categories of creation and doing. It is the site where creation opens up—that is, where a reading, as exemplified by Felman, can take place. Reading is then no longer a hermeneutic activity, a deciphering of meanings, but an activation of a space of creation.

With her trademark "and," Felman inaugurates this new form of pedagogy, which can be called a poetic pedagogy. Like Socrates and Freud, she is a teacher of nonknowledge. Her practice might be usefully compared to the practice of painting, where the painter's gestures are not intended to copy existing reality. Rather, these gestures or, in Felman's case, her actual practice of reading passages closely, are the tracing of a creative place of blindness within vision, or the space of nonknowledge within knowledge. The painter paints out of the invisible, here not understood in the sense of that which is hidden or subject to a failure of perception, but rather as the space where creation takes place. Similarly, Felman's creation takes place at the moments where a text, even at the moments of impasse, generates new meaning, rather than just presenting what has already been understood.

Shoshana Felman's writings challenge and even upend the conventional genres of literary, cultural, and film criticism. Uniquely, Felman's work does not position itself as a critical metalanguage in relation to an *object* of inquiry, for instance, a literary text, historical event, legal document or case, or personal testimony. Like all critics of significance, her work creates and constitutes its objects of inquiry as works to be studied by us; her readings do not take things apart or search for hidden meanings but bring texts to life as if for the first time. In this vein, she can declare Claude Lanzmann's *Shoah* to be a masterpiece and a work of art, and she can read a story by Balzac in a way that makes this reading unavoidable in the future.

Shoshana Felman is one of the most important literary critics in the world today. Her intellectual beginnings can be traced to at least two or three countries and languages. She studied French and English literature at Hebrew University in Jerusalem and French literature and thought in Geneva, Switzerland, and Grenoble, France. Felman arrived at Yale University in 1970, a year before the appointment of Paul de Man, which marked the beginning of the so-called Yale School, including Barbara Johnson, Geoffrey Hartman, J. Hillis Miller, Harold Bloom, and Jacques Derrida. Felman brought psychoanalysis into this group and created a connection between the philosophical, literary, and psychoanalytic concerns that inform literary criticism today. Like all original members of this constellation, Felman remained fiercely independent in her work, questions, and concerns. Her stay at Yale can be characterized by three main periods. In the beginning, she concentrated on reading mainly literary works. She then turned to the question of history, and in particular to the question of the philosophical significance of the Holocaust and other twentieth-century traumas. History, for her, is not the empirical change of meanings brought about by force. Against those who assume that deconstruction is not interested in history, history was from the very beginning at the heart of Felman's project. Precisely because she cannot simply accept history as something given or as the record of changes through time, she investigated this dimension under different names: madness, woman, trauma, childhood. Her recent work addresses law and justice, both historical and poetic. She has analyzed major legal trials and other historical events where cultural narratives are formed. In 2003, Felman moved to a new site of influence: Emory University in Atlanta, Georgia. Many of her colleagues are former Yale students who have taken the insights of the Yale School and applied them to new fields of inquiry. Felman is working on new projects.

Felman's work is characterized and appreciated—and widely assigned in coursework—for its pedagogical force. All of her essays take off from a very concrete, precisely phrased, and even commonsensical question or concern: What is a child? What is a woman? Who can bear witness? Where does madness begin? She then develops this deceptively simply question in a succession of logical steps, each of which seems inevitable but which succession somehow unfailingly arrives at an astonishing insight for which the reader is utterly unprepared. Reflecting back on the essay from this insight, the original question does not look so simple any more. What has happened is that the reader has been implicated in the process of her reading. Her work, possibly like that of no other contemporary theorist, succeeds in interrupting her readers' complacencies and transforming the reader via this unique, inimitable address.

Her procedure is to show that within every discourse there is a dimension in excess of this discourse. What is a discourse? A discourse is here understood as an established form of speaking and writing that delineates a territory or a field of objects that can then be investigated according to the rules of this discourse. There is always a double move at work in any given discourse, for example, history, sociology, or art criticism. On the one hand, the discourse examines objects that are presumed as already given, and on the other hand, it constitutes a certain class of objects that it then proceeds to investigate. This act of constitution, or of naming the objects of inquiry, is the opening up of a particular perspective within which one can then approach these objects. In these kinds of discourses, language tends to be reified in relation to the objects it designates. Shoshana Felman calls the dimension in excess of every discourse "literature." Literature, in Felman's practice as a reader, is that which is not a discourse. For her, there is no *object* such as literature because literature is that which resists the confusion of language with the objects that come under its sway. In this confusion, language tends to be understood in terms of the objects it designates. In her readings of texts, whether literary or belonging to other disciplines or genres, she reveals the powers of language. She demonstrates *par excellence* Lacan's dictum "There is no metalanguage."

Felman has an exceptionally subtle ear for the workings of language. Her listening is not thematic or aesthetic, in the sense of identifying sound patterns or matching themes, but rather attuned to what might be called, in order to avoid an overly philosophical terminology, the pain, affect, suffering, or joy of discourse. In taking recourse here to the categories of the passions, we want to point to Felman's conceptual achievement of bringing together bodily events and linguistic categories. For her, literature is, in this sense, a listening to what she calls "the scandal of the speaking body."

This listening to the speaking body receives in her later work on trauma, which points in psychoanalysis to a dimension between the body and the psyche, the name of "testimony." In Felman's understanding, in distinction to the prevailing discourses on the body, the human body is always already a body of language. It is not a material entity, object, animate thing, or realm outside of language, but has to be thought of as the opening up of sensibility. Another way of putting this is to say that the body is the opening of the world as sensation, that the body is an event or has to be thought of even as a *verb* of opening to something as sensation. The body is the possibility to touch or to be touched.

> If the problem of the human act thus consists in the relation between language and body, it is because the act is conceived — by performative analysis as well as by psychoanalysis — as that which problematizes at one and the same time the separation and the opposition of the two. The act, an enigmatic and problematic production of the speaking body, destroys from its inception the metaphysical dichotomy between the domain of the 'mental' and the domain of the 'physical,' breaks down the opposition between body and spirit, between matter and language.[1]

Felman's work does not articulate this concept but operates out of an implicit understanding of the relation between body and meaning in this way. This kind of listening is the lesson she draws out of psychoanalysis, and it constitutes her singular contribution to and transformation of the psychoanalytic way of listening. To some extent, this listening also separates her work from the more exclusively linguistic investigations undertaken by her colleagues in the Yale School. The fact that she draws on psychoanalysis as a revolutionary discourse that understood this new conception of the body as a linguistic body and not simply a somatic site of brute suffering sets her apart from the deconstructive critics that have also made such important contributions. Clearly, Felman's work shares with these critics the impetus to liberate marginalized, repressed, minoritized, and otherwise excluded dimensions of language and existence.

In her early work, *La folie dans l'oeuvre romanesque de Stendhal* (1971) and *Writing and Madness* (1978), she investigates this excess under the rubric of "madness." Madness, in these investigations of Stendhal,

Nerval, Flaubert, Lacan, Foucault, Derrida, and James, is precisely not a stable category or label that is the opposite of meaning, coherence, sense, and so on, but rather the event that unravels the self-certainty of philosophical, clinical, and other discourses. It is that which discourses banish, often simply by labeling and defining it as an outside that stands in opposition to a coherent inside. By addressing texts that deal with madness as a thematic concern, clinical category, or conceptual problem, Felman in fact shows how even those definitions are in themselves already the results of the separating operations that created the categories of madness versus sanity, sense versus unreason, health versus illness. She shows that this separation of discourses (of medicine, of psychology) is ultimately untenable, and that reading itself is the breaking down of the distinction between outside and inside. The reader, Felman shows, is not a given site of interpretive identity presumed in advance of his or her encounter with the text, as this figure is often constructed in contemporary criticism (the way a woman reads, a gay man may read, or a nineteenth-century person might have read). Rather, the reader is the one who responds or is the witness to the text's failure to constitute itself as unified and closed meaning.

For instance, in her widely cited and by now classic interpretation of Henry James's novella "The Turn of the Screw," Felman redefines what it means to read literature psychoanalytically. She shifts the focus from the biographically informed, author-oriented interpretations starting with Edmund Wilson and continuing through the early 1980s. In these readings, texts had been understood as passive objects of study subjected to a psychological explanation from which the reader is exempted. Felman moves beyond this model of the literary text to a dynamic model of literary criticism in which the reader is shown to be an effect of the linguistic structures of the text. With the invention of this dynamic, critical method, Felman charts a way for literary critics to address the ways in which texts have real effects in the world and how our quest for meaning is transformed in the encounter with a text that holds such a promise. In the same gesture, she also taught future critics how to read Freud with the help of the literary text. Instead of treating literature as an aesthetic object or the privileged locus of knowledge (communicated through symbolic forms), she explains how literature gives voice to precisely that which prevents other discourses from turning into totalizing, self-consistent bodies of knowledge or ways of knowing the world. This means, in essence, that literature, for Shoshana Felman, has no proper identity.

Extending from this inquiry into the concept of madness and its relation to literature, Shoshana Felman turns her critical attention to the linguistic and philosophical concept of the performative as defined by J. L. Austin. In a daring and utterly unexpected juxtaposition of Moliére's *Don Juan* and Austin's work in analytic philosophy, Felman reads the excessive dimension she earlier associated with madness now in relation to the two categories of promise and seduction. As Judith Butler observes in relation to this work, Felman "charts what is erotic for us in speech, producing an erotic even between cognitive and corporeal claims, finding the space between them that partakes of both and that is finally irreducible to either."[2] The discovery of this conjunction of Austin and Don Juan, as Stanley Cavell writes, "affords the most illuminating frame . . . against which to articulate the widespread sense and claim that the act and concept of promising is not just one more among performative utterances . . . but that promising— even especially the promise to marry—is somehow privileged in Austin's view, naming the fact of speech itself."[3]

A third major contribution made by Felman is the investigation of this excessive dimension under the rubric of trauma, and the figure of the witness—earlier conceptualized as the reader—as the one addressed by trauma. This does not mean that every reader is traumatized. Rather, Felman suggests that the experience of reading exposes us to an event that cannot be "known," that is, objectified and thematized, precisely because this experience of reading engages a logic that is simply the dimension of time and history as the opening of speech itself, in excess of meaning, knowledge, and information. The reader is now understood as a witness to a dimension of temporality or history, opening in the very failure of the text, or the occurrence, to have a unified meaning that can be grasped within the framework of one or another discourse.

In her book *Testimony* and her seminal essay on Claude Lanzmann's film *Shoah,* which triggered an intense, international debate in several fields of study, Felman extended her rethinking of the relation between discourses by analyzing what "witnessing" means in history, law, and literature. In the movement between literary, historical, and documentary testimonial texts, Felman finds that the occurrence can be witnessed. Her analysis of Lanzmann's cinematic techniques reveals precisely this kind of shuttling and destabilization of a single point of view to arrive, finally, at the Shoah as an event that cannot be reduced to one (historical, psychological, political, legal) meaning. Lanzmann's *Shoah* constituted an enormous provocation to other works in this area because he refused to obey the implicit mandates to curtail his own perspective and align it with a certain kind of ideological framework. Felman and Lanzmann shifted an understanding of ethics from a moralistic notion of identification with one position or the other (victim or perpetrator) to an imperative that emerges precisely from the loss of position experienced in this cinematic or critical movement between positions and also experienced by the historical subjects of his catastrophe. Importantly, this ethical imperative is also experienced by those of us who try to listen to this event—a fact that she allegorizes in an essay on a classroom experience at Yale University included in *Testimony*. In *Testimony*, Felman shows that no single conception of the witness can be arrived at within a single discipline. Rather, it becomes imperative to investigate how witnessing exceeds the conceptual limits of particular disciplines.

Another major area of Felman's investigations is the question of sexual difference. Her book *What Does a Woman Want?* asks whether Freud's notorious question can be asked at all from the position of a woman. Her contention is to understand difference as nonsubordinate to identity, so instead of privileging the figure of woman as a site of moral superiority and entitlement due to women's status as victim in the world, Felman tries to think through both the categories of men and women without assigning to them an a priori status within politics, history, and language. As in her incisive introduction to the thought of Jacques Lacan, Felman embarks on an analysis of the signifier ("woman," "man," "sex," "gender") as opposed to an analysis of the signified. In her work on sexual difference and the Lacanian revision of Freudian psychoanalysis, Felman explains how the significance lies not just in consciousness but specifically in its disruption, and that there is a possibility of interpreting the lack of meaning in a given text or in one's life without necessarily transforming this lack into meaning.

In her most recent book, *The Juridical Unconscious,* Felman examines the cultural conviction that the law sutures the wounds of collective violence. However, in her analysis of several paradigmatic scenes from major trials of the twentieth century, especially the Nuremberg Trials, the trial of Adolf Eichmann, and, in the American context, the trial of

O. J. Simpson, she shows how the narrative of trauma in the courtroom in fact inflicts with a particular kind of blindness the legal process that is meant to assign meaning to, resolve, and ultimately put to rest this trauma. Again, in this work Felman dexterously juxtaposes literary texts, legal documents, historical events, and courtroom scenes to show how the encounter between those discourses (history, law, art) can adequately testify to the opening and, therefore, possibility of meaning that is conventionally labeled "trauma." It is to this traumatic wounding, this failure of the transmission of meaning, that Felman gives speaking power.

Felman is a major contributing force in all the major developments in literary and cultural studies over the past three decades. At the same time, her essays reveal how all of these critical concerns (deconstruction, psychoanalysis, trauma studies, legal studies, and gender studies) are linked to a central problematic, which concerns the dimension that has remained unspoken under various names: woman, madness, trauma, and literature.

Shoshana Felman's work can be situated in a constellation of thinkers including Jacques Derrida, Michel Foucault, Jacques Lacan, Paul de Man, and Julia Kristeva, all of whom have exposed the claims for absolute authority and self-knowledge of the Western philosophical tradition as illusory at best and, although often necessary and unavoidable, repressive. Unlike these other thinkers, however, Felman does not make this conceptual problem her point of departure. Instead, all of her work originates in a concrete encounter with a literary text and the experience of reading it. This allows her not to be predetermined by a philosophical agenda but to arrive at her insights from an engagement with concrete reality. In the seminal interpretation of a famous story by Balzac, for example, Felman focuses on a character whose gender seems indeterminate. This very concrete thematic enigma occasions an investigation of the categories of gender as defined by psychoanalysis and feminist theory. Felman shows that the enigma in Balzac's text is not in the nature of a riddle or hermeneutic puzzle that can be resolved to yield the true meaning of gender. Instead, she shows how the question of gender is, in effect, the enigmatic unsettling of existing categories of knowledge, among which one is gender. This reading precedes by twenty years and still goes beyond the insights of even the most influential gender theorists, such as Judith Butler, Eve Sedgwick, and D. A. Miller.

The order of chapters here follows the itinerary of her thought. We try, for the first time, to offer a panoramic view and to bring to light the rigorous unity and continuity of Felman's work, which features are not always immediately apparent. The responses were invited by leading scholars from various fields who have engaged with her work. The book also includes transcripts from two of Felman's courses: one from one of her last classes at Yale, and the other from her first class at Emory University. These transcripts testify to Felman's power as a teacher, a role no less essential than that of her role as author.

PART 1 | Writing and Madness

SHOSHANA FELMAN

1 | Writing and Madness
From "Henry James: Madness and the Risks of Practice (Turning the Screw of Interpretation)"

What does the act of turning a screw have to do with literature?[1] What does the act of turning a screw have to do with psychoanalysis? Are these two questions related? If so, might their relationship help to define the status of literature? It is these rather odd questions that the present study intends to articulate, so as to give them a further turn, to investigate and interrogate them on the basis of Henry James's famous short novel, *The Turn of the Screw*.

I. An Uncanny Reading Effect

I didn't describe to you the purpose of it . . . at all, I described to you . . . the effect of it—which is a very different thing.
— HENRY JAMES, *The Sacred Fount*

The mental features discoursed of as the analytical are, in themselves, but little susceptible of analysis: we appreciate them only in their effects. — EDGAR ALLEN POE, *The Murders in the Rue Morgue*

The plot of *The Turn of the Screw* is well known: a young woman answering a want ad in a newspaper goes to meet a "perfect gentleman," a "bachelor in the prime of life," who hires her to take charge of his niece Flora and his nephew Miles, two little orphans who live in a secluded country house belonging to him. The young woman is to become the children's governess, but under the strict condition set down by her employer—"the Master"—that she assume "supreme authority" for her two charges, that is, that she solve singlehandedly any problems concerning them, without at any time turning to him for help or even contacting him for any reason. This condition is no sooner accepted than it begins to weigh heavily upon the governess (who is also the narrator)—especially when a letter arrives informing her, without giving the reason, that little Miles has been expelled from school: this unexplained punishment makes the child's apparent innocence seem somehow mysterious, suspect, ambiguous. In addition, the governess discovers that the house is haunted: several times she finds herself confronted by strange apparitions, whom, with the help of information about the house's past history gleaned from the housekeeper, Mrs. Grose, she finally identifies as the ghosts of two servants, Peter Quint and Mess Jessel, now dead, but formerly employed by the Master in this very house, and whose shady intimacy had, it seems, "corrupted" the children. The governess becomes steadily more convinced that the ghosts have come back to pursue their nefarious intercourse with the children, to take possession of their souls and to corrupt them radically. Her task is thus to *save* the children from the ghosts, to engage in a ferocious moral struggle against "evil," a struggle whose strategy consists of an attempt to catch the children in the very act of communing with the spirits, and thereby to force them to admit that communion, to confess their knowledge of the ghosts and their infernal complicity with them. Total avowal, the governess believes, would exorcise the children. The results of this heroic metaphysical struggle are, however, ill-fated: Flora, the little girl, caught by the governess in presence of the phantom of Miss Jessel, denies seeing the vision and falls seriously ill following the vehement accusations directed at her by the governess, whom she thenceforth holds in abhorrence; Miles, the little boy, on the other hand, having seemingly "surrendered" by pronouncing—under the governess's pressure—the *name* of Peter Quint face to face with his ghost, at that very moment dies in the arms of the governess as she clasps him to her breast in moral triumph. It is with this pathetically ironical embrace of a corpse that the story ends.

If the strength of literature could be defined by the intensity of its impact on the reader, by the vital energy and power of its *effect*, *The Turn of the Screw* would doubtless qualify as one of the strongest—i.e., most *effective*—texts of all time, judging by the quantity and intensity of the echoes it has produced, of the critical literature to which it has given rise. Henry James was himself astounded by the extent of the effect produced on his readers by his text, the generative potency of which he could measure only a posteriori. Ten years after the first appearance of *The Turn of the Screw*, in his New York Preface (1908), he writes:

> Indeed if the artistic value of such an experiment be measured by the intellectual echoes it may again, long after, set in motion, the case would make in favour of this little firm fantasy—which I seem to see draw behind it today a train of associations. I ought doubtless to blush for thus confessing them so numerous that I can but pick among them for reference.[2]

Few literary texts indeed have provoked and "drawn behind them" so many "associations," so many interpretations, so many energetic passions and energetic controversies. The violence to which the text has given rise can be measured, for example, by the vehement, aggressive tone of the first reactions to the novel, published in the journals of the period: "The story itself is distinctly repulsive," affirms *The Outlook* (LX, October 29, 1898: 537; *Norton*, 172). And *The Independent* goes still further:

> *The Turn of the Screw* is the most hopelessly evil story that we have ever read in any literature, ancient or modern. How Mr. James could, or how any man or woman could, choose to make such a study of infernal human debauchery, for it is nothing else, is unaccountable. . . . The study, while it exhibits Mr. James's genius in a powerful light, affects the reader with a disgust that is not to be expressed. The feeling after perusal of the horrible story is that one has been assisting in an outrage upon the holiest and sweetest fountain of human innocence, and helping to debauch—at least by helplessly standing by—the pure and trusting nature of children. Human imagination can go no further into infamy, literary art could not be used with more refined subtlety of spiritual defilement. (*The Independent*, LI, January 5, 1899: 73; *Norton*, 175)

The publication of *The Turn of the Screw* thus meets with a scandalized hue and cry from its first readers. But, interestingly enough, as the passage just quoted clearly indicates, what is perceived as the most scandalous thing about this scandalous story is that *we are forced to participate in the scandal,* that the reader's innocence cannot remain intact: there is no such thing as an innocent reader of this text. In other words, the scandal is not simply *in* the text, it resides in *our relation to the text,* in the text's *effect on us,* its readers: what is outrageous in the text is not simply that *of which* the text is speaking, but that which makes it speak *to us.*

The outraged agitation does not, however, end with the reactions of James's contemporaries. Thirty years later, another storm of protest very similar to the first will arise over a second scandal: the publication of a so-called Freudian reading of *The Turn of the Screw.* In 1934, Edmund Wilson for the first time suggests explicitly that *The Turn of the Screw* is not, in fact, a ghost story but a madness story, a study of a case of neurosis: the ghosts, accordingly, do not really exist; they are but figments of the governess's sick imagination, mere hallucinations and projections symptomatic of the frustration of her repressed sexual desires. This psychoanalytical interpretation will hit the critical scene like a bomb. Making its author into an overnight celebrity by arousing as much interest as James's text itself, Wilson's article will provoke a veritable barrage of indignant refutations, all closely argued and based on "irrefutable" textual evidence. It is this psychoanalytical reading and the polemical framework it has engendered that will henceforth focalize and concretely organize all subsequent critical discussion, all passions and all arguments related to *The Turn of the Screw.* For against Wilson, affirming or denying the "objectivity" of the reality of the ghosts, the critical interpretations have fallen into two camps: the "psychoanalytical" camp, which sees the governess as a clinical neurotic deceived by her own fantasies and destructive of her charges; and the "metaphysical," religious, or moral camp, which sees the governess as a sane, noble savior engaged in a heroic moral struggle for the salvation of a world threatened by supernatural Evil. Thus, as John Silver astutely puts it, "If the ghosts of 'The Turn of the Screw' are not real, certainly the controversy over them is."[3]

Would it be possible to say, indeed, that the *reality of the debate* is in fact more significant for the impact of the text than the reality of the ghosts? Could the critical debate itself be considered a *ghost effect?* Even more than the debate's content, it is its *style* that seems to me instructive: when the pronouncements of the various sides of the controversy are examined closely, they are found to repeat unwittingly—with a spectacular regularity—all the main lexical motifs of the text. Witness the following random examples, taken from a series of polemical essays:

—The motif of a danger that must be averted:

> The *danger* in the psychoanalytic method of criticism lies in its apparent plausibility. (Nathan Bryllion Fagin)[4]

—The motif of a violent aggression inflicted upon an object by injurious, alien force:

> The Freudian reading of Henry James' "The Turn of the Screw" . . . *does violence* not only to the story but also to the Preface. (Robert Heilman)[5]

—The motif of attack and defense, of confrontation and struggle: in a rebuttal to the Freudian reading, Oliver Evans proposes that Wilson's theory be

> *attacked* point by point. (Oliver Evans)[6]

—The motif of final victory, of the enemy's defeat:

> Here is one place where I find Freud completely *defeated.* (Katherine Anne Porter)[7]

It could perhaps be objected that a vocabulary of aggression, conflict, and maybe even danger is natural in a conflictive critical debate, and that it is just a coincidence that this vocabulary seems to echo and repeat the combative spirit that animates the text. Such an objection could not, however, account for some other, more specific, more peculiar stylistic echoes of the text that reemerge in the very language of the critics, in the very style of the polemic: the motif, for instance, of neurosis and of madness, of hysterical delusion. Robert Heilman thus accuses Wilson of alleged "hysterical blindness" (FR, *MLN,* 434), which alone would be able to account for the latter's errors in interpretation. Wilson, argues Heilman, is misreading James's use, in his New York Preface, of the word "authority." In Heilman's view, James's statement that he has given the governess "authority" is referring but to her *narrative* authority, to the *formal* fact that the story is being told *from her point of view,* and not, as Wilson would have it, to "the relentless English 'authority' which enables her to put over on inferiors even purposes which are totally deluded." How is this misreading possible? "Once again," explains Heilman, "the word *authority* has brought about, in an unwary liberal, an emotional spasm which has resulted in a kind of hysterical blindness" (FR, *MLN,* 434). Wilson's reading is thus polemicized into a *hysterical* reading, itself viewed as a neurotic symptom. What is interesting—and seems to me instructive—about this is that it is the very critic who *excludes* the hypothesis of neurosis from the *story* who is rediscovering neurosis in Wilson's critical *interpretation* of the story, an interpretation that he rejects precisely on the grounds that *pathology as such cannot explain the text:*

> It is probably safe to say that the Freudian interpretation of the story, of which the best known exponent is Edmund Wilson, no longer enjoys wide critical acceptance. . . . We cannot account for the evil by treating the governess as pathological . . .[8]

But the hypothesis of madness, or "pathology," which is indeed brought up by the governess herself, is not nearly so easy to eliminate as one might think since, expelled from the text, it seems to fall back on the text's interpreter, and thus ironically becomes, through the very critical attempt at its elimination, ineradicable from the critical vocabulary, be it that of the "Freudians" or that of the "metaphysicians."

Another textual motif that crops up unexpectedly in the very language of the critical controversy is that of *salvation.* While insisting on the fact that *The Turn of the Screw* is in truth a drama of salvation, that is, a rescue operation to save the children from the evil ghosts, Robert Heilman writes:

> *The Turn of the Screw* may seem a somewhat slight work to call forth all the debate. But there is something to be said for the debate. For one thing, it may point out the danger of a facile, doctrinaire application of formulae where they have no business and hence compel either an ignoring of, or a gross distortion of, the materials. But more immediately: *The Turn of the Screw* is *worth saving.* (FR, *MLN,* 443)

The rescue operation, the drama of salvation described by the text thus *repeats itself* in the critical arena. But *from what* must the text be saved? From being reduced, explains Heilman, to "a commonplace clinical record." But again, let us notice the terms of the objection, which associates the psychoanalytical reading's abuses with the more general abuses of science as such:

> We run again into the familiar clash between scientific and imaginative truth. This is not to say that scientific truth may not collaborate with, subserve, and even throw light upon imaginative truth; but it is to say that the scientific prepossession may seriously impede the imaginative insight. (FR, *MLN*, 444)

Another critic, repeating and emphasizing the term "prepossession," agrees: "We must agree, I think, that Freudian critics of the tale are *strongly prepossessed.*"[9] But what precisely is a "prepossessed" critic if not one whose mind is in advance in the *possession* of some demon, one who, like James's children, is himself *possessed*? Possessed—should we say—by the ghost of Freud? It is clear, in any case, that the urgency of rescuing, of *saving the text,* in a critical account like Heilman's, strongly resembles the exorcistic operations of the governess *vis-à-vis* her "possessed" charges, and that the critical confrontation appears itself as a kind of struggle against some ghost-effect that has somehow been awakened by psychoanalysis. The scene of the critical debate is thus a *repetition* of the scene dramatized in the text. The critical interpretation, in other words, not only elucidates the text but also reproduces it dramatically, unwittingly *participates in it.* Through its very reading, the text, so to speak, acts itself out. As a reading effect, this inadvertent "acting out" is indeed uncanny: whichever way readers turn, they can but be turned by the text, they can but *perform* it by *repeating* it. Perhaps this is the famous trap James speaks of in his New York Preface:

> It is an excursion into chaos while remaining, like Blue-Beard and Cinderella, but an anecdote—though an anecdote amplified and highly emphasized and returning upon itself; as, for that matter, Cinderella and Blue-Beard return. I need scarcely add after this that it is a piece of ingenuity pure and simple, of cold artistic calculation, an *amusette* to catch those not easily caught (the "fun"

of the capture of the merely witless being ever but small), the jaded, the disillusioned, the fastidious. (*Norton,* 120)

We will return later on to this ingenious prefatory note so as to try to understand the distinction James is making between naïve and sophisticated readers, and to analyze the way in which the text's return upon itself is capable of trapping *both*. Up to this point, my intention has been merely to suggest—to make explicit—this uncanny trapping power of Henry James's text as an inescapable *reading-effect*.

Taking such reading-effects into consideration, we shall here undertake a reading of the text that will at the same time be articulated with a reading of its readings. This two-level reading—which also must return upon itself—will be concerned with the following questions: What is the nature of a reading-effect as such? and by extension: what is a reading? What does the text have to say about its own reading? What is a "Freudian reading" (and what is it *not*)? What in a text *invites*—and what in a text *resists*—a psychoanalytical interpretation? In what way does literature *authorize* psychoanalysis to elaborate a discourse about literature, and in what way, having granted its authorization, does literature *disqualify* that discourse? A combined reading of *The Turn of the Screw* and of its psychoanalytical interpretation will here concentrate, in other words, not only on what psychoanalytical theory has to say about the literary text, but also on what literature has to say about psychoanalysis. In the course of this double reading, we will see how both the possibilities and the limits of the encounter between literature and psychoanalytical discourse might begin to be articulated, how the conditions of their meeting, and the modalities of their not meeting, might begin to be thought out.

II. What is a Freudian Reading?

The Freudians err in the right direction. — MARK SPILKA

I would like, as a starting point, to begin by subscribing to the following remarks by Mark Spilka:

My concern . . . is with the imaginative poverty of much Freudian criticism, its crudeness and rigidity in applying valid psychological insights, its narrow conception of its own best possibilities. . . .

> Over the past four decades Freudian critics have made James's tale
> a *cause célèbre*. The tale sustains the *"cause"* through erotic ambigu-
> ities. Since it also arouses childhood terrors, and perhaps arises
> from them, we may say that the Freudian approach works here or
> nowhere. Yet opponents charge that Freudian critics have reduced
> the tale to a "commonplace clinical record." Though they are per-
> fectly correct, my own charge seems more pertinent: these Freud-
> ian critics have not been sufficiently Freudian. (*Norton*, 245)

These subtle, challenging remarks err only in the sense that they consider as resolved, nonproblematic, the very questions that they open
up: how Freudian is a Freudian reading? Up to what point can one be
Freudian? As what point does a reading start to be "Freudian enough"?
What is Freudian in a Freudian reading, and in what way can it be
defined and measured?

The one characteristic by which a "Freudian reading" is generally
recognized is its insistence on the crucial place and role of sexuality in
the text. The focal theoretical problem raised by a psychoanalytical
reading would thus appear to be the definition of the very status of
sexuality as such *in a text*. Wilson's reading of *The Turn of the Screw* indeed follows the interpretative pattern of accounting for the whole
story in terms of the governess's sexual frustration: she is in love—says
Wilson—with the Master, but is unable to admit it to herself, and thus
obsessively, hysterically projects her own desires upon the outside
world, perceives them as exterior to herself in the hallucinated form
of fantasmatic ghosts.

> The theory is, then, that the governess who is made to tell the
> story is a neurotic case of sex repression, and that the ghosts are
> not real ghosts but hallucinations of the governess.[10]

In order to reinforce this theory, Wilson underlines the implicitly
erotic nature of the metaphors and points out the numerous phallic
symbols:

> Observe, also, from the Freudian point of view, the significance of
> the governess's interest in the little girl's pieces of wood and of
> the fact that the male apparition first takes shape on a tower and
> the female apparition on a lake. (*Wilson*, 104)

What, however, was it in James's text that originally called out for a "Freudian" reading? It was, as the very title of Wilson's article suggests, not so much the sexuality as "the *ambiguity* of Henry James." The text, says Wilson, is ambiguous. It is ambiguous, that it, its meaning, far from being clear, is itself a *question*. It is this question that, in Wilson's view, calls forth an analytical response. The text is perceived as questioning in three different ways:

(1) *Through its rhetoric:* through the proliferation of erotic metaphors and symbols *without* the direct, "proper" naming of their sexual nature.[11]

(2) *Through its thematic content*—its *abnormal* happenings and its fantastic, strange manifestations.[12]

(3) *Through its narrative structure,* which resembles that of an enigma in remaining, by definition, elliptically incomplete.[13]

Solicited by these three modes of textual questioning—narrative, thematic, and rhetorical—the "Freudian" critic, in Wilson's view, is called upon to *answer.* In the case of the narrative question of the elliptical, incomplete structure of the enigma, he answers with the riddle's missing word, with the mystery's solution: the governess's sexual desire for the Master. In the case of the thematic question of uncanny strangeness, of fantastic happenings, he answers with a *diagnosis:* the ghosts are merely the symptoms of pathological, abnormal sexual frustration and repression. In the case of the rhetorical question of symbolic ambiguity, he answers with the "proper name," with the *literal* meaning of the phallic metaphors.

Considered from the "Freudian point of view," sexuality, valorized as both the foundation and the guidepost of the critical interpretation, thus takes on the status of an *answer* to the *question* of the text. Logically and ontologically, the answer (of sexuality) in fact pre-exists the question (of textuality). The question comes to be articulated (rhetorically, thematically, and narratively) only by virtue of the fact that the answer is as such *concealed.* Indeed the question is itself but an answer in disguise: the question is the answer's hiding place. The Freudian critic's job, in this perspective, is but to pull the answer out of its hiding place—not so much to give an answer *to* the text as to answer *for* the text: to be *answerable for* it, to answer *in its place,* to replace the question with an answer. It would not be inaccurate, indeed, to say that the traditional analytical response to literature is to provide the literary question with something like a reliably professional "answering service."

Such an operation, however, invites two fundamental questions: Does "James" (or James's text) authorize this way of answering *for* him? Does "Freud" (or Freud's text) authorize this way of answering *through* him?

The question of the possibility of answering for the text, as well as that of the status of such an answer, is in fact raised by James's text itself in its very opening, when Douglas, having promised to tell his dreadful story, intimates that it is a *love story*, which was confided to him by the heroine (the governess):

> Mrs. Griffin, however, expressed the need for a little more light. "Who was it she was in love with?"
>
> "The story will tell," I took upon myself to reply. . . .
>
> "The story *won't* tell," said Douglas; "not in any literal, vulgar way." (Prologue, *Norton*, 3; James's italics)

In taking upon himself "to reply," to make *explicit* who it was the governess was in love with, in locating the riddle's answer in the governess's repressed desire for the Master, what then is Edmund Wilson doing? What is the "Freudian" reading doing here if not what the text itself, at its very outset, is precisely indicating as that which it *won't* do: "The story *won't* tell; not in any literal, vulgar way." These textual lines could be read as an ironic note through which James's text seems itself to be commenting upon Wilson's reading. And this Jamesian commentary seems to be suggesting that such a reading might indeed be inaccurate not so much because it is incorrect or false, but because it is, in James's terms, *vulgar.*

If so, what would that "vulgarity" consist of? And how should we go about defining not only an interpretation's accuracy, but what can be called its *tact?* Is a "Freudian reading"—by definition—tainted with vulgarity? *Can* a Freudian reading, as such, avoid that taint? What, exactly, makes for the "vulgarity" in Wilson's reading? Toward whom, or toward what, could it be said that this analysis lacks tact?

"The difficulty itself is the refuge from the vulgarity," writes James to H. G. Wells (*Norton*, 111). And in the New York Preface to *The Turn of the Screw*, he elaborates further the nature of that difficulty, of that tension which underlies his writing as a question:

Portentous evil—how was I to *save that,* as an intention on the part of my demon spirits, from the drop, the *comparative vulgarity,* inevitably attending, throughout the whole range of possible brief illustration, the offered example, the imputed vice, the cited act, the limited deplorable presentable instance? (*Norton,* 122)

What is vulgar, then, is the "*imputed* vice," the "offered example," that is, the explicit, the specific, the unequivocal and immediately referential "illustration." *The vulgar is the literal,* insofar as it is unambiguous: "the story won't tell; not in any *literal,* constitutive of meaning, because it blocks and interrupts the endless process of metaphorical substitution. The vulgar, therefore, is anything that misses, or falls short of, the dimension of the symbolic, anything that rules out, or excludes, meaning as a loss and as a flight—anything that strives, in other words, to eliminate from language its inherent silence, anything that misses the specific way in which a text *actively* 'won't tell.'" The vulgarity that James then seeks above all to avoid is that of a language whose discourse is outspoken and forthright and whose reserves of silence have been cut, that of a text inherently *incapable* of silence, inherently unable to hold its tongue.

If vulgarity thereby consists of the *reduction of rhetoric* as such, of the elimination of the indecision that inhabits meaning and of the *ambiguity* of the text, isn't that precisely Wilson's goal? Isn't Wilson's critical and analytical procedure that, precisely, of a *literalization* (i.e., in James's terms, of a "vulgarization") of sexuality in the text? Wilson, in fact, is quite aware of the text's rhetorical undecidable question:

The fundamental question presents itself and never seems to get properly answered: What is the reader to think of the protagonist? (*Wilson,* 122)

But he only points out that question in order to *reduce* it, *overcome* the difficulty of the ambiguity, *eliminate* the text's rhetorical indecision by supplying a prompt *answer* whose categorical *literality* cannot avoid seeming rudimentary, reductive, "vulgar." What are we to think of the protagonist?

We find that it is a variation on one of his [James's] familiar themes: the thwarted Anglo-Saxon spinster; and we remember unmistakable cases of women in James's fiction who deceive themselves and others about the origins of their aims and their emotions. . . .

James's world is full of these women. They are not always emotionally perverted. Sometimes they are apathetic. . . . Or they are
longing, these women, for affection but too inhibited or passive
to obtain it for themselves. (*Wilson*, 110–11)

Is this type of literalization of textual sexuality what a "Freudian
point of view" is really all about? Invalidated and disqualified by
James, would this "vulgarizing" literalization in truth be validated,
authorized, by Freud? If for James the *literal* is *vulgar,* can it be said that
from a Freudian point of view the *sexual* as such is *literal?* In order to
investigate this question, I would like to quote, at some length, Freud
himself, in a little-known text that appeared in 1910 under the title
"'Wild' Psychoanalysis":

A few days ago a middle-aged lady . . . called upon me for a consul-
tation, complaining of anxiety-states. . . . The precipitating cause
of the outbreak of her anxiety-states had been a divorce from her
last husband; but the anxiety had become considerably intensi-
fied, according to her account, since she had consulted a young
physician in the suburb she lived in, for he had informed her that
the *cause* of her anxiety was her *lack of sexual satisfaction.* He said
that she could not tolerate the loss of intercourse with her husband, and so there were only three ways by which she could recover her health — she must either return to her husband, or take
a lover, or obtain satisfaction from herself. Since then she had
been convinced that she was incurable. . . .

She had come to me, however, because the doctor had said that
this was a new discovery for which I was responsible, and that she had
only come to ask me to confirm what he said, and *I should tell her
that this and nothing else was the truth.* . . . I will not dwell on the
awkward predicament in which I was placed by this visit, but instead
will consider the conduct of the practitioner who sent the lady to
me . . . connecting my remarks about "wild" psycho-analysis with
this incident.[14]

It is tempting to point out the analogy between the rather comical
situation Freud describes and the so-called Freudian treatment of the
governess by Wilson. In both cases, the reference to Freud's theory is
brutally and crudely literal, reducing the psychoanalytical explanation
to the simple "lack of sexual satisfaction." Here, therefore, is Freud's

own commentary on such procedures. Curiously enough, Freud, like James, begins with a reminder that the validity of an interpretation is a function not only of its truth, but also of its *tact:*

> Everyone will at once bring up the criticism that if a physician thinks it necessary to discuss the question of sexuality . . . he must do so with tact. (*Standard,* 222)

But tact is not just a practical, pragmatic question of "couchside manner"; it also has a theoretical importance: the reserve within the interpretative discourse has to allow for and to indicate a possibility of error, a position of uncertainty with respect to truth.

> Besides all this, one may sometimes make a wrong surmise, and *one is never in a position to discover the whole truth.* Psycho-analysis provides these definite technical rules to replace the indefinable "medical tact" which is looked upon as a special gift. (*Standard,* 226)

The analysis of the "wild psychoanalyst" thus lacks the necessary tact, but that is not all.

> Moreover, the physician in question was ignorant of a number of *scientific theories* [Freud's italics] of psycho-analysis or had misapprehended them, and thus showed how little he had penetrated into an understanding of its nature and purposes. . . .
> The doctor's advice to the lady shows clearly in what sense he understands *the expression "sexual life"—in the popular sense,* namely, in which by sexual needs nothing is meant but the need for coitus. . . . *In psychoanalysis the concept of what is sexual comprises far more; it goes lower and also higher than its popular sense.* . . .
> Mental absence of satisfaction with all its consequences can exist where there is no lack of normal sexual intercourse. . . .
> By emphasizing exclusively the somatic factor in sensuality he undoubtedly simplifies the problem greatly. (*Standard,* 222–23)

Sexuality, says Freud, is not to be taken in its literal, popular sense: in its analytical *extension,* it goes "lower and also higher" than its literal meaning, it extends both beyond and below. The relation between the analytical notion of sexuality and the sexual act is thus not a relation of simple, literal adequation, but rather a relation, so to speak, of *inadequation:* the psychoanalytical notion of sexuality, says Freud, comprises both *more* and *less* than the literal sexual act. But how are we to understand an *extension* of meaning that includes not only *more,* but also *less* than the literal meaning? This apparent paradox, indeed, points to the specific complication that, in Freud's view, is inherent in human sexuality as such. The question here is less that of the meaning *of* sexuality than that of a complex *relationship between sexuality and meaning;* a relationship that is not a simple *deviation* from literal meaning, but rather a *problematization of literality as such.*

The oversimplifying literalization professed by the "wild psychoanalyst" thus essentially misconstrues and misses the complexity of the relationship between sex and sense. It entails, however, another fundamental error, which Freud goes on to criticize:

A second and equally *gross misunderstanding* is discernible behind the physician's advice.

It is true that psycho-analysis puts forward *absence of sexual satisfaction* as the cause of nervous disorders. *But does it not say more than this?* Is its teaching to be ignored as too complicated when it declares that *nervous symptoms arise from a conflict between two forces* — on the one hand, the libido (which has as a rule become excessive), and on the other, a rejection of sexuality, or a repression (which is over-severe)? No one who remembers this *second* factor, which is *by no means secondary in its importance,* can ever believe that sexual satisfaction in itself constitutes a remedy of general reliability for the sufferings of neurotics. *A good number of these people are, indeed . . . in general incapable of satisfaction.* (*Standard,* 223)

Nervous symptoms, Freud insists, spring not simply from a "lack of sexual satisfaction" but from a *conflict between two forces.* Repression is constitutive of sexuality: the *second* factor is by no means *secondary* in importance. But the second factor as such is precisely the *contradiction* of the first. Which means not only that the literal meaning — the first factor — is not simply first and foremost, but also, that its *priority,* the very *primacy* in which its literality is founded, its very *essence of literality,* is itself *subverted* and *negated* by the second, but not secondary, meaning. Indeed, sexuality being constituted by these *two* factors, *its meaning is its own contradiction:* the *meaning* of the sexual as such is *its own obstruction,* its own deletion.

The "lack of satisfaction," in other words, is not simply an *accident* in sexual life, it is essentially inherent in it: "All human structures," says Lacan, after Freud, "have as their essence, not as an accident, the restraint of pleasure—of fulfillment."[15]

Here, then, is another crucial point that Wilson misses, *opposing* as he does sexuality to the "lack of satisfaction," considering the frustration of the governess (defined as the "thwarted Anglo-Saxon spinster") as an abnormal *accident* to be treated as pathogenic. What would "the abnormal" be, however, in Wilson's view, if not precisely that which is *not literal,* that which *deviates* from the *literal?* Literal (normal) sex being viewed as a simple, positive *act* or *fact,* it is simply inconceivable that it would constitutively miss its own aims, include its own negation as its own inherent property. For Wilson, sex is "simple," i.e., adequate to itself.[16] Wilson can thus write of *The Sacred Fount,* another enigmatic Jamesian story—"What if the hidden theme of *The Sacred Fount* is *simply sex* again?" (*Wilson,* 115). But for Freud, as we have seen, not only is the status of sexuality not *simple:* composed as it is by two dynamically contradictory factors, sexuality is precisely *what rules out simplicity as such.*

It is indeed because sexuality is essentially the violence of its own nonsimplicity, of its own inherent "conflict between two forces," the violence of its own division and self-contradiction, that it is experienced as anxiety and lived as terror. The terrifying aspect of *The Turn of the Screw* is in fact linked by the text itself, subtly but suggestively, precisely to its *nonsimplicity.* After promising to tell his story, Douglas adds:

> "It's quite too horrible." . . ."It's beyond everything. Nothing at all that I know touches it."
> "For sheer terror?" I remember asking. He seemed to say *it was not so simple as that:* to be really at a loss how to qualify it. (Prologue, 1)

If, far from implying the simplicity of a self-present literal meaning, sexuality points rather to a multiplicity of conflicting forces, to the complexity of its own divisiveness and contradiction, its meaning can by no means be univocal or unified, but must necessarily be *ambiguous.*

It is thus not rhetoric that disguises and hides sex; sexuality *is* rhetoric, since it essentially consists of ambiguity: it is the coexistence of dynamically antagonistic meanings. Sexuality is the *division and divisiveness of meaning;* it is meaning *as* division, meaning *as* conflict.

And, indeed, what is the *subject* of *The Turn of the Screw* if not this very conflict that inhabits meaning, the inherent conflict that structures the relationship between *sex* and *sense?* "The governess," John Lydenberg pertinently writes, "may indistinctly consider the ghosts as the essence of evil, and, as Heilman points out, she certainly chooses words which identify them with Satan and herself with the Saviour. But our vantage point is different from the governess's: we see her as one of the combatants, and as the story progresses we become even more uncertain who is fighting whom."[17]

In thus dramatizing, through a clash of meanings, the very functioning of meaning as division and as conflict, sexuality is not, however, the "text's meaning": it is rather that through which meaning in the text *does not come off,* that which in the text, and through which the text, *fails to mean,* that which can engender but a *conflict of interpretations,* a critical debate and discord precisely like the polemic that surrounds *The Turn of the Screw* and with which we are concerned here. "If analytical discourse," writes Lacan, "indicates that meaning is as such sexual, this can only be a manner of accounting for its *limits.* Nowhere is there a last word. . . . Meaning indicates only the direction, points only at the sense toward which it fails."[18]

| | | |

IX. The Madness of Interpretation: Literature and Psychoanalysis

"Do you know what I think?"

"It's exactly what I'm pressing you to make intelligible."

"Well," said Mrs. Briss, "I think you are crazy."

It naturally struck me. "Crazy?"

"Crazy."

I turned it over. "But do you call that intelligible?"

She did it justice. "No; I don't suppose it can be so for you if you are insane."

I risked the long laugh which might have seemed that of madness. " 'If I am' is lovely." And whether or not is was the special sound, in my ear,

of my hilarity, I remember just wondering if perhaps I mightn't be.
— HENRY JAMES, *The Sacred Fount*

The indication that *The Turn of the Screw* is constructed as a *trap* designed to close upon the reader is in fact, as we saw earlier, explicitly stated by James himself:

> It is an excursion into chaos while remaining, like Blue-Beard and Cinderella, but an anecdote — though an anecdote amplified and highly emphasized and *returning upon itself;* as, for that matter, Cinderella and Blue-Beard return. I need scarcely add after this that it is a piece of ingenuity pure and simple, of cold artistic calculation, an *amusette** to *catch those not easily caught* (the "fun" of the *capture* of the merely witless being ever but small), the jaded, the disillusioned, the fastidious. (The New York Preface, *Norton*, 120; *James's italics; other italics mine)

What is interesting about this trap is that, while it points to the possibility of two alternative types of reading, it sets out, in capturing *both* types of readers, to eliminate the very demarcation it proposes.[19] The alternative type of reading that the trap at once elicits and suspends can be described as the *naïve* ("the capture of the merely witless") and the *sophisticated* ("to catch those not easily caught . . . the jaded, the disillusioned, the fastidious"). The trap, however, is specifically laid not for naïveté but for *intelligence* itself. But in what, indeed, does intelligence consist, if not in the determination to *avoid the trap?* "Those not easily caught" are precisely those who are *suspicious,* those who sniff out and detect a trap, those who refuse to be *duped:* "the disillusioned, the jaded, the fastidious." In this sense the "naïve reading" would be one that would *lend credence* to the testimony and account of the governess, whereas the "disillusioned" reading would on the contrary be one that would suspect, demystify, "see through" the governess, one that, in fact, would function very much like the reading carried out by Wilson, who in effect opens his discussion by *warning* us precisely against a *trap* set by the text, a "trick of James's":

> A discussion of Henry James's ambiguity may appropriately begin with *The Turn of the Screw.* This story . . . perhaps *conceals another horror behind the ostensible one. . . .* It is a not infrequent *trick of*

James's to introduce sinister characters with descriptions that at first sound flattering, so *this need not throw us off.* (*Wilson,* 102)

Since the trap set by James's text is meant precisely for "those not easily caught" — those who, in other words, watch out for, and seek to avoid, all traps — it can be said that *The Turn of the Screw,* which is designed to snare *all* readers, is a text particularly apt to catch the *psychoanalytic* reader, since the psychoanalytic reader is, *par excellence,* the reader who *would not be caught,* who would not be made a *dupe.* Would it be possible then to maintain that *literature,* in *The Turn of the Screw,* constitutes *a trap for psychoanalytical interpretation?*

Let us return, one last time, to Wilson's reading, which will be considered here not as a model "Freudian reading," but as the illustration of a prevalent tendency as well as an inherent temptation of psychoanalytical interpretation as it undertakes to provide an "explanation," or an "explication" of literary text. In this regard, Wilson's later semi-retraction of his thesis is itself instructive: convinced by his detractors that for James the ghosts were real, and that James's *conscious* project or intention was to write a simple ghost story and not a madness story, Wilson does not, however, give up his theory that the ghosts consist of the neurotic hallucinations of the governess, but concedes in a note:

One is led to conclude that, in *The Turn of the Screw,* not merely is the governess self-deceived, but that James is self-deceived about her. (*Wilson,* note added in 1948, 143)

This sentence can be seen as the epitome, and as the verbal formulation, of the desire underlying psychoanalytical interpretation: the desire to be a *non-dupe,* to interpret, i.e., at once uncover and avoid, the very traps of the unconscious. James's text, however, is made of traps and dupery: in the first place, from an analytical perspective, the governess is *self-deceived;* duping us, she is equally herself a *dupe* of her own unconscious; in the second place, in Wilson's view, James himself is self-deceived: the reader, in the third place, is in turn duped, deceived, by the very rhetoric of the text, by the author's "trick," by the ruse of his narrative technique that consists in presenting "cases of self-deception" "from their own point of view" (*Wilson,* 142). Following Wilson's suggestions, there seems to be only one exception to this circle of universal dupery and deception: the so-called Freudian literary critic himself. By avoiding the double trap set at once by the unconscious and by rhetoric, by remaining himself *exterior* to the reading-errors that delude and blind both characters and author, the critic thus becomes the sole agent and the exclusive mouthpiece of the *truth* of literature.

This way of thinking and this state of mind, however, strikingly resemble those of the governess herself, who is equally preoccupied by the desire, above all, not to be made a dupe, by the determination to avoid, detect, demystify, the cleverest of traps set for her credulity. Just as Wilson is distrustful of James's narrative technique, suspecting that its rhetoric involves a "trick," i.e., a strategy, a ruse, a wily game, the governess in turn is suspicious of the children's rhetoric: "'It's a game,' I went on, 'it's a policy and a fraud'" (chap. 12, p. 48). And just as Wilson, struck by the *ambiguity* of the text, concludes that the governess, in saying *less* than the truth, actually says *more* than she means — the governess herself, struck by the ambiguity of Mrs. Grose's speech, concludes in a parallel fashion that Mrs. Grose, in saying less than *all*, nonetheless says *more* than she intends to say:

> . . . my impression of her having accidentally said more than she meant . . .
>
> I don't know what there was in this brevity of Mrs. Grose's that struck me as ambiguous. (chap. 2, pp. 12–13)

> I was . . . still haunted with the shadow of something she had not told me. (chap. 6, p. 27)

Like Wilson, the governess is *suspicious* of the ambiguity of signs and of their rhetorical reversibility; like Wilson, she thus proceeds to *read* the world around her, to *interpret* it, not by looking *at* it but by seeing *through* it, by demystifying and *reversing* the values of its outward signs. In each case, then, it is *suspicion* that gives rise as such to *interpretation*.

But isn't James's reader-trap, in fact, a *trap set for suspicion?*

> . . . an *amusette** to catch those not easily caught. . . . Otherwise expressed, the study is of a conceived "tone," the tone of *suspected* and felt *trouble,* of an inordinate and incalculable sore — the tone

of tragic, yet of exquisite, mystification. (New York Preface, *Norton*, 120; *James's italics; other italics mine)

The Turn of the Screw thus constitutes a trap for psychoanalytical interpretation to the extent that it constructs a trap, precisely, for suspicion. It has indeed been said of psychoanalysis itself that it is a veritable "school of suspicion."[20] But what, exactly, is suspicion? "Oran," reads the opening line of Camus' *The Plague*, "was a city without suspicion." Brought by "the Plague," suspicion will then signify, in this case, the awakening of consciousness itself through its mêlées with death, with fear, with suffering—the acquisition of keen awareness of the imminence of a catastrophe of unknown origin, which has to be prevented, fought against, defeated. If it is thus the plague that brings about suspicion, it is well known, indeed, that Freud himself, at the historic moment of his arrival in the United States, said precisely that he had brought with him, ironically enough, "the plague". . . . Psychoanalysis, therefore, could very accurately be described as a "school of suspicion," a school that teaches an awareness of the Plague. What, however, is the alternative to suspicion? James's text can perhaps provide an answer. In the New York Preface, to begin with, the alternative to the suspicious reader was incarnated in the so-called witless reader ("the 'fun' of the capture of the merely witless being ever but small"); suspicion would thus seem to be equivalent to "wit," to the *intelligence* of the reader. In the text of *The Turn of the Screw* itself, moreover, the alternative to the suspicion of the governess is, symmetrically, the naïve *belief* of Mrs. Grose, who unsuspectingly lends credence to whatever the governess may choose to tell her. And, as if the very name of Mrs. Grose were not a sufficient clue to James's view of the attitude of *faith* that he thus opposes to suspicion, the fact that Mrs. Grose *does not know how to read* ("my counselor couldn't read!" chap. 2, p. 10) clearly suggests a parallel with the "witless" reader that the New York Preface in its turn opposes to the suspicious, unbelieving reader, the one who is precisely difficult to catch. Psychoanalysis, therefore, is strictly speaking a "school of suspicion" to the extent that it is, in effect, a *school of reading*. Practiced by Wilson as well as by the governess, but quite unknown to Mrs. Grose, "suspicion" is directed, first and foremost, toward the nontransparent, arbitrary nature of the sign: it feeds on the discrepancy and distance that separate the signifier from its signified. While suspicion constitutes, thereby, the very motive of the process of interpretation, the very moving force behind the "wit" of the discriminating reader, we should not forget, however, that readers are here "caught" or trapped, not *in spite of* but *by virtue of, because of* their intelligence and their sophistication. Suspicion is itself here part of the mystification ("the tone of *suspected* and felt trouble . . . the tone of tragic, yet of exquisite, *mystification*"): the alert, suspicious, unduped reader is here just as "caught" as mystified, as the naïve believer. Like faith (naïve or "witless" reading), suspicion (the intelligence of reading) is here a *trap.*

The trap, indeed, resides precisely in the way in which these two opposing types of reading are themselves inscribed and comprehended in the text. The reader of *The Turn of the Screw* can choose either to *believe* the governess, and thus to behave precisely *like the governess.* Since it is the governess who, within the text, plays the role of the suspicious reader, occupies the *place* of the interpreter, to *suspect* that place and that position is, thereby, *to take it.* To demystify the governess is only possible on one condition: the condition of *repeating* the governess's very gesture. The text thus constitutes a reading of its two possible readings, both of which, in the course of that reading, it deconstructs. James's trap is then the simplest and the most sophisticated in the world: the trap is but a text, that is, an invitation to the reader, a simple invitation to undertake its reading. But in the case of *The Turn of the Screw,* the invitation to undertake a reading of the text is perforce an invitation to *repeat* the text, to enter into its labyrinth of mirrors, from which it is henceforth impossible to escape.

It is in just the same manner as the governess that Wilson, in his reading, seeks to avoid above all being duped: to avoid, precisely, being the governess's dupe. Blind to his own resemblance to the governess, he repeats, indeed, one after the other, the procedures and delusions of her reading strategy. "Observe," writes Wilson, "from a Freudian point of view, the significance of the governess's interest in the little girl's piece of wood" (*Wilson,* 104). But to "observe" the *signified* behind the wooden *signifier,* to observe the meaning, or the significance, of the very *interest* shown for that signifier, is precisely what the governess herself does, and invites others to do, when she runs crying for Mrs. Grose, "They know—it's too monstrous: they know, they know!" (chap. 7, p. 30). In just the same manner as the governess, Wilson equally *fetishizes* the phallic simulacrum, delusively raises the mast in Flora's boat to the status of Master-Signifier. Far from following the incessant slippage, the unfixable movement of the signifying chain from link to link, from signifier to signifier, the critic, like the governess, seeks to *stop* the meaning, to *arrest* signification, by a grasp, precisely, of the Screw (or of the "clue"), by a firm hold on the Master-Signifier:

> What if the hidden theme . . . is *simply sex* again? . . . the *clue of experience* . . . (*Wilson*, 115)

> When one has once *got hold of the clue to this meaning* of *The Turn of the Screw,* one wonders how one could ever have missed it. (*Wilson,* 108)

Sharing with the governess the illusion of having understood *all,* of having *mastered* meaning by clutching at its clue, at its master-signifier, Wilson could have said, *with* the governess and *like* her, but *against* her: "I seemed to myself to have mastered it, to see it all" (chap. 21, p. 78). In Wilson's case as in the governess's, the move toward mastery, however, is an aggressive move, an "act of violence," which involves a gesture of repression and of *exclusion.* "Our manner of excluding," writes Maurice Blanchot, "is at work precisely at the very moment we are priding ourselves on our gift of universal comprehension." In their attempt to elaborate a speech of mastery, a discourse of *totalitarian* power, what Wilson and the governess both *exclude* is nothing other than the threatening power of rhetoric itself—of sexuality as *division* and as meaning's *flight,* as contradiction and as ambivalence; the very threat, in other words, of the unmastery, of the impotence, and of the unavoidable castration that inhere in *language.* From his very *grasp* of meaning and from the grasp of his interpretations, Wilson thus excludes, *represses,* the very thing that led to his analysis, the very subject of his study: the role of language in the text, "the ambiguity of Henry James":

> Henry James never seems aware of the amount of space he is wasting through the long abstract formulations that do duty for concrete details, the unnecessary circumlocutions and the gratuitous meaningless verbiage—the *as it were's* and *as we may say's* and all the rest—all the words with which he pads out his sentences and which themselves are probably symptomatic of a tendency to stave off his main problems. (*Wilson,* 129; Wilson's italics)

As Jean Starobinski puts it elsewhere, "The psychoanalyst, the expert on the rhetoric of the unconscious, does not himself wish to be a rhetorician. He plays the role that Jean Paulhan assigns to the terrorist as such: he demands that one speak in clear language."[21] In demanding that the text "speak in clear language," Wilson thus reveals the *terroristic status* of his psychoanalytic exegesis. But the governess as well demands "clear language": she terrorizes in effect the child into "surrendering the name," into giving, that is, to the ghost its *proper name.* Wilson's treatment of the text indeed corresponds point for point to the governess's treatment of the child: Wilson, too, forces as it were, the text to a *confession.* And what, in fact, is the main effort of the analytical interpreter as such, if not, at all events, to extort the *secret* of the text, to compel the language of the text—like that of the child—to confess or to avow: to avow its *meaning* as well as its *pleasure; to avow its pleasure and its meaning to the precise extent that they are *unavowable.*

It is thus not insignificant for the text's subtle entrapment of its psychoanalytical interpretation that the governess ends up *killing the child.* Neither is it indifferent to the textual scene that the Latin word for child, *infans,* signifies precisely, "one incapable of speaking." For would it not be possible to maintain that Wilson, in pressing the text to confess, in forcing it to "surrender" its *proper* name, its explicit, literal meaning, himself in fact commits a *murder* (which once more brings up the question of *tact*), by suppressing within language the very silence that supports and underlies it, the silence *out of which* the text precisely speaks?

> . . . a stillness, a pause of all life, that had nothing to do with the more or less noise we at the moment might be engaged in making . . . (chap. 13, p. 53)

As the figure of a *knowledge that cannot know itself,* that cannot reflect upon nor name itself, the child in the story incarnates, as we have seen, *unconscious* knowledge. To "grasp" the child, therefore, as both the governess and Wilson do, to press him to the point of suffocating him, of killing or of stifling the silence within him, is to do nothing other than to submit, once more, the silent speech of the unconscious to the very gesture of its *repression.*

Here, then, is the crowning aberration that psychoanalysis some-times unwittingly commits in its mêlées with literature. In seeking to "explain" and *master* literature, in refusing, that is, to become a *dupe* of literature, in killing within literature that which makes it litera-ture—its reserve of silence, that which, within speech, is incapable of speaking, the literary silence of a discourse *ignorant of what it knows*—the psychoanalytical reading, ironically enough, turns out to be a read-ing that *represses the unconscious,* that represses, paradoxically, the un-conscious it purports to be "explaining." To *master,* then (to become the Master), is, here as elsewhere, to *refuse to read* the letters; here as elsewhere, to "see it all" is in effect to "shut one's eyes as tight as possible to the truth"; once more, "to see it all" is in reality to *exclude;* and to exclude, specifically, the unconscious.

Thus repeated on all levels of the literary scene, by the governess as well as by her critics, in the story as well as in its reading, this basic gesture of repression, of exclusion, is often carried out under the aus-pices of a label that while naming that which is cast out, excluded, also at the same time sanctions the exclusion. That subtle label is the term "madness" used by the interpreter to mark what is repressed as indeed *foreclosed,* external to, shut out from, meaning. Wilson thus sug-gests that the governess is *mad,* i.e., that her point of view *excludes* her, and hence should be excluded, from the "truth" and from the meaning of her story. But the governess herself in her own reading, indeed, re-fers no less insistently to the question of insanity, of madness. She is preoccupied, as we have seen, by the alternative of madness and of sense as mutually exclusive; she is quite aware, in fact, that the possi-bility of her own madness is but the converse—the other side, the other turn—of her seizure and *control* of sense, of her "grasp" of and her firm "hold"[22] on meaning, a hold involving the *repression* of other-ness as such, an exclusion of the Other. To "grasp," "get hold" of sense will therefore also be to *situate* madness—*outside,* to shut it out, to *locate* it—in the Other: to cast madness as such onto the other insofar as the Other in effect *eludes one's grasp.* The governess indeed maintains that the children are no less than *mad;*[23] when Mrs. Grose urges her to write to the Master about the children's strange behavior, the governess demurs:

> "By writing to him that his house is poisoned and his little nephew and niece *mad?*"

"But if they *are*, Miss?"

"And if I am myself, you mean? That's charming news to be sent him by a person . . . whose prime undertaking was to give him no worry." (chap. 12, pp. 49–50)

It is thus *either* the governess or the children who are mad: if the children are *not* mad, the governess could well be; if the children *are* mad, then the governess is truly in the right, as well as in her right mind. Hence, to *prove* that the children *are* mad (that they are *possessed* by the Other—by the ghosts) is to prove that the governess is *not* mad: to point to the madness of the Other is to deny and to negate the very madness that might be lurking in the self. The Other's madness thus becomes a decisive proof and guarantee of one's own sanity:

> Miss Jessel stood before us. . . . I remember . . . my thrill of joy at having brought on a *proof.* She was there, and I was justified; *she was there, so I was neither cruel nor mad.* (chap. 20, p. 71)

Thus, for the governess to be in *possession* of her *senses,* the *children* must be *possessed* and *mad.* The governess's very *sense,* in other words, is founded on the children's *madness.* Similarly but conversely, the story's very *sense,* as outlined by Wilson, by the *logic* of his reading, is also, paradoxically, *based on madness*—but this time on the madness of the *governess.* Wilson, in other words, treats the governess in exactly the same manner as the governess treats the children. It is the governess's madness, that is, the exclusion of her point of view, that enables Wilson's reading to function as a *whole,* as a system at once *integral* and *coherent*—just as it is the *children's* madness, the exclusion of *their* point of view, that permits the governess's reading, and its functioning as a *totalitarian* system.[24]

"It is not by locking up one's neighbor," as Dostoevsky once said, "that one can convince oneself of one's own soundness of mind." This, however, is what Wilson seems precisely to be doing, insofar as he is duplicating and *repeating* the governess's gesture. This, then, is what psychoanalytical interpretation might be doing, and indeed is doing whenever it gives in to the temptation of *diagnosing* literature, of indicating and of *situating madness* in a literary text. For in shutting madness up in literature, in attempting not just to explain the literary symptom, but to explain away the very symptom of literature itself, psychoanalysis, like the governess, only diagnoses literature so as to *justify itself*, to insure its own *control* of meaning, to deny or to negate the lurking possibility of its own madness, to convince itself of its own incontrovertible soundness of mind.

The paradoxical trap set by *The Turn of the Screw* is therefore such that it is precisely by proclaiming that the governess is mad that Wilson inadvertently *imitates* the very madness he denounces, unwittingly *participates in it.* Whereas the diagnostic gesture aims to situate the madness in the other and to disassociate oneself from it, to exclude the diagnosis from the diagnosed, here, on the contrary, it is the very gesture of exclusion that includes: to exclude the governess—as mad— from the place of meaning and of truth is precisely to repeat her very gesture of exclusion, to *include oneself,* in other words, within her very madness. Unsuspectingly, Wilson himself indeed says as much when he writes of another Jamesian tale: "The book is not merely mystifying, but maddening" (*Wilson,* 112).

Thus it is that *The Turn of the Screw* succeeds in *trapping* the very interpretation it in effect *invites* but whose authority it at the same time *deconstructs.* In inviting, in *seducing* the psychoanalyst, in tempting him into the quicksand of its rhetoric, literature, in truth, only invites him to *subvert himself,* only lures psychoanalysis into its necessary self-subversion.

In the textual mechanism through which the roles of the governess and of the children become reversible, and in the text's tactical action on its reader, through which the roles of the governess and of her critic (her demystifier) become symmetrical and interchangeable—the textual dynamic, the rhetorical operation at work consists precisely in the *subversion* of the *polarity* or the *alternative* that opposes as such analyst to patient, symptom to interpretation, delirium to its theory, psychoanalysis itself to madness. That psychoanalytical theory itself occupies precisely a symmetrical, and hence a specular, position with respect to the madness it observes and faces, is in fact a fundamental given of psychoanalysis, acknowledged both by Freud and by Lacan. Lacan as well as Freud recognize indeed that the very value—but equally the risk—inherent in psychoanalysis, its insightfulness but equally its blindness, its truth but also its error, reside precisely in this turn of the screw: "The discourse of the hysteric," writes Lacan, "taught [Freud] this other substance which entirely consists in the fact that such a thing as a signifier exists. In taking in the effect of this signifier, within the hysteric's discourse, [Freud] was able to give it that *quarter-turn* which was to turn it into analytical discourse" (*Encore*, 41). Freud, in turn, acknowledges a "striking similarity" between his own psychoanalytical theory and the delirious ravings of President Schreber: "It remains for the future to decide," writes Freud, "whether there is more delusion in my theory than I should like to admit, or whether there is more truth in Schreber's delusion than other people are as yet prepared to believe."[25]

It is doubtless no coincidence, therefore, that the myth of Oedipus — the psychoanalytical myth *par excellence* — should happen to recount not only the *drama of the symptom* but equally the very *drama of interpretation*. The tragedy of Oedipus is, after all, the story no less of the analyst than of the analysand: it is specifically, in fact, the story of the deconstruction, of the subversion of the polarity itself that distinguishes and opposes these two functions. The very *murder* that Oedipus commits is indeed constitutive in the story, just as much of the impasse of the interpreter as of the tragedy of the interpreted. For it is the murder that founds the rhetorical movement of substitution as a *blind* movement, leading blindly to the communication, or to the switch between interpreter and interpreted: it is by murdering that the interpreter takes the place, precisely, of the symptom to be interpreted. Through the blind substitution in which Oedipus unwittingly takes the place of his victim, of the man he killed, he also, as interpreter (as the detective attempting to solve the crime), and equally unwittingly, comes to occupy the place and the position of the very *target* of the blow that he *addresses to the Other*. But Wilson also is precisely doing this, unknowingly assuming the position of the target, when he inadvertently repeats the gesture of the governess at whom he aims his blow, thereby taking her *place* in the textual structure.

It is through *murder* that Oedipus comes to be *master*. It is by *killing literary silence*, by stifling the very silence that inhabits literary language as such, that psychoanalysis *masters* literature, and that Wilson claims to *master* James's text. But Oedipus becomes master only to end up *blinding himself*. To blind oneself: the final gesture of a master, so as to delude himself with the impression that he still is in control, if only of his self-destruction, that he still can master his own blindness (whereas his blind condition in reality preexisted his self-inflicted blindness), that he still can master his own loss of mastery, his own castrations (whereas he in reality *undergoes* it, everywhere, from without); to blind oneself, perhaps, then, less so as to punish, to humiliate oneself than so as to persist, precisely, in *not seeing,* so as to deny, once more, the very truth of one's castration, a castration existing outside Oedipus's gesture, by virtue of the fact that his conscious mastery, the mastery supported by his consciousness, finds itself subverted, by virtue of the fact that the person taken in by the trap of his detection is not the Other, but he himself—by virtue of the fact that he *is* the Other. And isn't this insistence on not seeing, on not knowing, precisely what describes as well the function of the Master in *The Turn of the Screw?* In its efforts to master literature, psychoanalysis—like Oedipus and like the Master—can thus but blind itself: blind itself in order to deny its own castration, in order not to see, and not to read, literature's subversion of the very possibility of psychoanalytical mastery. The irony is that, in the very act of judging literature from the height of its masterly position, psychoanalysis—like Wilson—in effect rejoins within the structure of the text the masterly position, the specific place of the Master of *The Turn of the Screw:* the place, precisely, of the textual *blind spot.*

Now, to occupy a blind spot is not only to be blind, but in particular, to be blind to one's own blindness; it is to be unaware of the fact that one occupies a spot *within* the very blindness one seeks to demystify, that one is *in* the madness, that one is always, necessarily, *in* literature; it is to believe that one is on the *outside,* that one *can* be outside: outside the traps of literature, of the unconscious, or of madness. James's reader-trap thus functions by precisely luring the reader into attempting to avoid the trap, into believing that there *is* an outside to the trap. This belief, of course, is itself one of the trap's most subtle mechanisms: the very act of trying to escape the trap is the proof that one is caught in it. "The unconscious," writes Lacan, "is most effectively misleading when it is caught in the act."[26] This, precisely, is what James suggests in *The Turn of the Screw.* And what James in effect *does* in *The Turn of the Screw,* what he undertakes through the performative action of his text, is precisely to mislead us, and to catch us, by on the contrary inviting us to *catch the unconscious in the act.* In attempting to escape the reading-error constitutive of rhetoric, in attempting to escape the rhetorical error constitutive of literature, in attempting to master literature in order *not to be its dupe,* psychoanalysis, in reality, is *doubly duped:* unaware of its own inescapable participation *in* literature and *in* the errors and the traps of rhetoric, it is blind to the fact that it itself exemplifies no less than the *blind spot* of rhetoricity, the spot where any affirmation of mastery in effect amounts to a self-subversion and to a self-castration. *"Les non-dupes errent"* (non-dupes err), says Lacan. If James's text does not explicitly make such a statement, it enacts it, and acts it out, while also dramatizing at the same time the suggestion that this very sentence—which entraps us in the same way as does the "turn of the screw"—this very statement, which cannot be affirmed without hereby being negated, whose very diction is in fact its own contradiction, constitutes, precisely, the position *par excellence* of *meaning* in the *literary utterance:* a rhetorical position, implying a relation of mutual subversion and of radical, dynamic contradiction between utterance and statement.

The fact that literature has no outside, that there is no safe spot assuredly outside of madness, from which one might demystify and judge it, locate it in the Other without oneself participating in it, was indeed ceaselessly affirmed by Freud in the most revealing moments of his text (and in spite of the constant opposite temptation—the mastery temptation—to which he at other times inevitably succumbed). Speaking of *The Sandman* and of Nathanael's uncanny madness—a madness textually marked, in Hoffmann's rhetoric, by the metaphor of Nathanael's distorted vision, due to the glasses bought from the Sandman (from the optician Coppola) and through which Nathanael at times chooses to behold the world that surrounds him; glasses through which he looks, at any rate, before each of his attacks of madness and of his attempts at murder—Freud emphasizes the fact that the reader is rhetorically placed *within* the madness, that there is no place from which that madness can be judged *from the outside:*

> . . . We perceive that he [Hoffmann] means to *make us, too, look through the fell Coppola's glasses . . .*
>
> We know now that we are not supposed to be looking on at the products of a madman's imagination behind which we, with the superiority of rational minds, are able to detect the sober truth . . .[27]

In a parallel manner, *The Turn of the Screw* imposes the governess's distorted point of view upon us as the rhetorical *condition* of our perception of the story. In James's tale as in Hoffmann's, madness is uncanny, *unheimlich,* to the precise extent that it *cannot be situated,* coinciding, as it does, with the very space of reading. Wilson's error is to try to *situate* madness and thereby situate *himself outside it*—as though it were possible, *in* language, to *separate* oneself from language; as though readers, looking through the governess's madness and comprehended by it, could situate *themselves* within it *or* outside it with respect to it; as though readers could indeed know *where* they are, what their place is and what their position is with respect to the literary language that itself, as such, does not know what it knows. Thus it is that when, in another of James's novels, *The Sacred Fount,* the label "madness" is ironically applied to the narrator as the last word—the last judgment in the book, "You *are* crazy, and I bid you good night"[28]—the narrator, indeed, experiences this last word as the loss of his capacity to situate himself: "Such a last word," he remarks, ". . . put me altogether nowhere."[29]

"It's a game," says the governess of the behavior of the children that in her turn she claims to be "mad"—"It's a *game,* it's a *policy* and a *fraud*" (chap. 12, p. 48)—"It's all a mere mistake and a worry and a joke" (chap. 20, p. 72), answers, indirectly, Mrs. Grose, when she realizes that it is the governess who is mad, and that the children are but the victims of her delirium. The "mistake," the "worry," and the "joke," in Mrs. Grose's mouth, refer to, and affirm, the nonexistence of the ghosts; they thus describe, accuse, excuse, the governess's madness. This ambiguous description of the error at the heart of *The Turn of the Screw* as at once tragic and comic, as both a "worry" and a "joke," is also implicit in James's statement in the New York Preface:

> The study is of a conceived "tone," the tone of suspected and felt trouble, of an inordinate and incalculable sore—*the tone of tragic, yet of exquisite, mystification.* (120)

The mystification is indeed exquisitely sophisticated, since it *comprehends* its very *de-mystification.* Since Wilson's gesture repeats the governess's, since the critic here participates in the madness he denounces, the psychoanalytical (or critical) *demystification,* paradoxically enough, ends up reproducing the literary *mystification.* The very thrust of the mystification was, then, to make us believe that there is a radical difference and opposition between the turn of the screw of mystification and the turn of the screw of demystification. But here it is precisely literature's mystification that demystifies and catches the "demystifier," by actively, in turn, *mystifying him.* Thus, paradoxically enough, it is mystification that is here demystifying, while demystification itself turns out to be but mystifying. The demystifier can only err within his own mystification.

"We could well wonder," writes Lacan of Poe's *Purloined Letter* but in terms applicable equally to *The Turn of the Screw*, "whether it is not precisely the fact that *everyone is fooled* that constitutes here the source of our pleasure."[30] If the literary mystification is, in James's term, "exquisite," it is indeed because it constitutes a source of pleasure. The mystification is a game, a joke; to play is to be played; to comprehend mystification is to be comprehended *in* it; entering into the game, we ourselves become fair game for the very "joke" of *meaning*. The joke is that, by meaning, everyone is fooled. If the "joke" is nonetheless also a "worry," if, "exquisite" as it may be, mystification is also "tragic," it is because the "error" (the madness of the interpreter) is the error of life itself. "Life is the condition of knowledge," writes Nietzsche; "Error is the condition of life—I mean, ineradicable and fundamental error. The knowledge that one errs does not eliminate the error."[31]

X. A Ghost of a Master

The whole point about the puzzle is its ultimate insolubility. How skillfully he managed it. . . . The Master indeed. — LOUIS D. RUBIN, JR., *One More Turn of the Screw*

Note how masterly the telling is . . . still we must own that something remains unaccounted for. — VIRGINIA WOOLF, *Henry James's Ghosts*

The postbag . . . contained a letter for me, which, however, in the hand of my employer, I found to be composed but of a few words enclosing another, addressed to himself, with a seal still unbroken. "This, I recognize, is from the head-master, and the head-master's an awful bore. Read him, please; deal with him; but mind you, don't report. Not a word, I'm off!" — HENRY JAMES, *The Turn of the Screw*

Thus it is that within the space of a joke that is also a worry, within the space of a pleasure that is also a horror, Henry James, Master of ceremonies, himself takes pleasure in turning the screw, in tightening the spring of our interest:

That was my problem so to speak, and my *gageure*— . . . to work my . . . *particular degree of pressure on the spring of interest.* (Preface to "The Golden Bowl," *AN*, 331)

—"You almost *killed* me,"

protests, in Mozart's opera *Don Giovanni,* the valet of Don Giovanni, Leporello;

—"Go on,—You are mad,
It was only a *joke.*"

replies his Master with a laugh. If the joke in *The Turn of the Screw* is equally a deadly, or a ghostly one, it is because the author—the master-craftsman who masters the "turns" of the game—had chosen indeed to *joke with death* itself. It is in his capacity as master of letters that James turns out to be a master of ghosts. Both ghosts and letter are, however, only "operative terms": the operative terms of the very movement of death within the signifier, of the capacity of *substitution* that founds literature as a paradoxical space of pleasure and of frustration, of disappointment and of elation:

What would the operative terms, in the given case, prove, under criticism, to have been—a series of *waiting satisfactions* or an array of *waiting misfits?* The misfits had but to be positive and concordant in the special intenser light, to represent together (*as the two sides of a coin show different legends*) just so many *effective felicities* and *substitutes.* . . . Criticism after the fact was to find in them arrests and surprises, emotions alike of disappointment and of elation: all of which means, obviously, that the whole thing was a *living**
affair. (Preface to "The Golden Bowl," *AN,* 341–42; *James's italics; other italics mine)

If death is but a joke, it is because a death is, in a sense, as Georges Bataille has put it, "an imposture." Like the ghosts, death is precisely what cannot die: it is therefore of death, of ghosts, that one can literally say that they are "a *living* affair," an affair of the living, the affair, indeed, of living.

Master of letters and of ghosts alike, James, in contrast to his interpreters, lets himself become as much as possible a *dupe,* precisely, of their literality. It is as the dupe of the very letter of his text that James remains the Master, that he deflects all our critical assaults and baffles all our efforts to master him. He proclaims to know nothing at all about the content—or the meaning—of his own letter. Like the letters in the very story of *The Turn of the Screw,* his own letter, James insists, contains precisely *nothing*. His text, he claims, can, to the letter, be taken as

> a poor pot-boiling *study of nothing* at all, *qui ne tire pas à conséquence.**
> It is but a monument to my fatal technical passion, which pre-
> vents my ever giving up anything I have begun. So that when *some-*
> *thing that I have supposed to be a subject turns out on trial to be none, je*
> *m'y acharne d'autant plus.** (Letter to Paul Bourget, August 19, 1898;
> *Norton*, 109; *James's italics; other italics mine)

> As regards a presentation of things so fantastic as in that wanton
> little tale, I can only blush to see real substance read into them.
> (Letter to Dr. Waldstein, October 21, 1898; *Norton*, 110)

> My values are positively all blanks save so far as an excited horror,
> a promoted pity, a created expertness . . . proceed to read into
> them more or less fantastic figures. (New York Preface, *Norton*, 123)

Master of his own fiction insofar as he, precisely, *is* its dupe, James, like
the Master in *The Turn of the Screw*, doesn't want to *know* anything about
it. In his turn, he refuses to read our letters, sending them back to us
unopened:

> I'm afraid I don't quite *understand* the principal question you put
> to me about "The Turn of the Screw." However, that scantily mat-
> ters; for in truth I am afraid . . . that I somehow can't pretend to
> give any coherent account of my small inventions "after the fact."
> (Letter to F. W. Myers, December 19, 1898, *Norton*, 112)

Thus it is that James's very mastery consists in the denial and in the
deconstruction of his own mastery. Like the Master in his story with
respect to the children and to Bly, James assures the role of Master only
through the act of claiming, with respect to his literary "property," the
"license," as he puts it, "of disconnexion and disavowal" (Preface to
"The Golden Bowl," *AN*, 348). Here as elsewhere, "mastery" turns out
to be self-dispossession. Dispossessing himself of his own story, James,
more subtly still, at the same time dispossessed his own story of its
master. But isn't this precisely what the Master does in *The Turn of the*
Screw, when, dispossessing the governess of her Master (himself), he
gives her nothing less than "supreme authority"? It is with "supreme

authority" indeed that James, in deconstructing his own mastery, vests his reader. But isn't this gift of supreme authority bestowed upon the reader as upon the governess the very thing that will precisely *drive them mad?*

> That one should, as an author, *reduce one's reader . . . to such a state of hallucination* by the images one has evoked . . . — nothing could better consort than *that . . .* with the desire or the pretension to cast a literary spell. (Preface to "the Golden Bowl," *AN,* 332)

It is because James's mastery consists in knowing that mastery as such is but a *fiction,* that James's law as master, like that of the Master of *The Turn of the Screw,* is a law of flight and of *escape.*[32] It is, however, through his escape, through his *disappearance* from the scene, that the Master in *The Turn of the Screw,* in effect, *becomes a ghost.* And indeed it could be said that James himself becomes a phantom master, a Master-Ghost *par excellence* in terms of his own definition of a ghost:

> Very little appears to be [done] — by the persons appearing; . . . This nega-*tive quantity* is large— . . . Recorded and attested "ghosts" are in other words . . . above all, *as little continuous and conscious and respon-sive,* as is consistent with their taking the trouble — and an immense trouble they find it, we gather — to appear at all. (The New York Preface, *Norton,* 121)

Now, to state that the Master has become himself a ghost is once again to repeat the very statement of *The Turn of the Screw:* there are *letters* from the moment there is no Master to receive them — or to *read* them: letters exist because a Master ceases to exist. We could indeed advance this statement as a definition of literature itself, a definition implicated and promoted by the practice of Henry James: literature (the very literality of letters) is nothing other than the Master's death, the Master's transformation into a ghost, insofar as that death and that transformation define and constitute, precisely, *literality* as such; literality as that which is essentially impermeable to analysis and to interpretation, that which necessarily remains unaccounted for, that which, with respect to what interpretation does account for, consti-tutes no less than *all the rest:* "All the rest is literature," writes Ver-laine.[33] "The rest," says the dying artist in James's novel *The Middle*

Years, "the rest is the madness of art": the *rest,* or literality, that which will forever make us *dupes* insofar as the very knowledge it conveys but cannot know, the knowledge that *our* knowledge cannot integrate, *dispossesses* us both of our mastery and of our Master. "That all texts see their literality increase," writes Lacan, "in proportion to what they properly imply of an actual confrontation with truth, is that for which Freud's discovery demonstrates the structural reason" (*Ecrits,* 364). To quote James again:

> It's not that the muffled majesty of authorship doesn't here *ostensibly** reign; but I catch myself again shaking it off and disavowing the pretence of it while I get down into the arena and do my best to live and breathe and rub shoulders and converse with the persons engaged in the struggle that provides for the others in the circling tiers the entertainment of the great game. There is no other participant, of course, than each of the real, the deeply involved and immersed and more or less bleeding participants. (Preface to "The Golden Bowl," *AN,* 328; *James's italics)

The deeply involved and immersed and more or less bleeding participants are here indeed none other than the members of the "circle round the fire" that we ourselves have joined. As the fire within the letter is reflected on our faces, we see the very madness of our own art staring back at us. In thus mystifying us so as to demystify our errors and our madness, it is we ourselves that James makes laugh—and bleed. The joke is indeed on us; the worry, ours.

SHOSHANA FELMAN

2 | Foucault/Derrida: The Madness of the Thinking/Speaking Subject

Madness/Philosophy/Literature

The belief in truth is precisely madness. — NIETZSCHE, *Das Philosophenbuch*

"Blindness,"[1] says the entry of the *Encyclopédie* under the word "Folie," "blindness is the distinctive characteristic of madness":

> To deviate from reason knowingly, in the drop of a violent passion, is to be weak; but to deviate from it confidently and with the firm conviction that one is following it, is to be what we call *mad*.[2]

What characterizes madness is thus not simply blindness, but a blindness *blind to itself,* to the point of necessarily entailing an *illusion of reason.* But if this is the case, how can we know where reason stops and madness begins, since both involve the pursuit of some form of reason? If madness as such is defined as an *act of faith* in reason, no reasonable conviction can indeed be exempt from the suspicion of madness. Reason and madness are thereby inextricably linked; madness is essentially a phenomenon of thought, of thought that claims to denounce, in another's thought, the Other of thought: that which thought is not. Madness can only occur within a world in conflict, within a conflict of thoughts. The question of madness is nothing less than the question of thought itself: the question of madness, in other words, is that which turns the essence of thought, precisely, *into a question*. "The capacity for self-reflection is given to man alone," writes Hegel: "that is why he has, so to speak, the privilege of madness."[3] Nietzsche goes still further:

> There is one thing that will forever be impossible: to be reasonable!
> A bit of reason though, a grain of wisdom . . .—that leaven is mixed in with everything: for the love of madness wisdom is mixed with all things![4]

Whereas Hegel places madness inside thought, Nietzsche places thought inside madness. In Pascal's conception, these contradictory positions could amount to the same. "Men," says Pascal, "are so necessarily mad that not to be mad would only be another form of madness." Rousseau, it seems, would agree: "Nothing resembles me less than myself";

> I am subject to two principal dispositions which change quite regularly . . . and which I call my weekly souls, one finds me wisely mad and the other madly wise, but in such a way that madness wins out over wisdom in both cases . . .[5]

One could indeed go on reciting a whole series of aphoristic statements issued by philosophers on madness. A question could be raised: Are these pronouncements *philosophical*, or *literary*? Is their effect as aphorisms ascribable to a rhetorical device, or to the rigor of a concept? Do they belong in literature, or in philosophy? If madness so remarkably lends itself to aphoristic statements, to plays of language and effects of style, it could be said that, even in philosophy, its function is rhetorical or literary. But on the other hand, if one turns now to literature in order to examine the role of madness there (in Shakespeare's works, for instance), one realizes that the literary madman is most often a disguised philosopher: in literature, the role of madness, then, is eminently philosophical. This paradox of madness, of being literary in philosophy and philosophical in literature, could be significant. The notions of philosophy, of literature, of madness, seem to be inherently related. And madness, in some unexpected way, could thus elucidate the problematical relationship between philosophy and literature.

Previously confined almost exclusively to the domain of literature, or to the brevity of aphoristic thought, madness, in the modern world, has become a major philosophical preoccupation. It is doubtless no coincidence that in a figure such as Nietzsche, madness invades not only the philosophy, but also the philosopher himself. The impact of Nietzsche, as a figure in which poet, philosopher, and madman coincide, is crucial in the intensification of the interest in madness, as well as in the recently increased proximity between philosophy and literature. Nietzsche's madness stands before the modern world as both an invitation and a warning, as the danger on which the condition of its very possibility is built. To reflect on the significance of "Nietzsche's madness"[6] is thus to open up and to interrogate the entire history of Western culture. Nothing less, indeed, is undertaken by Michel Foucault's important study, *Folie et déraison. Historie de la folie à l'âge classique.*[7]

The History of Madness

> *Ils ont enfermé Sade; ils ont enfermé Nietzsche; ils ont enfermé Baudelaire.* — BRETON, *Nadja*

> *It is not just the wisdom of the ages but also their madness that bursts out in us. It is dangerous to be an heir.* — NIETZSCHE, *Thus Spoke Zarathustra*

Foucault's main object—and the challenge of his study—is to contend that anthropology, philosophy, psychology, psychiatry, are built upon a radical misunderstanding of the phenomenon of madness and a deliberate *misapprehension* of its language. The entire history of Western culture is revealed to be the story of Reason's progressive conquest and consequent repression of that which it calls madness. The turning point occurs, as Foucault sees it, in the Cartesian *Cogito:* in his first *Méditation,* Descartes expels madness from the confines of culture and robs it of its language, condemning it to silence. Descartes encounters the phenomenon, the possibility of madness, right at the beginning of his quest for truth, through his methodical pursuit of doubt. The doubt strikes first at the senses as a foundation of knowledge. At this elementary stage of the method, the closest and most evident certainties communicated by the senses are not, however, submitted to doubt:

to cast doubt on the obvious, one would indeed have to be mad. How, writes Descartes, can I doubt "that I am here, sitting beside the fire, in my dressing-gown, holding this paper in my hands, and the other things of that sort?"

> And how shall I deny that these hands and this body are mine? unless perhaps I were to compare myself to those lunatics whose brains are so disturbed and blurred by their black bilious vapors that they go around calling themselves kings, while they are very poor, and saying that they are clothed in gold and crimson, while they are completely naked, or imagining that they are jugs or have a body of glass. . . . But then, they are madmen, and I would hardly be less demented if I followed their example.

This, as Foucault sees it, is the decisive sentence: the statement of a break with madness, a gesture of exclusion that expels it from the very possibility of thought. Indeed, Descartes does not treat madness in the same way as he treats other illusions, dreams, or errors of the senses: in contrast to mistakes in sense perception and to dream illusions, madness is not even allowed to serve as an instrument of doubt; if even dreams, even perceptual errors contain some elements of truth, the same cannot be said of madness: "If its perils do not compromise the method nor the essence of truth, it is not because such and such a thing, even in the thought of a madman, cannot be false, but because *I who am thinking cannot be mad*. . . . It is an impossibility of being mad inherent not in the object of thought, but in the subject who thinks. . . . Dreams or illusions are overcome in the very structure of truth; but madness is excluded by the subject who doubts. Just as it will soon be excluded that he does not think, that he does not exist" (*HF,* 57). A man can still be mad, but thought cannot. Thought is, by definition, the accomplishment of reason, and exercise of sovereignty of a subject capable of truth. I think, therefore I am not mad; I am not mad, therefore I am. The being of philosophy is thenceforth located in non-madness, whereas madness is relegated to the status of non-being.

The Cartesian gesture is symptomatic of the oppressive order, of the monarchic and bourgeois regime that was at that time being organized in France. The philosophical decree of exclusion anticipates the political decree of the "great internment" (*le grand renfermement*), by which, one morning in Paris, 6,000 people were taken—fools, mad-men, loiterers, drunks, tramps, paupers, and profaners—to be con-fined: that is how, in 1657, the General Hospital was created. The General Hospital, however, was not a medical institution: it was "the third force of repression" (*HF,* 61), a semijudiciary structure that, work-ing alongside the law and the police, had the power to try, to convict, and to execute—outside of court. Internment is thus an invention of Classicism, an invention that assigns to madmen the status of outcasts, which had, in the Middle Ages, been reserved to lepers. The medieval conception of madness as something cosmic, dramatic, and tragic loses, in the Classical age, its quasi-religious mystery: madness is now desacralized, and through its exclusion takes on a political, social, and ethical status.

In 1794 begins a new era: the enchained madmen of Bicêtre are liber-ated by Pinel; psychiatry is constituted, madness is released from its physical chains. But this liberation, in Foucault's eyes, masks a new form of confinement: madness is now reduced to the diminished status of "mental illness," to be caught in the positivistic net of erudite determinism. The binary, metaphysical structure of the Classical age: Being and Non-being, Error and Truth, is now replaced by a three-term anthropological structure: Man, his madness, and *his* truth. Madness sheds the negative foreignness by which, for the Classical mind, it eluded an objective grasp, so as to become an object among others, submitted to the process of knowledge and rational understanding. Science thereby takes up where the Cartesian *ratio* left off: in the very acquisition of its specificity, madness, according to Foucault, is still excluded, still a prisoner, bound now by the chains of its objectifica-tion, still forbidden the possibility of appearing in its own right, still prevented from speaking for itself, in a language of its own.[8]

The Philosophy of Madness

Comment Dieu ne deviendrait-il pas malade à découvrir devant lui sa rai-sonnable impuissance à connaître la folie? — BATAILLE, *La Folie de Nietzsche*

Tâche doublement impossible. — FOUCAULT, *Histoire de la folie*

For historians whose task it is to narrate—and denounce—the way in which the history of culture has throughout excluded madness, the problem is how to avoid repeating, in their own historical accounts, the very gesture of excluding madness that is constitutive of history as such. In other words, the historian's problem is that of finding a language: a language other than that of reason, which masters and represses madness, and other than that of science, which transforms it into an object with which no dialogue can be engaged, *about* which monologues are vacantly expounded — without ever disclosing the experience and the voice of madness in itself and for itself. The aim, the challenge, the ambitious wager of Foucault's endeavor is thus to say madness itself, to open our ears to "all those words deprived of language" — forgotten words on whose omission the Western world is founded: "all those words deprived of language whose muffled rumbling, for an attentive ear, rises up from the depths of history, the obstinate murmur of a language which speaks by itself, uttered by no one and answered by no one, a language which stifles itself, sticks in the throat, collapses before having attained formulation and returns, without incident, to the silence from which it had never been freed. The charred root of meaning."[9]

> The language of psychiatry, which is a monologue of reason *about* madness, could only be founded on such a silence. I did not want to write the history of that language, but rather the archeology of that silence.
>
> . . . The object, that is, is to write not a history of knowledge, but the rudimentary movements of an experience. A history, not of psychiatry, but of madness itself, before it has been captured by knowledge.[10]

In a sense, the study of Foucault involves, but at the same time puts in question, the very nature of discursive thought and philosophical inquiry. The fundamental question that, though not enunciated, is implicitly at stake, is: What does understanding mean? What is comprehension? If to comprehend is, on the one hand, to grasp, to apprehend an object, to objectify, Foucault's implicit question is: how can we comprehend *without* objectifying, without *excluding*? But if to comprehend is, on the other hand (taken in its metaphorical and spatial sense), to enclose in oneself, the embrace to *include*, i.e., to contain within certain limits, the question then becomes: how can we comprehend *without* enclosing in ourselves, without *confining*? How can we understand the

Subject, without transforming him (or her) into an object? Can the Subject comprehend itself? Is the Subject *thinkable,* as such? To put the question differently: is the Other thinkable? Is it possible to think the Other, not as an object, but as a subject, a subject who would not, however, amount to the same?

For the historian and the philosopher of madness the problem then is how, while analyzing History's essential structure of muffling madness, to give it voice, restore to madness both its language and its right to speak; how to say madness itself, both as Other and as Subject; how to speak from the place of the Other, while avoiding the philosophical trap of dialectic *Aufhebung,* which shrewdly reduces the Other into a symmetrical same; while rejecting all discourses *about* madness, how to pronounce the discourse *of* madness. Is such a discourse possible? Precisely how can one *formulate* a "language which sticks in the throat, collapsing before having attained any formulation"? How can one *utter* a "language that speaks by itself, uttered by no one and answered by no one"? How can madness as such break through the universe of discourse?

It can now be seen that what is at stake, in Foucault's historical study, is in fact the philosophical search for a *new status of discourse,* a discourse which would undo both exclusion and inclusion, which would obliterate the line of demarcation and the opposition between Subject and Object, Inside and Outside, Reason and Madness. To enounce Difference as language and language as Difference; to say inside language the outside of language; to speak, in a philosophical way, from within what is outside philosophy; this is what Foucault conceives of as a *problem of elocution,* in which he sees the major difficulty of his enterprise: the elocutionary difficulty of what he calls a "relativity without recourse," of a language deprived of the foundation of any absolute truth.

> . . . it was necessary to maintain a kind of relativity without recourse . . .
>
> An ungrounded language was thus required: a language which played the game, but which authorized exchanges. It was essential at all costs to preserve the *relative,* and to be *absolutely* understood.
>
> There, hidden and expressed in a simple problem of elocution, lay the major difficulty of the enterprise.[11]

This "simple problem of elocution" becomes at times for Foucault an impossibility inherent in the very terms of this project.

> But the task is no doubt doubly impossible: since it would have us re-constitute the dust of actual suffering, of senseless words an-chored by nothing in time; and especially since that suffering and those words can only exist and be offered to themselves and to others in an act of division which already denounces and masters them. . . . The perception which seeks to seize them in their natu-ral state belongs necessarily to a world which has already cap-tured them. The freedom of madness can only be heard from the top of the fortress which holds it prisoner.[12]

The Madness of Philosophy

> Ce qui m'oblige d'écrire, j'imagine, est la crainte de devenir fou.
> — BATAILLE, Sur Nietzsche

> Though this be madness, yet there is method in't. — SHAKESPEARE, Hamlet

That any *translation* of madness is already a form of its repression, a form of violence against it, that the praise of folly can only be made in the language of reason, this fundamental insight is in turn developed by Jacques Derrida in his critique of Foucault.[13] Not only, remarks Der-rida, does madness remain necessarily confined in the fortress that holds it prisoner, but Foucault's own enterprise is itself imprisoned by the conceptual economy it claims to denounce:

> Can an archeology, even of silence, be anything but a form of logic, that is, an organized language, . . . and order . . . ? Would not the archeology of silence end up being the most effective, the most subtle renewal, the *repetition* . . . of all that has been perpe-trated against madness, in the very act of denouncing it?
>
> It is perhaps not enough to do without the conceptual tools of psychiatry in order to disculpate our own language. The whole of European language . . . has participated . . . in the adventure of Occidental reason. *Nothing* in that language and *no one* among those who speak it can escape the historical guilt which Foucault seems to want to put on trial. But this is perhaps an impossible

trial, since the hearing and the verdict are an endless reiteration of the crime by the simple act of their elocution. (*ED*, 57–58)

Foucault, of course, was fully aware of the impossibility of his task. Derrida however would like to go beyond that awareness, by reflecting on the significance of the impossibility itself. How can the very *possibility* of Foucault's book be situated with respect to its impossible aim? For Derrida, the relationship of mutual exclusion between language and madness, exclusion that Foucault's own discourse cannot avoid perpetuating, is not *historical,* but *economical,* essential to the economy of language as such: the very status of language is that of a break with madness, of a protective strategy, of a difference by which madness is deferred, put off. With respect to "madness itself," language is always *somewhere else.* The difficulty of Foucault's task is thus not contingent, but fundamental. Far from being a historical accident, the exclusion of madness is the general condition and the constitutive foundation of the very enterprise of speech.

> Sentences are normal by nature. They are impregnated with normality, that is, with meaning. . . . They contain normality and meaning, no matter what the state of health or madness of their utterer may be . . .
> So that . . . any philosopher or any speaking subject (and the philosopher is merely the epitome of the speaking subject) who is trying to evoke madness *inside* of thought . . . can only do so in the dimension of *possibility* and in the language of fiction or in the fiction of language. In doing so, his own language reassures him against the threat of actual madness. (*ED*, 84–85)

> But this is not a failing or a search for security belonging to any one particular historical language . . . , it is inherent in the essence and intent of all language in general. (*ED*, 84)

Descartes' exclusion of madness proceeds then not from the *Cogito* but from his very intention to *speak.* Derrida in fact proposes a somewhat different interpretation of the first *Méditation*: in *his* reading, the disqualification of delirium is quoted in the text ironically, as the objection of the nonphilosopher, which is temporarily accepted by Descartes, only to be surpassed by the hypothesis of universal sleep and constant dream. Far from excluding madness, Descartes fully accepts it in assuming, at a later stage, the possibility of absolute delusion through the hyperbole of the *malin génie,* a demon who distorts and twists not only sense perceptions but intelligible truth itself. Whereby Descartes' proceeding does not imply, as Foucault would have it, "I who am thinking *sum*" (*ED,* 86); "even if the whole of what I am thinking is tainted with falsehood or madness. . . . I think, I am *while* I am thinking" (*ED,* 87). By straining toward the undetermined, toward the sense of nonsense, the Cartesian Cogito is itself a "crazy project" (*ED,* 87) strangely similar to Foucault's (impossible) undertaking. Of course, the discourse of Descartes insures itself against the kind of "madness" from which it springs, as does the discourse of Foucault. In this sense indeed Foucault's book, itself "a powerful gesture of protection and confinement," is nothing less than "a Cartesian gesture for the twentieth century" (*ED,* 85). And the History of Madness would thus peculiarly resemble the History of Philosophy.

> To define philosophy as wanting-to-say-hyperbole is to admit — and philosophy is perhaps that gigantic admission — that within the pronouncements of history, in which philosophy recovers its equanimity and excludes madness, philosophy betrays itself . . . ; it breaks down, forgets itself and enters into a phase of crisis which is essential to its movement. I can only philosophize in *terror,* but in the *avowed* terror, of going mad. The avowal is there, present as both an unveiling and a forgetting, a protection and an exposition: an economy. (*ED,* 96)

By thus reformulating Foucault's thought, but with a change of emphasis and with a different punctuation, Derrida elaborates a textual chiasmus, which he does not articulate as such but which sums up the scheme of his argumentation: any Philosophy of Madness can only bear witness to the Reason of Philosophy; philosophical reason itself, however, is but the *economy* of its own madness. The impossible *philosophy of madness* becomes, in Derrida's reading, the inverted and irrefutable sign of the constitutive *madness of philosophy.*

Philosophy and Literature

Language is a sweet madness. While speaking man dances over all things.
— NIETZSCHE, *Thus Spoke Zarathustra*

In this theoretical confrontation between Derrida and Foucault, the problem, of course, is not that of deciding which way of reasoning is "correct." The question "whose reasoning does justice to madness?" is in any case an absurd question, a contradiction in terms. It is clear, at the same time, that the thoughts on both sides, although no doubt governed by different desires, in fact enrich, reinforce, and illuminate each other. I do not intend, for that reason, to side with one or the other of the two respective positions, but rather to seek to examine what is the *issue* of the debate, what is *at stake* in the argumentation.

Even while attesting to the madness of philosophy, Derrida then judges contradictory and logically impossible any philosophy of madness (of "madness in itself"), since the phenomenon of madness, being in its essence *silence*, cannot be rendered, *said* through *logos*. This impossibility is twice enounced by Derrida, articulated in two different contexts, which I would here like to juxtapose:

(1) Speaking of Descartes:

So that, to come back to Descartes, any philosopher or any speaking subject (and the philosopher is merely the epitome of the *speaking subject*), who is trying to evoke madness *inside of* thought (and not just in the body or in some extrinsic form), can only do so in the dimension of *possibility* and in the language of fiction or in the fiction of language. (*ED,* 84)

(2) Speaking of Foucault:

What I mean is that the silence of madness is not *said,* cannot be said in the *logos* of this book, but is indirectly made present, metaphorically, if I may say so, in the *pathos*—I take the word in its best sense—of this book. (*ED,* 60)

In both cases, madness escapes philosophy (philosophy in the strict sense of the word), but in both cases madness by no means disappears, it takes refuge in something else: in the first case it is the principle of *fiction,* "the language of fiction or the fiction of language," which harbors madness; in the second case, it is the *pathos* of its *metaphoric* evocation. Metaphor, *pathos,* fiction: without being named, it is *literature* that surreptitiously has entered the debate. The discussion about madness and its relation to philosophy has thus indirectly led us to the significant question of literature, and the way in which madness displaces, blocks, and opens up questions seems to point to the particular nature of the relationship between literature and philosophy.

In Derrida's discourse, an opposition, then, is sketched out between *logos* and *pathos*. The silence of madness, he writes, is not *said* in the *logos* of the book but *rendered present* by its *pathos,* in a *metaphorical* manner, in the same way that madness, *inside of thought,* can only be evoked through *fiction*. What then is the meaning of this opposition between *logos* and *pathos?* Does it amount to the opposition between metaphor and literal meaning, or between figure and concept? How does the pathos of figurative *language* relate to the *silence* of madness? In what way can silence be conveyed by literature? Why is it to literature that the task of "saying madness" is entrusted? What kind of relationship interconnects madness with "the language of fiction"? In what way can madness "inside of thought" be evoked by "the fiction of language"? What is, precisely, the status of fiction "inside of thought"? In what way does literature attest to the intercourse between thought and madness? In what way, "in the language of fiction or in the fiction of language," and to what extent can thought maintain itself in Difference? Can thought maintain itself as thought within the difference that pertains to madness?—All these questions assail the debate: questions Derrida does not ask, but that are suggested by his objections, in his response to Foucault; questions that Foucault does not raise, but that nevertheless underlie his book.

Literature and Madness

> *Dans la folie . . . il nous faut reconnaître . . . un discours où le sujet, peut-on dire, est parlé plutôt qu'il ne parle.* — JACQUES LACAN, *Ecrits*

On the idea that literature, fiction, is the only possible meeting place between madness and philosophy, between delirium and thought, Foucault would doubtless agree with Derrida. It is in fact to *literature* that Foucault turns in his search for the authentic voice of madness—to the *texts* of Sade, Artaud, Nerval, or Hölderlin. The essential connection between madness and literature in Foucault's study present itself from two different perspectives: (1) *in a metonymic manner,* by the constant reference to the theme of madness *inside* literature; (2) *in a metaphoric manner,* as Derrida suggests, by the "literarity" of Foucault's book itself, its *pathos:* the intensity and the emotion that pervade its style. It thus seems that literature is there to *re-place* madness: metaphorically (substitutively) and metonymically (contiguously).

Derrida and Foucault thereby agree on the existence of a literary buffer zone between madness and thought. This literary zone does not, however, play for each the same role, in relation to philosophy. For Foucault, literature gives evidence *against* philosophy; this is not the case for Derrida. For Foucault, the fictions of madness undermine, *disorient* thought. For Derrida, on the contrary, at least in the case of Descartes, the fiction of madness has as its end to *orient* philosophy. As we have seen, Descartes, attempting to "evoke madness *inside of* thought (and not just in the body or in some extrinsic form), can only do so in the dimension . . . of fiction," by inventing a *malin génie,* a mysterious demon who may perhaps deceive us in all things, imbue with errors and illusions not only the perception of the senses but also the truths of mathematics, distorting intelligibility itself. Through this fiction of the *malin génie* Descartes, in Derrida's account, assumes the hypothetic possibility of his own madness, but continues nonetheless to *think,* to *speak,* to live. Fiction being thus the means by which the philosophic subject takes on madness—in order to protect himself against it, to exclude it (or to put it off) in the act of speaking—literature for Derrida, or rather intraphilosophic fiction, itself becomes a metaphor of the madness of philosophy.

Foucault maintains a different view, and contests in turn Derrida's account of Descartes. For Foucault indeed, the fiction of the *malin génie* is "anything but madness":

All is, perhaps, illusion, but with no credulity. The *malin génie* is doubtless much more deceitful than an obstructed mind; he can conjure up all the illusory trappings of madness; he is anything but madness. One could even say that he is just the opposite: since madness makes me *believe* that my nudity and my misery are robed in illusory crimson, whereas the hypothesis of the *malin génie* enables me *not to believe* that these hands and this body exist. As far as the extent of the delusion is concerned, the *malin génie* indeed is not less powerful than madness; but as for the position of the subject with respect to the delusion, *malin génie* and madness are rigorously opposed. . . .

The difference is clear: when confronted with the shrewd deceiver, the meditating mind behaves, not like a madman panic-stricken in the face of universal error, but like an equally shrewd adversary always on the alert, constantly reasonable, and never ceasing to be the master of his fiction.[14]

The philosopher ends up getting his bearing, *orienting himself* in his fiction: he only enters it in order to abandon it. The madman, on the other hand, is engulfed by his own fiction. As opposed to the subject of logos, the subject of *pathos* is a subject whose position with respect to fiction (even when he is the author) is not one of mastery, of control, of sovereign affirmation of meaning, but of *vertigo*, of *loss of meaning*. It could then be said that madness (as well as pathos and, perhaps, literature itself) is the *nonmastery of its own fiction;* it is a blindness to meaning. In contrast, the discourse of philosophy (for example, in the figure of Descartes) is precisely distinguished by its control, its position of mastery, of domination with respect to its own fiction.

By thus acknowledging that the relationship between philosophy and madness cannot be separated from literature's essential questions, that the communication between thought and madness cannot be direct, but necessarily must pass through fiction, the focus of the debate has shifted, the accent falling now on the specific nature of the relationship between madness and fiction, and on the *status of fiction* in relation to philosophy. The question here emerges: if "the language of fiction," in Derrida's terms, is thus distinguished from the language of philosophy *per se,* determined therefore as its Other, as its *outside,* how can it at the same time be "confined, enclosed *within* philosophy? Is the literature *within* philosophy inside or out? To state, as does Foucault, that the mad subject cannot situate himself within his fiction; that, *inside* literature, he knows no longer *where* he is, is to imply indeed that fiction may not exactly be located "*inside of* thought," that literature cannot be properly enclosed *within* philosophy, present, that is, to itself and at the same time present *to* philosophy: that the fiction is not always where we think, or where it thinks it is; that if, excluded from philosophy, madness is indeed to some extent *contained* in literature, it by no means constitutes its *content.* All this can be summed up by saying that the role of fiction in philosophy is comparable to that of madness inside literature; and that the status, both of fiction in philosophy and of madness inside literature, is not *thematic.* Literature and madness by no means reside in theme, in the content of a statement. In the play of forces underlying the relationship between philosophy and fiction, literature and madness, the crucial problem is that of the subject's *place*, of his *position* with respect to the delusion. And the position of the subject is not defined by *what* he says, nor by what he talks *about*, but by the place—unknown to him—*from which* he speaks.

Literature's Reason

We work in the dark—we do what we can—we give what we have. . . . The rest is the madness of art.
— HENRY JAMES, *The Middle Years*

The question now is to examine whether, with respect to the delusion, the position of the subject and the content of his statement can coincide, whether the subject and the theme of madness can become present to each other, establish a synonymous, symmetrical relationship. Literature could very simply serve as a transparent intermediary between madness and philosophy, it could indeed succeed in *saying* madness *inside* of philosophy, if it could have with madness on the one hand and with philosophy on the other, a pure relationship of symmetry and of homologous equivalence. But for Foucault the History of Madness is, on the contrary, the story of a radical *dissymmetry:* of something that occurs, precisely, in the gap, in the discrepancy between the history of philosophy and that of literature. Foucault's own discourse tried to situate itself within this very gap that history has opened up between philosophy and literature, *logos* and *pathos.* In relation to philosophy, literature is, for Foucault, in a position of excess, since it includes that which philosophy excludes by definition: madness. Madness thus becomes an overflow, that which remains of literature after philosophy has been subtracted from it. The History of Madness is the story of this surplus, the story of a literary residue.

In the beginning of the Classical period, it is true, literature itself is silent: "Classical madness belonged to the realm of silence . . . : there is no literature of madness in the Classical period" (*HF,* 535). Descartes' decree succeeded then in silencing—along with madness—a certain type of literature as well. This is not the last on Foucault's list of grievances against Descartes: "Descartes, in the very movement of proceeding toward truth, *renders impossible the lyricism* of unreason" (*HF,* 535;

my italics). Madness, however, starts to reappear in the domain of literary language with Diderot's *Neveu de Rameau,* and continues to gain strength and ground in Romanticism. As a "lyrical explosion" (*HF,* 537), insanity, in nineteenth-century literature, is given as a "theme for recognition" (*HF,* 538), a theme in which the reader is called upon to recognize himself; but philosophical cognition still continues to exclude this literary recognition: "embraced by lyrical experience, this recognition is still rejected by philosophical reflections" (*HF,* 538). If Foucault denounces, then, "the modern world's effort to speak of madness only in the serene, objective terms of mental illness and *to obliterate its pathos*" (*HF,* 182; my italics), what he most decries indeed is this *obliteration of the pathetic resonance,* this suppression, by philosophy and science, of the literary overflow. The History of Madness, for Foucault, is nothing but the story of this obliteration: "Madness, *the lyric glow of illness,* is ceaselessly snuffed out."[15]

This is a crucial point. Madness, for Foucault, is nothing but that which the history of madness has *made possible precisely by suppressing it:* the "lyric glow of illness." Madness, which is *not* simply mental illness, *not* an object, is nothing other than the excess of its *pathos,* a "lyrical explosion" (*HF,* 537), a "torn presence"; it is precisely this capacity for suffering, for emotion, for *vertigo,* for *literary* fascination. Madness, in other words, is for Foucault *pathos* itself, a *metaphor of pathos,* of the unthought residue of thought. And if, as Derrida asserts, madness can only be made present "metaphorically," through the very *pathos* of Foucault's book—then the *pathos* of the book is a metaphor of *pathos. Pathos* thus turns out to be a metaphor of itself, caught in the movement of its own metaphoric repetition. Madness, in other words, is for Foucault (like *pathos*) a notion that does not *elucidate* what it connotes, but rather *participates* in it: the term madness is itself *pathos,*[16] not *logos;* literature, and not philosophy. And if pathos can refer us only to itself, is its own metaphor, then madness, in Foucault's book, like literature itself, becomes a metaphor whose referent is a metaphor: *the figure of a figure.*

How is this possible? Foucault's reference to Nietzsche can perhaps enlighten us:

The study which follows would be but the first . . . in that long inquiry, which, under the sun of the great Nietzschean search, would try to confront the dialectics of history with the immobile structure of tragedy.

> . . . At the center of these borderline-experiences of the Western world bursts out . . . that of tragedy itself—Nietzsche having shown that the tragic structure from which the history of the Western world proceeds is nothing other than the refusal, the forgetting, and the silent fall of tragedy through history.[17]

The tragic structure of history proceeds from the obliteration of tragedy by history. The pathetic resonance of madness proceeds from history's obliteration of the pathetic resonance of madness. Madness as *pathos* is, in other words, the metaphor of the erasing of a metaphor; the history of madness is the story of the metaphor of history's forgetting of a metaphor.

Placing Foucault's failure (not the failure of his enterprise but that of his declared ambition to say "madness itself") in his necessary and unavoidable recourse to metaphor, Derrida objects to the absence of a guiding definition in Foucault's book, the lack of a clear concept delimiting madness:

> . . . the concept of madness is never submitted to a thematic examination on the part of Foucault; but isn't this concept—outside of everyday popular language which always drags on longer than it should after being put in question by science and philosophy—isn't this concept today a *false concept,* a concept so disintegrated that Foucault, by refusing psychiatric or philosophic tools, which have done nothing but imprison madmen, ends up making use—and he has no alternative—of a *common, equivocal notion,* borrowed from a *fund beyond control.*[18]

The very rigor of the objection begs the question: for what Foucault intends in fact to put in question is the way in which philosophy and science precisely do *put into question* "everyday popular language"; and particularly the *control* that they claim to exert over this "fund beyond control." Madness cannot constitute a concept, being a metaphor of metaphor. The requirement of Derrida (that of the madness of philosophy) is the philosophical requirement *par excellence:* that of a concept, of a maximum of *meaning.* But the requirement of Foucault (that of the impossible philosophy of madness: of *pathos*) is the requirement of literary *par excellence*—the search for metaphor and for a maximum of *resonance*. It goes without saying that both Derrida and Foucault are powerful writers, and as such, inhabited by language: they both find themselves, in one way or another, *up against* literature. But in this theoretical debate over the status of the term "madness," it turns out that one is clearly enouncing the demand for a *concept* of metaphor, whereas the other solicits and pleads for a *metaphor* of the concept.

A double paradox, then, two philosophically untenable philosophical positions; indeed not one but *two "tâches doublement impossibles,"* two "doubly impossible tasks," both contradicted by their own language, in which the *content* of the statement can never coincide with the *position* of a subject who, in both cases, oversteps himself, passes out into the other. Perhaps the madness of philosophy and the philosophy of madness are, after all, each but the figure of the other? Which in no way implies that they are coextensive, that they amount to the same thing; but rather, that if each is eccentric to the other, both of them are, in addition, eccentric to the very framework of their opposition, rebellious to the very structure of their alternative.

That madness is at once a "common notion" and a "false concept," Foucault would but agree; in order to repeat it, differently. For in Foucault's conception, the proper meaning of the notion "madness" is precisely that it has no proper meaning, that it is, and rigorously, "a false concept," a metaphor indeed—of the radical metaphoricity that corrodes concepts in their essence, a metaphor of literature, from whose obliteration philosophy proceeds. Madness—or literature: this "equivocal and common notion," to use the terms of Derrida, this "false concept," is necessarily, inevitably "borrowed from a fund beyond control," a fund unfounded and whose sole foundation is indeed the loss, the absence of control: loss of the relation to the mastery of meaning that ceaselessly transforms itself, offers itself but to be misunderstood, misapprehended. It becomes thus clear that this unfounded fund can by no means be *thematic* apprehension, it is *rhetorical,* that is, consisting in the very principle of *movement,* in an endless, metamorphic transformation. It was then inevitable that Foucault would not submit this fund, as Derrida suggests, to "a thematical examination": any examination of its theme can but reveal its fusion with another, its energetic alteration, its endless metamorphosis; any examination of its *place,* of its conceptual center, encounters only the decentralizing energy of its *displacement*. The answer here can but disseminate the question.

If it is true then that the question underlying madness *cannot be asked*, that language is not *capable* of asking it; that through the very formulation of the question the *interrogation* is in fact excluded, being necessarily a confirmation, and *affirmation*, on the contrary, of reason: an affirmation in which madness does not question, is not *in question*; it is, however, not less true that, in the fabric of a text and through the very act of writing, the question is *at work*, stirring, changing place, and wandering away: the question underlying madness *writes*, and writes itself. And if we are unable to locate it, read it, except where it already has escaped, where it has moved—moved *us—away*—it is not because the question relative to madness does not question, but because it questions *somewhere else:* somewhere at that point of silence where it is no longer we who speak, but where, in our absence, we are *spoken.*

SHOSHANA FELMAN

3 "You were right to leave, Arthur Rimbaud": Poetry and Modernity

Rimbaud with Mallarmé: Modernity, Poetry, Translation (Postface, December 2005)

The following essay on Rimbaud, translated here for the first time, is my earliest piece included in this Reader. I wrote it in my youth, in 1973. At the time, I meant it to be a text on the relation between language, poetry, and Rimbaud's (rhetorical and philosophical) preoccupation with modernity. Today, I see this essay slightly differently, as a text mostly concerned with the significance of Rimbaud's destiny, a mysterious destiny inscribed by—and within—his poetry.

I wrote this text in Paris, and I took for granted the notoriety of Rimbaud in France as one of France's greatest poets, and consequently every Frenchman's (schooldays) familiarity both with Rimbaud's life and with his verses. Because such familiarity does not exist in the United States, this text—rooted in Frenchness—seemed untranslatable, and thus I did not include it in the selection of chapters that constitutes *Writing and Madness*, the abridged English version of my *La Folie et la chose littéraire* (Paris, Seuil: 1978). The essay on Rimbaud is, moreover, a text on poetry, and Rimbaud is basically, as Mallarmé calls him, "a singer"—a musical, acoustic poet. Thus his poetry, his rhymes, and his semantics play on signifiers and on sounds (the sounds of fragmented syllables) in a way that is inherently dependant on the aural specificity of the French language. My own French style, especially in those years of the seventies, was also quite playful in its language, resonating with Rimbaud's linguistic ironies and puns, and underscoring, in its turn, Rimbaud's own constant plays with the sonorous materiality of the French signifiers. Thus, it was extremely difficult to translate this text into a plausibly poetic, sonorously resonant, semantically nuanced, and yet neither artificial nor mechanical, but fluent, natural, and polished English. This task, almost impossible—this transference or translation from the soul and body of one language to the soul and body of another—was here nevertheless accomplished, thanks to the uncommon writerly linguistic genius of Barbara Johnson, whose outstanding verbal ingenuity and fluency, delicate poetic sensitivity, and discriminating critical ear could tap right into the French signifiers, receive their wealth of meanings, and brilliantly render for the English-speaking reader not only the poetic resonances of the French, but also the historically specific conceptual and critical nuances of the French context of those years, with which she was herself acquainted.

Simultaneously with her work on the translation of my essay, Barbara Johnson was also at work on a far more difficult job of creative translation and poetic rendition—translating into English for the first time the whole corpus of Mallarmé's poetic prose, including the evocative poetic portrait Mallarmé draws of Rimbaud in his "Medallions and Portraits."[1] By chance, I revisited my own essay in its English version side by side with Johnson's fluent and rich English rendition of Mallarmé's poetic evocation of Rimbaud. This parallel, coincidental reading on my part of these two interpretations of Rimbaud (Mallarmé's and mine) and the spark of the encounter between these two French poets and between their two stunning poetic languages, in a language that was not French, was for me like an epiphany, which helped me at the same time to understand Rimbaud much better and to understand myself. I felt that Mallarmé shed light, in retrospect, on the elliptical significance of my own essay. His exquisite prose powerfully concretized for me, with the inspired pathos of a poet, insights I had tried more awkwardly and more abstractly to articulate about Rimbaud, from my own historically inflected 1973 Parisian stance as a literary critic. Since this encounter of translations was for me a revelation, I wish to share it with my readers, adding to my own article this Postface, in which I hope to make as evocative as possible what I later understood from Mallarmé, as an added dimension to my own vision of Rimbaud—as a belated, chance illumination juxtaposed to the meaning of my essay. This sketch will underscore what I believe to be the essence or quintessence of Rimbaud, which Mallarmé saw and depicted in a flash through the poetic touch and visionary power of his extraordinary language: a language that for me rendered more palpable, gave flesh and life to, the emotion underlying the conceptual insights of my own analysis.

Rimbaud is first of all, says Mallarmé, a striking physical emergence: a striking body, a beautiful and very striking face, of which the famous photo (by Carjat, 1870), and the famous painting (by Fantin-Latour, 1872), are unforgettable and well known.

"I did not know him," Mallarmé says, "but I saw him, once, at one of those literary banquets, arranged in haste, at the end of the War— *the Dinner of Naughty Goodfellows*—named by an antithesis, and made famous by the painting and by Verlaine's description, in *Les Poètes maudits*, of Rimbaud": "He was tall," Verlaine writes, "well built, almost athletic, with the perfectly oval face of an exiled angel, with disorderly

brown hair and pale blue eyes that were disquieting" (p. 513). Mallarmé now adds to Verlaine's words his own testimonial reminiscences, his own visual and visceral impressions of Rimbaud, accompanied by his own sense of surprise, of wonderment, and, as he puts it, of "unfinished admiration" at what he feels to be the ambiguities, the contradictions of Rimbaud, displayed already without words, in this physique whose muteness teases an amazing poetry, a poetry seductively communicative and seductively withheld. Mallarmé remembers:

> With a mysterious something about him either proudly or meanly flaunted, he recalled a daughter of the people, and his laundrywoman's appearance, because of his enormous hands, reddened with chilblains because of rapid changes of temperature, which might have indicated even more terrible jobs, since they belonged to a boy. I later learned that they had signed some beautiful poems, unpublished; in any case his sardonic mouth, with its pouting and mocking expression, had never recited one. (p. 513)

"Maybe you want to know what the person was like," Mallarmé says: "but at least we have the published works—*A Season in Hell, Illuminations*, and the volume of *Poems* published long ago" (p. 512). "Maybe you want to know what the person was like": Mallarmé entices us, intimating that Rimbaud can be known only through his poetry, known only poetically; and even then it would be impossible fully to know Rimbaud, because, says Mallarmé, Rimbaud is that unique phenomenon of poetry which has *an impact*, and which exercises an ongoing powerful, irresistible, and indeed indelible *influence* on poets, only insofar as Rimbaud remains, and will continue to remain, profoundly (paradoxically) *unassimilable*. Not even Verlaine, Mallarmé suggests, has fully understood Rimbaud, fully assimilated his poetic innovation, his pathbreaking modernity. Or perhaps—Mallarmé's syntax is ambiguous on this point, he hesitates—perhaps Verlaine, "the magnificent elder, who raised the baton," was the only exception to the fact that Rimbaud's novelty could not be assimilated. Probably not even Verlaine had truly assimilated the significance of Rimbaud's dazzling poetic emergence:

> Maybe you want to know what the person was like: but at least we have the published works—*A Season in Hell, Illuminations*, and the volume of *Poems* published long ago, which henceforth exercise,

on recent poetic events, an influence so particular that, once one has mentioned him, one can but keep an enigmatic silence, and reflect, as if a lot of silence and reverie imposed themselves, as if one were struck by some unfinished admiration.

You can doubt, my dear host, whether the principal innovators at the present time, even the one, indeed, or perhaps, mysteriously, with the exception of, the magnificent elder, *who raised the baton*, Verlaine, you can doubt whether all these have really undergone, in any depth or directly, Arthur Rimbaud. Nor does the freedom now allowed to verse, or better, springing out of it, claim derivation from him who, except for his stuttering very last verses or his absolute cessation, strictly observed the official forms. . . . He burst on the poetic scene like a meteor, ignited by no motive other than his presence, streaking alone in the sky, and extinguished alone. (p. 512)

Mallarmé has this incredible and surprising insight: the more unassimilable Rimbaud is, the more he influences; the more he influences, the more he is emulated, followed, adulated, the more his novelty and his originality remain inimitable, his modernity intact and his innovation (paradoxically) unrepeatable.

This, says Mallarmé, is what it means to be a meteoric poet: "He burst on the poetic scene like a meteor, ignited by no motive other than his presence, streaking alone in the sky, and extinguished alone" (p. 512). This image of the meteor encapsulates a profound insight into the catastrophic human and poetic cost of Rimbaud's strength, into the tragic price exacted by his poetry. Rimbaud shines in his meteoric aloneness. "You can doubt, my dear host, whether the principal innovators at the present time, even the one, indeed, or perhaps, mysteriously, with the exception of, the magnificent elder, *who raised the baton*, Verlaine, you can doubt whether all these have really undergone, in any depth or directly, Arthur Rimbaud." Tragically and fatally, perhaps not even Verlaine—Rimbaud's lover, his companion and poetic partner, and later his editor and publisher, has really understood Rimbaud. Rimbaud, says Mallarmé, has a tremendous influence on the current poetic generation and all the "principal innovators" claim themselves from him, but no innovator, neither Verlaine nor any other poet, "has really undergone, in any depth or directly, Arthur Rimbaud." Mallarmé is a profound thinker and a deep observer. His poetic prose is a thinking prose, which cuts sharp, like a diamond. Rimbaud's influence is stunning, but no one has truly "undergone" Arthur Rimbaud.

Maybe that is why Rimbaud was predestined, so to speak, in the end to leave Verlaine, who was unable really to accompany him or truly "undergo" him ("directly or in any depth"), unable, that is, to be inflected, changed, transformed by Rimbaud's language or by his love, take in his irresistible yet unassimilable influence, truly receive his magnetic, violent originality.

"Cheap anecdotes," continues Mallarmé, "are not lacking around someone who had lost the thread of his existence; they fell naturally into the newspapers" (p. 514).

Thereupon follows Mallarmé's description of the events leading to the famous Brussels breakup, the dramatic and explosive scene of separation between the two great tragic poets, following upon the arrival in Brussels of Verlaine's young wife, recently become mother to his child. This explosive breakup scene will have catastrophic consequences for both poets: Verlaine will be imprisoned; Rimbaud will disappear into the deserts of Arabia and North Africa, lost at once to poetry and to "civilization." Mallarmé narrates:

> When the prestige of Paris was about used up, and Verlaine was beginning to have marital problems, . . . it didn't take much to convince Rimbaud to visit London. The couple led there an existence of orgiastic poverty, breathing the free smoke of coal fires, drunk on reciprocity. A letter from France to one of the fugitives [Verlaine] said that all was forgiven as long as he abandoned his companion. The young wife, between mother and mother-in-law, expected a scene of reconciliation when she arrived at the appointed place. Here I refer to the story as delicately traced by M. Berrichon,[2] the most poignant scene in the world, given that its two heroes, one wounded and the other delirious, were two poets roaring in agony. Entreated by all three women together, Verlaine had renounced his friend, but saw him, by accident, at the hotel room door, flew into his arms to follow him, ignored the chilly requests by the latter to do nothing of the sort, "swearing that their affair was forever dissolved"—"even without a penny," although they had come to Belgium just in order to make money for the return trip, "he was leaving." That attitude repulsed Verlaine, who pulled the trigger of a pistol he happened to have on

him, before he dissolved into tears at Rimbaud's feet. It was said that things couldn't remain, as it were, all in the family. Bandaged, Rimbaud, still determined to leave, came back from the clinic, and was shot again, in the street. The shooting, decidedly public now, earned the faithful friend [Verlaine] two years in the prison of Mons. Alone, after this tragic incident, one can say that nothing enables us to decipher him [Rimbaud] in his ultimate crisis, which interests us because he ceased everything literary: friends and works. Facts? He is said to have gone to England. . . . then he went to Germany, where he held teaching posts, and used his gift for languages, which he collected, having sworn off any heightening of his own; went to Italy . . . first by train . . . , then on foot; he crossed the Alps . . . and, finally . . . allowed himself to be officially repatriated.

Not before he had been brushed by a breeze from the East.

Somewhere in there is the mysterious yet natural date [of his departure, a date] on which we must agree that he rejected dreams—through his fault or theirs—and amputated from himself, alive and wide awake, all trace of poetry, later being able to find only far away, very far away, a new state of being . . . civilization failing to outlast, in the individual, the call of a supreme sign.

An unexpected report, in 1891, circulated in the journals: that he who was for us and always will remain a poet, landed in Marseille with a fortune, and, world traveler, arthritic, he let himself be operated on and had just died. . . . I feel, however, that prolonging the hope of a mature work is harmful, here, toward the exact interpretation of a unique adventure in the history of art. That of a child too precociously and peremptorily touched by the wings of literature, who, barely having had the time to live, used up its stormy and magisterial destiny, without recourse to any possible future. (pp. 515–18)

Thus Rimbaud, "one who was violently ravaged by literature" (p. 514), "he who was for us and always will remain a poet"(p. 517), "burst upon the poetic scene like a meteor, ignited by no motive other than his presence, streaking alone in the sky, and extinguished alone"(p. 512), "civilization failing to outlast, in the individual, the call of the supreme sign"(p. 517): "Everything would have remained the same since then without this considerable passage, just as no literary circumstance prepared for it: but the personal case remains, indelible" (p. 512).

"Cheap anecdotes," said Mallarmé, "are not lacking around someone who had lost the thread of his existence; they fell naturally into the newspapers": "But your ambition would be to see, in this mass of details, the *broad outlines* of a significant destiny; which, even in its apparent deviations, ought to maintain the rhythm of a singer along with a strange simplicity" (pp. 514–15).

This is, in my view, Mallarmé's second great insight and his final unexpected paradox, another stroke of genius in his vision of Rimbaud: Even when he sings of his own extinction, the meteor, says Mallarmé, remains a singer. Rimbaud's complexity and contradictions do not prevent, and should not hide from view, his power of melodious singing and its "strange simplicity". Simplicity is power of expression, of condensation and concision, a power of reduction of complexity—to basics of sonority and rhythm. These basics do not just govern Rimbaud's poetry: they predominate his destiny as well, a destiny in which the "broad outlines" are always visible: "But your ambition would be to see, in this mass of details, the *broad outlines* of a significant destiny." Despite its great complexity and its resistance to intelligibility, Rimbaud's destiny preserves the musical eloquence and the melodic rhythm of a singer. Rimbaud, says Mallarmé, is and remains "a singer," even when he becomes tragic, even when he, irreversibly, leaves the song behind, even when the song is covered and engulfed by the poet's final silence, which exceeds the song toward the singer's disappearance, toward the poet's meteoric act of vanishing. The meteoric destiny inscribed in Rimbaud's poetic words is still a destiny that sings. And this is—Mallarmé implies—the true miracle of Rimbaud's poetry and of Rimbaud's inimitable performance as a poet. In Rimbaud's meteoric rise and fall, it is not only the fall which strikes and inscribes itself in memory, as the momentum, the velocity, and the path of light that are Rimbaud's own and that no one else can follow: it is the physical and the poetical emergence of that path of sound and light that cannot be forgotten and remains indelible. Rimbaud remains forever this incomprehensible emergence, and its mysterious force—its stunning, enigmatic gift—of singing, and of singing with "a strange simplicity."

Everything would have remained the same since then without this *considerable passage*, just as no literary circumstance prepared for it: but the personal case remains, indelible.

Cheap anecdotes are not lacking around someone who had lost the thread of his existence; they fell naturally into the newspapers.

But your ambition would be to see, in this mass of details, the *broad outlines* of a significant destiny; which, even in its deviations, ought to maintain the rhythm of a singer along with a strange simplicity. (Mallarmé, April 1896)

"You were right to leave, Arthur Rimbaud": Poetry and Modernity (1973)

One must be absolutely modern. — RIMBAUD, *Adieu*[1]

To be modern is to tinker with the incurable.
— CIORAN, *Syllogisms of Bitterness*[2]

"Rimbaud," writes René Char, "is the first poet of a civilization that has not yet appeared. . . . But if I knew what Rimbaud is for me, I would know what poetry is ahead of me, and I would no longer have to write. . . ."[3] While the name of Rimbaud has been justly linked, since the Surrealists, with an unprecedented enterprise of rupture, and consequently, with an innovative kind of linguistic and poetic "departure,"[4] the testimony of Rimbaud himself about his own departure has been little studied: what Rimbaud has said about his own "modernity" remains essentially unread.

"You were right to leave, Arthur Rimbaud," says Char. In the name of poetry and of poetic language, Rimbaud is hailed for his audacity of innovation, and it is felt that his modernity, linguistically and existentially, is related to the courage of his act of leaving, and leaving behind. What is it that Rimbaud leaves? At the beginning of his history or his prehistory, Rimbaud, still only a precocious child with an unusual gift for languages and with uncommon talents and truly extraordinary critical intelligence, leaves his native town Charleville to escape his family, to run away from an unhappy and abusive mother and from the absence of a father (who had in turn left his wife and children when Rimbaud was six), to go to Paris, to join the society (or the fraternity) of poets, and to unite there with a famous host — and a poetic mentor — who will soon become his lover and his literary sponsor: the older and established master-poet and spellbinding poetic musician-singer, whom Mallarmé describes for his contemporaries as "the Great Verlaine."[5] This initial flight from home, and this inaugural departure toward new meaning, will be followed by a whole series of ruptures and departures, increasingly more radical ones. At the beginning of his own career as poet, Rimbaud deliberately and provocatively leaves, abandons commonsense and Reason, leaves social and linguistic rules and breaks away with customary codes and Bourgeois moral standards, in order to become, in his own terms, a "seer" and a visionary, an "objective poet," as opposed to a romantic or "subjective" one.[6] At the end of his too-short career as poet, which spans less than five years of explosive youthful productivity, he once again repeats the act of leaving: he leaves Verlaine, his lover and his mentor (who tries to shoot him to prevent his leaving, but to no avail), and consequently, leaves France, leaves French, his native tongue, leaves Europe, leaves the West, and goes to live in foreign landscapes and in foreign tongues, to work as a colonial trader and wander as a nomad in the deserts of Arabia and North Africa, renouncing and erasing his vocation as a writer, and leaving poetry and literature behind. At the very end of his young life, Rimbaud, having returned to Marseille to be operated on for knee cancer and having undergone a dramatic and traumatic operation that amputates his leg, still dreams of leaving France immediately and going back to Africa, but at this point can only (suddenly) depart from life, in prematurely dying, unexpectedly, at 37. At the end of this uncanny, powerful, and catastrophic life, departure therefore seals the poet's speechlessness, his voluntary abdication of his gifts as poet, and his enigmatic, tragic, unintelligible final silence. But at the beginning, Rimbaud writes with his departure, as with a pen. To put it differently, Rimbaud's departure is what constitutes him as a writer. Rimbaud's departure writes: it writes language; it writes life; it writes poetry; it writes a destiny. The spell Rimbaud has cast on us is linked to his departure. The departure in itself remains a mystery. Yet it is certain that this enigmatic fact (of language and of life: the fact of leaving), this fact that writes both poetry and silence, is connected at the same time to Rimbaud's unique and unrepeatable modernity, *and* to our own premature *loss* of his modernity, our premature loss of Rimbaud himself as poet, through his final act of leaving poetry itself, and leaving it behind. It is also certain that whatever is poetic in Rimbaud—the fatality of the poetic in Rimbaud—is related to this act of leaving: to the fact that his modernity—his vocation as a poet—remains uncompromising, and uncompromised.

This essay will attempt to analyze the link between Rimbaud's departure, his poetry, and his modernity by analyzing Rimbaud's language, and by listening to his own poetic words as a compelling, lyric, and dramatic *testimony*: testimony to the riddle of his life; testimony to the tensions of his writing; testimony to what one might call his oath to—his vocation of—modernity; testimony to what one might call (and this would be today my definition of Rimbaud): *modernity as destiny.*[7]

| | | |

"One must be absolutely modern," says Rimbaud. Too many would-be writers from today and yesterday are in a rush to acquiesce, to jump onto the Modernist bandwagon; too many "flags of ecstasy"[8] are waved for this slogan-idea, which crowns at once self-serving ads and "trendy" publications, and shares the urgency both of commercial and of cultural terrorism. Modernity sells: whether it be commodities, discourses, or ideas.

This inflationist marketing and commoditization of the new is, of course, far from anything Rimbaud had in mind. The poet's irony dismissed and parodied the "modern Ecclesiastes" of his era:

> "Rien n'est vanité; à la science, et *en avant!*" crie l'Ecclésiaste moderne, c'est-à-dire Tout le monde.[9]

> ["Nothing is vanity; science reigns; forward *march!*" cries the modern Ecclesiastes, that is, *Everyone.*]

From his earliest texts, Rimbaud as an apprentice-visionary and a would-be seer always marked his distance from the trendy fashions of his day. While he requires of poets "something new—ideas and forms," he immediately adds: "Every clever writer would think he has satisfied this requirement.—*That's not it.*"[10]

"One must be absolutely modern" ("*il faut être absolument moderne*"): this quintessential and defining sentence, in Rimbaud's text, is neither simple nor transparent. First of all, it is a paradoxical imperative, an oxymoron, defined by a contradiction in terms. What does it mean, "to be *absolutely* modern"? How can the *modern,* which is by definition *relative* (being historical through and through)—escape both history and time, and claim the status of the *absolute*? How, more generally, can something that belongs to the process of *becoming* achieve *being*—let alone "absolute" being? And since the French expression—"*il faut être absolument moderne*"—connotes at once necessity and lack ("*il faut*" can come from either the verb *falloir* ["to be necessary"] or from the verb *faillir* ["to lack, to fall short of"] and can thus mean either "we must" or "we lack"), the invitation to be modern right away contradicts itself.

What does the imperative *"il faut"* mean if it immediately puts itself in question, if it announces—on the level of its very language—that the modernity it asks for is rigorously, simultaneously impossible? What sense can we make of a normative ethical imperative we can't follow?

To tease out the problematics and the tensions through which Rimbaud's language at once calls for and condemns, precludes the concept of modernity, is not simply to show, by means of Rimbaud, how the concept contradicts itself, but rather to explore the ways in which Rimbaud's poetic quest for absolute modernity unsettles and shakes up the very text that writes it, in endowing Rimbaud's writing with its own concrete modes of production, and with its own singular poetic style and rhythm.

The attribute of contradiction has itself been defined by later poets as a modern attribute, a modern question par excellence: "What we propose," writes Char, "is that the modern question of incompatibilities be examined attentively, *modern* because it acts on the conditions of existence of our time . . . at once effervescent and ominous."[11]

It is instructive to observe how, out of its own contradictions, modern thought has thematized itself into a thought about the modern. Thus, Paul Valéry, reflecting on "the crisis of the [modern] mind," theorizes and conceptualizes the modernity of the crisis:

> And of what does the disorder of European thought consist? Of the free coexistence in all cultivated minds of the most dissimilar ideas, of the most opposite principles of life and knowledge. That is what characterizes a *modern* era.
>
> I don't hesitate to generalize the concept of the modern and to give that name to a certain kind of existence, and not treat it as a simple synonym for *contemporary*.[12]

But is it not already contradictory to *theorize* modernity both through and beyond the given specificity of its historic situation, to think poetically and theoretically, in general, not about "*the* modern era" but about "*a* modern era," not about "modern life," but about "*a* modern life that would be more abstract" (Baudelaire)[13]—to abstract, that is, a *concept* of modernity itself? Thus Baudelaire's ambition is nothing less than, as he puts it, to "draw the eternal out of the transitory."[14]

"Baudelaire is the first seer, king of poets, a real God,"[15] writes the young Rimbaud, who soon follows in Baudelaire's footsteps by proposing his own staggering, iconoclastic vision of modernity.

"One must be absolutely modern"; "I don't hesitate to generalize the concept of the modern." But the question is *how* one is to generalize precisely *such a* concept, such a designation of the particular. And why does such a generalization—so contradictory in purpose and by definition so "untimely"—seem so urgent and so *timely* for contemporary literature? Out of what space and what duration does one "draw the eternal out of the transitory"? Out of what historic moment does the untimely become timely? *Who* is speaking, *who* is generalizing, and with what kind of *authority*?

The pro-nouns of modernity

"One must be absolutely modern"; "*il faut être absolument moderne*": this categorical statement stresses the predicate of "*falloir*" but de-emphasizes the subject. "*Il*" in the "*il faut*" is a neutral subject, an empty sign. Logically, the verb has no subject: whether we translate "one must" or "it is necessary"—"*il faut*"—there is no *person* in the requirement to "be absolutely modern." Modernity has an absent subject. The utterance seems to be an impersonal truth, floating above the head of any speaking subject, beyond any narcissistic or egocentric "I."

But, on the other hand, the "modern" by definition seems to imply a *subjective* relation to time and language, to insert itself between the time of the statement and the time of the enunciation. The word's etymology goes back to the low Latin *modernus* (1361), from *modo,* "recently." From which comes "modern: that which takes into consideration recent developments in its field; is of its time," says the *Petit Robert,* or more precisely: "Which is of the time of the speaker, or of a relatively recent period." Which is *of the time of the speaker.* And even if "modern" were used in the Nietzschean sense meaning not "of one's time" but "against one's time,"[16] modernity would still be a function of "the speaker's time." "He's our affection and our present . . . He's our affection and our future . . . O *he and us!* O world!" cries Rimbaud in "Génie" ["Genius"].

Et si l'Adoration s'en va, sonne, sa promesse sonne: "Arrière ces superstitions, ces anciens corps, ces ménages et ces âges." C'est *cette époque-ci* qui a sombré![17]

[And if Adoration goes away, resounds, her promise resounds: "Get back, old superstitions and former bodies, old ménages and ages." It's *this* era right here that is sinking!]

However decentered the call for modernity appears, it depends on the voice of the speaking subject: he who says *modern* says "I." "This world in which *I* experience what *I* experience," writes Breton,

> this *modern* world, finally, blast! What do you want me to do about it? The surrealist voice will perhaps disappear. . . . I've lost count of all my disappearances.[18]

Whether I appear or disappear, collect myself or scatter myself, include or exclude myself, I say "*modern*" and thus I speak, and thus I say "I am speaking."

Modernity therefore belongs, linguistically, to the grammatical category of the first person. Although it is substantivized, it retains a certain pronominal logic. Like the "I," it functions as a linguistic "shifter"[19] that includes, each time it is used, both its own verbal sign and its user. Theoretically and generally, then, the "modern" is a vacant sign, ready to be occupied by anyone who picks it up and assumes and appropriates it in the very act of speaking. Modernity can only be defined in terms of *locution*—not in terms of an object, as an authentically nominalized sign would be. It refers not to some "objective" spatiotemporal reality but to the reality of discourse, to the very act of using language. As a self-referential shifter, modernity—in its most rigorous sense—can neither be denied nor verified. It escapes the truth-claims it both calls for and announces.

"One must be absolutely modern": as a discursive void that claims and reaches toward the fullness and the plenitude of "being," modernity is situated at the very heart of literary "truth." It is above all a structure of pathos, and designates only a certain *relation to the speaking subject.*

Concretely, then, our task is to engage in an analysis of the subject of the text. What does the *je* who would be modern have to say about himself?

But that's precisely the point: he says that he is not; he says that he is not the "I" we think he is.

Too bad for the wood that finds it has become a violin . . .

> Car Je est un autre. Si le cuivre s'éveille clairon, il n'y a rien de sa faute. Cela m'est évident: j'assiste à l'éclosion de ma pensée: je la regarde, je l'écoute: je lance un coup d'archet: la symphonie fait son remuement dans les profondeurs, ou vient d'un bond sur la scène.[20]

> [For I is an other. If the brass wakes up a bugle, it is not responsible for it. This seems obvious to me: I witness the unfolding of my thought: I look at it; I listen to it; I raise my baton: the symphony murmurs in the depths or bounds onto the stage.]

As a spectator rather than an actor in "the unfolding" of his own thought, the *je* is witness to it, *undergoes* it: the act of thinking imprints itself on a receptive subject, who feels its effects rather than possessing its keys.

> C'est faux de dire: Je pense. On devrait dire: On me pense. Pardon du jeu de mots.
> Je est un autre. Tant pis pour le bois qui se trouve violon, et nargue aux inconscients, qui ergotent sur ce qu'ils ignorent tout à fait.[21]

> [It's false to say: I think. One should rather say: I am thought. Excuse my play on words.
> I is an other. Too bad for the wood that finds it has become a violin; the unconscious *savants* are ridiculous, constantly *ergoting* on what they know nothing about.]

It is fascinating and surprising to note the rigor with which Rimbaud inscribes, rewrites, and deconstructs another text that can dimly be made out through his epigrammatic text: the Cartesian Cogito. *Cogito ergo sum: Cogito*—I think; "it's false to say: I think"; *ergo*—therefore: "the unconscious *savants* are ridiculous, constantly *ergoting* [reasoning] on what they know nothing about"; *sum*—I am: "I is an other." Not even "I *am* an other," which would make that other only a double or reflection of the same Cartesian "I," assured of being—of being in its proper place—, assured of inhabiting an "I am." No; in place of "I am," this text says "I is." Its deconstruction of the subject is both violent and rigorous.

"I am thought." ("*On me pense*"). In the twist of the French expression, the traditional subject, the Cartesian subject, becomes here the direct object [*me*], undergoing rather than controlling his own thought, acted upon rather than actor, passive rather than active, while the grammatical, syntactic subject is the "one" who is no-one, an "indefinite personal pronoun ["*on*": *on me pense*]." Through the "on," individuation becomes the result of an impersonal force, or rather, the person becomes unindividuated. It is an anonymous force that escapes the condition of person: whether it be the Freudian unconscious (what Freud calls *id* and what Lacan would call "*le ça*": another indefinite pronoun), or more generally language, the social body of discourse, the scripts of the culture that bespeak me and that speak *through* me: "I am thought." As Samuel Beckett will later put it, "I am of words, I am made out of words, other people's words . . . I am all those words, all those strangers, that verbal dust."[22] Thought is not the attribute of a self—spontaneous, substantive, self-present—but rather an effect inscribed on a passive object, who feels that his own intelligence, his own faculty of speaking—through which he learns to say "I"—works in and upon him, not *by means of* him. What results from thought, the "work" of art, is thus inhabited by impersonal forces, and often unbeknownst to the author:

Si le cuivre s'éveille clair-ON, il n'y a rien de sa faute.[23]
Tant pis pour le bois qui se trouve viol-ON . . .[24]

[If the brass wakes up as a bugle (*clair-ON*), it is not responsible for it.
Too bad for the wood that finds it has become a violin (*viol-ON*)] . . .

Several times, Rimbaud traces his "thought," his "talents," back to an impersonal source, an "indefinite pronoun," which functions like the null set of the person: "one [*on*]," "another" or "an other," "someone," "no one [*personne*]."

Je vais dévoiler tous les mystères . . .
Écoutez! . . .
J'ai tous les talents.—Il n'y a *personne* ici et il y a *quelqu'un*. [25]

[I'm going to unveil all the mysteries . . .
Listen! . . .
I possess all the talents. — There is *no one* here and there's *someone*.]

"No one," "someone." But there still remain authors who believe in their "creative selves," and who, blind to their relation to language, caught in the lure of their mirror image, think they are the origin of their complete works, instead of understanding that they themselves are its *effects*. Those are the "subjective poets," the opposite of the modern poet, whose "objectivity" consists in his impersonality. "Objective poetry" or just "Poetry" period, belongs to "one [*on*]"; it lies beyond the murmurs centered on a self; it speaks beyond any narcissistic self-complacency.

Tant d'égoïstes se proclament auteurs; il en est bien d'autres qui s'attribuent leur progrès intellectuel.[26]

[There are so many egoistic scribblers who call themselves authors; others attribute to themselves all intellectual progress!]

Si les vieux imbéciles n'avaient pas trouvé du Moi que la signification fausse, nous n'aurions pas à balayer ces millions de squelettes qui, depuis un temps infini, accumulent les produits de leur intelligence borgnesse, en s'en clamant les auteurs![27]

[If those old imbeciles hadn't found only the false significance of the Self, we wouldn't have to sweep away so many skeletons, which, from time immemorial, have gathered up the products of their half-baked intelligence and proclaimed themselves authors!]

"For I is an other." In spite of its apparent pronominal logic, the "I" is here, like modernity itself, made into a noun ("I *is*"), but not in order to become, like the Self, a substance which is self-identical and present to itself: I is — another. It is not just that the "I" is in this way *doubly subverted* (first, because he says he is "an other," and second, because he is dislodged from the "I am," dispossessed of the verbal form "proper" to him, and is thus not in *his own* "being"), but also, and more radically, in this opposition-equivalence Rimbaud surprisingly sets up between the "I" and "another," it is "being" itself that is pulverized, the *copula* itself that bursts: the very principle of identity no longer resembles itself. Identity is alterity.

The text in which Rimbaud writes this subversion of the "I" for the first time, this breakup of identity through the "I is an other [I is an-other]," is a letter he sends to his teacher, Izambard, which serves as a commentary and as an introduction to a poem he also sends along. To analyze and measure the complexity of Rimbaud's speech, we should attempt to read here the poem in the context of the letter.

"The Tortured Heart," which will later be re-entitled "The Stolen Heart," describes explicitly a scene of homosexual rape in a military barrack. This is perhaps something that happened to Rimbaud during the Commune. But the autobiographical referent does not really matter. The problem the text poses, glossed in the letter, is that of knowing how a *fantasy* or an event of rape (understand: of the raped subject) is transformed into a *poetics* of rape, in order to sustain and animate the prestigious "I is an other [I is another]."

Mon triste coeur bave à la poupe
Mon coeur couvert de caporal:
Ils y lancent des jets de soupe,
Mon triste coeur bave à la poupe:
Sous les quolibets de la troupe
Qui pousse un rire général,
Mon triste coeur bave à la poupe,
Mon coeur couvert de caporal!

. . . .

Quand ils auront tari leurs chiques,
Comment agir, ô coeur volé?
Ce seront des hoquets bachiques
Quand ils auront tari leurs chiques:
J'aurai des sursauts stomachiques,
Moi, si mon coeur est ravalé:
Quand ils auront tari leurs chiques
Comment agir, ô coeur volé?[28]

. . . .

[My sad heart foams at the stern,
My heart covered with tobacco spit:
They even spew soup on it in turn,
My sad heart foams at the stern:

Hearing the troop's jeers, my ears burn,
And they break out in general laughter.
My sad heart foams at the stern,
My heart covered with tobacco spit!

. . . .

When they have finally emptied their cheeks,
How will you act, o stolen heart?
When you are racked with Bacchic hics,
When they have finally emptied their cheeks,
And, as for me, my stomach churns and creaks.
If my heart is abased and swollen
When they have finally emptied their cheeks,
How will you act, o heart so stolen?]

The third-person plural, the "They," plays in this drama the syntactic role of "one [*on*]" — the role of an indefinite subject pronoun — whereas the speaking subject, metonymically designated by the "tortured heart," is reduced to the status not only of an object, but of a *stolen* object, taken away from its owner. The violated subject is thus dispossessed of what is *proper* to it: at once the cleanliness, the intactness of his body [*la propreté de son corps*] and the possession, the propriety of his heart [*la propriété de son coeur*]. The "heart" here can symbolize the Narcissistic, fictive image of the "Self," the professions of a romantic "beautiful soul." If the "heart" here regrets its lost purity, it is because the rape has robbed him of his dream-identity: that identity was no less false for that, propped up by bourgeois idealism. Dispossessed of his own mastery and of his own self-image, the subject, now dis-heartened [*é-coeuré*], his heart and body violated, awakens to the consciousness that "I" is "another." "Too bad for the wood that finds itself a VIOL-in; the unconscious *savants* are ridiculous, *ergoting* [reasoning] on things they know nothing about." The violence undergone changes into the violence of thought: "The violence of the poison distorts my members."[29] "All types of *violent* monstrosities *violate* the atrocious gestures of Hortense."[30] Every thought, then, becomes "vol" and "*viol*" ("theft" and "rape"), every thought becomes a newly ravished proof of the dislocation of a system recognized to be false. And since every theft (*vol*) is, at the same time, a violation (*viol*) of the bourgeois code, a *coup* against the regime of the authoritative, self-possessed, proprietary Subject, the theft—on the level of pragmatics and of politics, as well as on the level of ideologies in general—becomes a necessary and euphoric "Song of War."

> Le printemps est évident, car
> Du Coeur des Propriétés vertes
> *Le vol* de Thiers et de Picard
> Tient des splendeurs grandes ouvertes! [31]

> [Springtime is everywhere, for
> Out of the heart of the greening Properties,
> The theft from Thiers and from Picard
> Has released the landscape's liberties and open splendors!]

But the *Stolen Heart* will have to be changed into a *Drunken Boat* in order for the *linguistic* resources of the rape to be fully tapped, in order for the text itself to elucidate and measure the distance traveled by the "I" become "another": from the "stolen heart" to the "violated boat,"[32] a biographical given becomes a theory of poetic language. The story of the boat begins, as is well known, with an act of violence (*vol, viol*): the "taking" or hijacking (theft or rape) of the boat-subject by Indian pirates ("loud-mouthed redskins"):

> Comme je descendais des Fleuves impassibles,
> Je ne me sentis plus guidé par les haleurs:
> Des Peaux-Rouges criards les avaient pris pour cibles,
> Les ayant cloués nus aux poteaux de couleurs.
>
> . . . .
>
> Plus douce qu'aux enfants la chair des pommes sures,
> L'eau verte pénétra ma coque de sapin
> Et des taches de vins bleus et des vomissures
> Me lava, dispersant gouvernail et grappin.
> Et dès lors, je me suis baigné dans le Poème
> De la Mer . . .[33]

> [As I descended the impassive Water,
> I felt I was no longer guided by the haulers' lines:

Loud-mouthed redskins had used them for practicing slaughter,
And had nailed them naked to totem-pole-ready pines.

. . . .

Mellower than the flesh of sour apples to little tots,
The green water seeped into my hull,
Washing away the blue wine and vomit spots,
Scattering my rudder, and making my hooks dull.
Since then, I've bathed in the Poem
Of the Sea . . .]

The metaphor of the boat-body dispossessed of its Guides signifies, here
again, the subversion of Mastery, of all illusions of authority and
"proper"-ness that the subject might entertain. But propriety has a particular significance here: what is "stolen" from the boat is the *sense* it
had of its own aims: the goals proper to it, the *direction* it was going in,
the sense of its itinerary. It is through a *loss* of sense, and not through
an *increase* in sense, that the subject undergoes his own inscription
into a text.

Ce Charme! il prit âme et corps
Et dispersa tous efforts.

Que comprendre à ma parole?
Il fait qu'elle fuie et *vole!* [34]

[That Charm! It took on body and soul,
And all efforts against it, it dispersed whole.

What can be understood from what I say?
That it must flee and fly and steal away!]

The stolen heart is transformed into a poetic word that ravishes its
subject, gives him wings with which to fly up:

— Des écumes de fleurs ont bercé mes dérades
Et d'ineffables vents m'ont ailé par instants. [35]

[— The foam of flowers rocked my driftings,
And ineffable winds sometimes gave me wings and buoyed
me up.]

Adrift on desires, *possessed* by the resources and potencies of language, the boat is violently caulked and violently thought (*panés — pensé*) by the sea. This dissolution of the subject within the words that write him is the condition of poetic language: it is only by losing all sense of direction that the drunken boat can bathe in the "Poem of the Sea." Writing is experienced as a violent process of *vol* (theft) and of *viol* (rape) of meaning. Poetry becomes identified with the linguistic process of the subject's dispossession.

Rimbaud's "Coup de 'dés'": de-regulation, de-lirium, de-parture

Violence to or from the subject is generalized and systematized into a theory of poetic language:

> Le poète se fait voyant par un long, immense et raisonné dérègle-
> ment de tous les sens.[36]

> [The poet becomes a seer through a long, immense, and reasoned
> deregulation of all senses.]

The "reasoned" deregulation of all senses arises out of a "system,"[37] "study,"[38] "work":[39] it is supported by a whole lineage of textual notions, whose presence is marked by "Des Coups de 'Dé-'s:"[40] "de-regulations [*dé-reglement*]," "dis-placements [*dé-placements*]," "dis-coveries [*dé-couvertes*]," "de-luges [*dé-luges*]," "de-liria [*dé-lires*]," "de-partures [*dé-parts*]," etc. The frequency and insistence of negative prefixes starting with "d," the constant sonorous, phonetic hammering of these de-s and dis-es [French *dé*], makes explicit what the poetic "work" consists of: a *general* enterprise of de-*construction*. "Lightning and thunder, — arise and roll, — Water and sadness, arise and bring back the Floods."[41]

> Mes faims, tournez. *Paissez, faims,*
>   *Le pré des sons* . . .
> Mangez les *cailloux qu'on brise,*
> Les vielles pierres d'églises;
> Les galets des vieux *dé-luges* . . .[42]

> [My hungers, spin. *Graze, my hungers,*
>   *In the field of sounds* . . .
> Eat the *pebbles* that are split,

And the old church *stones;*
And the *boulders* of former floods . . .]

We are witnessing, indeed, the "de-regulation" of all senses, in all the senses of the word "senses." One remembers the sharp retort Rimbaud gave his mother when she asked him what he could have possibly meant in *A Season in Hell:* "I meant what it says, literally and in all senses." The deregulation, then, of all *senses:* (linguistic) *significations,* (geographical) *directions,* and (corporeal, physiological) *sensations,* — one and all without exception are subjected to a trial by reversal, in search of dis-equilibrium; the enterprise of perverting, de-viating, making a de-tour, precisely, from the "correct" path (Latin *pervertere* — "to in-vert," "to turn around") — pertains as much to language as to the body; the classical system of ethical, linguistic, ideological, and methodological prohibitions is methodically dis-organized: "All the forms of love, suffering, madness,"[43] a "demonic"[44] attempt to drive the usual codes crazy.

Je finis par trouver sacré le *dés-ordre* de mon esprit.[45]
Jamais *dé-lires* ni tortures semblables.[46]

[I ended up finding the *dis-order* of my spirit sacred.
Never have there been such *de-liriums* and tortures.]

"De-lirium": from Latin "delirare," to be deranged, from *de-,* "down" + *lira,* "furrow"; in French, "de-lire" sounds like "un-read" [de-, *un-,* + lire, *to read*]: to de-code the "Vowels" (the *corpus delicti*) in order to vio-late, de-tatch,[47] dis-perse the code; to dis-mantle and dis-articulate the classical way of reading that is linear and oriented around sense, to dis-lodge it and dis-seminate it "literally and in all senses." It is to become systematically un-educated in reading in the classic sense: "It began as a course of study."[48] To un-learn existing literature:

Je trouvais *dé-risoires* les célébrités de la peinture et de la poésie moderne. J'aimais les peintures idiotes . . . ; la littérature *dé-modée* . . .[49]

[I considered all the celebrities of modern painting or writing *de-risory.* I liked idiotic paintings . . . ; *un-fashionable* literature . . .]

Functioning as a de-lirium, "deliria too big for our lyrics," too big for "our *lyres*,"[50] Rimbaud's modernity "un-reads," "de-lyricizes" the fashionable lyric, and actively "un-fashions" so-called modern poetry.

If the new "deliria" are "too big for our lyres," then un-tying tongues is also un-leashing them; "The search for a [new] language"[51] is the ultimate aim of poetic deregulation; "inventing a poetic word that would some day be accessible *to all senses*."[52]

> J'écrivais des silences, des nuits, je notais l'inexprimable.
>   Je fixais des vertiges.[53]
>
> [I wrote down silences, I wrote down nights; I noted the inexpressible, I pinned down dizziness.]

To re-write the codes, to re-read or un-read them starting from "silence" and "night" is to push back the limits of language. To dis-place limits is in fact Rimbaud's general ambition here:

> Je rêvais voyages de *dé-couvertes* dont on n'a pas de relations, républiques sans histoires, . . . *dé-placements* de races et de continents . . .[54]
>
> [I dreamt of voyages of dis-covery we have heard nothing about; republics with no history; . . . the dis-placements of races and continents . . .]

The writing of the limit also necessarily becomes a writing of de-parture. For someone who feels, to borrow Mallarmé's verse, like a "solitary captive of the threshold," displacements become an obsession, a haunted and persistent thought:

> Parce qu'il faudra que je m'en aille, très loin, un jour.[55]
>
> [For I'll have to go away, very far away, some day.]

To be haunted by de-parture is another de-lirium, a frenzy of de-tachment: it un-ties the subject from any belonging to a place, to a family. De-regulation is a de-racination: the "I" who is "another" or "an other" recognizes himself to be essentially a nomad, a de-centered subject:

Ah! Cette vie de mon enfance, la grande route par tous les temps;
plus *dés-intéressé* que le meilleur des mendiants, fier de n'avoir ni
pays, ni amis.[56]

[Ah! My childhood life, the open road in any weather, more *dis-interested* than the best of beggars, proud of having neither country nor friends.]

And if departures tear apart and "de-stroy hearts,"[57] destruction is also
a force: a force of rupture, of dis-junction and de-tachment. The act
of leaving—the departure, repeatedly begun again—tries to keep on
moving, and in so doing, to conjure itself: to conjure, master, and control the very *stops of life.*

> Assez vu . . .
> Assez eu . . .
> Assez connu. Les arrêts de la vie . . .
> *Départ* dans l'affection et le bruit *neufs!*[58]

> [Seen enough . . .
> Had enough . . .
> Known enough. The stops of life . . .
> Departure into *new* affections and *new* sounds!]

"A-dieu"

> *Un Ennui, désolé par les cruels espoirs.*
> *Croit encore à l'adieu suprême des mouchoirs.*
>
> [Boredom, desolated by the cruel hopes,
> Still believes in a handkerchief's supreme farewell.]
> — MALLARMÉ, *"Brise marine"*

"In poetry," writes René Char, "one lives only in the places one
leaves."[59] Which is to say that displacement, departure—or modernity,
if you wish—far from being an accident, a possibility, is on the contrary an essential necessity inherent in poetry itself. Which is also to
say that poetry has never *finished* leaving. The problem of departure for
Rimbaud is precisely that of understanding the end: in leaving, Rimbaud envisions some definitive accomplishment of rupture, the radical

writing of an "adieu." The whole writing effort of *A Season in Hell* is meant to lead up to that "Adieu";[60] to leave *once and for all;* to escape the "seasons";[61] to get out of the cyclical, repetitive temporal scheme; to be without memory, or, better, to be "absolutely modern."

> Oui, l'heure nouvelle est au moins très sévère.
> Car je puis dire que la victoire m'est acquise . . . Tous les souvenirs
>   immondes s'effacent . . .
> Il faut être absolument moderne.[62]

> [Yes, the new hour is at least very harsh . . .
>   For I can say that my mission is victoriously accomplished . . .
> All the horrible memories are fading . . .
>   One must be absolutely modern.]

What Rimbaud is searching for, in the text that he calls "Adieu" and that closes *A Season in Hell,* is thus a "way out" of the past that will emerge into an inaugural and originary present. The "Adieu" is an act of erasure; a radical effort of forgetting designed to render one radically contemporary.

But this obsession with the farewell and the "adieu" carries within it an impossible desire; the very insistence on the "Adieu" testifies at the same time to an inherent incapacity to detach oneself or to forget:

> Je disais adieu au monde dans d'espèces de romances.[63]

> [I used to say farewell to the world in romance-like poems].

"I was always saying farewell [*je disais adieu*]": that the word of farewell (*adieu*) — the word that defies repetition — is here constantly being repeated, points to the problem of a departure caught within a repetitive structure. However radical the break, it is never — and cannot be — absolutely modern. The search for an originary and nonrepetitive modernity is itself structured like paradox and repetition. The last word is precisely what never stops recommencing. Departure is an endless task, and constantly needs to be begun again. The "Adieu" thus signifies not the ultimate leave-taking, the definitive break, but the open system of the repetition of breaks and ruptures.

What is the place of modernity in this signifying chain of repetitions? It is the question Baudelaire asks in his poem, "Le Voyage" ("The Voyage"):

> Singulière fortune où le but se déplace,
> Et, n'étant nulle part, peut être n'importe où![64]

> [It is an odd destiny, where the end keeps shifting,
> And, being nowhere, could in fact be anywhere!]

Modernity occupies a non-place. Departures are thus, at the same time, the unsettling revelation of the impossibility of leaving. As Rimbaud puts it: "One does not leave."[65]

> La même magie bourgeoise à tous les points où la malle nous déposera![66]

> [The same old bourgeois magic wherever the suitcase sets us down!]

As soon as one has understood that, the only possible response to Baudelaire's question "Must one leave? Stay?" (*Faut-il partir, rester?*") is the answer given by the poem:

> . . . Si tu peux rester, reste;
> Pars, s'il le faut . . .[67]

> Mais les vrais voyageurs sont ceux-là seuls qui partent
> Pour partir; . . .
> De leur fatalité jamais ils ne s'écartent.[68]

> [. . . If you can stay, stay.
> Leave, if you must . . .

> But the genuine travelers are those only who leave
> So as to leave . . .
> From their destiny they never stray . . .]

Perhaps it is not possible truly to *leave*. But for Rimbaud, neither is it possible to *not leave*.

Je ne puis plus, baigné de vos langueurs, ô lames,
Enlever leur sillage aux porteurs de cotons,
Ni traverser l'orgueil des drapeaux et des flammes,
Ni nager sous les yeux horribles des pontons.[69]

[I am no longer able, once I've bathed in your languorousness,
    waves,
To follow the wakes of the cotton-haulers,
Nor to move through the pride of flags and flames,
Nor swim beneath the horrid eyes of pontoons.]

"I am no longer able": the "drunken boat" assumes, not without regret, its paradoxical fatality: its inability to *not* leave, its *impotence* to
not go in search of a "future *vigor*." Modernity pulls the subject toward
a fated departure: but a departure that compulsively repeats itself.

Un pas de toi c'est la levée des nouveaux hommes et leur en
    marche.
    Ta tête se détourne: le nouvel amour! Ta tête se retourne:—le
nouvel amour![70]

[Just one of your steps raises new men and sets them marching.
    Your head is turned: a new kind of love! Your head turns back:
    a new kind of love!]

"L'amour est à réinventer, on le sait." Love—"affection and the present"[71]—is always "to be *re*-invented, as we know."[72] What can a head *do*
besides *turn* and *re-turn* to hail each new love? The illusion of modernity is repeated; but there is no new *sense* (direction or signification) to
the movements of the head, unless it be energetic movement in itself,
the energy of life itself, of the repetition as perpetual movement.

If the "new love" unmasks the illusion, the error or the lie of former
loves, it cannot avoid but repeat the error, indulge again in the fascination by a new illusion, heading straight for the catastrophe of a new
unmasking.

Il est l'affection et le présent . . . Il est affection et l'avenir . . .
Il est l'amour, mesure parfaite et réinventée . . .
    Ô monde! et le chant clair des malheurs nouveaux.[73]

[He's affection and the present . . . He's affection and the future . . .
He's love, a perfect, reinvented measure . . .
   O world! And the clear melody of new catastrophes . . .]

Modernity's "Adieu" is thus a farewell to love; a new farewell to an old
love.

Un bel avantage, c'est que je puis rire des vieilles amours men-
songères, et frapper de honte ces couples menteurs.[74]

[One beautiful advantage is that I can now laugh at the old deceptive loves, and hit with shame all those lying couples.]

Rimbaud's originality was to have sensed that modernity itself could
be viewed as a problem of coupling: of the *couple,* on the double level
of desire and of language; whether the couple be of actual lovers, or of
signifier and its signified, of a word and its (referential, truthful) meaning. For the same duality between emotion (on the one hand) and language (on the other), the same duplication that exists between the two
poems *Deliria* ("Delirium I: The Foolish Virgin and the Infernal Spouse"
and "Delirium II: The Alchemy of the Word") is once again repeated
and narrated in "Adieu," but as a double error and a double abdication. Modernity arises as an awareness of the inadequation and
illusion at the heart of the couple: the nonresemblance and noncoinci-
dence between a signifying system and a signified system. Modernity
is thus the recognition of the necessity and of the inescapability of the
arbitrary: a recognition of the arbitrary nature of the sign, certainly;
but also, of the constant temptation to fill in the void of desire—to
breach over the semiotic gap—only to recognize each time the constitutional bad fit between "the time of desire" and that of "essential
satisfaction."[75] It is in this gap (in the sign, between signifier and signified; in the couple, the split occasioned by the unseen differences)—as
opposed to the identity, the adequation and compatibility asked of
both the couple and the sign—it is in this gap within both the couple
and the sign that the "lie" slips in, in the form of illusion and suspicion, and in the inevitability of interpretation. The arbitrariness of the
sign necessitates its *reading.* Modernity is in effect itself, above all else,
a *reading act.* The text of "Adieu" is an *interpretation,* a demystification,
i.e., a questioning of the previous concept of modernity, and of its driving forces—love, and literature itself. "Adieu" thus establishes the

whole poetic volume of *A Season in Hell* as a reading of itself: as the resurgence of its own singular modernity, in and through the repetition of its own acts of rereading.

Through the functioning of the interpretive process in "Adieu," and through the hall of mirrors and reflections between love and literature, Rimbaud discovers, on the one hand, that desire is language and desire for language, that love is a discourse, *is only literature;* and, on the other hand, that literature itself is but a simulacrum: only an illusion of love. If *everything* turns out to be literature, that does not mean that literature itself has the key to truth. The "Adieu" of modernity becomes then the symbolic locus where literature becomes conscious of its exile from reality, of its existence as an irremediable structure of error.

To say good-bye to error is, henceforth, for Rimbaud, to say good-bye to literature. The ultimate form of literary break would be that through which literature detaches itself from literature. Thus it is that with Rimbaud "literature annexes its own absence," "establishes itself on a refusal."[76] But refusing poetry is still poetry. Turning away from literature, modernity is still moved by a *literary* energy, a *textual* force of difference and of decentering: an energy through which writing keeps going even as it attempts to erase itself, and literature is repeated while turning itself upside down. It is this refusal and these rhetorical reversals that explain the paradoxical statements of modern poets: "Poetry is inadmissible; besides, it does not exist."[77] These statements can only be read as *denials* proffered by poets, that is, as statements in the highest degree *poetic.* But the text of modernity, haunted by its own silence and by its own refusals, destabilizes and unsettles the security, the safety, and the innocence of its own utterances, and challenges and undercuts the comfort and legitimacy of its strange status as "poetry" or "literature." "What is unique about poetry," notes Georges Bataille, thinking about Rimbaud and Lautréamont: "What is unique about poetry inheres in those moments that are farthest away from its most beautiful finds: compared to its defeat, poetry crawls on the ground. Thus, people agree to set these two poets apart, because both add to the gleam of their poems the blinding light of their failure. Ambiguity is linked to their names, but both of them exhausted the sense of a poetry that turns into its opposite, arising out of hatred for poetry. Any poetry that does not rise to the non-sense of poetry embodies just the emptiness of poetry — pretty poetry."[78]

Je dois enterrer mon imagination et mes souvenirs.
Une belle gloire d'artiste et de conteur emportée![79]

[I have to bury my imagination and my memories.
Another glorious, beautiful career as an artist and storyteller carried away!]

Adieu, chimères, idéals, erreurs.[80]

[Adieu, illusions, ideals, errors!]

. . . je puis . . . frapper de honte ces couples menteurs . . . et il me
sera loisible *de posséder la vérité dans une âme et un corps.*[81]

[I can . . . hit with shame those lying couples . . . and I'll have time
to *possess the truth in a soul and in a body.*]

To get outside of literature is still to want to have it; to "hit with shame
those lying couples" is to thirst for their truth. There is only one
way—a radical way—to escape the past: to get outside of language altogether. To "possess the truth," for Rimbaud, is to repudiate language,
to understand that the truth cannot be possessed. "Absolutely modern," literature will henceforth dwell in its own silence.

Il faut être absolument moderne.
Point de cantiques: tenir le pas gagné.[82]

[One must be absolutely modern.
No celebratory songs: one should simply hold the line one
    reaches, hold one's step as won.]

No celebratory songs: the ultimate farewell rejoins, in the text of
"Adieu," the etymological sense of this final word: "À-Dieu," "to God."
The march toward modernity is a "hard night" comparable to the
night Christ spent on the cross.

Dure nuit! Le sang séché fume sur ma face et je n'ai rien derrière
moi que cet horrible arbrisseau! . . .[83]

[Hard night! Dried blood steams on my face, and I have nothing
behind me but this horrible shrub! . . .]

The horrible shrub is of course the cross:

> ... l'ivresse, les mille amours qui m'ont crucifié.[84]

[... intoxications, the thousand loves that have crucified me.]

> Le combat spirituel est aussi brutal que la bataille d'hommes; mais la vision de la justice est le plaisir de Dieu seul.[85]

[The spiritual fight is as brutal as a fight between men, but the vision of justice is enjoyed by God alone.]

To be human is to be condemned to error: the vision of justice is not to be had. The only relation one can have with God (that "vision of justice," that ultimate principle of Truth, Meaning, and Being) is the one that leads Christ to accept God's disappearance or desertion. To be Christ (the Word) is precisely, in this text, to learn that God does not exist: to recognize that language does not coincide with truth. And Rimbaud's Christ, like Nerval's *Christ Among the Olive Trees,* could indeed cry out:

> Frères, je vous trompais: Abîme! abîme! abîme!
> Le dieu manque à l'autel où je suis la victime ...
> Dieu n'est pas ! Dieu n'est plus ...
>
> En cherchant l'oeil de Dieu, je n'ai vu qu'une orbite
> Vaste, noire et sans fond, d'où la nuit qui l'habite
> Rayonne sur le monde et s'épaissit toujours ...[86]
>
> [My Brothers, I misled you: Abyss! Abyss! Abyss!
> God is missing from the altar on which I sacrifice myself ...
> God is not! God is no longer! ...
>
> While seeking God's eye, I found only an eye-hole—
> Vast, black, and bottomless—from which the night it contains
> Sheds onto the world growing thicker and thicker ...]

Future Vigor, Bottomless Nights

> ... *parce qu'en raison d'un événement toujours que j'expliquerai, il n'est pas de Présent, non—un présent n'existe pas. ... Mal informé celui qui se crierait son propre contemporain.*

[. . . because in function of an event that I still have to explain, there is no Present, no — the present does not exist. . . . He who would proclaim himself his own contemporary is badly informed.] — MALLARMÉ, *"L'Action Restreinte"*

The farewell of Christ to God constitutes the prolongation of the anguished question asked by the Drunken Boat:

Est-ce ces nuits sans fond que tu dors et t'exiles;
Million d'oiseaux d'or, ô future Vigueur?[87]

[Is it in those bottomless nights that you sleep and withdraw,
O flock of golden birds, O future Vigor?]

As the capital letter in the last verse indicates, modernity is an allegory: the allegory — and the vision — of a "future Vigor." The dreamed future potency is first of all a *figure,* whose form shifts places and repeats itself along a chain of substitutions, but whose sense is destined to be exiled and withdrawn. The *"future* Vigor" is by definition what cannot present itself, what is never present, what has no *proper* meaning: instead it constantly backs farther away into a vanishing point, a "bottomless night." Dizzy with the loss of balance that constitutes it, modernity, once nevertheless sought as a point of origin, a new beginning and a founding principle, swerves and dissolves into a bottomless night. It is as though modernity were aspired by its own illimitation. "I get close to poetry," writes Bataille, "but in order to just miss it."[88] Isn't what we can learn from Rimbaud similar? Doesn't Rimbaud precisely teach us that we always approach modernity — or poetry — so as to miss them? Poetry announces its own lack; it is entirely constituted by its own deficiency. Isn't modernity, too, an excess of itself built on its own lack? It has too much of its own absence; it is a void open to the excess of desire, always at odds with itself, always displaced in relation to its center, lacking its own balance and falling short of its own identity.

Modernity inheres, thus, in its own problematic status. The energy that destabilizes it is the energy of a relentless, never-ending question. Rimbaud has left us; the poet is gone, but his interrogation does not cease. The question that his poetry articulates remains, and is only perpetuated, amplified, and powerfully echoed by his final silence:

Est-ce en ces nuits sans fond que tu dors et t'exiles,
Million d'oiseaux d'or, ô future Vigueur?

[Is it in those bottomless nights that you sleep and withdraw,
O flock of golden birds, O future Vigor?]

Structuring itself around this central question, Rimbaud's text, instead of answering it, radically shakes up the question's context. "The
modern," writes C. G. Jung, "is the man who has just appeared; a modern problem is a question that has just been raised and whose answer
is still in the future. So doesn't the psychic problem of modern man,
even in the best of cases, consist in asking questions that might be
entirely different if we had the vaguest idea of what the future answer
might be?"[89] The modern is a question whose answer is missing. But
wandering around in the absence of an answer keeps the question
moving. In fact, the question of the modern turns out to be the very
question of the text, and the question of the text is—*pour qui la lit,*
for whoever is reading it. The text is essentially modern in Rimbaud's
sense—it too has no present; its golden birds scatter in all directions;
they are disseminated (as Rimbaud would say) *literally and in all senses;*
the Vigor of the text is always in the *future,* since no reading can ex-
haust—or even tackle—the bottomlessness of its nights.

"One must be absolutely modern"

"He who is satisfied with nothing, how could we be satisfied with him?"
— RENÉ CHAR, *Recherche de la Base et du Sommet*

With Rimbaud gone and his pen abdicated, we have nevertheless inherited, along with his tormented question, an imperative, a sort of
ethics: "One must be absolutely modern." A rule that is all the more
ambiguous for casting doubt on the very possibility of its fulfillment;
an imperative all the more complex insofar as Rimbaud's text inscribes
modernity not only as the very locus of the inaccessible, but as an
attempt whose mandatory failure determines the specific modes of its
pathbreaking, dazzling utterance. The—absolute—modernity of Rimbaud is precisely that impasse, that tension through which the literary
text discovers its own radical inability to be "absolutely modern." How
should we account, therefore, for the imperative nature of this rule?

How can modernity—which signs itself "impossible"—nevertheless announce itself as a command?

It is the prose poem "Genius" that gives perhaps the best account of the complex nature of Rimbaud's commanding and compelling invitation to modernity. Who, or what, is the poetic "Genius" that invites us to be "absolutely modern"?

Il est l'affection et le présent . . . , lui qui est le charme des lieux fuyants et le délice surhumain des stations. Il est l'affection et l'avenir, la force et l'amour que nous, debout dans les rages et les ennuis, nous voyons passer dans le ciel de tempête et les drapeaux d'extase.

  . . . .

Il nous a connus tous et nous a tous aimés. Sachons, cette nuit d'hiver, de cap en cap . . . forces et sentiments las, le *héler* et le voir, et le *renvoyer,* et sous les marées et au haut des déserts de neige, *suivre* ses vues, ses souffles, son corps, son jour.[90]

[He's affection and the present . . . , he who is the charm of evanescent places and the superhuman delight of stations. He's affection and the future, the strength and love that we, in rage and boredom, see passing in the stormy sky or in the banners of ecstasy.

  . . . .

He has known all of us and loved us all. Let us be able, on this winter night, from cape to cape . . . , our strength and feelings tired, to *hail* him, *see* him, and *dismiss* him, and, beneath the tides and at the tops of wastelands of snow, to follow his visions, his breath, his body, his day.]

What is remarkable is the wide-open closure of this text, the last of the *Illuminations.* "Let us be able to . . . hail him, see him, . . . *dismiss* him . . . and *follow* him." We are at once to "dismiss" and to "follow" the Genius of modernity. The ironic and lucid gaze that animates the text of "Genius" is a disillusioned gaze, but one that has not for all its disillusionment lost its enthusiasm: an enthusiastic gaze, but one that has not, for all its enthusiasm, lost its awareness of the inevitable disenchantment. Neither mystified nor demystifying, Rimbaud's gaze is situated neither *in* illusion nor *outside* it, neither *within* literature nor *outside of* literature, but all at once inside and out. It is a gaze wholly animated by the pathos of modernity; that is, it knows that it dwells in literature, not truth: it recognizes that it is itself a compound of pathos and error. That is why we have to learn to *dismiss* that "genius" with no name (no name that is proper to it), and that is also why we have to learn to *hail* him and to *see* him (recognize and witness him) and *follow* his vision. For modernity is not only the excess of its own lack. It is the extra empty space that makes the literary system function, the necessary absence, the essential gap that is constitutive of the fact of literary or poetic structure. The "lack" ("*il faut*" in the expression "*il faut être absolument moderne*"; "*il faut*": that which is lacking, *wanting*) is thus reinvested with the weight of its own structural necessity: we *want* illusion, we *want* modernity, we *want* that which is lacking, wanting (*il faut* la modernité, il *faut* l'illusion, il *faut* la faille). *Il faut*—"It is wanting," "One wants," "One must"—is the only thing modernity can say in the present tense. "*Faillir*" ["to lack, to fall short of"] and "*falloir*" ["to be necessary, to have to"] are, as we know, historical doublets:[91] that is what binds necessity so tightly to lack. "One must be absolutely modern": the "absolutely modern" is what *fails to be*. It is thus that modernity inscribes its break, its rupture—and its opening: the necessity—and the fatality—of its unfulfillable but incessant command. "One must be absolutely modern."

> Les philosophes: Le monde n'a pas d'âge. L'humanité se déplace, simplement. Vous êtes en Occident, mais libre à vous d'habiter dans votre Orient, quelque ancien qu'il vous le *faille*.[92]
>
> [Philosophers have said: the world has no age. Humanity just changes places, that's all. You are in the West, but you're free to live in your East, however ancient *you must* have it . . .]
>
> Parce qu'il *faudra* que je m'en aille, très loin, un jour.[93]
>
> [Because I'll *have to* go away, very far away, some day.]
>
> Voyez comme le feu se relève! Je brûle comme il *faut*.[94]
>
> [Watch how the fire gets hotter! I'm burning as *one should*.]

Je le suivais, il le faut: "I followed him, one *had to*," says the Foolish Virgin of the Infernal Spouse:

Je vais où il va, il le faut.[95]

[I go where he goes; *one has to.*]

Thus it is that literature—the *Foolish Virgin*—keeps moving and constantly repeats its impossible marriage ceremony with a modernity it "follows" and "dismisses," and that is none other than its *Infernal Spouse.*

Translated by Barbara Johnson

PART 2 | The Literary Speech Act

SHOSHANA FELMAN

4 | From *The Scandal of the Speaking Body: Don Juan with J. L. Austin, or Seduction in Two Languages*

Preface: The Promising Animal

> How am I to promise as if there were still in me something left of my own? — CLAUDEL, *The Satin Slipper*
>
> To breed an animal with the right to make promises — is not this the paradoxical problem nature has set itself with regard to man? And is it not man's true problem? — NIETZSCHE, *Genealogy of Morals*

If promising can in some way, as Nietzsche suggests, define the problematics of the human, if it can *situate* what makes for *problems* in man, it is not surprising that promising should have come recently to occupy center stage in linguistic and philosophical theory. Current research on the performative[1] is very often organized around promising, which is taken as the exemplary model of speech acts in general. "I shall take promising as my initial quarry," writes John Searle, for one, "because as illocutionary acts go, it is fairly formal and well articulated; like a mountainous terrain, it exhibits its geographical features starkly. But we shall see that it has more than local interest, and many of the lessons to be learned from it are of general application."[2] Owing to their stark contours, these mountainlike promises doubtless cast shadows in one direction or another, shadows that, paradoxically, may be as illuminating as the light of the performative itself. The exploration of these shadows is the task this book will undertake.

What, then, is a promise? What exactly are we doing when we say "I promise," and what are the consequences? All these questions are addressed by the logicians of language who deal with the performative. But here I should like to displace the findings of linguistic and logical analysis somewhat, in order to bring to bear upon them the Nietzschean question: In what way does a promise constitute a paradox, a problem? In what way is the very logic of promising a sign of a fundamental contradiction that is precisely the contradiction of the human? These latter questions, although they are implied by the performative, do not lie strictly within the domain of formal linguistic research; they emerge again, on the other hand, at the heart of a famous literary myth that raises the problem of the performative in a spectacular way: the myth of Don Juan.[3]

Don Juan, in fact, lavishes promises right and left, and breaks them repeatedly. "I *repeat the promise* I made you," he says to Charlotte (II, ii) but he is soon whispering to Mathurine: "I *bet* she's going to tell you that I *promised* to marry her"; and then, to Charlotte, "*Let's bet* she'll argue that I *gave her my word* I'd marry her." "He saw me . . . and *promised* to marry me," Charlotte maintains. But Mathurine protests: "It's me and not you he *promised* to marry." "Sir, did you *promise* to marry her?" asks Charlotte. And Mathurine: "Is it true, sir, that you *promised* to be her husband?" And Don Juan replies: "Both of you claim I *promised* to marry you. . . . Shouldn't the girl I really *promised* be able to ignore what the other one says? What does she have to worry about, *provided that I keep my promise?* All the discussion in the world won't help matters. We have to act, not talk; actions speak louder than words" (II, iv). Don Juan obviously abuses the institution of promising. But what does this abuse signify about promising itself? The scandal of seduction seems to be fundamentally tied to the scandal of the broken promise. *Don Juan* is the myth of scandal precisely to the extent that it is the myth of violation: the violation not of women but of promises made to them; in particular, promises of marriage. The question that this book will raise is thus twofold: how does research on the performative shed light on the myth of Don Juan? But also, on the other hand, what light does the Don Juan myth shed on performative theory? Our reading of Molière's *Don Juan* in the light of the writing of J. L. Austin and Emile Benveniste will be followed — paralleled and exceeded — by a reading of the Austin/Benveniste polemic, itself in turn illuminated by the text of *Don Juan*. On the basis, then, of a triple reading — of a literary text, a linguistic text, and a philosophical text — I want to undertake a meditation on promising, in such a way that the place of the literary will become the meeting and testing ground of the linguistic and the philosophical, the place where linguistics and philosophy are interrogated but also where they are pushed beyond their disciplinary limits.

Now it is at the very moment of this overreaching or outdistancing that the literary, producing analytic effects and thus giving rise to the necessity—and the possibility of a theoretical articulation between psychoanalysis and the performative (an articulation that brings both theories out into a new light), opens onto an irreducible *scandal:* the scandal (which is at once theoretical and empirical, historical) of the incongruous but indissoluble relation between language and the body; the scandal of the *seduction* of the human body insofar as it speaks—the scandal of the promise of love insofar as this promise is *par excellence* the promise that cannot be kept; the scandal of the promising animal insofar as what he promises is precisely the *untenable.*

To write the scandal of the speaking body, to speak the scandal of seduction, that which grounds, in my view, the literary order, the theoretical order, and the historical order in turn, to do this here will thus mean attempting to articulate something at the crossroads of several disciplines (the point where psychoanalysis, linguistics, philosophy, literature, etc., meet and fail to meet . . .) and at the crossroads of language (where English and French, or theoretical language and literary, rhetorical language, meet and fail to meet); attempting to articulate not so much what is *said* or could be said but what is happening, taking effect, producing acts, what is being *done* or could be done between speaking bodies, between languages, between knowledge and pleasure.

To speak and act: can this be done? Is it possible to speak seduction—the always scandalous intervention of love in theory, of pleasure in knowledge?

Perhaps I have only spoken the seduction exercised on me by certain texts, certain theories, certain languages; perhaps I have in turn, in this book, only perpetrated scandal, only articulated my own promise. Perhaps I have spoken here only the unknown of my own pleasure. May readers, in any case, find their own pleasure here—that is my hope.

The Reflections of J. L. Austin: Between Truth and Felicity

The English philosopher J. L. Austin, who initiated speech-act research and introduced the term "performative," began by demystifying—in a thoroughly Nietzschean manner, moreover—the illusion upheld by the history of philosophy according to which the only thing at stake in language is its "truth" or "falsity."[1] If the attribute of truth or false-hood is indeed applicable to the category of utterances that Austin labels *constatives*, that is, to descriptive utterances, to sentences that set forth *statements* of fact, that report a state of affairs, true or false, this attribute is inapplicable, on the other hand, to another category of utterances, henceforth christened *performatives*: expressions whose function is not to inform or to describe, but to carry out a "perform-ance," to accomplish an *act* through the very process of their enuncia-tion. The first example chosen (and this choice will turn out to be significant for us later on) to illustrate the performative is the linguis-tic act by means of which a marriage is performed: according to Aus-tin, when I respond in the affirmative to the ritual and legal question posed during a marriage ceremony—"Do you take this woman to be your lawful wedded wife?" I am not *describing* what I am doing, I am *acting*; by saying "I do," I am accomplishing the marriage. Likewise, when I say "I promise," "I swear," "I apologize," I am not describing my act but accomplishing it; by speaking, by pronouncing these words, I produce the *event* that they designate: the very act of promising, swearing, apologizing, and so forth. And since, in this case, to speak is to act, performative utterances, inasmuch as they produce actions and constitute operations, cannot be logically true or false, but only suc-cessful or unsuccessful, "felicitous" or "infelicitous." Thus in place of the truth/falsity criterion, essential to constative language, Austin sub-stitutes in the case of performative language the criterion of felicity as opposed to infelicity, that is, the success or failure of the act or opera-tion in question.

After listing the ways in which the performative can fail,[2] Austin sets out to find a specifically linguistic criterion that would make it possible to identify and recognize the performative, and would thus formally consolidate the opposition established between performative and constative. It is here that the philosopher's reflections, reaching an impasse, change direction. For although linguistic criteria that might formalize the distinction do exist, they prove to be neither exhaustive nor at all absolute. The principal grammatical criterion is the asymmetry that occurs, in certain verbs (henceforth recognized as "performative verbs"), between the first person of the present indicative, active voice, and the other persons and tenses of the verb: whereas the first person, by uttering the verb in the present tense, effectively carries out the designated act ("I *promise*," "I *swear*," "I *guarantee*," "I *name* this ship the *Liberty*," "I *call* the meeting *to order*"—said by the presiding officer), all other forms of the verb are descriptions, not acts; they only state or report the event ("I promised," "he swears," "he names this ship . . . ," "she called the meeting to order," and so on). But this criterion is insufficient, for we find other expressions that do not include an explicit performative verb and yet still belong to the category of the performative because they too accomplish an action and lie outside the reach of the truth/falsity criterion. The imperative, for example, "Go away!", may be seen as an ellipsis of the performative "I *order* you to leave." Or the sign "Beware of the dog" can be translated by the performative "I warn you that this dog bites." Thus we have to distinguish between explicit and implicit performatives. But as soon as we acknowledge the existence of implicit performatives, it is difficult to find any sentence that would not fall into this category. For even constative utterances might imply the ellipsis of "I note," "I affirm," "I declare": these expressions too, in the last analysis, do no more than carry out linguistic *acts* that are neither true nor false but that on the other hand may be successful or unsuccessful, felicitous or infelicitous. "What we need to do for the case of stating, and by the same token describing and reporting," Austin writes, "is to take them a bit off their pedestal, to realize that they are speech-acts no less than all these other speech-acts that we have been mentioning and talking about as performative."[3] "If, then, we loosed up our ideas of truth and falsity we shall see that statements, when assessed in relation to the facts, are not so very different after all from pieces of advice, warnings, verdicts, and so on" (*PP*, 251).

The original distinction between performative and constative is thus weakened, and indeed dislocated. What is needed in its place, Austin concludes, is a general theory of speech acts as such.

Austin provides this general theory in his doctrine of illocution. Encompassing and broadening the concept of performance examined with reference to the *context* of the interlocution, to the concrete and conventional discursive situation in which speech acquires, above and beyond its meaning, a certain force of utterance (the force of warning, commitment, plea, command, and so on). In his analysis of language, Austin thus distinguishes *meaning* and *force*: the two almost always co-exist in the production of speech. He labels the production of *meaning* a "*locutionary* act," and opposes this to the power plays of the "*illocutionary* act." These two types of speech acts are both contrasted, in turn, with a third type, called "*perlocutionary* acts," consisting in the production of *effects* on the *interlocutor* (surprising, convincing, deceiving, misleading, and so on). This "he said to me: 'Shoot her!' meaning by 'shoot' shoot and referring by 'her' to *her*" is a locutionary act; "he urged (or advised, ordered, &c.) me to shoot her" is an illocutionary act; "he persuaded me to shoot her" or "he got me to (or made me, &c.) shoot her" is a perlocutionary act (*HT*, 101–2).

The performative as such thus takes its place within a general doctrine of illocution and of enunciatory forces, which Austin divides into five categories:

1. The category of verdicts (*verdictives*): speech acts that constitute the exercise of judgment (condemning, acquitting, estimating, evaluating, etc.).

2. The category of orders (*exercitives*): speech acts that constitute assertions of authority or the exercise of power (commanding, giving an order, naming, advising, pardoning, etc.).

3. The category of commitments (*commissives*): speech acts that consist in the assumption of an engagement with respect to a future action (promising, contracting, espousing, enrolling, swearing, betting, etc.).

4. The category of behaviors (*behabitives*): speech acts linked to a social posture (congratulating, apologizing, greeting, etc.).

5. The category of expositions (*expositives*): speech acts that consist in a discursive clarification (affirming, denying, questioning, asking, remarking, etc.). (*HT*, 151–63).

Emile Benveniste's Modifications: Felicity and Legitimacy

Recognizing the importance of the category of the performative for linguistics itself, Emile Benveniste opposes the broadening of this category, and consequently dissociates himself from the general doctrine of illocutionary acts. "We see no reason for abandoning the distinction between the performative and the constative. We believe it justified and necessary. . . . If one does not hold to precise criteria of a formal and linguistic order, and particularly if one is not careful to distinguish between sense and reference, one endangers the very object of analytic philosophy; the specificity of language in the circumstances in which the linguistic forms one chooses to study are valid."[4]

Setting out to provide a more precise description of the performative from a strictly linguistic standpoint, Benveniste's critical reassessment of Austin's theory turns out to include—when we attempt to summarize it analytically—three subtractions (exclusions) and four additions (specifications, definitional elements).

The three subtractions, or exclusionary moves, are presented in the form of secondary methodological notes, but in fact they constitute three analytical principles:

1. *The exclusion of the general theory of illocutionary forces*: this serves to safeguard the formal purity of the constative/performative opposition.

2. *The exclusion of the theory of failure or infelicities ("unhappinesses") of the performative*: "We have taken . . . only the most salient points of the line of reasoning and those arguments in the demonstration which touched upon facts which are properly linguistic. Thus we [shall not] examine the considerations of the logical 'unhappiness' which can overtake and render inoperative either type of utterance" (Benveniste, 234). Later on, discussing the "unhappiness" of an unrealized performative, Benveniste explains that such an utterance simply does not exist as a performative; thus it is excluded from the category: "Anybody can shout in the public square, 'I decree a general mobilization,' and as it cannot be an *act** because the requisite authority is lacking, such an utterance is no more than *words;** it reduces itself to futile clamor, childishness, or lunacy. *A performative utterance that is not an act does not exist*" (236; *Benveniste's emphasis).[5]

Beyond the Felicity Principle: The Performance of Humor

In the eyes of one who has all knowledge and all power, the comic door does not exist.
— BAUDELAIRE, "On the Essence of Laughter"

Alice said rather impatiently: "I don't belong to this railway journey at all—I was in a wood just now—and I wish I could get back there!"
"You might make a joke on that," said the little voice close to her ear: "something about 'you would if you could,' you know."
"Don't tease so," said Alice, looking about in vain to see where the voice came from. "If you're so anxious to have a joke made, why don't you make one yourself?"
The little voice sighed deeply. It was very unhappy, evidently. . . .
— LEWIS CARROLL, *Through the Looking-Glass*

The act of *failing* thus leads, paradoxically, to an *excess* of utterance: manifest through its pleasure, independent of the "felicity" of its search for knowledge, the Austinian "force of utterance" is constantly in excess over the *meaning* of the theoretical statement. It is precisely this excess of energy that is continually discharged through humor. "[Some] French authors," writes Freud, "describe laughter as a *détente*. . . . We should say that laughter arises if a quota of psychical energy . . . has become unusable, so that it can find free discharge."[1]

Humor indeed is preeminently not a "saying" but a "doing": a "making (someone) laugh." If Austin is continually taking and giving the pleasure of jokes, it is because, paradoxically, the supreme performance of the *body's* failing itself is that of making jokes (*faire de l'esprit*).

To be sure, the "joke" participates in the "doing" of seduction, stemming in its turn, like the banquet Don Juan offers, from the gratuitousness of the gift of pleasure. As Freud writes, "the psychical process in the hearer . . . can scarcely be more aptly described than by stressing the fact that he has bought the pleasure of the joke with very small expenditure on his own part. *He might be said to have been presented with it*" (*Jokes,* 148). However, Austin's invitation to laughter is not just (yet another) invitation to the *pleasure of scandal:* "we shall most interestingly," as Austin put it, "have committed the act of bigamy." The laughter provoked by a joke turns the reader into an *accomplice*: an accomplice precisely in scandal. As Freud writes: "I am merely a listener who has not assisted in this functioning of [the criminal's] sense of humor, but I feel its effect, as it were from a distance. I detect in myself a certain humorous satisfaction, possibly much as he does."[2]

Scandal, of course, is never thematized or articulated, never explicitly denoted; it is nonetheless insidiously connoted by the oblique, always maliciously aberrant insistence on the humor — the incongruous humor — of *examples*. Consider, for example, the humor of scandal or the scandal of humor in the following examples, which are quite characteristic of Austin's style:

Examples of intentionality:

> Suppose I tie a string across a stairhead. A fragile relative, from whom I have expectations, trips over it, falls, and perishes. Should we ask whether I tied the string there intentionally? Well, but it's hard to see how I could have done such a thing unintentionally. . . . You don't do that sort of thing — by accident? By mistake? Inadvertently? On the other hand, would I be bound to admit I did it "on purpose" . . . ? That has an ugly sound. What could the purpose have been if not to trip at least someone? Maybe I had better claim I was simply passing the time . . . practising tying knots. (*PP*, 274–75)

Examples of excuses:

> We may plead that we trod on the snail inadvertently: but not on a baby — you ought to look where you are putting your great feet. (*PP*, 194)

Examples of infelicities:

> Suppose, for example, I see a vessel on the stocks, walk up and smash the bottle hung at the stem, proclaim "I name this ship the *Mr. Stalin*" . . . : but the trouble is, I was not the person chosen to name it (whether or not — an additional complication — *Mr. Stalin* was the destined name; perhaps in a way it is even more of a shame if it was). We can all agree:
> 1) that the ship was not thereby named;
> 2) that it is an infernal shame.

. . . It is a mockery, like a marriage with a monkey. (*HT*, 23–24)

When the saint baptized the penguins, was this void because the procedure of baptizing is inappropriate to be applied to penguins, or because there is no accepted procedure of baptizing anything except humans? (*HT*, 24)

What makes us laugh, in the examples, is the unexpectedness of their at once incongruous and trivial character, which brings to mind the figures of speech and the rhetorical strategies of the heroï-comic genre, in which the comic is based, in fact, on the incongruous mix of the sublime and the ridiculous. "Laughter," Baudelaire writes, "is essentially contradictory; that is to say that it is at once a token of an infinite grandeur and an infinite misery. . . . It is from the perpetual collision of these two infinites that laughter is struck."[3] Consider, again, in Austin, the following example (of an excuse) that, using the most characteristic of the heroï-comic figures,[4] might well be one of Don Juan's remarks, so well does it reflect a lucid view of the inherent incongruity of the speaking body:

If I have broken your dish or your romance, maybe the best defence I can find will be clumsiness. (*PP*, 177)

"Laughter," writes Freud, quoting Herbert Spencer, "naturally results only when consciousness is unawares transferred from great things to small—only when there is what we may call a *descending* incongruity" (*Jokes*, 146). Through the shock effect of the laughter that it provokes, the descending incongruity of Austin's examples seems to institute, as it were, triviality itself as a philosophy—as a method.[5]

The more we imagine the situation in detail, with a *background of story*—and it is worth employing *the most idiosyncratic* . . . means to stimulate and to discipline our wretched imaginations—the less we find we disagree about what we should say. (*PP*, 184)

Austin's "example" is thus a "story," a case history—and the case is "idiosyncratic," trivially and derisorily incongruous. Now what is trivial is only what is peripheral to the center: to the center of (conscious) attention. Austin's humor in his choice of examples thus produces, in the theoretical space, a decentering effect that we may call analytic.

In general, the relation of Austin's methodical "philosophy" of language to the triviality of his "examples" is strangely like the relation of psychoanalytic theory to the triviality of "case histories." With Austin as with psychoanalysis, the irreducible triviality of the idiosyncratic is that of a *practice* of the singular.

Of a practice, that is, of what belongs to the order of *doing.* For unlike saying, doing is always trivial: it is that which, by definition, cannot be generalized. As Benveniste says with respect to the performative, the act "has the property of being *unique.* It cannot be produced except in special circumstances, at one and only one time, at a definite date and place. It does not have the value of definition or prescription but, once again, of performance. This is why it is often accompanied by indications of date, of place, of names of people, witnesses, etc." (236). Thus true History, belonging to the order of acts or of practice, is always — however grandiose it may be — made up of trivialities.

The same is true of writing. Barthes writes:

A writer — by which I mean . . . the subject of a praxis — must have the persistence of the watcher who stands at the crossroads of all other discourses, in a position that is *trivial* in respect to purity of doctrine (*trivialis* is the etymological attribute of the prostitute who waits at the intersection of three roads). ("Lecture," 37; Barthes's emphasis)

Now at the intersection of three paths it is not simply the prostitute — or sex, always illicit — that is waiting or that one is meeting, but also the murder of the father — of Laius, still unknown. Hence a murder that is, literally and in every sense of the words, peripheral and trivial.

Indeed, however trivial it may be, the often black humor of Austin's examples abounds in images of murders and of monstrous marriages ("marriage with a monkey," "bigamy," etc.). The triviality of the witty example is thus incongruous only because it belongs to a radically heteronomous space, because it brings about the intervention, on the homogenous place of the theoretical stage, of the heroï-comic heterogeneity of the *Other Stage.*

||||

Thus there exists, in Austin's text, a *disparity of levels* between the theo-retical statement and the presence — which is all the more pronounced in that it is incongruous — of that Other Stage, a disparity of levels be-tween theory and humor, between meaning and pleasure. Now the passage from one level to another is not harmonious, gradual, continu-ous; on the contrary, it is — like laughter — convulsive and brutal. Mean-ing, in fact, can be accompanied by pleasure only on condition that it *fall* from one level to another. In other words, the passage from one textual plane to another is on the order of a skid or a fall.

Now the fall is the supreme example of what provokes laughter. "What is there," Baudelaire asks, "so delightful in the sight of a man falling on the ice or in the street, or stumbling at the end of a pave-ment?" ("Laughter," 139).

> SIGNARELLE: My reasoning is that there is something admirable in man, whatever you may say. . . . Isn't it wonderful that I am here, and that I have something in my head that thinks . . . and makes my body do whatever it wants . . . ? (*He drops dizzily to the ground.*)
> DON JUAN: There! Your reasoning has fallen flat on its face! (III, i)

Austin's humor is the humor of the fall — a humor that is closely tied to the performative, since falling is an *act*: *the* act, indeed, in so far as it is a failure — the very prototype of the *acte manqué*. In English, more-over, a "lapsus" is commonly called a "slip," a "slip of the tongue."

Indeed Austin, like a good skier, delights in slides and slips — and his awareness of them, as his vocabulary attests, is very highly developed:

> It's very easy to *slip* into this view. (*PP*, 236)

> We have discussed the performative utterance and its infelicities. That equips us . . . with two *shining new skids* under our metaphysi-cal feet. (*PP*, 241)

> It is a matter of unpicking, one by one, a mass of *seductive* (mainly verbal) fallacies. . . . We may hope to learn something . . . about the meanings of some English words . . . philosophically *very slippery*.[6]

What is dangerously "slippery" is thus seduction itself ("a mass of seductive fallacies"); what *causes skidding*, in language, is especially pleasure itself, inasmuch as it surreptitiously causes one to slide—without being aware of it—outside the realm of meaning, outside the terrain of knowledge.

"Vainly I strive against it," writes Kierkegaard. "My foot slips. My life is still a poet's existence."[7] The seduction of slipping is thus the seduction of poetry, of the *poetic* functioning of language. "Stumbling over words like cobblestones" is, in one of Baudelaire's definitions, the nature of the poetic act.[8] The Austinian performance thus participates, in a way, in poetic performance.

Now if to give pleasure (poetic or humorous) is to seduce or to lead the reader—unbeknownst to himself—onto essentially *slippery* ground, the performance of humor, or the act accomplished by a joke, is not simply the act of provoking laughter, but also that of tripping. "What could the purpose have been in not to trip at least someone?" Austin asked in his insidiously oblique fashion, playing on his favorite rhetoric of first-person "examples": "Maybe I had better claim I was simply passing the time, playing . . . , practising tying knots" (*PP*, 275). Tripping someone, however, is obviously much more than a "pastime": it is not simply a *pleasurable* act, it is also, and especially, a *subversive* act.

In fact, humor in Austin intervenes very often only to subvert knowledge, to call it into question, to cast doubt upon it. For Baudelaire, "laughter is only an expression, a symptom, a diagnostic. Symptom of what? That is the question" ("Laughter," 143). "We do not know," Freud says, similarly, "what is giving us enjoyment and what we are laughing at. This uncertainty in our judgment, which must be assumed to be a fact, may have provided the motive for the construction of jokes in the proper sense of the word" (*Jokes*, 132). Pleasure is pleasure only in not knowing where it comes from; the comic is comic only in that it does not know its own nature.[9] Jokes achieve, in this way, an unsettling effect with respect to knowledge: according to Freud, "they [set] themselves up against . . . critical judgment" (*Jokes*, 133). The entire effort of the Austinian enterprise of performative theory is directed at subverting the *cognitive evidence* inherent in the constative. This general problematization of the presumption of "knowing" is constantly enacted through the nervous energy of humor:

Of course philosophers have been wont to talk as though you or I or anybody could just go round stating anything about anything and that would be perfectly in order, only there's just a little question: is it true or false? But besides the little question, is it true or false, there is surely the question: is it in order? Can you go round just making statements about anything? Suppose for example you say to me, "I'm feeling pretty mouldy this morning." Well, I say to you, "You're not," and you say "what the devil do you mean, I'm not?" I say, "Oh, nothing — I'm just stating you're not, is it true or false?" And you say, "Wait a bit about whether it's true or false, the question is what did you mean by making statements about somebody else's feelings? I told you I'm feeling pretty mouldy. You're just not in a position to say, to state that I'm not." This brings out that you can't just make statements about other people's feelings (though you can make guesses if you like); and there are very many things which, having no knowledge of, not being in a position to pronounce about, you just can't state. (PP, 249)

Still, humor constitutes not only an assault on knowledge but also an assault on power, on repression in every sense of the word — political or analytical. Freud explains:

The main characteristic of the joke-work [is] that of liberating pleasure by *getting rid of inhibitions*. . . . [The power of jokes] lies in the yield of pleasure which they draw from the sources of play upon words and of liberated nonsense. (*Jokes,* 134)

An examination of the determinants of laughing will perhaps lead us to a plainer idea of what happens when a joke affords assistance against suppression. (*Jokes,* 136)

In fact, the Austinian performance of humorous *slipping* aims above all at shaking the institution of prejudice itself, the institution of beliefs or received ideas: "To feel the firm ground of prejudice slipping away is exhilarating . . ." (*HT,* 61). Thus the act of provoking laughter (of provoking pleasure), by causing a slip (by tripping) leads to the act of *exploding.* If laughter is, literally, a sort of explosion of the speaking body, the act of exploding — with laughter — becomes an explosive performance in every sense of the word.

What we need to do for the case of stating, and by the same token describing and reporting, is to *take them a bit off their pedestal.* (PP, 249–50)

I distinguish five very general classes. . . . They are . . . quite enough to *play Old Harry with two fetishes* which I admit to an inclination to play Old Harry with, viz. (1) the true/false fetish, (2) the value/fact fetish. (*HT,* 151)

The subversive performance of laughter rejoins the performance—a supremely Donjuanian performance—of the iconoclast. Like Don Juan, Austin takes pleasure—to use his own terms—in *playing old Harry,* playing the devil.[10] The comic, as Baudelaire, too, says, is "of diabolic origin" ("Laughter," 137).

Now to "play the devil" is above all to renounce playing God; that means—in Don Juan's fashion—not believing in the promise of Heaven as the power that underwrites the promising animal; not believing, by the same token, in the promise of the promising animal, even if that animal is oneself.

If Austin, like Don Juan, is constantly making promises in order not to keep them, this self-subversion of his own promise is achieved—through humor—at the very outset, in the witty play of his titles. If Austin's humor, as a whole, has managed to go unnoticed by commentators and interpreters, who have never *taken it into consideration,* it is nevertheless surprising to see to what an extent the world of theory has managed to remain blind to the fact that Austin's titles are, above all, jokes.

How to Do Things with Words exploits in an ironically witty fashion the conventional formula of how-to manuals, of practical guides: "How to Make Money," "How to Make Love," "How to Repair Your House," or, better still, *How to Win Friends and Influence People, How to Stop Worrying and Start Living.*[11] How to do things with words: practical recipes for the speaking body: "everything you need to *know* in order to *be able . . .*"; *scilicet*—"you can know" (when you have read this book) how to do this with words; nothing is simpler, nothing easier. . . . The pernicious humor of the title is directed against its author, against his *promise of teaching:* it suggests, by antiphrasis, that we are perhaps dealing here with the *unteachable,* with the noncognitive, with the heteronomy of "things."

Or another famous title: "A Plea for Excuses," which might be paraphrased "an excuse for excuses." When Austin was being questioned at Royaumont on the necessity for types of research other than his own (psychological research, for example), he, as usual, responded with a joke:

> I favor that sort of research, and I can only refer you to an article of mine in which I have formulated my credo on this point: an article very aptly entitled "Excuses"; since my credo amounts in the end to excusing myself for not doing what I have no intention of doing. (*CR,* 375)

"A Plea for Excuses" begins with a play on its title:

> The subject of this paper, *Excuses,* is one not to be treated, but only to be introduced, within such limits. . . . What, then, is the subject? I am here using the word "excuses" *for a title,* but it would be unwise to freeze too fast to this one noun. . . . The field . . . includes "plea," "defence," "justification" and so on. (*PP,* 175; Austin's emphasis)

"I am . . . using the word 'excuses' for a *title*": this may mean either that "the word 'excuses' indeed appears in the title of this essay," or "I am speaking *in the name of excuses.*" Thus Austin's self-subverting humor manages from the outset to enact the subject of excuses: I am introducing, says, Austin, the (new) subject of excuses; although this subject has been neglected up to now, I find it very important, it deserves an apology, a defense; I am thus about to excuse (or justify) excuses; I apologize, however, for being unable to do it in a satisfactory way within the limits of this essay, thus I am excusing excuses, but I excuse myself for failing to excuse them as I ought.

Perhaps the richest title, the one whose humor is most subtle and most sophisticated, is "Three Ways of Spilling Ink," the title of a study presented as a lecture in a colloquium entitled "Responsibility" organized by the American Society of Political and Legal Philosophy. "Three Ways of Spilling Ink" takes on the study of three ways of expressing intention in English: "intentionally," "deliberately," and "on purpose." Austin's title, in the context of "political and legal philosophy," seems somewhat irreverent, but we quickly discover that the title "merely" alludes to an *example* in the text, an example Austin uses to get his study off the ground. The triviality of his title is thus explained—at least apparently—by the triviality of the example.

A schoolteacher may ask a child who has spilled the ink in class: "Did you do that intentionally?" or "Did you do that deliberately?" or "Did you do that on purpose . . . ?" They appear to mean the same. But do they really? (*PP*, 274)

Let us distinguish between acting *intentionally* and acting *deliberately* or *on purpose*, as far as this can be done by attending to what language can teach us. (*PP*, 273)

Given the example of the child, the "three ways" — the three accredited ways — of "spilling ink" may have a double meaning: they are either the three ways in which the child carries out the action of spilling the ink — *three ways of acting* designated by the three expressions of intention; or *three linguistic ways of speaking* of the child's act, of describing its intentionality; in this latter case, it is Austin himself who is the ink-spiller, as he studies the three expressions and *writes his article* on the child's "three ways." The humorous play of the title thus suggests that writing itself (in this case, Austin's writing on the theory of language or of acts) is in some way of the same order of "responsibility" or of intentionality as the child's play or as his act (pleasure-seeking? insolent? gratuitous? — in any case, enigmatic) of spilling ink.

Humor, as Freud rightly says, goes back to the pleasure — again, an "irresponsible" pleasure — of child's play. Beginning with a reference to Bergson's *Le Rire,* Freud stresses the fact that Bergson

endeavours to explain the comic as an after-effect of the joys of childhood. "Peut-être même devrions-nous . . . chercher dans les jeux qui amusèrent l'enfant la première ébauche des combinaisons qui font rire l'homme. . . . Trop souvent surtout nous méconnaissons ce qu'il y a d'encore enfantin, pour ainsi dire, dans la plupart de nos émotions joyeuses." (Bergson, 1900, 68ff.)[12] Since we have traced back jokes to children's play with words and thoughts which has been frustrated by rational criticism . . . we cannot help feeling tempted to investigate the infantile roots . . . in the case of the comic as well. . . . Children themselves do not strike us as in any way comic, though their own nature fulfills all the conditions which, if we compare it with our own nature, yield a comic difference. . . . A child only produces a comic effect on us when he conducts himself not as a child but as a serious adult. . . .

But so long as he retains his childish nature the perception of him affords us a pure pleasure, perhaps one that reminds us slightly of the comic. We call him naive, in so far as he shows us his lack of inhibition, and we describe as naively comic those of his utterances which in another person we should have judged obscenities or jokes. (*Jokes*, 222–23)

"Three ways of spilling ink," Austin's title said, putting on an equal footing — through its malicious humor — the child's activity and that of the philosopher-writer who is studying, in fact, the intentionality of this activity. Austin's text never *answers* the question "why did the child spill ink?" It only enumerates, inventories the variety of possible questions — a list that one might be tempted to prolong: Did the child spill the ink maliciously? spitefully? just for fun? or *simply* because he was clumsy? We shall never know. The schoolteacher's questions are doomed to remain unanswered.

A schoolteacher may ask a child who has spilled the ink in class: "Did you do that intentionally?" or "Did you do that deliberately?" or "Did you do that on purpose (or purposely)?"

"Why do you spill ink?" Austin was asked — in another style — at Royaumont.

So, to go back to the questions which seemed to be addressed more particularly to me. . . . We are dealing once again with the method of analytic philosophy. We are asked why we are doing what we are trying to do when we behave as we do. When I am asked this question, I find myself rather in the position of one of my colleagues who had some children and, whenever he was about to punish one of them, was restrained by the fact that he couldn't manage to remember any of the reasons one has for punishing children. The same is true for me. When I am asked why I do what I do, I remain silent. (*CR*, 348)

"Three ways of spilling ink":

To write —
The inkwell, crystal like a consciousness, with its drop, at the bottom, of darkness . . . sets aside the lamp.

You noticed, one does not write, luminously, on a dark field . . . ;
man pursues black on white.
The writer, of his troubles . . . or of a gladness, must make of
himself, in the text, the spiritual histrion.[13]

By making ink flow, Austinian humor, as Mallarmé would say, "pursues black on white," and making of itself, in the text, the spiritual histrion, *sets aside the lamp.*

"How to do things with words," "a plea for excuses," "three ways of spilling ink": what Austin's titles do, through humor, is to suspend their own entitlement—their own authority. The titles, as titles, are promises (promises of new subjects, promises of authorial authority, promises of knowing or learning: "How to do . . ."; "we could scarcely hope for a more promising exercise than the study of excuses" [*PP*, 184])—and, at the same time, in the same breath, the titles call into question their own right to promise, subvert their own promise. This amounts to saying that the titles, drops of spilled ink, only *do* something—with wit—by suspending their own authority to *say* something.

"The man who trips," writes Baudelaire, "would be the last to laugh at his own fall, unless he happened to be a philosopher, one who had acquired by habit a power of rapid self-division and thus of assisting as a disinterested spectator at the phenomena of his own *ego*" ("Laughter," 141). Austin in fact never stops laughing at his own fall, never ceases to make a *philosophic joke* of the performance of his own slipping:

> So far then we have merely felt the firm ground of prejudice slide away beneath our feet. But now how, as *philosophers,* are we to proceed? One thing we might go on to do, of course, is to take it all back: another would be to *bog, by logical stages, down.* But all this must take time. (*HT,* 13)

> (I must explain again that we are floundering here. To feel the firm ground of prejudice slipping away is exhilarating, but brings its revenges.) (*HT,* 61)

Austin's humor stems, in this way, not only from the *subversive* performance inherent in the unconscious, but also from the *self-subverting* performance inherent in the superego. As Freud writes:

The joke, it may be said, is the contribution made to the comic from the realm of the unconscious. . . . (*Jokes,* 208)

In just the same way, *humor would be a contribution to the comic made through the agency of the super-ego. . . .*

In other respects, we know that the super-ego is a stern master. It may be said that it accords ill with its character that it should wink at affording the ego a little gratification. . . . The principal thing is the intention which humour fulfils, whether it concerns the subject's self or other people. Its meaning is: "Look here! This is all that this seemingly dangerous world amounts to. Child's play—the very thing to jest about!"

If the super-ego does try to comfort the ego by humour and to protect it from suffering, this does not conflict with its derivation from the paternal function.

If it is really the super-ego which, in humour, speaks such kindly words of comfort to the intimidated ego, this teaches us that we still have very much to learn about the nature of that energy. ("Humour," 268–69)

Thus the fun-loving Austin is not simply a man of pleasure, not simply, either, a man who takes pleasure in laughing; he is also, and especially, someone who, as a philosopher, takes pleasure in laughing, above all, *at pleasure,* someone whose philosophical performance indeed never stops laughing at its own pleasure. The constitutive relationship of theory and jokes in Austin's work suggests at every turn that the apparent convergence of pleasure and rigor is only a decoy [*leurre*],[14] but at the same time, that "those who are not duped err."[15] If Austin's Gay Science is finally, as Proust would say, the science "of that perpetual error that is known, precisely, as 'life,'" the seductive coincidence between cognitive rigor and performative pleasure points ceaselessly, through humor, toward its residue:

In philosophy it is *can** in particular that we seem so often to uncover, just when we had thought some problem settled, *grinning residually* up at us like the frog at the bottom of the beer mug. (*PP,* 231; *Austin's emphasis)

The *residual* smile of humor thus makes concrete the theory's problematics of "can" as leaving an irreducible remainder: what, from the theoretical performance—performance of the incongruence between knowledge and pleasure—emerges as that which is present at once, irreducibly, as *more* and *less* than "felicity."

Response: STANLEY CAVELL

Foreword to *The Scandal of the Speaking Body*

Rationalists would eat sombreros. — WALLACE STEVENS,
"Six Significant Landscapes"

As one for whom the encounter with J. L. Austin's writing and
teaching almost half a century ago was formative and remains
inspiring, I say at once that Shoshana Felman's (playfully serious) description of Austin's (seriously playful) work as scandalous strikes me as accurate to something of Austin's own sense
of it—although I would add that his work also conveys the
sense that it is philosophy's own scandal that what he says is,
or seems to be, news to it. This compound of attitudes has
not always been found endearing in professional philosophy,
which has meant that in these circles *The Scandal of the Speaking
Body*—one of the most brilliant and daring and disturbing
works of its period, which appeared in English translation in
1984, during the furor over the reception of so-called French
theory in American literary and cultural studies—has never
found the full radius of readers it assumes and deserves. Bearing in mind Felman's location of the literary as the place
where philosophy (with linguistics) is "interrogated but also
. . . pushed beyond [its] disciplinary limits" (5), I offer in what
follows some opening responses to her text, which may be of
use in locating certain likely disciplinary points of resistance
to her thoughts, and suggest lines along which to use these
points to better effect than, to my knowledge, they have so far
had.

Felman continuously redescribes the task of her text throughout the writing of it, quite as if saying what she is doing is the principal task of what she is doing. A dominant way her task has presented itself to me is as, still, the most extended and sustained effort I know to represent, or rather—out of, let's say, a style of thinking inherited from the poorly named "continental" philosophy—to respond to an influential text from the opposed style of thinking of the equally poorly named "analytical" philosophy. Such a task is, to my mind, as important as it is difficult, since I regard these styles or voices or signatures of philosophy as forming the contesting, all but exhaustive senses of the present, hence of the foreseeable future, of philosophy. Here are instances of how Felman formulates her task:

> I had better declare at once that I am *seduced* by Austin. I like not only the openness that I find in his theory, but the theory's potential for scandal; I like not only what he says, but what he "*does* with words." . . . For it seems to me that the history of linguistic philosophy . . . reflects an appropriation of the constative aspect of the theory, but hardly at all of its performative aspect. (48)

> Perhaps I have only spoken the seduction exercised on me by certain texts, certain theories, certain languages; perhaps I have in turn, in this book, only perpetrated scandal, only articulated my own promise. Perhaps I have spoken here only the unknown of my own pleasure. May readers, in any case, find their own pleasure here—that is my hope. (5)

What Felman calls the "performative aspect" of Austin's theory is its presentation in a style of writing that essentially and insistently includes jokes, puns, literary allusions, and the general, repeated invitation to have fun in philosophizing, so in a sense it is no wonder that—in its philosophical inheritance—its performative aspect has not only been appropriated, but must be regarded (apart from some private moments of enjoyment, providing topics of chats after work, like Austin's hobby of raising pigs), as philosophically strictly impertinent. One might accordingly say that Felman's book is not meant for philosophers who think this way, but is, on the contrary, so to speak, a free response to Austin's practice meant for someone already convinced, for example, of Lacan's theoretical and psychological acumen, of the pertinence of philosophy and literature to one another, of the relevance, but inaccuracy, of what Derrida had to say about Austin. A limitation of this response is that (apart from the fact that it fails to respond to the chic of Felman's own performance) it neglects Felman's strength as a reader of Lacan, so that one less than convinced by Lacan's feats of articulation — characteristically in confronting psychoanalysis (that is, confronting his readings of Freud's texts) with philosophy and with theology and with literature — may want to try them further, prompted by the clarity and surprises of pertinence in Felman's juxtaposition of moments of Lacan with, among others, moments of Austin.

Take the dominating coup of Felman's reading — the alignment of Austin's inventing of the performative utterance in *How to Do Things with Words* with the figure of Don Juan in Molière's *Don Juan* and in Mozart's and Da Ponte's *Don Giovanni*. This ironic conjunction affords the most illuminating frame known to me against which to articulate the widespread sense, and claim, that the act and concept of promising is not just one more among performative utterances, as these are characterized by Austin in contrast to constative utterances (those defined as being true or false), but that promising — even especially the promise to marry — is somehow privileged in Austin's view, naming as it were the fact of speech itself. This privilege is suggested in Austin's major essay "Other Minds," where he compares "I know" with "I promise" (stopping short of claiming that knowing is performative), and is virtually said out loud when in *How to Do Things with Words* Austin identifies speaking as *giving one's word,* as if an "I promise" implicitly lines every act of speech, of intelligibility, as if it were a condition of speech as such. (Kant held that "I think" is such a lining.)

But why does Felman take it that the wonderful connection with *Don Juan,* the compulsive promise maker and promise breaker, shows Austin to be "like Don Juan" (a phrase Felman uses repeatedly of Austin) rather than showing Don Juan to be Austin's nemesis, a figure for the chaos awaiting a social order forgetful of Austin's monitions? An answer is that, appealing to the more familiar telling in *Don Giovanni,* Don Giovanni's nemeses are the "serious" characters of the otherwise *buffa* opera, whereas Austin assigns to himself the jokes, etc., in an otherwise mad world endlessly tempted to promise breaking, marriage mocking, bet evading, gift revoking, etc. But is it not worth trying to distinguish the laughter — and the attendant anxiety — caused in one who, like Austin, senses the bond of our words apt to be loosened beyond understanding, from the laughter caused in another who, like Don Juan, finds the bond of our words apt to be tightened beyond reason, in each case destroying both obligation and pleasure?

A principal preparation for Felman's project is given in Lacanian formulations such as:

> A body is speech arising as such. (65)

> Misfiring is the object. . . . *The object is a misfire. The essence of the object is misfiring.* (56)

> A body is that which enjoys itself. That which enjoys itself only through incorporating its enjoyment in a signifying manner. (71)

> For what we have in the discovery of psychoanalysis is an encounter, an essential encounter—an appointment to which we are always called with a real that eludes us. (63)

And her project is colored by remarks like Claudel's "That promise which my body made you I am powerless to fulfill" (42). When Felman articulates related thoughts in such observations as "Like Don Juan, Austin suspects in his turn that the promise will not be kept, the debt not paid" (46) and "If the capacity for misfire is an inherent capacity of the performative, it is because the act as such is defined, for Austin, as the capacity to *miss its goal* and to *fail to be achieved,* to remain *unconsummated*" (55–56), she is, as I understand her, fairly explicitly challenging Derrida's virulently influential reading of Austin's sense of language as one precisely that fails to recognize the inherent, say, internal, possibility of its failure(s). I think Felman's perception of Austin is more faithful to his sense of things than Derrida's is on this point, but it runs its own dangers of denying something in Austin.

I have in mind Austin's horror of using, not to say constructing, some metaphysical discovery as a comic excuse for moral chiseling, as in his example that takes a remark of Euripides' Hippolytus, "My tongue swore but my heart did not," as a way of keeping a promise.[1] (Austin is perhaps falsely remembering Hippolytus's later behavior.) It seems no harder to picture Austin's imagining someone's using the idea of "the act as such is defined as the capacity to miss its goal" as an excuse for having failed in a given case to do the best one might have done under the circumstances.

Yet I share the desire in Felman's meditation to preserve Austin's text against attempts (not only by philosophers) merely to pluck from it a technical result within, let us call it, philosophical linguistics: Austin does say (and do) the things she says he says and does—he jokes, makes puns, identifies himself as Old Harry, sets off fireworks, offers words as food and theories as remunerative, etc. If (or to the extent that) one feels, as I do, that this is a remunerative way to read Austin (valuable, especially, in the virtuosic detail that Felman's superb powers as a reader prompt her to), feels indeed that ways of reading him that ignore his playful "manner" are ignoring something essential to his philosophical seriousness, then if one finds oneself sometimes at odds with the interpretative morals Felman draws from her reading, one will thereupon be committed to account otherwise for the details and strata of the text she has claimed and shown to be essential to it. Here are two examples.

First, Felman notes that while "Austin does not speak . . . explicitly . . . of 'misfires' in the specifically [psycho-]analytical sense of parapraxis," "one can see how his grasp of the referential aspect of the act in negative terms is close . . . to the Freudian concept of slip and parapraxis, and to the Lacanian concept of the differential referential" (56). But just because I would like comparing Austin and Freud on the subject of slips to be an uncontroversially welcome idea, I do not want it to carry the price of having to accept controversial theories of reference (Benveniste's linguistic [re]interpretation of Austin's characterization of the performative; Lacan's idea of the real)—though of course for Felman these are not prices but rewards. That is not something I want here to deny, but merely not to have to count on. An Austinian "misfire" is not a Freudian slip, because it is not essentially motivated. Yet Austin does investigate slips; that forms the project of his rediscovery of the importance of the concept of excuses, sketched in his notes called "A Plea for Excuses." There what emerges is that, in contrast to Freud's vision of the human being as a field of significance whose actions express wider meaning than we might care to be questioned about, Austin's vision is of the human being as a field of vulnerability whose actions imply wider consequences and effects and results—if narrower meaning—than we should have to be answerable for. But then of what use is the difference without the sameness between them? And the sameness has to do with what might be seen as versions or visions of the speaking body.

Second, noting that Don Juan is pestered about his failure to pay his servant his wages, Felman adduces (46) Austin's suggestion that his invoking notions of the performative, the infelicity, and the forces of utterances may seem "a little unremunerative." Felman takes this to allude to Austin's apparent refusal of a linguistic payoff (namely, of his initial distinction between constative and performative, which the linguist Benveniste wishes to preserve). Without denying this, there seems to me a plainer, more pertinently aggressive tone to this nonchalant declaration, namely, that rather than offering remuneration in the coin philosophy recognizes well—too well—Austin is, on the contrary, depriving philosophy of full credit in that coin, namely, in the notion that the full meaningfulness of speech is tied to utterances that are true or false. The theoretical collapse of the initial or general distinction between the performative and the constative is, seen so, not an intellectual failure but a signal success, showing the performative (namely, a form of utterance neither true nor false) to be fully as meaningful as the constative; it thus deprives positivism (together with an important strain of the literary New Criticism of Austin's period, as prompted in the work of I. A. Richards) of a place for the imagined distinction between what was called "emotive meaning" as opposed to "cognitive (or scientific) meaning." Yet who but Shoshana Felman would have found a door to such thoughts in Austin's use of "unremunerative"? And I am not prepared to doubt but that there are further thoughts in store there. (If Don Juan's servant's anxiety about not receiving his wages is not simply mercenary, but rather an anxiety that he will lack this mark of exit from his relation with Don Juan, hence that the relation will seem something more than mercenary, then Austin's wish to withhold remuneration may signal that he is greedy in wanting our relation to his text not to provide an early exit from what it provides.)

Other doors may seem harder, or less promising, to try. When, for example, Felman speaks of what "Austin christens [as] 'illocutionary force' or 'force of utterance'" as an "excess of utterance over the statement" and goes on to speak of this "referential excess of utterance" as the "referential residue of meaning" (52), it is hard to determine whether this is meant to deny or to affirm that statements and performatives differ in their powers of referring to the world. A writer such as Paul de Man influentially takes the difference precisely to be that performatives do not refer. What I have urged is that it is essential to Austin's achievement to have shown that the distinction between, for example, betting and stating is not that betting fails to refer (say to a particular horse) or that stating fails to do something (say inform or alarm you). But the very difficulty in Felman's articulation (locating Austin's idea of force not as a function of a power—call it intention— either opposed to or identical with its referent, but as a function of language itself) seems to me a protective response to the early moment in Austin's expositing at which he opens himself (who will guess with what deliberateness, or daring?) to such an interpretation as Derrida initiated of *How to Do Things with Words*. According to that interpretation, Austin assures the authority of speech (substituting, as it were, the presence of intention for the absence of reference) by ruling out essentially undermining possibilities of its authority (joking, playacting, etc.) as "nonserious," hence as inessential, uses of language. Derrida has picked up here Austin's rebuttal of the imagined (and doubtless also actual) charge against the view of performativity he has just announced, namely, the charge that the view amounts simply to saying that "To marry is to say a few words" or "Betting is simply saying something" (*HT*, 7). Austin had sensibly conceded: "Such a doctrine sounds odd or even flippant at first," and he adds, "but with sufficient safeguards it may become not odd at all." Yet when, two pages later, Austin guards against the sound of flippancy by declaring that "Surely the words must be spoken 'seriously' and so as to be taken 'seriously,'" it turns out that his scare quote around "seriously," far from helping to provide safeguards against flippancy, are symptoms that he has, and knows he has, turned away from the founding question he has raised concerning what it is to say something.

This is not the moment to try to trace how Derrida has determined that Austin's casual, deflected (with scare quotes) concession about seriousness, which in appearance is directed to a possible (prejudicial or argumentative) formulation of Austin's own theory—or rather, to his own proof by example, not argument, of the existence of a common form of utterance that is neither true nor false, and that no one will call nonsense, which accordingly proposes a direct and massive region of counterexample to logical positivism's proclamation of the nonsense, or meaninglessness, of "value judgments" (utterances it held to be strictly meaningless *because* neither true nor false)—is instead, in reality, an announcement by Austin of the nature of speech as such.[2] But even without an account of Derrida's determination, I think it can be said that Austin at this early point in his exposition had distracted himself into a half-hearted, routine glance at "seriousness," whereas every gesture of his philosophizing can be taken as a tracking of false seriousness. And he has evidently been drawn away from assessing the significance of his demonstration that saying something is doing something—for example, it provides a novel way of assigning the seriousness of an utterance, namely, that an utterance without performative (illocutionary or, I would add, perlocutionary) force says nothing, is in that sense not serious—and drawn away perhaps from ever considering that saying something is also *not* simply, just, exactly, merely, quite, only, purely (what you might call) doing something (a point Austin takes note of in *HT*, 5).

Again, when Felman says, winningly, "To seduce is to produce felicitous language" (15), one devoted to Austin might wish to reply, pulling a long face, "Well, the quasi-technical use of 'felicitous' fashioned by Austin applies only to what emerges as illocutionary acts (what is done in saying something), not to perlocutionary acts (what is done by saying something), and the quasi-utterance 'I seduce you,' as its very unsayability displays, is not illocutionary, hence it cannot be evaluated either as felicitous or as infelicitous." But Felman's formulation raises the question why Austin does not go on to attempt to define felicity for the perlocutionary, and I am indebted to her insistence for having helped to prompt, in my own case, a continuing effort to pursue that question, which has meant, in effect, to follow my intuition that Austin's uncharacteristic outburst, shortly after introducing the distinction between illocutionary and perlocutionary acts, "For clearly *any*, or almost any, perlocutionary act is liable to be brought off, in sufficiently special circumstances, by the issuing, with or without calculation, of any utterance whatsoever" (*HT*, 110) is not to be trusted. Illocutions, we might say, can name what they do (to say "I promise, bet, wed, announce," etc., is to promise, wed, etc.); perlocutions cannot in this way name what they do. If apparently perlocutionary acts (uttering "I deter, punish, alarm, amaze, disgust, seduce, delight, etc. you") were *eo ipso* (as Austin likes to say) to deter, punish, alarm, disgust, seduce, delight you, speech would essentially, over an unsurveyable field, be a form of magic (as if it were throughout that field set to unheard and irresistible music). While I may often, or characteristically, alarm or delight you inadvertently or accidentally, it does not

follow that I therefore cannot (that there are not ways, call them conditions of felicity, I might recur to or discover in which to) alarm or
delight you intentionally, foreseeably. (I do not conceive that Wallace
Stevens has asked us to consider his rationalist's sombrero as the cover
exclusively of gaiety or of somberness. But who would take this to
mean that the figure is particularly out of control?)

An indication of what I mean may be brought out as follows. Austin
says of performative utterances—or of illocutionary acts, which for
him track performativity when he resets the theoretical table of his
study—that the "I" comes essentially into the picture (even when the
grammatical form of the utterance is not explicitly cast in the first
person). That is to say, I have to do my own promising, marrying, betting, etc.; moreover, no one is on the whole better placed than I to
determine whether I have (felicitously) promised, married, bet, etc., no
one upon whom I can pass off my responsibilities for assessment here.
In the case of perlocutionary acts, on the contrary, especially those
that track what I have come to call passionate utterances ("You delight
me," "I intimidate you, I hear"), you are better placed than I to determine whether the act has been accomplished; indeed it is part of the
conditions of felicity of the perlocutionary act that (there being no
standing conditions for its felicity) it demands of you to say (and that
you in fact say) what its accomplishment (felicity) has been. I mark this
difference between performative and passionate utterances by saying
that with the latter the "you" comes essentially into the picture. The
perlocutionary is the field of human interaction, which is not governed by the conventions or conditions or rituals Austin invokes, but
represents the complementary field occupied by or calling for improvi-
sation and passion and aggression. It is the region Austin backs away
from in backing away from investigating the perlocutionary.

I sketch here this step beyond what Austin actually goes into, but
which is implied there, in order to highlight Felman's insight in invoking the work of Antonin Artaud ("Everything that acts is a cruelty,"
28) to characterize "Donjuanian perversity." It is to the field of the
perlocutionary, not to performativity as Austin declares it, marked by
the illocutionary, that Artaud's work can be seen incontestably (to my
mind) to apply. (I do not deny that the work can be shown to have
application to promising, etc., but only that in that application Austin's work as it stands is left behind. This may shed its own slant of

illumination.) If Felman's invocation of Artaud lacks philosophical decorum, so much the worse for philosophical decorum.

But I am back at my beginning, remembering Shoshana Felman's declaration, "I am *seduced* by Austin." Have I responded to that? According to my way of thinking, it is a speech act in the field largely undefined in Austin's theory of the performative, a perlocutionary act that, directed, for example, to me, demands a response to a seductive declaration of attraction to another man, another philosopher. It is up to me how to respond to it; no response is dictated by antecedent rules or conditions of the sort Austin shows to be invoked by illocutionary acts. If I have no response to it (neither caution nor alarm nor approval, for example), I had better make that explicit, since I might otherwise be taken to be rejecting the demand as impertinent, indecorous, overbearing, and that is not what I wish to convey. But haven't I responded to it? Shoshana Felman says it is her hope that her readers find their own pleasure here, in her (and presumably, among other's, also in Austin's) text. I have modified, or extended, that description of her motivation in identifying her speech act also as demanding a response to her pleasure. That is a cruelty, as her view implies. That it is at the same time a pleasure I hope I have shown in what I have been saying and doing. For in sharing the sense, and valuing Felman's riskiness in enacting it, of festival in Austin's text, I share further the sense, even in these days when theories of seduction are more common, and more suspect, than when her book first appeared, that philosophy's cruelty is inherently seductive, or said otherwise, that philosophers have to bear the recognition that in their defense of reason they may not know why one guise of reason has come to attract them more than another to a life's work.

Response: J U D I T H   B U T L E R

Afterword to *The Scandal of the Speaking Body*

A body is speech arising as such. — L A C A N

Originally titled *Le Scandale du corps parlant,* Shoshana Felman's English book (titled *The Literary Speech Act*) lost the body in its initial translation. It regains its body with this publication, which is just, since the body is crucial. There is no speech act without the body, and at the same time the body limits the role of intention in the speech act. Performative speech acts are forms of doing, often spoken ones, and they draw upon the body to articulate their claims, so institute the realities of which they speak. The speech act thus draws as well on philosophical approaches to language, especially to the effectivity of performative language, and to more general theories of language that situate the utterance within a wider ambit of discursive aims exceeding the intentions of the subject. *The Scandal of the Speaking Body* is known as the most important and trenchant effort to bring together the literary and philosophical dimensions of the speech act, unparalleled in its ability to sustain a discourse that works at once comparatively and critically across these domains and within their interstices. So, does the text aim to specify a "literary" speech act? Or is it, all along, shuttling between philosophy and literature, staging a certain dramatic tension between them and showing how a reading that insists on both can and must take place? If this text is about the relation of the body to the speech act, on the one hand, and the relation of philosophy and literature, on the other, then its earlier English title belies two of its central claims, making it perhaps more "disciplinary" (literary) than it ought to be and more cognitive and disembodied (philosophical) than its argument would allow.

Originally published in 1980 in France, it offers a deconstructive approach to the theory of the speech act that differs remarkably from Derrida's "Limited Inc. *a b c . . .*" (1977).[1] Derrida recasts the speech act as a function of writing, not speech. Arguing against the presumption in Austin that subjective presence offers the spoken word a legitimating effect, he shows that the spoken word, to have performative force, must be subject to a logic of iterability that belongs to the transposability of the written word. Felman returns deconstructive reading to the question of voice and to speaking, not to defend a "sovereign" subject as its guarantor, but to remind us that speaking is, in part, a *bodily* act. As bodily, the speech act loses its claim to sovereignty in a different way than it does when recast as writing. The speech act "says" more than it can ever intend or know. Indeed, as bodily, the speech act never had the sovereignty it sometimes tries to claim for itself. In this way, Felman offers a deconstructive approach to the speech act that realigns deconstruction with psychoanalysis and with the theory of speech that emerges in the context of the transference.

At the same time, she refuses certain disciplinary and subdisciplinary feuds, and inaugurates a life for speech-act theory that will resonate throughout the disciplines, even at times providing a crucial rallying point for cross-disciplinary work. Since 1977 (Derrida) and 1980 (Felman), the speech act has been appropriated in many ways. Felman's text prefigured and sometimes prompted the cross-disciplinary travels of the speech act: in legal and literary works, performance studies, queer theory, political theory, and ethnography. Could Eve Sedgwick's reading of the performativity of the marriage ceremony have taken place without Felman's work?[2] And would those trained in the tradition of continental philosophy have thought to turn to Austin for intellectual resources without this book, in conjunction with Derrida's engagement with speech-act theory?

Whereas the philosophy of language has for the most part waned in U.S. philosophy departments, ceding terrain to new forms of cognitivism traveling under the rubric of "philosophy of mind," speech-act theory has found increasing popularity in several fields outside the purview of academic philosophy. At the time of its publication, Felman's book might have been nearly unreadable to philosophers who knew Austin only in the context of the Anglo-American philosophical tradition (even though it explicates one of the most important exchanges on the speech act for Austin, namely, the colloquy with Benveniste in France). The book buoyantly scandalizes these disciplinary boundaries, posing the question of how Austin might be read in conjunction with Molière's *Don Juan,* or what he might have to do with psychoanalysis, a persistent "third" in the relation between Austin and Don Juan. Or, again, those philosophers and literary theorists schooled in the continental tradition might have been interested in the conjunction of psychoanalysis with deconstruction but would find it difficult to engage the literary readings here, the sense of comedy emerging from the Donjuanian promise, much less the Oxbridge irony of J. L. Austin. But the text shows, even if it does not state, that deconstructive reading can take different forms, and that Austin himself can become the occasion for divergent deconstructions. In Felman's reading, Austin imperils the disciplinary boundaries by which he has, more or less successfully, been contained. Don Juan exemplifies not only the misfires of the performative, its failed instances along with its constitutive failure, but how the theorization of the speech act is tied to the viability and frailty of the promise, to marriage vows and their constitutive comedy, and to the always limited and errant way that speech might knowingly stand for the body and its sexuality. It will turn out that the body in its sexuality guarantees the failure of the speech act. Here Felman supplements Austin with Don Juan through Lacan, whom she cites, adding her own synonym within parentheses: "Failure (misfire) itself can be defined as what is sexual in every human act" (78).

When the body speaks, it fails to fulfill the claims made on behalf of consciousness. But the body is not "outside" the speech act. At once the organ of speech, the very organic condition of speech, and the vehicle of speech, the body signifies the organic conditions for verbalization. So if there is no speech act without speech, and no speech without the organic, there is surely no speech act without the organic. But what does the organic dimension of speech do to the claims made in speech, and on behalf of speech? If one assumes that speech reflects consciousness and, in particular, the "intention" of the speaker, then the intention is isolated as a cognitive moment represented by speech, and speech is understood as corresponding to this prior cognitive content. But if speech is impossible without the organic, even as speech claims to represent a cognitive intention—as in the case of the promise—then the speech act cannot circumvent the organic, the bodily, at the moment in which it appears to represent or correspond to an intention. Indeed, it turns out that the only way to produce the appearance of a speech act that represents an intention is by using, and so validating, the invariably organic conditions of speech itself. One could argue logically that the organic conditions of speech do not in themselves compromise the cognitive content represented by speech. And surely Felman's point is not to vitiate all claims of consciousness and turn all effects of consciousness into so many epiphenomenal manifestations of a prior materialism. She is not making a metaphysical argument of that kind. But if the point is to think about the speech act, what it does when it assumes the form of a promise, then a certain set of metaphysical conditions are presupposed. And it turns out that these premises are not compatible with one another.

Indeed, coming up with a metaphysics for the speech act turns out to yield insuperable paradoxes. If the explicit claim that a promise makes is not only to represent an intention, and to represent it continuously through time ("I will do this, and I will do it despite what happens tomorrow or the next day"), then the promise assumes that language can and does represent intention or, in this instance, "will" in a transparent, adequate, and sustaining way. This is, as it were, the implicit metaphysics of a sustainable promise. What Felman argues is that the "I" who is understood by Austin to be the presumption of all illocutionary utterances is presumed to be a pure consciousness, a will, an intention, cognitive in content, adequately and transparently represented by language in time. But if we reconsider the "I" as that which represents its bodily life in language, we see a different notion of representation at work or, rather, a relation between body and language that puts into crisis the very relation of representation presumed by the sovereign and intentional "I." If one makes a promise, one is performing an act and not, as Austin makes clear, communicating something that is "true." It is a performative rather than a constative claim. But if, as Austin claims, every performative can be reduced to the referential capacity of a sovereign subject not only to make a promise, but to represent itself in the promise, then a constative condition is presumed, namely, that language can and does adequately represent intention. So language must represent this truth, and it must represent

it truthfully—and so function constatively in its transparent and referential capacities. But it must do this at the very moment in which it
performs its act, and so it functions performatively.

If we ask what it means for language to perform or, rather, for language to exemplify its performativity at the moment in which a speech
act is uttered, we find that the very notion of performance requires
the body because a speech act is a vocalization, which requires the
mouth as its organ and its vehicle. What is the mouth doing in this
cognitive scene? That we offer promises with the mouth has some bearing on the promises we make. But what is this bearing? Felman suggests: "one might say that the Don Juan myth of the mouth is the
precise *place of mediation between language and the body.* Don Juan's
mouth is not simply an organ of pleasure and appropriation, it is also
the speech organ *par excellence,* even the organ of seduction" (37).

Felman points out that the promise functions in the service of seduction for Don Juan: it is made and broken innumerable times; it does
not represent an inner and enduring truth, or insure a future action.
The promise, for Don Juan, is an act that refers only to its own doing
and that seeks to alter something in the speech-act situation in which
it takes place: "Saying, for him, is in no case tantamount to knowing,
but rather to *doing: acting* on the interlocutor, modifying the situation
and the interplay of forces within it" (14). So a certain action is performed with the mouth, but this still does not show us that the content or force of what is said is in any way modified by the organic basis
of the utterance.

The connection between the two becomes clear only once we understand the relations among promising, seduction, and marriage. Felman shows this deftly by considering the many times that Don Juan
proposes and demonstrating how the proposal functions in the service
of an infinitely promiscuous seduction that never materializes in marriage. Austin similarly uses marriage as one of his key examples. For
Felman, marriage becomes exemplary for the speech act. The promise
is the speech act that stands for intention across time, and marriage is
the speech act that stands for the disposition of the sexual body in
conformity with consistency and loyalty. If the promise is not merely
associated with marriage but is essential to the marriage vow, then the
speech act in that instance not only stands for the body, but is the very
action of the body as it dedicates itself through time to the one to
whom and with whom it takes the vow. But does language have the

power to comport the body in the way that it decides? Can language not only represent the body, but exercise a power over the body to keep it constant? The language of the promise does not reflect an intention or, rather, does not gain its efficacy by virtue of a stated relation to intention. The promise is the speech act that is understood to compel the body to comport itself, in constancy, toward the other. Seduction, which, for Don Juan, foils marriage again and again, or even makes the marriage vow into a transient strategy of seduction, potentially infinite in its displacements, is a way of enacting desire in language, or of using language to compel erotic submission. It works, when it works, precisely because the word that is spoken (and thus is already a bodily act) is directed toward the body of the addressee. Here speech becomes the enactment of desire. It does what it says insofar as the body is doing it, and it is the action of the body for which it stands. The speaking body functions as a chiasmic relay between the promise and the disposition of the sexual body that the promise is meant to bind.

The body functions here in at least two ways. First, it is the ineluctable vehicle for the performance of the speech act, considered as a verbalization. Second, the body is sexuality, understood not as an "intentional" disposition, but as unconscious fantasy structuring bodily desire. In the first instance, we find that the very meaning of the promise references the body: invariably, a promise commits the body to an enduring or repeated action of some sort. But if we consider the body as bearing unconscious fantasy, it works precisely against intention. In this second sense, the body signifies what is unintentional, what is *not* admitted into the domain of "intention," primary longings, the unconscious and its aims. Unconscious aims, although precisely not "intentional," belong to the "I." Being an unintegrated assemblage of conscious and unconscious, the "I" cannot stand knowingly for itself. Or when it claims to stand for itself, in the instance of promising, it finds that it has not taken stock of the full range of aims by which its actions are motivated, and it cannot.

The "I" is thus embarrassed by its proclamations because it seeks to represent itself, but finds that it is more than can be represented. To the extent that this "more" is signified by the body, it follows that the body interferes with every promise. The body is at once the organic condition of promise making and the sure guarantor of its failure. If the promise relays an intention and the body signifies the unintentional, then the body, which is presupposed by the promise, is also the occasion of the promise's necessary failure.

The promise thus "does" something other than what it explicitly claims to do. Instead of binding the body of the speaker to the one to whom the promise or vow is made, it prefigures the possibility of such a tie. It can, as in the case of Don Juan, do this infinitely without ever making good on what it produces as pure possibility. This is so because the body is the vehicle for the speech act. Because the body already participates in seductive speech and speech cannot be seductive — indeed, cannot be speech — without a body (somewhere), the body is at once the precondition for the speech act and that which is indexed in the act itself, without which the act could not be the act at all. Seductive speech is what the body does, is a present action of the body, at the same time that it portends what the body will do. This it is, as it were, the body on its way, figured in its possibilities.

Since the body cannot be fully known or represented by the promise, the promise cannot be kept, or, rather, it is always a question whether the promise can be kept, whether its "intentions" will be derailed along the way. Although Felman is explicitly reading Austin with Molière's Don Juan, she is also reading both of them against the background of psychoanalysis, in particular, the theory of transference. What happens to speech in transference? "A body," writes Lacan, cited by Felman, "is speech arising as such" (65). Something is said, and it appears that an intention is being represented in speech, that correspondence is intact, that the sovereign "I" is the ground of the utterance. But the speech act is a form of address, and it is addressed to one who is not transparently there, who is known only in profile or through the voice, someone never properly introduced. Thus a statement about the "I" is offered into this scene, though every statement is also a way of asking, "Who are you?" The analyst is addressed, but the analyst is not known. A certain address is sent in the direction of the unknown; it returns from there, if it does, as a partially unrecognizable reflection of oneself. Whose speech is it anyway? Is that my voice returning from elsewhere? Is it the voice of another? Has my own voice returned as the Other?

Those who enter analysis may seek to recover some knowledge about who they are, but it seems more likely that the cognitive recovery of knowledge suffices. In transference, aims that the intending speaker does not fully know or control become articulated in the ways speech (whose speech?) is enacted in the course of the interlocutory exchange between analyst and patient. The language may be saying something, claiming to express what it knows, but it may also be doing something else with the claim that it makes, riding the wave of an aim that is known only in the effects it seeks to achieve, in an utterance from "the other scene," in the particular ways it attempts to modify the interlocutory situation at hand. Indeed, a claim to express what one knows may well display an unknowingness in the very saying. Or a speech act may explicitly claim to be trying to produce one set of effects (flattery, for instance), but effectively be producing another (cruelty). And insofar as a speech act knows not what it does, the claim is a kind of performative, a form of doing, that is clearly not the product of the sovereign "I," a doing at odds with an intending, in persistent divergence from itself.

Felman reads in this way, showing us yet another way that texts we would have never thought to put together already comment upon one another, allowing a certain association among the texts to display the way in which they already, without knowing it, presuppose one another. Austin himself is unknowing about the ways his own views are implicated in psychoanalysis, especially in his use of the language of satisfaction, which presupposes a drive or desire and which has a questionable and tenuous relation to any claims of truth. Felman does not take Austin to be a sovereign subject, precisely because she takes him at his word. It would make no sense to try to verify what he could have meant or intended. On the contrary, his own claims, attended closely, display his unknowingness, and his own irony and compulsive efforts to scrap the latest conceptual architectonic in favor of a new one attest to this. He is not sure of his way, and he leaves the legacy of his misfires on the page for us to read. Felman is shrewd to discover that for Austin, as for psychoanalysis, the question is always one of an aim that fails to find the satisfaction that is intentionally sought. For Austin, performatives satisfy or do not; they are felicitous, or are not; but they are neither true nor false. Thus Austin identifies for us a realm of pleasure and displeasure that can be thought outside the framework of truth and falsity. And like a good analyst, who suspends the question of reality to interrogate the psychic meaning in play, Austin circumscribes a performative capacity of the speech act in which the value of its doing is in no way linked to the question of its capacity to correspond to reality.

For Felman, this does not mean that the performative is nonreferential. She writes: "Referential knowledge of language is not knowledge *about* reality (about a separate and distinct entity), but knowledge that *has to do with reality,* that acts within reality, since it is itself—at least in part—what this reality is made of. The referent is no longer simply a preexisting *substance,* but an *act,* that is, a dynamic movement of modification of reality" (51).

I would put this differently, suggesting, not that the referent *is* an act, but that an act refers only insofar as it presumes a situation upon which to act. Thus, although the referent institutes reality rather than describing it, the referent always institutes reality within an already constituted field. It is not God's performative, which brings into being what it names and thereby exercises the performative in a creation *ex nihilo.* The performative, understood as illocutionary, indicates reality, even transforms it, as a matter of course; it seeks to modify a situation, to have certain effects. It therefore has this situation as its necessary, if not constitutive, referent. (The phenomenological word "horizon" perhaps describes this better than "referent.") Indeed, the instituting act cannot be conceived without this indicating function.

We might also say that, just as the performative presupposes a referential field to act upon and transform, so it also seeks to transform that field in accord with wishes and desires that are carried in language, that precede and exceed the strategic intentions of the speaker. At a key juncture, Felman tries to explain how language exceeds the utterance, relaying desire in relation to a subject, but not as its property. She cites Lacan: "What am I aiming at, if not at convincing you that what the unconscious brings back for us to study is the law according to which utterance can never be reduced to the statement of any discourse?" (52). The utterance is part of a language that exceeds the statement, but, most importantly, language has aims of its own that exceed the aims represented by a statement. Felman speculates that nonsemantic excess, which Austin calls "force," is the pulsional character of desire in language, the insistence of the body as it both motivates and derails the workings of speech. A speech act is reducible neither to the body nor to a conscious intention, but becomes the site where the two diverge and intertwine. In this sense, the speaking body scandalizes metaphysics, in particular, its penchant for clear dichotomies:

> If the problem of the human act thus consists in the relation between language and body, it is because the act is conceived—by performative analysis as well as by psychoanalysis—as that which problematizes at one and the same time the separation and the opposition between the two. The act, an enigmatic and problematic production of the *speaking body,* destroys from its inception the metaphysical dichotomy between the domain of the "mental" and the domain of the "physical," breaks down the opposition between body and spirit, between matter and language. (65)

That *The Scandal of the Speaking Body* brings us up against this insuperable paradox in shifting and related contexts is the sign of its enormous, ambitious intellectual success. According to its own terms, however, "failure, to be sure, pervades every performance, including even that of theory, which in turn becomes erotic for being nothing but a failed act, or an act of failing" (79). This text charts what is erotic for us in speech, producing an erotic event between cognitive and corporeal claims, finding the space between them that partakes of both and that is finally irreducible to either. It does this by manifesting the shrewd humor of the one (which is everyone) for whom failure is the condition of the speech act, the risk that permits us to act with language, and to find that our acts, precisely when they are made of language, carry the force of more knowledge than we can know.

PART 3 | Reading and Sexual Difference

SHOSHANA FELMAN

5 | Textuality and the Riddle of Bisexuality: Balzac, "The Girl with the Golden Eyes"

Rereading, an operation contrary to the commercial and ideological habits of our society, which would have us "throw away" the story once it has been consumed . . . so that we can then move on to another story, buy another book . . . rereading is here suggested at the outset, for it alone saves the text from repetition (those who fail to reread are obliged to read the same story everywhere). —
ROLAND BARTHES

"The Riddle of Femininity"

"Today's lecture," wrote Freud in 1932, "may serve to give you an example of a detailed piece of analytic work, and I can say two things to recommend it. It brings forward nothing but observed facts . . . and it deals with a subject which has a claim on your interest second almost to no other":

> Throughout history people have knocked their heads against the riddle of the nature of femininity. . . . Nor will *you* have escaped worrying over this problem—those of you who are men; to those of you who are women this will not apply—you are yourselves the problem.[1]

Intended for "an audience gathered from all the Faculties of the University,"[2] the lecture, entitled "Femininity," was in fact never delivered. Having undergone an operation for mouth cancer, its author was no longer in a condition to deliver

155

public lectures. And thus he wrote, prefacing his own unspoken lecture:

> A surgical operation had made speaking in public impossible for me. If, therefore, I once more *take my place in the lecture room* during the remarks that follow, it is only by an artifice of the imagination; it may help me not to forget to *bear the reader in mind* as I enter more deeply into my subject.[3]

I would here like to take my place as reader—as a reader of "Femininity" and as a reader of femininity—by reflecting, first, on its relation to Freud's place: to Freud's place in the lecture room, at once real and imaginary, of the University of Vienna; the place he addresses and from which he asks the question of femininity. In quoting Freud's introductory remarks as an introduction to this essay—itself originally delivered as a public talk—I have displaced, however, the locus of the question to another lecture room and to another structure of address. Thus, when I said along with Freud, "Today's lecture . . . has a claim on your interest second almost to no other," and, "I can say two things to recommend it," "today" was not 1932 but 1989; the "you" addressed was not the Viennese university public but a contemporary American audience gathered for a feminist colloquium; and my usage of the first person *I* introduced into the quotation a discrepancy of genders, since Freud's *I* implied the male gender, whereas I addressed the public as a woman. Consequently, when I then went on to quote, "throughout history men have knocked their heads against the riddle of femininity. . . . Nor will *you* have escaped worrying over this question—those of you who are men; to those of you who are women this will not apply—" the audience—as I had expected—did not fail to laugh.

What are the implications of this laughter? It was brought about by an awareness—at once spontaneous and historical—of the spatial, temporal, and sexual displacement that my enunciation operated in Freud's statement. But this historical awareness—the discrepancy named "history" that my reading introduced into Freud's text as a difference from itself—only made apparent the inherent textual discrepancy between Freud's *statement,* opening up the question *of* the Woman, and his *utterance,* closing it *for* women, excluding women from the question: "to those of you who are women, this will not apply—you are yourselves the problem."

"Those of you who are men," on the other hand, will not "have escaped worrying over this problem." A question, Freud thus implies, is always a question of desire; it springs out of a desire that is also the desire for a question. Women, however, are considered merely as the *objects* of desire, and as the *objects* of the question. To the extent that women "*are* the question," they cannot *enunciate* the question; they cannot be the speaking *subjects* of the knowledge or the science that the question seeks.

In assuming here my place as a speaking subject, I have then *interfered*, through female utterance and reading, in Freud's male writing. I have *enacted* sexual difference in the very act of reading Freud's interrogation of it; enacted it as precisely difference, with the purpose not of rejecting Freud's interrogation, but of displacing it, of carrying it beyond its *stated* question, by disrupting the transparency and misleadingly self-evident universality of its male enunciation.

Freud, indeed, in spite of his otherwise radical approach, still articulates "the riddle of femininity" in typical nineteenth-century terms. His question: "What is femininity?" in reality asks: "What is femininity—for *men*?" My simple (female) reiteration of Freud's question— with the rhetorical effect of the public's laughter—has somewhat redefined the "riddle" and implied a slightly different question: What does the question, "What is femininity—*for men*?" mean *for women*?

It is this question that I propose to address in the present chapter, through a reading of an ingenious text by Balzac, which, in its turn, dramatizes the "riddle of femininity" as the double question of the reading of sexual difference and of the intervention of sexual difference in the very act of reading.

I. "Gold and Pleasure": Social Classes and Sex Roles

The text in question, Balzac's short novel entitled "The Girl with the Golden Eyes,"[4] is in fact literally a provocative erotic *riddle*, specifically addressing the question of sexual difference: dramatizing, in a triangular complication, the interferences of an affair between a man and a woman with an existing affair between two women, depicting both the interplay and the conflict between homosexual and heterosexual loves, the text at once explores and puts in question the very structure of opposition between the sexes, as well as the respective definitions of masculinity and femininity.

The erotical narrative, however, is preceded by a long discursive pre-amble in which the narrator depicts a panoramic analytical picture of Paris and its social classes. The classes are separated, economically distinguished, according to their material wealth, according to the amount of gold that they possess or do not possess; but they are also united by their common desire for "gold" and for "pleasure": the self-destructive drive for ever-increasing amounts of money and enjoyment canalizes the social energies on all class levels. Paris is thus viewed by Balzac as a battlefield of interests and passions in which "everything stimulates the upward march of money" (318), each "sphere" throwing its "spawn into a superior one," each class endeavoring to rise to a higher social rank, in order "to obey that universal master, gold or pleasure" (316, TM). "Who . . . is dominant in this country . . . ? Gold and pleasure. Take these two words as a light," says Balzac (310–11, TM).

What is then the connection, the question arises, between Balzac's "light" and Balzac's darkness, between this discursive sociological trea-tise on Parisian society and the rather obscure erotical narrative that follows? How does that *class struggle* depicted in the prologue relate to the *sex struggle* around which the story revolves?

It would seem, at first sight, that what is common to the two strug-gles is the very structure of *division* from which they spring, as well as the principle of *hierarchy,* which in both cases organizes the division as an authoritative order. The prologue's hierarchical division of social classes would thus correspond to the story's hierarchical division of sexual roles, according to which, in Balzac's society as well as in ours, the female occupies the inferior position, whereas the male, in much the same way as the class possessing the gold, occupies the superior, ruling position.

It is no coincidence that the feminine heroine, Paquita, is a slave whose origin is "a country where women are not human beings, but chattels. One does what one likes with them, sells them, buys them, kills them. In fact one uses them to indulge one's whims, just as here you make use of your furniture" (390). The alibi of a foreign country's cultural manners should not, however, mislead us, since it is in Paris that Paquita is thus disposed of, being sexually used and unscrupu-lously murdered. It is equally in Paris that Henri de Marsay pronounces his contemptuous verdict on women:

And what then is woman? a little thing, a bunch of twaddle. With two words spoken in the air, can't she be made to work for four hours? She is sure that the fop will take care of her, because he does not think of great things. . . . Indeed, a fop cannot help being a fop if he has a reason for being one. It's the women who give us this rank. The fop is the colonel of love, he is a lady killer, he has his regiment of women to command. . . . So therefore foppishness . . . is a sign of an unquestionable power conquered over the female population. (348–49, TM)

It is in these terms, by this verdict on women, that Henri de Marsay defines his own foppishness as well as his male role in the story, the typical male role of the Parisian civilization. According to these well-defined masculine/feminine social roles, the relationship between man and woman is one of sexual hierarchization, in which the man is the master, whereas the woman is reduced to the state of a mere slave, at once man's pleasure object and his narcissistic assurance of his own importance, value, and power.

GOLD AND FEMININITY

This culturally determined male attitude can also, more subtly, be analyzed, not through Henri's contempt for "the female population" of Paris but through his admiration for an exceptional woman—the girl with the golden eyes—whose desirable image strikes him as his feminine ideal, the very incarnation of the woman of his dreams:

Last Thursday . . . I was strolling about . . . , I found myself face to face with a woman. . . . This was no case of stupefaction, nor was she a common streetwalker. Judging from the expression on her face, she seemed to be saying: "What! you are here, my ideal, the being I have thought of, dreamed of night and morning! . . . Take me, I am yours. . . ." And so on. . . . So I looked at her closely. My dear fellow, from a physical standpoint, this incognita is *the most adorably feminine woman I have ever met.* . . . *And what most struck me straightaway,* what I still find fascinating, is *her two eyes,* yellow as a tiger's; yellow as *gleaming gold; living gold, brooding gold, amorous gold, gold that wants to come into your pocket.* . . . Ever since I have taken interest in women, my unknown *she* is the only one whose

virginal bosom, whose ardent and voluptuous curves have realized for me the unique woman of my dreams. . . . *She is the very
essence of woman,* an abyss of pleasure whose depths may never be
sounded: *the ideal woman.* (337–39, TM, emphasis mine)

Clearly Henri is here attracted to the girl's golden eyes because they
are for him the sign of feminine desire and sexuality, the very incarnation of femininity per se. However, what are the connotations of the
metaphor of gold that, through her eyes, comes to symbolize the girl
and, thus, to embody ideal femininity? By virtue of its very brilliance,
the "gleaming gold" ("*jaune d'or qui brille*") is essentially a *reflective*
substance, which reflects a source of light external to itself; the light
reflected comes indeed from the object contemplated by the woman—
Henri himself: the golden eyes of femininity are fundamentally a *mirror* in which the male—Henri—can contemplate his own idealized self-
image so as to admire himself: "Judging from the expression on her
face, she seemed to be saying: 'What! you are here, my ideal, the being
I have thought of, I have dreamed of night and morning!'" (338).

The golden brilliance of the girl with the golden eyes is fascinating,
says Henri, because it is an "amorous gold, gold that wants to come
into your pocket." Paradoxically, gold as the metaphor of the utmost
value is an image, at the same time of *possession* and *appropriation,*
through which the ideal woman is again reduced to a mere *object,*
whose sole function is to be possessed and owned by a man. But the
metaphor evoked by Henri of the gold that wants to come into his
pocket is even more ambiguous than that, since, carrying a clear erotic
connotation suggestive of the sexual act, it grants the golden eyes of
femininity a phantasmic masculine—phallic—role. Ironically enough,
femininity itself thus turns out to be a metaphor of the phallus. To the
extent that the girl with the golden eyes is here viewed by Henri as the
tool for his purely narcissistic satisfaction, Henri's desire for the ideal
woman can be said to be a sort of masturbation fantasy: his own phallus is indeed the prize he seeks. In much the same way as, in the prologue, gold was said to be the ruling principle, a principle of
domination and of hierarchy, so the gold phallus in the story, beckon-
ing from behind the mask of woman's beauty, is to be wishfully recuperated and restored to its proper place: man's pocket.

The girl with the golden eyes is thus the very name of woman and
of femininity *as a fantasy of man.* The name, indeed, was given to the

girl by a group of men—Henri's friends. Defined by man, the conventional polarity of masculine and feminine names woman as a *metaphor of man.* Sexuality, in other words, functions here as the sign of a rhetorical convention, of which woman is the *signifier* and man the *signified.* Man alone has thus the privilege of proper meaning, of *literal* identity: femininity, as a signifier, cannot signify *itself;* it is but a metaphor, a figurative substitute; it can but refer to man, to the phallus, as its proper meaning, as its signified. The rhetorical hierarchization of the opposition between the sexes is then such that woman's *difference* is suppressed, being totally subsumed by the reference of the feminine to masculine identity.

II. A Question of Address

When Henri decides to possess, that is, to place in his pocket, the gold of the girl with the golden eyes, he has first to find out who she is. Having followed the girl to the house where she lives, he charges his valet to spy on the mailman and shrewdly extort from him the name of the target of his desire. In order to ward off the mailman's suspicion, the valet is furnished with a false package, which he supposedly has to deliver to the golden-eyed girl. Having learned from the mailman that the house belongs to Don Hijos, Marquis de San Réal, the valet mistakenly concludes that the woman desired by his master must be the marquis's wife. "My package," he thus tells the mailman, "is for the Marquise" (342). But he soon realizes his mistake when the mailman, responding to a bribe offer, informs him of the presence of still another woman in the Marquis's house. The mailman then shows him the address on a letter he has to deliver: the real name of the golden-eyed girl is Paquita Valdès. On the basis of this information, the valet, and Henri in his turn, will make a second mistake, assuming that Paquita must then be the mistress of the marquis. The drama of desire being a triangular one, the marquis, Henri mistakenly thinks, must therefore be his rival and his enemy.

> The report made by his valet Laurent had enormously enhanced the value of the girl with the golden eyes. Battle had to be given to some secret antagonist, as dangerous, it seemed, as he was cunning. To gain the victory all the forces at Henri's command would not be superfluous. He was about to act the eternally old, eternally

new comedy with three characters: an old man, Don Hijos, a girl, Paquita, and a suitor, de Marsay. (347)

If Henri's story seems, at its outset, to follow indeed the conventional triangular pattern of erotic competition, of rivalry in desire, the seemingly banal triangle is an uncanny one to the extent that Henri has no real knowledge, in fact, of his partners in the triangle. Engaged as he is in the very act of desiring and of struggling, of opposing, Henri does not really know who it is that he truly desires, who it is that he truly opposes, who are the two other poles of the triangle that implicates him and structures his own sexual involvement. The episode with the mailman, more crucial than it appears to be, outlines thus the basic unconscious inquiry that governs Henri's adventure: the question is indeed one of *addresses*. Through his valet, Henri asks the mailman: what is the real address of the message of my desire? Whom do I really desire? For whom, in fact, is my package? And what, on the other hand, is the true address (the true addressee) of my hostility, of my aggressivity? Who is my real enemy? These two basic questions, pertaining to the address of desire and to the identity of the enemy, immediately translate themselves into two *interpretative mistakes:* "My package is for the marquise," says Laurent; the enemy is the marquis, thinks Henri. Whereas the first mistaken assumption is quickly dispelled and corrected, the second mistake is there to stay, in Henri's interpretation as well as in that of the reader, until the dénouement of the story, in which Henri, along with the reader, discovers that Henri's rival is not the *marquis* but the *marquise.* The mistake, in other words, consists in the substitution of the *masculine* for the *feminine.* It is therefore governed by the logic of the rhetorical hierarchy of the polarity masculine/feminine, according to which the signified (i.e., meaning) is as such necessarily *masculine,* can only be read in the masculine. But the story on the contrary shows the rhetorical presupposition to be indeed an ironic error. Henri, as well as the reader, has to learn, as the text puts it, to "read this page, so brilliant in its effect, and guess its hidden meaning" (376, TM). If Henri's drama springs from a *misreading of femininity,* consisting in a blind substitution of the masculine for the feminine, what Henri has to learn is precisely how to read femininity; how to stop reading through the exclusive blind reference to a masculine signified, to phallocentric meaning.

The substitution, by Henri, of the masculine for the feminine in his attempt to read the proper name of his enemy, is by no means the only error in the story. Ironically enough, Paquita commits a strikingly similar, although diametrically opposed, mistake. In much the same way as Henri—a typical ideological product of the ruling male civilization—is unable to read in the feminine, Paquita, by reason of the coercive and restrictive education to which she has been subjected, is unable to read in the masculine. Having been confined as a slave since the age of twelve in sexual bondage to the marquise, Paquita—in the most literal manner—does not know what a man is, before her encounter with Henri. That is why her understanding of the opposition masculine/feminine takes the feminine as its point of reference. When she sees Henri for the first time, she is struck by his resemblance to the *woman* she knows and loves—the marquise—who, we will later learn, is really Henri's sister. "It's the same voice," said Paquita in a melancholy tone, "and the same ardent passion" (361). Paquita then falls in love with Henri because of his very resemblance to the woman she knows. In their first sexual scene, Paquita makes Henri dress as a woman, so that he might better resemble the original model, the feminine referent: a wish that Henri unsuspectingly obeys as a pure fantasy. Paquita's very innocence thus becomes an ironic reversal of the conventional functioning of the polarity masculine/feminine: like the feminine for Henri, the masculine for Paquita signifies not itself but its symmetrical, specular opposite. The feminine is at first for Paquita the *proper meaning* of the masculine. Whereas Henri's ideal woman is a metaphor of the phallus, Paquita's ideal man is a metaphor of a woman.[5]

Since Paquita makes Henri wear a woman's dress, Henri, unwittingly, becomes a transvestite. Balzac's text could be viewed, indeed, as a rhetorical dramatization and a philosophical reflection on the constitutive relationship between transvestism and sexuality, that is, on the constitutive relationship between sex roles and clothing. If it is clothes, the text seems to suggest, if it is clothes alone, that is, a cultural sign, an institution, which determine our reading of the sexes, which determine masculine and feminine and insure sexual opposition as an orderly, hierarchical polarity; if indeed clothes make the *man*—or the woman—are not sex roles as such, inherently, but travesties? Are not sex roles but travesties of the ambiguous complexity of real sexuality, of real sexual difference? Paquita's ideal man is but a travesty of feminine identity, in much the same way as Henri's ideal woman is a travesty of masculine identity. Henri's masculine sex role for Paquita and Paquita's feminine sex role for Henri are thus but transvestisms of the other sex's deceptively unequivocal identity; that is, they are travesties of a travesty.

If transvestism then refers sexuality to clothes, to the cultural institution of the sign, travesty is possible because signs function not just grammatically, according to a norm, but rhetorically, through substitutions. Transvestism is indeed an arbitrary sign whose signifier is displaced onto a signified not "its own," an exiled signifier that no longer has, in fact, a "proper" signified, a "proper" meaning, a claim to literality. Transvestism, in Balzac's story, links sexuality to rhetoric, and rhetoric to sexuality: *"Tu travestis les mots"* ("You disguise—you travesty—your words") (337), says Henri to his friend Paul de Manerville, unwittingly suggesting that transvestism as well as travesty are conditioned by the functioning of language; that sexes can be substituted, that masculine and feminine can be exchanged, or travestied, because words can be.

ACTIVE DISCRETION

Henri, indeed, exposes a whole theory of rhetoric relating sexuality to language through two principles of "discretion":

> When you find yourself in need of discretion, learn this: there are *two kinds, one active, one negative. Negative discretion* belongs to the dolts who have recourse to *silence, denial,* frowning faces, the discretion which takes effect behind closed doors—sheer impotence! *Active discretion proceeds by blunt assertion.* (375, emphasis mine)

Active discretion, in other words, consists not in denying what one wants to hide, nor in simply keeping silent about it, but in positively saying something else, in making a concrete erotic *affirmation* altogether different, so as to displace the focus of attention, to divert suspicion from the fact to be concealed. Of active discretion, Henri says, "The best kind of discretion . . . consists of compromising a woman we're not keen on, or one we don't love or possess, in order to preserve the honor of the one we love sufficiently to respect her. The former is what I call the *screen-woman*" (375, TM). The rhetoric of sexuality is thus a rhetoric of screens: of what Henri calls "negative discretion"—euphemisms and understatements—or of what he calls positive, "active discretion," the ostentatious use—in a kind of erotic overstatement—of a *screen-woman*.

The question here arises: if a woman can as such be but a screen, what can she screen? Is there, in Balzac's text, a screen-woman? Who is she? Where are the screens? And what is being screened? Can the polarity of masculine and feminine itself be modified, affected by the screen procedure, by the potentiality of transvestism built into language?

A screen can have a triple function: it can serve to divide or separate, to conceal or hide, to protect or shield. In a sense, it could be said that the marquise, Henri's sister, is the screen-woman, since she literally tries to screen Paquita—to hide Paquita from the world and to hide the world from Paquita. In so acting, she constitutes a screen between Paquita and Henri. Henri's attempt, of course, is to break through, to traverse that screen. But the marquise inadvertently reemerges as a screen—as a barrier—between the lovers when Paquita, by mistake, cries out her name at the very height of her ecstatic sexual intercourse with Henri.

> At the very moment when de Marsay was forgetting everything and was minded to take possession of this creature for ever, in the very midst of ecstasy, a dagger-stroke was dealt him which pierced his heart through and through: the first mortification it had ever received. Paquita, who had found strength enough to lift him above her as if to gaze upon him, had exclaimed: "Oh! Mariquita!"
>
> "Mariquita!" the young man roared out. "Now I know all that I didn't want to believe." (383–84)
>
> Paquita's exclamation was the more hateful to him because he had been hurled down from the sweetest triumph which had ever exalted his masculine vanity. (385)

Paquita's exclamation is a double insult to Henri, and a symbolic emasculation, first, because the name she calls out in her ecstasy is not his own, and second, because not only is he a mere substitute, but he is obviously being substituted for a *woman*. It is thus the very name Mariquita that becomes a screen between the lovers: a screen because it separates them; a screen in that it is a substitute, a *proper* name that names *improperly:* the very name, indeed, of impropriety.

The screen is thus a *signifier,* and the signifier's implications could extend beyond its simple referent, the woman it refers to. Mariquita, indeed, is not just a woman's name; it also means, in Spanish, an effeminate man; its implicit connotation of homosexuality, although obviously linked to the marquise's name as well as to her sexual mores, cannot but reflect back upon Henri, whom it renames. Furthermore, the name *Mariquita* can be read as a composite, either of *marquise* and *Paquita* or of *Marsay* (Henri) and *Paquita;* as a signifier, the word *Mariquita* thus names both Paquita's ambiguity as a part of two different couples and the linkage of de Marsay and Paquita in Mariquita, that is, the triangular linkage that ties together de Marsay, Paquita, and Mariquita. Paradoxically, the screen between the lovers, the name *Mariquita,* while it separates them, also metonymically links them to each other. The screen is a triangle. And the triangle is a screen in that it cancels out, precisely, the propriety of its three proper names, setting them in motion, as interchangeable, in a substitutive signifying chain that subverts, along with their propriety, their opposition to one another, subverting, by the same token, the clear-cut polarity, the symmetrical, dual opposition, of male and female, masculine and feminine.

III. Effects of Impropriety

No longer pointing to opposed *"proper* places," to literal referential points, but to successive *roles* in a triangular, dynamic spatial figure, to respectively opposed but interchangeable positions in a structure that subverts propriety and literality, the polarity of masculine and feminine itself becomes dynamic and reversible. However, the substitutions of woman for man and of man for woman, the interchangeability and the reversibility of masculine and feminine manifests a discord that subverts the limits and compromises the coherence of each of the two principles.

The male-centered cultural division of sex roles, the hierarchical model of male domination that conventionally structures the relationship of man and woman, through which Henri indeed expects to dominate Paquita, is thereby equally subverted or unsettled, since the master-slave relation of male to female presupposes the transparent, unified identity of each, and particularly, the coherent, unequivocal *self-identity* of the ruling male. This male self-identity, however, and the mastery to which it makes a claim, turns out to be a sexual as well as a political fantasy, subverted by the dynamics of bisexuality and by the rhetorical reversibility of masculine and feminine. If Paquita is indeed a slave, she nonetheless undermines Henri's delusion that he is her master when it turns out that she has still another master. But the marquise is not Paquita's real master either, since her hierarchical claim as Paquita's owner is equally frustrated by Paquita's love affair with Henri. If both Henri and the marquise treat Paquita as an object (be it a precious object—gold—to be owned and guarded in one's pocket), Paquita usurps the status of a subject from the moment that she takes *two lovers*—has two masters. The golden eyes of ideal femininity thus turn out to be deceptive: having two lovers, subject to a double visual fascination and infatuation, the mirroring, brilliant golden vision no longer reflects the idealized *unified* self-image of the lover but his *division*, his fragmentation. The golden eyes do not keep their phantasmic promise: the gold is not to be possessed; all it does is *disown* the marquise and *dispossess* Henri of the illusion of his self-identical master-masculinity. The signifier "femininity" no longer fits in the code of male representation or in any representative unequivocal code; it is no longer representative of the signified masculinity, nor is it any longer representative of *any* single signified. It is precisely constituted in *ambiguity*, it signifies itself in the uncanny space *between two signs, between* the institutions of masculinity and femininity. It is thus not only the conventional authority of sovereign masculinity that Paquita's femininity threatens, but the authority of any representative code as such, the smooth functioning of the very institution of representation.

THE SECRET ENEMY

It is this threat that Henri plots to eliminate through Paquita's murder: the physical suppression of Paquita's life, repressing femininity as a difference, as otherness, would eliminate ambiguity as such, stabilize the suddenly drifting cultural signs, ensure the principle of hierarchy and of representation, reestablish the univocality of the political institution of sexuality, that is, of culture.

It is, however, once again the marquise who precedes Henri and kills Paquita. Henri arrives at the murder scene only to find the dagger—an obvious phallic symbol—already thrust into Paquita's chest; the masculine sign of power has once again been usurped by a woman. "'Ah!'

de Marsay cried. . . . 'This woman will even have robbed me of my revenge!'" (387). In the very moment of his attempt to deny, through an act of violence, woman's power, Henri finds himself in the dénouement, once again, face to face with its castrating image. But most uncannily, this terrifying image has suddenly become his own.

> Faced with the spectacle that offered itself to his eyes, Henri had more than one cause for astonishment. The marquise was a woman. . . . The girl with the golden eyes lay dying. . . . The marquise was still holding her blood-stained dagger . . . . The marquis was about to fling herself on the divan, . . . stricken with despair. . . . This movement enabled her to notice Henri de Marsay.
>
> "Who are you?" she said, rushing upon him with raised dagger.
>
> Henri seized her by the arm, and thus they were able to look at each other face to face. A shocking surprise chilled the blood in the veins of both of them and they stood trembling like a pair of startled horses. In truth, the two Menaechmi could not have been more alike. In one breath they asked the same question: "Is not Lord Dudley your father?"
>
> Each of them gave an affirmative nod.
>
> "She remained true to the blood line," said Henri, pointing to Paquita.
>
> "She was as free of guilt as it is possible to be," replied Margarita-Euphemia-Porraberil, throwing herself on Paquita's body with a cry of despair. (388–90, TM)

This recognition scene finally provides the answer to the question that has obsessed Henri throughout the story: who is the secret enemy? What is the identity of the rival, of the third term in the triangular drama of desire? But the answer, at last revealed and clarified, is by no means a simple one, since Henri's enemy is his duplicate in every sense: in this uncanny mirror game of doubles over the corpse of their mutual victim, Henri beholds in his enemy the exact reflection of his own desire and of his own murderous jealousy; the enemy has his own voice, his own face; the enemy, in other words, is *himself.* The recognition scene thus meets and illustrates, in a striking, unexpected manner, Freud's psychoanalytic definition of the "uncanny" (*das Unheimliche*) as the anxiety provoked through the encounter with something that, paradoxically, is experienced as at once foreign and familiar, distant and close, totally estranged, unknown, and at the same time strangely recognizable and known. What, indeed, could be more distant from oneself, more foreign and estranged, than one's very enemy? What, on the other hand, is closer to oneself than oneself? But Balzac's text, in much the same way as Freud's text, postulates the meeting of extremes. The enemy—the embodiment of foreignness and distance—here uncannily turns out to be the very image of familiarity and closeness.

> "We will meet again," said Henri. . . .
> "No, brother," she said. "We shall never meet again. I shall return to Spain and enter the convent of Los Dolores."
> "You are too young and beautiful for that," said Henri, taking her in his arms and kissing her. (391)

What could be suspected in the recognition scene, and becomes apparent in these lines, is the connotation of incestuous desire between the brother and the sister. Narcissistic incest is indeed the implied logical consequence of the narcissistic structure of their mutual desire for Paquita; it is the secret figure that, throughout the novel, this particular triangle geometrically builds up to: since Paquita's golden eyes are but a mediating mirror in which the brother and sister, each in his and her turn, behold his or her own idealized self-images, fall in love with his or her own reflection, it is but natural that they would equally desire *his or her own image* in each other, each being an exact *reflection* of the other.

THE PURLOINED PACKAGE

What the dénouement reveals, then, is that, paradoxically enough, it has been Paquita—the apparent female center of the story—who has in fact all along been the *screen-woman*, screening an incestuous (unconscious) narcissistic fantasy. The golden eyes themselves were thus the screen: the screen has been a mirror, blinding in its refractions, dazzling in its bright intensity, screening through its very golden brilliance and its play of rays deflections and reflections. It is therefore through Paquita's murder—through the physical annihilation of the screen—that the face-to-face encounter between the brother and the sister is made possible.

In this manner, the dénouement provides a second unexpected answer to the second question outlined by the story: what is the true *address* of Henri's desire? Looking back again at the initial scene in which Henri's valet interrogates the mailman in the hope of finding out the true address of Henri's false package, the name of the desired woman, the true address, in other words, of Henri's message of desire, we can now fully understand the dramatic irony and symbolic impact of the valet's mistake, in saying: "My package is for the marquise." For as it turns out, Henri's package is, indeed, unwittingly *for the marquise*. Let it be recalled, in this conjunction, that the mailman shows the valet Paquita's name and address on the envelope of a letter sent from London, sent—as we will later gather—by the marquise. Symbolically, it is therefore from the start the marquise who *gives* Henri the *address* of his desire; and indeed, materially and literally, Paquita's address and the address of the marquise are the same. Furthermore: the phonetic resonance of the name Paquita resembles the phonetic resonance of the French word *paquet*, "package." In much the same way as the true address of Henri's message of desire is mediated by the false package, Paquita herself, as the screen-woman, turns out to be but a false package whose function ultimately is to be eliminated, having brought together brother and sister, the addressor and his real addressee. Paquita, in other words, can be said to be, ironically, Henri's uncanny *purloined package*.

IV. The Father's Name

The narrative's completion of the suggestive figure of incestuous desire brings back to the text the forgotten father figure of Lord Dudley. This rhetorical return of the father, both doubled and materialized by the actual return of the marquise from England, the father's country, illustrates again Freud's definition of the uncanny as a return of the repressed, as the recurrence of "something familiar and old-established in the mind that has been estranged only by the process of repression."[6] Lord Dudley has indeed *rhetorically* been repressed at the beginning of the story, where he is mentioned, as it were, for the last time, as *that of which the text will speak no more:*

But *let us finish with Lord Dudley* [*Lord Dudley,* pour n'en plus parler]: he came and took refuge in Paris in 1816 in order to escape from English justice, which gives its protection to nothing exotic except

merchandise [*qui, de l'Orient, ne protége que la marchandise*]. The itin-
erant lord saw Henri one day and asked who the beautiful young
man was. On hearing his name, he said: "Ah! He's my son. What a
pity!" (331)

This euphemistic passage seems to point to Lord Dudley's homosexuality: Dudley must have fled to Paris to escape prosecution for his homosexual mores, euphemistically referred to as an Oriental import
outlawed by the English courts. Lord Dudley's cynical understatement,
"He's my son. What a pity!" seems to imply that, having come across
Henri in Paris, the father has unwittingly lusted after his own hand-
some son. The rhetorical return in the dénouement of the rhetorically
repressed Lord Dudley thus connotes the return both of incest and of
homosexuality.

But Lord Dudley, let us not forget, is equally involved with women:
it is indeed his unwanted, multiplied, and disseminated fatherhood
that accounts for the story: "To make this story comprehensible, we
must at this point add that Lord Dudley naturally found many women
ready enough to strike a few copies of so delightful a portrait. His second masterpiece of this kind was a girl called Euphémie. . . . Lord Dudley gave his children no information about the relationships he was
creating for them here, there, and everywhere" (331). If, therefore, in
the recognition scene between the brother and the sister, the father's
name suddenly emerges in the very place of the erased name of the
girl with the golden eyes, it is not just because both names evoke bisexuality, but because they both occupy a symmetrical place in two symmetrical triangles: in much the same way as Paquita, having two love
affairs, occupies the midposition between her first love and her second, between Euphémie and Henri, Lord Dudley, in the primal scene
triangle, occupies the midposition between his first love affair, Henri's
mother, and his other love affair, Euphémie's mother, and consequently also between Henri and Euphémie. Furthermore, being a for-
eigner in Paris, as is the father, Paquita can only speak to Henri and
communicate with him in English: his father tongue.

Occupying thus the same position in the symbolic structure, Paquita's gold ultimately comes to symbolize the father. The signifier *gold* is
itself inscribed in the father's name: the French pronunciation of the
word *Lord* (lor') would phonetically resemble, be in fact a homonym of,
the word *l'or* (gold). The desired golden eyes turn out to be, indeed, the

family jewels. And just as in Paquita's case, the golden eyes themselves ultimately constitute a screen, so in the father's case it is gold that *screens* the *father's name,* which conceals the fatherhood, since it is gold that buys the "artificial" father, the parental substitute, de Marsay, who, for the money he is paid by Dudley, accepts to act as father, to recognize Henri as his son and give Henri his name.

The return of the lost *name of the father* in the dénouement therefore strips Henri of his (adoptive) proper name, de Marsay, leaving him, indeed, with *no name* that he can claim to be *his own,* that he can claim to be his *proper* name. The cultural procedure of name giving as insuring representative authority is no longer valid in the story: the (male) authority of name givers, customarily father and husband, is here disrupted: the father is no longer truly and legitimately *represented* by the son, in much the same way as the masculine is no longer truly and legitimately represented by the feminine. The Name of the Father, which traditionally is supposed to symbolize and to guarantee both propriety (proper name) and property (gold), here turns out to symbolize both *impropriety,* loss of proper name, and *dispossession,* loss of gold: it emerges in the very place of the symbolic loss of the golden eyes.

GOLD AND MEANING, OR THE PATERNITY OF THE PROLOGUE

Gold itself, the very fetish of desire, the very principle the prologue establishes as that which makes society go round, no longer incarnates the economic principle of *property* and of possession but rather the economic principle of *substitution* and replacement, the very principle of endless circulation of screening substitutes and their blind fetishization.

It is because the fetish is a screen, the very screen of substitution, the screen of screening, that Henri, so as to join the girl with the golden eyes, had to agree to be blindfolded, and that he has symbolically to lose the golden eyes so as to face the gold inscribed—as signifier, not as signified—in the father's name.

The opposition between *gold* as signified and *gold* as signifier, the displacement and disruption of the one by the other, was indeed prefigured at the outset by the *narrative's first word:* the word that serves as a *transition* between the prologue and the story. It is noteworthy and quite striking that, right after the prologue has established the word *or* ("gold") as an all-encompassing explanatory guiding "light," as the authoritative sign of meaning, the narrative is in its turn, introduced by the word *or*. This *or*, however, is just a homonym, and not a synonym, of the prologue's "gold": since it is used as a *coordinating conjunction*, it is a signifier not of the (luminous) precious substance but of the *logical relation* between the prologue and the story, a logical relation that is by no means clear and whose meaning (although ironically articulated by the signifier *or*) can no longer be "taken as light":

> *Or*, par une de ces belles matinées du printemps . . . , un beau jeunne homme . . . se promenait dans la grande allée des Tuileries.

> [*Now* (thus? however?), on one of those beautiful spring mornings . . . , a handsome young man . . . was sauntering along the main avenue of the Tuileries gardens.] (327, TM)

Constituting the ambiguous *transition* between the introductory authoritative discourse and the narrative, joining the prologue's gold and the story of the girl with the golden eyes, does the signifier, the conjunction *or*, mean "thus" (logically introducing an argument in support of a thesis), or does it mean "however" (logically introducing an objection)? Through this conjunction, does the story serve to *illustrate* the prologue, as a slave would serve its master[7] (*or* = "thus"), or is the story, on the contrary, a rhetorical *subversion* of the authority (of the paternity or consciousness) of the prologue (*or* = "however")?

NARRATIVE INSUBORDINATION

It could be said that, through the chiasmus, the reversal operated by the story's dénouement within the very import and significance of the sign "gold," the narrative indeed ends up subverting, to some extent at least, the "guiding light" of the prologue, the authoritative truth that was supposed to be its "proper" meaning and that it had to "demonstrate" as a self-evident principle of identity and value that, while distinguishing between the social classes, organizes Paris as a social universe of *order* and of ascending *hierarchy*. But in the narrative, on all three levels of the story—the level of the economical class struggle, of the political sex struggle, and of the rhetorical sense struggle—the signifier *gold* turns out to be no longer a principle of identity, of order, and of hierarchy but rather, on the contrary, a principle of universal economical *equivalence* that subverts the "proper" in every sense and thus upsets the hierarchical coherence and legitimacy of classification and of class, whether political (social classes, poor as opposed to rich), rhetorical (substitutive metaphorical as opposed to literal, figurative as opposed to "proper" meaning), or sexual (female as opposed to male). The prologue can no longer be *represented* by the narrative, in much the same way as, in the story's dénouement, the father can no longer be represented by the son, or the signified "gold" by its signifier, or the signified "male" by the signifier *female*.

DIFFERENCE

The principle of identity is subverted along with the principle of opposition when Henri discovers, in the recognition scene, that the Same is uncannily Other and that the Other is uncannily the Same: what he had expected to be Other—his rival's face—is Same; what he had expected to be Same—his rival's sex—is Other. Difference, Henri thinks, is determined by sexual identity. As it turns out, identity itself is determined by sexual difference. What the uncanny mirror game of the recognition scene suddenly reveals to Henri is womanhood, not as manhood's specular reflection but as the disorienting incarnation of real sexual difference: "Faced with the spectacle which offered itself to his eyes, Henri had more than one cause for astonishment. The marquise was a woman" (388, TM). What is the significance of this final revelation of the woman to Henri, as the ultimate signifier of the story?

The incestuous desire for the feminine sisterly double can be read as a fantasy of a return to the womb, to femininity as mother, a fantasy that Freud precisely mentions in his discussion of "The Uncanny": "It often happens," writes Freud, "that male patients declare that they feel that there is something uncanny about the female":

> This *unheimlich* place, however, is the entrance to the former *heimat* [home] of all human beings, to the place where everyone dwelt once upon a time and in the beginning. There is a humorous saying, "Love is a home-sickness," and whenever a man dreams of a place or a country and says to himself, still in the dream, "this place is familiar to me, I have been there before," we may interpret the place as being his mother's . . . body. In this case, too, the *unheimlich* is what was once *heimisch,* homelike, familiar; the prefix "un" is the token of repression. (153)

Since Henri's sister is a marquise, she can equally evoke Henri's mother, who was also a marquise. Henri's entire drama within the close interiority of the boudoir of the San Réal mansion betrays a womb nostalgia, a nostalgia for the woman as a familial and familiar essence, a nostalgia for femininity as snug and canny, *heimlich,* that is, according to Freud's definition, "belonging to the *house* or to the *family,*" "tame, companionable to man" (126).

Paquita, however, let us not forget, must be sacrificed, eliminated, killed, so that this incestuous return to the womb can occur. The nostalgia for *heimlich* femininity, for the woman as the tame, domesticated essence of domesticity and homeliness turns out to be a deluded, murderous narcissistic fantasy that in reality represses femininity as difference, kills the real woman.

Furthermore, the narcissistic *heimlich* union with familial and familiar femininity itself turns out to be un*heimlich* and uncanny. For in the mirror, Henri has to recognize incarnated by his double — by his sister — his own feminine reflection: he sees *himself* as a woman. Henri uncannily thus finds himself face to face with his own castration, symbolized at once by this reflection of his woman's face and by his loss of the golden eyes, through which he could complacently behold his own idealized male self-image, his univocal masculine literality. Dethroned from the privilege of unequivocal self-present literality, the masculine can no longer signify itself with a sign of plenitude. If femininity becomes indeed a signifier of castration, it is by no means here the embodiment of *literal castration,* the literalization of the figure of castration (as it sometimes is in Freud), but rather (as I understand the most radical moments of Freud's insight — as well as of Balzac's text), castration as a differential process of substitution, subverting, on the contrary, literality as such.

Masculinity, Henri discovers, is not a substance of which femininity would be the *opposite,* that is, at once the *lack* and the negative *reflection.* Since Henri himself has a woman's face, the feminine, Henri discovers, is not *outside* the masculine, its reassuring canny *opposite,* it is *inside* the masculine, its uncanny *difference from itself.*

THE UNCANNY AND THE WOMAN

"What interests us most in this long extract," writes Freud in his study on "The Uncanny," after having examined the lexicological and philological implications of the term, of the word *unheimlich* as opposed to *heimlich,*

What interests us most . . . is to find that among its different shades of meaning the word *heimlich* exhibits one which is identical with its opposite, *unheimlich*. What is *heimlich* thus comes to be *unheimlich*. . . . In general we are reminded that the word *heimlich* is not unambiguous, but belongs to two sets of ideas . . . on the one hand, it means that which is familiar and congenial, and on the other, that which is concealed and kept out of sight. The word *unheimlich* is only used . . . as the contrary of the first signification and not of the second. (18)

Thus *heimlich* is a word the meaning of which develops towards an ambivalence, until it finally coincides with its opposite, *unheimlich*. (131)

One might say, following Freud's analysis, that what is perhaps most uncanny about the uncanny is that it is not the opposite of what is canny but, rather, that which uncannily *subverts the opposition* between "canny" and "uncanny," between "*heimlich*" and "*unheimlich*." In the same way, femininity as real otherness, in Balzac's text, is uncanny in that it is not the opposite of masculinity but *that which subverts the very opposition of masculinity and femininity*.

Masculinity is not a substance, nor is femininity its empty complement, a *heimlich* womb. Femininity is neither a metonymy, a snug container of masculinity, nor is it a metaphor—its specular reflection. Femininity *inhabits* masculinity, inhabits it as otherness, as its own *disruption*. Femininity, in other words, is a pure difference, a signifier, and so is masculinity; as signifiers, masculinity and femininity are both defined by the way they differentially relate to other differences. In "The Girl with the Golden Eyes," femininity, indeed, is rigorously *the substitutive relationship between different screens*.

The dynamic play of sexuality as *difference* in the recognition scene between the brother and the sister takes place, indeed, not only *between* man and woman, between Henri and Euphémie, but between the masculinity and femininity of each. If the girl with the golden eyes was thus a *screen* between Henri and Euphémie, her symbolic screening function was not just to screen the other woman but to be a screen between Henri and his own femininity, to travesty, disguise, or hide from Henri's eyes his own split otherness, his own division as a subject, his own castration, reassuringly projected outside of himself onto his external female partner. Paquita, in other words, was a screen to the extent that she embodied the bar of censorship that separates consciousness from the unconscious. The golden eyes therefore function precisely as the prefix *un* in *unheimlich,* a prefix that Freud defines as the very "token of repression," screening the unconscious differential energy. Paquita as the bar of censorship insures the deceptively unequivocal ideological functioning of the phantasmically reified and fetishized *institutions* of masculinity and femininity.

THE COVER-UP

With Paquita's death, the golden veil is torn, the bar of censorship is for a moment lifted, Henri and Euphémie can see into their own difference from themselves, into their own constitutive division and castration; but this uncanny moment of intolerable insight and of terrifying knowledge will itself be soon repressed with the cover-up of Paquita's murder and the new linguistic screen, the final euphemism that commits the murder—and the whole adventure—to forgetfulness:

> A week later Paul de Manerville met de Marsay in the Tuileries Gardens. . . .
> "Well now, you rascal, what has become of our lovely GIRL WITH THE GOLDEN EYES?"
> "She's dead."
> "Of what?"
> "A chest ailment [*De la poitrine*]." (391)

"*La poitrine,*" or the ailing "chest"—a euphemism for consumption—is of course a lie, a social cover-up, which at the same time euphemistically and cynically describes the truth of Paquita's death through the dagger thrust into her chest; it can also euphemistically mean that Paquita has indeed died of the heart, as a metaphor for her love; she has died of her emotional and passionate involvement with Henri. The chest, however, can also euphemistically, through a dramatic textual irony, point to a sign of female difference, a signifier of femininity. In this sense, the text could here be answering that the girl with the golden eyes has died *because she is a woman;* she was sacrificed, repressed, because she incarnated femininity as otherness, as real sexual difference.

Paquita's death is thus a rhetorical transition from "active discretion" to a passive, "negative discretion," from an erotical affirmation, from the overstatement of a screen-woman, to an erotical negation, to euphemistic understatements. It is no coincidence that Henri's sister, the woman who is revealed to Henri through Paquita's murder, though the erasure of the screen-woman, is called Euphémie, Euphemia, Euphemism.[8] Femininity is in this text at once the relationship and the difference between "positive" and "negative" discretion, between a screen-woman and a euphemism. Ultimately, femininity itself becomes a euphemism, a euphemism at once for difference and for its repression, at once for sexuality and for its blindness to itself; a euphemism for the sexuality of speaking bodies and their delusions and their dreams, determined by a signifier fraught with their castration and their death. With the novel's final euphemism, however, with Paquita's death of "a chest ailment"—*de la poitrine*—femininity becomes indeed a *euphemism of euphemism*, a figure of the silencing of the very silencing of woman, of the repression of the very functioning of repression. The text, nonetheless, through its very silencing of death by language, opens up an ironic space that articulates the force of the question of femininity as the substitutive relationship between blind language and insightful, pregnant silence—between a language threatened and traversed by silence, and the silence out of which language speaks.

SHOSHANA FELMAN

6 From "Competing Pregnancies: The Dream from Which Psychoanalysis Proceeds (Freud, *The Interpretation of Dreams*)"

I

PSYCHOANALYSIS AND FEMINISM: QUESTIONS OF APPROACH

"The greatest part of the feminist movement," writes Juliet Mitchell, "has identified Freud as the enemy":

> It is held that psychoanalysis claims women are inferior and that they can achieve true femininity only as wives and mothers. . . . I would agree that popularized Freudianism must answer to this description, but the argument of this book is that a rejection of psychoanalysis is fatal for feminism. However it may have been used, psychoanalysis is not a recommendation *for* patriarchy, but an analysis *of* one. If we are interested in understanding and challenging the oppression of women, we cannot afford to neglect it.[1]

Like Mitchell, I am concerned with the misguided feminist belief that identifies Freud as the enemy of women: I take this attitude to be a grave misreading that fundamentally misconstrues both psychoanalysis and its as yet unexplored potentialities for a feminist reflection. Like Mitchell, I believe that feminism—the struggle toward a new feminine awareness fighting sex discrimination and redefining male and female sex roles—cannot afford to disregard psychoanalysis. I also believe, however, that psychoanalysis cannot afford to disregard—as Mitchell ultimately does—the feminist critique of

179

psychoanalysis. I agree that psychoanalysis is not a recommendation or normative prescription for, but rather an analysis of, the patriarchal symbolic system in which we live. I am not as sure, however, that *as* an analysis of patriarchy, Freudian psychoanalysis is entirely transparent to itself, entirely conscious of its full ideological implications. Thus, although I basically agree with most of the specifics of Mitchell's corrective readings of the feminist *misreadings* of psychoanalysis, and although in practice I admire and endorse Mitchell's paradoxical position as a feminist advocate of Freud, I cannot endorse, in theory, the unbreachable totality of the advocacy, that is, its implicit theoretical assumption that Freud, because he was the genius that he was, was inherently incapable of error, prejudice, or oversight: that Freud is thus by definition innocent of *any* feminist critique. To the feminist charge that Freud's view of femininity was tainted, or distorted, by the sexual ideology of his times, Mitchell answers: "As Octave Mannoni says, Freud made history, he was not made by it" (328).

Freud did make history. But does the experience of making history entirely exclude that of being made by it? Do we really have here a symmetrical alternative, a simple binary opposition of active/passive, either/or? "The setting or personality of a scientist," writes Mitchell, "by definition of his work, is largely irrelevant; if it becomes relevant, then we have to question whether it is a science that he is working in" (323). Can we be so sure that we *do not* have to put in question the particular scientific status of psychoanalysis? Freud himself, who referred to many of his theories as "his mythologies," was far less optimistic and far less apt to take for granted the scientific purity of his new method of investigation and of his innovative theoretical speculation. Perhaps a book like Mitchell's shows, indeed—because of the admirable, unflinching rigor of its psychoanalytic argument countering the feminist critique—why psychoanalysis is *not* a science: because it is, precisely, *irrefutable.* To suggest, however, that psychoanalysis is not—or may not be—a simple science is by no means to disqualify the truth inherent in its theory or the efficiency proceeding from its practice. "Psychoanalysis," says Lacan, "has to be taken seriously, even though it is not a science. It is not a science because—as Karl Popper has amply demonstrated—it is irrefutable. It is a *practice.* . . . All the same, psychoanalysis has consequences."[2]

BEYOND REVERSED POLARIZATIONS

Even though I sympathize with Mitchell's paradoxical position as a feminist advocate of Freud, then, I feel the need to advocate a different kind of advocacy. I cannot, psychoanalytically speaking, endorse the totality of the defense, that is, Mitchell's total rejection of the feminist critique of Freud, in much the same way as I cannot endorse the feminist critique's total rejection of Freud's theories and texts. "What all these [feminist] writers share," writes Mitchell pertinently, "is . . . a fundamental rejection of the two crucial discoveries of psychoanalysis: the unconscious and with it infantile sexuality. . . . Of course without [these two basic psychoanalytic concepts], Freud's theories of sexual difference become far easier to attack—for then, *robbed of their entire significance,* they are only prejudices." "My concern here," Mitchell perspicaciously goes on, "is in the main with the [feminist] denial of the unconscious" (352). And yet, does not Mitchell's symmetrical reversal of the feminist critique, her absolute rejection of what this critique points to as Freudian oversights, itself partake—ironically enough—of a *denial of the unconscious,* to the extent that it implicitly assumes, in the claim it makes to Freud's total awareness and total lucidity, that Freud himself had no unconscious—no (possible, conceivable) blind spots?

An absolute loyalty to Freud's consciousness is, paradoxically enough, a disloyalty to—a denial of—his theory of the unconscious. Perhaps we cannot avoid denying the unconscious, whatever we may choose to say, and in particular in any polemical pronouncement. Perhaps every *defense* entails such a *denial,* whether the defense is that of feminism against what it takes to be the aggression of psychoanalysis on the interests of women, or (as in Mitchell's case) that of psychoanalysis against what it takes to be the aggression of the feminist critique on its theoretical integrity (in both senses of the word).

But psychoanalysis precisely teaches us that every human knowledge has its own unconscious, and that every human search is blinded by some systematic oversights of which it is not aware. This is true as well of psychoanalysis itself, which cannot except itself from its own teaching. And, of course, it is also true of feminism. The unconscious means that every insight is inhabited by its own blindness, which pervades it: you cannot simply polarize, oppose blindness and insight (whether such polarization then equates blindness with feminism and insight with psychoanalysis, or on the contrary puts the insight on the side of feminism and the blindness on the side of psychoanalytic theory). Unfortunately, Mitchell's attitude only *reverses* the polarization but does not restructure, undermine, the illusory polarities.

The need for a restructuring of the symmetrically antagonistic, polar structure that has defined (delimited and limited the possibilities of) the feminist debate has been well seen, and quite incisively articulated, in Betty Friedan's book *The Second Stage*.[3] While I do not necessarily endorse Friedan's political solutions nor adhere to the specifics of her choices and ideological positions, I think she masterfully points out, and analyzes, the methodological impasse that the feminist critique has reached in many areas through a stereotyping of its own polarized positions.

> The feminine mystique[4] was obsolete. . . . It was, is, awesome — that quantum jump in consciousness. A whole new literature, a new history, new dimensions in every field are now emerging, as the larger implications of women's personhood and equality are explored. The women's movement, which started with personal truth not seen or understood by the experts, or even by the women themselves, has, in the span of one generation, changed life, and the accepted image. (31)

> Saying no to the feminine mystique and organizing to confront sex discrimination was only the first stage. We have somehow to transcend the polarities of the first stage, and even the rage of our own "no," to get to the second stage. (40)

> The first stage, the women's movement, was fought within, and against, and defined by that old structure of unequal, polarized male and female roles. But to continue reacting against that structure is still to be defined and limited by its terms. What's needed now is to transcend those terms, transform the structure itself. (40)

Again, it is not the pragmatic answers but the methodological questions of Friedan's (feminist self-) critique which I find compelling, and most eloquently pertinent to a rethinking of the woman question.

For my part, I would like to channel Friedan's appeal — as she does not — to the specific topic of the relationship between psychoanalysis and feminism. I would like to propose an approach that would take into account both what we can learn (far beyond what has been learned) from psychoanalysis about femininity and what we can learn from the feminist critique about psychoanalysis, in a way that would transcend the reified polarization of these two (as yet unfinished) lessons.

II

FREUD AND THE WOMAN QUESTION

Freud knew, and said, that his speculative theories of femininity were but provisional. For him, psychoanalysis was not so much an answer (the answers were provisional), as the constant and unfinished struggle to articulate—to open up—a question; a question whose revolutionary implications I believe neither women nor psychoanalysis has as yet measured; a question that he was the first to ask, the first not to take for granted: "What does a woman want?"[5]

Let us pause a moment and reflect: let us try to grasp the creatively outrageous, visionary, revolutionary imagination that it must have taken to historically articulate this question as a *serious* question. Let us listen to the question. Let us listen to its unheard confession and to its unheard of challenge.

What does a woman want? Doesn't everybody *know* what a woman wants? Doesn't what a *woman* wants go without saying? In a patriarchal society, what *can* a woman want except—as everybody knows—to be a mother, daughter, wife? What *can* a woman want except to be protected, loved by man? And what can a woman want in Freud's own eyes except—as every feminist well knows—to have and/or be the phallus, to realize—in one way or another—her *Penisneid?* And yet, Freud asks. Freud asks, and for the first time in the history of ideas, not just the commonsense–defying question: "What *is* a woman?" telling us for the first time that we *do not know* what a woman is, that, counter to all conventional expectations, "what constitutes masculinity or femininity is an unknown characteristic which anatomy cannot lay hold of."[6] Freud also puts in question, puts in focus, woman's *want* as the unresolved problem of psychoanalysis and, by implication, as the unresolved problem of patriarchy, telling us, again, that *we do not know* what a woman really wants. Presumably what a woman wants is of utmost importance. Presumably what a woman really wants is something altogether different than what patriarchy prescribes for her, assumes to be her "natural" desire: otherwise, there is no room for such a question.

"The great question," says Freud to Marie Bonaparte, "the great question that has never been answered and which I have not been able to answer, despite my thirty years of research into the feminine soul, is 'What does a woman want?'"

I propose now to explore, in Freud's text, not so much the answers (tentative and speculative) but the very crisis, the very critical explosion of the question. I propose to search the way Freud *lived* the question, and lived out its crisis, by turning, now, not to any speculative essay on femininity or female sexuality, not to any Freudian theoretical pronouncement, but to a *dream:* Freud's dream of Irma, reported and interpreted in chapter 2 of *The Interpretation of Dreams.* It was the very first dream Freud submitted to detailed interpretation, and he historically derived the theory of dreams from it.[7] I turn to this dream, which, in yielding thus a key to dreams, in triggering Freud's greatest insight into dream interpretation, can be said to be the very dream from which psychoanalysis proceeds, because it also is a dream about femininity, and about Freud's relationship—professional and personal—to femininity. It is thus the singular confession of a singular male dream of singular theoretical and pragmatic consequences. Perhaps it is significant that the relationship of Freud to women is precisely questioned in, and is the focus of, the very crisis dream from which psychoanalysis proceeds.

In turning to this dream, however, I do not mean simply to seize upon a "royal road" to Freud's unconscious so as to attempt reductively—as has become quite fashionable—to "outsmart" Freud in his own psychoanalysis, to psychoanalyze the dream and use it against Freud in a demystifying manner,[8] but rather, and quite differently, I mean to follow up on Freud's advice given in another context: "This," wrote Freud at the end of his theoretical essay on femininity, "is all I have to say to you about femininity. It is certainly incomplete and fragmentary and does not always sound friendly. . . . *If you want to know more about femininity, enquire from your own experiences of life, or turn to the poets, or wait until science can give you deeper and more coherent information*" (22:135).

I do indeed want to know more, and I propose to learn more—from Freud himself. In turning here to Freud not as theoretician but as dreamer, and as interpreter of his own dream, it seems to me I am precisely taking Freud's advice to interrogate at once experience,[9] poetry, and science: I am precisely turning to a poet (writer), to a scientist (dream interpreter), and to the life experience of a man who lives out (dreams, and dreams of solving) the questions and contradictions of sexual difference in the concrete dailiness of his material—and creative—life.

Let us now refresh our memory of the dream itself and of its circumstances. The evening before the dream was dreamed (July 23, 1895), Freud met a colleague and friend, Otto, who had just returned from a summer resort where he had met a young woman called Irma, who was Freud's patient. Irma's treatment had been partially successful: she was cured of hysterical anxiety but not of certain somatic symptoms. Before going on vacation Freud had offered Irma an interpretation—a "solution"—of the riddle of her symptoms, but Irma had been unwilling or unable to accept it; and the symptoms persisted. To Freud's question about how Otto had found the patient in that summer resort, Otto replied: "Better, but not quite well," words in which Freud detected a reproach. So as to justify himself, Freud that evening wrote out an explanation of his views on Irma's illness, in the form of a case history addressed to Dr. M., the leading figure in the medical circle at the time and a common friend of Otto and Freud. These circumstances were followed by the dream:

> A large hall—numerous guests, whom we were receiving.—Among them was Irma. I at once took her on one side, as though to answer her letter and to reproach her for not having accepted my "solution" yet. I said to her: "If you still get pains, it's really only your fault." She replied: "If you only knew what pains I've got now in my throat and stomach and abdomen — it's choking me" — I was alarmed and looked at her. She looked pale and puffy. I thought to myself that after all I must be missing some organic trouble. I took her to the window and looked down her throat, and she showed signs of recalcitrance, like women with artificial dentures. I thought to myself that there was really no need for her to do that.—She then opened her mouth properly and on one side I found a big white patch; at another place I saw extensive whitish grey scabs upon some remarkably curly structures which were evidently modelled on the turbinal bones of the nose.—I at once called in Dr. M., and he repeated the examination and confirmed it. . . . Dr. M. looked quite different than usual; he was very pale, he walked with a limp and his chin was clean shaven. . . . My

friend Otto was now standing beside her as well, and my friend Leopold was percussing her through her bodice and saying: "She has a dull area low down on the left." He also indicated that a portion of the skin on the left shoulder was infiltrated. (I noticed this, just as he did, in spite of her dress.) . . . M. said: "There's no doubt it's an infection, but no matter; dysentery will supervene and the toxin will be eliminated." . . . We were directly aware, too, of the origin of the infection. Not long before, when she was feeling unwell, my friend Otto had given her an injection of a preparation of propyl, propyls . . . propionic acid . . . trimethylamin (and I saw before me the formula for this printed in heavy type). . . . Injections of that sort ought not to be made so thoughtlessly. . . . And probably the syringe had not been clean. (4:107)

The pragmatic interpretation of the dream — through the chain of associations it evokes in Freud — is oriented toward the pathbreaking theoretical conclusion posited, at the end, as the basic thesis of Freud's book: that dreams have a meaning, and that their meaning is the fulfillment of a wish. "I became," writes Freud,

aware of an intention which was carried into effect by the dream and which must have been my motive for dreaming it. The dream fulfilled certain wishes which were started in me by the events of the previous evening (the news given me by Otto and my writing out of the case history). The conclusion of the dream, that is to say, was that I was not responsible for the persistence of Irma's pains, but that Otto was. Otto had in fact annoyed me by his remarks about Irma's incomplete cure, and the dream gave me my revenge by throwing the reproach back onto him. The dream acquitted me of the responsibility for Irma's condition by showing that it was due to other factors — it produced a whole series of reasons. The dream represented a particular state of affairs as I should have wished it to be. *Thus its content was the fulfillment of a wish and its motive was a wish.* (4:119)

Let us now return to our central question here, concerning the relationships of Freud to women and, through them, his relation to the question of femininity. Apparently, Irma is the only female figure in the dream. But as the chain of associations reveals, Irma is in fact the condensation of three different women representing, with respect to Freud, three different sorts of feminine relations. I will now try to organize the associative material related to these three female figures in a somewhat more coherent and more structured manner than the one immediately apparent in Freud's own haphazard, chronological exposition. As I relay this more consistent narrative of the dream's associations, many interpretative connections that Freud deliberately chooses to leave in the dark and not to comment on, not to make explicit, will become apparent. This exposition of the dream material will thus anticipate already, in a sketchy manner, the outline for a possible interpretation. Here, then, is the structured female trio condensed in Irma and the related interpretive information that comes up in Freud's associations.

The First Female Figure: The Young, Recalcitrant Woman

PATIENT—IRMA HERSELF Irma, a young widow, is characterized in the dream by her complaint (her pains), and her resistance, her unwillingness to accept Freud's solution. Through her "recalcitrance" she is doubled, however, by the image of another young woman patient, a governess who "seemed a picture of youthful beauty, but when it came to opening her mouth she had taken measures to conceal her plates" (4:109). It is thus the incongruous feature of the false teeth and examination of Irma's oral cavity that brings to Freud's mind the past examination of the governess, as well as "recollections of other medical examinations and of little secrets revealed in the course of them" (4:109).

The feature of the masculine medical examination of female cavities, unveiling and penetrating female secrets, can be related to the later part of the dream, in which Irma is examined and percussed by a group of male doctors, and her symptoms—this time an infection, and "infiltration" in the shoulder—are perceived and diagnosed through, "in spite of her dress." Follow the associations:

> *In spite of her dress.* . . . We naturally used to examine the children in the hospital undressed: and this would be a contrast to the manner in which adult female patients have to be examined. I remembered that it was said of a celebrated clinician that he never made a physical examination of his patients except through

their clothes. Further than this I could not see. Frankly, I had no desire to penetrate more deeply at this point. (4:113)

Later still, when it is discovered that Irma's infection or "infiltration" was caused by an injection given her by Otto with a dirty syringe, Freud's associations evoke two contradictory experiences in his medical treatment of women patients: on the one hand, his tragic, guilty experience with a woman patient named Mathilde (like his eldest daughter), whom Freud had inadvertently killed by prescribing a remedy that was at the time regarded as harmless; and on the other hand, his innocent, felicitous experience with an old lady to whom for two years Freud had given injections with no ill effect. Having learned by chance, the day before the dream, that the old lady was now suffering from phlebitis, Freud at once assumes that "it must be an infiltration caused by a dirty syringe," and is proud that he himself was never guilty of such malpractice: "I was proud of the fact that in two years I had not caused a single infiltration; I took constant pains to be sure that the syringe was clean" (4:118).

The Second Female Figure behind Irma: The Ideal, Phantasmic

WOMAN PATIENT—IRMA'S FRIEND "The way in which Irma stood by the window," writes Freud, "reminded me of another experience":

Irma had an intimate woman friend of whom I had a very high opinion. When I visited this lady one evening I had found her by a window in the situation reproduced in the dream, and her physician, the same Dr. M., had pronounced that she had a diphteric membrane. . . . It now occurred to me that for the last few months I had had every reason to suppose that this other lady was also a hysteric. Indeed, Irma herself had betrayed the fact to me. What did I know of her condition? One thing precisely: that, like my Irma of the dream, she suffered from hysterical choking. So in the dream I had replaced my patient by her friend. I now recollected that I had often played with the idea that she too might ask me to relieve her of her symptoms. I myself, however, had thought this unlikely, since she was of a very reserved nature. She was *recalcitrant,* as was shown in the dream. Another reason was that *there was no need for her to do it:* she had so far shown herself strong enough to master her condition without outside help. . . . What could the reason have been for my having exchanged her in the dream for her friend? Perhaps it was that I should have *liked* to exchange her: either I felt more sympathetic towards her friend or had a higher opinion of her intelligence. For Irma seemed to me foolish because she had not accepted my solution. Her friend would have been wiser, that is to say she would have yielded sooner. She would have then *opened her mouth properly,* and have told me more than Irma. (4:110)

Like Irma, Irma's friend is "also a young widow" (4:117).

The Third Female Figure behind Irma: Freud's Wife

There still remained a few features that I could not attach either to Irma or to her friend: *pale; puffy; false teeth.* . . . I then thought of someone else to whom these features might be alluding. She again was not one of my patients, nor should I have liked to have her as a patient, since I had noticed that she was bashful in my presence and I could not think she would make an amenable patient. She was usually pale, and once, while she had been in specially good health, she had looked puffy. Thus I had been comparing my patient Irma to two other people who would also have been recalcitrant to treatment. (4:110)

The text does not spell out the identity of this "someone else," this third female figure who "again was not one of my patients"; but a footnote called forth by the nostalgic mention "once, while she had been in specially good health, she had looked puffy" reads: "The person in question was, *of course,* my own wife" [emphasis mine]. In the footnote, too, another unexplained complaint of Irma finds explanation (it is, in fact, the wife's complaint), although the explanation itself is not explicated:

The still unexplained complaint about *pains in the abdomen* could also be traced back to this third figure. The person in question was, of course, my own wife; the pains in the abdomen reminded me of one of the occasions on which I had noticed her bashfulness. I was forced to admit to myself that I was not treating either Irma or my wife very kindly in this dream; but it should be observed by way of excuse that I was measuring them both by the standard of the good and amenable patient. (4:110)

What Freud omits to tell us, here, is the crucial fact that his wife is, at the time of the dream, *pregnant*,[10] a predicament that can perhaps better explain her "complaint" of "pains in the abdomen and in the stomach."

Although his wife's current pregnancy is never mentioned by Freud, her pregnant condition reappears in a different context of the dream's associations, in connection with the dirty syringe. Immediately after having congratulated himself on the clean syringe with which he gave injections to the old lady, who now was suffering from phlebitis due, perhaps, to the dirty syringe of another doctor, Freud notes: "The phlebitis brought me back once more to my wife, who had suffered from thrombosis during one of her pregnancies" (4:118). The wife is also present in the beginning of the dream, implicit in the words "we were receiving." The dream was dreamed, as the associations tell us, "a few days before my wife's birthday" (4:108), anticipating the birthday party. The birthday celebrated in the background is perhaps implicitly related, in its turn, to the experience of *giving birth*, that is, to the wife's unmentioned pregnancy and to the birth the wife will soon give to Freud's child.

"LADIES AND GENTLEMEN": FREUD'S STRUCTURE OF ADDRESS

What, then, is the dream telling us about Freud and women? It is easy—all too easy and too tempting—to submit the dream to the traditional hostile and antagonistic feminist approach to Freud, that is, to submit to a *critical* interpretation—to submit to our new feminine awareness and self-awareness—Freud's positions and propositions with respect to the women of the dream. I will first outline this kind of reading below and then attempt to show the limitations of such a traditional feminist approach. I outline, in other words, the critical *first stage* of a feminist interpretation, only with a view toward the further possibilities of a *second-stage* (or a third-stage) approach.

"Ladies and Gentlemen," wrote Freud, at the well-known opening of his theoretical lecture on "Femininity,"

Today's lecture . . . deals with a subject which has a claim on your interest second almost to no other. Throughout history people have knocked their heads against the riddle of the nature of femininity. . . .

Nor will *you* have escaped worrying over this problem, those of you who are men; as for the women among you this will not apply—they *are* themselves this riddle. (22:113)[11]

In the previous chapters, I have discussed the problematic contradiction inherent in this male structure of address, the discrepancy between Freud's statement opening up the question *of* the woman and his utterance closing it *for* women, excluding women from the question. Freud's address is obviously a rhetorical tease, but Freud is blind to the fact that his tease—his enunciation—unwittingly *represses* what his statement strives to *liberate,* to open up against so many prejudiced and conventional expectations. Freud's rhetorical address seems to imply that the question of femininity, while *involving* women ("they *are* themselves this riddle"), in effect *addresses* only men. The question of femininity becomes thus, in effect, a question of *complicity* among men: a question of the complicity of men about the fact that the question of the Woman is *their* exclusive question.

It is interesting to note that, in its very different setting, the Irma dream inscribes, dramatically, the very same *male* structure of address that "Femininity" inscribes theoretically and pedagogically.

It is to Dr. M.—"the leading figure in our circle"—that Freud, in waking life, addresses Irma's case report; and in the dream, when Irma's suffering defies and threatens Freud's "solution," it is to male authority that Freud appeals: "I at once called in Dr. M., and he repeated the examination and confirmed it." The riddle of the woman— Irma's body, or Irma's riddle—is thus submitted to an exclusively male examination: "My friend Otto was now standing beside her . . . and my friend Leopold was percussing her through her bodice. . . . M. said: 'There's no doubt it's an infection. . . .' We are directly aware, too, of the origin of the infection." Here again the question of femininity becomes a question of male knowledge, a knowledge whose authority is ratified by male complicity. Irma does not speak, whereas the male group speaks *about* her, but not *to* her. The riddle, it would seem, "does not apply" to Irma *because* "she herself is the riddle."

THE QUESTION OF MALE INSIGHT

Commenting on "the habitual masculine bias of Freud's own terms and diction,"[12] Kate Millet notes very judiciously, in reference to the whole corpus of Freud's writing:

> One is struck by how thoroughly the subjectivity in which all these events are cast tends to be Freud's own, or that of a strong masculine bias, even of a rather gross male supremacist bias. (247)

> [Freud] himself seemed incapable of *imagining objectivity* as a non-masculine related quality. (273)

This is absolutely true and probably has not been, and is not, sufficiently acknowledged by mainstream psychoanalysis to date. There is a basic given of psychoanalytic theory that psychoanalytic theory has as yet to learn how to take into account: Freud's is a *male genius*. Freud is a male genius.

This may sound like a simple statement. Yet I contend that we do not yet know what this statement really means. It certainly *does not mean* that Freud's stupendous insight is disqualified as far as women are concerned, or that his genius is irrelevant to women (or to feminism); it *does mean* (but in what way?) that his insight is inhabited by certain systematic oversights, and that the light it sheds also casts shadows.

The question, then, the real challenge that will keep confronting feminists who wish to be informed — or inspired — by psychoanalysis, is how to work *with* Freud's male genius, and not simply *against* it, as the feminist tradition felt compelled to do in its beginnings: whereas the first-stage feminism simply blocked, *foreclosed* male insights because of the (necessarily prejudicial) bias of their male enunciation, what we have not finished learning and what, in my view, we will never finish learning is, on the contrary, how to *relate* — in ever new ways — to a male genius: how to work *within* male insights so as to displace their oversights not from without, but from within, in such a way as to learn from their inspiration, and thus derive fresh (female) insights from their past conceptions.

THE ANXIETY OF PATERNITY

Let us, then, return to the dream and to its "first-stage"[13] feminist interpretation. We have seen that in the dream Irma's riddle is submitted to a male examination. But Freud had told us, in that crucial and peculiar footnote, that his wife is also present behind Irma. What is then the role, and the significance, of Freud's wife in and for the dream? Monique Schneider, one of the subtlest French interpreters of

Freud among those who submit Freud to a feminist critique, suggests that if the "possible allusion to the unborn child as the fruit of the unclean syringe" links the whole dream to the idea of maternity, then the expression "the toxin will be eliminated" is "disquieting," because the "purgative elimination" can be symbolically equated with "infanticide."[14] "Freud," writes Schneider, "had doubtless the feeling of having abandoned, inside the body of his wife, a part of his own substance, of his own 'solution'" (143). The dream is thus "the expression of a refused paternity, a paternity cleaned away" (133). "How," asks Monique Schneider, "could paternity be transformed into an infanticidal operation?" And she answers: "In the dream, the necessity of a maternal mediation—the patient has to 'accept the solution'—may account for the vindictive movement which would like to liquefy the belly interposing itself, in paternity, between the action proper of the father and the product of his action. . . . The woman constitutes a screen, an obstacle in the realization of a creative omnipotence; the wife as well as the patient are accused of not offering themselves as purely receptive matrixes" (134). Thus, the dream's purgative intention stands, in Schneider's interpretation, for a "matricidal and infanticidal fury" (133).

Perhaps Schneider's interpretation can explain the fact that Freud took such care to repress rhetorically, never to mention, his wife's pregnancy. "I have now completed the interpretation of the dream," writes Freud, and in a footnote (written ten years later) adds: "Though it will be understood that I have not reported everything that occurred to me during the process of interpretation" (4:118). "I will not pretend," Freud recapitulates toward the chapter's end,

> that I have completely uncovered the meaning of the dream or that its interpretation is without a gap. I could spend much more time over it, derive further information from it and discuss fresh problems raised by it. I myself know the points from which further trains of thought could be followed. But considerations which arise in the case of every dream of my own restrain me from pursuing my interpretive work. If anyone should feel tempted to express a hasty condemnation of my reticence, I would advise him to make the experiment of being franker than I am. (4:121)

If Schneider perhaps uncovers what Freud hides, it is, however, in the tradition of the feminist approach, so as to reverse, symmetrically, the image of Freud the hero into that of Freud the villain. The interpretation is not carried out so as to explore an insight (for instance, the significance of infanticidal fantasies in mental life, or the complexity and ambiguity of human creativity) but rather so as to pronounce a moral condemnation, to set Freud on trial and to set up a Manichaeistic world picture in which human beings are divided into two clearly defined, symmetrically and diametrically opposed camps: men/women; aggressors/victims; villains/heroines; "the bad"/"the good." Indeed, in spite of her remarkable finesse and penetrating analytic mind, Monique Schneider cannot but fall into this Manichaeistic trap. To borrow, once again, Betty Friedan's pertinent expressions, this is doubtless not "the feminine mystique"; but is it not a *feminist mystique?*

COMPETING PREGNANCIES

In the same line of interpreting the pregnancy—and the presence of Freud's wife—as the dream's center, Erik Erikson proposes a different reading,[15] more sympathetic to the dreamer's male point of view. "Freud," writes Erikson, "had the Irma dream when he was about to enter the fifth decade of his life, to which he would ascribe the generativity crisis" (IYC 197), the crisis of middle age: "an age when he seemed to notice with alarm the first signs of aging, and in fact, of disease; burdened with the responsibility for a fast-growing family" (IYC 199):

> [It was] a time when his wife was again expecting and when he himself stood before a major emancipation as well as the "germination" of a major idea. (DS 41)

> At the time of this dream, then, he knew that he would have to bear a great discovery—and "bear" here has a "pregnant" double meaning. (IYC 199)

> The Irma dream is concerned with a middle-aged man's cares, with the question of how much of what he has started he can also take care of, and whether or not he is not at times too careless to be able to sustain his ambitions. (IYC 197)

Erikson's interpretation is indeed ingenious: the Irma dream is dealing with the *competing pregnancies* of Freud—pregnant with psychoanalysis—and of his wife—pregnant with their child.

However, Erikson relates, still more ingeniously and through an absolutely brilliant insight, the paradoxical predicament of Freud's own pregnancy with the presence, in the dream, of Freud's friend and supporter, Fliess, evoked by Freud in association with the formula of trimethylamine.[16] (It should be remembered—in the background—that it is from Fliess that Freud derived the theory of bisexuality.) Here then is Erikson's interpretation:

> The "mouth which opens wide" . . . is not only the oral cavity of a patient and not only a symbol of woman's procreative inside, which arouses horror and envy because it can produce new "formations." It is also the investigator's oral cavity, opened to medical inspection; and it may well represent, at the same time, the dreamer's unconscious, soon to offer insights never faced before to an idealized friend with the hope that (here we must read the whole dream backwards) *wir empfangen:* we receive, we conceive, we celebrate a birthday. That a man may incorporate another man's spirit, that a man may conceive from another man, and that a man may be reborn from another, these ideas are the content of many fantasies and rituals which mark significant moments of male initiation, conversion and inspiration; and every act of creation, at one stage, implies the unconscious fantasy of inspiration by a fertilizing agent of a more or less deified, more or less personified mind or spirit. (DS 48)

But if, as Erikson magnificently analyzes, the Irma dream is transferentially *addressed* to Fliess; if Freud is seeking to conceive psychoanalysis from Fliess—or with Fliess—rather than to concentrate on his child's conception with his wife, then the dream repeats, once more, the exclusion of the woman, the homosexual complicity, the male supremacist structure of address, even with respect to this most female theme of pregnancy, of *conception.*

"Women," as indeed Freud writes in *Civilization and Its Discontents,*

> represent the interests of family and the sexual life; the work of civilization has become more and more men's business; it confronts them with ever more difficult tasks and compels them to carry out instinctual sublimations of which women are little capable. Since a man does not have unlimited quantities of psychical

energy at his disposal, he has to accomplish his tasks by making an expedient distribution of his libido. What he employs for cultural aims he to a great extent withdraws from women and sexual life. His constant association with men, and his dependence on his relation with them, even estrange him from his duties as a husband and father. Thus the woman finds herself forced into the background by the claims of civilization and she adopts a hostile attitude towards it. (21:103–4)

This sexual separation—this mutual discontent of the sexes toward each other within the normative prescriptions of a patriarchal social structure—may be seen as the very issue of the Irma dream.

The claims of patriarchal structure are, indeed, dramatized by the dream not just on the personal-familial level, but on the professional-medical level as well. Not only are all the doctors male and all the patients female: the "recalcitrant" female patient is treated by the self-righteous and paternalistic doctor like a stubborn child. The rapport between doctor and patient thus perpetuates the hierarchical male/female, father/child subordinating opposition in a medical frame apparently structured by a master-slave relationship. On this basis, Sarah Kofman, still another French feminist interpreter of Freud, writes, in reference to the Irma dream: "The irreducible women who refuse to open up their mouth"—their oral cavity—"because they do not accept the pernicious 'solution' of their psychoanalyst, will be . . . soon abandoned by him, quickly substituted by this man whose tenderness is reserved only to 'sympathetic,' likable women, those who properly open their mouth, those whom he finds 'wiser,' 'more intelligent' because they better know how to follow his advice, accept his solutions. . . . It is always the ladies' fault. . . . The dream is a veritable defense counsel's speech in favor of Freud's innocence."[17]

"But if Freud experiences such a need to disculpate himself," Kofman argues, "it is because he is, himself, the criminal. Not only because he has not yet cured Irma, but . . . because he has himself (a fault which is displaced in the dream and its interpretation onto his friend Otto) rendered her ill, because he has himself infected her with his symbolico-spermatic solution of . . . trimethylamine injected with a dirty syringe. . . . If Irma and all the irreducible women refuse to open their mouth and genitals, it is because Freud has already . . . closed their mouth, rendered them frigid, by injecting them with an erudite and malignant male solution. What else would they still have to say or to reveal, if not . . . that they were contaminated by him who, under the pretext of curing them, constrains them to collaborate, because he needs their complicity in order to believe, himself, in the value of his 'solution'" (56–57).

"The psychoanalytic solution," Kofman concludes, "restores speech to the woman only in order then better to despoil her of it, better to subjugate this speech to the discourse of the master" (57).

READING AND ANGER

Again, we are confronted, in this single-minded feminist interpretation, on the one hand, with an angry female reading and, on the other hand, with a Freud who has become, once more, a villain and a culprit.

Such rage, unfortunately, is self-blinding. As a woman, I cannot but understand the anger. But as a reader, I cannot but deplore the way in which I see the anger miss its mark, miss its own critical objectives in sliding toward a caricature—both of Freud and of itself.

The trouble with such mystifying demystifications is that they do to Freud precisely what they claim Freud does to women: they close the mouth of Freud's text: they judge, but they do not listen. Having decided in advance upon the "closure" of Freud's text, they paradoxically realize this closure through their own impermeability to the male insight of the text. "Battles won or lost," writes Betty Friedan, "are being fought in terms that are somehow inadequate, irrelevant. . . . And yet the larger revolution, evolution, liberation . . . has hardly begun. How do we move on? What are the terms of the second stage?" (*Second Stage*, 27).

To restate the question in terms of my own concerns here: how can we account *at the same time* for the text's *male blindness* and for the text's *male insight* (its very textual otherness to its blindness)? How can we engage in a dialogue at once with the blindness *and* with the insight of Freud's text?

A SELF-IRONIC STATEMENT

What, indeed, does the traditional feminist critique fail to see, above all, in the Irma dream? It fails to see the fact (which, like "The Purloined Letter," is "a little too self-evident" to be perceived)[18] that Freud has made it all too easy for us women to attack him in this way because *he said it all himself,* explicitly. The text *invites* this feminist critique, invites it not through its blind spots but, on the contrary, through its most conscious, and self-conscious, statements. The "first-stage" feminist critique, in other words, is first and foremost Freud's male *self-critique.*

Indeed, the first-stage feminist critique precisely fails to read, in Freud, that very aspect of his text that should, in my opinion, be regarded as his greatest—his most inspiring and thought-provoking—contribution to a feminist reflection: the crucially self-critical, self-questioning, and self-ironical potential, and activity, of his text. The Irma dream is, on the whole, a *self-ironic* statement: Freud's subtle but ever present irony toward himself constantly calls into question his own assumptions, his own certainties, his own male consciousness—and consciousness as such.

> *I reproached Irma for not having accepted my solution; I said: "If you still get pains, it's your own fault."* . . . It was my view at the time (though *I have since recognized it was a wrong one*) that my task was fulfilled when I had informed a patient of the hidden meaning of his symptoms: I considered that I was not responsible for whether he accepted the solution or not—though this was what success depended on. *I owe it to this mistake,* which I have now *fortunately corrected, that my life was made easier* at a time when, in spite of all my inevitable ignorance, I was expected to produce therapeutic successes. (4:108; emphasis mine)

Kofman's reading does not in effect analyze the dream but paraphrases it—incompletely, echoing but one of its many voices. Paradoxically enough, in blaming Freud for his repressive and reductive male *appropriation* of female speech, what Kofman is precisely doing is (selectively, reductively) *appropriating* Freud's own words.

But the symmetry, here as elsewhere, is misleading. For in seemingly reversing Freud's appropriative gesture, Kofman fails to see that the Irma dream is not simply a description of Freud's attempt at mastery; it is a description, a dramatization, of the necessary failure of such an attempt: the Irma dream is, on the contrary, a recognition of the *impasse* (medical and sexual) inherent in the very impulse to appropriate, to forcefully reduce the otherness of the other.

And this is why the Irma dream is a key dream that, in the search that was to be psychoanalysis, yields the fruit of the discovery not just of wish fulfillment and of the theory of dreams, but of the question of *resistance* as a psychoanalytic question (as yet unexplored, unformulated, but obscurely grasped, intuited). The dream's discovery, in other words, is that of the necessity, precisely, of *transforming,* in psychoanalysis, the master-slave relationship. The dream articulates the necessity of breaking away from the prescriptions of the medical patriarchal frame and the conventional professional relationship that structure it.

AN ONEIRIC LESSON OF SELF-DIFFERENCE

In waking life, Freud indeed desired to *reduce resistance* and specifically, resistance to his male or medical or intellectual "solutions." But the dream, precisely, dramatizes, through the insistent "recalcitrance" of women both as lovers and as patients, something like a *resistance of resistance:* it is the dream itself that seems to be resisting Freud's daytime, waking attitudes; it is not simply women but the dream, Freud's dream, which seems to be resisting Freud's solutions, as well as Freud's resistance to resistance. The solutions *of* the dream are, in other words, altogether different from the solutions *in* the dream. The dream is looking for a solution altogether different from the imposition of solutions that it dramatizes.

If the dream comes up, precisely, with the notion of *wish fulfillment* as the meaning (the *solution*) of the dream—of any dream—it is perhaps because Freud realizes that his past solutions were but wish fulfillments, dream solutions. "The unconscious," says Lacan, "is precisely the hypothesis that one does not dream only when one sleeps" (5). But, says Freud, if we do indeed have an unconscious, if we do not dream only when we are asleep, is it possible that the dream itself could have a *waking function?* Is it possible that sleep itself could *wake us up* from our daily dream of wakefulness? Is it possible, in other words, that a dream—in sleep—would sound the alarm of daytime false solutions?

This, it seems to me, is what is at stake in the Irma dream, dealing as it does with the inadequacy of waking (sexual and medical) male solutions. The dream—and this is why it is a dream of genius: a dream that speaks *beyond* Freud's ego, beyond Freud's present knowledge, beyond Freud's narcissistic male self-consciousness and consciousness—the dream is *critical* of Freud's life attitudes: but critical in a creative way: a way that opens up a "royal road" to a pathbreaking innovation, a way whose very *dead end*—the deadlock dramatized by the dream—will bring about a revolutionary *breakthrough*. And this is why the Irma dream—the dream, precisely, of the awkwardness of Freud's patriarchal encounter with feminine resistance, the very dream of the inadequacy of Freud's male solutions to the feminine complaint—will end up giving birth to the *displaced* solution of a revolutionary kind of listening: of listening—differently and differentially—at once to others and to oneself; of listening—differently and differentially—to one's own dream. And Freud, indeed, had listened to the crisis, to the question of the dream. And this is why the Irma dream—this critical, historical inscription of male blindness and male genius—will end up giving birth to the displaced solution of a revolutionary theory of sexual difference, that is, of sexuality not just as difference but as *self-difference*. And this is why the Irma dream—Freud's dream of femininity, of sexuality, of difference—has turned out to be, in all the senses of the word, the very *dream* from which, in an undreamed of manner, psychoanalysis was born.

On Asking Again:
What Does a Woman Want?

My memory may not be quite accurate, but I believe I heard the earliest version of Shoshana Felman's beautiful and important essay on Freud's dream of Irma's injection one evening in early autumn, 1983, read by her at—was it?—the Kanzer Seminar, anyway, upstairs in the Whitney Humanities Centre, Yale University. The date and occasion may be vague, but the experience is not. Elegantly, she gave an immaculate presentation. The room divided as though some grand canyon had opened up down the middle of the large room. On one side sat clinicians, on the other, academics. Only on one level could they really share an idiom, and that idiomatic unity was achieved by isolating Shoshana as a woman. It was courteously done—but I remember her bemused look as she assured her questioners she was familiar with the well-known texts on the topic to which they had thought they were introducing to her.

On my most recent visit to Yale some twenty years later, I had the privilege of attending a class Felman was giving on Balzac. It stands for me as a unique instance of remarkable pedagogic excellence: it was inspiring. The young woman speaker of the early eighties and the mature woman teacher of today were equally brilliant, but something more than the confidence of age and the authority of academic success had brought about a sea change in the presentation. How far is such a change a reflection of, or caused by, a shift from first-stage to second-stage feminism? From either/or sexual antago-nism to an understanding of gender as "self-difference," as

Felman evokes it here, along with the transcendence of the either/or of psychoanalysis and its feminist opposition into "an approach that would take into account both what we can learn from psychoanalysis about femininity and what we can learn from the feminist critique about psychoanalysis, in a way that would transcend the reified polarization of these two (as yet unfinished) lessons" (72).

The chapter—"Competing Pregnancies: The Dream from Which Psychoanalysis Proceeds"—engages with what feminists have perceived as Freud's male blindness and simultaneously with what psychoanalysis offers as the dream text's male insight. This beautifully articulated enquiry leads Felman to a point where she is able to bring the two strands together as a foundational and exemplary postmodern perception, asking, can we find a way in which "the unknown . . . the genuine unknown of gender and of gender difference—the radical unknown of sexuality as difference—*fecundates* at once Freud's dream and the unprecedented theory to which the dream historically gives birth?" (116).

After the Kanzer Seminar, Shoshana and I continued to meet occasionally and to become friends. She generously used my own work in *Psychoanalysis and Feminism*[1] as a new starting point for this essay. My work is, quite rightly, regarded by her as an instance of first-wave either/or-ism: *either* Freud *or* his feminist critics, but not both, are right. There can be no fecundating relationship—for which Shoshana's essay sets the agenda. Similarly, in the seminar of 1983, *either* the clinicians *or* the academic practitioners of psychoanalytic criticism were correct. Let us look at this again.

Of either/or positions, Freud writes: "If . . . in reproducing a dream, its narrator feels inclined to make use of an either-or—e.g. 'it was either a garden or a sitting-room'—what was present in the dream thoughts was not an alternative but an 'and,' a simple addition. An 'either-or' is mostly used to describe a dream-element that has a quality of vagueness—which, however, is capable of being resolved. In such cases the rule for interpretation is: treat the two apparent alternatives as of equal validity and link them together with an 'and.'"[2] The "and" of my book, *Psychoanalysis and Feminism*, was made famous by a lengthy critique from Jane Gallop.[3] The book is, of course, no dream. However, something of this relationship of "either/or" to its origin and subsequent translation as "and" pertains: women and men are of equal validity, as are feminism and psychoanalysis, but to express that equality of two different objects, one resorts to "either/or." The old question: How can two apparent un-alikes be equal?

My own background had been in Marxist-Feminism; dialectically the thesis and antithesis move into a position of synthesis—war becomes peace, and this new unity, in which each have changed into the other, becomes a new point of antithesis or thesis. The theory implicates movement and change; the practice was one of polemic and argument between those with the same concerns. There has to be some common ground to start with; a giraffe and a stone can never form any part of a dialectical relationship. I was, perhaps, seeing women and men, psychoanalysis and feminism on a par with war and peace (rather than as a giraffe and a stone, whose equal status is meaningless); these also have to be expressed as *either* war *or* peace. This "either/or" as meaning "and" is not the same as the postmodern possibility explored by Shoshana, in which she finds that Freud gives birth to psychoanalysis through the critique of women; that men find themselves in women—the rheumatic pain in Freud's shoulder is dreamed as an illness in the upper chest of his patient, Irma. Quoting Freud on the either/or of the dream, Shoshana omits the "and": "In confronting Freud, however, with the either-or alternatives and symmetrical dichotomies of a Manicheastic worldview, and in taking literally the oneiric statement of Freud's wish fulfillment as the homogeneously one-sided, self-identical statement of the dream, the first-stage feminist critique precisely misses the wish fulfillment's—and the text's—status as a joke" (93). And: "Unfortunately, Mitchell's attitude only *reverses* the polarization but does not restructure, undermine, the illusory polarities" (71). Having largely accepted Felman's criticism hitherto, I am now somewhat less sure. I think Shoshana's analysis is superb, but I want to argue that there is a place for oppositional perspectives that respect each other but also can confront each other. There is something necessarily different about both psychoanalysis and feminism, and a particular (a very particular) difference between men and women; to transcend these loses the dynamic of historical change that only comes about through their confrontation. In *Psychoanalysis and Feminism* I was harsher in my critique of feminists than of Reich and Laing simply because their work was more important to my project of using the different perspective of psychoanalysis to confront the demands of feminism for a theory and practice based on an analysis of sexual difference. Could there not be both Shoshana's postmodern perspective and one in which an either/or indicates an "and"—her viewpoint and mine? In some, perhaps important, perhaps residual respects, psychoanalysis and feminism, women and men are polarities that can find a meeting point and then enter into a new opposition. A confrontational difference between clinicians and academics seems to me often more fruitful than an apparent transcendence of these disciplines, one of which uses people, the other texts, as its material resource.

However we understand the written text of a dream, not a single subtle addition can ever tell us anything more about Freud than he has already told us himself. Texts are not people and, though they have blind spots, they cannot reply to an interpretation with free associations, that is, with responses that, because they have escaped censorship, can open up some further unconscious meanings relevant to the life history of the person. One can enrich the text and one can use the dream to tell us more about something else. In this sense, all the interpretations—Erikson's, Schneider's, Kofman's, Felman's, the one I am about to offer, and the hundreds of others—are equally valid as interpretations of Freud's dream, although some may tell us more than others about the text and also use the text to explore something else with greater or less efficacy. Because Shoshana and I have the same project of using psychoanalysis to understand sexual difference, it is this other question of sexual difference for which I am going to use Freud's dream in the hopes of furthering our enquiry. I do not disagree with Felman's insights, quite the contrary. However, only to praise can truly be to bury—I want to continue the discussion.

Throughout *The Interpretation of Dreams*, the figure of Irma stands as an exemplary instance of both condensation and multiple determination—both these are major means of dream construction. From his associations, Freud makes it clear that Irma stands for several, if not many, women in his life and thought. However, Freud and, more emphatically, Felman select three women as key figures in the dream—for Felman these are: Freud's eponymous patient, Irma; Irma's intelligent, unnamed friend whom Freud would prefer for a patient; and Freud's pregnant, here unnamed, wife. Freud's three are different: "the phlebitis (of an old lady, another patient) brought me back to my wife, who had suffered from thrombosis during one of her pregnancies; and now three similar situations came to my recollection involving my wife, Irma and the dead Mathilde. The identity of these situations had evidently enabled me to substitute the three figures for one another in the dream" (SE 4:118). The trio for Freud is Irma, his wife, and not Irma's friend but the named Mathilde. Names are important in dreams, as they act as bridges. Mathilde was a patient of Freud's who died from his prescription of sulphonal, a poison considered safe at the time. Mathilde is also the name of Freud's oldest daughter, who nearly died of diphtheria two years before the dream. At the time of the dream, the Freuds have five children, and there is every evidence from the letters that Freud adores his wife and their "brats." But dead Mathilde must play her part.

Thirteen years after the publication of this foundational dream of psychoanalysis and eighteen years after it was dreamt, Freud published an essay on "The Theme of the Three Caskets," finding that, in common with many fairy tales and much literature, these caskets stood for three women and the need for a man to choose between them. A man's choice falls on the third, who, from the symbolic *pale* lead of the casket that Bassanio in *The Merchant of Venice* selects to the silent daughter whom King Lear favors, through many other examples, represents death, although she may also appear as love or beauty. The three women are the Fates, a man's destiny; the essay ends: "We might argue that what is represented here are the three inevitable relations that a man has with a woman—the woman who bears him, the woman who is his mate and the woman who destroys him; or they are the three forms taken by the figure of the mother in the course of a man's life—the mother herself, the beloved one who is chosen after her pattern, and lastly the mother earth who receives him once more. But it is in vain that an old man yearns for the love of woman as he had it first from his mother; the third of the Fates alone, the silent Goddess of Death, will take him into her arms" (SE 12:301).

Death and maternity are both strong features of the earlier dream that, no less than the later essay, would have been informed by the mythology of three women/the Fates. First—Death: *Irma*, Freud's patient and his wife's friend, to whom he will give an injection that reminds him that it was injecting the cocaine he had recommended that had killed one of his closest friends (the story of cocaine also implicated his feelings about his wife); his patient *Mathilde*, dead from his prescription of sulphonal; his daughter, also *Mathilde*, who at the time of her last sibling's birth nearly died of diphtheria: "It had never occurred to me before, but it struck me now almost like an act of retribution on the part of destiny. It was almost as though the replacement of one person by another was to be continued in another sense: this Mathilde for that Mathilde, an eye for and eye and a tooth for a tooth" (SE 4:112). Childbirth is also, at least ultimately, the replacement of one generation by another; thus, it brings intimations of mortality. It is the third of Freud's trio of women, dead Mathilde, who brings the second, his endangered (thrombosis) pregnant wife to mind. Freud's wife is puffy and pale (Dr. M. and Freud's elderly sick brother are likewise pale); pale as death. She also hides her false teeth—it was said that for every child conceived, a tooth was lost. Life and death are either/or.

Next—Maternity: In a letter two months before the dream, Freud had excitedly congratulated his great friend Fliess for the possible discovery of the periods when conception would take place—joking it was some months too late this time but would be useful if the Freuds were to avoid conception the following year. Martha would have been about two months pregnant; they would have known this only because she would have missed menstruating. Irma's complaints about her abdominal pains will also have been period pains, her actual complaint of nausea, morning sickness; the various chest infections and pains of the dream's actors could have to do with other fantasies of conception: Eve from Adam's rib and so on. The male patient to whom Freud associates is suffering from hysterical dysentery; although Freud only mentions the man's defecatory problems, he would most likely have been bleeding anally. In Western cultures, men can only be pregnant or menstruate if they are hysterics.

Freud doesn't want to be responsible for the dangers of his wife's condition, including the dangers that might arise from his own ambivalence toward her and her pregnancy—he has killed other people (von Markow and Mathilde) inadvertently. To Freud's considerable anxiety, Martha Freud was in great discomfort in the last months of her pregnancy (as she may well have been in previous pregnancies); however, there is no reason why she would have been suffering at two months, the time of the dream. But there was a considerable risk of death in childbirth; abortions of fetuses were common enough. The three caskets: the mother as death. One fears that one's unconscious wish to kill may bring the retribution of being killed.

Are the pains in the stomach Martha's or Sigmund's—it is, after all, his dream? A patient of mine took until the eighth month to grasp that the ulcer and then possible stomach cancer from which he suffered belonged to the painful, murderous anxiety he felt about the growth not in his but in my pregnant "stomach." This is a separate and simpler point than Felman's establishment of Freud's ability to dream of Irma's pain because of his own pain and his discovery of self-difference. It is once more to suggest that, on one level, this is not only a dream that wishes Freud's understanding of hysteria is correct, not only a dream about hysterical patients, but the dream of a hysteric—Freud's own *petite hystérie* (manageable, like that of Irma's unnamed friend), which he was to analyze in the years between the dream and its publication. Identifications with another can be a means to understanding—they can also be a defense against the recognition that the other is not the same as the self. Felman argues for the first—I believe the second also pertains: only in hysteria do men get pregnant; who can be pregnant is an either/or condition.

Hysterics, according to Lacan, ask perpetually: what is a woman? However, I believe Lacan is conflating women and mothers. The received wisdoms of what, for want, as yet, of subtler distinctions we must call "patriarchy," consider that reproduction produces the "essential difference"[4] between women and men. However, the role of female ova and male sperm in reproduction are, in fact, not an essential difference but, so far at least, an irreducible difference. Until now, pregnancy, although now not impregnation, has likewise been an irreducible particularity. Even a surrogate mother is a woman. However, that a mother is a woman does not mean that woman is a mother. What our ideologies conflate is first female/male with reproduction and then with women and men. There are many other aspects to being female and male than reproduction. The difference between women and men is neither essential nor irreducible. The either/or with which I started, is, I would argue, the irreducible binary/polarity of reproduction.

Hysterics are, I believe, only stuck with everybody's first question about the origin of babies—hysteria is therefore a useful aid to understanding mental processes as their neurosis paints the general scene in brighter, clearer colors. As Freud was to put it, when small children want to know where babies come from, what they have in mind is— where does this particular intruder (sibling or substitute) originate? Just so, do hysterics ask with the same, original, indeed desperate insistence? It is the hysteric who exaggerates everyone's ignorance by his determination quite madly to find out what it means to be a mother— and not to take on board that children can't be pregnant. A Lacanian reading makes a hysteric such as Dora not know that woman is that sex that has babies.[5] The normativity of heterosexuality[6] rests on what is proclaimed as the hysteric's cure. But the hysteric is being wrongly cured, or cured within patriarchal conflations of women and motherhood and thus binary sexual polarities. It is not that reproduction will have no effect on human sociopsychology, it is just that its effect should be seen as one among others.

The question of Freud's dream is not "what is a woman?" but "where do babies come from?" "what is a mother?" "what is a man's role in pregnancy?" It is a dream about reproduction. Except from the viewpoint of childhood or hysteria, there are no competing pregnancies — this is, like life and death, the irreducible problem. From the symbolism of the great hall where, for his wife's birthday, together they are receiving the hysterics, doctors, friends, and family of Freud's dream, we have an investigation into the dividing line of reproduction. What it reveals, among other things, is that women and men can, both equally and in the same way, not grasp it. Motherhood is not the cure for hysteria because mothers are as liable as anyone else not to understand reproduction. Is there anything to understand other than its irreducibility? Like death.

Felman has importantly celebrated that Freud puts in question the patriarchal assumption that all a woman "wants" is to be a daughter, a wife, and a mother. She focuses on the radical brilliance of Freud's later question, of his not knowing: what does a woman want? This, she argues, sublates the conventional: what is a woman? She asks: "What is, then, the question that the dream discovers, the question that the specimen dream is quite literally *engrossed with?* Is there a different, nonreductive way in which the unknown, the dream's navel, can be, not accounted for, explained away, subsumed by what is known, but rather thought out as the way in which the genuine unknown of gender and of gender difference — the radical unknown of sexuality as difference — *fecundates* at once Freud's dream and the unprecedented theory to which the dream historically gives birth?" (116).

I would argue that, at least by the time of Freud's question, "The Three Caskets" demonstrates that he knows that the usual answer is a patriarchal vision — it is what a man wants a woman to want. And the answer is that woman wants to be what she is, the mother. In other words, Freud may ask a new question, but it is framed with the equation of woman and motherhood, which is what the little boy learns when he can't make a baby like the one his mother has produced. Nor of course can the little girl. If they were to realize not that that is what women do, but that that is what mothers do, we might be outside a patriarchal framework to our enquiry. Neither feminism nor psychoanalysis has followed through on the radical insight of the *Three Essays on the Theory of Sexuality* that sexuality and reproduction are not the same.

"The radical unknown of sexuality as difference," writes Felman. But is sexuality constructed as difference? Surely not. Freud discovered that there is only one libido for women and men (called "male" under patriarchy). Sexuality can be "about" anything—that is the meaning of its "polymorphous perversity." The pathbreaking discovery of the *Three Essays on the Theory of Sexuality* was to demonstrate that reproduction was only tacked on to sexuality. It is reproduction, not sexuality, which is unknown in its irreducible difference. To confuse the two is to subscribe to the ideology of "patriarchy." That is one of the problems addressed in Freud's dream. The either/or belongs to reproduction—it is vague because, although we understand it scientifically, somewhere conception remains the miracle it seemed to us as small children—where on earth *has* this intruder come from? Could it magically vanish as it magically appeared? The either/or is the *and* of ova and sperm. The variousness of sexuality and of gender is another matter altogether.

PART 4 | Psychoanalysis and the Question of Literature

SHOSHANA FELMAN

7 | To Open the Question

"Love," says Rimbaud, "has to be reinvented." It is in much the same spirit that we would like here to reinvent the seemingly self-evident question of the mutual relationship between literature and psychoanalysis. We mean indeed to suggest that not only the approach to the question, but also the very relationship between literature and psychoanalysis — the way in which they inform each other — has in itself to be reinvented.

Let us outline this suggestion in a series of programmatic remarks, the purpose of which would be to put in question the apparently neutral connective word, the misleadingly innocent, colorless, meaningless copulative conjunction *and,* in the title "Literature and Psychoanalysis." What does the *and* really mean? What is its conventional sense, its traditional function, in the usual approach to the subject? In what way would we like to *displace* this function (to reinvent the "and"), — what would we like it to mean, how would we like it to *work,* in this issue?

Although "and" is grammatically defined as a "coordinating conjunction," in the context of the relationship between "literature and psychoanalysis" it is usually interpreted, paradoxically enough, as implying not so much a relation of coordination as one of *subordination,* a relation in which literature is submitted to the authority, to the prestige of psychoanalysis. While literature is considered as a body of *language* — to *be interpreted* — psychoanalysis is considered as a body of *knowledge,* whose competence is called upon to *interpret.* Psychoanalysis, in other words, occupies the place of a *subject,* literature

that of an *object;* the relation of interpretation is structured as a relation of master to slave, according to the Hegelian definition: the dynamic encounter between the two areas is in effect, in Hegel's terms,
a "fight for recognition," whose outcome is the sole recognition of the
master—of (the truth of) psychoanalytical theory; literature's function, like that of the slave, is to *serve* precisely the *desire* of psychoanalytical theory—its desire for recognition; exercising its authority and
power over the literary field, holding a discourse of masterly competence, psychoanalysis, in literature, thus seems to seek above all its
own *satisfaction.*

Although such a relationship may indeed be satisfying to psychoanalytical theory, it often leaves dissatisfied the literary critic, the reader
of a text, who feels that, in this frame of relationship, literature is in
effect *not recognized* as such by psychoanalysis; that the psychoanalytical reading of literary texts precisely *misrecognizes* (overlooks, leaves
out) their literary specificity; that literature could perhaps even be defined as that which remains in a text precisely *unaccounted for* by the
traditional psychoanalytical approach to literature. In the literary critic's perspective, literature is a subject, not an object: it is therefore not
simply a body of knowledge to interpret, since psychoanalysis itself is
equally a body of language, and literature is also a body of knowledge,
even though the mode of that knowledge may be different from that
of psychoanalysis. What the literary critic might thus wish is to initiate
a real exchange, to engage in a real *dialogue* between literature and
psychoanalysis, as between two different bodies of language and between two different modes of knowledge. Such a dialogue has to take
place outside of the master-slave pattern, which does not allow for
true dialogue, being, under the banner of competence, a unilateral
monologue of psychoanalysis *about* literature.

In an attempt to disrupt this monologic, master-slave structure, we
would like to reverse the usual perspective, and to consider the relationship between psychoanalysis and literature *from the literary point of
view.* We would not presuppose, as is often done, that the business of
defining, of distinguishing, and of relating literature and psychoanalysis belongs, as such, to psychoanalysis. We would like to suggest—and
the following articles will try to demonstrate this proposition each in
its specific manner—that in much the same way as literature falls
within the realm of psychoanalysis (within its competence and its
knowledge), psychoanalysis itself falls within the realm of literature,

and its specific logic and rhetoric. It is usually felt that psychoanalysis has much or all to teach us about literature, whereas literature has little or nothing to teach us about psychoanalysis. If only as a working hypothesis, we will discard the presupposition. Instead of literature being submitted, as is usually the case, to the authority and to the knowledge of psychoanalysis, psychoanalysis itself would then here be submitted to the literary perspective. This reversal of the perspective, however, does not intend to simply reverse the positions of master and slave in such a way that literature now would *take over* the place of the master, but rather its intention is to disrupt altogether the position of mastery as such, to try to avoid *both* terms of the alternative, to deconstruct the very structure of the *opposition* mastery/slavery.

The odd status of what is called a "literary critic" indeed suffices to mix and shuffle the terms of the alternative. It could be argued that people who choose to analyze literature as a profession do so because they are unwilling or unable to choose between the role of the psychoanalyst (he or she who analyzes) and the role of the patient (that which is being analyzed). Literature enables them not to choose because of the following paradox: (1) the work of the literary analyst resembles the work of the psychoanalyst; (2) the status of what is analyzed—the text—is, however, not that of a patient, but rather that of a master: we say of the author that he is a master; the text has for us authority—the very type of authority by which Jacques Lacan indeed defines the role of the psychoanalyst in the structure of transference. Like the psychoanalyst viewed by the patient, the text is viewed by us as "a subject presumed to know"—as the very place where meaning and *knowledge* of meaning reside. With respect to the text, the literary critic opposes thus at once the place of the psychoanalyst (in the relation of interpretation) *and* the place of the patient (in the relation of transference). Therefore, submitting psychoanalysis to the *literary* perspective would necessarily have a subversive effect on the clear-cut polarity through which psychoanalysis handles literature as its other, as the mere object of interpretation.

There is another point on which literature can inform psychoanalytical discourse in such a way as to deconstruct the temptation of the master's position and the master-slave pattern. There is one crucial feature that is constitutive of literature but is essentially lacking in psychoanalytical theory, and indeed in theory as such: irony. Since irony precisely consists in dragging authority as such into a scene that it cannot master, of which it is *not aware* and that, for that very reason, is the scene of its own self-destruction, literature, by virtue of its ironic force, fundamentally deconstructs the fantasy of authority in the same way, and for the same reasons, that psychoanalysis deconstructs the authority of the fantasy—its claim to belief and to power as the sole window through which we behold and perceive reality, as the sole window through which reality can indeed reach our grasp, enter into our consciousness. Psychoanalysis tells us that the fantasy is a fiction, and that consciousness is itself, in a sense, a fantasy-effect. In the same way, literature tells us that authority is a *language effect,* the product or the creation of its own *rhetorical* power: that authority is the *power of fiction;* that authority, therefore, is likewise a fiction.

The primacy granted here to the literary point of view would therefore not simply mean that literature, in its turn, would claim—as has been done—priority and authority over psychoanalysis as its influential *historical source,* as its ancestor or its predecessor in the discovery of the unconscious; but rather, the reversal of the usual perspective is here intended to displace the whole pattern of the relationship between literature and psychoanalysis from a structure of rival claims to authority and to priority to the scene of this structure's deconstruction.

In view of this shift of emphasis, the traditional method of *application* of psychoanalysis to literature would here be in principle ruled out. The notion of *application* would be replaced by the radically different notion of *implication:* bringing analytical questions to bear upon literary questions, *involving* psychoanalysis in the scene of literary analysis, the interpreter's role would here be not to *apply* to the text an acquired science, a preconceived knowledge, but to act as a go-between, to *generate implications* between literature and psychoanalysis—to explore, bring to light, and articulate the various (indirect) ways in which the two domains do indeed *implicate each other,* each one finding itself enlightened, informed, but also affected, displaced, by the other.

In its etymological sense, "implication" means "being folded within" (Latin: im-plicare = in + fold): it indicates, between two terms, a spatial relation of *interiority.* Application, on the other hand, is based on the presumption of a relation of exteriority; a presumption that, in the case of literature and psychoanalysis, can be shown to be a deceptive one. From the very beginning, indeed, literature has been for psychoanalysis not only a contiguous field of external verification in which to test its hypotheses and to confirm its findings, but also the constitutive texture of its *conceptual* framework, of its theoretical body. The key concepts of psychoanalysis are references to literature, using literary "*proper*" names—names of fictional characters (Oedipus complex, Narcissism) or of historical authors (masochism, sadism). Literature, in other words, is the language that psychoanalysis uses in order to *speak of itself,* in order to *name itself.* Literature is therefore not simply *outside* of psychoanalysis, since it motivates and *inhabits* the very names of its concepts, since it is the *inherent reference* by which psychoanalysis names its findings.

However, the relation of *interiority* conveyed by the interimplication of literature and psychoanalysis is by no means a simple one. Since literature and psychoanalysis are *different* from each other, but, at the same time they are also "enfolded within" each other, since they are, as it were, at the same time outside and inside each other, we might say that they compromise, each in its turn, the interiority of the other. The cultural division, in other words, of scholarly "disciplines" of research is by no means a natural geography: there are no *natural* boundaries between literature and psychoanalysis, which clearly define and distinguish them; the border between them is undecidable since they are really *traversed* by each other.

Each is thus a potential threat to the interiority of the other, since each is contained in the other as its *otherness-to-itself,* its *unconscious.* As the unconscious traverses consciousness, a theoretical body of thought always is traversed by its own unconscious—its own "unthought," of which it is not aware, but which it contains in itself as the very conditions of its disruption, as the possibility of its own self-subversion. We would like to suggest that, in the same way that psychoanalysis points to the unconscious of literature, *literature, in its turn, is the unconscious of psychoanalysis;* that the unthought-out shadow in psychoanalytical *theory* is precisely its own involvement with literature; that literature *in* psychoanalysis functions precisely as its "*unthought*": as the condition of possibility *and* the self-subversive blind spot of psychoanalytical *thought.*

The articles that follow are heterogeneous, varied in their interests and in their insights. What they have in common is that none of them simply takes for granted the relationship between literature and psychoanalysis: they all reflect upon the textual and theoretical encounter between literature and psychoanalysis not as an answer, but as a question, questioning at once its possibilities and its limits. They thus suggest, each in its specific, different manner, how the question of the relationship between literature and psychoanalysis might begin to be articulated—*otherwise:* how psychoanalysis and literature might indeed begin to be rethought, both in their otherness and in their common wisdom.

SHOSHANA FELMAN

8 | From "Beyond Oedipus: The Specimen Text of Psychoanalysis"

I

WHAT IS A KEY NARRATIVE?

"Only one idea of general value has occurred to me. I have found love of the mother and jealousy of the father in my own case too." From the *Letters to Fliess* to *The Interpretation of Dreams*, what Freud is instituting is a new way of writing one's autobiography, by transforming personal narration into a pathbreaking theoretical discovery. In the constitution of the theory, however, the discovery that emerges out of the narration is itself referred back to a story that confirms it: the literary drama of the destiny of Oedipus, which, in becoming thus a reference or a key narrative—the specimen story of psychoanalysis—situates the validating moment at which the psychoanalytic storytelling turns and returns upon itself, in the unprecedented Freudian narrative-discursive space in which narration becomes theory.

> This discovery is confirmed by a legend which has come down to us from classical antiquity: a legend whose profound and universal power to move can only be understood if the hypothesis I have put forward in regard to the psychology of children has an equally universal validity. What I have in mind is the legend of King Oedipus and Sophocles' drama which bears his name. . . .

The action of the play consists in nothing other than the process of revealing, with cunning delays and ever-mounting excitement—a process that can be likened to the work of a psycho-analysis—that Oedipus himself is the murderer of Laius, but further that he is the son of the murdered man and of Jocasta. . . .

If *Oedipus Rex* moves a modern audience no less than it did the contemporary Greek one . . . there must be something which makes a voice within us ready to recognize the compelling force of destiny in the Oedipus. . . . His destiny moves us because it might have been ours—because the oracle laid the same curse upon us before our birth as upon him. It is the fate of all of us, perhaps, to direct our first sexual impulse towards our mother and our first hatred and our first murderous wish against our father. Our dreams convince us that this is so. Kind Oedipus, who slew his father Laius and married his mother Jocasta, merely shows us the fulfillment of our childhood wishes. . . . While the poet . . . brings to light the guilt of Oedipus, he is at the same time compelling us to recognize our own inner minds, in which those same impulses, though suppressed, are still to be found. (SE 4:261–63)

Freud's reference to the Oedipus as a key narrative is structured by three questions that support his analytical interrogation:

The question of the effectiveness of the story. Why is the story so compelling? How to account for the story's practical effect on the audience—its power to elicit affect, its symbolic efficacy?

The question of the recognition. The story has power over us because it "is compelling us to recognize" something in ourselves. What is it that the story is compelling us to recognize? What is at stake in the recognition?

The question of the validity of the hypothesis or theory. "A legend whose profound and universal power to move can only be understood if the hypothesis I have put forward in regard to the psychology of children has an equally universal validity."

Any further inquiry into the significance of the Oedipus story in psychoanalytic theory and practice would have to take into account the implications of those three questions: the narrative's practical efficacy (and hence, its potential for a clinical efficacy: its practical effect on us, having to do not necessarily with what the story means but with what it does to us); the meaning of the theoretical recognition (what do we recognize when we recognize the Oedipus?); and the very status of the theoretical validation through a narrative, that is, the question of the relationship between truth and fiction in psychoanalysis.

I would suggest now that Lacan's reading of Freud renews each of these questions in some crucial ways; and that an exploration of this renewal—an exploration of the way in which the Oedipus mythic reference holds the key to a Lacanian psychoanalytic understanding—may hold the key in turn to the crux of Lacan's innovative insight into what Freud discovered and, consequently, into what psychoanalysis is all about.

THE COMPLEXITY OF THE COMPLEX

Nowhere in Lacan's writing is there any systematic exposition of his specific understanding of the significance of Oedipus. As is often the case, Lacan's insight has to be derived, through a reading labor, from an elliptical and fragmentary text, from sporadic comments, from episodic highlights of (often critical and corrective) interpretations, and from the omnipresent literary usage of the reference to the Oedipus myth in Lacan's own rhetoric and style. My attempt at a creative systematization of what may be called Lacan's revision of the Oedipus mythic reference would organize itself, in a structure of its own, as a relation between three dimensions. (1) *The purely theoretical dimension:* How does Lacan understand the basic psychoanalytic concept of "the Oedipus complex"? (2) *The practical and clinical dimension:* What is, in Lacan's eyes, the practical relevance of Oedipus to the clinical event, to practical dealings with a patient? (3) *The literary dimension:* How does Lacan understand the way in which Sophocles' text informs psychoanalytic knowledge?

Traditionally, the Oedipus complex is understood to mean the literal genesis and the literal objects of man's primordial desire: an incestuous sexual love for the mother and a jealous, murderous impulse toward the father. In this view, what Freud discovered in the Oedipus is a universal *answer* to the question: What does man unconsciously desire? This answer guarantees a knowledge—psychoanalytic knowledge—of the instinctual content of the human unconscious, which can be found everywhere. Any Freudian reading is bound to uncover the same meaning, the ultimate signified of human desire: the Oedipus complex.

This is not the way Lacan understands the gist of Freud's discovery. For Lacan, the Oedipus complex is not a signified but a signifier, not a meaning but a structure. What Freud discovered in the Oedipus myth is not an answer but *the structure of a question,* not any given knowledge but a structuring positioning of the analyst's own ignorance of his patient's unconscious. "If it is true," writes Lacan, "that our knowledge comes to the rescue of the ignorance of the analysand, it is no less true that we too are plunged in ignorance, insofar as we are ignorant of the symbolic constellation underlying the unconscious of the subject. In addition, this constellation always has to be conceived as structured, and structured according to an order which is *complex*" (S 1:78–79). What is essential, in Lacan's eyes, is the key word "complex" in the notion of the Oedipus complex. The fecundity of Freud's paradigmatic schema lies precisely in its irreducible complexity.

> When we go toward the discovery of the unconscious, what we encounter are situations which are structured, organized, complex. Of these situations, Freud has given us the first model, the standard, in the Oedipus complex. . . . [What we have to realize is] the extent to which the Oedipus complex poses problems, and how many ambiguities it encompasses. The whole development of analysis, in fact, was brought about by the successive emphases placed upon each of the tensions implied in this triangular system. This alone forces us to see in it an altogether different thing than this massive bloc summed up by the classical formula— sexual desire for the mother, rivalry with the father. (S 1:79)

The triangular structure, crucial to Lacan's conception, is not the simple psychological triangle of love and rivalry, but a socio-symbolic structural positioning of the child in a complex constellation of alliance (family, elementary social cell) in which the combination of desire and a Law prohibiting desire is regulated, through a linguistic structure of exchange, into a repetitive process of replacement—of substitution—of symbolic objects (substitutes) of desire.

In this symbolic constellation, the mother's function differs from the father's function. The mother (or the *mother's image*) stands for the first object of the child's narcissistic attachment (an object and an image of the child's self-love, or love for his own body—for his own image), inaugurating a type of mirroring relationship that Lacan calls "the Imaginary." The father (or the *father's name*), as a symbol of the

Law of incest prohibition, stands on the other hand for the first author-itative "no," the first social imperative of renunciation, inaugurating, through this castration of the child's original desire, both the necessity of repression and the process of symbolic substitution of objects of desire, which Lacan calls "the Symbolic." While the child is learning how to speak, signifiers of incestuous desire are repressed, become un-speakable, and the desire is displaced onto substitutive signifiers of desire. This is what the Oedipus complex mythically, schematically, accounts for: the constitution of the Symbolic, through the coinci-dence of the child's introduction into language and of the constitution of his (linguistic) unconscious.

The triangularity of the Oedipal structure is thus crucial in Lacan's perception in that it implies a radical asymmetry between the Imagi-nary (archetypal relation to the mother) and the Symbolic (archetypal relation to the structure of alliance between mother, father, and child). The Imaginary is the dual perspective (narcissistic mirroring, ex-changeability of self and other); the Symbolic is the triangular perspec-tive. Both are encompassed by the Oedipal structure and will continue to define different registers of human experience and relationships.

> You are familiar with the profoundly asymmetrical character . . .
> of each of the dual relations which the Oedipal structure encom-
> passes. The relation which links the subject to the mother is dis-
> tinct from the relation which links him to the father, the
> narcissistic or imaginary relation to the father is distinct from the
> symbolic relation, and is also distinct from the relation which we
> must call real—and which is residual with respect to the architec-
> ture which interests us in analysis. All this is enough of a demon-
> stration of the complexity of the structure. (S 1:79)

What matters, in Lacan's perception of the Oedipus as constitutive of the qualitative difference between the Imaginary and the Symbolic, is the fact that the triangularity of the Symbolic narratively functions as the story of the subversion of the duality of the Imaginary. The Oedi-pus drama mythically epitomizes the subversion of the mirroring illu-sion through the introduction of a difference in the position of a Third: Father, Law, Language, the reality of death, all of which Lacan desig-nates as the Other, constitutive of the unconscious (otherness to one-self) in that it is both subversive of, and radically ex-centric to, the narcissistic, specular relation of self to other and of self to self.

In his first Seminar, Lacan reviews a clinical case history reported by Melanie Klein.[1] The reinterpretation he then offers of Klein's narrative sheds light not just on his particular conception of the Oedipus, but on the clinical relevance of this theoretical conception to psychoanalytic practice. First I will sum up the case by quoting from Klein's own report.

> [The case] is that of a four-year-old boy who, as regards the poverty of his vocabulary and of his intellectual attainments, was on the level of a child of about . . . eighteen months. . . . This child, Dick, was largely devoid of affects, and he was indifferent to the presence or absence of mother or nurse. From the very beginning he had only rarely displayed anxiety, and that in an abnormally small degree. . . . He had almost no interests, did not play, and had no contact with his environment. For the most part he simply strung sounds in a meaningless way. . . . When he did speak he generally used his meagre vocabulary in an incorrect way. But it was not that he was unable to make himself intelligible: he had no wish to do so. . . .
>
> [In the first visit] he had let his nurse go without manifesting any emotion, and had followed me into the room with complete indifference . . . just as if I were a piece of furniture. . . . Dick's behaviour had no meaning or purpose, nor was any affect or anxiety associated with it . . .
>
> But he was interested in trains and stations and also in doorhandles, doors and the opening and shutting of them. . . .
>
> I took a big train, and put it beside a smaller one and called them "Daddy train" and "Dick-train." Thereupon he picked up the train I called "Dick" and made it roll to the window and said "Station." I explained: "The station is mummy; Dick is going into mummy." Meantime he picked up the train again, but soon ran back into the space between the doors. While I was saying that he was going into dark mummy, he said twice in a questioning way: "Nurse?" I answered: "Nurse is soon coming," and this he repeated and used the words later quite correctly, retaining them in his mind. . . . In the third analytic hour he behaved in the same way,

except that besides running into the hall and between the doors, he also ran behind the chest of drawers. There he was seized with anxiety, and for the first time called me to him. . . . We see that simultaneously with the appearance of anxiety there had emerged a sense of dependence . . . and at the same time he began to be interested in the soothing words "Nurse is coming soon" and, contrary to his usual behaviour, had repeated and remembered them. . . .

It had been possible for me to gain access to Dick's unconscious by getting into contact with such rudiments of phantasy-life and symbol-formation as he displayed. The result was a diminution of his latent anxiety, so that it was possible for a certain amount of anxiety to become manifest. But this implied that the working-over of this anxiety was beginning by way of the establishment of a symbolic relation to things and objects, and at the same time his epistemophilic and aggressive impulses were set in action. Every advance was followed by the release of fresh quantities of anxiety and led to his turning away to some extent from the things with which had therefore become objects of anxiety. As he turned away from these he turned towards new objects and his aggressive . . . impulses were directed to these new affective relations in their turn. . . . He then transferred his interest from them to fresh things. . . . As his interests developed he at the same time enlarged his vocabulary, for he now began to take more and more interest not only in the things themselves but in their names. . . .

Hand in hand with this development of interests and an increasingly strong transference to myself, the hitherto lacking object-relation has made its appearance. . . .

In general I do not interpret the material until it has found expression in various representations. In this case, however, where the capacity to represent it was almost entirely lacking, I found myself obliged to make my interpretations on the basis of my general knowledge. . . . Finding access in this way to his unconscious, I succeeded in activating anxiety and other affects. The representations then became fuller and I soon acquired a more solid foundation for the analysis. (238–46)

What Lacan seeks to understand in Klein's narrative is, specifically, her clinical usage of Oedipus in the originating moment of the therapeutic intervention. This clinical usage, however, strikes him as highly problematic and ambiguous. Lacan is shocked by the reductive crudity of the initial Oedipal interpretation and, as a clinician, disapproves in principle of such "symbolic extrapolations" (S 1:101), of interpretations having the character of a mechanical imposition by the interpreter. And yet this crude originating moment turns out to have been clinically insightful, since it brought about a spectacular therapeutic process. How can that be understood?

> She sticks symbolism into him, little Dick, with the utmost brutality, that Melanie Klein! She begins right away by hitting him with the major interpretations. She throws him into a brutal verbalization of the Oedipus myth, almost as revolting to us as to any reader whatever — *You are the little train, you want to fuck your mother.*
>
> This procedure obviously lends itself to theoretical discussions. . . . But it is certain that, as a result of this intervention, something happens. This is what it's all about. . . .
>
> This text is precious because it is the text of a therapist, of a woman of experience. She senses things, she cannot be blamed if she cannot always articulate what she senses. (S 1:81)

> We have to take Melanie Klein's text for what it is, namely, the account of an experience. (S 1:95)

How does one read, how does one listen to, the practical account of an experience? Lacan's reply is: as an analyst, as a practitioner. Indeed, the paradox of the clinical success of a reductive, elementary interpretation, not only triggers Lacan's interest, but actively enhances his attention to a level that is properly, for him, the analytic level. As a clinician, Lacan is always listening, in the discourse that recounts an experience, for its discrepancies, its ambiguities, its paradoxes. The analytic path is always opened up by something that resists, something that disrupts the continuity of conscious meaning and appears to be incomprehensible.

> What counts, when one attempts to elaborate an experience, is less what one does understand than what one does not understand. . . . Commenting on a text is the same as doing an analysis. How many times have I pointed it out to those I supervise when they say to me — *I thought I understood that what he meant to say was*

this, or that—one of the things we should be watching out for most, is not to understand too much, not to understand more than what there is in the discourse of the subject. Interpreting is an altogether different thing than having the fancy of understanding. One is the opposite of the other. I will even say that it is on the basis of a certain refusal of understanding that we open the door onto psychoanalytic understanding. (S 1:87–88)

It is indeed on the basis of Lacan's own *analytical refusal of understanding*—both of the apparently transparent meaning of the Oedipal clinical intervention and of what it is that Klein does understand—that Lacan will shed new light, both on what the Oedipus myth and on what the clinical event are all about.

In much the same way as Freud, dealing with Oedipus, interrogates specifically the practical effect, the narrative efficacy, of the myth, Lacan, withholding understanding of the meaning of Klein's Oedipal intervention, interrogates specifically its narrative-symbolic efficacy: its productive practical and clinical effect. Why is the story of Oedipus—in the clinical experience as in literature—so effective? The question here again is not what does the story *mean,* but what does the story *do?* Not what is the clinician's statement, but what is the clinical significance, the actual principle of functioning, of her performance? Suspending thus what Klein believes she understands, Lacan asks: What is it that Klein does? What does the clinical event—the clinical advent—consists of? What *happens,* in effect, with Dick?

What then has Melanie Klein in effect done? (S 1:99)

What is the specific function of the Kleinian interpretation which presents itself with this character of intrusion, of imposition on the subject? (S 1:88)

PROJECTION/INTROJECTION: THE CLINICAL INTERVENTION

In her own account of what happens in the therapeutic process, Melanie Klein talks about Dick's development in terms of his projections and his introjections:

As his analysis progressed it became clear that in thus throwing [objects] out of the room he was indicating an expulsion, both of the damaged object and of his own sadism . . . which was in this manner projected into the external world. Dick had also discovered the wash-basin as symbolizing the mother's body, and he displayed an extraordinary dread of being wetted with water. He anxiously wiped it off his hand and mine, which he had dipped in as well as his own, and immediately afterwards he showed the same anxiety when urinating. Urine and faeces represented to him injurious and dangerous substances.

It became clear that in Dick's phantasy faeces, urine and penis stood for objects with which to attack the mother's body, and were therefore felt to be a source of injury to himself as well. These phantasies contributed to his dread of the contents of his mother's body, and especially of his father's penis which he phantasied as being in her womb. We came to see this phantasied penis and a growing feeling of aggression against it in many forms, the desire to eat and destroy it being specially prominent. For example, on one occasion Dick lifted a toy man to his mouth, gnashed his teeth and said "Tea Daddy," by which he meant "Eat Daddy." He then asked for a drink of water. The introjection of his father's penis proved to be associated with the dread both of it, as of a primitive, harm-inflicting super-ego, and of being punished by the mother thus robbed: dread, that is, of the external and the introjected objects. (243–44)

It should be remembered that, in Klein's conception, the child's mental universe is produced as a relation to a container — his mother's body — and to the imagined contents of this container. During the progress of his instinctual relationship with his mother, the child proceeds through a series of imaginary incorporations. He can, for example, bite or absorb his mother's body: the style of this incorporation implies the destruction of the object incorporated. Within the maternal body, on the other hand, the child expects to encounter a certain number of objects that he projects as dangerous, because he imaginarily invests them with the same capacity for destruction that he experiences in himself. This is why he will need to emphasize their exteriority by expelling them, rejecting them as dangerous entities, bad objects, feces. But still they will appear threatening to him. In order, then, to overcome the threat, the child will reincorporate or introject the dangerous objects, substituting other objects toward which he will deflect his interest. Different objects of the external world, gradually more diversified and more neutralized, will emerge as the equivalents of the first. These imaginary equations between objects will thus produce, in the child's mental functioning, an alternative mechanism of projection and introjection, expulsion and absorption: an imaginary play between contents and container, inside and outside, inclusions and exclusions.

It would seem that the mechanisms of projection and introjection, based as they are on the play of symmetry (the mirroring, reversibility, and exchangeability) between inside and outside, are themselves basically symmetrical, inverted mirror images of each other. In her account of Dick's alternative projections and introjections, Klein seems to use the terms in this oppositional-symmetry way, which is in fact the way they are routinely understood in psychoanalytic theory.

Lacan, however, points out a radical asymmetry between projection and introjection, and this asymmetry, in his view, holds the key to the very essence of the therapeutic process and is thus crucial to an understanding of what Klein does as a clinician.

> Dick plays with the container and the contents. . . . He envisions himself as a little train. . . . The dark space is immediately assimilated to the inside of his mother's body, in which he takes refuge. What does not happen is the free play, the conjunction between the different forms — real and imaginary — of the objects. . . .
>
> We are here in a mirroring relation. We call it the level of projection. But how should we indicate the correlative of projection? It is necessary to find another term than introjection. In the way we use it in analysis, introjection is not the opposite of projection. It is practically employed, you will notice, only when what is at stake is symbolic introjection. It is always accompanied by a symbolic denomination. *Introjection is always the introjection of the discourse of the Other,* and this fact introduces a dimension altogether different from the dimension of projection. It is around this distinction that you can separate, and see the difference, between the function of the ego, which is of the order of the dual register, and the function of the superego [pertaining to the triangular register]. (S 1:97)

In other words, projection is identified by Lacan with what he calls the (dual) order of the Imaginary. Introjection is understood as pertaining to the (triangular) order of the Symbolic. Projection and introjection are not symmetrical because there is a *qualitative difference* between the Imaginary and the Symbolic. What the therapist does is to introduce this qualitative difference into the child's life, to introduce Dick into the Symbolic (into a symbolic world whereby difference is articulated in a linguistic system), by promoting in the child, all at once, the capacity of *speaking* and the capacity of *substituting* objects of desire, thus permitting him to articulate reality into a symbolic network of differentiated meanings and differentiated object relations.

> You have noticed the lack of contact which Dick experiences. . . . This is why Melanie Klein distinguished him from the neurotics, because of his profound indifference, his apathy, his absence. It is clear, in fact, that in Dick what is not symbolized is reality. This young subject is entirely in crude reality, reality unconstituted. He is entirely in the undifferentiated. (S 1:81)

> Anxiety is what is not produced in this subject. . . . In Melanie Klein's office, there is for Dick neither other nor self; there is reality pure and simple. The interval between two doors is his mother's body. The trains and all the rest are something, without doubt, but something which is neither nameable nor named.
>
> It is against this background that Melanie Klein, with this brute's instinct which characterizes her and which has, incidentally, made her perforate a sum of knowledge hitherto impenetrable, dares to speak to him—speak to a being who . . . in the symbolic sense of the term, does not answer. He is there as if she did not exist, as if she were a piece of furniture. And nevertheless she speaks to him. She literally gives name to what—until then has been, for this subject, nothing but reality pure and simple— certainly, he already has a certain apprehension of some syllables, but . . . he does not assume them. (S 1:82–83)

What drives a child to assume—that is, to endorse, make his, to take upon himself—the vocables of language? In Lacan's conception, the Symbolic—the desire and ability to symbolize—hinges on the more fundamental *need to call:* the need to *address* the other, to attempt to draw the attention of the other toward something that the caller, the addressor, lacks.

> If we sum up everything that Melanie Klein describes of Dick's attitude, the significant point is simply this—the child does not address any call to anybody.

The call takes its value within a system of language which is already acquired. Now, what is here at stake is that this child emits no call. The system by means of which the subject comes to situate himself in language is interrupted, at the level of speech. Speech and language are not the same; this child is, to a certain extent, master of language, but he does not speak. It is a subject who is there and who, literally, does not answer.

Speech has not come to him. Language has not encroached on his imaginary system. . . . For him, the Real and the Imaginary are the same. . . .

Melanie Klein does not proceed here—and she is aware of it—to any interpretation. She starts out, as she tells us, with ideas that she has, and which are known. . . . Let me make no bones about it, I tell Dick, *Dick-little train, Daddy-big train.* Thereupon, the child begins to play with his little train, and he says the word *station.* This is a crucial moment, in which what is beginning to take place is the encroachment of language on the imaginary of the subject.

Melanie Klein sends him back this—*The station is mummy; Dick is going into mummy.* As of this moment, everything is set in motion. She will give him only statements of this kind, and not others. And very quickly the child progresses. It's a fact.

What then has Melanie Klein in effect done? Nothing other than to provide verbalization. She has symbolized an effective relation, the relation of being, named, with another. She has applied—indeed mechanically imposed—the symbolization of the Oedipus myth, to call it by its name. It is as a result of that that, after a first ceremony in which the child seeks shelter in the dark space in order to renew contact with the container, something new awakens in him.

The child verbalizes a first call—a spoken call. He asks for his nurse, with whom he had entered and whose departure he had taken as though nothing were the matter. For the first time, he produces a reaction of appeal, of call—a call which is not just an emotional address . . . but a verbalized address, and which henceforth entails an answer.

Things develop consequently to a point where, in a situation henceforth organized, Melanie Klein can bring about the intervention of other situational elements, including that of the father, who comes to play his role. Outside of the sessions, Klein tells us, the relationship of the child develops on the level of Oedipus. The child symbolizes the reality surrounding him out of this kernel, of this palpitating cell of symbolism which Melanie Klein has provided him with.

This is what she calls, later on, "having opened the doors of his unconscious." (S 1:98–100)

The important point, in Lacan's account of the clinical event, is the following: the initial sentence of the clinician ("Dick-little train, Daddy-big train, Dick is going into mummy") does not function *constatively* (as a truth report, with respect to the reality of the situation) but *performatively* (as a speech act). The success of the interpretation, its clinical efficacy, does not proceed from the accuracy of its meaning ("You want to fuck your mother") but from the way this discourse of the Other situates the child, in language, in relation to the people who surround him, are close to him. This is what the Oedipal intervention is all about. "Melanie Klein does not proceed here to any interpretation," insists Lacan. What the preconceived and heavy-handed interpretation does is to give the child — through the verbalized Oedipal constellation — not a meaning but a *structure,* a linguistic structure by which to relate himself to other human beings; a structure, therefore, in which meaning — sexual meaning — can later be articulated and inscribed.

Let me try to recapitulate the complexity of Lacan's restatement of Klein's clinical account, by stating Lacan's insight in my own terms. After Klein, after Lacan, in the space of insight opened up by the (analytic?) dialogue between their different terminologies, I will sum up in yet another narrative voice the crux of the encounter between Dick and Oedipus.

THE STORY OF THE INTRODUCTION OF A DIFFERENCE

Dick's recovery is the story of his development, his passage, from projection to introjection, from the Imaginary to the Symbolic, from a stage that precedes the primary identification of the "mirror stage,"[2] to a stage in which the secondary identification of the Oedipus is accomplished, through the child's introjection of the "father's name" and the constitution thereby of his superego.[3]

What Klein describes as projection — the *equation,* in her terms, *between "bad objects" and their substitutes* — Lacan designates as the Imaginary. The Symbolic, as opposed to this, would be the *network of equations between these substitutes.* Language is, precisely, a relation between substitutes. Thus, while projection is always in Lacan's conception the displacement of an image from the "inside" to the "outside," that is, a displacement of any one given object with respect to the ego, introjection is not simply the symmetrical displacement of an object from the outside to the inside, but a movement from the outside to the inside of an object's name, that is, the assumption by the ego of a *relation* between a named object and a system of named objects. Introjection, says Lacan, is always a *linguistic* introjection, in that it is always *the introjection of a relation.*

This is why projection is "imaginary," dual ("here" equals "there," "inside" equals "outside"), whereas introjection is "symbolic," triangular (the relation between "inside," "outside," and "myself"). Since naming an element relates it to a *system*—language—and not simply to *me,* who becomes yet another element in the same system, the Symbolic is the differential situating of the subject in a *third position;* it is at once the place *from which* a dual relation is apprehended, the place *through which* it is articulated, and that which makes the subject (as, precisely, this symbolic, third place) into a linguistic signifier in a system, which thereby permits him to relate symbolically to other signifiers, that is, at once to relate to other humans and to articulate his own desire, his own unconscious, unawares.

What, then, is Dick's story in this conception? Initially, Dick has a separate relation (a relation of projection) to each of his imaginary objects. What Klein does is to articulate the relations of the objects among themselves, Dick being one of the objects in the system: Dick learns to assume himself as such, to assume himself as a signifier.

"Dick-little train, Daddy-big train, Dick is going into mummy." In saying this, Klein takes the relation between Dick and the train and articulates it as a relation between two trains. In this way she introduces Dick into the Symbolic through the constellation of the Oedipal triangle and brings about Dick's secondary (Oedipal) identification. Here is what happens:

I. *Primary Identification* (Imaginary realm of the Mirror Stage)

Projection	Two elements are seen as
here = there	equivalent from the point of view
inside = outside	of one of the elements (visual
container = contents	metaphors, specular fascination).

my body = my mother's body
       = my mirror image
self = other

II. *Secondary Identification* (Oedipus, introduction into the Symbolic realm)
Introjection
Incorporation of the father's name, constitution of superego
Setting in motion of the mechanism of repression through a chain of displacement of signifiers
Dick is to Mummy what Daddy is to Mummy
"Little train" is to "station" what "big train" is to "station"
"A" is to "B" what "C" is to "B"
Me : mother :: father : mother
A : B :: C : B
The equivalence is not between two objects but between two relations, in which the substitution of A (Dick) and C (Daddy) is not accomplished by resemblance (projective identity) but by a parallel position in a structure (metonymy, desire).

How should we account now for the salutary emergence of Dick's anxiety? Anxiety is linked to the Symbolic: it is the way in which the introjection of the symbolic system *as a whole* makes itself felt in the subject, when any element in it is disturbed or displaced. There is no relation at first for Dick between the train and the space between the doors, until Klein establishes — through discourse — this relation. The rising anxiety in Dick embodies his nascent intuition that, in a symbolic system, any element or change has repercussions in the whole. Dick thus develops anxiety, as he passes from *indifference* (everything is equally real) to *difference* (everything is not equally real; there is imaginary; where the imaginary is, is undecidable).

Dick Initial Indifference	*The Advent of Difference*
Lack of affect	Difference emerges and is
Lack of anxiety	articulated as sexual difference.
Lack of difference	Everything is not the same. A
No change in any element	change in any element changes
changes anything because	the givens of a situation. The
everything is the same.	subject is subject to the givens of

his situation, starting with the fact that his sex is one sex and not another.

Anxiety occurs with the assumption of difference (castration), not simply because of the imaginary fear that something (death, or loss of bodily integrity) might happen to the subject, but because of the symbolic recognition that, since everything is not the same and since every disturbance is reverberated in the whole symbolic constellation, the situational givens that affect the subject do make a difference (meaning).

Dick's story is thus Oedipal, in that it is at one and the same time the story of the child's birth into symbolism (language), the story of the human genesis of anxiety (and thus of meaning), and the story of the introduction of articulated difference.

THE ANALYTICAL SPEECH ACT

"It had been possible for me, in Dick's analysis, to gain access to his unconscious," writes Melanie Klein. What, asks Lacan, is the key—the practical, clinical key—to that access? Unlike Klein, who proposes as the key a whole cognitive theory of the child's Oedipal sadism and of the maturation of his instincts, Lacan believes the key is not cognitive but performative.[4] The key is not in the clinician's understanding, or her meaning, but in her actual speech act:

Is it not insofar as Melanie Klein speaks that something happens? (S 1:88)

She sticks symbolism into him, little Dick, with the utmost brutality. . . . But it is certain that, as a result of this intervention, something happens. This is what it's all about.

What is at stake in this whole observation — what you have to understand — is the virtue of speech, insofar as *the act of speech* functions in coordination with a preestablished, typical, and in advance, significant, symbolic system. (S 1:103)

What does Klein's speech act consist of if it works in the context of a preestablished, typical symbolic meaning? It consists precisely in effectively producing in the child the call that was lacking, the address that then becomes his motivation for the introjection of human discourse (language).

And how does Klein's speech act produce the call in Dick? By calling him ("Dick-little train"), by naming him within the constellation of a symbolic structure, by thus performatively constituting him, through her own discourse, as a subject.

Ask yourselves what the call represents in the field of speech. It represents — the possibility of a refusal. (S 1:102)

But if I call the person to whom I am speaking by whatever name I choose to give him, I intimate to him the subjective function that he will take on again in order to reply to me, even if it is to repudiate this function. (E 300, N 86–87)

What I seek in speech is the response — the reply — of the other. What constitutes me as a subject is my question. In order to be recognized by the other, I utter what was only a function of what will be. In order to find him, I call him by a name that he must assume or refuse in order to reply to me. (E 299, N 86; translation mine)

In order to find Dick, Klein calls him by a name that he must then acknowledge — assume or refuse in order to reply to her. And Dick indeed replies, first with a call and later with the articulation of his desire. But the call and the desire, the address and the response, the question and the answer, are not statements (meanings), but performances, speech acts. It is thus not on the level of its statements but on the level of its illocutionary forces that the analytic dialogue takes place between the therapist and Dick. But this is, in Lacan's conception, the true thrust of any analytic dialogue: fundamentally, the dialogic psychoanalytic discourse is not so much informative as it is performative.

Whether it sees itself as an instrument of healing, of training, or of exploration in depth, psychoanalysis has but a single medium: the patient's speech. That this is self-evident is no excuse for our neglecting it. Now, speech is what calls for a reply. (E 247, N 40; tm)

A reaction is not a reply. . . . There is no reply except for *my* desire. . . . There is no question except for my anticipation. . . .

Henceforth, the decisive function of my own reply [as analyst] appears, and this function is not, as has been said, simply to be received by the subject as acceptance or rejection of his discourse, but really to recognize him or to abolish him as subject. Such is the *responsibility* of the analyst, each time he intervenes by means of speech. (E 300, N 86–87; tm; original italics)

THE ANALYST'S RESPONSIBILITY, OR THE FUNCTION OF INTERPRETATION

Each time the analyst speaks, interprets in the analytic situation, he gives something asked of him. What he gives, however, is not a superior understanding, but a reply. The reply addresses not so much what the patient says (or means), but his call. Being fundamentally a reply to the subject's question, to the force of his address, the interpretive gift is not constative (cognitive) but performative: the gift is not so much a gift of truth, of understanding or of meaning: it is, essentially, a gift of language. This is how Lacan accounts for the theoretical clarifications Freud gives to the Rat Man, when the patient had to be "guaranteed before pursuing his discourse":

> The extremely approximative character of the explanations with which Freud gratifies him, so approximative as to appear somewhat crude, is sufficiently instructive: at this point it is clearly not so much a question of doctrine, nor even of indoctrination, but rather of a symbolic gift of speech, pregnant with a secret pact. (E 291, N 78–79)

Speech is in effect a gift of language, and language is not immaterial. It is a subtle body, but body it is. (E 301, N 87)

If interpretation is a gift of language — that is, a reply to the analysand's address — rather than a gift of truth, how does interpretation function? If, moreover, in Lacan's conception, "the question of correctness" or the psychoanalytical interpretation "moves into the background" (E 300, N 87), how does the analyst's interpretive intervention bring about the desired therapeutic, clinical effect? Lacan's reply is twofold.

First, since the analyst's interpretation has to be not necessarily correct but *resonant* (ambiguous, symbolically suggestive), since "we learn that analysis consists in playing in all the many staves of the score of speech in the registers of language" (E 291, N 79), "every spoken intervention is received by the subject in terms of his structure" (E 300, N 87). The stake of analysis is precisely to identify the symbolic structure in whose terms the interpretations are received, that is, to identify the structure into which the gift of language is translated, to identify the question in whose terms the reply is sought and heard.

> The stake of analysis is nothing other than this—to recognize what function the subject assumes in the order of symbolic relations which cover the whole field of human relations, and of which the initial cell is the Oedipus complex, where the assumption of sex is decided. (S 1:80)

This is, then, the first Oedipal stake of analytical interpretation, whereby the analyst's reply to the analysand is not an answer concerning the initial sexual or incestuous relations of the subject (the Oedipus as answer, as a meaning), but a search for the initial question of the subject (the Oedipus question, as the constitutive speech act of the patient). Since any spoken intervention or interpretation is "received in terms of the subject's structure," the analytical reply thus seeks the structure of the subject's question. This is what the Oedipus consists in, as an object of the analytical interpretation: it defines the analysand's initial *structure of address:*

> In order to know how to reply to the subject in analysis, the procedure is to recognize first of all *the place* where his ego is . . . in other words, to know *through whom and for whom the subject poses his question.* So long as this is not known, there will be the risk of a misunderstanding concerning the desire that is there to be recognized and concerning the object to whom this desire is addressed. (E 303, N 89)

In her first spoken intervention, Melanie Klein, to return to her, has precisely defined this initial structure of address for Dick: "she has symbolized an effective relation, that of a being, named, with another" (S 1:100). Let us not forget, however, that Dick's problem as a child was his failure to address: "If we sum up everything that Melanie Klein describes of Dick's attitude, the significant point is simply this—the child does not address any call to anybody." What Klein in effect does through her first spoken intervention (Oedipal interpretation) is thus not simply to identify the child's initial structure of address, but to create it.

This brings us to the second Oedipal stake of the analyst's spoken intervention and to the second function of interpretation in Lacan's conception.

"Not only is every spoken intervention received by the subject in terms of his structure, but the intervention takes on a structuring function in him, by dint of its symbolic form" (E 301, N 87; tm). Thus not only is the analytic dialogue essentially performative (acting through its illocutionary force) rather than informative (acting through its statements or its meanings); the analytical interpretation in itself is a performative (not cognitive) interpretation in that it has a fundamental structuring, transforming function. If analysis is necessarily always a reference to some "other scene," it is to the extent that it takes place on the performative, other scene of language.

> For in its symbolizing function, the intimation of speech is moving towards nothing less than a transformation of the subject to whom it is addressed by means of the link that it establishes with the one who emits it—or, to put it differently, by means of the introduction of a signifier effect. (E 296, N 83; tm)

This is precisely what Klein has accomplished in the Dick case through her spoken intervention, in spite of the "brutality" of her "symbolic extrapolations." The question then becomes how to account for the spectacular clinical success *in spite of* the symbolical extrapolation, *in spite of* what might be seen as the heavy-handedness of the approach, *in spite of* the mechanical character of the interpretive intervention. Who, or what, is responsible for the therapy's success?

THE UNCONSCIOUS IS THE DISCOURSE OF THE OTHER

Let me quote at some length the suggestive way in which Lacan specifically addresses the question of Klein's clinical success:

In what way has Melanie Klein done anything whatsoever which manifests a grasp of any process whatsoever which would be, in the subject, his unconscious?

She admits it right away: she has done it—she has acted—*out of habit*. Reread this observation and you will see in it a spectacular demonstration of the formula I am always repeating to you—*the unconscious is the discourse of the Other*.

Here is a case in which it is absolutely manifest. In this subject [Dick], there is no unconscious whatsoever. It is Klein's discourse which brutally grafts upon the initial egotistic inertia of the child the first symbolization of the Oedipal situation. . . .

In a dramatic case, in this subject who has not acceded to human reality because he emits no call, what are the effects of the symbolizations introduced by the therapist? They determine an initial position out of which the subject can put into play the imaginary and the real, and conquer his development. . . .

The development takes place only insofar as the subject is integrated into a symbolic system, which he practices and in which he asserts himself through the exercise of an authentic speech. It is not even necessary, you will notice, for this speech to be his own. In the couple instantaneously formed—though in its least affective form—between the therapist and the subject, an authentic speech can be generated. Not any speech will do, of course—this is where we see the virtue of the symbolic situation of the Oedipus.

It is really the key—a very reduced key, I would think—as I have already indicated to you—that there is probably a whole set of keys. . . . When we study mythology . . . we see that the Oedipus complex is but a tiny detail in an immense myth. The myth enables us to collate a series of relations between subjects, in comparison with whose complexity and wealth the Oedipus appears to be such an abridged edition that, in the final analysis, it is not always utilizable.

But no matter. We analysts have so far contented ourselves with it. We are totally mixed up, however, if we do not distinguish between the imaginary, the symbolic, and the real. (S 1:100–101)

In this "reduced key" that Freud has named after the story of Oedipus, it is important to distinguish the Symbolic from the Real and from the

Imaginary because psychoanalytic practice—that is, psychoanalytic *work*—has to do with the Symbolic. The narrative symbolic efficacy of the Oedipal reference in the psychoanalytic situation and the therapeutic, practical felicity of the analyst's speech act are accounted for by the resonant and enigmatic formula: "the unconscious is the discourse of the Other." What, precisely, does that mean? And how, specifically, does this formula account for what happens in the Dick case?

In general, when Lacan repeats this formula, what he wants to emphasize, by way of "intimation," are the following key points:

The unconscious is a discourse. Freud is not the first to have discovered the unconscious, but the first to have discovered the essential fact that *the unconscious speaks*: in slips of the tongue, in dreams, in the symbolic language of the symptoms. The unconscious is not simply a forgotten or rejected bag of instincts, but a indestructible infantile desire whose repression means that it has become symbolically unrecognizable, since it is differentially articulated through rhetorical displacements (object substitutions). Repression is, in other words, the rejection not of instincts but of symbols, or of signifiers: their rejection through their replacement, the displacement or the transference of their original libidinal meaning onto other signifiers.

The unconscious is a discourse that is other, or ex-centric, to the discourse of a self. It is in effect a discourse that is other to itself, not in possession of itself; a discourse that no consciousness can master and that no speaking subject can assume or own.

The unconsciousness is a discourse that is radically intersubjective. Since it is a discourse that no consciousness can own, the only way a consciousness can hear it is as coming from the Other. In this way, the formula describes the analytic situation as coincident with the radical structure of the unconscious, that is, the analytic (dialogic) situation as the condition of possibility for the production of psychoanalytic truth (an audible speech of the unconscious). "The Other" thus stands in the psychoanalytic dialogue both for the position of the analyst, through whom the subject hears his own unconscious discourse, and for the position of the subject's own unconscious, as other to his self (to his self-image and self-consciousness).

In language, our message comes to us from the Other, in a reverse form. (E 9)

The unconscious is that discourse of the Other by which the subject receives, in an inverted form, his own forgotten message. (E 439)

In what sense, then, does Lacan say that the Dick case is a spectacular demonstration of his formula of "the unconscious is the discourse of the Other"? Even as applied to this specific case, the Lacanian utterance has many resonances. In a first sense, it is in effect Klein's discourse (her initial Oedipal interpretation) that actively constitutes Dick's unconscious, that is, determines "an initial [symbolic] position out of which the subject can put into play the imaginary and the real, and conquer his development." The constitution of Dick's unconscious (mental functioning necessitating and enabling the substitution of objects of desire) is coincident, moreover, with Dick's own introduction into language—a language that precedes him and that comes to him from the Other (represented, here, by the therapist); a language that articulates a pre-established sociocultural symbolic system governed by a Law that structures relationships and into which Dick's own relations must be inscribed.

> The development takes place only insofar as the subject is integrated into a symbolic system, which he practices and in which he asserts himself through the exercise of an authentic speech. It is not even necessary, you will notice, for this speech to be his own.

For Dick, then, the unconscious is the discourse of the Other since it is, quite literally, constituted by Klein's discourse.

But, whereas the key to Dick's unconscious is in Klein's performative interpretation, Klein's interpretation is in turn *not her own.*

> In what way has Melanie Klein done anything whatsoever which manifests a grasp of any process whatsoever which would be, in the subject, his unconscious?
>
> She admits it right away: she has done it—she has acted—*out of habit.* (51: 100)

Klein has in effect done nothing other than "mechanically apply" (*plaquer*) "the symbolization of the Oedipus myth." If Klein rejoins, thus, Dick's unconscious, it is not because she truly understands its messages or directly hears its discourse, but because she is herself inhabited by the discourse of the Other—inhabited by the discourse of the Oedipus myth—of which she is herself nothing but an unconscious medium when, at a loss with respect to any understanding of the child and "out of habit," she quasi-automatically ventures her mechanical interpretation.

> Here we are then, up against the wall, up against the wall of language. We are there exactly in our place, that is to say, on the same side as the patient, and it is on this wall—the same for him as for us—that we are going to attempt a reply to the echo of his speech. (E 316, N 101; translation mine)

For Klein too, then, even as she acts as therapist, the unconscious is the discourse of the Other: the practitioner speaks out of her own unconscious, out of her own inscription into language. And this is always true in Lacan's conception: the psychoanalytical interpreter is not, himself, in possession of the truth of his interpretation, does not possess, in other words, the unconscious discourse he delivers, because the truth of this unconscious discourse is, as such, radically dialogic (it can only come about, discursively, in analytic dialogue; it is neither in, or of, the analyst, nor in, or of, the patient). "In the couple instantaneously formed . . . between the therapist and the subject [Dick], an authentic speech can be generated."

The unconscious is the discourse of the Other, therefore, to the extent that the "authentic speech of the unconscious" is neither Dick's nor Klein's. The Other is in a position of a Third, in the structure of the psychoanalytic dialogue: it is a locus of unconscious language, sometimes created by the felicitous encounter, by the felicitous structural, verbal coincidence between the unconscious discourse of the analyst and the unconscious discourse of the patient. It is a third, not only because it is neither of the two participants in the analytic dialogue but because, with respect to each of these participants, it is also not the imaginary "other" whom each faces. "The unconscious is the discourse of the Other"—of a Third—in that it is ex-centric to, and subversive of, the specular duality (the seductive, narcissistic mirroring) between analyst and analysand.

This is the field that our experience polarizes in a relation which is only apparently two-way, for any positing of its structure in merely dual terms is as inadequate to it in theory as it is ruinous for its technique. (E 265, N 56)

It is to this Other beyond the other that the analyst yields his place by means of the neutrality with which he makes himself . . . neither one nor the other of those present; and if the analyst keeps silent, it is precisely in order to let the Other speak. (E 459)

It is therefore in the position of a third term that the Freudian discovery of the unconscious becomes clear as to its true grounding. This discovery may simply be formulated in the following terms:

The unconscious is that part of concrete discourse in so far as it is transindividual, that is, not at the disposal of the subject in reestablishing the continuity of his conscious discourse. (E 258, N 49)

Although Lacan elliptically passes over the relation between the paradoxical triangularity of the psychoanalytic dialogue (a triangularity that distinguishes the psychoanalytic dialogue from any other dialogue), and the structural triangularity he insists on in the Oedipus (as constitutive of the Symbolic), it is clear that the *thirdness* of the term that materializes, in the analytic dialogue, the unconscious as the "discourse of the Other" is itself an implicit, subtle reference to the Oedipus. The paradoxical triangularity of the analytic dialogue is Lacan's elliptical, sophisticated, and profound way of *referring* the significance of the psychoanalytic situation to the structural significance he has shed new light on in the Oedipus.

This structural significance can be told as *a narrative of the discovery, precisely, of this structure:* a narrative of the discovery of the structure of the psychoanalytic situation, and this, indeed, is Lacan's specific psychoanalytic story.

This Lacanian story, this particular conception of the narrativity of the psychoanalytic dialogue, is, however, very different from the usual one, which attributes the narration in the analytic dialogue respectively, or successively, to the two agents of the dialogue. Such, for instance, is Roy Schafer's story:

I shall now attempt to portray this psychoanalytic dialogue in terms of two agents, each narrating or telling something to the other in a rule-governed manner. Psychoanalysis is telling and re-telling along psychoanalytic lines: this is the theme and form of the present narration. It is, I think, a story worth telling.[5]

But the Lacanian psychoanalytic story is an altogether different story because the narration happens not between two agents but between three terms, and since it takes place (takes effect) only *through* the emergence of this third—this Other; since the subject of the psychoanalytic narration, in all senses of the word (both its speaking subject and what is being spoken of), is neither the analysand nor the analyst, but the discourse of the Other. The psychoanalytic narrative is nothing other, for Lacan, than the story of, precisely, the discovery of the third participant in the structure of the dialogue. And this dramatic, narrative, and structural discovery implicitly refers to Oedipus.

As in Freud's case, though in a somewhat different manner, the (elliptical) Lacanian Oedipus emerges, in its peculiar double status as a psychoanalytic key and as a reference story, as an original relation between narrative and theory, between the static, spatial schema of a structure and the dynamic, temporal movement of a story. For Lacan, in much the same way as for Freud, the Oedipus embodies an unprecedented, revolutionary moment of coincidence between narration and theorization.

But if for Freud the Oedipus embodies the insightful moment of discovery at which the psychoanalytic narration—in passing through the analytic practice and in turning back upon itself—becomes theory, it could be said that for Lacan the Oedipus embodies the insightful moment of discovery at which the psychoanalytic theory—in passing through the analytic practice and in turning back upon itself—becomes narration: unfinished analytic dialogue, or an ongoing story of the discourse of the Other.

III

THE LITERARY REFERENCE: OEDIPUS THE KING

Thus it is that, while Freud reads Sophocles' text in view of a confirmation of his theory, Lacan rereads the Greek text, after Freud, with an eye to its specific pertinence not to theory but to psychoanalytic practice. Freud had already compared the drama of Oedipus to the process of a practical psychoanalysis:

> The action of the play consists in nothing other than the process of revealing, with cunning delays and ever-mounting excitement—a process that can be likened to the work of a psychoanalysis—that Oedipus himself is the murderer of Laius, but further that he is the son of the murdered man and of Jocasta. (SE 4:262)

But while this comparison between the literary work and the work of the analysand leads Freud to the confirmation of his *theory*—a theory of wish, of wish fulfillment, and of primordial Oedipal desires (incestuous and parricidal)—Lacan's different analytic emphasis on the relevance of Oedipus to the clinician's practice is not so much on wish as on the role of speech, of language, in the play.

As we have seen, what Freud discovered in the Oedipus—the unconscious nature of desire—implies, in Lacan's view, a structural relation between language and desire: a desire that articulates itself, substitutively, in a symbolic metonymic language that is no longer recognizable by the subject.

> The relations between human beings are truly established below the level of consciousness. It is desire which accomplishes the primitive structural organization of the human world, desire inasmuch as it is unconscious. (S 2:262)

> It is always at the juncture of speech, at the level of its apparition, its emergence . . . that the manifestation of desire is produced. Desire emerges at the moment of its incarnation into speech—it is coincident with the emergence of symbolism. (S 2:273)

No wonder, then, that *Oedipus the King*, dramatizing as it does the *primal scene* of desire, in effect takes place on the *other scene* of language. Even more than Klein's case history, *Oedipus the King* is in its turn a spectacular demonstration of the Lacanian formula, "the unconscious is the discourse of the Other": for Oedipus' unconscious is quite literally embodied by the discourse of the Oracle.

Oedipus' unconscious is nothing other than this fundamental discourse whereby, long since, for all time, Oedipus' history is out there—written, and we know it, but Oedipus is ignorant of it, even as he is played out by it since the beginning. This goes way back—remember how the Oracle frightens his parents, and how he is consequently exposed, rejected. Everything takes place in function of the Oracle and of the fact that Oedipus is truly other than what he realizes as his history—he is the son of Laius and Jocasta, and he starts out his life ignorant of this fact. The whole pulsation of the drama of his destiny, from the beginning to the end, hinges on the veiling of this discourse, which is his reality without his knowing it. (S 2:245)

The unconscious is this subject unknown to the self, misapprehended, misrecognized, by the ego. (S 2:59)

The Oedipal question is thus that the center of each practical psychoanalysis, not necessarily as a question addressing analysands' desire for parents but as a question addressing analysands' misapprehension, misrecognition (*méconnaissance*) of their own histories.

The subject's question in no way refers to the results of any specific weaning, abandonment, or vital lack of love or affection; it concerns the subject's history inasmuch as the subject misapprehends, *misrecognizes,* it; this is what the subject's actual conduct is expressing in spite of himself, insofar as he obscurely seeks to *recognize* this history. His life is guided by a problematics which is not that of his life experience, but that of his destiny—that is, what is the meaning, the significance, of his history? What does his life story mean?

SHOSHANA FELMAN

9 Flaubert's Signature: The Legend of Saint Julian the Hospitable

An uncanny superimposition of the myths of Oedipus and Christ, *The Legend of Saint Julian the Hospitable* is the strange story of Christ the murderer and/or of Oedipus the saint: the story of a child who kills his parents only to be sainted by this very deed, which turns out to be at once his fated cross and his redeeming Calvary.

The tale, divided into three parts strictly calculated in conception and composition, does not articulate a simple chronology or succession of events, but a veritable narrative logic, a *structural necessity* that links, through the central murder of the parents (chapter 2), the initial story of the child (chapter 1) and the final legend of the saint (chapter 3). The parents' murder, by its mediate position, would appear, then, as the paradoxical transition, as the unexpected necessary juncture between the *birth of a child* and the *birth of a legend*. Through the mediating gap thus structurally produced by the murder, two underlying questions seem to be concurrently inscribed in—and articulated by—Flaubert's text:

What is a child?
What is a legend?

I

JULIAN'S DESTINY

What is a child? A child, the text seems to suggest, is first of all a dream: the combined dream of his two parents.

Rejoice, oh mother! Your son will be a saint![1]

says the apparition of a hermit to the mother; and to the father, a beggar looming up from the mist predicts:

Ah! Ah! Your son! . . . Much blood! . . . Much glory! . . . Always happy! An emperor's family. (178)

What is the meaning of these two prophecies regarding Julian's destiny? In what way do the oracles reveal the origin, at once of the child's fate and of the legend's meaning?

We may note, to begin with, the way in which the oracle of Julian's destiny significantly differs from the oracle concerning Oedipus. In the Oedipus myth, the parents receive—by way of a divine *curse*—a *single* oracular message warning them of the *misfortune* their son will bring them. Here, the parents receive two separate messages—*two* oracles—which they perceive, not as a curse, but on the contrary as a *blessing*. Their son appears in the oracular message, not as an agent of misfortune, but as a promise of good fortune:

He was dazzled by the splendors destined for his son, even though the *promise* of these splendors was not clear. (179)

The underlying Flaubertian question, *What is a child?* here translates textually into the following question: Why does the promise of good fortune the child embodies prove to be, as such, incapable of fulfillment? Why can't Julian keep the promise he is supposed to be except by transforming its good fortune into bad? How—and why—is the blessing changed into a curse?[2]

If the destiny of Oedipus—the fatal curse uttered to the parents—is here ironically believed to be a blessing, and if the divine message concerning Julian divides itself into two distinct predictions separately given to the mother and the father, it is because Flaubertian oracle in reality only returns to each parent *his* own unconscious message, his own *desire* for the child.

In both cases, in effect, the text discreetly puts in question the objective reality of the oracle: no one but the father and the mother sees the respective apparitions.

The next day, all the servants questioned said that they had seen no hermit. (178)

The good nobleman looked right and left, called out as loudly as he could. No one! The wind was whistling, and the morning mists were clearing away. (179)

The ambiguous status of the oracle—real or fantasized—does not, moreover, escape the notice of the parents themselves, who very much suspect, each in his turn, the hallucinated, dreamlike nature of the message that so gratifies them. "Dream or reality," the mother tells herself, "it must have been a message from heaven" (178). As for the father, "He attributed the vision to his mental fatigue from having slept too little" (179).

Thus not only are the oracles themselves of different substance for the mother and the father, but the two parental *readings* of the oracles are in turn diametrically opposed: while the mother chooses to interpret what could be her symptom as no less than a supernatural sign, the father, for his part, chooses to interpret what could be a supernatural sign as nothing but a symptom; while the mother chooses to reduce the very ambiguity of the vision to a single, mystical meaning (religious or transcendental), the father chooses to reduce the ambiguity of the vision to a single, realistic meaning (psychological or pathological). On one side, an absolute passion for mysticism; on the other, an absolute passion for realism; on one hand, a fantastic reading; on the other, a phantasmic reading of the legendary element of the oracle: two antithetical interpretations, mutually exclusive, and yet whose destiny it is to coexist, to coincide throughout the tale—two schemes of meaning whose dynamic contradiction fights over—and within— Julian himself.

This is, in Flaubert, the fateful secret of the oracle: the two distinct fates prophesied for Julian correspond to the two ambitions that the father and the mother secretly nurture for their son.[3] The father, a veteran of war who regularly and nostalgically takes pleasure in "regaling . . . his old battle companions" (179), wishes for his son heroic distinction and military fame ("Much blood! . . . Much glory!"); the mother, religiously ascetic, and whose household is "governed like the inside of a monastery" (178), hopes her son will be "a saint": two heterogeneous ambitions, two irreconcilable parental desires whose difference is determined not just by two scales of value, by two different *ethics,* but, above all, by two distinct *self-images,* two narcissistic constellations radically foreign to each other. Each parent, in effect, projects onto the son his own idealized self-image. On both sides, the child is imagined, dreamed, desired as a double — as a narcissistic reflection.

Torn, from before his birth, between two narcissistic programmings, caught between two laws, between two unconscious minds, between two projects for his future, Julian will be called upon to satisfy two radically contradictory parental wishes. "What is a child?" asks the text. The answer, ironically outlined by the very silence of the narrator, arises out of that which can be articulated, not by words, but only by events: a child is, paradoxically enough, nothing other than the embodiment of the *contradiction between his parents.*

THE BLANK, THE SILENCE, THE GAP

The problem for Julian — the model child, "a little Jesus" (179) — is thus the following: how can he *live* the contradiction that has begotten him? How can he conform to the double, contradictory model ordained by his two parents?

> Often, the nobleman would regale his old battle companions. As they drank, they would recall their wars, the assaults on fortresses with the clash of armor and the prodigious wounds. Julian, listening to them, would let out cries at this; then his father had no doubt that he would later be a conqueror. But in the evening, as the Angelus drew to a close, when he would pass between the bowing poor, he would dip into his purse with such modesty, with such noble air, that his mother was convinced she would eventually see him an archbishop.
>
> His place in the chapel was at his parents' side. (179)

The silence of the narrator (of the story) is audible only in the blank that separates and links the two indented paragraphs so as to situate — to mark — Julian's "place." It is important to note that this paragraph immediately precedes Julian's first act of violence: the murder of the mouse. The succession of the paragraphs suggests that, in some way, the murder — as dissonant as it may be — comes out of Julian's place: Julian's place, precisely, in the chapel. But what is, strictly speaking, this place beside his parents, one of whom envisions him as an archbishop and the other — as a conqueror? It is a middle place, but a place—an *in-between space*—that is totally contradictory, impossible: a place that, like the blank of the indented paragraph that introduces it, is the silent locus of *discontinuity*, the very place of a division, of a gap. Julian's problem, his tragic dilemma, is, precisely, *how to assume the lapse* of that location, the hiatus of that place. How can he respond to the *division* between the two demands addressed to him? How can he take on, how can he realize the gap between his parents?

Two parents that the text, from its first words, simultaneously *juxtaposes* and *opposes:*

The *father* and the *mother* of Julian lived in a castle. (178)

Two parents that the text, once again, carefully juxtaposes and opposes in the two contiguous paragraphs that describe them for the first time. The contrast between the father and the mother is not spelled out: the opposition comes out of a concerted technique of juxtaposition. As always with Flaubert, it is the last sentence of the paragraph that *punctuates* the latter (gives it a *point*), while also making it ambiguous. That is, it at the same time gives the paragraph all its meaning and suspends the meaning: it makes the meaning veer toward the silence of the blank space, which it overloads with the unsaid. Now the parallel structure of the two paragraphs describing the parents is punctuated by two concluding sentences between which a dissonance begins ironically to resonate from one paragraph to the other:

Always wrapped up in a fox fur, he would walk about his house, give justice to his vassals, arbitrate his neighbors' quarrels. . . . *After many adventures, he had taken as his wife a maiden* of high birth.

She was very white, somewhat proud and serious. . . . Her household was governed like the inside of a monastery. . . . *By dint of praying to God, a son came unto her.* (178)

What is striking is the *nonencounter* between the two paragraphs, both of which, however, point toward the *encounter* that will give birth to a son. "After many adventures, he had taken as his wife a maiden . . .";
"By dint of praying to God, a son came unto her." Like the contrast that will later be brought out by both the oracles and the parental readings of the oracles, these initial descriptions already prefigure the

dichotomy between the paternal order—secular, assertive, realistic, and the maternal order—mystical, religious, and ascetic.

Still, the semantic overload, the ironic tinge of the sentence that concludes the description of the mother—"By dint of praying to God, a son came unto her"—does more than just oppose the mother's religious and the father's secular disposition. By making quite plainly an allusion to the Immaculate Conception, it connotes a *nonrelation of the mother to the actual father* of her son. The mother's mystical perception thus involves not simply faith but a subtle syntax of denial, of negation: a denial—conscious or unconscious—of the sexual act that necessarily preceded the child's birth, a denial, therefore, of the mother's own sexuality as what motivated—and made possible—her maternity. Julian, then, will also have to consummate a double bind—to live out an aporia—between two paradigms of which one, the paternal, is a model of self-assertion and sensual affirmation, whereas the other, the maternal, is a model of self-denial and sexual negation.

The contradiction is, however, neither simply the result of the mother's faith nor a simple accident of psychology: it corresponds to the stereotypical sex roles of the man (Patriarch-Adventurer) and the woman (always, in some sense, Virgin-Mother) in Western culture. The mother's *mysticism* is, indeed, the *feminine mystique* par excellence. Thus the contradictions of which Julian is the incarnation are also, among other things, the symptom of a culture. However, Julian is a symptom only insofar as he is the very offspring of the gap, the very child of the discrepancy between his father and his mother insofar as, paradoxically enough, he is *begotten by the nonrelation between the sexes*. What, indeed, could be more strikingly ironic than this version of an *aporetic sexual act?*

The implicit motif of the nonrelation between the mother and the father is taken up again in a more explicit form in the scene of the oracular apparitions—solitary visions that the two spouses keep above all from communicating to each other. Thus the very image of the child stays with each parent as a private, unshared fantasy: the discontinuity between the father and the mother, the nonrelation between the two sexes, are thematized and sealed by the nondialogue—the silence—between the two partners of the couple whose child becomes, ironically, the figure, not of what they share, but of what they *do not share*. The child of contradiction and division, Julian is the offspring, above all, of silence.

Dream or reality, it must have been a message from heaven; but she took care to say nothing about it, for fear of being accused of pride. . . .

He attributed this vision to his mental fatigue from having slept too little. "If I speak of it, I will be ridiculed," he told himself.

The spouses hid their secret from each other. But both cherished the child with equal love. (178–79)

This silence that unites and separates the parents—and that makes the child into a *guilty secret*—is prolonged, extended, deepened, later on, by the child's own guilty silence sealing his first murder: the murder of the mouse in the church:

A drop of blood stained the flagstone. He wiped it up quickly with his sleeve, threw the mouse outside, and *said nothing about it to anyone.* (179)

The silence of the child about the mouse—the real murder he has committed—is in turn prolonged by the silence of Julian's wife concerning the obsession that haunts her husband: the fantasy of the murder of his parents. But it is precisely *by keeping silent* to Julian's parents about their son's imaginary secret that Julian's wife brings about the fantasy's realization:

They asked a thousand questions about Julian. She replied to each one, but *took care to keep silent about the ominous idea concerning them.* . . .

Julian had crossed the park. . . . Everywhere there hung a great silence. . . .

. . . .

His father and his mother were before him, lying on their backs with holes in their chests; and their faces, with a gentle majesty, seemed to be keeping an eternal secret. (183–85)

From the "secret" of the oracle that the spouses hid from each other, to the "eternal secret" that the parents' corpses seem to keep, *The Legend of Saint Julian the Hospitable* can be read as *the story of a silence.* "Man," writes Freud in a formula itself oracular and lapidary, "man speaks in order not to kill." It is out of the reversal of this formula that Flaubert's narrative is written: Julian *kills because he does not speak;* in his legend, it is silence that engenders, motivates, unleashes murder.

Paradoxically, however, it is also *what withholds speech* in the legend that constitutes the very energy of its narration: it is *out of Julian's silence* that Flaubert *writes,* that the text *speaks,* that the tale is indeed *telling.*

THE INK STAIN

The symbolism of color contrast draws out at yet another level the opposition between the mother and the father. Thus the mother, who "was very *white*" (178), is repeatedly associated with the signifier of the color white. When the mother is by mistake all but murdered by her son, it is "two white wings" that Julian sees and at which he throws his javelin, thinking he has seen a stork.

> A piercing cry was heard.
> It was his mother, whose bonnet . . . remained pinned to the wall.
> (182)

In the same way, the "little *white* mouse" (179) killed in church—the mother's space—is doubtless also a substitutive figure for the mother.

The father, on the other hand, is symbolically associated with the signifier black. So the prodigious stag that, "solemn like a patriarch and like a judge," curses Julian for killing him and predicts he will one day "assassinate his father and his mother," "was *black* and monstrous in stature" (181).

It is doubtless not by accident that the contradiction of black and white turns out to be the very one that produces writing. As Mallarmé suggestively puts it:

> You have remarked, one does not write, luminously, on an obscure background, the alphabet of the stars alone is thus indicated, sketched, or interrupted; *man pursues black on white.*[4]

What, then, is the *writing* that the contradiction between black and white—between the mother and the father in Flaubert's text—in effect produces, if not Julian himself as the very *text of contradiction,* as a marked, imprinted page?

The spouses hid their secret from each other. But both cherished the child with equal love; and regarding him as *marked by God,* they bestowed infinite respect and care on his beloved person. (179)

Produced by contradiction, difference, and alterity, the *mark*—at once the counterpart and the obverse of silence—is nothing other than a written letter. But what is, here, the page on which the mark is to be printed, the page on which the stained destiny of contradiction is to be inscribed and literally written down "black on white," if not, precisely, Julian's very body? Thus, in the metaphorical deer family, white the stag-"patriarch" is "black" and the doe-mother is "fair," the little fawn—obviously Julian's own reflection—is significantly "spotted" (181).

But Julian's own skin is itself literally spotted, marked. It is indeed these very marks or spots that serve as signs of recognition by which Julian's aged parents, who are unknown to his wife, are able to identify their son for her:

Nothing could convince the young woman that her husband was their son.

They provided proof by describing *particular signs* he had on his skin. (183)

Julian is thus "marked by God" very much like Cain, bearing in his turn the concrete inscription of a *writing*—of distinctive marks or signs—printed or imprinted on his very skin.

It is therefore not surprising that this legend of marked skin—of the epidermal stain and of writing in the flesh—should reach its pinnacle, or its epiphany, in the dramatic figure of the leper.

Julian saw that a hideous leprosy covered his body. . . . His shoulders, his chest, his skinny arms disappeared into *slabs* of scaly pustules. Enormous *wrinkles* dug into his forehead.

"I'm hungry!" he said. Julian gave him what he had, an old chunk of lard and a few crusts of dark bread.

When he had devoured them, the table, the bowl, and the handle of the knife bore *the very same spots that were visible on his body.* (186–87)

Just like the spotted fawn and the signs marking Julian's skin, the leper's spotted skin is, once again, nothing other than a metaphorical image of Julian himself. But whereas Julian kills the fawn and plans to kill himself, he accepts—and saves—the leper: the ending of the tale marks the climactic moment at which Julian (at the actual point of dying—that is, of becoming in effect a saint) for the first time *forgives himself*—and accepts himself: forgives himself his spotted, tainted skin; forgives himself, in other words, for being *marked* by his own *otherness to himself*; accepts himself, therefore, as a stained, marred text, at once black and white, innocent and guilty: a text of contradiction he will no longer struggle to suppress (as he had attempted through the various killings), but to which he will henceforth submit, endeavoring to *pass through*, to traverse, to *pass beyond*. The crossing of the river, among other things, is also the symbolic crossing of his own division and his own contradiction.

II

THE VOICE CAME FROM THE OTHER SIDE

> Since the passage became known, travelers presented themselves. They would hail him from the other bank. . . .
> . . . The . . . voice . . . came from the other side. . . . The shadows were deep, and here and there *torn by the whiteness* of cresting waves. . . .
>
> With each thrust of the oar, the backwash raised [the boat] in front. The water, *blacker than ink,* flowed furiously on each side of the vessel. (186–87)

Why is the river's water said to be "blacker than ink"? In what way are we meant to read the crossing of the river as a metaphor of writing? And what, if so, is writing all about?

Navigating in the midst of "*shadows . . . torn* by the *whiteness* of cresting waves," passing through the *ink-black* river, Julian, struggling to survive division, crosses the contradiction between black and white (father and mother, innocence and guilt, sameness and otherness, consciousness and the unconscious). From one side of the ink-black river to the other, writing is this passage for survival, this constant shuttle movement between life and death. It is thus that Julian struggles to *traverse the ink stain,* to survive, pass through, and pass across the writing on his very flesh.

This struggle, this necessity of crossing, this agonizing passage through the ink stain is, indeed, Julian's predicament. But it is also the predicament of Flaubert who, elsewhere, writes in turn, for his part, to Louise Colet:

> I fret, I itch. . . . I've got stylistic abscesses, and the sentence itches and cannot be quelled. What a heavy oar the pen is, and what a hard current is the idea, when one digs into it![5]

But what, then, is Flaubert's place in the legend of the Other, in the story of Saint Julian—which he writes?

The place from which the legend is enunciated is itself *marked* in the last paragraph of the tale:

> And that's the story of Saint Julian the Hospitable, as one can find it—more or less—on a stained-glass window of a church, in my country. (187)

It is out of this concluding, final sentence that the second question of the tale emerges: What, in the last analysis, is a legend?

A double blank, a silent gap marking a break in tone and a change of perspective, separates this final sentence from the narrative that precedes it. However, in order to attempt to grasp the import of the final sentence and the way it can shed light on what a legend is, we must try to look beyond—in fact across—this gap, for the *relation*—the articulation—on the contrary, between the apparently removed last sentence and the main (narrative) bulk of the text.

What is remarkable about this sentence—which is indeed unique in Flaubert's work—is the peculiar fact that it refers the text to a *first person* ("*my* country"), which could well be not (fictitiously) the narrator's, but perhaps also (referentially) the author's. Even aside from the specific reference to the church window whose historical existence in Rouen did in reality motivate and trigger the writing of the tale,[6] the closing sentence—at least fictitiously—designates the narrator as the actual author. Placed just above the proper name "Flaubert," the "I" that so unexpectedly emerges in the closing sentence *in excess of the story,* so as to punctuate the text and bring it to a close, appears indeed to be, in relation to the (written story), not just its narrator but its *signatory*. It therefore, in some sense, inscribes within the text the very signature of Flaubert.

The signature, however, says: *It isn't me,* it's not my person, that is the tale's originator: it's not from me that the narration springs, but from my homeland, from "my country." The question then becomes: what, exactly, is a country?

THE STORY OF A COUNTRY

I have in me that melancholy of the barbarian races, with its migratory instincts and innate disgust with life that made them leave their country as if they were leaving themselves. — FLAUBERT, *Letters*

Julian crossed in this way an interminable plain, and at last he found himself on a plateau dominating a great expanse of country. Flat rocks were scattered among vaults in ruins. One would stumble over dead men's bones; here and there, worm-eaten crosses slanted lamentingly. But there were shapes moving about in the uncertain shadows of the tombs.
— FLAUBERT, *The Legend of Saint Julian*

What is a country? The answer to this question is, indeed, suggested in the tale: suggested by the way in which the signatory, final sentence implicitly rejoins the narrative's first sentence, which it remotely echoes; the ending is thus structured as a subtle counterpart to the tale's opening:

The father and the mother of Julian lived in a castle, in the middle of the woods, on the slope of a hill. (178)

Much could be said about this sentence, which, like the closing sentence, is rich in implications—beyond its innocuous appearance. One could stress the opposition it draws out between the *castle* and the *wood* (the animals' space, which will grow to be important in the story): an opposition between inside and outside, between the space of nature and the protected space of culture; "the slope of a hill" foreshadows, on the other hand, the possibility of a fall; and since this spatial description does not directly situate Julian himself, the implicit question that is left hanging is that of knowing, what space will belong to Julian? Indeed, as we will later learn, Julian will turn out to be the natural inhabitant of the woods and of the slope—far more than of the castle. What I wish to stress, however, is the fact, crucial in its simplicity, that the legend's opening—the very first sentence of the tale— gives information as to *where the hero's parents live.* The first sentence speaks, in other words, of Julian's country—of Julian's homeland, whereas the last sentence speaks of Flaubert's country—of the signatory's homeland.

What, then, is a country, if not, as the text suggests, the country where one's parents live? So, too, in the closing sentence, "my country" means *my parents' country;* that is to say, the country, at the same time, of the *cultural heritage* my parents have passed on to me.

But in this text "the country of my parents" necessarily implies the country of the *contradiction* that inhabits the relationship of those who have a child: the country of the gap, of the discontinuity that, paradoxically, is enacted by the very act of procreation. "My country," therefore, is the country of the contradictions embodied by the burden of the cultural heritage within which I am born, and with which my birth afflicts me.

The question of the meaning of a country thus begins to answer the initial question, concerning the nature of a legend. A legend is, precisely, the unconscious of the contradictions that beget us: the unconscious of the cultural heritage, articulating its *discontinuity with itself* in the form of this contradiction we, in turn, have to live, and to live out.

As if we didn't have enough of our own past, we chew over that of humanity in its entirety.[7]

In fact, beneath the allegoric figure of the very story of *birth into consciousness,* it is humanity's entire cultural and mythic past that Flaubert condenses into the *legend.* Almost all of the myths of the Western heritage are present in it: the Greek and Latin myths of Oedipus, Narcissus, Ajax, Charon, the biblical myths of Adam, Noah, and Cain, the evangelical myths of the life of Christ and the trials of the saints.[8] "The story found in my country" being that of Occidental culture as a whole, "my country" is not simply France of Rouen, but rather Babel: the very Babel of the West.

But the Flaubertian inscription of this mythic Babel ruptures and subverts, for each myth, its autonomy of sense and its semantic unity and integrity. Out of the Western Babel of the myths, Flaubert's ironic writing registers precisely the contradictions that, opposing the myths to one another, oppose them—and make them discontinuous—to themselves.

Thus Julian, Christ and Oedipus,[9] is *crucified,* irreverently, not over his own death, but over someone else's death: over the corpses of two goats—prefiguring those of his parents—that the text specifically describes as his *cross.*[10]

Incarnating, in this way, the very irony—the very aberration—of the contradictory coincidence of Oedipus and Christ, Julian is also, at the same time, the embodiment of the conflicting myths of Adam and of Noah:

> Sometimes, in a dream, he saw himself as *our father Adam* in the midst of paradise, among all the animals; stretching out his arms, he would make them die; or they would file two by two . . . as on the day they entered *Noah's ark.* (183)

Adam, in the myth, did not *kill* animals: he *named* them. The Flaubertian distortion of the myths suggests, in a revealing way, a textual correlation between *naming* and *killing.* In the case of Julian, the act of killing is suggestively substituted for the act of naming or of speaking, implying, once again, a relationship between silence and murder. Julian *kills* because he does not name; Flaubert, for his part, *names*—in order not to kill? Or perhaps rather to kill *by naming* him "our father Adam," to implicate himself in turn in the very parricide of myths? "The distortion of a text," writes Freud, "is not unlike a murder, in its implications. The difficulty resides not so much in perpetrating the crime, but in covering up its traces."[11]

What is there to cover up, however, if not the fact that the murdered father had already—from the outset—been dead, that there had always been *too many fathers,* too many myths?[12] What *The Legend of Saint Julian the Hospitable* reveals is, paradoxically enough, that *parricide is fundamentally impossible.*

Too many fathers, too many myths: behind "our father Adam" is already profiled, in the same breath (in the same paragraph), this other father of the human race, whose mythic function was, precisely, to start it over: "The animals would file two by two, . . . as on the day they entered Noah's ark." Noah, Adam: in coupling those two fathers of humanity, what is at stake in Flaubert's text is, once again, the inscription of a (yet another) contradiction between our parents. Whereas Adam, perpetrator of original sin, is the embodiment of guilt and of its irreducible human inheritance, Noah is, in contrast, the very figure of innocence par excellence: far from killing animals, he is rather their savior, the one who gives them life. The superimposition of these two myths in the same paragraph suggests that Julian—the very text of contradictions—is *at once* innocent and guilty: he who is most guilty, he from whom descends mankind's heritage of sin, and he who, of all mankind, is the sole innocent. Innocence is here no longer, in effect, *opposed* to guilt.

In this way Flaubert, inscribing "black on white" the myths of stain upon the myths of purity, writes innocence into the myths of guilt and guilt into the myths of innocence.

> And that's the story of Saint Julian the Hospitable, as once can find it—more or less—on a stained-glass window of a church, in my country. (187)

The story of a country: a story of the relation between Flaubert's land—that of the closing sentence—and Julian's (parents') land—that of the opening sentence. A tale of the relationship between where Flaubert comes from and where Julian comes from, between the country that locates the hero at the contradictory crossroads of conflicting dreams and parents, and the country that locates the signatory or the signature—the very energy of the writing—at the contradictory crossroads of conflicting myths.

INSIDERS AND OUTSIDERS: HOSPITALITY

Since the native country of the signatory is thus related to the legendary country where "the father and the mother" live,[13] it should be stressed that Julian, nonetheless, is by definition one who cannot say "my country": his story is that of an *exile,* endlessly renewed. Structurally, the repeated scansion of Julian's displacement—his departure into exile—in effect constitutes the very punctuation of the three parts of the tale: each chapter ends with the hero leaving. Thus, at the end of the first chapter, Julian flees the parental castle and leaves his native country; at the end of the second chapter, he flees his own castle and leaves the country of his wife, which, through marriage, had become his own; at the end of the third chapter, he leaves this world to ascend to heaven—the wayfarer's ultimate departure.

Since Julian is, by definition, he who has no land, but who nonetheless *inhabits my land*—lives in "my country" as the host of a church window, what else is a country if not, precisely, that which is *constituted by legends of exile?* If Julian, all the same, is defined as the story of "my country," then the story of "my country" is the story of an exile situated, not outside, but, paradoxically, *inside* my land.

This commingling of the inside and the outside of the tale itself, this relation adumbrated by the closing sentence between the (intrinsic) legendary hero and the (extrinsic) narrative first person of the signatory—between the legend and Flaubert's self-referential signing of the legend—suggests that writing is itself in fact an *inside job:* a relation—far more complex than we might think—between being an insider and being an outsider, between the stance of being in and the stance of being out of what one writes about.

Writing—but also murder. Julian consummates, indeed, his destiny as a murderer both by virtue of his being an insider and by virtue of his being an outsider. On the one hand, it is because Julian has left his country that he—like Oedipus—ends up unwittingly killing his parents: the tragic mistake would not have happened had Julian not exiled himself out of his home and family, had he not cast himself on the outside.

But on the other hand, ironically enough, Julian kills in order to eliminate outsiders, to *protect the inside* of his home and of his family: finding his parents in his own bed, offered them—without his knowledge—by his wife, and tragically confusing his mother and his wife—whom he believes to have caught with a lover, Julian commits the double murder of his parents in a fit of jealousy that is clearly, in a metaphoric manner, Oedipal. But if Julian kills because he takes his own father for a stranger—an outsider—he kills because he in effect radically *confuses inside and outside* and thus mistakenly strives to protect what is *within* against what he believes to be an *intrusion from without.*

The attitude of the murderer, who endeavors to protect the inside from the outside and hence casts on the outside what is really only an

unrecognized part of his inside, is diametrically opposed to the attitude of the Hospitable, who opens himself up to the outside and actually welcomes the outsider into his own home. It is not by chance,
indeed, that "the Hospitable" figures in the legend's title. Hospitality,
though hardly obvious or explicit — except precisely in the title — in effect plays in the tale an absolutely crucial role: crucial for an understanding of the way Flaubert *rewrites* the legend and of the irony with
which he writes *into* the legend his sophisticated signature.

While it is true that Flaubert's title is no more than a recapitulation
of the traditional title of the saint, as well as of the saint's title to
sainthood — *Saint Julian the Hospitable* — Flaubert's writing does not fail
to introduce *into the very title* (of the saint, as of the tale) an ironic split:
the ambiguous tension, once again, of contradiction and division.

Hospitality itself, it turns out, is ironically divided in Flaubert's text:
the title in effect refers not to just one but to *two* occurrences, to two
displays of hospitality in the tale. The most obvious is that of Julian
welcoming the leper and offering him everything he has, right down
to his very body. That is, by all accounts, the ultimate in hospitality:
the kind of hospitality that leads to sainthood. But the other textual
occurrence of hospitality is when Julian's wife generously welcomes
into her own bed the two strange visitors — the two impoverished and
aged nomads — that the very parents of her husband have over the
years become.

The symbolic link between these two narrative occurrences of hospitality is effected through the signifier of the bed: in both cases, the
hospitable welcome is enacted by the gesture of *giving one's own bed:*

Julian's wife persuaded them not to wait up for him. *She herself put
them in her bed,* then closed the window; they fell asleep. (184)

The leper shook from limb to limb . . . and, in an almost silenced
voice, he murmured: "Your bed!" Julian gently helped him drag
himself to it. (187)

Thus it is the bed that twice becomes the quintessential site of hospitality. But to what is the bed hospitable — what does a bed host? Sleep,
of course, and dreams, and desire, and the erotic mingling of bodies
("Undress, so I can have the warmth of your body!" says the leper). But
in the *legend,* the bed also becomes a tomb, since it is in bed that Julian

kills his parents. The bed is thus equally hospitable to the murder of one's parents.

The ultimate gesture of welcome—*offering one's bed*—leads, then, on the one hand, to the sainthood of Saint Julian the Hospitable, yet on the other hand it leads to murder.

But it is precisely to the coincidence of these two scenes—to the ironic contradiction between these two displays of hospitality *taken together* and together issuing either in murder or in sainthood—that Flaubert's writing, in its turn, means to be hospitable. Hospitable to contradiction: hospitable to the voice of the Other, to a constant *countercurrent of meaning;* hospitable to silence, sleep, to its own silence, its own sleep, to its own difference from itself—hospitable, then, to a maximal number of mutually exclusive points of view within the same narrative statement, to a maximal number of opposed, conflicting readings (maternal/paternal, religious/sexual, supernatural-fantastic and/or natural-phantasmic, and so forth) within a single enunciation.

In the story as in its narration, on the inside as on the outside, what is at stake in hospitality is, therefore, not the simple gesture of inviting the outsider in—the welcoming of the outside inside—but, much more radically, the subversion of the very limit that distinguishes them from each other: the discovery that the outside is already within, but that what is within is, in effect, without—outside—itself.

MUCH BLOOD, MUCH GLORY; OR, THE STAINS OF THE STAINED-GLASS WINDOW

A double, triple irony: not only is hospitality what leads at once to sainthood and to murder, but the Hospitable is, paradoxically enough, a man who has, himself, no country—no home of his own,[14] a man, moreover, who is himself received or welcomed by no one, and whose narrative—or message—will elicit nothing other than an absolute refusal of hospitality:

> Out of the spirit of humility, he would tell his story: then everyone would flee him, making the sign of the cross. In the villages he had been through before, as soon as he was recognized, *the doors were shut,* threats were yelled out at him, and stones were thrown at him. The most charitable people set a bowl on their windowsill, then closed the shutters to avoid seeing him. (185)

How is it that Flaubert can tell Julian's story while Julian himself *cannot tell*—or get anyone to listen to—his story? It must be because Julian's story is by definition the story of the Other—the story of no one: a tale in some way without language, which can be articulated in effect only by the *silence* of the stained-glass window. If Flaubert speaks, tells the deaf, mute story of the stained-glass visual image, he can only read, *translate* it. For his own protection, he is screened, precisely, by the stained-glass window, whose function is indeed to separate him from his own tale.

It is thus the stained-glass window of the church that can alone be host—hospitable—to Julian's story; but Flaubert's tale can in turn be hospitable to—host—the stained-glass window.

> And that's the story . . . as one can find it on a stained-glass window of a church, in my country. (187)

Is the window *hosted* by the tale inside or outside? What is the significance of the inscription of the window in the closing sentence? In what way does Flaubert's stained glass in effect partake of the very nature of a signature?

The tale, quite literally, is *the legend of the stained-glass window,* since the word *legend* can also mean "any text that accompanies an image and gives it its meaning."[15] If the tale—like the account or interpretation of a dream—thus consists in the verbal translation of pictorial images into narrative, the stained-glass window constitutes a *legend* in the etymological sense as well: *legenda*—"what must be read." How, then, does the text define—or concretize—this figure of "what must be read?"

A stained-glass window is a painting; but it is also, at the same time, just a window; as such, it is, once more, a boundary, a limit that not only separates what is within from that which is without but also sets up the dependence of the inside on the outside: indeed, we could not see the painting on the inside were it not for the light that filters in from the outside. The stained glass thus enacts an ambiguous relationship of nontransparency, and yet of interfusion, between what is in and what is out. The outside—behind the painted window—is what the eye looking at the painting *does not see,* but it is also, at the same time, *what enables it to see.*

All these connotations of the stained-glass window are put into play by the tale itself. For the closing sentence, with its signatory gesture toward the referential church window that the narrator has just translated, is not the only mention of a stained-glass window in the legend. From within this signatory, painted window that in some sense frames the tale—apparently from outside the tale—another stained-glass window is outlined—and framed—inside the tale, in the very heart of the narrative itself. The story speaks, indeed, no fewer than three times of another stained-glass window: not that of Flaubert's home church, but that of Julian's castle. It must be significant that the three occurrences of this other stained-glass window all appear in proximity to the parental murder, which they literally frame.

The first appearance of the window introduces into the tale's silence a signatory note of tragic irony that mutely *signs* the parents' last sleep—the sleep from which they will never again awaken:

Julian's wife persuaded them not to wait up for him. She put them herself in her bed, then closed the window; they fell asleep. *Day was about to break,* and *behind the stained-glass window,* little birds began to sing. (184)

In the bedroom, *in front of the window,* the invisible narrator seems to contemplate the parents' sleep—their unawareness. But what is there *behind the stained-glass window?* Apparently, behind the window day is breaking. But in reality, day will, for the parents, dawn no more: behind the stained-glass window it is nothing other than eternal night— and death—which in effect await them. The window, then, embodies here the very ambiguity of day and night: the ambiguous borderline that at the same time separates and links sleeping and waking, death and life, without our being able to know for sure which is inside, which is outside—what, exactly, lies behind the window.

The second textual inscription of the stained-glass window can be found just before the murder, when Julian, harassed and frustrated by the final hunt, returns home:

Having taken off his sandals, he gently turned the key, and went in. *The stained-glass windows adorned with lead obscured the light of dawn.* Julian . . . made his way towards the bed, lost in the shadows spreading deep into the room. When he was at the bedside, in order to embrace his wife, he bent over the pillow, where two heads were resting side by side. Then, he felt against his mouth the sensation of a beard. . . . Definitely it was a beard . . . and a man! A man in bed with his wife!

Bursting with inordinate anger, he leapt at them, stabbing them repeatedly with his dagger. (185)

The signifying chain of the stained-glass windows that constructs a link between the narrative and its frame, that subtly binds the windows framed by the legendary story and the framing window of the narrator-signatory, here takes on a curiously ironic tinge. For while the stained-glass window contemplated by the narrator is *what makes us see* the legend, giving the story visibility, the window at the same time turns out to be *that which obscures,* creates a blindness: it is because of the window that Julian, seeing nothing, kills his parents. The window thus maintains an ambiguous relation with light: its function is not just—by letting in the rays of light—to *produce representation,* but also—by screening them off—to *distort perception.* The stained-glass window, or "what must be read," at once gives sight and blinds.

And if, unlike those who "closed their doors" so as *not to see* Julian, so as not to look at—listen to—his story (185), we agree to look at the stained-glass window, to listen to the legend, is it not precisely because of the blinding power of what a stained-glass window—or a legend— lets us see? Doesn't Flaubert suggest that the property of a legend (of a window) is to make us look, to make us see, while at the same time blinding us to the way the window in effect reflects on—has to do with—us?

The third occurrence of the stained-glass window takes place right after the murder. As day breaks, the rebus of the window lights up:

His father and mother were before him, stretched out on their backs with holes in their chests. . . . Splashes and *pools of blood* spread over the middle of their *white skin,* onto the bedsheets, onto the ground. . . . *The scarlet reflection of the stained glass window, now struck by the sun, lit up these red stains, and cast many more of them around the whole room.* (185)

At its last appearance within the legend, the stained-glass window—hit by light—becomes itself a rhetorical figure of writing: a figure of the optical prism of language as what determines, motivates, compels, the performance of "the pen-man."[16] "Style being, in itself, an absolute way of *seeing* things,"[17] it is indeed the window that is writing: it is the window that, *multiplying stains of red* throughout the room, brings back the motif of color contrast—the textual inscription of the stain, the mark. "The scarlet reflection of the stained-glass window, now struck by the sun, lit up these red stains, and cast many more of them around the whole room."

In this way, the stained-glass window turns out to be *hospitable* to *blood:* hospitable, ambiguously, both to what in blood is most uncanny, most unsettling—the blood of mortal injury, of murder—but also, at the same time, to what in blood is most familiar, reassuring: the blood-line of the family, the very familiarity of heritage. Uncannily familiar and familiarly uncanny, the stained-glass window is inscribed throughout the text as a writing that consists, precisely, of staining white surfaces: a writing—a play of colors and a play of light, a chiaroscuro—that consists of tinting the white pages of the text with ink that, in effect, is blood, with blood that, in effect, is ink.

It is thus that, when the signatory brings the legend to a close by bringing out his own relation to the stained-glass window in his home-land, the referential, outside window is already *signed* from inside the text: signed, precisely, by the blood stain changed into an ink stain.

"Of all writing," asserts Nietzsche through the mouth of Zarathus-tra, "I love but that which one has written with one's blood. Write with blood, and you will learn that blood is spirit."[18] Has Flaubert told the story of, precisely, writing with one's blood?

> It was a Bohemian with a braided beard. . . . With an inspired air,
> he stammered these disconnected words:
>   Ah! Ah! . . . Much blood! . . . Much glory! (178)

In the end, what is the connection that uncannily emerges from be-hind these words' apparent disconnection? In telling us, along with Julian's story, the very story of the stained (glass) signature, the tale can give a different, unexpected insight both into the Bohemian's "in-spiration" and into the nature of the "glory" he predicts. If the art of disconnection here turns out, indeed, to be inspired, if blood issues in glory and if the very glory of the "inspiration" is necessarily tied up with blood, the glory—like the blood as well—is Flaubert's.

"Almost everyone dies," writes Flaubert, "without knowing his proper name, unless he is a fool." A signature, indeed, is not the simple writing down of a proper name. A signature is nothing other than the story of one's writing with one's blood: the story of how *one does not know one's own name* and how, not knowing one's own name, one signs, instead, with one's own blood.

I, THE UNDERSIGNED

It would be quite pleasant to spell out my thought in order to relieve Sir Gustave Flaubert by means of sentences; but what importance does this honorable Sir have? — FLAUBERT, *Letters*

As for disclosing my own personal opinion of the people I put on stage, no, no, a thousand times no! I don't grant myself the right to do so.
— FLAUBERT, *Letters*

And that's the story of Saint Julian the Hospitable, as one can find it — more or less — on a stained-glass window of a church, in my country. (187)

This highly complex signature in effect says in one breath: I am external to my text (an outsider); I am internal to my text (an insider). There is a gap separating me from my tale: the wall of the church window, for which I am not responsible. But on the other hand, it is only "more or less" that my text duplicates the stained-glass window: so I am also, at the same time, responsible for the discrepancy — the gap — that separates the stained-glass window from my tale. Just as the stained-glass window stands between my text and me, (the) "I" in turn stand(s) between the window and my text. Where, then, does the legend come from? With respect to it, I am at once responsible and not responsible, guilt and innocent.

To *Georges Charpentier. Croisset, Sunday (16 February 1879)*. . . . I wanted to put the stained-glass window of the Rouen cathedral after *Saint Julian*. It was a matter of adding colors to the plate that's found in Langlois's book, nothing more. And this illustration pleased me precisely because it was not an illustration, but a historical *document*. In comparing the image to the text, one would have said to oneself "I don't understand any of it. How did he get this out of that?"

All illustrations exasperate me, . . . and while I am alive none will be made. . . . The same is true of my portrait.[19]

Just as Julian's "I" enacts the gap—the *relationless relation* that at the same time separates and links his parents—the signatory's "I" enacts the relationless relation that at the same time separates and links the window and the tale. "And that's the story . . . more or less": the expression of approximation—more or less (*à peu près*)—marks the "I" as the play, precisely, of the undecidability between distance and proximity.

However the very play of undecidability is itself decided and overdetermined: it is a play the "I" does not—cannot—decide.

One morning as he was returning through the colonnade, he saw on the crest of the rampart a large pigeon. . . . Julian stopped to look at it; since there was a breach in the wall at that point, *a splinter of stone met his fingers.* He cocked his arm, and *the stone knocked down the bird,* which fell straight into the ditch. (179)

Just as the stone *meets* Julian's fingers—of its own accord, it seems—the stained glass window—"as one can find it" in the church—*meets* Flaubert's eye. The signatory's "I" itself is therefore nothing other than the acting out of the encounter between necessity and chance: the very writing of the unavoidable necessity of a chance encounter. Flaubert is the *instrument of the window,* just as Julian is the instrument of the stone.

Art has but the form we can give it: we are not free. Each follows his path, despite his own will.[20]

I've always guarded against putting anything of myself into my works, and yet I've put in a great deal.[21]

It is noteworthy that Flaubert, whose writing effort always tended toward the suppression of the "I," the effacement of the author's voice, nonetheless signs one of his last works by referring it back to the realm—discreet as it may be—of the first person, a first person, it is true, whose silent, subtle presence is denied and masked by an indefinite third person:

And that's the story of Saint Julian the Hospitable, as *one* can find it [telle qu'*on* la trouve] . . . in *my* country [dans *mon* pays]. (187)

To understand the implications of this *mon* ("my")—beyond its contradiction, its denial by the *on* ("one")—it is revealing to relate the signatory silence of this first person ("my") to all the other instances of the discourse of an "*I*" in the legend of Saint Julian. When we extract from the legend's narrative, told in the third person, the few fragments of *direct speech*—the several quotations reported in the first person—what we come up with is a stupefying textual precipitate that reads as follows:

CHAPTER 1	I cannot kill them!
(Julian's discourse)	What if I wanted to, though? (181)
CHAPTER 2	It's to obey you! At sunrise I'll be back.
(Julian's discourse)	(183)
(Julian's wife's discourse)	It's my father. (183)
CHAPTER 3	I'm hungry.
(The leper's discourse)	I'm thirsty.
	I'm cold.
	Undress, so I can have the warmth of
	your body.
	I'm going to die. (187)

This then, what the "I" says, what the "I" *can* say, *all* the "I" can say—a quintessence of the discourse of the "I," an abstract of that, precisely, which Flaubert will never say in his own name, in his own right, with his own voice. Literature is, for Flaubert, *about the silence* of this discourse: the art of writing, in Flaubert's conception, is, precisely, the production of such silence.

What Flaubert will never say; what literature is all about:

I cannot kill them. What if I wanted to, though?
It's to obey you . . . I'll be back.
It's my father.
I'm hungry, thirsty, cold.
Undress, so I can have the warmth of your body.
I'm going to die.

This muted discourse of the "I," this summarily exhaustive spectrum of complaint, appeal, anxiety, protest, interrogation, and the demand of the first person, is, however, what the undersigned—the signatory "I" of the legend of Saint Julian—in the very gesture of denying it his own voice, at the very moment of his own lapse into silence, nonetheless refers back to his space—"finds in *his* country."

> "And that's the story of Saint Julian the Hospitable, as one can find it—more or less—on a stained-glass window of a church, in my country."

Flaubert's signature: I, the undersigned, have found in my country that which I can tell, but which I cannot say—that which I deny myself the right to say.

> "I, the undersigned, am going to die."

> I am getting lost in my childhood memories like an old man. I expect of life nothing more than a succession of sheets of paper to stain with black ink. I seem to be traversing a loneliness with no end, to go I don't know where. And I myself am all at once the traveler, the desert and the camel.[22]

> I feel mortally wounded. . . . I'll soon be fifty-four years old. At that age one does not redo one's life, one does not change habits. I'm devoured by the past, and the future has nothing good to offer me. I think of nothing other than of the days past and of the people that cannot come back. Sign of old age and of decadence. As for literature, I no longer believe in myself, and I feel empty. . . . In the meantime, I'm going to begin writing the legend of *Saint Julian the Hospitable,* just to occupy myself with something and *to see whether I am still able to craft a sentence,* which I sincerely doubt.[23]

Flaubert's signature: this is what *I* will not say.

> I'm cold, I'm thirsty.
> I, the undersigned, am going to die.

What Flaubert will never say, he nonetheless—in his own sophisticated, silent way—will *sign:* a crafted sentence. A sheet of paper stained with black ink.

"And that's the story." The legend of Saint Julian. The story of the ink /
blood stain. As one can find it in my country.

Were it necessary to be moved in order to move others, I could
write books that would make hands tremble and hearts pound,
and, since I'm sure I'll never lose this capacity for emotion which
the pen gives me of its own accord without my having anything
to do with it, and which happens to me in spite of myself in a way
that's often disturbing, I don't preoccupy myself with it, and what
I look for, on the contrary, is not *vibration* but *design.*
  Signed: Gustave Flaubert[24]

Hölderlin's Sapphic Mode: Revising the Myth of the Male Pindaric Seer

The following essay treats, via a reading of Hölderlin's poetry, simultaneously two powerful forms of female symbolic authority: the poet Sappho and Plato's Diotima. It is my contention that any attempt to describe the work and lessons of Shoshana Felman cannot be done without considering what female intellectual authority means in the past as well as today. In this sense my essay lays the foundations for a story that belongs for me to the horizon of a portrait of Shoshana Felman. In its description of a traumatic break in Hölderlin's language which is read as abrupt silencings in the sapphic mode, the essay also makes direct use of Shoshana Felman's techniques of reading such "unreadable" phenomena.

Twentieth-century Hölderlin scholarship has revealed with overwhelming success that Pindar was the key ancient model for Hölderlin's so-called "late" poems, i.e. the ones which were written between 1800 and 1805 and are widely considered his most outstanding works of art. Until very recently, however, little comparative attention has been paid to the fact that Pindar's odes were the preeminent authority in the genre of poetry not just from Plato to Quintilian, but likewise from the Renaissance editions of Pindar's works through Ronsard's *Odes Pindariques* (1550),[1] the English "Pindaricks" of the seventeenth century[2] and Opitz's dictum "O meine lust / Pindarisiren [Oh what a joy to Pindarize]"[3] all the way up to Klopstock who was Hölderlin's most direct model for Pindarizing in the German language. Yet at the very moment—in or around 1800—when Hölderlin is about to continue this tradition, a fundamental change occurs, or is felt to have occurred, as a result of which Pindar's work abruptly loses its significance. The constitutive linking of lyrical expression to great deeds and model heroes with mythical genealogies—and to reinforcing social and religious hierarchies—has ceased to be a part of the notion of the "lyrical," which for modern readers is very much a "Romantic" concept. Thus, when Hölderlin devotes a great portion of the years 1801–4 to translating and making "free adaptations" of Pindar, he does so against the prevailing decline of his model, thus accepting and embracing a potentially anachronistic stance.

In the critical discourse on poetry, most notably from Herder through Schlegel to Hegel, Sappho serves as the ancient model for the modern concept of lyric poetry which stresses the expression of subjective "passions." Sappho's dedication to the sufferings and pathographies of erotic obsessions, to experiences of emotional loss as well as of the decline of one's own beauty through aging, appears to be much closer to the modern canon of the lyrical genre than does the Pindaric celebration of heroism, success and victory. The purpose of my essay is to show that Hölderlin's poems also contain a substantial Sapphic legacy and bear many traces of the elaborate discourse on Sappho from Ancient rhetoric to eighteenth-century poetics. The image of the (male-connoted) prophet and poet-seer is thus opened to a counterpoint which relates both the historical Sappho and the symbolic coordinates of the "lyrical" around 1800 to imaginations of "femininity"—not at least of a kind that subverts or transgresses the traditional gender roles. Sappho, it turns out, is of outstanding importance for the definition of what passes as "lyrical" since the end of the 18th century, and Hölderlin has a considerable share in this self-definition of "lyric poetry" through reference to the lesbian poetess. Sappho is also—and the two overlap—*the* historical name for the precarious position of female authority in art and thought, just as Diotima is *the* mythical name for this authority.

My argument will focus almost entirely on a close reading of the famous poem "Hälfte des Lebens" (Half of life). Written between 1800 and 1803, "Hälfte des Lebens" appeared at the end of 1804 in Friedrich Wilman's *Pocket Almanac for the Year 1805*. It is one of a group of nine poems which were the last ones to be sent to the printer by Hölderlin himself. Uncannily, the writing of the poem "Hälfte des Lebens" marks in fact the very half of Hölderlin's life. After its publication, Hölderlin was clinically determined mad and spent another thirty-seven years of his life in what most scholars believe was a state of schizophrenia.

Sappho and Adonis in Hölderlin

THE SAPPHIC ADONEUS AS THE METRICAL SIGNATURE OF THE POEM

The first observation I would like to take as the starting point of my lecture is a metrical one. Whatever the title "Hälfte des Lebens" may mean, its formal properties resonate throughout the entire poem. Roughly equally distributed, rhythmically analogous word groups recur: as verse fragments in the expressions "trúnken von Küssen" (drunk with kisses), "nüchterne Wásser" (sober waters), "Schátten der Érde" (shades of earth); and finally as an integral verse in the closing line "klírren die Fáhnen" (the banners flap). The rhythmic match between title and closing line—"Hälfte des Lébens," "klírren die Fáhnen"—sets the strongest stress. In rhetoric this five-syllable pattern has a suggestive name: *adoneus*. The name is derived from the ritual lament *o ton Adonin* (woe to Adonis),[4] which is found among the fragments of Sappho's odes. In the first book of her *Songs* the close of the Sapphic strophe generally follows the metrical pattern of this lament on the death of beautiful Adonis, which is why ancient grammarians gave the name *adoneus* to this group of syllables.[5] The name is well chosen: Sappho is by far the oldest known source for the Adonis cult, and her extant verses on Adonis suggest that she composed one or more songs for the Lesbic Aphrodite cult,[6] the annually recurring part of which was the lament over Adonis' early death. Making free use of Saussure's term, as further developed by Jean Starobinski, Michael Riffaterre, and Paul de Man, the Adonic verse pattern in Hölderlin's poem could be called a metrical "hypogram" discretely inscribed in the series of words.[7]

The emergence of lyrical language in modern German poetry heavily depended on very elaborate metrical experiments which took the ancient Greek ode meters as their starting point. From the very beginning, these efforts did not aim at returning to an ancient ideal, but at liberating the German verse from the total predominance of the alexandrine verse as shaped after French models. The free adaptation of Greek forms very successfully introduced new flavors and new charms into the German language. Goethe disliked the metrical experiments, but he profited from them to a high degree. It was primarily Klopstock's achievement to open up to the German poetic language an abundance of new metrical and rhythmic possibilities by freely drawing on the ancient ode meters. Hölderlin explicitly used Klopstock's metrical devices of adopting the Greek modes as a key starting point of his own poetical work. In Hölderlin, however, the whole range of Ancient Greek meters as canonized by Horace is largely reduced to the duality of the Asclepiadean and the Alcaic strophe.[8] Sappho's most famous strophic meter reappears just once in Hölderlin's odes, namely in "Unter den Alpen gesungen" (Sung beneath the Alps) (II 44; 1801).[9] Even in Klopstock's extensive output of odes the Sapphic meter appears very rarely. Among his three isolated Sapphic odes, however, there is one that belongs to his outstanding achievements: "Furcht der Geliebten" [*Fear of the Beloved*] (1753).[10] As in "Hälfte des Lebens," this poem uses the adoneus both as clausula ("Weíne nicht, Cídli."), which conforms to Sappho, and as title, which is a feature altogether absent in Melic poetry.

In his only Sapphic ode Hölderlin has — through the mere displacement of two unstressed syllables — modified the Sapphic meter in such a fashion that the Adonic pattern is not only doubled at the end of the strophe, but also opens the very first line. The adoneus becomes a frame, with respect to the clausula, even a double frame of the entire Sapphic meter:

Sappho	Hölderlin
–u–*u*–uu–u–*u*	(**–uu–u**)–u–u–u
–u–*u*–uu–u–*u*	–u–uu–u–u–u
–u–*u*–uu–u–*u*	–u–u–u(**–uu–u**)
(**–uu–u**)	(**–uu–u**)

Metrical analysis thus reveals the Adonic pattern which frames "Hälfte des Lebens" likewise to frame Hölderlin's version of the Sapphic strophe. This coincidence clearly indicates that of all features of the Sapphic strophe the adoneus attracted Hölderlin's most marked attention and therefore also deserves a similar degree of critical attention.

Apart from "Unter den Alpen gesungen" Hölderlin seems to have intended Sappho's integral strophic meter for the poem "Thränen"

(Tears) (II 58). At least he noted the scheme of the strophe on the reverse of the sheet on which he wrote the poem (II 516). In its first two variants this poem bore a title which probably also motivated the metrical sketch: "Sapphos Schwanengesang" (Sappho's swan song) (II 515). In the third variant, however, the Alcaic form definitely prevails, and the new title erases any direct echo of a Sapphic ode. For "Hälfte des Lebens" this poem is all the more suggestive as it not only dates from the same period, but was prepared for the printer and published by Hölderlin together with "Hälfte des Lebens." Both poems take the form of a "swan song" conjuring up a beauty and love which is past; both poems bear traces of a self-effacing preoccupation with the Sapphic form.

This formal feature constitutes a highly distinctive philological datum of some significance. Sapphic odes which reproduce the ancient meter in the German language are extremely rare phenomena; those that erase their Sapphic references as soon as they make them are even rarer.

SAPPHO AND DIOTIMA

Hölderlin's novel *Hyperion* expressly mentions "Sappho" as the poetess about whom Diotima and Hyperion "spoke a lot" (III 168). Herder and Schlegel also have only one answer to the question of who is *the* lyrical poetess: "Sappho."[11] She figures in the poetry of the period around 1800 — as she did in ancient rhetoric — as the epitome of the great poetess. Sappho is, as Rilke was later to say, "the small figure reaching out to the infinite that everyone [. . .] had in mind when speaking of *the* poetess [*die kleine, ins Unendliche hinaus gespannte Gestalt, die alle* [. . .] *meinten, wenn sie sagten: die Dichterin*]."[12] Schlegel extolled Sappho both as a model of the independent, "free" woman and as the historical model of Plato's mythical Diotima.[13] According to Aelianus, no less an authority than Plato called the poetess from Lesbos "the Wise Woman"[14] — another bridge between Sappho and the Platonic Diotima. For Schlegel, Diotima was as "necessary an idea for Socratic philosophy as the Madonna is to the Catholic religion."[15] Something analogous goes for Hölderlin's poetry. Diotima-Sappho is the Laura, the standard female reference in his poetry. While the typical muses make the male poets speak, yet themselves remain silent — at least not a single saying of a muse is on record — Diotima and Sappho not just make listen and speak, but have left behind a powerful legacy of thought, speech, and poetry. They were genuine teachers as well as admired models of authoritative language, while topical muses were only the mute imaginary sources of male poiesis. Sappho, said Hölderlin in confirmation of the ancient tradition, was the "tenth Muse" (IV 196)—and hence a muse in excess of the nine proper muses, an excessive muse—and Diotima "the silent union of our thought and poetry" (III 221). While Freud and Lacan see the position of authority as a male gender role or, more precisely, as male power over the symbolic; while Kristeva's introduction of a female (counter)authority is entirely confined to the pre- or transsymbolic "corps maternel,"[16] Schlegel's and Hölderlin's quest related to the names of "Sappho" and "Diotima," is aimed at the—apparently impossible—position of a female authority in the symbolic sphere. Although it is only Diotima that Hölderlin evokes in his poems by name, Sappho's presence in them is not confined to the Sapphic strophe or the Sapphic adoneus. The "Hymne an die Menschheit" (Hymn to humanity) and the "Hymne an den Genius der Jugend" (Hymn to the genius of youth) refer to the concept of "Lesbic *Gebilde*" (Lesbic works of art)" (I 147) or "Lesbic Gestalt" (I 147) and link it to poetic "enthusiasm" and "der Schönheit Allgewalt" (the supreme power of beauty). Since the days of Horace if not earlier, the poetic modes of Sappho and Alcaeus are described as "Lesbic" or "eolic modes." Sappho's songs are indeed devoted to "der Schönheit weitem Lustgefilde" [the realm of pleasures derived from beauty] (I 147): to the creative arts, beautiful customs, scented ointments, ornamental objects, beautiful movements and—not least—the beautiful bodies of young women (and occasionally of young men as well). The desire for this beauty is nearly always colored by melancholy, even despair. Either the beautiful object of desire has eluded the "I" whose ardor it has aroused, or it resists attempts to woo it, or again it is presented as one who is just about to abandon Sappho; or it is imagined by the poetess, as a woman in her mid-thirties, as something basically over and done with, consigned only to memory. Thus the ritual lament for Adonis, which provides the model for the clausula of the Sapphic strophe, is in fact a key figure of Sapphic poetry altogether.

FROM ADONEUS TO ADONIS: "HÄLFTE DES LEBENS" AS A REWRITING OF THE ANCIENT MYTH OF BEAUTY

The two polar strophes of "Hälfte des Lebens" correspond exactly to the polarity in Adonis' life as reported by Panyassis (a Greek poet of the fifth century B.C.). After his birth, Aphrodite had taken Adonis under her protection because of his beauty. But immediately afterwards she entrusted his upbringing to Persephone. The latter, however, was reluctant to surrender Adonis when he had grown up to become a beautiful youth. Finally Zeus had to resolve the dispute: for a part of the year he awarded Adonis to Persephone, and hence to the underworld, and for the rest of the year to Aphrodite.[17] The feast of Adonis in the Aphrodite cult marks the annually recurring end of the Aphroditian' half of his life; it also laments the bitter necessity of another "half of life." Seen in this light, Adonis is a figure who arrives at the "half of life" not just once, but periodically. In Latin antiquity, the two polar regions and seasons of Adonis were explicitly identified with summer and winter.[18] The feast of Adonis, like Hölderlin's poem, commemorates, indeed performs the switch from one to the other: at the height of summer, the flora of the Adonis gardens and the images of the beautiful youth are borne down to the water. *Ausführen.* The act of throwing them into the water is a symbolic funeral that announces, with the loss of Adonis' beauty, the imminent onset of winter. Cries of woe accompany this symbolic change, in which the surface of the water marks the boundary between the upper and the underworld. The ritual Adonis lament and Hölderlin's poem also concur in making the absence of flowers symbolize the loss of both Adonis and the beauty of late summer.

The rhythmic pattern thus overlaps in several respects with its mythical horizon: in the medium of the adoneus the myth of Adonis, of the shining presence and the melancholy absence of beauty, is "recounted" anew. To this extent the metrical hypogram can be read not only as the inscription of *an* adoneus, but more precisely of *the* eponymous Adoneus—namely Sappho's verse *ō ton Adōnin* ("wéhe Adónis").[19] Apart from the metrical allusion to Aphrodite's mourning of Adonis, Hölderlin has referred several times explicitly to this myth. There is, in fact, from Schlegel and Creuzer through Shelley and Keats, a plethora of rewritings of the Adonis myth in Hölderlin's times. Particularly in the German context, the romantic "Adonis" and the romantic "Sappho" are correlated in multiple ways. In fact, their presence or absence—be it separately or in an associated fashion—amounts to a topical indicator of the distance between Schlegel's and Hölderlin's take on the Greeks on the one hand, and Winckelmann, Goethe, and

Schiller on the other hand who do not grant any significance to Adonis or Sappho, in fact barely even mention them.

Beyond the metrical and thematic patterns, the references to both Sappho and Adonis share a marked emphasis on female license in terms of sexual and gender roles. With regard to Sappho, this requires no further elaboration, as she notoriously represents the classic case of a female teacher having highly sexualized relations with her much younger disciples. Something similar holds, and less ambiguously so, for the female rites of Adonis: they were perhaps the most conspicuous acts of female dissatisfaction and resistance to Athenian gender rules. These rules implied that women had no say at all in public matters and had to accept the fact that their husbands routinely directed their sexual and also emotional attention both to the vast number of available prostitutes of various kinds and to young men. In the context of the Adonic rites, the widely neglected and even routinely mistreated Athenian spouses publicly expressed their desire for a beautiful and tender young lover. No wonder, therefore, that these rites were not part of the official Athenian calendar, but only barely and unofficially tolerated. The references to these rites in Aristophanes[20] and Plato[21] make it crystal clear that men perceived them as an outrageous attack on male authority, something amounting to a serious threat not only to the gender order, but literally to the security of the state. For these reasons, the Adonic rite has—over the past two decades—attracted substantial attention from scholars of Greek antiquity interested in gender issues.[22] The discourse on Sappho and Adonis around 1800 very much prefigures this recent scholarly interest by essentially stressing the same agenda of gender conflict, female sexual license, and—last, but not least—female symbolic authority.

ADONIS UND NARCISSUS

Although no beautiful youth appears on the scene of "Hälfte des Lebens," the specific features of the lament for Adonis also conjure up another key figure among mythological narratives of beauty, one that was already associated with Adonis in ancient times and even more so in Shakespeare's verse epic *Venus and Adonis*: Narcissus. Narcissus' bending down to the water—beauty which inclines toward the surface of water—is the key image in Ovid's famous narrative. Narcissus is not standing at the immaculate well, he is bending down to it. In Hölderlin a similar downward movement determines a whole series of phenomena: yellow pears, wild roses, indeed the "land" itself and the "holden Schwäne" (graceful swans). To the extent that all "objects" in the first strophe show an inclination toward the surface of the lake, the swans dipping (*tunken*) their heads in the water—their touching and crossing of the boundary between the surface and the underworld with their heads (*Haupt*)—is the *telos* and outstanding event of the first half of the poem. Rhythmically, there is likewise a special stress on *tunkt* (dips): It opens the first and only line in the whole strophe not to begin with an anacrusis.

Compared to Ovid, Hölderlin reinforces the gesture of inclining downward to the lake by extending it to a multitude of natural phenomena. This creates awareness of an undertow, a force of attraction emanating from beneath the surface of the lake, an assumed force which ever since Frazer's *Golden Bough* has been associated with the fear—well documented by ethnologists—of seeing one's own reflection in water.[23] It is a fear based on the assumption that reflections, like shadows, are not just metaphorical simulacra, but real and vulnerable metonymic parts of the person reflected. More than that, they were considered to be the person's soul, which was in danger of being pulled below the surface of the water by evil spirits, causing the death of the reflected person. The presence of such a potentially dangerous undertow down toward the reflecting surface of the lake permeates the radiance of the golden late summer or early autumn day in Hölderlin's poem. The gesture of 'hanging down' into the water thus endows the image of perfect beauty with a tendency toward a fatal outcome. Here again, as with Adonis and Narcissus, a short life and imminent death are an inherent feature in the depiction of supreme beauty.

As the (imagined) *telos* that governs the direction of all stooping and dipping, the "water" literally receives the last word in the first strophe. It conforms to the allusions to Narcissus' stooping over the spring that the impact on the water destroys the beautiful and desired image and hence is directly followed by a mournful "Weh" (woe). When Narcissus touched the water with his arms, all the beauty of the reflective image imploded and dissipated. Narcissus responded to this with gestures of mourning a deceased person and accompanied them with a sorrowful "eheu" (alas) that the nymph Echo instantly reinforced with another "eheu."[24] *"Hälfte des Lebens"* translates this lament into German: "Eheu" becomes "Weh." The disintegration of the total image and of the desire that is directed at it is further reflected in the staccato-like interruptions which shape the flow of the sentence in the first line of the second strophe: "Weh mir, wo nehm ich, wenn."

The catastrophic change thus takes place in the vacant line between the words "Wasser" [water] and "weh"—and hence literally in the empty "half" of the poem. Much as Walter Benjamin has suggested, the caesura—whose significance lies in marking the absence of a positive signifier in the sequence of signs—becomes the critical moment where an expressionless "truth" intervenes.[25] Only out of this moment of crisis, of a potentially traumatic turnaround does the very position of the speaking "I" emerge. It first appears both grammatically and as the subject of speech when the caesura is explicitly lamented. Echoed in a sequence of further *w* assonances, the caesura occurring between "Wasser" and "weh" switches the focus of the poem from overripe summer to piercing cold winter. The purely negative characterization with which the second strophe operates initially, resembles the famous *ekphrasis* that Ovid gives of the spring in which the fatal reflection of Narcissus occurs. This spring is surrounded by so thick a wood that no sunbeam can penetrate it. The Latin *nullo sole* directly prefigures the situation of the unavailability of sun to which Hölderlin's "I" sees himself exposed. I am confining myself here to these very brief remarks on the Narcissus analogy in the imagery of the poem. A further elaboration of this topic could show that around 1800 the myth of Narcissus was central to reflecting the predicament of the poet and that Hölderlin's evocation of Narcissus has in fact some bearing on this topos of poetic self-reflection. The swan perfectly blends with this line of reading Hölderlin's poem, as the swan has a rich tradition both as the poet's image of himself and as an emblem of narcissistic self-centeredness.

The "Melting Pot" of Hölderlin's Poetical Language: The Interplay of Sapphic, Alcaic, and Pindaric Features

In Hölderlin studies the first and to date only metrical interpretation of "Hälfte des Lebens" is now tactfully referred to as a curiosity. In an anthology of German poetry entitled *Ewiger Vorrat deutscher Poesie* (Eternal stock of German poetry) (1926) Rudolf Borchardt rendered "Hälfte des Lebens," in a remarkable distortion of its graphic representation, as a fragment of a failed attempt at an Alcaic ode.[26] According to Borchardt, only madness prevented Hölderlin from writing the whole poem in the manner of the Alcaic ode.[27] Borchardt's explanation is all the less convincing as Hölderlin when working on "Hälfte des Lebens" simultaneously edited and sent to the printers five complete Alcaic odes, some of them newly written. Nevertheless, Borchardt's bizarre commentary contains an important insight into Hölderlin's poem.[28] As meanwhile has been shown for many of Klopstock's and Hölderlin's other "free" verse poems, "Hälfte des Lebens" can indeed at least partly be read as a recombination of fragments taken from the Alcaic ode.[29] Seen in this light, "Hälfte des Lebens" represents a mixture—or in Hölderlin's words: an "interchange" of "tones" (III 148, VI 339)—which metrically refer both to the Adonic clausula of the Sapphic strophe and to fragments taken from the Alcaic strophe. In this highly specific blend of metrical features "Hälfte des Lebens" resembles no other poem so much as "Hyperions Schicksalslied" (The song of Hyperion's fate), the second outstanding short poem by Hölderlin.[30]

Nevertheless both poems are in free rhythms in the full sense of the word, and "Hälfte des Lebens" also shares important rhythmic features of the great Pindaric *Gesänge*: above all the tendency to accumulate strong word stresses using techniques of isolating the words against the flow of the sentence, especially by inserting multiple breaks between sentence, rhythm and line caesuras.[31] As these features of Hölderlin's language have been elaborately discussed elsewhere—though not specifically with regard to "Hälfte des Lebens"—I need not go into any detail here and return right again to the metrical quotations that Hölderlin blends into his free rhythms. The combination of fragmented Sapphic and Alcaic patterns in his two outstanding short poems has a striking theoretical resonance in that contemporary poetics defines the strophic ode, indeed the lyrical muse itself, precisely in terms of the polarity of Sappho and Alcaeus. In his pivotal essay on the two authors from Lesbos, Herder wrote: "Alcaeus and Sappho, the man and woman from Lesbos, can be valued as the original models of the ode in its two main variants, the bold and the tender."[32] The Sapphic and Alcaic odes differ from the strophic meters "invented" by Pindar a good hundred years later not only in their lesser extent and lower degree of metrical complexity, but also in giving another role to the (imaginary) voice. Pindar's songs, as Friedrich Schlegel pointed out, always give voice to a "public feeling," a collective content. They are lyrics for a choir, even "if they have never been sung by a choir."[33] Sappho's and Alcaeus' imaginary voices, on the other hand, represent strictly themselves: they make it "a principle" to stress the "singularity" (*Einzelheit*) they are voicing and "usually seek only to give the strongest and clearest expression to individual feelings."[34] This distinction formulates in the language of a contemporary known to Hölderlin the eccentric position that Pindar's poetry occupies in relation to the (modern) concept of the Lyrical. Hegel too identified—with all due respect for Hölderlin's revered authors Pindar, Klopstock and Schiller—the melic lyric (Sappho and Alcaeus) as the model of the lyrical mode as such: "Genuine lyrical reflection and passion develop in the so-called melic lyric."[35] In view of all this, the discovery of Sapphic and Alcaic verses and verse fragments in Hölderlin's "Hälfte des Lebens" has rich implications. It relates the poem, by virtue of its formal properties, to a contemporary poetics which identifies Sappho and Alcaeus as the "original models" of lyrical "beauty" altogether. Hölderlin's subtle configuration of fragments taken from the meters of these model authors introduces new modes of meaning into the play of meter and rhythm that cannot sufficiently be grasped using the influential poetics of his predecessor Klopstock. Klopstock remained true to the ancient theory of rhythm in that he saw in the temporal and stress patterns of syllable groups—i.e. in their purely material properties—an immediate expression of "passions."[36] The content of a poem may force us to make hermeneutical efforts at comprehension and for this reason take longer to reach us than the declamation itself. The rhythmic form, on the other hand—its time, stress and caesura patterns—always affects our emotions instantaneously, "schnell,"[37] as Klopstock says, and can also impart a great deal that is not contained in the words and is thus "unsaid." The clear semiotic distinction between these modes of meaning inspired Klopstock to come up with a wonderful formulation: "In einem guten Gedicht geht das Ungesagte umher wie in Homers Schlachten die nur von wenigen gesehenen Götter [In a good poem the Unsaid wanders about like in Homer's battles the gods who are seen by but a few]."[38] This finding applies as much to Hölderlin's poems as to Klopstock's, yet the way the unsaid is generated is fundamentally different. Although Klopstock's poems— beginning with the unique practice of schematically exhibiting their metrical pattern between the title and the first line—often create an impression of purely intellectual experimentation and excessively contrived rhythms, his theory is still aimed at the immediate "expression" of something that is not described and is not fully sayable either and hence—as Goethe famously put it—at "symbolic" correspondences of material linguistic patterns and emotions. By contrast, Hölderlin's late manner of using metrical allusions also has some markedly "allegorical" features. For the fragmented metrical quotations are not just juxtaposed and contrasted for the sake of their material properties and their immediate expressive values, they are also designed to evoke fragments of historical knowledge from a period extending from the remote context of their first use to the contemporary debate on Sappho's and Alcaeus' odes as the basic models of the Lyrical. The metaphorical correspondences between rhythmic structures and emotion are thus superimposed by metonymic contiguity associations which charge the rhythm with semantic resonances of mythical, historical, and theoretical significance. Making a free use of Klopstock's beautiful sentence about the unsaid, one might say that these metrical allegories have something ghostly about them, all the more so from a historical distance; for they discreetly wander through the poems, almost incognito and invisible "like in Homer's battles the gods who are seen by but a few."

The poems written after 1805, indeed Hölderlin's entire work after the last publication taken care of by himself, mark a radical break with these metrically supported appearances of canonical Greek forms which were simultaneously adopted as models for the Romantic lyric. Against the background of this late *tabula rasa*, the pain of parting expressed in "Hälfte des Lebens" entails an autoreflective dimension in that the idealized patterns of the lyrical, before altogether disappearing from Hölderlin's work, are granted a final appearance as barely discernible metrical ghosts—just as the pluralized swans are hardly recognizable anymore as icons of the self-confident poet.[39] This notion of a final appearance on a stage about to be abandoned blends perfectly with the fact that the adoneus owes its name to a rite which mourns and laments a terrible loss. By paradoxically using the feature of the Adoneic clausula already for the title, Hölderlin immerges the entire scene from the very beginning in the prevailing sentiment of a mournful farewell. Henceforth, right after this final staging in "Hälfte des Lebens," the grand lyrical modes of Greek antiquity fall silent.

The traumatic catastrophe that permeates the often praiseful and wholly affirmative iambic-trochaic lines Hölderlin kept writing for much of the remaining "half of (his) life" (until his death in 1843), gains its full poetic momentum only if one senses the shadows these often forcedly banal rhymes conceal: their eradicating, denying, and silencing of the revered lyrical modes Hölderlin had consistently drawn and elaborated on. "Hälfte des Lebens" engages in a complex final interplay what afterward is only negatively audible through its absence and hence "expressionless" in Benjamin's sense: the icons (swan), historical model-heroes, and formal modes of what was called "lyrical," especially in Germany circa 1800. Reading "Hälfte des Lebens" in this light, exposes the reader to a catastrophic breach in the very system of the language of poetry.

If the Adonic rites perform a mournful burial of the object of desire, the Sapphic-Adonic verse in Hölderlin's "Hälfte des Lebens" anticipates, and in fact seals, the future absence of what in the preceding years used to be the position of love, female symbolic authority, and the mode of the "Romantic" lyrical. Indeed, if there is a genuine poetical measurement of Hölderlin's much discussed "madness" throughout the second half of his life, it is the absence of the Sapphic mode right after the publication of the poem "Hälfte des Lebens" — a publication which literally coincides with the end of the first half of Hölderlin's life. While both the Alcaic and the Pindaric mode occasionally reappear in Hölderlin's writing before he finally settles for rhymes and iambo-trochaic verses only, the Sapphic mode remains silenced once and forever, with no transition period and no exception. The disappearance of Sappho from Hölderlin's writing is concomitant with clinical madness becoming permanent.

It appears to be a worthy desideratum to think of a new sub-discipline of rhetoric — one I am tempted to call "allegorical metrics" — that might account for phenomena like the ones I am addressing here. Like Benjamin's readings of other allegorical structures, such allegorical metrics depend on extensive studies in historical semantics. In the case I am considering here, for instance, there is no direct way at all between identifying the pattern of an adoneus and determining its allegorical significance. Rather, my interpretation rests on an extensive study of Sappho's role in late-eighteenth-century poetics and hence of the issues involved when referring to her poetry in a specific moment of literary history. What I present here, is just a small amount of these historical references which bring together questions of meter, rhythm, style, a strong interest in questions of gender and gender-crossing (the sublime poetess), and a highly specific notion of the "lyrical."

The Antagonism Within the Poem Itself – A Sapphic Element in Hölderlin's Pindaric Hymns?

Hölderlin's explicit poetics from the period of the poems discussed here entails a radical break with any correspondence of form and content, any rhetorical *aptum* and any classical-aesthetic notion of the harmony of structure of a work of art. According to Hölderlin, the achievement of artistic form does not consist in the brilliant presentation of its content, but in the compensatory overcoming of what it lacks most. While the preeminent experience of the Greeks — their "natural" and "inborn" inclination, according to Hölderlin — was "the fire from heaven," the "sacred *pathos*," their artistic aspiration went in the opposite direction of a striving to achieve the very qualities that were "alien" to them: namely, "precision," "clarity of presentation," and "sobriety" (VI 425–26). For the moderns Hölderlin diagnosed the opposite predicament, namely the striving for pathos against a given background of a sobriety of thought. In both cases, art achieves its mastery only against a force operating in the opposite direction, by constituting what Hölderlin called an "Umkehr,"[40] an inversion of its own basis.[41] The negative reflection, the sudden change from beauty and abundance to barrenness and want, that takes place in the myths of Adonis and Narcissus as it does in Hölderlin's poem, is at the same time a basic figure of Hölderlin's poetics.

This figure very much anticipates Nietzsche's interpretation of the Apollonian beauty of the work of art — as a dream-like figure designed to subdue and even consign to oblivion an underlying Dionysian experience with the very opposite features.[42] In fact, Hölderlin has even used the strong concept of denial (*Verleugnung*) in order to emphasize the negativity at work in the apparent form of an artwork. He succinctly stipulated that the "ground" or experiential fundament of a poem be "denied" by its "artistic character (*Kunstkarakter*)" (IV 150). As a result, the "ground" of any given poem must be sought in something that is almost made to disappear. The almost unreadable quality of the Adoneus-Adonis in "Hälfte des Lebens" and of the Sapphic dimension of Hölderlin's poetry in general may well be part of this necessary trajectory of "inversion" in which Hölderlin ultimately saw the decisive achievement of artistic form. The almost complete "denial" of the Sapphic meter and of all direct references to Sappho in the final version of the ode "Thränen" which was first entitled "Sapphos Schwanengesang" might serve as an example directly highlighting a logic of this kind. Following this line of thought, the suspicion arises that likewise in Hölderlin's great Pindaric cantos the effort of poetic negativity is aimed at working its way through opposite and almost "denied" features as well. Since any "denial" retains traces of what is denied, Hölderlin's texts, by virtue of the theory they are based on, require us to be on the alert for effects based on tipping over into something else, for discreet breaches of their own tone. And indeed: many of the Pindaric hymns — nearly all of them, in fact — are pervaded by an obstinate recurrence of the (Sapphic) adoneus. The first five strophes of the "Pindaric" hymn "Der Einzige" (The only one) all end in an adoneus: "únter den Ménschen" (among men), "bín ich gegángen" (I went), "Gáste verbérget" (harbor ye guests), "ándere féhlet," "zähmte der Völker" (tamed the nations). At the end of the fourth strophe of "Patmos" the adoneus occurs in a similarly massive accumulation: "Großen das Große" [to the great what is great], "Níe eine Waíde," "Bleíbet im Ánfang," "Géht dieses wíeder." In his famous poem "Andenken" (Remembrance) Hölderlin used several discreetly inserted adonei to pave the way to what is perhaps his best known adoneus of all, one which closes not only the strophe but also the poem and is moreover the gnomic node of the composition: "Was bleibet aber, *stíften die Díchter* [But what persists is founded by the poets]" (II 189). It testifies to Hölderlin's mastery of the self-denying form, that the free verse "Was bleibet aber, stiften die Dichter" could become a veritable commonplace without anyone noticing that the second half of the line is a perfect German adoneus.[43] The metrical hypogram quite literally gives the great Pindaric forms a Sapphic-Adoneic signature.

Pindar's own poems, by changing one or two verse positions, often modulate eolic into dactylic or iambic-trochaic meters, and vice versa. The use of eolic meters with subsequent "modulation out of them" is more "common" than the modulation of other metres into the eolic ones.[44] While employing analogous devices, Hölderlin's Adoneic strophe endings reverse the direction predominant in Pindar's modulation: they modulate *into* the eolic meter. It was Sappho and Alcaeus, who paved the way for Pindar's technique of varying and mixing traditional meters.[45] They did so by adding the older iambic and dactylic meters to the stock of eolic forms and applying methods of mutual reworking: Sapphos used elements of the alcaic meter, and Alcaeus borrowed from the Sapphic meter.[46,47] Polymetry is the very essence of

Greek melopoeia from Sappho to Pindar: meters are introduced, varied, mixed with counter tones, allowed to flow into one another—this is the rhythmical basis of the lyrical *mousiké*. Thus the discovery of a mixture of Sapphic, Alcaic and Pindaric patterns in *Hälfte des Lebens* can no longer be seen as a pathological indication of progressive disintegration, as Rudolf Borchardt would have us believe. Rather, Hölderlin appears to have understood perfectly well that the lyrical languages of his Greek models were already themselves polymetrical cantos (*Gesänge*), full of "switching tones" and of employing metrical cross-references rich in associations.

The male Hölderlin as a Pindaric poet-seer is a product of 20th century reception which began with Hellingrath and was based on the concepts of "austere harmony" and "vaterländische Gesänge" (which may be approximately translated as "fatherlandish cantos," but not as "patriotic songs"). Throughout the nineteenth century, the prevailing image of the poet was that of an all too sensitive, all too "soft" and moreover ethereally beautiful youth.[48] By declaring the great hymns in the Pindaric style to be Hölderlin's "genuin legacy" and seeing them as the "Word of God"[49] spoken in "austere harmony," Hellingrath opened the way to a comprehensive recoding of Hölderlin which resulted in the Sapphic element being lost to view behind the overambitious male prophet-seer. In the previously prevailing "soft" and in fact explicitly 'female' image of Hölderlin the masculinity cult of the George circle has left very strong and lasting traces. Without this gender reversal, Hölderlin would barely have ended up becoming a pocketbook companion of German soldiers.

Even the triumphal career of the concepts of "austere harmony" and "parataxis" (as one out of several syntactic devices for austere harmony) may be largely due to Hölderlin's symbolic gender change. Heidegger, Adorno, and most "deconstructive" readings of Hölderlin have in a variety of ways reinforced this trend inaugurated by Hellingrath. The result has been a tendency in the last hundred years to forget what for Hölderlin's Romantic contemporaries was self-evident: namely that Hölderlin was also, if not primarily, an unsurpassed master of the smooth harmony (*harmonía glaphyrá*). What is so unmistakable and irresistible in poems like *Heidelberg* or *Andenken*, remains to various degrees and in various combinations an integral part of the other late poems as well. Sappho herself was considered by the most outstanding literary critics of Latin antiquity—Dionysius, Demetrius, and Pseudo-Longinus—as much a mistress of smooth harmony[50] as she was praised as a sublime poetess who forced together opposing elements within the narrow confines of a verse.[51] An eye for the balance between the "austere" and "smooth" factors in Hölderlin's work can only be (re)-gained, if the extremely successful demonstration of Hölderlin's succession to Pindar is restored to its proper proportion. The presence of the Sapphic adoneus in the middle of the "austere" hymns is but one of many elements pointing in this direction.

—Translated from the German by Ian W. Taylor

PART 5 | Trauma and Testimony

SHOSHANA FELMAN

10 | From "The Return of the Voice: Claude Lanzmann's *Shoah*"

I

HISTORY AND WITNESS, OR THE STORY OF AN OATH

"If someone else could have written my stories," writes Elie Wiesel, "I would not have written them. I have written them in order to testify. My role is the role of the witness. . . . Not to tell, or to tell another story, is . . . to commit perjury."[1]

To bear witness is to take responsibility for the truth: to speak, implicitly, from within the legal pledge and the juridical imperative of the witness's oath.[2] To testify—before a court of law or before the court of history and of the future; to testify, likewise, before an audience of readers or spectators—is more than simply to report a fact or an event or to relate what has been lived, recorded, and remembered. Memory is conjured up essentially in order to *address* another, to impress upon a listener, to *appeal* to a community. To testify is always, metaphorically, to take the witness stand, or to take the position of the witness insofar as the narrative account of the witness is at once engaged in an appeal and bound by an oath. To testify is thus not merely to narrate but to commit oneself, and to commit the narrative, to others: to *take responsibility*—in speech—for history or for the truth of an occurrence, for something that, by definition, goes beyond the personal, in having general (nonpersonal) validity and consequences.

But if the essence of the testimony is impersonal (to enable a decision by a judge or jury—metaphorical or literal—about the true nature of the facts of an occurrence; to enable an objective reconstruction of what history was like, irrespective of the witness), why is it that the witness's speech is so uniquely, literally irreplaceable? "If someone else could have written my stories, I would not have written them." What does it mean that the testimony cannot be simply reported, or narrated by another in its role as testimony? What does it mean that a story—or a history—cannot be told by someone else?

It is this question, I would suggest, that guides the groundbreaking work of Claude Lanzmann in his film *Shoah* (1985), and constitutes at once the profound subject and the shocking power of originality of the film.

A VISION OF REALITY

Shoah is a film made exclusively of testimonies: first-hand testimonies of participants in the historical experience of the Holocaust, interviewed and filmed by Lanzmann during the eleven years which preceded the production of the film (1977–1985). In effect, *Shoah* revives the Holocaust with such a power (a power that no previous film on the subject could attain) that it radically displaces and shakes up not only any common notion we might have entertained about it, but our very vision of reality as such, our very sense of what the world, culture, history, and our life within it are all about.

But the film is not simply, nor is it primarily, a historical document on the Holocaust. That is why, in contrast to its cinematic predecessors on the subject, it refuses systematically to use any historical, archival footage. It conducts its interviews, and takes its pictures, in the present. Rather than a simple view of the present, the film offers a disorienting vision of the present, a compellingly profound and surprising insight into the complexity of the *relation between history and witnessing*.

It is a film about witnessing: about the witnessing of a catastrophe. What is testified to is limit-experiences whose overwhelming impact constantly puts to the test the limits of the witness and of witnessing, at the same time that it constantly unsettles and puts into question the very limits of reality.

ART AS WITNESS

Second, *Shoah* is a film about the *relation between art and witnessing*, about film as a medium that *expands* the capacity for witnessing. To understand *Shoah*, we must explore the question: what are *we* as spectators made to witness? This expansion of what we in turn can witness is, however, due not simply to the reproduction of events, but to the power of the film as a work of art, to the subtlety of its philosophical and artistic structure and to the complexity of the creative process it engages. "The truth kills the possibility of fiction," said Lanzmann in a journalistic interview.[3] But the truth does not kill the possibility of art—on the contrary, it requires it for its transmission, for its realization in our consciousness as witnesses.

Finally, *Shoah* embodies the capacity of art not simply to witness, but to *take the witness stand:* the film takes responsibility for its times by enacting the significance of our era as an *age of testimony,* an age in which witnessing itself has undergone a major trauma. *Shoah* gives us to witness a *historical crisis of witnessing,* and shows us how, out of this crisis, witnessing becomes, in all the senses of the word, a *critical* activity.

On all these different levels, Claude Lanzmann persistently asks the same relentless question: what does it mean to be a witness? What does it mean to be a witness of the Holocaust? What does it mean to be a witness to the process of the film? What does testimony mean, if it is not simply (as we commonly perceive it) the observing, the recording, the remembering of an event, but an utterly unique and irreplaceable topographical *position* with respect to an occurrence? What does testimony mean, if it is the uniqueness of the *performance of a story* that is constituted by the fact that, like the oath, it cannot be carried out by anybody else?

THE WESTERN LAW OF EVIDENCE

The uniqueness of the narrative performance of the testimony in effect proceeds from the witness's irreplaceable performance of the act of seeing—from the uniqueness of the witness's "seeing with his/her own eyes." "Mr. Vitold," says the Jewish Bund leader to the Polish courier Jan Karski, who reports in his cinematic testimony thirty-five years later, in narrating how the Jewish leader urged him—and persuaded him—to become a crucial witness: "I know the Western world. You will be speaking to the English. . . . It will strengthen your report if you will be able to say: '*I saw it myself*'"(171).[4]

In the legal, philosophical, and epistemological tradition of the Western world, witnessing is based on, and is formally defined by, first-hand seeing. "Eyewitness testimony" is what constitutes the most decisive law of evidence in courtrooms. "Lawyers have innumerable rules involving hearsay, the character of the defendant or of the witness, opinions given by the witness, and the like, which are in one way or another meant to improve the fact-finding process. But more crucial than any one of these—and possibly more crucial than all put together—is the evidence of eyewitness testimony."[5]

Film, on the other hand, is the art par excellence that, like the courtroom (although for different purposes), calls upon a *witnessing* by *seeing*. How does the film use its visual medium to reflect upon eyewitness testimony both as the law of evidence of its own art and as the law of evidence of history?

VICTIMS, PERPETRATORS, BYSTANDERS: ABOUT SEEING

Because the testimony is unique and irreplaceable, the film is an exploration of the *differences* between heterogeneous points of view, between testimonial stances that can neither be assimilated into, nor subsumed by, one another. There is, first of all, the difference of perspective between three groups of witnesses, or three series of interviewees: the real characters of history who, in response to Lanzmann's inquiry, play their own role as the singularly real actors of the movie, fall into three basic categories:[6] those who witnessed the disaster as its *victims* (the surviving Jews), those who witnessed the disaster as its *perpetrators* (the ex-Nazis), those who witnessed the disaster as *bystanders* (the Poles). What is at stake in this division is not simply a diversity of points of view or of degrees of implication and emotional involvement, but the *incommensurability* of different topographical and cognitive positions, between which the discrepancy cannot be breached. More concretely, what the categories in the film give to see is *three different performances of the act of seeing*.

In effect, the victims, the bystanders, and the perpetrators are here differentiated not so much by what they actually see (what they all see, although discontinuous, does in fact follow a logic of corroboration), as by what and how they *do not see*, by what and how they *fail to witness*. The Jews see, but they do not understand the purpose and the destination of what they see: overwhelmed by loss and by deception, they are blind to the significance of what they witness. Richard Glazar strikingly narrates a moment of perception coupled with incomprehension, an exemplary moment in which the Jews fail to read, or to decipher, the visual signs and the visible significance they nonetheless see with their own eyes:

Then very slowly, the train turned off the main track and rolled
... through a wood. While he looked out — we'd been able to open
a window — the old man in our compartment saw a boy . . . and he
asked the boy in signs, "Where are we?" And the kid made a funny
gesture. This: (draws a finger across his throat) . . .

And one of you questioned him?

Not in words, but in signs, we asked: "what's going on here?"
And he made that gesture. Like this. We didn't really pay much
attention to him. We couldn't figure out what he meant. (34)

The Poles, unlike the Jews, *do* see, but, as bystanders, they do not
quite *look,* they avoid looking directly, and thus they *overlook* at once
their responsibility and their complicity as witnesses:

You couldn't look there. You couldn't talk to a Jew. Even going
by on the road, you couldn't look there.

Did they look away?

Yes, vans came and the Jews were moved farther off. You could
see them, but on the sly. In sidelong glances. (97–98)

The Nazis, on the other hand, see to it that both the Jews and the
extermination will remain unseen, invisible: the death camps are surrounded, for that purpose, with a screen of trees. Franz Suchomel, an
ex-guard of Treblinka, testifies:

Woven into the barbed wire were branches of pine trees. . . . It was
known as "camouflage." . . . So everything was screened. People
couldn't see anything to the left or right. Nothing. You couldn't
see through it. Impossible. (110)

It is not a coincidence that as this testimony is unfolding, it is hard
for us as viewers to see the witness, who is filmed secretly.

As is the case for most of the ex-Nazis, Franz Suchomel agreed to
answer Lanzmann's questions, but not to be filmed; he agreed, in other
words, to give a testimony, but on the condition that, as a witness *he*
should not be seen:

*Mr. Suchomel, we're not discussing you, only Treblinka. You are a very
important eyewitness, and you can explain what Treblinka was.*

But don't use my name.
No, I promised . . . (54)

In the blurry images of faces taken by a secret camera that has to shoot through a variety of walls and screens, the film makes us see concretely, by the compromise it unavoidably inflicts upon our act of seeing (which, of necessity, becomes materially an act of *seeing through*), how the Holocaust was a historical assault on seeing and how, even today, the perpetrators are still by and large invisible: "Everything was screened. You couldn't see anything to the left or right. You couldn't see through it."

FIGUREN

The essence of the Nazi scheme is to make itself—and to make the Jews—essentially invisible. To make the Jews invisible not merely by killing them, not merely by confining them to "camouflaged," invisible death camps, but by reducing even the materiality of the dead bodies to smoke and ashes, and by reducing, furthermore, the radical opacity of the *sight* of the dead bodies, as well as the linguistic referentiality and literality of the *word* "corpse," to the transparency of a pure form and to the pure rhetorical metaphoricity of a mere *figure:* a disembodied verbal substitute that signifies abstractly the linguistic law of infinite exchangeability and substitutability. The dead bodies are thus verbally rendered invisible, and voided both of substance and specificity, by being treated, in the Nazi jargon, as *figuren:* that which, all at once, *cannot be seen* and can be *seen through.*

> The Germans even forbade us to use the words "corpse" or "victim." The dead were blocks of wood, shit. The Germans made us refer to the bodies as *figuren,* that is, as puppets, as dolls, or as *Schmattes,* which means "rags." (13)

But it is not only the dead bodies of the Jews that the Nazis, paradoxically, do not "see." It is also, in some striking cases, the living Jews transported to their death that remain invisible to the chief architects of their final transportation. Walter Stier, head of Reich Railways Department 33 of the Nazi Party, chief traffic planner of the death trains ("special trains," in Nazi euphemism), testifies:

But you knew that the trains to Treblinka or Auschwitz were—

Of course we knew. I was the last district. Without me the trains couldn't reach their destination . . .

Did you know that Treblinka meant extermination?

Of course not. . . . How could we know? I never went to Treblinka. (135)

. . . .

You never saw a train?

No, never. . . . I never left my desk. We worked day and night. (132)

In the same way, Mrs. Michelshon, wife of a Nazi schoolteacher in Chelmno, answers Lansmann's questions:

Did you see the gas vans?

No. . . . Yes, from the outside. They shuttled back and forth. I never looked inside; I didn't see Jews in them. I only saw things from outside. (82)

THE OCCURRENCE AS UNWITNESSED

Thus, the diversity of the testimonial stances of the victims, the bystanders, and the perpetrators have in common, paradoxically, the incommensurability of their different and particular positions of not seeing, the radical divergence of their topographical, emotional, and epistemological positions not simply as witnesses, but as witnesses who *do not witness,* who let the Holocaust occur as an event essentially unwitnessed. Through the testimonies of its visual witnesses, the film makes us see concretely—makes us *witness*—how the Holocaust occurs as the unprecedented, inconceivable historical advent of *an event without a witness,*[7] an event that historically consists in the scheme of the literal *erasure of its witnesses* but that, moreover, philosophically consists in an accidenting of perception, in a *splitting of eyewitnessing* as such; an event, thus not empirically, but cognitively and perceptually without a witness both because it precludes seeing and because it precludes the possibility of a *community of seeing:* an event that radically annihilates the recourse (the appeal) to visual corroboration (to the commensurability between two different seeings) and thus dissolves the possibility of any *community of witnessing.*

Shoah enables us to see—and gives us insight into—the occurrence of the Holocaust as an absolute historical event whose literally *overwhelming evidence* makes it, paradoxically, into an *utterly proofless* event whose magnitude of reference is at once below and beyond proof.

THE MULTIPLICITY OF LANGUAGES

The incommensurability between different testimonial stances, and the heterogeneous multiplicity of specific cognitive positions of seeing and not seeing, is amplified and duplicated in the film by the multiplicity of languages in which the testimonies are delivered (French, German, Sicilian, English, Hebrew, Yiddish, Polish), a multiplicity that necessarily encompasses some foreign tongues and that necessitates the presence of a professional translator as an intermediary between witnesses and Lanzmann as their interviewer. The technique of dubbing is not used, and the character of the translator is deliberately not edited out of the film—on the contrary, she is quite often present on the screen, at the side of Lanzmann, as another one of the real actors of the film, because the process of translation is itself an integral part of the process of the film, partaking both of its scenario and of its own performance of *its* cinematic testimony. Through the multiplicity of foreign tongues and the prolonged *delay* incurred by the translation, the splitting of the eyewitnessing that the historical event seems to consist of, the incapacity of seeing to translate itself spontaneously and simultaneously into a meaning, is recapitulated on the level of the viewers of the film. The film places us in the position of the witness who *sees* and *hears,* but *cannot understand* the significance of what is going on until the later intervention, the delayed processing and rendering of the significance of the visual/acoustic information by the translator, who also in some ways distorts and screens it, because (as is attested by those viewers who are native speakers of the foreign tongues that the translator is translating, and as the film itself points out by some of Lanzmann's interventions and corrections), the translation is not always absolutely accurate.

The palpable foreignness of the film's tongues is emblematic of the radical foreignness of the experience of the Holocaust, not merely to us, but even to its own participants. Asked whether he has invited the participants to see the film, Lanzmann answered in the negative: "In what language would the participants see the film?" The original was a French print: "They don't speak French."[8] French, the native language of the filmmaker, the common denominator into which the testimonies (and the original subtitles) are translated and in which the film is thought out and gives, in turn, its own testimony happens (not by chance, I would suggest) not to be the language of any of the witnesses. It is a metaphor of the film that its language is a language of translation, and, as such, is doubly foreign: that the occurrence, on the one hand, happens in a language foreign to the language of the film, but also, that the significance of the occurrence can only be articulated in a language foreign to the language(s) of the occurrence.

The title of the film is, however, not in French and embodies thus, once more, a linguistic strangeness, an estrangement, whose significance is enigmatic and whose meaning cannot be immediately accessible even to the native audience of the original French print: *Shoah,* the Hebrew word that, with the definite article (here missing), designates "the Holocaust" but that, without the article, enigmatically and indefinitely means "catastrophe," here names the very foreignness of languages, the very namelessness of a catastrophe that cannot be possessed by a native tongue and that, within translation, can only be named as the *untranslatable:* that which language cannot witness; that which can be articulated in *one* language; that which language, in its turn, cannot witness without *splitting.*

THE HISTORIAN AS A WITNESS

The task of the deciphering of signs and of the processing of intelligibility—what might be called the *task of the translator*[9]—is, however, carried out within the film not merely by the character of the professional interpreter, but also by two other real actors—the historian (Raul Hilberg) and the filmmaker (Claude Lanzmann)—who, like the witnesses, in turn *play themselves* and who, unlike the witnesses and like the translator, constitute *second-degree witnesses* (witnesses of witnesses, witnesses of the testimonies). Like the professional interpreter, although in very different ways, the filmmaker in the film and the historian on the screen are in turn catalysts—or agents—of the process of *reception,* agents whose reflective witnessing and whose testimonial stances aid our own reception and assist us both in the effort toward comprehension and in the unending struggle with the foreignness of signs, in processing not merely (as does the professional interpreter) the literal meaning of the testimonies, but also, (some perspectives on) their philosophical and historical significance.

The historian is, thus, in the film, neither the last word of knowledge nor the ultimate authority on history, but rather, one more topographical and cognitive position of yet *another witness*. The statement of the filmmaker—and the testimony of the film—are by no means *subsumed* by the statements (or the testimony) of the historian. Though the filmmaker does embrace the historical insights of Hilberg, which he obviously holds in utter respect and from which he gets both inspiration and instruction, the film also places in perspective—and puts in context—the discipline of history as such, in stumbling on (and giving us to see) the very limits of historiography. "*Shoah*," said Claude Lanzmann at Yale, "is certainly not a historical film. . . . The purpose of *Shoah* is not to transmit knowledge, in spite of the fact that there is knowledge in the film. . . . Hilberg's book *The Destruction of the European Jews* was really my Bible for many years. . . . But in spite of this, *Shoah* is not a historical film, it is something else. . . . To condense in one word what the film is for me, I would say that the film is an *incarnation,* a *resurrection,* and that the whole process of the film is a philosophical one."[10] Hilberg is the spokesman for a unique and impressive knowledge on the Holocaust. Knowledge is shown by the film to be absolutely necessary in the ongoing struggle to resist the blinding impact of the event, to counteract the splitting of eyewitnessing. But knowledge is not, in and of itself, a sufficiently active and sufficiently effective act of seeing. The newness of the film's vision, on the other hand, consists precisely in the surprising insight it conveys into the radical ignorance in which we are unknowingly all plunged with respect to the actual historical occurrence. This ignorance is not simply dispelled by history—on the contrary, it *encompasses* history as such. The film shows how history is used for the purpose of a historical (ongoing) *process of forgetting* that, ironically enough, *includes* the gestures of historiography. Historiography is as much the product of the passion of forgetting as it is the product of the passion of remembering.

Walter Stier, former head of Reich Railways and chief planner of the transports of the Jews to the death camps, can thus testify:

> *What was Treblinka for you? . . . A destination?*
> Yes, that's all.
> *But not death.*

No, no. . . .

Extermination came to you as a big surprise?

Completely. . . .

You had no idea.

Not the slightest. Like that camp—what was its name? It was in the Oppeln district. . . . I've got it: Auschwitz.

Yes, Auschwitz was in the Oppeln district. . . . Auschwitz to Krakow is forty miles.

That's not very far. And we knew nothing. Not a clue.

But you knew that the Nazis—that Hitler didn't like the Jews?

That we did. It was well known. . . . But as to their extermination, that was news to us. I mean, even today people deny it. They say there couldn't have been so many Jews. Is it true? I don't know. That's what they say. (136–38)

To substantiate his own amnesia (of the name of Auschwitz) and his own claim of essentially *not knowing,* Stier implicitly refers here to the *claim of knowledge*—the historical authority—of "revisionist historiographies," recent works published in a variety of countries by historians who prefer to argue that the *number* of the dead cannot be *proven* and that since there is no scientific, scholarly hard evidence of the *exact extent* of the mass murder, the genocide is merely an invention, an exaggeration of the Jews and the Holocaust, in fact, never existed.[11] "But as to their extermination, that was news to us. I mean, even today, people deny it. They say there could not have so many Jews. Is it true? I don't know. That what they say." I am not the one who knows, but there are those who know who say that what I did not know did not exist. "Is it true? I don't know."

Dr. Franz Grassler, on the other hand (formerly Nazi commissioner of the Warsaw Ghetto), comes himself to mimic, in front of the camera, the very gesture of historiography as an alibi to *his* forgetting.

You don't remember those days?

Not much. . . . It's a fact: we tend to forget, thank God, the bad times. . . .

I'll help you to remember. In Warsaw you were Dr. Auerswald's deputy.

Yes. . . .

Dr. Grassler, this is Czerniakow's diary. You're mentioned in it.

It's been printed. It exists?

He kept a diary that was recently published. He wrote on July 7, 1941 . . .

July 7, 1941? That's the first time I've relearned a date. May I take notes? After all, it interests me too. In July I was already there! (175–76)

In line with the denial of responsibility and memory, the very gesture of historiography comes to embody nothing other than the blankness of the page on which the "notes" are taken.

The next section of the film focuses on the historian Hilberg holding, and discussing, Czerniakow's diary. The cinematic editing that follows shifts back and forth, in a sort of shuttle movement, between the face of Grassler (which continues to articulate his own view of the ghetto) and the face of Hilberg (which continues to articulate the content of the diary and the perspective that the author of the diary—Czerniakow—gives of the ghetto). The Nazi commissioner of the ghetto is thus confronted structurally, not so much with the counter-statement of the historian, but with the first-hand witness of the (now dead) author of the diary, the Jewish leader of the ghetto whom the ineluctability of the ghetto's destiny led to end his leadership—and sign his diary—with suicide.

The main role of the historian is, thus, less to narrate history than to *reverse the suicide,* to take part in a cinematic vision that Lanzmann has defined as crucially an "incarnation" and a "resurrection." "I have taken a historian," Lanzmann enigmatically remarked, "so that he will incarnate a dead man, even though I had someone who had been a director of the ghetto."[12] The historian is there to embody, to give flesh and blood to, the dead author of the diary. Unlike Christian resurrection, though, the vision of the film is to make Czerniakow *come alive precisely as a dead man.* His "resurrection" does not cancel out his death. The vision of the film is at once to make the dead writer come alive as a historian, and to make, in turn, history and the historian come alive in the uniqueness of the living voice of a dead man, and in the silence of his suicide.

THE FILMMAKER AS A WITNESS

At the side of the historian, *Shoah* finally includes among its list of characters (its list of witnesses) the very figure of the filmmaker in the process of making—or the creation—of the film. Traveling between the living and the dead and moving to and fro between the different

places and the different voices in the film, the filmmaker is continuously—though discreetly—present in the margin of the screen, perhaps as the most silently articulate and as the most articulately silent
witness. The creator of the film speaks and testifies, however, in his
own voice, in his triple role as the *narrator* of the film (and the signatory—the first person—of the script), as the *interviewer* of the witnesses
(the solicitor and the receiver of the testimonies), and as the *inquirer*
(the artist as the subject of a quest concerning what the testimonies
testify to, the figure of the witness as a questioner, and of the asker
not merely as the factual investigator but as the bearer of the film's
philosophical address and inquiry).

The three roles of the filmmaker intermix and in effect exist only in
their relation to each other. Since the narrator is, as such, strictly a
witness, his story is restricted to the story of the interviewing: the narrative consists of what the interview hears. Lanzmann's rigor as narrator is precisely to speak strictly as an interviewer (and as an inquirer),
to abstain, that is, from narrating anything directly in his own voice,
except for the beginning—the only moment that refers explicitly the
film to the first person of the filmmaker as narrator:

> The story begins in the present at Chelmno. . . . Chelmno was the
> place in Poland where Jews were first exterminated by gas. . . . Of
> the four hundred thousand men, women and children who went
> there, only two came out alive. . . . Srebnik, survivor of the last
> period, was a boy of thirteen when he was sent to Chelmno. . . . I
> found him in Israel and persuaded that onetime boy singer to re-
> turn with me to Chelmno. (3–4)

The opening, narrated in the filmmaker's own voice, at once situates
the story in the present and sums up a past that is presented not yet as
the story but rather as a pre-history, or a pre-story: the story proper is
contemporaneous with the film's speech, which begins, in fact, subsequent to the narrator's written preface, by the actual song of Srebnik
resung (reenacted) in the present. The narrator is the "I" who "found"
Srebnik and "persuaded" him to "return with me to Chelmno." The
narrator, therefore, is the one who *opens,* or reopens the story of the past
in the present of the telling: But the "I" of the narrator, of the signatory of the film, has no voice: the opening is projected on the screen as

the silent text of a mute script, as the narrative voice-over of a *writing* with no voice.

On the one hand, then, the narrator has no voice. On the other hand, the continuity of the narrative is insured by nothing other than by Lanzmann's voice, which runs through the film and whose sound constitutes the continuous, connective thread between the different voices and the different testimonial episodes. But Lanzmann's voice — the active voice in which we hear the filmmaker speak — is strictly, once again, the voice of the inquirer and of the interviewer, not of the narrator. As narrator, Lanzmann does not speak, but rather vocally recites the words of others, *lends his voice* (on two occasions) to read aloud two written documents whose authors cannot speak in their own voice: the letter of the Rabbi of Grabow, warning the Jews of Lodz of the extermination taking place at Chelmno, a letter whose signatory was himself consequently gassed at Chelmno with his whole community ("Do not think" — Lanzmann recites — "that this is written by a madman. Alas, it is the horrible, tragic truth"; 83–84), and the Nazi document entitled "Secret Reich Business" and concerning technical improvements of the gas vans ("Changes to special vehicles . . . shown by use and experience to be necessary"; 103–5), an extraordinary document that might be said to formalize Nazism as such (the way in which the most perverse and most concrete extermination is abstracted into a pure question of technique and function). We witness Lanzmann's voice modulating evenly — with no emotion and no comment — the perverse diction of this document punctuated by unintentional, coincidental irony embodied by the signatory's name: "Signed: Just."

Besides this recitation of the written documents, and besides his own mute reference to his own voice in the written cinematic preface of the silent opening, Lanzmann speaks as the interviewer and as an inquirer, but as narrator he keeps silent. The narrator lets the narrative be carried on by others — by the live voices of the various witnesses he interviews, whose stories must be able to *speak for themselves,* if they are to testify, that is, to perform their unique and irreplaceable first-hand witness. It is only in this way, by this abstinence of the narrator, that the film can in fact be a narrative of testimony: a narrative of that, precisely, which can neither be reported, nor narrated, by another. The narrative is thus essentially a narrative of silence, the story of the filmmaker's *listening:* the narrator is the teller of the film only insofar as he is the bearer of the film's silence.

In his other roles, however, that of the interviewer and of the inquirer, the filmmaker, on the contrary, is by definition a transgressor, and a breaker, of silence. Of his own transgression of the silence, the interviewer says to the interviewee whose voice cannot be given up and whose silence must be broken: "I know it's very hard. I know and I apologize" (117).

As an interviewer, Lanzmann asks not for great explanations of the Holocaust, but for concrete descriptions of minute particular details and of apparently trivial specifics.[13] "Was the weather very cold?" (11). "From the station to the unloading ramp in the camp is how many miles? . . . How long did the trip last?" (33). "Exactly where did the camp begin?" (34). "It was the silence that tipped them off? . . . Can he describe that silence?" (67). "What were the [gas] vans like? . . . What color?" (80). It is not the big generalizations but the concrete particulars that translate into a vision and thus help both to dispel the blinding impact of the event and to transgress the silence to which the splitting of eyewitnessing reduced the witness. It is only through the trivia, by small steps — and not by huge strides or big leaps — that the barrier of silence can be in effect displaced, and somewhat lifted. The pointed and specific questioning resists, above all, any possible canonization of the experience of the Holocaust. Insofar as the interviewer challenges at once the sacredness (the unspeakability) of death and the sacredness of the deadness (of the silence) of the witness, Lanzmann's questions are essentially desacralizing.

> How did it happen when the women came into the gas chamber? . . . What did you feel the first time you saw all these naked women?
>
> . . . .
>
> But I asked you and you didn't answer: What was your impression the first time you saw these naked women arriving with children? How did you feel?
>
> I tell you something. To have a feeling about that . . . it was very hard to feel anything, because working there day and night between dead people, between bodies, your feeling disappeared, you were dead. You had no feeling at all. (114–16)

Shoah is the story of the liberation of the testimony through its desacralization; the story of the decanonization of the Holocaust for the sake of its previously impossible historicization. What the interviewer above all avoids is an alliance with the silence of the witness, the kind of emphatic and benevolent alliance through which interviewer and interviewee often implicitly concur, and work together, for the mutual comfort of an avoidance of the truth.

It is the silence of the witness's death that Lanzmann must historically here challenge, in order to revive the Holocaust and to rewrite the *event-without-a-witness* into witnessing, and into history. It is the silence of the witness's death, and of the witness's deadness, which precisely must be broken and transgressed.

> *We have to do it. You know it.*
> I won't be able to do it.
> *You have to do it. I know it's very hard. I know and I apologize.*
> Don't make me go on please.
> *Please. We must go on.* (117)

What does *going on* mean? The predicament of having to continue to bear witness at all costs parallels, for Abraham Bomba, the predicament faced in the past of having to continue to *live on,* to survive in spite of the gas chambers, in the face of the surrounding death. But to have to *go on* now, to have to keep bearing witness, is more than simply to be faced with the imperative to replicate the past and thus to replicate his own *survival.* Lanzmann paradoxically now urges Bomba to break out of the very deadness that enabled the survival. The narrator calls the witness to come back from the mere mode of surviving into that of living—and of living pain. If the interviewer's role is thus to break the silence, the narrator's role is to insure that the story (be it that of silence) will go on.

But it is the inquirer whose philosophical interrogation and interpellation constantly reopen what might otherwise be seen as the story's closure.

> *Mrs. Pietyra, you live in Auschwitz?*
> Yes, I was born there. . . .
> *Were there Jews in Auschwitz before the war?*
> They made up eighty percent of the population. They even had a synagogue here. . . .
> *Was there a Jewish cemetery in Auschwitz?*

It still exists. It's closed now.
Closed? What does that mean?
They don't bury there now. (17–18)

The inquirer thus inquires into the very meaning of *closure* and of narrative, political and philosophical *enclosure*. Of Dr. Grassler, the ex-assistant to the Nazi "commissar" of the Jewish ghetto, Lanzmann asks:

My question is philosophical. What does a ghetto mean, in your opinion? (182)

DIFFERENCES

Grassler of course evades the question. "History is full of ghettos," he replies, once more using erudition, "knowledge," and the very discipline of history to avoid the cutting edge of interpellation: "Persecution of the Jews wasn't a German invention, and didn't start with World War II" (182). Everybody knows, in other words, what a ghetto is, and the meaning of the ghetto does not warrant a specifically *philosophical* attention: "history is full of ghettos." Because "history" knows only too well what a ghetto is, this knowledge might as well be left to history, and does not need in turn to be probed by us. History is thus used both to deny the *philosophical* thrust of the question and to forget the specificity—the *difference*—of the Nazi past. Insofar as the reply denies precisely the inquirer's refusal to *take for granted* the conception—let alone the preconception—of the ghetto, the stereotypical, preconceived answer in effect *forgets* the asking power of the question. Grassler essentially forgets the difference: forgets the *meaning* of the ghetto as the first step in the Nazi overall design precisely of the framing—and of the enclosure—of a difference, a difference that will consequently be assigned to the ultimate enclosure of the death camp and to the "final solution" of eradication. Grassler's answer *does not meet* the question, and attempts, moreover, to *reduce* the question's difference. But the question of the ghetto—that of the attempt at the containment (the reduction) of a difference—perseveres both in the speech and in the silence of the inquirer-narrator. The narrator is precisely there to insure that the question, in its turn, will *go on* (will continue in the viewer). The inquirer, in other words, is not merely the agency that asks the questions, but the force that takes apart all previous answers. Throughout the interviewing process the inquirer-narrator, at the side of Grassler as of others, is at once the witness of the question and the witness of the gap—or of the difference—between the question and the answer.

Often the inquirer bears witness to the question (and the narrator silently bears witness to the story) by merely recapitulating word by word a fragment of the answer, by literally repeating—like an echo—the last sentence, the last words just uttered by the interlocutor. But the function of the echo—in the very resonance of its amplification—is itself inquisitive, and not simply repetitive. "The gas vans came in here," Srebnik narrates: "there were two huge ovens, and afterwards the bodies were thrown into these ovens, and the flames reached to the sky" (6). "To the sky [*zim Himmel*]," mutters silently the interviewer, opening at once a philosophical abyss in the simple words of the narrative description of a black hole in the very blueness of the image of the sky. When later on, the Poles around the church narrate how they listened to the gassed Jew's screams, Lanzmann's repetitious echoes register the unintended irony of the narration:

> *They heard screams at night?*
> The Jews moaned. . . . They were hungry. They were shut in and starved.
> *What kind of cries and moans were heard at night?*
> They called on Jesus and Mary and God, sometimes in German. . . .
> *The Jews called on Jesus, Mary and God!* (97–98)

Lanzmann's function as an echo is another means by which the voice-lessness of the narrator and the voice of the inquirer produce a *question* in the very answer, and enact a *difference* through the very verbal repetition. In the narrator as the bearer of the film's silence, the *question* of the scream persists. And so does the *difference* of what the screams in fact call out to. Here as elsewhere in the film, the narrator is, as such, both the guardian of the question and the guardian of the difference.

The inquirer's investigation is precisely into (both the philosophical and the concrete) particularity of difference. "*What's the difference* between a special and a regular train?" the inquirer asks of the Nazi traffic planner Walter Stier (133). And to the Nazi teacher's wife, who in a Freudian slip confuses Jews and Poles (both "the others" or "the foreigners" in relation to the Germans), Lanzmann addresses the following meticulous query:

> Since World War I the castle has been in ruins. . . . That's where the Jews were taken. This ruined castle was used for housing and delousing the Poles, and so on.
> *The Jews!*
> Yes, the Jews.
> *Why do you call them Poles and not Jews?*
> Sometimes I get them mixed up.
> *There's a difference between Poles and Jews?*
> Oh yes!
> *What difference?*
> The Poles weren't exterminated, and the Jews were. That's the difference. An external difference.
> *And the inner difference?*
> I can't assess that. I don't know enough about psychology and anthropology. The difference between the Poles and the Jews? Anyway, they couldn't stand each other. (82–83)

As a philosophical inquiry into the ungraspability of difference and as a narrative of the specific differences between the various witnesses, *Shoah* implies a fragmentation of the testimonies—a fragmentation both of tongues and of perspectives—that cannot ultimately be surpassed. It is because the film goes from singular to singular, because there is not possible *representation* of one witness by another, that Lanzmann needs us to sit through ten hours of the film to begin to witness—to begin to have a concrete sense—both of our own ignorance and of the incommensurability of the occurrence. The occurrence is conveyed precisely by this fragmentation of the testimonies, which enact the fragmentation of the witnessing. The film is a gathering of the fragments of the witnessing. But the collection of the fragments does not yield, even after ten hours of the movie, any possible totality or any possible totalization: the gathering of testimonial incommensurates does not amount either to a generalizable theoretical statement or to a narrative monologic sum. Asked what was his concept of the Holocaust, Lanzmann answered: "I had no concept; I had obsessions, which is different. . . . The obsession of the cold. . . . The obsession of the first time. The first shock. The first hour of the Jews in the camp, in Treblinka, the first minutes. I will always ask the question of the first time. . . . The obsession of the last moments, the waiting, the fear. *Shoah* is a film of fear, and of energy too. You cannot do such a film theoretically. Every theoretical attempt that I tried was a failure, but these failures were necessary. . . . You build such a film in your head, in your heart, in your belly, in your guts, everywhere" (*Interview,* 22–23). This "everywhere" that, paradoxically, cannot be totalized, and that resists theory as such, this corporeal fragmentation and enumeration that describes the "building"—or the process of the generation—of the film while it resists any attempt at conceptualization, is itself an emblem of the specificity—of the uniqueness—of the mode of testimony of the film. The film testifies not merely by collecting and by gathering fragments of witnessing, but by actively exploding any possible enclosure—any conceptual frame—that might claim to *contain* the fragments and to fit them into one coherent whole. *Shoah* bears witness to the fragmentation of the testimonies as the radical invalidation of all definitions, of all parameters of reference, of all known answers, in the very midst of its relentless affirmation—of its materially creative validation—of the absolute necessity of speaking. The film puts in motion its surprising testimony by performing the historical and contradictory double task of the breaking of the silence and of the simultaneous shattering of any given discourse, of the breaking—or the bursting open—of all frames.

For Shoshana Felman: Truth and Art

Shoshana Felman's writing accompanies Claude Lanzmann's film *Shoah* with such intelligent complicity that it succeeds in creating a new object, which it is appropriate to call the "Lanzmann-Felman duo."[1] This Lanzmann-Felman duo encompasses two enigmas that continue to confront us: What was the aim of the Final Solution? What art is possible after Auschwitz?

The brutal evidence of the response to the first question — the final solution directed against the Jews — is burdened with meaning: the systematic extermination of living bodies; the ritual obliteration of all traces of the crime; the "scientific" eradication of the visible, of speech, of thought, of communication. The monstrous Nazi mystique betrays itself in the form of a fierce engagement in a destruction obsessed with a Biblical message. It would obliterate the foundations on which the identity of the Jewish people is built in these terms: to perpetuate living bodies, "to affect the one who listens,"[2] to communicate the meaning of human desire as the desire for meaning.

It was necessary that Claude Lanzmann's talent transform the philosophical seizure of this unprecedented horror in a *cinema of the invisible* in order for Shoshana Felman's elucidation to reveal why the Nazi crime was an attempt to destroy, along with the Jewish people, this Gordian knot that constitutes the human, and which is nothing other than the *indivisible unity of life-look-speech*. In refusing to exhibit the horror visually ("absence of corpses on the screen"),[3] the film confronts us, the spectators, with the *result* of the real and symbolic putting to death perpetuated by the Nazis — the difficulty of bearing witness. However, in the course of this investigation, this *result* reveals itself as the *source* of this same crime: one did not want to, or could not, watch, speak, or communicate.

The "Final Solution" reveals itself as a "historical attack" against bearing witness, in the double sense of the term: to begin with, the act of looking truth in the face and, simultaneously, the translation of this vision into meaning.[4] In order to understand that *life-vision-meaning are inseparable,* Claude Lanzmann the philosopher transforms himself into a paradoxical film maker: in giving himself the task of filming the "fatal secret," he produces this tension that is necessarily a contradiction—the rendering of the invisible into image. The film *Shoah* reveals simultaneously the putting to death of the human and the "explosion of visual testimony"[5] as two sides of the same crime against humanity. In the same way, it opens an epochal interrogation which has nothing to do with the aesthetic, but which concerns the survival of civilization: What art is possible for the invisible? For the unthinkable?

Figuren

In effect, the desire for extermination that mobilizes the Nazis aims simultaneously at the *genetic survival* of the living bodies and *the possibility of representing* this annihilation and its goal. The genetic destruction is immediately accompanied by a destruction of words and images: at the same time that the Shoah banishes living beings it banishes the terms "dead" and "victims." These human beings who are declared "superfluous"—following the analysis of Hannah Arendt—become no more than " billots of wood," "marionettes," "dolls," *Figuren,* or *Schmatten,* rags, nothing. This lexical purification betrays the extent of the "historical attack": it is a question of the exclusion of a people not only from the human domain, but from the domain of the living as such. No more than inanimate objects, the Jews are excluded—by the same mortifying gesture that excludes them from the domain of human time—from the time of language, from the time of signification.

To Make Trauma Visible

How to make visible the varied difficulties of bearing witness after this catastrophe—this *Shoah*—without precedent? Neither as an image of horror—a monstrosity of compassionate melancholy—nor as an entry in a history book. The Lanzmann-Felman duo reveals the defensive amnesia of the survivors, points out the denials and the criminal complicity of the "outside"[6] (the "oblique" look of the Polish). Lanzmann points to the cruel irony that underlies the "will to silence" of the Nazis when he insists[7]: "My question is a philosophical question: In your opinion, what does a ghetto signify?" Lanzmann's *enormous* question reveals the narrow-minded perversity of Dr. Grassler who, "starting the game," prefers to evoke History in lieu of responding to the interrogator-philosopher, thus avoiding signification as well as responsibility. But the Lanzmann-Felman duo does not forget the rare "Justes," such as the messenger Jan Karski, who acts as a relay between the "outside" and the "inside" and, in this role of visiting angel, breaks the wall that separates those who do not want to know and those who are condemned to the powerlessness of putting words to this horror, with the "orphic reiteration of his spectral visit" equivalent to "a sermon of love."[8]

The multiple impossibilities of testifying to the horror confront the spectators, the readers that we are—and those who come after us—with the profundity of the *trauma* that "the Final Solution" inflicts on the entirety of humanity. Jan Karski's voyage in the ghetto of Warsaw reveals this trauma with the maximum of economy and intensity. "What has happened to them?" demands this man to his friend Bundiste. "They died," he responds, and Jan Karski sees, that is to say, he understands.[9] And only in this way does he become a messenger: one who by seeing and questioning reveals the trauma. But he does not stop here. Karski internalizes the trauma, so that from this moment forth he takes part in the trauma: his speech is not an act of compassion, but of passion itself. He returns in order to see once more those who die. The messenger has made nothing more than a "relation": that is not much, that is everything. He cannot "recount memories" because the trauma has contaminated him. He dies with this "they" who die. Of "this" Jan Karski cannot speak except in negative phrases: "This was not humanity! . . . This was not a world. I was not there. I was not part of that."[10] The trauma as such cannot be spoken.

The Question and Its Languages
And yet, confronted with this trauma, the film gambles on two modes of discourse to communicate the trauma to us: *investigation* and the *multiplicity of languages.*

The truth of the trauma destroys all possibility of narration, and of all imaginary speech, even the most enigmatic poetry. The Lanzmann-Felman duo conveys this conviction with insistence. "Truth kills the possibility of art," insists Claude Lanzmann. "But truth does not kill the possibility of art."[11]

The filmic art merges with the art of the investigation, which comes extremely close to psychoanalytic amnesia. But it distinguishes itself at the same time because, contrary to the psychoanalyst, the film-maker of the invisible does not interpret: he contents himself with making visible the simultaneity of the putting to death of bodies *and* the putting to death of vision-speech-memory. He does this obstinately, with a cold irony that freezes us before the sight of these human beings who were stripped of all that we believe constitutes humanity. It is this irony of intelligence on which the Lanzmann-Felman duo bets, and which communicates to us the hope of surpassing the trauma. Obstinately, Lanzmann insists, to the point of exhorting Bomba "to shake himself out of the lethargy that has permitted him to survive,"[12] so that with him we are forced to return from a rough "survival" to a "vital suffering."

But which "we"? We, the inheritors of a Biblical message that binds life to vision and to communication? We, the civilization of the Book that speaks and reveals the truth? Or what remains of it?

But one does not break the silence surrounding a trauma without "opening, by breaking them open, all of the secrets."[13] In what language can we speak the invisible? An other language searches for its identity before the camera. Immersed in a Babel of foreign languages, it avoids at great pains the familiar chatter full of amnesia, of the desire to not know, even of incisive judgments that bring together the denials, the crimes, the bandages of forgetfulness, and often the inexpressible sadness itself

Several languages: German, Polish, Yiddish, cut through the language of the director-interrogator, French, so that it is the *translation* that imposes itself as the only language of the film: "It is a metaphor of film that its language must be a language of translation and, in such a way, doubly strange: that the event happens in languages foreign to that of film, but also, that the signification of the event cannot articulate itself save in a language foreign to the languages of the event."[14]

To Translate: All Languages Are "Languages of the Event"

I am not sure that French was foreign to the event of the Shoah. In fact, I am sure of the opposite. I recall that when we commemorated the creation, after the Second World War, of the Faculty of Letters at Georgetown University in Washington, the Jesuit president of this faculty declared in substance that there was no other response to the murder of men and memory than to keep alive the memory of languages, to convene all languages *in the event*. And I share with the Lanzmann-Felman duo the conviction that the presence of a professional translator in the film, placed between the witnesses and the interviewer, incarnates, in an indelible fashion, the impossibility of finding meaning in the trauma other than through a mosaic of languages: dialogue in the abyss between our opaque idiolects and yet nevertheless comprehensible, defensive national languages that are yet no less receptive to the broken process of signification, divided, shattered, stupefying, and yet, on the whole, possible.

An Incarnation

Thus, this paradoxical film not only allows us to see, but replaces the narrator with an interviewer who is also a translator. And, although it fragments the narration of events in order to make us feel the single event that is worth the trouble — the trauma of the historical attack against life-vision-communication — a virtual film nevertheless emerges. This is the film of incarnation.

Through the thread that weaves together this arrangement of fragments, interviews and images, faces, questions, responses, and by the tireless recommencement of an inquest that dedicates itself, by its very recommencement, infinite, in-finite — an *incarnation* is produced, a *resurrection:* of the dead author of a journal (Czerniakow),[15] of the singing child (Simon Srebnik), and of the "last Jew of the Warsaw Ghetto" (Simha Rottem, called Kajik),[16] who become the protagonists in the retrieved memory of the spectator. They become one with the intention of the film and take up residence within us.

Claude Lanzmann wins his bet: in place of the radical impossibility of witness, his "art" substitutes the possibility "to reach people through their own intelligence":[17] to communicate not only a constant, but an open question, without response; to arouse us in order to move us. Not to conclude, but to leave the question wide open. This eternal ambition of philosophy becomes an artistic, cinemagraphic ambition. An exception? A utopia? Let us see.

Lanzmann the Messenger

Claude Lanzmann takes on the role of Jan Karski, the messenger from "outside" who sees the "inside," revisits, and bears witness.[18] Even if the testimony of this "most honest outside witness"[19] does not change the politics of the Allies, as his Zionist friends wished, an essential breach is accomplished in the project of the "Final Solution": failing to save the lives of the Jews, Jan Karski saves the vision and its communication and, with these, the hope of putting an end to barbarism. Is this the role of Lanzmann's film *Shoah,* of art after Auschwitz? Such seems the message of the Lanzmann-Felman duo.

But their vigilance does not stop there. Shoshana Felman returns to the question of the history of this enigmatic cinematographer himself, and does not avoid recalling his biography: an "assimilated" French Jew, and not always content to be so, a philosopher at ease with the German language and Sartrean existentialism. In other words, could we not say that he is a man of the "outside" who accedes to the "inside," a sort of Karski? A man that European history has cut into two — one side "inside," the other "outside" — on one side trauma, on the other the desire for *universal communication.* To save the Jews and to save thought. To begin with this incarnated thought that is art. "To condense in a word what this film is for me, I would say that it is an *incarnation,* a *resurrection,* and that its entire approach is philosophical," Lanzmann declared at a gathering at Yale.[20]

Art as a philosophical intervention that transverses the traumatic truth, by opening the possibility of resurrection, of incarnation. Lanzmann is decidedly a messenger: he attempts a transmission between Europe as the inheritor of the Greeks and the Evangelicals, Europe as philosophical and humanist, the Europe that "shattered" itself by perpetuating a historical attack against life-vision-communication, and the people who were murdered. An uncomfortable position. A promising position. A hypothesis.

Lanzmann does not deceive himself with an easy solution. What is signified by this "last Jew," Simha Rottem, a member of the insurrection that awaited the Germans in the Warsaw ghetto?[21] The last one to revolt? Or the last to be threatened with extermination? For, from this moment forward, no Jew will be shut away in ghettos by the Germans or by their eventual imitators. Is it a question of the last persecuted Jew, of the end of the Shoah? Lanzmann hopes so, and the film hopes the same. Nothing is absolutely sure, however, insofar as the unity of life-vision-communication continues to be threatened. "Then, I decided that the last image of the film would be a train in movement, a train in movement . . . forever," declares Lanzmann, reprised through the voice of Shoshana Felman.[22]

The Shoah continues? Yes? No? How to be sure?

I watch the television transmissions of the Tsunami: absolutely no relation to the "Final Solution." And yet, the flood of mediatized images, while evidence of the triumph of an over-sated technology that takes pleasure in the good conscience of its general gifts, strangely renders death less real. The third millennium begins with the incapacity to think the meaning of human life; we evacuate all meaning in images and monetary transactions. We watch, certainly, but who sees? Where are the "messengers"?

Have we taken the measure of the historical catastrophe that the Shoah has inflicted on us? We have reacted with a counter-investment in the visible: the look is everywhere at once; there is not a single event that escapes the register of the visible. But this inflation of vision is deprived of *intelligence*. Is this privation perhaps the most insidious endurance of the *catastrophe*, of the *Shoah*? This train in motion, without end. . . .

The art of the truth waits to be accomplished. We revisit the Lanzmann-Felman duo, and find that the Shoah has not finished revealing to us its ravages. Only a philosophical art capable of incarnating the message of the Bible can save us now.

February 2005

SHOSHANA FELMAN

11 From "The Storyteller's Silence: Walter Benjamin's Dilemma of Justice"

> *One can ask oneself whether the relationship of the storyteller to his material, human life, is not itself a craftsman's relationship . . . exemplified by the proverb, if one thinks of it as an ideogram of a story.* — WALTER BENJAMIN, "The Storyteller"

> *Death is the sanction of everything that the storyteller has to tell. He has borrowed his authority from death.*
> — WALTER BENJAMIN, "The Storyteller"

> *No justice . . . seems possible without the principle of some responsibility, beyond all living present, before the ghosts of those who are not yet born or who are already dead, be they victims of wars, political or other kinds of violence, nationalist, racist, colonialist, sexist or other kinds of extermination.*
> — JACQUES DERRIDA, *Specters of Marx*

Why start a book on trials with the story of the life and of the thought of Walter Benjamin? The story, I would argue, is a parable for the twentieth century, a parable that a sophisticated literary author could perhaps entitle "Before the Law": before the law both in the temporal and in the spatial sense.[1]

"Kafka does not use the word 'justice,'" writes Walter Benjamin, "yet it is justice which is the point of departure of his critique."[2] In the same way, one could say: Benjamin seldom uses the word "justice," yet it is justice that is the point of departure for his critique. The story of the life and of the work of Walter Benjamin (the only chapter in this book that is not about a trial) is, I would propose, a story about the relation between silence and justice. It is a story that achieves the status of what Benjamin will call "a proverb": "A proverb, one might say, is a ruin which stands on the site of an old story and in which a moral twines about a happening like ivy around a wall."[3]

Part One: Benjamin's Justice

I

Two stories here will therefore intersect and, through their intersection, shed light on each other: the story of the life of Walter Benjamin and the story of his writing.

Although Benjamin does not write about trials, he does write about history as the arena of a constant struggle between justice and injustice. He does write about the relation between history and justice. In the wake of Benjamin, this chapter is dedicated to an exploration and (after Benjamin) an attempt at conceptualization of this central relation, which, as I will later show, similarly governs trials. The chapters that follow illustrate concretely how the questions Benjamin identified as central (as constitutive within the relation between history and justice) nowadays emerge as haunting questions at the center of contemporary trials.

History, Justice, and the Law

Trials have always been contextualized in—and affected by—a general relation between history and justice. But they have not always been judicially concerned with this relationship. Until the middle of the twentieth century, a radical division between history and justice was in principle maintained. The law perceived itself either as ahistorical or as expressing a specific stage in society's historical development. But law and history were separate. The courts sometimes acknowledged they were part of history, but they did not judge history as such. This state of affairs has changed since the constitution of the Nuremberg tribunal, which (through the trial of the Nazi leaders as representatives of the historical regime and the historical phenomenon of Nazism) for the first time called history itself into a court of justice.[4]

In the wake of Nuremberg, a displacement has occurred in the relationship between history and trials.[5] Not only has it become thinkable to put history on trial, it has become judicially necessary to do so. Nuremberg did not intend, but has in fact produced, this conceptual revolution that implicitly affects all later trials, and not only the tradition of war crimes and of international criminal law. In the second half of the twentieth century, it has become part of the function of trials to repair judicially not only private but also collective historical injustices.[6]

History on Trial

Thus, the Eichmann trial puts on trial the whole history of the Nazi persecution and genocide of the European Jews.[7] Decades later, the defense in the O. J. Simpson trial puts on trial the whole history of lynching and of the persecution of American blacks, while the prosecution puts concurrently on trial the historical injustices inflicted with impunity on battered women and on murdered wives. This book explores these two paradigmatic legal examples among the many other trials (civil as well as criminal) that judge history as such: the *Brown v. Board of Education* case in the United States, the *Irving v. Lipstadt* British libel case, the French Klaus Barbie trial, the trials of the officers and torturers of the "Dirty War" in Argentina, the Turkish trial of those accused of having committed genocide against the Armenians in 1921, the international ad hoc war crimes tribunals for Rwanda and for the former Yugoslavia. In this last case of Bosnia and the former Yugoslavia, the crime of history consists (again) both in human murder and in gendered murder, both in the crime of genocide itself and in the companion outrage targeted at women. What the war crimes tribunal in The Hague for the first time puts on trial as a crime against humanity is not just the ethnic crime (the genocidal history) of massacres and ethnic cleansing but also the sexual crime (the sexualized genocidal history) of systematic and collective rape.

The significance of all these legal cases that put history on trial—a significance this book proposes to extract and to explore—is not only that they are revolutionary in the sense that what they judge is both "the private" and "the public," but also, even more significantly, that in them the court provides a stage for the expression of the persecuted. The court allows (what Benjamin called) "the tradition of the oppressed"[8] to articulate its claim to justice in the name of a judgment— of an explicit or implicit prosecution—of history itself. *The court helps in the coming to an expression of what historically has been "expressionless."*

In this chapter I will analyze how, *in anticipation of developments in law and in advance of history*, Benjamin gives voice precisely to this claim to justice in the name of the tradition of the oppressed. I argue that Benjamin is the philosopher and the conceptual precursor, the herald of this claim to justice. His theories are allegorical of the necessity of recovering the silence of the oppressed in the name of a judgment of history itself. In this he is inscribed prophetically in relation to contemporary trials. Benjamin's reflections on history predict, or at the very least anticipate, what will actually happen in the realm of the law in the second half of the twentieth century.

The Expressionless

The court, I claimed, gives a stage to "the tradition of the oppressed," in helping the "expressionless" of that tradition (the silence of the persecuted, the unspeakability of the trauma of oppression) to come into expression.

Walter Benjamin originally coined the term *expressionless* (*das Ausdruckslose*) as an innovative literary concept,[9] a concept that essentially links literature and art to the (mute yet powerful) communication of what cannot be said in words[10] but what makes art belong in "the true world," what "shatters" art, says Benjamin, into "the torso of a symbol," into a "fragment" of the real world (Benjamin, "GEA," 340). The expressionless in literature (and, I will later show, in law) is thus an utterance that signifies although and because it has no possibility of statement.

But in linking literature through the expressionless not only to a stillness and a speechlessness but also to a moment that connotes death, trauma, and petrification—"the moment in which life is petrified, as though spellbound in a single moment" ("GEA," 340)—Benjamin created, I will argue, a groundbreaking concept that can be applied as well to political phenomena, and that in particular sheds new light on twentieth-century *critiques of history*[11] and on contemporary historical developments, including late legal developments.[12]

I use the word *expressionless* throughout this book in Benjamin's pathbreaking sense,[13] but also in the sense of Levinas[14] (whose added resonance is here included in the Benjaminian sense):[15] expressionless (*das Ausdruckslose*) are those whom violence has deprived of expression; those who, on the one hand, have been historically reduced to silence, and who, on the other hand, have been historically made faceless, deprived of their *human* face—deprived, that is, not only of a language and a voice but even of the mute *expression* always present in a *living* human face.[16] Those whom violence has paralyzed, effaced, or deadened, those whom violence has treated in their lives as though they were *already dead*, those who have been made (in life) without expression, without a voice and without a face have become—much like the dead—historically (and philosophically) expressionless (*das Ausdruckslose*).

This book proposes to explore precisely the status of the expressionless in court, and the legal modes by which the expressionless of history finds an expression in trials that judge history itself and in legal proceedings that deal with (and try to repair) the crimes of history.

In the cases that this book discusses and in others like them, the court either intentionally gives a stage to the expressionless of history or unintentionally and unconsciously enacts that expressionlessness and is forced to witness it and to encounter it legally to deal with it. Through the proceedings, the expressionless at least partially recovers the living humanity and the *expression* of a human face. In the courtroom (to put one against the other two key Benjaminian concepts), the *expressionless* turns into *storytelling*.

I argue that Benjamin claims in advance this type of exercise of justice and this court that judges history.

He grasps ahead of others the significance of the relationship between history (oppression, trauma, violence) and silence. He sees ahead of others the necessity for justice to repair this silence by dragging history itself to court.

Benjamin sees in advance, I argue (ahead of what will happen in the second half of the twentieth century) at once the urgent need for the repair of collective historical injustices, and the abhorrent acts of "barbarism"—the barbaric *crimes—that* are constitutive of history as such.[17] He analyzes in advance at once the reasons for and the imperative historical necessity of putting history as such on trial, of bringing history as such and most of all, contemporary history into a court of justice.

II

"Hope in the Past," or Justice for the Dead

History in Benjamin's reflections is related not just to the structure of a trial but, more radically, to "Judgment Day": the day on which historical injustice will be cancelled out precisely through the act of judgment; the day on which justice and memory will coincide (perhaps the day on which the court will be redeemed from its inherent political *forgetfulness*). Only on Judgment Day will the meaning of history (a meaning that cannot be mastered or possessed by "man or men")[18] emerge from the political unconscious[19] and come to light. Only on Judgment Day will the past come into full possession of its meaning: a meaning in which even the expressionless of history (the silence of the victims, the muteness of the traumatized) will come into historical expression. "To be sure, only a redeemed mankind receives the fullness of its past which is to say, only for a redeemed mankind has its past become [legally] citable in all its moments. Each moment it has lived becomes a *citation à l'ordre du jour*—and that day is Judgment Day" (Benjamin, "Theses," 254). The invocation of a Judgment Day to which history itself is destined is often read as testimony to Benjamin's involvement with—or act of faith in—a Messianic eschatology. I read it secularly as the (revolutionary, legal) day that will put history itself on trial, the day in which history will have to take stock of its own flagrant injustices.

Judgment Day implies a necessary reference of history and of historical justice to a reawakening of the dead;[20] and justice is, indeed, for Benjamin, above all justice (and, quite paradoxically, life) for the dead. Life for the dead resides in a remembrance (by the living) of their story; justice for the dead resides in a remembrance (by the living) of the injustice and the outrage done to them. History is thus, above and beyond official narratives, a haunting claim the dead have on the living, whose responsibility it is not only to remember but to protect the dead from being *misappropriated:* "Only that historian will have the gift of fanning the spark of hope in the past who is firmly convinced that even the dead will not be safe from the enemy if he wins" ("Theses," 255).

Critique of Violence

What the dead will one day put on trial is the violence of history: the violence of "the triumphal procession in which the present rulers step over those who are lying prostrate" ("Theses," 256); the violence by which the rulers institute their own rule (their own violence) as law: usurpers, they hold themselves to be proprietors of justice. "Walter Benjamin noted," writes Mariana Varverde, "that every philosophical reflection on justice can be recuperated by questionable political projects, as part of the bourgeois appropriation of all manner of 'cultural treasures.' . . . The appropriation of philosophies of justice by the ruling classes of each generation was the greatest concern of Benjamin's thoughts on history."[21] Only the dead can judge the sheer violence of the historical appropriation of philosophies of justice: only from the perspective of the dead can this violence disguised as justice and cloaked as law be seen in its nakedness and put on trial.

The law—and the court itself—are therefore not entirely (and not by definition) on the side of justice; they partake of the violence of history. The law must thus stand trial along with history itself. Like history, the law has an inherent relationship to death. It is precisely this constitutive relationship of law to violence and death that must be laid bare and in turn indicted. "The task of a critique of violence"— Benjamin observes—"can be summarized as that of expounding its relation to law and justice":[22]

> For if violence, violence crowned by fate, is the origin of law, then it may be readily supposed that where the highest violence, that over life and death, occurs in the legal system, the origins of law jut manifestly and fearsomely into existence. . . . For in the exercise of violence over life and death more than in any other legal act, law reaffirms itself. But in this very violence something rotten in law is revealed. . . . Law . . . appears . . . in so ambiguous a moral light that the question poses itself whether there are no other violent means for regulating conflicting human interests. (Benjamin, "Critique," 286–87)[23]

This radical critique of violence is born (Benjamin explains) from the unmatched catastrophe and the unparalleled ideological and technological violence of the First World War: a twentieth-century watershed event that encapsulates the undreamt-of aggression and brutality revealed in the contemporary world. It is precisely this epiphany of violence, which has deceptively paraded as civilization, that it is urgent to unmask, demystify, and bring to trial. After the First World War, it is no longer possible to speak of violence naively.

> If in the last war the critique of military violence was the starting point for a passionate critique of violence in general—which taught at least one thing, *that violence is no longer exercised or tolerated* naively—nevertheless violence was not only subject to criticism for its lawmaking character, but was also judged, perhaps more annihilatingly, for another of its functions. For a duality in

the function of violence is characteristic of militarism, which could only come into being through general conscription. Militarism is the compulsory, universal use of violence to the ends of the state. . . . For the subordination of citizens to laws—in the present case, to the law of general conscription—is a legal end. If that first function of violence [militarism] is called the lawmaking function, this second [conscription] will be called the law-preserving function. Since conscription is a case of law-preserving violence . . . a really effective critique of it is far less easy than the declamations of pacifists and activists suggest. Rather, such a critique coincides with the *critique of all legal violence*—that is, with the critique of legal or executive force—and cannot be performed by any lesser program. ("Critique," 284, emphasis mine)

Violence is lawmaking when it institutes itself as law and creates new legal norms and new prescriptive standards. Such, for instance, was the case of the precedent-setting court of the victorious at Nuremberg:[24] it was the violence of victory that enabled the Nuremberg proceedings to take place and enabled the victorious Western Allies (and their tribunal) to set up a groundbreaking legal precedent and institute for the whole legal future: the new justiciability and the new jurisprudential concept of "crimes against humanity." When violence is not at the origin of legitimation as lawmaking (when it does not institute a new law that legitimates it ex post facto), it is legitimated as law—preserving, it is in the service of a preexisting law. Such, as Benjamin points out, is the case of the institution of compulsory conscription in the First World War, or, to take a more extreme and more obvious example, the case of the Nazi violence deployed in the service of the Nuremberg laws. "All violence as a means is either lawmaking or law-preserving. If it lays claim to neither of these predicates, it forfeits all validity. It follows, however, that all violence as a means, even in the most favorable case, is implicated in the problematic nature of law itself" ("Critique," 287).

On Judgment Day, *the law will therefore judge the law*: the Western law (the International Military Tribunal) will judge the Nazi law; the Russian law will judge the Soviet law, and will free, amnesty, and rehabilitate the victims of the Moscow trials. In this respect, the most characteristic trial of history is the third of the Nuremberg trials, the so-called Justice Case, in which the Nazi judges (and civil servants) were put on trial and convicted.

Law itself is therefore both redemptive and oppressive, and so is in potential every trial. Every trial can be both at the same time, or it can be rather the one or the other. Benjamin's concern for justice derives precisely from this contradiction—from this suspension between redemption and oppression—inherent in the very nature of the law. It is because redemption is impossible that there is a demand for justice and an imperative of justice. One longs for justice and one hopes in legal justice because the only secular redemption comes from the law.[25] Yet the law offers no ultimate redemption and no final day of judgment.[26] "Justice," writes Levinas, "is always a revision of justice and the expectation of a better justice."[27] Judgment Day is both concrete (particular, political, historical) and doomed to remain historically, eternally deferred.

III

Justice, Death, Silence, and the Unappropriated

When Benjamin claimed justice for the dead, he did not yet foresee himself as dead. Or did he? Did he know that he himself would one day be a victim of the violence of history exhibiting its mad injustices as law? Did he already know that, under such circumstances, he would rather take his own life than submit to the delusions and the distortions of such history? When this book will in its turn—after Benjamin—claim justice for the dead, it will claim it quite concretely first of all for Walter Benjamin himself: for the *private story* of his life and of his death, and for the *public story*—henceforth the collective legacy—of his reflective and imaginative work. To do justice to Benjamin, however, it will talk about his silence.

While Benjamin's philosophy of history incorporates a vision of redemptive justice that, in bringing the "expressionless" into expression, will recover and restore the missing, silenced history of the oppressed and of the disenfranchised, the life of Benjamin as an oppressed and disenfranchised German-Jewish refugee encapsulates, in contrast, a drama of *distorted justice* very similar (in its precise factual details) to the realities of Kafka's trial. If Kafka's apparently fantastic novel in effect prophetically depicts the future legal tragedy of Walter Benjamin and the array of possible and actual totalitarian *perversions* of the law, could it be said that Kafka's trial is, indeed—above all legal tri-als—the ultimate trial of the century (the one that truly puts the cen-tury on trial)? Like K. in Kafka's trial, Benjamin is harassed by the law. Like K., he is finally silenced by legal means. Indeed, the drama of his final fall to silence illustrates, in contrast to his hopes, at once the failure of civilization to redeem the silenced and the silencing capacity of law itself in its potential (and in its totalitarian reality) as civiliza-tion's most pernicious and most brutal tool of violence. Like K., in Kaf-ka's trial, Benjamin ends up being himself a murdered victim of a persecutory culture that masquerades itself as trial and of a law that masquerades its crimes as questions of procedural legalities and legal technicalities.

"On September 26, 1940," writes Hannah Arendt, "Walter Benjamin, who was about to emigrate to America, took his life at the Franco-Spanish border":

> There were various reasons for this. The Gestapo had confiscated his Paris apartment, which contained his library . . . and many of his manuscripts. . . . Besides, nothing drew him to America, where, as he used to say, people would probably find no other use for him than to cart him up and down the country to exhibit him as "the last European." But the immediate occasion for Benjamin's sui-cide was an uncommon stroke of bad luck. Through the armistice agreement between Vichy France and the Third Reich, refugees from Hitler Germany . . . were in danger of being shipped back to Germany. . . . To save this category of refugees . . . the United States had distributed a certain number of emergency visas through its consulates in unoccupied Europe. . . . Benjamin was among the first to receive such a visa in Marseilles. Also, he quickly obtained a Spanish transit visa to enable him to get to Lisbon and board a ship there. However, he did not have a French exit visa . . . which the French government, eager to please the Gestapo, invariably denied the German refugees. In general this presented no great difficulty, since a relatively short and none too arduous road to be covered by foot over the mountains to Port Bou was well known and was not guarded by the French border police. Still, for Benja-min apparently suffering from a cardiac condition . . . even the shortest walk was a great exertion, and he must have arrived in a state of serious exhaustion. The small group of refugees that he

had joined reached the Spanish border town only to learn that Spain had closed the border that same day and that the border officials did not honor visas made out in Marseilles. The refugees were supposed to return to France by the same route the next day. During the night Benjamin took his life, whereupon the border officials, upon whom this suicide had made an impression, allowed his companions to proceed to Portugal. A few weeks later the embargo on visas was lifted again. One day earlier Benjamin would have got through without any trouble; one day later the people in Marseilles would have known that for the time being it was impossible to pass through Spain. Only on that particular day was the catastrophe possible.[28]

"Before the Law," writes Kafka, "stands a doorkeeper. To this doorkeeper there comes a man from the country who begs for admittance to the Law."

But the doorkeeper says that he cannot admit the man at the moment. The man, on reflection, asks if he will be allowed, then, to enter later. "It is possible," answers the doorkeeper, "but not at this moment." Since the door leading into the Law stands open as usual and the doorkeeper steps to one side, the man bends down to peer through the entrance. When the doorkeeper sees that, he laughs and says: "If you are so strongly tempted, try to get in without my permission. But note that I am powerful . . . this door was intended for you, and I am now going to shut it."[29]

The truth of Benjamin's life as a harassed German-Jewish refugee, as a running, stateless person, as an illegal border crosser, and as a would-be immigrant to the free world is the truth of Kafka's trial. Like K., Benjamin "has actually become a mute figure in the shape of the accused man, a figure (Benjamin insists) of the most striking intensity."[30] Like K., Benjamin is fundamentally and radically *a subject under a regime on trial.*

But in this era in which law becomes culture's most blatant tool of violence, in this totalitarian world of the Nuremberg laws and of the Moscow trials, Benjamin (like K. and unlike K.) does not even stand trial. He simply is excluded from the Law. He merely does not have an exit visa from the country (France) into which he fled from Nazi Germany and in which he took unwelcome refuge as a stateless, segregated, disenfranchised, and interned German refugee. Like K., Benjamin dies at the hands of officials, of representatives of the law: in the (Spanish) policemen that arrest him for his missing exit visa (from Occupied France), Benjamin confronts, like K., the guardians of procedures and the guardians of boundaries, the gatekeepers that deny admittance and forbid entrance to the Law. Benjamin's last moments, therefore, strikingly and eerily resemble K.'s last moments.

After an exchange of courteous formalities regarding which of them was to take precedence in the next task—these emissaries seemed to have been given no specific assignment in the charge laid jointly upon them. . . . The two of them laid K. down on the ground, propped him against the boulder, and settled his head upon it. But in spite of the pains they took and all the willingness K. showed, his posture remained contored and unnatural-looking . . . Once more, the odious courtesies began, the first handed the knife across K. to the second, who now handed it across K. back again to the first. *K. now perceived clearly that he was supposed to seize the knife himself, as it traveled from hand to hand above him, and plunge it into his own breast. . . . He could not completely rise to the occasion, he could not relieve the officials of their tasks. . . .* His glance fell on the top story of the house. . . . With a flicker of a light going up, the casements of a window there flew open; a human figure, faint and insubstantial at that distance and that height, leaned abruptly far forward and stretched both arms still farther. Who was it? A friend? A good man? Someone who sympathized? Someone who wanted help? Was it one person only? Or was it mankind? Was help at hand? Were there arguments in his favor that had been overlooked? Of course there must be. Logic is doubtless unshakeable, but it cannot withstand a man who wants to go on living. Where was the Judge whom he had never seen? Where was the high Court, to which he had never penetrated? He raised his hands and spread out his fingers.

But the hands of one of the partners were already at K.'s throat, while the other thrust the knife deep into his breast and turned it there twice. With failing eyes K. could still see the two of them immediately before him . . . watching the final act. "Like a dog!" he said; it was as if the shame of it must outlive him.[31]

There is, however, one essential difference between Benjamin and K.: K. submits himself to the "procedure" and collaborates with it. Benjamin, in contrast, makes good on what K. would like to do but fails to do: he dies by his own hand, he "relieves the officials of their tasks." He *sentences himself* to death in order to avoid precisely the execution of the verdict by officials — the (Nazi) officials of the era. In K. there is indeed a hidden element of *identification* with the law, and *with officials* — an element, thus, of collaboration with the executioners. It is precisely this "cooperation" between the victim and the executioner that Hannah Arendt will define years later, on the occasion of the Eichmann trial, as "the totality of the moral collapse the Nazis caused in respectable European society, not only in Germany but in almost all countries, not only among the persecutors but also among the victims."[32] K. knows that his murder by the law constitutes "a shame" that "will outlive him," but the shame is also his *distortion* — his "contortion" — by the law.[33] Benjamin says *no* to the distortion. He will not let history as violence appropriate him and appropriate his death. He will die not at the hands of others — of the officials of the law — but rather at his own hands. He will fall silent by his own decision.

Silence, Benjamin knows well, is the essence of oppression and traumatization, but it is also something that escapes (resists) the master. This mute refusal of cooperation (and of identification) with the master — this mute resistance to his own appropriation by the (fascist) forces of historical distortion — is the ultimate significance of Benjamin's own self-inflicted death. This death (to borrow words from Levinas) is "a breach made by the human in the barbarism of being."[34] Benjamin creates this *breach*. He will not let history erase his final cry for justice, even if this cry must be "expressionless" and must remain forever a mute cry. Silenced by law, he will not let history appropriate the *meaning* of his silence.

"Conversation," Benjamin always remembered, "strives toward silence, and the listener is really the silent partner. The speaker receives meaning from him; the silent one is the unappropriated source of meaning."[35]

Through his choice of death and through his self-inflicted fall to silence, Benjamin remains, like justice, an unappropriated source of meaning. His life becomes a parable of the relation between history and silence.

Part Two: Benjamin's Silence

Nothing more desolating than his acolytes, nothing more godforsaken than his adversaries. No name that would be more fittingly honored by silence. — WALTER BENJAMIN, "Monument to a Warrior," *One-Way Street*

Expect from me no word of my own. Nor should I be capable of saying anything new; for in the room where someone writes the noise is so great. . . . Let him who has something to say step forward and be silent! — KARL KRAUS, cited by Walter Benjamin

I propose now to address—and listen to—that element in Benjamin's own language and writing that specifically, decisively remains beyond appropriation and beyond communication. "In all language and linguistic creations," Benjamin has said, "there remains in addition to what can be conveyed something that cannot be communicated. . . . It is the task of the translator to release in his own language that pure language which is exiled among alien tongues, to liberate the language imprisoned in a work."[36] In Benjamin's own work, in his abbreviated, cryptic style and in the essentially elliptical articulation of his thought, a surcharge of meaning is quite literally "imprisoned" in instances of silence. It is the task of the translator of Benjamin's own work to listen to these instances of silence, whose implications, I will show, are at once stylistic, philosophical, historical, and autobiographical. "Midway between poetry and theory,"[37] my critical amplification of this silence—my own translation of the language that is still imprisoned in Benjamin's work—will thus focus on what Benjamin himself has underscored but what remains unheard, unheeded in the critically repetitive mechanical reproduction of his work: "that element in a translation that goes beyond transmittal of subject-matter."[38]

IV

Wars and Revolutions

Nothing is understood about this man until it has been perceived that, of necessity and without exception, everything—language and fact—falls for

him within the sphere of justice. . . . For him, too, justice and language
remain founded in each other. — WALTER BENJAMIN, "Karl Kraus"

It is customary to view Benjamin essentially as an abstract philosopher, a critic and a thinker of modernity (and/or of postmodernity) in culture and in art. In contradistinction to this dominant approach, I propose now to view Benjamin—far more specifically and more concretely—as a thinker, a philosopher, and a narrator of the wars and revolutions of the twentieth century. "Wars and revolutions," writes Hannah Arendt, "have thus far determined the physiognomy of the twentieth century. And as distinguished from the nineteenth century ideologies—such as nationalism and internationalism, capitalism and imperialism, socialism and communism—which, though still invoked by many as justifying causes, have lost contact with the major realities of our world, war and revolution . . . have outlived all their ideological justifications."[39]

> The seeds of total war developed as early as the First World War, when the distinction between soldiers and civilians was no longer respected because it was inconsistent with the new weapons then used. . . . The magnitude of the violence let loose in the First World War might indeed have been enough to cause revolutions in its aftermath even without any revolutionary tradition and even if no revolution had ever occurred before.
>
> To be sure, not even wars, let alone revolutions, are ever completely determined by violence. Where violence rules absolutely, . . . everything and everybody must fall silent.[40]

In my reading, Walter Benjamin's life's work bears witness to the ways in which events outlive their ideologies and consummate, dissolve, the grounding discourse of their nineteenth-century historic and utopian meanings. Benjamin's texts play out, thus, one against the other and one through the other, both the "constellation that poses the threat of total annihilation through war against the hope for the emancipation of all mankind through revolution,"[41] and the deadly succession of historical convulsions through which culture—in the voice of Benjamin, who is its most profound witness—must fall silent.

Theory and Autobiography

Silence can be either the outside of language or a position inside language, a state of noiselessness or wordlessness. Falling silent is, however, not a state but an event. It is the significance of the event that I will underscore and try to further understand in what will follow. What does it mean that culture—in the voice of its most profound witness—must fall silent? What does it mean for culture? What does it mean for Benjamin? How does Benjamin come to represent and to incorporate concretely, personally, the physiognomy of the twentieth century? And how in turn is this physiognomy reflected, concretized, in Benjamin's own face?

In searching for answers to these questions, I will juxtapose and grasp together theoretical and autobiographical texts. Benjamin's own work includes a singular record of an autobiographical event that, to my mind, is crucial to the author's theories as much as to his destiny (although critics usually neglect it). Benjamin narrates this event in one of his rare moments of personal directness, in the (lyrical) auto-biographical text entitled *A Berlin Chronicle*. I will interpret this event together with, and through, two central theoretical essays that consti-tute the cornerstones of Benjamin's late work: "The Storyteller" and "Theses on the Philosophy of History." In reading the most personal, the most idiosyncratic autobiographical notations through the most far-reaching, groundbreaking theoretical constructions, my effort is to give Benjamin's theory a face.[42] The conceptual question that will over-ride and guide this effort will be: what is the relation between the theory and the event (and what, in general, is the relationship between events and theories)? How does the theory arise out of the concrete drama (and trauma) of an event? How does the concrete drama (and trauma) of an event become theory? And how do both event and theory relate to silence (and to Benjamin's embodiment of silence)?

v

Theories of Silence

Because my sense is that in Benjamin, the theory is (paradoxically) far less obscure than the autobiography, I will start my close reading of Benjamin by addressing first the two theoretical essays—perhaps the best known abstract texts of Benjamin—of which I propose to under-score the *common* theoretical stakes. I will argue that both "The Story-teller" and the "Theses on the Philosophy of History" can be construed as two theories of silence derived from, and related to, the two world wars: "The Storyteller," written in 1936, is retrospectively, explicitly connected with the First World War; "Theses on the Philosophy of History," written shortly before Benjamin's death in 1940, represents his ultimate rethinking of the nature of historical events and of the task of historiography in the face of the developments of the beginning of the Second World War.

I suggest that these two texts are in effect tied up together. I propose to read them one against the other and one through the other, as two stages in a larger philosophical and existential picture, and as two variations of a global Benjaminian theory of wars and silence. I argue therefore that "The Storyteller" and "Theses" can be viewed as two theoretical variations of the same profound underlying text. My methodology is here inspired by the way in which Benjamin himself discusses — in his youth — "Two Poems by Friedrich Hölderlin,"[43] in analyzing in the two texts (as he puts it) "not their likeness which is nonexistent" but their "comparability,"[44] and in treating them — despite their distance — as two "versions" (or two transformations) of the same profound text.

The End of Storytelling

"The Storyteller" is presented as a literary study of the nineteenth-century Russian writer Nikolai Leskov, and of his striking art of storytelling. But the essay's main concern is in depicting storytelling as a *lost art*: the achievements of the nineteenth-century model serve as the background for a differential diagnosis of the ways in which *storytelling is lost to the twentieth century*. Something happened, Benjamin suggests, that has brought about the death — the agony — of storytelling, both as a literary genre and as a discursive mode in daily life. Benjamin announces thus a historical drama of "the end of storytelling" — or an innovative cultural theory of the collapse of narration — as a critical and theoretical appraisal (through Leskov) of a general historical state of affairs.

The theory, thereby, is Benjamin's way of grasping and bringing into consciousness an unconscious cultural phenomenon and an imperceptible historical process that has taken place outside anyone's awareness and that can therefore be deciphered, understood, and noticed only retrospectively, in its effects (its symptoms). The effects, says Benjamin, are that today, quite symptomatically, *it has become impossible to tell a story*. The art of storytelling has been lost along with the ability to share experiences.

Less and less frequently do we encounter people with the ability to tell a tale properly. . . . It is as if something that seemed inalienable to us . . . were taken from us: the ability to exchange experiences.[45]

Among the reasons Benjamin gives for this loss—the rise of capitalism, the sterilization of life through bourgeois values, the decline of craftsmanship, the growing influence of the media and the press—the first and most dramatic is that people have been struck dumb by the First World War. From ravaged battlefields, they have returned mute to a wrecked world in which nothing has remained the same except the sky. This vivid and dramatic explanation is placed right away at the beginning of the text, like an explosive opening argument or an initial shock or blast inflicted on the reader, with whose shock the whole remainder of the text will have to cope and to catch up. The opening is, indeed, as forceful as it is ungraspable. The text itself does not quite process it, nor does it truly integrate it with the arguments that follow. And this ungraspability or unintegratability of the beginning is not a mere coincidence; it duplicates and illustrates the point of the text, that the war has left an impact that has struck dumb its survivors, with the effect of interrupting now the continuity of telling and of understanding. The utterance repeats in act the content of the statement: it must remain somewhat unassimilable.

In Benjamin, however, it is productive to retain what cannot be assimilated. And it is crucially important in my view that what cannot be assimilated crystallizes around a date. Before it can be understood, the loss of narrative is *dated.* Its process is traced back to the collective, massive trauma of the First World War.

With the [First] World War a process began to become apparent which has not halted since then. Was it not noticeable at the end of the war that men returned from the battlefield grown silent— not richer, but poorer in communicable experience? What ten years later was poured out in the flood of war books was anything but experience that goes from mouth to mouth. And there was nothing remarkable about that. For never has experience been contradicted more thoroughly than strategic experience by tactical warfare, economic experience by inflation, bodily experience by mechanical warfare, moral experience by those in power. A generation that had gone to school on a horse-drawn streetcar now stood under the open sky in a countryside in which nothing remained unchanged but the clouds, and beneath these clouds, in a field of force of destructive torrents and explosions, was the tiny, fragile human body. ("St.," 84)

Thus, narration was reduced to silence by the First World War. What has emerged from the destructive torrents—from the noise of the explosions—was only the muteness of the body in its absolutely helpless, shelterless vulnerability. Resonating to this dumbness of the body is the storyteller's dumbness.

But this fall to silence of narration is contrasted with, and covered by, the new loudness, the emerging noise of information—"journalism being clearly . . . the expression of the changed function of language in the world of high capitalism."[46]

In a world in which public discourse is usurped by the commercial aims and by the noise of information, soldiers returning from the First World War can find no social or collective space in which to integrate their death experience. Their trauma must remain a private matter that cannot be symbolized collectively. It cannot be exchanged, it must fall silent.

The Unforgettable

Gone are the days when dying was "a public process in the life of an individual and a most exemplary one" ("St.," 93). Irrespective of the battlefield experience, mortality is self-deceptively denied in sterilized bourgeois life, which strives to keep death out of sight symbolically and literally.[47] Narration was, however, born from the pathos of an ultimate exchange between the dying and the living. Medieval paintings represent the origin of storytelling: they show the archetypal or inaugural site of narration to be the deathbed, in which the dying man (or the original narrator) reviews his life (evokes his memories) and thus addresses the events and lessons of his past to those surrounding him. A dying speaker is a naturally authoritative storyteller: he borrows his authority from death.[48]

Today, however, agonizers die in private and without authority. They are attended by no listeners. They tell no stories. And there is no authority—and certainly no wisdom—that has survived the war. "We have no counsel either for ourselves or for others. After all, counsel is less an answer to a question than a proposal concerning the continuation of a story which is just unfolding" ("St.," 86).

It is not simply that there is no longer a proposal for historical or narrative continuation. The First World War is *the first war that can no longer be narrated*. Its witnesses and its participants have lost their stories. The sole signification that "The Storyteller" can henceforth articulate is that of mankind's double loss: a loss of the capacity to symbolize and a loss of the capacity to moralize.[49]

A Philosophy of History

The outbreak of the Second World War in 1939 (three years after the publication of "The Storyteller") brings Benjamin to write, in 1940—in the months that were to be the last ones of his life—what I have called his second theory of silence, entitled "Theses on the Philosophy of History." At first, this text seems altogether different from "The Storyteller." Its topic is not literature but history, of which the essay offers not a diagnosis but a theory. The theory is programmatic: its tone is not descriptive but prescriptive. The "theses" are audaciously abbreviated and provocatively dogmatized. They do not explicitly reflect on silence. The essay focuses rather on (scholarly and scientific) *discourses* on history. The word *silence* does not figure in the text.

And yet, speechlessness is at the very heart of the reflection, and of the situation, of the writer. Like the storyteller who falls silent or returns mute from the First World War, the historian or the theorist of history facing the conflagration of the Second World War is equally *reduced to speechlessness*: no ready-made conceptual or discursive tool, no discourse about history turns out to be sufficient to explain the nature of this war; no available conceptual framework in which history is customarily perceived proves adequate or satisfactory to understand or to explain current historical developments. Vis-à-vis the undreamt-of events, what is called for, Benjamin suggests, is a *radical displacement of our frames of reference,* a radical transvaluation of our methods and of our philosophies of history. "The current amazement that the things we are experiencing are 'still' possible in the twentieth century is *not* philosophical. This amazement is not the beginning of knowledge—unless it is the knowledge that the view of history which gives rise to it is untenable" (VIII, in Benjamin, *Ill.,* 257).

History is now the property and the propriety of Nazis (of those who can control it and manipulate its discourse). It is by virtue of a loyalty to history that Hitler is proposing to avenge Germany from its defeat and its humiliation in the First World War. All the existing discourses on history have proven ineffective either to predict or to counteract the regime and the phenomenon of Hitler.[50]

History in Nazi Germany is fascist. Fascism legitimates itself in the name of national identity on the basis of a unity and of a continuity of history. The philosophical tenets of this view are inherited from nineteenth-century historicism, which has equated temporality with progress, in presupposing time as an entity of natural development, progressively enhancing maturation and advancing toward a betterment as time (and history) go by. Benjamin rejects this view, which has become untenable vis-à-vis the traumas of the twentieth century. It is the victor who forever represents the present conquest or the present victory as an improvement in relation to the past. But the reality of history is that of those traumatized by history, the materialist reality of those who are oppressed by the new victory. Historicism is, however, based on an unconscious identification with the discourse of the victor, and thus on an uncritical espousal of the victor's narrative perspective. "If one asks with whom the adherents of historicism actually empathize," Benjamin writes,

> The answer is inevitable: with the victor. . . . Empathy with the victor inevitably benefits the ruler. Historical materialists know what that means. Whoever has emerged victorious participates to this day in the triumphal procession in which the present rulers step over those who are lying prostrate. According to traditional practice, the spoils are carried along in the procession. They are called cultural treasures, and a historical materialist views them with cautious detachment. For without exception the cultural treasures he surveys have an origin which he cannot contemplate without horror. They owe their existence not only to the efforts of the great minds and talents who have created them, but also to the anonymous toil of their contemporaries. There is no document of civilization which is not at the same time a document of barbarism. And just as a document is not free of barbarism, barbarism taints also the manner in which it was transmitted from one owner to another. (VII, *Ill.*, 256)

Historicism is thus based on a perception of history as victory. But it is blind to this presupposition. So blind that it does not see the irony with which this axiom has been borrowed — taken to extremes — by the discourses of fascism. Fascism is, indeed, quite literally, a *philosophy of history as victory*. Unlike historicism, it is not unconscious of this prejudice: it is grounded in a cynical and conscious *claim* of this philosophy of history.[51]

Historicism is thus based on a confusion between truth and power. Real history is, on the contrary, the ineluctable discrepancy between the two.[52] History is the perennial conflictual arena in which collective memory is named as a *constitutive dissociation* between truth and power.

What, then, is the relation between history and silence? In a (conscious or unconscious) historical philosophy of power, the powerless (the persecuted) are constitutionally deprived of voice.

Because official history is based on the perspective of the victor, the voice with which it speaks authoritatively is *deafening:* it makes us unaware of the fact that there remains in history a claim, a discourse, that we *do not hear.* And in relation to this deafening, the rulers of the moment are the heirs of the rulers of the past. History transmits, ironically enough, a legacy of deafness in which historicists unwittingly share. What is called progress, and what Benjamin sees only as a piling of catastrophe upon catastrophe, is therefore the transmission of historical discourse from ruler to ruler, from one historical instance of power to another. This transmission is constitutive of what is (misguidedly) perceived as continuity in history. "The continuum of history is that of the oppressors." "The history of the oppressed is a discontinuum."[53]

If history, despite its spectacular triumphal time, is thus barbarically, constitutively conflict-ridden, the historian is not in possession of a space in which to be removed, detached, "objective"; the philosopher of history cannot be an outsider to the conflict. In the face of the deafening appropriation of historical philosophy by fascism, in the face of the Nazi use of the most *civilized* tools of technology and law for a most barbaric racist persecution, "objectivity" does not exist. A historical articulation proceeds not from an epistemological "detachment" but, on the contrary, from the historian's sense of urgency and of emergency.[54]

The tradition of the oppressed teaches us that the "state of emergency" in which we live is not the exception but the rule. We must attain to a conception of history that is in keeping with this insight. Then we shall clearly realize that it is our task to bring about a real state of emergency, and this will improve our position in the struggle against Fascism. (VIII, *Ill.*, 257)

The theory of history is thus itself an *intervention in the conflict;* it is itself historical. In the middle of a cataclysmic world war that shifts the grounds from under our very feet, danger, Benjamin implies, is what triggers the most lucid and the most clairvoyant *grasp* of history. Historical insight strikes surprisingly and unexpectedly in "moments of sudden illumination" in which "we are beside ourselves."[55] Danger and emergency illuminate themselves as the conditions both of history (of life) and of its theory (its knowledge). New, innovative theories of history (such that enable a displacement of official history) come into being only under duress.

To articulate the past historically does not mean to recognize it "the way it really was" (Ranke). It means to seize hold of a memory as it flashes up at a moment of danger. Historical materialism wishes to retain that image of the past which unexpectedly appears to man singled out by history at a moment of danger. (VI, *Ill.*, 255)

In Benjamin's own view, history—a line of catastrophe—is not a movement toward progress but a movement toward (what Benjamin calls enigmatically) redemption. Redemption—what historical struggles (and political revolutions) are about—should be understood as both materialist (Marxist, political, interhistorical) and theological (suprahistorical, transcendent). "Redemption" is discontinuity, disruption. It names the constant need to catch up with the hidden reality of history that always remains a debt to the oppressed, a debt to the dead of history, a claim the past has on the present.

Redemption is the allegory of a future state of freedom, justice, happiness, and recovery of meaning. History should be assessed only *in reference* to this state, which is its goal. Historical action should take place as though this goal were not utopian but pragmatic. Yet it can never be decided by a mortal if redemption, ultimately, can be immanent to history or if it is doomed to remain transcendental, beyond history. "This world," Benjamin has written elsewhere, "remains a mute world, from which music will never ring out. Yet to what is it dedicated if not redemption?"[56]

Dedicated to Redemption

When, therefore, will redemption come? Will there be a redemption after the Second World War? Will there ever be redemption *from* the Second World War? Benjamin foresees the task of the historian of the future.

> He will be sad. His history will be the product of his sadness.
>
> Flaubert [Benjamin writes], who was familiar with [the cause of sadness], wrote: "*Peu de gens devineront combien il a fallu être triste pour ressusciter Carthage*" [Few will be able to guess how sad one had to be in order to resuscitate Carthage]. (VII, *Ill.*, 256)

Before the fact, Benjamin foresees that history will know a holocaust. After the war, the historian's task will be not only to "resuscitate Carthage" or to *narrate extermination* but, paradoxically, to *save the dead:*

> Nothing that has ever happened should be regarded as lost to history. (III, *Ill.*, 254)
>
> Only that historian will have the gift of fanning the spark of hope in the past who is firmly convinced that *even the dead* will not be safe from the enemy if he wins. (VI, *Ill.*, 255; Benjamin's italics)

Thus, the historian of the Second World War will be sad. Beyond sadness, he will have to be intently vigilant. In this war, particularly, the conceptual question of the historian's identification with the victor inadvertently evolves into a graver, far more serious question of political complicity.

The task of the historian of today is to *avoid collaboration* with a criminal regime and with the discourses of fascism. Similarly, the historian of tomorrow will have to be watchful to avoid complicity with history's barbarism and with culture's latent (and now patent) crimes. Benjamin's text, I argue, is the beginning of the critical awareness of the treacherous questions of collaboration that so obsessively preoccupy us to this day. It is still early in the war. Benjamin intuitively senses the importance of this question, as it will arise precisely, later, *out of* the Second World War. The historian, Benjamin suggests, must be revolutionary lest he be unwittingly complicit. And complicity, for Benjamin, is a graver danger, a worse punishment than death.

> Historical materialism wishes to retain the image of the past which unexpectedly appears to man singled out by history at a moment of danger. The danger affects both the content of the tradition and its receivers. The same threat hangs over both: that of becoming a tool of the ruling classes. In every era the attempt must be made to wrest tradition away from a conformism that is about to overpower it. (VI, *Ill.*, 255)

The historian, paradoxically, has no choice but to be a revolutionary if he does not want to be a collaborator.[57]

History and Speechlessness

Benjamin advances, thus, a theory of history as trauma—and a correlative theory of the historical conversion of trauma into insight. History consists in chains of traumatic interruptions rather than in sequences of rational causalities. But the traumatized—the subjects of history—are deprived of a language in which to speak of their victimization. The relation between history and trauma is speechless. Traditional theories of history tend to neglect this speechlessness of trauma: by definition, speechlessness is what remains out of the record. But it is specifically to this speechless connection between history and trauma that Benjamin's own theory of history intends now to give voice.

He does so by showing how the very discipline, the very "concept of history"[58] is constituted by what it excludes (and fails to grasp). History (to sum up) is thus inhabited by a historical unconscious related to—and founded on—a double silence: the silence of "the tradition of the oppressed," who are by definition deprived of voice and whose story (or whose narrative perspective) is always systematically reduced to silence; and the silence of official history—the victor's history—with respect to the tradition of the oppressed. According to Benjamin, the hidden theoretical centrality of this double silence defines historiography as such. This in general is the way in which history is told, or rather, this is in general the way in which history is silenced. The triumph of fascism and the outbreak of the Second World War constitute only the most climactic demonstration, the most aberrant materialization or realization of this historiography.

Whereas the task of the philosopher of history is thus to take apart "the concept of history" by showing its deceptive continuity to be in fact a process of silencing, the task of the historian is to reconstruct what history has silenced, to give voice to the dead and to the vanquished and to resuscitate the unrecorded, silenced, hidden story of the oppressed.

PART 6 | Beyond the Law

SHOSHANA FELMAN

12 | A Ghost in the House of Justice: Death and the Language of the Law

> *Justice requires and establishes the state. . . . But justice itself cannot make us forget the origin of the right or the uniqueness of the other, henceforth covered over by the particularity and the generality of the human. It cannot abandon that uniqueness to political history, which is engaged in the determinism of powers, reasons of state, totalitarian temptations and complacencies. It awaits the voices that will recall, to the judgments of the judges and statesmen, the human face.* — EMMANUEL LEVINAS, "Uniqueness"

A witness faints on the stand during the Eichmann trial. This chapter will explore the meaning of this unexpected legal moment, and will ask: is this witness's collapse relevant—and if so, in what sense—to the legal framework of the trial? How does this courtroom event affect the trial's definition of legal meaning in the wake of the Holocaust? Under what circumstances and in what ways can the legal default of a witness constitute a legal testimony in its own right?

I will present, first, Hannah Arendt's reading of this episode (in *Eichmann in Jerusalem*), and will then contrast her reading with my own interpretation of this courtroom scene. Next I will analyze the judges' reference to this scene in their opinion. I will return in the end to Walter Benjamin, with whom this book began, who will become relevant again at once as part of Arendt's story (as a subtext of Arendt's text: a hidden presence in *Eichmann in Jerusalem*) and as a guide for my own reading of the trial.

These different and successive analytical and textual vantage points will be systematically and commonly subordinated to the following three overriding theoretical inquiries:

1. What is the role of human fallibility in trials?
2. Can moments of disruption of convention and of discourse—moments of unpredictability that take the legal institution by surprise—nevertheless contribute to the formulation of a legal meaning?
3. How can such moments shed light on (what I set out to highlight as) the key structural relation between law and trauma? What tools does the law have—and what are the law's limits—in adjudicating massive death and in articulating legal meaning out of massive trauma?

Part One: Death and the Language of the Law

I

Two Visions of Historic Trial

In the postwar trials that attempted to judge history and to resolve the horrors of administrative massacre in the wake of the unprecedented trauma of the Second World War, two antithetic legal visions of historic trials have emerged: that of the Nuremberg trials in 1945–46, and that of the Eichmann trial in 1961. The difference between these two paradigms of historic trial derived from their divergent evidentiary approach: the Nuremberg prosecution made a decision to shun witnesses and base the case against the Nazi leaders exclusively on the documents, whereas the prosecution in the Eichmann trial chose to rely extensively on witnesses as well as documents to substantiate its case. While both prosecutors similarly used the trial to establish what in Nietzsche's term can be called a "monumental [legal] history,"[1] Nuremberg was a monumental testimonial case (despite its equally substantial use of documents). In 1954, the chief prosecutor and the architect of Nuremberg, Justice Robert Jackson, retrospectively explained the grounds for his choice of proof:

The prosecution early was confronted with two vital decisions. . . . One was whether chiefly to rely upon living witnesses or upon documents for proof of the case. The decision . . . was to use and rest on documentary evidence to prove every point possible. The argument against this was that documents are dull, the press would not report them, the trial would become wearisome and would not get across to the people. There was much truth to this position, I must admit. But it seemed to me that witnesses, many of them persecuted and hostile to the Nazis, would always be chargeable with bias, faulty recollection, and even perjury. The documents could not be accused of partiality, forgetfulness, or invention, and would make the sounder foundation, not only for the immediate guidance of the tribunal, but for the ultimate verdict of history. The result was that the tribunal declared, in its judgment, "the case, therefore, against the defendants rests in a large measure on documents of their own making."[2]

Fragile Evidence

The documentary approach matched the bureaucracy of the Nazi regime and was particularly suitable to the exposure of the monstrous bureaucratic nature of the crime and of its alibis. The testimonial approach was necessary for the full disclosure of the thought-defying magnitude of the offense against the victims, and was particularly suitable to the valorization of the victims' narrative perspective.

The reason he decided to add living witnesses to documents, the Israeli prosecutor Gideon Hausner in his turn explained, was that the Nuremberg trials had *failed to transmit*,[3] or to impress on human memory and "on the hearts of men," the knowledge and the shock of what happened. The Eichmann trial sought, in contrast, not only to establish facts but to transmit (transmit truth as event and as the shock of an *encounter* with events, transmit history as an experience). The tool of law was used not only as a tool of *proof* of unimaginable facts but, above all, as a compelling *medium of transmission* — as an effective tool of national and international *communication* of these thought-defying facts. In comparing thus the evidentiary approach of Nuremberg to his own legal choices, the Israeli prosecutor wrote:

There is an obvious advantage in written proof; whatever it has to convey is there in black and white. . . . Nor can a document be . . . broken down in cross-examination. It speaks in a steady voice; it may not cry out, but neither can it be silenced. . . .

This was the course adopted at the Nuremberg trials. . . . It was . . . efficient. . . . But it was also one of the reasons why the proceedings there failed to reach the hearts of men.

In order merely to secure a conviction, it was obviously enough to let the archives speak. . . . But I knew we needed more than a conviction; we needed a living record of a gigantic human and national disaster. . . .

In any criminal proceedings the proof of guilt and the imposition of a penalty, though all-important, are not the exclusive objects. Every trial also . . . tells a story. . . . Our perceptions and our senses are geared to limited experiences. . . . We stop perceiving living creatures behind the mounting totals of victims; they turn into incomprehensible statistics.

It was beyond human powers to present the calamity in a way that would do justice to six million tragedies. The only way to concretize it was to call surviving witnesses, as many as the framework of the trial would allow, and to ask each of them to tell a tiny fragment of what he had seen and experienced. . . . Put together, the various narratives of different people would be concrete enough to be apprehended. In this way I hoped to superimpose on a phantom a dimension of reality.[4]

Because of the difference in their evidentiary approach, the Nuremberg trials made a more solid contribution to international law, in setting up a blind legal precedent of "crimes against humanity"; the Eichmann trial made a greater impact on collective memory. The two trials dramatize the difference between human and nonhuman evidence. Jackson desires to exclude human vulnerability both from the process of the law and from the exercise of judgment. He thus protects the courtroom from the death it talks about. Because Jackson wants his legal evidence to be literally invulnerable, he has to give preference to nonhuman and nonliving evidence. "The documents could not be accused of partiality, forgetfulness, or invention." "Witnesses," on the other hand, "many of them persecuted," "would always be chargeable with bias, faulty recollection, and even perjury."

In choosing, on the contrary, to include as evidence the previously excluded, fragile testimony of the persecuted, the Eichmann trial quite specifically gives legal space to the potential legal failings and shortcomings Jackson fears. It consciously *embraces* the vulnerability, the legal fallibility, and the fragility of the human witness. It is precisely the witness's fragility that paradoxically is called upon to testify and to bear witness.[5]

An Oath to the Dear (A Pseudonym)

Nowhere was this fragile essence of the human testimony more dramatically exemplified and more acutely tested than when, in one of the most breathtaking moments of the trial, a witness fainted on the stand.

He was called to testify because he was a crucially relevant eyewitness: he had met Eichmann in Auschwitz.[6] But he collapsed before he could narrate this factual encounter. His testimony thus amounted to a legal failure, the kind of legal failure Jackson feared. And yet this legal moment of surprise, captured on film,[7] left an indelible mark on the trial and has impressed itself on visual and historic memory. This courtroom scene has since been broadcast many times on radio and television. Despite the repetition, the power of this legally compelling moment does not wane, and its force of astonishment does not diminish and does not fade. It has remained a literally unforgettable key moment of the trial, a signal or a symbol of a constantly replayed and yet ungrasped, ungraspable kernel of collective memory.[8] I propose to try to probe here the significance of this mysteriously material kernel.

Who was this witness? He happened to be a writer. He was known under the pseudonym Ka-Tzetnik (K-Zetnik).[9] He saw himself as a messenger of the dead, a bearer of historical meaning he had the duty to preserve and to transmit. K-Zetnik is a slang word meaning a concentration camp inmate, one identified not by name but by the number the Nazis tattooed on each inmate's arm. "I must carry this name," K-Zetnik testified during the Eichmann trial, "as long as the world will not awaken after the crucifying of the nation . . . as humanity has risen after the crucifixion of one man."[10] K-Zetnik had published, prior to the Eichmann trial, several books that were translated into many languages and that had gained a celebrity on both sides of the Atlantic. Describing human existence in the extermination camps, they were all published as the successive volumes of what the author calls "the Chronicle of a Jewish Family in the Twentieth Century." The name K-Zetnik was selected almost automatically. The author began writing soon after he was liberated from Auschwitz, in a British army hospital in Italy. He asked the Israeli soldier who was taking care of him to bring him pen and paper: he had made an oath to the dead, he said, to be their voice and to chronicle their story; since he felt his days were numbered, he had to hurry up; from the beginning his writing was racing against death. For two and a half weeks he hardly got up, writing in one fit his first book. He asked the soldier who was taking care of him to transfer the finished manuscript to Israel. Reading the title "Salamandra" on the first page, the soldier whispered: "You forgot to write the name of the author." "The name of the author?" the surviving writer cried out in reply: "They who went to the crematories wrote this book; write their name: Ka-Tzetnik."[11] Thus the soldier added in his handwriting the name that soon was to acquire world fame.

II

The Collapse

"What is your full name?" asked the presiding judge.[12]

"Yehiel Dinoor,"[13] answered the witness. The prosecutor then proceeded.

"What is the reason that you took the pen name K-Zetnik, Mr. Dinoor?"

"It is not a pen name," the witness (now seated) began answering. "I do not regard myself as a writer who writes literature.

"This is a chronicle from the planet Auschwitz. I was there for about two years. Time there was different from what it is here on earth. Every split second ran on a different cycle of time. And the inhabitants of that planet had no names. They had neither parents nor children. They did not dress as we dress here. They were not born there nor did anyone give birth. Even their breathing was regulated by the laws of another nature. They did not live, nor did they die, in accordance with the laws of this world. Their names were the numbers 'K-Zetnik so and so.' . . . They left me, they kept leaving me, left . . . for close to two years they left me and always left me behind. . . . I see them, they are watching me, I see them—"

At this point, the prosecutor gently interrupted: "Mr. Dinoor, could I perhaps put a few questions to you if you will consent?"

But Dinoor continued speaking in a hollow and tense voice, oblivious to the courtroom setting, as a man plunged in hallucination or in a hypnotic trance. "I see them. . . . I saw them standing in the line. . . ."

Thereupon the presiding judge matter-of-factly intervened: "Mr. Dinoor, please, please listen to Mr. Hausner; wait a minute, now you listen to me!"

The haggard witness vacantly got up and without warning collapsed into a faint, slumping to the floor beside the witness stand.

Policemen ran toward Dinoor to lift his collapsed body, to support him and to carry him out of the courtroom.[14] The flabbergasted audience remained motionless, staring in disbelief. "Quiet, quiet, quiet!" ordered the presiding judge: "I am asking for silence." A woman's cry was heard from the direction of the audience. A woman wearing sunglasses was coming from the audience toward the unconscious human body held by the policemen, saying she was the witness's wife. "You may approach," the bench conceded. "I do not believe that we can go on." The witness was still limp and lifeless, plunged in a deep coma. "We shall take a recess now," declared the presiding judge. "Beth Hamishpat" ("the House of Justice") shouted the usher, as the audience rose to its feet and the three judges in their black robes were going out. An ambulance was called and rushed the witness to the hospital, where he spent two weeks between life and death in a paralytic stroke. In time he would recover.

The Legal Versus the Poetical

The Israeli poet Haim Gouri, who covered the trial, wrote:

> What happened here was the inevitable. [K-Zetnik's] desperate attempt to transgress the legal channel and to return to the planet of the ashes in order to bring it to us was too terrifying an experience for him. He broke down.
>
> Others spoke here for days and days, and told us each his story from the bottom up. . . . He tried to depart from the quintessential generalization, tried to define, like a meteor, the essence of that world. He tried to find the shortest way between the two planets among which his life had passed. . . .
>
> Or maybe he caught a glimpse of Eichmann all of a sudden and his soul was short-circuited into darkness, all the lights going out. . . .
>
> *In a way he has said everything.* Whatever he was going to say later was, it turns out, superfluous detail.[15]

This empathetic description, which took the testimony on its terms and which, examining it from the vantage point of its own metaphors, poetically reflected back the shock and the emotion of the audience, was a poet's coverage of a fellow poet's testimony. The legal coverage of this episode that Hannah Arendt sent to the *New Yorker* and later published in *Eichmann in Jerusalem* was much harsher and much less forgiving.

Arendt disputed fundamentally the way in which the prosecution framed the trial, in narratively focusing it on the victims. The state sought to narrate a unique legal story that had never before been told and that had failed to be articulated by the Nuremberg trials. To do so, it sought to reconstruct the facts of the Nazi war against the Jews from the victims' point of view and to establish for the first time in legal history a "monumental history" not of the victors but of the victims. But Arendt argued that the trial should be focused on the criminal, not on the victim; she wanted it to be a cosmopolitan trial rather than a Jewish nationalist one; she wanted it to tell the story of the Jewish tragedy and of the crime against the Jewish people. She thus felt impelled to fight Jewish self-centeredness on every point (and on every legal point), and systematically to deconstruct and to decenter the prosecution's monumentalizing victim narrative. In her role as legal reporter for the *New Yorker,* Arendt finds a stage for exercising her ironic talents not only to dispute the story of the prosecution but to narrate a contrapuntal legal narrative and to become in turn an ironic or a *contrapuntal prosecutor*—a prosecutor or (in Nietzsche's terms) a critical historian of the monumental trial.[16]

When she was first confronted with the Nazi crimes during the Nuremberg trials, Arendt believed the magnitude of the phenomenon and the abyss it opened in perception could not be apprehended by the law, except in rupturing its legal framework. She thus wrote in 1946 to Karl Jaspers, her ex-teacher and the continued German friend and interlocutor whom she refound at the end of the war and through whose sole agency she has now reconnected with her own disrupted German youth:

> Your definition of Nazi policy as a crime ("criminal guilt")[17] strikes me as questionable. The Nazi crimes, it seems to me, *explode the limits of the law;* and that is precisely what constitutes their monstrousness. For these crimes, no punishment is severe enough. . . .

That is, this guilt, in contrast to all criminal guilt, oversteps and shatters any and all legal systems. That is the reason why the Nazis in Nuremberg are so smug. . . . And just as inhuman as their guilt is the innocence of the victims. Human beings simply can't be as innocent as they all were in the face of the gas chambers (the most repulsive usurer was as innocent as a newborn child because no crime on a human, political level, compared with a guilt that is beyond crime and an innocence that is beyond goodness or virtue). This is *the abyss* that opened up before us as early as 1933 . . . and into which we have finally stumbled. I don't know how we will ever get out of it, for the Germans are burdened now with . . . hundreds of thousands of people who cannot be adequately punished within the legal system; and we Jews are burdened with millions of innocents, by reason of which every Jew alive today can see himself as innocence personified.[18]

Jaspers does not agree with Arendt. Her attitude, he says, is *too poetical.* But poetry, he emphasizes, is a much more inadequate, a much less sober tool of apprehension than the law. Poetry by definition is misguided because, by its very nature, it is made to *miss the banality* of the phenomenon. And the banality, in Jasper's eyes, is the constitutive feature of the Nazi horror, a feature that should not be mystified or mythified.

You say that what the Nazis did cannot be comprehended as "crime"—I'm not altogether comfortable with your view, because a guilt that goes beyond all criminal guilt inevitably takes on a streak of "greatness"—of satanic greatness—which is, for me, as inappropriate for the Nazis as all the talk about the "demonic" element in *banality,* in their prosaic triviality, because that's what truly characterizes them. . . . I regard any hint of myth and legend with horror. . . . Your view is appealing—especially as contrasted with what I see as the false inhuman innocence of the victims. But all this would have to be expressed differently. . . . The way you express it, *you've almost taken the path of poetry.* And a Shakespeare would never be able to give adequate form to this material—his instinctive aesthetic sense would lead to falsification of it. . . . There is no idea and no essence here. Nazi crime is properly a subject for psychology and sociology, for psychopathology and jurisprudence only.[19]

From its inception, the future concept of the "banality of evil" emerges as a concept that defines itself by its methodological invalidation of the "the path of poetry," and the sobering path of the law (and of the social sciences). "I found what you say about my thoughts on 'beyond crime and innocence' half convincing," Arendt replies at first ambivalently, but she concedes: "We have to combat all impulses to mythologize the horrible."[20]

When the Eichmann trial is announced fifteen years later, Jaspers and Arendt switch positions. Jaspers maintains that Israel should not try Eichmann, because Eichmann's guilt—the subject of the trial—is "larger than law."[21] Arendt insists that only law can deal with it: "We have no tools to hand except legal ones," she says.[22] By now, the tool of law is in her hands, par excellence, *a tool of apprehension of banality,* a tool specifically of *demythologization* and of deliberate, sobering reduction. And if the perpetrator must be banalized and demythologized to be understood in his proper light, so does the victim. No longer can the victim's innocence be allowed to burst the legal frame or to explode the tool of law. No longer can the victim be spared the banality of innocence.

III

Arendt's Contrapuntal Tale

Arendt reserves some of her harshest language and some of her fiercest irony in *Eichmann in Jerusalem* for the description of K-Zetnik's unsuccessful court appearance. Indeed, nowhere is Arendt's role as contrapuntal, critical historian of the trial more clearly and more blatantly expressed than in her narration of this episode. Arendt views K-Zetnik's failure on the stand as symptomatic of the general misfire of the trial. She blames this general misfire on the misdirections and the blunders of the prosecution, whose witness has symbolically defaulted through its own fault.

Generally, Arendt makes three objections to the prosecution's choice of witnesses:

1. Contrary to legal rules of evidence, the witnesses are not selected for their relevance to Eichmann's acts but for the purposes of the depiction of a larger picture of the Nazi persecution of the Jews. "This

case"—writes Arendt disapprovingly—"was built on what the Jews had suffered, not on what Eichmann had done" (EiJ, 6). This depiction by the victims of the persecution they had suffered and their reconstruction of the global history of their victimization is irrelevant in Arendt's eyes. K-Zetnik as a witness seems to Arendt to exemplify the witnesses' irrelevance.

2. Contrary to Arendt's judgment and to her taste, the prosecution prefers witnesses of prominence. It has a predilection, in particular, for famous writers, such as K-Zetnik and Abba Kovner. The former's testimony was a fiasco. The latter, Arendt caustically notes, "had not so much testified as addressed an audience with the ease of someone who is used to speaking in public and resents interruptions from the floor" (EiJ, 230). In Arendt's eyes, a witness's fame is a corrupting element of the judicial process. The writer's professional articulateness compromises the truth of the testimony in turning testimonies into speeches. Such is K-Zetnik's case.

3. The prosecution's choice of witnesses is guided—Arendt charges— by theatrical considerations. The witnesses are called for the sensational effects provided by their "tales of horror." K-Zetnik's breakdown is an accidental yet consistent illustration of this logic that transforms testimony into a theatrical event that parasitizes the trial.

> At no time [Arendt writes] is there anything theatrical in the conduct of the judges. . . . Judge Landau . . . is doing his best, his very best to prevent this trial from becoming a show trial under the influence of the prosecutor's love of showmanship. Among the reasons he cannot always succeed is the simple fact that the proceedings happen on a stage before an audience, with the usher's marvelous shout at the beginning of each session producing the effect of the rising curtain. Whoever planned this auditorium . . . had a theater in mind. . . . Clearly, this courtroom is not a bad place for the show-trial David Ben Gurion, Prime Minister of Israel, had in mind when he decided to have Eichmann kidnapped in Argentina and brought to the district court of Jerusalem to stand trial for his role in "the final solution to the Jewish question. . . ."
>
> Yet no matter how consistently the judges shunned the limelight, there they were, seated at the top of the raised platform, facing the audience as from the stage in a play. . . . The audience

was supposed to represent the whole world. . . . They were to watch a spectacle as sensational as the Nuremberg Trials, only this time "the tragedy of Jewry as a whole was to be the central concern . . ."

It was precisely the play aspect of the trial that collapsed under the weight of the hair-raising atrocities. . . .

Thus, the trial never became a play, but the show trial Ben Gurion had had in mind . . . did take place. . . . (EiJ, 4–9)

Most of the witnesses, Arendt narrates, were Israeli citizens who "had been picked from hundreds and hundreds of applicants" (EiJ, 223). But Arendt is suspicious of witnesses who volunteer. She is allergic to the narcissism she keeps spying both in the legal actors (the chief prosecutor in particular) and in the witnesses, whom she suspects of seeking or being complacent with the elements of spectacle that parasitize and compromise the trial. K-Zetnik is for her a case in point. The narrative of his collapse becomes, in Arendt's hands, not an emotional account of human testimonial pathos but a didactic tale that illustrates ironically what accidents can happen when a witness is, quite paradoxically, too eager to appear. It is thus with her most sarcastic, her most undercutting and most funny style that Arendt will approach this testimony.

How much wiser it would have been to resist these pressures altogether . . . and to seek out those who had not volunteered! As though to prove the point, the prosecution called upon a writer, well known on both sides of the Atlantic under the name K-Zetnik . . . as the author of several books on Auschwitz which dealt with brothels, homosexuals, and other "human interest stories." He started off, as he had done at many of his public appearance, with an explanation of his adopted name. . . . He continued with a little excursion into astrology: the star "influencing our fate in the same way as the star of ashes at Auschwitz is there facing our planet, radiating toward our planet." And when he arrived at "the unnatural power above Nature" which had sustained him thus far, and now, for the first time, paused to catch his breath, even Mr. Hausner felt that something had to be done about this "testimony," and very timidly, very politely interrupted: "Could I perhaps put a few questions to you if you will consent?" Whereupon the presiding judge saw his chance as well: "Mr. Dinoor, please, please listen to Mr. Hausner and me." In response, the disappointed witness, probably deeply wounded, fainted and answered no more questions. (*EiJ*, 223–24)

Even Mr. Hausner felt that something had to be done about this "testimony." For Arendt, this is a "testimony" only in quotation marks. It is an aberration of a testimony. Arendt's derision is, however, not directed personally at K-Zetnik but derives from an impersonal black-humorous perception of the ludicrous, hilarious way in which the courtroom as a whole could be mistaken, at this legally surprising moment, for a theater of the absurd. The buffoonery comes from the situation, not from the people: the farcical or comic element derives from the discrepancy and from the total incommensurability between the two dimensions that the testimony inadvertently brings into dialogue: the natural and the supernatural, the rationality and discipline of courtroom protocols and the irruption of irrationality through delirious ramblings or what Arendt calls an "astrological excursion" (the witness's voyage into "other planets"). I would agree differently than Arendt that the courtroom in its very legal essence here flirts with madness and with nonsense. For some, this courtroom drama and the suffering it unfolds both in the past and in the present of the courtroom constitute a tragedy, a shock. For Arendt, this is a comedy. Pain is translated into laughter. If this is theater, sometimes potentially sublime or tragic, it is a Brechtian theater. Keeping her distance is for Arendt key. The ludicrous example of K-Zetnik's fainting and his default as a witness illustrates, for Arendt, not the proximity uncannily revealed between madness and reason, not the profound pathos of a cognitive abyss abruptly opened up inside the courtroom and materialized in the unconscious body of the witness, but the folly of the prosecution in both its disrespect for legal relevance and in its narcissistic and misguided predilection for witnesses of prominence. This double folly of the prosecution gets both its poetic justice and its comic punishment when its own witness faints outside the witness stand and inadvertently becomes an inert, hostile witness who "answers no more questions."

Evidentiary Misunderstandings

Looking at the facts, Arendt's fierce irony, ironically, is based on two erroneous assumptions.

1. Contrary to what Arendt presumes, Dinoor did not volunteer to share his "tale of horror" on the witness stand but, on the contrary, was an involuntary and reluctant witness. As a writer, he had always shunned in principle public appearances. In consequence, he had at first refused to testify. He had to be pressured by the chief prosecutor to consent (reluctantly) to appear before the court.

2. Among the trial's testimonies, Arendt depicts K-Zetnik's as the one that is self-evidently the most crazily remote from facts.[23] She thus regards this testimony as the most grotesque and hyperbolic illustration of "the right of the witnesses to be irrelevant" (EiJ, 225) and presumes it could not possibly bear any legal relevance to Eichmann's case. What Arendt does not know and does not suspect is that Dinoor was one of the very few survivors known to have actually met Eichmann at Auschwitz.[24] Had he been able to complete his testimony, he would have turned out to be a material eyewitness.

Yet what K-Zetnik wants is not to prove but to transmit. The language of the lawyer and that of artist meet across the witness stand only to concretize within the trial their misunderstanding and their *missed encounter*.[25]

In what follows, I explore this "missed encounter" (the way in which K-Zetnik's language fails the prosecutor and the way in which the courtroom and the trial fail K-Zetnik). I will view this missed encounter as exemplary, on the one hand, of a dimension (of reality, of death, and of disaster) that the law has to confront but is structurally bound to miss. On the other hand, I will show how the very moment of incongruity—the enacted drama of misunderstanding and the missed encounter between the artist and the law—nevertheless impacts upon the structures of the law and in the end endows the Eichmann trial with an unprecedented jurisprudential dimension. The missed encounter allows for insights that an encounter, or a cohesive moment, might have foreclosed.

| | | |

"When the prosecutor invited me to come and testify at the Eichmann trial," writes K-Zetnik more than twenty years after the trial,

> I begged him to release me of this testimony. The prosecutor then said to me: Mr. Dinoor, this is a trial whose protocol must put on

record testimony providing that there was a place named Auschwitz and what happened there. The mere sound of these words made me sick to my stomach, and I said: Sir, describing Auschwitz is beyond me! Hearing me, his staff eyed me with suspicion. You, the man who wrote these books, you expect us to believe you can't explain to the judges what Auschwitz was? I fell silent. How could I tell them that I am consumed by the search for the word that will express the look in the eyes of those who headed toward the crematorium, when they passed me with their gaze inside my eyes? The prosecutor was not convinced, and I appeared at the Eichmann trial. Then came the judges' first question about Auschwitz and no sooner did I squeeze out a few miserable sentences than I dropped to the floor and was hospitalized half-paralyzed and disfigured in my face.[26]

Trauma and the Language of the Law

"Mr. Dinoor," goes Arendt's contrapuntal narrative,

"please, please listen to Mr. Hausner and to me."
    In response, the disappointed witness, probably deeply wounded, fainted and answered no more questions. (*EiJ*, 224)

Follows Arendt's serious commentary on her sarcastic and laughingly didactic take:

This, to be sure, was an exception, but if it was an exception that proved the rule of normality, it did not prove the rule of simplicity or of ability to tell a story, let alone of the rare capacity for distinguishing between things that had happened to the storyteller more than sixteen, and sometimes twenty, years ago, and what he had read and heard and imagined in the meantime. (*EiJ*, 224)

For these very reasons, Nuremberg at the war's end excluded living witnesses and limited the evidence to documents, opting for a case of legal invulnerability that only the nonhuman and nonliving paper evidence could guarantee. "The documents," said Jackson, "could not be accused of partiality, forgetfulness, or invention;" "witnesses," on the other hand, "many of them persecuted and hostile to the Nazis, would always be chargeable with bias, faulty recollection, and even perjury." In a similar vein, Arendt disqualifies K-Zetnik as a witness because his testimony fails to meet legal criteria and fails to be contained by the authority of the restrictive safeguards of the legal rules. In Jackson's spirit, out of concern for the law as representative of culture and as the arbiter of truth in history, Arendt excludes K-Zetnik's discourse because it stands for the *contamination between fact and fiction* — for the confusion and the interpenetration between law and literature — that the law in principle cannot accept and has to resolutely, rigidly rule out.

By legal standards, K-Zetnik represents for Arendt a communicative failure. I will argue here that Arendt in her turn represents, in more than one sense, in her stance toward K-Zetnik, *the limits of the law* in its encounter with the phenomenon of *trauma*.

I would like now to contrast Arendt's interpretation of K-Zetnik's legal failure with my own reading of this courtroom scene.

IV

Intrusions

What Arendt's irony illuminates is how the law is used as a straitjacket to tame history as madness.

Arendt's sarcastically positivistic view of K-Zetnik's failure makes a positivistic recourse to a summarily explanatory psychological vocabulary, through which legal vision overrides (and Arendt condescendingly dismisses) the witness's (narcissistic) subjectivity. "In response, the disappointed witness, probably deeply wounded, fainted and answered no more questions" (*EiJ,* 224).

Against this oversimplifying psychological vocabulary, I propose to use a psychoanalytical vocabulary informed by jurisprudential trauma theory.[27] I will combine thereby a psychoanalytic reading with a philosophical and legal reading of this courtroom scene.

Out of the witness stand falls, in my vision, not a "disappointed witness" but a terrified one. The witness is not "deeply wounded" but is *re-traumatized.* The trial reenacts the trauma.

I have argued in chapter 2 that the law is, so to speak, professionally blind to its constitutive and structural relation to (both private and collective, cultural) trauma, and that its "forms of judicial blindness" take shape wherever the structure of the trauma unwittingly takes over the structure of a trial and wherever the legal institution, unawares, triggers a legal repletion of the trauma that it puts on trial or attempts to cure. In K-Zetnik's case, this happens punctually.

When the judge admonishes Dinoor from the authoritarian position of the bench, coercing him into a legal mode of discourse and demanding his cooperation as a witness, K-Zetnik undergoes severe traumatic shock in reexperiencing the same terror and panic that dumbfounded him each time when, as an inmate, he was suddenly confronted by the inexorable Nazi authorities of Auschwitz. The judge's words are heard not as an utterance originating from the present of the courtroom situation but as a censure uttered from within "the other planet," as an intrusive threat articulated right out of the violence of the traumatic scene that is replaying in K-Zetnik's mind.[28] The call to order by the judge urging the witness to obey—strictly to answer questions and to follow legal rules—impacts the witness *physically* as an invasive call to order by an SS officer. Once more, the imposition of a heartless unbending rule of order violently robs him of his words and, in reducing him to silence, once more threatens to annihilate him, to erase his essence as a *human* witness. Panicked, K-Zetnik loses consciousness.[29]

> In a trembling [he will later write about his unrelenting Auschwitz nightmares] I lift my eyes to see the face of God in its letters, and see in front of me the face of an SS man.[30]
>
> I grow terrified. . . . The rules here are invisible. . . . No telling what's permitted and what's prohibited.[31]
>
> I was seized by fear and trembling. I am crying of dread. I want to hide my face and not be seen. But there is no escape from Auschwitz. There is no hiding place in Auschwitz.[32]

Between Life and Death: Frontier Evidence

The objectivity of justice—whence its rigor—[is] offending the alterity of the face that originally signifies or commands outside the context of the world, and keeps on, in its enigma or ambiguity, tearing itself away from, and being an exception to, the plastic forms of the presence and objectivity that it nonetheless calls forth in demanding justice.
— EMMANUEL LEVINAS, "Alterity and Diachrony"

Prior to his fainting spell, at the point where the prosecutor interrupts him, K-Zetnik tries to define Auschwitz by re-envisaging the terrifying moment of selection, of repeated weekly separation between inmates chosen for an imminent extermination and inmates arbitrarily selected for life. This moment is ungraspable, the witness tries to say.

> And the inhabitants of the planet had no names. They had neither parents nor children. . . . They did not live, nor did they die, in accordance with the laws of this world. Their names were the numbers. . . . They left me, they kept leaving me, left . . . for close to two years they left me and always left me behind. . . . I see them, they are watching me, I see them.

What K-Zetnik keeps reliving of the death camp is the moment of departure, the last gaze of the departed, the exchange of looks between the dying and the living at the very moment in which life and death are separating but are still tied up together and can for the last time see each other eye to eye.

> Even those who were there don't know Auschwitz [writes K-Zetnik in a later memoir]. Not even someone who was there for two long years as I was. For Auschwitz is another planet, whereas we humankind, occupants of the planet Earth, we have no key to decipher the code-name Auschwitz. How could I dare defile the look in the eyes of those who head toward the crematorium? They passed me, they knew where they were going, and I knew where they were going. Their eyes are looking at me and mine are looking at them, the eyes of the going in the eyes of the remaining, under silent skies above the silent earth. Only that look in the eyes and the last silence. . . .
>
> For two years they passed me and their look was inside my eyes.[33]

A Community of Death, or Giving Voice to What Cannot Be Said

In constantly reliving through the moment of departure the repeated separation between life and death, what K-Zetnik testifies to is, however, not the separation or the difference between life and death but, on the contrary, their interpenetration, their ultimate resemblance. On the witness stand, he keeps reliving his connection to the dead, his bond to the exterminated. His loyalty to them is symbolized by his adopted name, K-Zetnik, with which he signs, he says, the stories that in fact are theirs:

> Since then this name testifies on all my books. . . . I am a man! . . . A man who wants to live! . . ."You have forgotten to write your name on the manuscript . . ." "The nameless, they themselves! The anonymous! Write their name: K-Zetnik."[34]
>
> How could I explain it was not me who wrote the book; they who went to the crematorium as anonymous, they wrote the book! They, the anonymous narrators. . . . For two years they passed before me on their way to the crematorium and left me behind.[35]
>
> All of them are now buried in me and continue to live in me. I made an oath to them to be their voice, and when I got out of Auschwitz they went with me, they and the silent blocks, and the silent crematorium, and the silent horizons, and the mountains of ashes.[36]

In a way K-Zetnik on the witness stand is not alone. He is accompanied by those who left him but who live within him. "I made an oath to them to be their voice." The writer K-Zetnik therefore could symbolically be viewed as the most central witness to the trial's project to *give voice to the six million dead*. K-Zetnik's testimony and his literary project pick up on the prosecutor's legal project.

> When I stand before you, Judges of Israel, in this court [the prosecutor said in his opening address] . . . I do not stand alone. With me . . . stand six million prosecutors. But alas, they cannot rise to level the finger of accusation in the direction of the glass dock and cry out "J'accuse" against the man who sits there. For their ashes are piled in the hills of Auschwitz. . . . Their blood cries to Heaven, but their voices cannot be heard. Thus it falls to me to be their mouthpiece and to deliver the awesome indictment in their name.[37]

Between Two Names

Because he is in turn speaking for the dead, K-Zetnik must remain, like them, anonymous and nameless. He must testify, that is, under the name K-Zetnik.[38] His memory of Auschwitz is the oblivion of his name.

But in a court of law, a witness cannot remain nameless and cannot testify anonymously. A witness is accountable precisely to his legal, given name.

"*Mr. Dinoor,* please, please listen to Mr. Hausner and to me," says the presiding judge impatiently, putting an end to the account that the witness gives his adopted name.

K-Zetnik faints because he cannot be interpellated at this moment by his legal name, Dinoor: the dead still claim him as *their* witness, as K-Zetnik who belongs to them and is still one of them. The court reclaims him as *its* witness, as Dinoor. He cannot bridge the gap between the two names and the two claims. He plunges into the abyss between the different planets. On the frontier between the living and the dead, between the present and the past, he falls as though he were himself a corpse.

v

Unmastered Past

Having no interest in sociopsychological or psychoanalytical phenomena, Arendt has neither a profound insight into nor an interest in trauma. She has an interest, however, in its *legal remedy*—in the trial as a means to *overcome* and to subdue a traumatic past. But K-Zetnik does not seize his legal chance to overcome the trauma on the witness stand. He is, rather, once more overcome by it. What is worse, he makes a spectacle of his scandalous collapse within the legal forum. K-Zetnik thus defeats the purpose of the law, which is precisely to *translate the trauma into consciousness.* He loses consciousness and loses his self-mastery, whereas the purpose of the law is, on the contrary, to get under control and to regain a conscious mastery over the traumatic nightmare of a history whose impact, Arendt recognizes in her nonpathetic, understated style, continues to have repercussions in the world's consciousness and thus remains with all of us precisely as the world's, Israel's as well as Germany's, "unmastered past."[39]

At the heart of the unmastered past, the trial tries to master an abyss.[40]

Trial and Abyss

K-Zetnik's loss of consciousness materializes in the courtroom what the trial cannot master: at once an abyss of trauma and an epistemological abyss, a cognitive rupture that Arendt unrelatedly will theorize and underscore in her political and philosophical account of the Nazi genocide.[41] Arendt herself experienced this epistemological abyss when the news of Auschwitz reached her for the first time as a shock that could not be assimilated. "What was decisive," Arendt confides to Günter Gaus in a German radio interview in 1964,

> What was decisive was the day we learnt about Auschwitz. That was in 1943. And at first we didn't believe it . . . because militarily it was unnecessary and uncalled for. My husband . . . said don't be gullible, don't take these stories at face value. They can't go that far! And then, a half-year later we believed it after all, because we had the proof. That was the real shock. Before what we said: Well one has enemies. That is entirely natural. Why shouldn't a people have enemies? But this was different. *It was really as if an abyss had opened.*[42]

But despite the shock, despite the cognitive rupture and the epistemological gap in history and in historical perception, Arendt's life consists in crossing the abyss and overstepping it, going beyond the rupture it has left. It later seems to Arendt, as she says to Günter Gaus, that "there should be a basis for communication precisely in the abyss of Auschwitz."[43] The law provides a forum and a language for such a communication.

I would argue that the Eichmann trial is, for Arendt, quite precisely what she calls "the basis for communication" in and over the abyss of Auschwitz. But K-Zetnik's plunge into a coma interrupts the process of communication painstakingly established by the law. K-Zetnik has remained too close to the reality and to the shock of the event, perhaps too close for Arendt's comfort. He is still a captive of the planet of the ashes. He is still *in* the Holocaust, still on the brink of the abyss, which he unwittingly reopens in the courtroom when the law has barely started to construct its legal bridge.

The law requires that the witness should be able to narrate a story in the past, to recount an event in the past tense. K-Zetnik is unable to regard the Holocaust as a past event but must relive it in the present, through the infinite traumatic repetition of a past that is not past, that has no closure and from which no distance can be taken.

Law, on the contrary, requires and provides distance from the Holocaust. Its inquiry and judgment are contingent on a separation between past and present. Law requires and brings closure and totalization of the evidence and of its meaning. This is why K-Zetnik's testimony, which defies at once legal reduction and legal closure, must remain unrealized, unfinished.

Part Two: Evidence in Law and Evidence in Art

VI

Between Law and Art

In 1964, a leading avant-garde literary critic in America, Susan Sontag, in a discussion of a German literary work about the role played by the pope during the Holocaust, surprisingly and quite provocatively argued that the Eichmann trial was "the most interesting and moving work of art of the past ten years."[44]

> We live in a time [she wrote] in which tragedy is not an art form but a form of history. Dramatists no longer write tragedies. But we do have works of art (not always recognized as such) which attempt to resolve the great historical tragedies of our time. . . . If then the supreme tragic event of modern times is the murder of six million Jews, the most interesting and moving work of art of the past ten years is the trial of Adolf Eichmann in Jerusalem in 1961.[45]

I do not believe, for my part, that the Eichmann trial—or any trial— can be reduced to, or subsumed in, the performance or the drama of a work of art. There is at least one crucial difference between an event of law and an event of art, no matter how dramatic they both are: a work of art cannot sentence to death. A trial, unlike art, is grounded in the sanctioned legal violence it has the power (and sometimes the duty) to enact.[46]

While it cannot be accepted at face value, Sontag's paradoxical remark about the Eichmann trial is nevertheless illuminating, not as a comment about trials but as an observation about art's relation to (juridical) reality. While the Eichmann trial can under no circumstances be regarded as a work of art, works of art have come today to imitate, to replicate or mimic, the legal structures of the Eichmann trial.

The strongest and most eloquent example of this trend (that reached its climax decades after Sontag's article) can be seen in the film *Shoah* by Claude Lanzmann, a work of art made of reality, whose legal, testimonial format is informed (and perhaps inspired) by the Eichmann trial[47] and of which it could indeed be said, in Sontag's words, "the most interesting and moving work of art of the past years."[48]

I speak here of *Shoah* as emblematic of art after the Holocaust and as *paradigmatic* of the work of art of our times. I argue that the Eichmann trial is the complementary event (the legal correlative) of the contemporary process of art's invasion by the structures of the trial and of its transformation into testimony, a process by which writers like K-Zetnik (and like Elie Wiesel, Celan, Camus, and others) have precisely vowed to make of art itself a witness — to present, that is, historical and legal evidence by means of art. What, then, is the difference between law and art when both are underwritten by the legal process and when both vow to pursue reality? "Reality," says Arendt, "is different from, and more than, the totality of facts and events, which anyhow is unascertainable. Who says what is . . . always tells a story."[49] In Arendt's words, I argue that *law's story focuses on what is different from, and more than,* that totality. I argue that the breakdown of the witness in the Eichmann trial was (unwittingly) at once part of the totality of facts and part of what was different from, and more than, that totality. In that sense, it was *law's story* and *art's story* at the same time. "The truth," says Lanzmann, "kills the possibility of fiction."[50] In the same way that art is today transpierced, invaded by the language and the structures of the trial, the Eichmann trial — through K-Zetnik's court appearance — was transpierced, invaded by the artist's language, by the artist's testimony, and by the artist's astonishing collapse.

The artist's language cannot relegate traumatic suffering to the past. "The worst moral and artistic crime that can be committed in producing a work dedicated to the Holocaust," says Lanzmann, "is to consider the Holocaust as past. *Either the Holocaust is legend or it is present: in no case is it a memory.* A film devoted to the Holocaust . . . can only be an investigation into the present of the Holocaust or at least into a past whose scars are still so freshly and vividly inscribed in certain places and in the consciences of some people that it reveals itself in a *hallucinated timelessness.*"[51] In a similar way, K-Zetnik does not treat the Holocaust as past but lives it as a present that endlessly repeats itself in a hallucinated timelessness. The hallucinated timelessness — the time of traumatic repletion and of the time of art—is the precise time of K-Zetnik's legal testimony. But legal temporality cannot admit, cannot include, cannot acknowledge timelessness except as a rupture of the legal frame. K-Zetnik's court appearance marks, thus, an invasion of the trial and of legal temporality by the endless, timeless temporality of art.

Law is a language of abbreviation, of limitation and totalization. Art is a language of infinity and of the irreducibility of fragments, a language of embodiment, of incarnation, and of embodied incantation or endless rhythmic *repetition*. Because it is by definition a discipline of limits, law distances the Holocaust; art brings it closer. The function of the judgment in the Eichmann trial was paradoxically to *totalize* and *distance* the event: the trial *made a past out of the Holocaust*.[52] And yet, within the courtroom, in the figure of K-Zetnik, the Holocaust returned as a ghost or as an incarnated, living present.

K-Zetnik's discourse in the trial has remained unfinished and, like art, interminable. In the courtroom, its lapse into interminability—into unconsciousness and silence—was paradoxically a physical reminder of the real, a physical reminder of a bodily reality that fractured the totality of facts sought by the law. But the testimonial power of this real, of this irreducible bodily presence of the witness, lay precisely in the pathos—in the crying power—of its legal muteness.

"But what can I do when I'm struck mute?" K-Zetnik will write almost thirty years after the Eichmann trial, in trying to explain at once the legal failure of his testimony and the very principle of interminability and inexhaustibility of his continued testimonial art:

But what can I do when I'm struck mute? I have neither word nor name for it all. Genesis says: "And Adam gave names . . ." When God finished creating the earth and everything upon it, Adam was asked to give names to all that God had created. Till 1942 there was no Auschwitz in existence. For Auschwitz there is no name other than Auschwitz. My heart will be ripped to pieces if I say, "In Auschwitz they burned people alive!" Or "In Auschwitz people died of starvation." But that is not Auschwitz. What, then, is Auschwitz? I have no words to express it; I don't have a name for it. Auschwitz is a primal phenomenon. I don't have the key to unlock it. But don't the tears of the mute speak his anguish? And don't his screams cry his distress? Don't his bulging eyes reveal the horror? I am that mute.[53]

Muteness in a courtroom is normally negative or void, devoid of legal meaning. Muteness in art, however, can be fraught with meaning. It is *out of its muteness* that K-Zetnik's writing in this passage *speaks*. It is out of its silence that his testimonial art derives its literary power. *Art is* what makes silence speak.

I would argue that it was precisely through K-Zetnik's *legal muteness* that the trial inadvertently *gave silence a transmitting power,* and — although not by intention — managed to transmit the legal meaning of collective trauma with the incremental power of a work of art. Once the trial gave transmissibility to silence, other silences became, within the trial, fraught with meaning.[54] At the limit of what could be legally grasped, something of the order of K-Zetnik's mute cry — something of the order of the speechlessness and the interminability of art — was present in the courtroom as a silent shadow of the trial or as a negative of the proceedings. It was in the interstices of the law as a ghost inside the house of justice. The poet Haim Gouri noted in his coverage of the trial:

> With an unmatched force, the court has managed to restrain the crushing power of the cry that burst out, now as if for the first time, and to transmit it partially into a language of facts and numbers and dates, while letting the remains of that cry float over the trial like a ghost.[55]

VII

The Judgment

Unlike K-Zetnik's testimony, the Eichmann trial did have closure. For his crimes against the Jewish people, his war crimes, and his crimes against humanity, the judges sentenced Eichmann to "the greatest penalty known to the law."[56] The judgment totalized a statement of the evidence. Like Arendt, the judges underscored the fact that their authority of doing justice (and of making justice seen) was contingent on the *force of limitation* of the law. "The judgment in the Eichmann case," Arendt reports, for once approvingly, "could not have been clearer":

All attempts to widen the range of the trial had to be resisted, because the court "could not allow itself to be enticed into provinces which are outside its sphere. . . . The judicial process [wrote the judges] has ways of its own, which are laid down by the law, and which do not change, whatever the subject of the trial may be." The court, moreover, could not overstep these limits without ending "in complete failure." Not only does it not have at its disposal "the tools required for the investigation of general questions, *it speaks with an authority whose very weight depends upon its limitation.*" (*EiJ*, 253–54; my emphasis)[57]

And yet, even the judges felt the need to point to the fact that there was something in the trial that went beyond their jurisdiction and beyond the jurisdiction of the law.

If these be the sufferings of the individual [wrote the judges], then the sum total of the suffering of the millions — about a third of the Jewish people, tortured and slaughtered — is certainly beyond human understanding, and who are we to try to give it adequate expression? This is a task for the greatest writers and poets. *Perhaps it is symbolic that even the author who himself went through the hell named Auschwitz, could not stand the ordeal in the witness box and collapsed.*[58]

What the judges say is not simply that law and art are two modes of transmission of the Holocaust, two languages in which to translate the incomprehensible into some sort of sense, two modes of coping with collective trauma and crossing the abyss of a mad and nightmarish history.

The judges recognize that even in the legal mode, within the language of the trial, the collapse of the writer and his breakdown as a witness was endowed with meaning. They further recognize that when the artist lapsed into unconsciousness, a dimension of infinitude and interminability registered itself within the trial *as what was uncontainable by its containment,* as what remained untotalizable precisely by and in the law's totalization, within the very legal text of totalization that constitutes their judgment.

The judgment in the Eichmann trial takes note of the fact that, in the meeting point between law and art with which the courtroom was unwittingly confronted through K-Zetnik's testimony, *the law had a dialogue with its own limits* and touched upon a boundary of meaning in which sense and senselessness, meaning and madness seriously, historically commingled and could not be told apart. The court acknowledges, however, that this surprising legal moment that unsettled legal norms and threw the courtroom into disarray was profoundly meaningful and not a senseless moment of the trial.

Part Three: Traumatic Narratives and Legal Frames

VIII

Story and Anti-Story: Between Justice and Impossibility of Telling

I want now to return to Arendt's story, but to return to Arendt's story differently: to listen not just to her statement, but to her utterance; to seek to understand not only her juridical critique, but her own inadvertent testimony as a writer. I propose to show how Arendt's legal narrative in *Eichmann in Jerusalem* unwittingly encapsulates not only the reporter's critical account, but the thinker's own (erased) artistic testimony and the writer's own traumatic narrative.[59]

Like the judges, Arendt views K-Zetnik's fainting as a symbol.[60] But while for the judges, the writer's collapse encapsulates—within the trial and beyond it—the *collapse of language* in the face of uncontainable and unintelligible suffering, for Arendt, the writer's collapse encapsulates the *legal failure* of the trial. While for the judges, the collapse is a dramatization of *a failure of expression,* for Arendt, the collapse is a dramatization of *a failure of narration.*

"This," says Arendt, "to be sure, was an exception, but if it was an exception that proved the rule of normality, it did not prove the rule of simplicity or of ability to tell a story" (*EiJ*, 224). As an exception that confirms the rule of normality—that is, as a symbol of the legal abnormality of the trial as a whole—Arendt faults K-Zetnik for his *inability to tell a story* and thus to testify coherently. "Who says what is . . . always tells a story, and in this story the particular facts lose their contingency and acquire some humanly comprehensible meaning," Arendt will write in "Truth and Politics,"[61] doubtless remembering unconsciously the unforgettable essay called "The Storyteller" written by her dead friend Walter Benjamin, whose name she will in 1968—five years after the Eichmann book—redeem from anonymity and namelessness by publishing his work in the United States, but whose lost friendship she will silently mourn all her life as an intimate grievance, a wordless wound, a personal price that she herself has secretly paid to the Holocaust.[62] I hear a reference to "The Storyteller" in the conclusion of Arendt's account of K-Zetnik's testimony: "[I]t did not prove the rule of simplicity or of *ability to tell a story*." There are several other references in *Eichmann in Jerusalem* to storytelling and to "The Storyteller."[63] While Benjamin's name is never mentioned and his text is never cited in the book, Benjaminian words and formulations unwittingly pervade its pages like stylistic echoes that form an impassioned philosophical *subtext* under and through the irony, the wryness, and the dryness of the legalistic text. At stake in this subtext is a relation between death and writing, an intimately personal relation that the writing "I" cannot possess or formulate directly, but can relate to indirectly through Benjamin's reflection on the relation between death and storytelling. Benjamin's memory and presence—the presence of his death and of his text—unwittingly yet hauntingly, persistently inform Arendt's style and permeate her writing and her utterance. "Death," wrote Benjamin precisely in his essay, "is the sanction of everything that the storyteller has to tell. He has borrowed his authority from death" ("St.," 94).

Has Arendt in her turn borrowed her authority as storyteller of the trial from a legacy of death of which she does not speak and cannot speak? I would suggest indeed that, through its understated but repeated reference to the storyteller, *Eichmann in Jerusalem* is also Arendt's book of mourning.[64] It is, in other words, a book—an unarticulated statement—on the *relation between grief and justice,* as well as on the counterparts of grief in narrative and storytelling. "It is perfectly true," Arendt will write in "Truth and Politics," that "all sorrows can be borne if you put them into a story or tell a story about them."[65] Both the Eichmann trial and Arendt's critical rehearsal of it are preoccupied—albeit in different styles—with the translation of grief into grievance as what underlies precisely the capacity and the significance of saying "I accuse," of crying out "J'accuse" in the name of those who can no longer say it.[66]

Eichmann in Jerusalem, I would suggest, is inhabited by Arendt's mourned and unmourned ghosts. Benjamin is one of those. (Another ghost, I would suggest, is Heidegger, but I will not dwell here on his ghostly significance in *Eichmann in Jerusalem*.)[67]

In all language, Benjamin has argued, there is a lament that mutes it out.[68] "In all mourning there is an inclination to speechlessness, which is infinitely more than the disinclination or the inability to communicate."[69] Benjamin's unmentioned name and subterranean presence as an inadvertent and complex subtext of *Eichmann in Jerusalem* is linked, I argue, both to Arendt's testimony in this book and to her silence, a silence that in turn is linked not just to her discretion but to her speechlessness, that is, to her own *inability to tell a story*. There is, in other words, a crucial story Arendt does not tell and cannot tell that underlies the story of the trial she does tell.[70]

"Familiar though his name may be to us," wrote Benjamin, "the storyteller in his living immediacy is by means a present force. He has already become something remote from us and something which is getting even more distant":

> Less and less frequently do we encounter people with the ability to tell a tale properly. . . . It is as if something that seemed inalienable to us . . . were taken from us: the ability to exchange experiences. ("St.," 83)

Benjamin intuitively knew that the inability to tell a story was related to the essence of traumatic experience.[71] Specifically, he linked this inability to tell to the collective, massive trauma of the war.

> Was it not noticeable at the end of the war that men returned from the battlefield grown silent—not richer, but poorer in communicable experience? ("St.," 84)

Benjamin spoke of the First World War.[72] K-Zetnik's testimony at the Eichmann trial showed how people had returned even more tongue-tied—even poorer in communicable experience, grown even more silent—from the death camps and from the traumatic nightmare of the Second World War.

> When I got out of Auschwitz [writes K-Zetnik] they went with me, they and the silent blocks, and the silent crematorium, and the silent horizons, and the mountain of ashes.[73]

| | | |

I would argue differently from Arendt (and with hindsight she could not possess) that (unpredictably, unwittingly) it was the *inadvertent legal essence* and legal innovation and uniqueness of the Eichmann trial, and not its testimonial accident, to voice the muteness generated by the Holocaust and to *articulate the difficulty of articulation* of the catastrophic story, the difficulty of articulation and the tragic unnarratability of the ungraspability of the ungraspable disaster and of its immeasurably devastating, unintelligible trauma. The impossibility of telling is not external to this story: it is the story's heart.[74] The trial shows how the inherent inability to tell the story is itself an integral part of the history and of the story of the Holocaust. The function of the trial thus becomes precisely to articulate the impossibility of telling through the legal process and to convert this *narrative impossibility* into *legal meaning.*[75]

| | | |

My conception of the trial is, then, fundamentally different from that of Arendt. Logically speaking, it is, however, Arendt's text that has enabled me to read the trial differently from her. It is precisely Arendt's own surprised insistence on "how difficult it was to tell the story" (*EiJ,* 229) and her own *excessive* utterance — her own haunted allusions to Benjamin and to "The Storyteller" — that have contributed to shape my perspective. All along, I have been reading Arendt's text in an attempt to understand what was peculiar and unique about the trial. My own effort was to listen to the trial with the help of Arendt, to gain an insight into what in 1961 was happening in the courtroom through the magnifying lens of Arendt's sharp and critically insightful eyes. In this last chapter, I have suggested that besides the criticism there is also an unspoken element of grief in Arendt's text, that a relation between grief and justice indirectly and unconsciously informs Arendt's text, that a relation between grief and justice indirectly and unconsciously informs Arendt's utterance, and that it is precisely this excessiveness of Arendt's utterance over her statement that gives her book authority and gives her text a literary depth, an existential density, and a political and legal-philosophical charisma that go beyond the conscious terms of her spoken argument.

I wish now to draw out this unspoken potential of Arendt's text and to pursue it further in my own way. In the remainder of my argument, I will go farther than Arendt does in drawing on the haunting relevance of Benjamin to *Eichmann in Jerusalem* and, more generally, in using Benjamin's reflection to highlight important aspects of the trial. Although I will, from this point on, use Benjamin to read the trial differently from Arendt (to argue with and argue *beyond* Arendt), my different understanding and my different proposition, to the extent that they rely in turn on Benjamin's authority and on his haunting presence, will also paradoxically be speaking *with* Arendt's text and *from her storyteller's silence:* from the unconscious pathos of her own excessive and yet silenced, *muted,* self-erased, and self-transcendent utterance.

IX

The Dramatic

In the wake of Benjamin, I argue therefore that the testimonial muteness underlying (and exceeding) Arendt's legal story reenacts, ironically enough, the literary muteness of K-Zetnik's story, and that K-Zetnik's *legal muteness*—his inability to tell a story in the trial—is part of the impossibility of telling that is at the trial's heart. Indeed, K-Zetnik's discourse prior to his fainting strive to *thematize* precisely the impossibility of telling, both in its use of the figure of "the other planet," testifying to the utter foreignness of Auschwitz and trying to convey the astronomic scale of distance separating its ungraspability and unnarratability from the narration in the courtroom in Jerusalem, and in its effort to narrate the scene of the extermination as a repeated scene of parting and of silence, a primal scene of silence whose sole meaning wordlessly resides in the exchange of looks between the living and the dying: between the not-yet-dead and the not-yet-surviving who remain behind for no other purpose than to tell and to retell the story that cannot be told.

But K-Zetnik's testimony does not simply tell *about* the impossibility of telling: it dramatizes it—*enacts it*—through its own lapse into coma and its own collapse into silence. "It was the most *dramatic* moment of the trial," writes Tom Segev, "one of the most dramatic moments in the country's history."[76]

For Arendt as a critical legal observer and as a conscious representative of the tradition conception of the law, however,[77] *the dramatic* as such is by definition *immaterial* and extraneous to the trial. Arendt's view follows the classical axioms of jurisprudential thought. "The process," says Justice Oliver Wendell Holmes in one of the most authoritative statements of Anglo-Saxon jurisprudence in the twentieth century, "the process [of the law] is one, from a lawyer's statement and of the case, eliminating as it does all the dramatic elements . . . , and retaining only the facts of legal import, up to the final analyses and abstract universals of theoretical jurisprudence."[78] This precisely is what Arendt tries to do, in discarding the dramatic and in theorizing in her legal proposition about the Eichmann trial the "abstract universal" of a new crime and of a new criminal without *mens rea*—without motive. "The banality of evil" is, in fact, strictly a "theoretical jurisprudential" concept: an *antiseptic* legal concept that is formed by the strict *reduction of the drama* that has given rise to its conceptual necessity. "If a man goes into law," says Holmes, "it pays to be a master of it, and to be a master of it means to look straight through all the dramatic incidents."[79]

Arendt therefore unambiguously discards the dramatic in the trial and denies it legal meaning. I would argue her, in contrast, that the dramatic *can be* legally significant. I submit that in the Eichmann trial (as the passing comment of the judges has in fact conceded) the dramatic *was* indeed endowed with *legal meaning,* meaning that the classical jurisprudential, legalistic view was programmed to miss and that Arendt consequently overlooked.

"As Hannah Arendt and others have pointed out," writes Susan Sontag, "the juridical basis of the Eichmann trial, the relevance of all the evidence presented and the legitimacy of certain procedures are open to question on strictly legal grounds":

> But the truth is that the Eichmann trial did not, and could not, have conformed to legal standards only. . . . The function of the trial was rather that of the tragic drama: above and beyond judgment and punishment, catharsis.
>   . . . [T]he problem with the Eichmann trial was not its deficient legality, but the *contradiction between its juridical form and its dramatic function.*[80]

Arendt herself acknowledged in the epilogue of *Eichmann in Jerusalem* that, as the saying goes, "justice must not only be done but must be seen to be done" (*EiJ*, 277). The legal function of the court, in other words, is in its very *moral essence a dramatic* function: not only that of "doing justice" but that of *"making justice seen"* in a larger moral and historically unique sense.[81] It was through the perspective of this larger cultural and *historic visibility* the trial gave dramatically, historically, to justice that the Eichmann trial was (I would propose) *jurisprudentially dramatic.*

In a different context, Walter Benjamin in turn defines the dramatic:

> The mystery is, on the dramatic level, that moment in which it juts out of the domain of language proper to it into a higher one unattainable for it. Therefore, this moment cannot be expressed in words but is expressible solely in representation: it is the "dramatic" in the strictest sense.[82]

Law in principle *rules out* what cannot be disclosed in words. In contrast, the dramatic, Benjamin says, is beyond words. It is a physical gesture by which language points to a meaning it cannot articulate.

Such is K-Zetnik's fall outside the witness stand. It makes a corpse out of the living witness who has sworn to remain anonymous and undifferentiated from the dead.

The witness's body has become within the trial what Pierre Nora would call *"a site of memory."*[83] In opposition to the trial's effort to create a conscious, totalizing memory and a totalizing historical consciousness, the site of memory is an unintegratable, residual, unconscious site that cannot be translated into legal consciousness and into legal idiom. This site materializes in the courtroom memory of death both as a physical reality and as a limit of consciousness in history.

On this legal site, the witness testifies through his unconscious body. Suddenly, the testimony is invaded by the body. The speaking body has become a dying body. The dying body testifies dramatically and wordlessly beyond the cognitive and the discursive limits of the witness's speech.

The body's testimony thus creates a new dimension in the trial, a *physical legal dimension* that dramatically expands what can be grasped as legal meaning. This new dimension in its turn transforms and dramatically reshapes not just the legal process of the Eichmann trial, but the conception and the very frameworks of perception of the law as such.

The Caesura of the Trial: The Expressionless

How is it that the body can unconsciously transform the parameters of Law as such? The witness's fainting—the body's dramatic collapse in the midst of the witness's verbal testimony—could strikingly exemplify *within the structure of the trial* what Walter Benjamin calls "the expressionless":

> The life undulating in it [Benjamin writes, and I would specify: the life undulating in the trial] must appear petrified and as if spellbound in a single moment. . . . What . . . spellbinds the movement and interrupts the harmony is the expressionless. . . . *Just as interruption by the commanding word is able to bring the truth out of the evasions . . . precisely at the point where it interrupts, the expressionless compels the trembling harmony to stop.* . . . For it shatters whatever still survives of the legacy of chaos . . . the false, errant totality, the absolute totality. Only the expressionless completes the work [completes the trial], by shattering it into a thing of shards, into a fragment of the true world, into the torso of a symbol.[84]

To borrow Benjamin's inspired terms to describe the trial, I would argue that K-Zetnik's fainting and his petrified body stand for the "expressionless"—*das Ausdruckslose*—that suddenly erupts into the language of the law and *interrupts* the trial. In Benjamin's terms, K-Zetnik's collapse can be defined as "the caesura" of the trial:[85] a moment of petrifaction that interrupts and ruptures the articulations of the law, and yet that grounds them by shattering their false totality into "a fragment of the true world"; a sudden "*counter-rhythmic rupture*" in which (as Benjamin has put it) "every expression simultaneously comes to a standstill, in order to give free reign to an expressionless power."[86]

The fainting that cuts through the witness's speech and petrifies his body interrupts the legal process and creates a moment that is *legally traumatic* not just for the witness, but chiefly for the court and for the audience of the trial. I argue in effect that, in the rupture of the witness's lapse into a coma, it is the law itself that for a moment loses consciousness. But it is through this breakdown of the legal framework that history emerges in the courtroom and, in the legal body of the witness, exhibits its own inadvertently dramatic (nondiscursive) rules of evidence. It is precisely through this breach of consciousness of law that history unwittingly and mutely yet quite resonantly, memorably *speaks*.[87]

And it is for these moments in which history as injury dramatically, traumatically spoke—these moments that combined the legal, the dramatic, and the legally traumatic, yet whose eloquence and legal meaning could not be translated into legal idiom—that the Eichmann trial is remembered. It is precisely through these moments that the Eichmann trial has impressed itself on memory, as a remarkable legal event in which the law itself was shattered into a new level of perception and into a new historical and legal consciousness.

Part Four: Conclusion

This chapter has dealt with a legal moment that took the legal institution by surprise and stupefied at once the judges and the audience of the trial. In their written opinion, the judges marked the unique evidentiary position of this moment in the trial. They thought it was significant that it was here a literary writer who collapsed, and that it was an artist's testimony that the trial had exploded. Indeed, law has exploded here the literary framework. In turn, the conflation of the writer's literary testimony with the law has brought about a parallel explosion of the legal framework. Both the legal and the literary frameworks came apart as a result of their encounter in the trial. I argue that this breakdown—this caesura—was legally significant although (and because) it was legally traumatic.

This moment in which the human witness, flabbergasting both the audience and the judges, plunges into the abyss between the different planets and falls as though he were himself a corpse, is internal to the trial. I argue that it is a moment *inside law,* although its power comes from its interruption of the law, its interruption of discourse by what Walter Benjamin calls "the expressionless." The expressionless, I argue, grounds both the legal meaning of the trial and its inadvertent literary and dramatic power.

For the purpose of transmission of the Holocaust, literature and art do not suffice. And yet, a trial equally is insufficient. I believe that only the *encounter between law and art* can adequately testify to the abyssal meaning of the trauma.

It is remarkable that such an encounter between trauma, law, and art happens inside a trial. Inside the trial, in *the drama of the missed encounter* between K-Zetnik and the legal actors (judge and prosecutor), there is a unique confrontation between literature and law as two vocabularies of remembrance. The clash between these two dimensions and these two vocabularies brings about a breakdown of the legal framework through the physical collapse of the witness. Yet, through this inadvertent breakdown of the legal framework, history uncannily and powerfully speaks. "Everything," said Benjamin,

> Everything about history that, from the very beginning, has been untimely, sorrowful, unsuccessful, is expressed in a face,[88] or rather in a death's head.[89]

This death's head emerges in the trial as history is uncannily transmitted through K-Zetnik's fainting and through his endlessly reverberating courtroom silence.

On "Missed Encounter(s)": Law's Relationship to Violence, Death, and Disaster

What K-Zetnik wants is not to prove but to transmit. The language of the lawyer and that of the artist meet across the witness stand only to concretize within the trial their misunderstanding and their missed encounter. . . . I view this missed encounter as exemplary . . . of a dimension (of reality, of death, of disaster) that the law has to confront but is structurally bound to miss.
— SHOSHANA FELMAN, "A Ghost in the House of Justice: Death and the Language of Law"

"I do not believe, for my part, that the Eichmann trial — or any trial — can be reduced to, or subsumed in, the performance or drama of a work of art. There is at least one crucial difference between an event of law and an event of art, no matter how dramatic they both are: a work of art cannot sentence to death. A trial, unlike art, is grounded in the sanctioned legal violence it has the power (and sometimes the duty) to enact. — SHOSHANA FELMAN, "A Ghost in the House of Justice: Death and the Language of Law"

Shoshana Felman's "The Ghost in the House of Justice: Death and the Language of Law" brilliantly and subtly explores law's limits in its confrontation with the most extreme kinds of violence and violation.[1] Felman invites her readers to think about law through the lens of trauma, seeing the latter as disrupting the formality of the legal trial and exposing the fragility of its ordering efforts. Her work is a critical intervention in contemporary jurisprudence, pointing to new ways of thinking about the limits of law and about law's relationship to violence, death, and disaster.

Felman focuses on a crucial moment in the trial of Adolph Eichmann, when a Holocaust survivor known as K-Zetnik faints as he tries to testify about his experience in the camps. She uses it to consider "a dimension (of reality, of death, and of disaster) that the law has to confront but is structurally bound to miss."[2] But, for her, this "missed encounter" is not so much a failure of law as constitutive of it. This missed encounter, Felman argues, "is a moment *inside* the law, although its power comes from its interruption of law."[3]

Exploring law's adequacy as a vehicle for responding to the Holocaust is, of course, not new.[4] Over fifty years ago, at the time of the Nuremberg Trial before the International Military Tribunal, Hannah Arendt observed:

> The Nazi crimes, it seems to me, explode the limits of law; and that is precisely what constitutes their monstrousness. For these crimes, no punishment is severe enough. It may well be essential to hang Göring, but it is totally inadequate. That is, this guilt, in contrast to all criminal guilt, oversteps and shatters any and all legal systems. That is the reason why the Nazis in Nuremberg are so smug. . . . We are simply not equipped to deal, on a human, political level, with a guilt that is beyond crime.[5]

Although Arendt's claim remains somewhat opaque—she never specifies exactly *how* Nazi crimes "explode the limits of law"—it has been widely cited as giving voice to a critical insight regarding the limited capacity of law to respond to horrific crimes, specifically when it comes to the question of shaping an adequate punishment. The two most common justifications for punishing criminals—deterrence and retribution—seem oddly weak if not irrelevant when it comes to dealing with mass crimes. It is hard to imagine any architect of genocide or would-be suicide bomber being deterred by any legal sanction, even the most extreme. Likewise, if the notion of retribution contemplates a legal evening of the scales, it seems that no amount of juridically authorized violence could ever balance out the burden of genocide or mass atrocities. Legal responses to mass crimes are, then, at best symbolic gestures—and, if we accept Arendt's observation, they symbolize little besides their own impotence.

Robert Jackson, who took an unprecedented leave from his post on the Supreme Court to head the prosecution at Nuremberg, was likewise sensitive to the question of law's structural limits as they apply to mass crimes. At the beginning of his address to the International Military Tribunal, Jackson observed:

> The commonsense of mankind demands that law shall not stop with the punishment of petty crimes by little people. It must also reach men who possess themselves of great power and make deliberate and concerted use of it to set in motion evils which leave no home in the world untouched.[6]

Jackson returned to this theme at the conclusion of his opening statement: "Civilization asks whether law is so laggard as to be utterly helpless to deal with crimes of this magnitude by criminals of this order of importance."[7] Yet it would be grotesque, Jackson suggests, to hold that law is adequate to the task of condemning the isolated killer but powerless to respond to the perpetrator of genocide. Such atrocities *must* avail themselves of legal response; to think otherwise is to make a travesty of the idea of submitting human conduct to the rule of law.

For present purposes, it is not critical to take sides in the debate between Arendt and Jackson. Rather, it suffices to note that both agree that mass atrocities — such as genocide, crimes against humanity, or acts of global terrorism — pose unique challenges to the rule of law, and usher law toward the frontier of its substantive efficacy. Yet, for Felman, the Arendt-Jackson debate is, in an important sense, the wrong one. For her, the Eichmann trial reveals less about law's substantive limits than its inability to capture and represent the nature of trauma and traumatic experience, its limitation as a medium through which to "transmit" death and disaster.

K-Zetnik's testimony and his collapse, in Felman's rendering, stand in for law's simultaneous attraction to the catastrophic and yet its inadequacy in the face of catastrophe. Catastrophes, like the Nazi genocide, "are not," Linda Meyer contends,

> just bad events in the world, but events that call into question our normative ground and cause radical normative disorientation. They are events that cause us to feel "unheimlich" — not at home in the world. Everything we took for granted is open to question.

Everything we counted on is missing. We are plunged into an alien, senseless wasteland of the sort Kafka or T. S. Eliot describe. Importantly, when we confront the failure of our normative ground, the edge of reason, we also experience our own lack of control. Where reason fails, so does prediction. The future is suddenly dark and uncertain. We here face our own limits, our own mortality. In Heidegger's terms, we experience "being-toward-death." We run aground on our own individuality, and for the first time, know in a more than merely intellectual way that the "I" must experience death, alone. The experience of senselessness, lack of control, and mortality that catastrophe turns up is profoundly uncomfortable and demands a response.[8]

It is the distinctive work of law to confront the catastrophic and to try to restore sense to a shattered world. Trials, like Eichmann's, seek to "deny that the event is a challenge to our normative structures, and . . . reframe it as injustice, not catastrophe. This is modern law's specialty. Modern law is constantly colonizing catastrophe, reframing it as injustice, expanding the bounds of law and, consequently, human control and responsibility. . . . In these reframings, the catastrophic norm-overturning nature of the event hides itself and catastrophe is reread as conventional injustice."[9]

K-Zetnik's loss of consciousness undoes these efforts, suggesting, as Peter Fitzpatrick puts it, that, as law confronts catastrophe, it is "stretched between stable determinism and responsive change. . . . A complete determination of position and a responsiveness to what is beyond position are antithetical things, but there can be neither position without responsiveness to what is always beyond it nor responsiveness without a position from which to respond."[10] K-Zetnik's collapse is law's collapse in the face of death and disaster, and it marks death as both "supreme stasis" and "the opening to all possibility that is beyond affirmed order."[11]

Felman's essay examines both law's attraction to the catastrophic and its inability to provide an adequate medium for its transmission, and it reminds us that law is saturated in, as well as surrounded by, violence and death. "A work of art cannot sentence to death," she writes. "A trial, unlike art, is grounded in the sanctioned legal violence it has *the power* (and sometimes the duty) to enact."[12] Here Felman joins with others who focus on the violence that is done every day with the explicit authorization of legal institutions and officials or with their tacit acquiescence.[13] Some of this violence is done directly by legal officials, some by citizens acting under a dispensation granted by law, and some by persons whose violent acts subsequently will be deemed acceptable.[14] Moreover, the pain that these violent acts produce is everywhere, in the ordinary lives of those subject to legal regulation, but also in law's occasional life-and-death decisions. Indeed, the original definition of sovereignty in the West comes from the Roman law maxim — *vitae et necis potestatem* — the power over life and death. Thus the opening sentence of Foucault's final section of volume 1 of his *History of Sexuality* says that "for a long time, one of the characteristic privileges of sovereign power was the right to decide life and death."[15] Law asserts its sovereignty and responds to the catastrophe of the Holocaust by deciding life and death. While much has been said and written about the power to kill within the confines of modern law,[16] the punishment given to Eichmann has been regarded as of a different order, as the most robust and terrifying of law's power, of its essential dealings in pain and violence.[17]

Yet because the bloodletting done, authorized or condoned by law's institutions, occurs with all the normal abnormality of bureaucratic abstraction, the blood spilled is often untraceably dispersed, and in this dispersal we see evidence of the "missed encounter" that is law's relationship to violence. Every decision according to rule is a cutting, wrenching, excision of law from its social context; every judicial decision and legislative act privileges some voices and silences others. This symbolic violence is, however, presented as a routine act of rule following, and, as a result, it is sometimes difficult to trace the human agency involved. Indeed, it is this distinctive combination of bloodletting and bureaucracy that makes law possible, and insures its continuous presence in our minds and also that the law/violence relationship is something of a "missed encounter."[18] Thus, while in the exercise of the power over life and death, more than in any other legal act, law reaffirms itself, "in this very violence something rotten in law is revealed, above all to a finer sensibility, because the latter knows itself to be infinitely remote from conditions in which fate might imperiously have shown itself in such a sentence."[19]

As Robert Cover observes, despite its significance, law's relationship to violence, death, and disaster has played little role, and occupied little space, in legal theory and jurisprudence.[20] Or, when it is present, awareness of the violence done or authorized by officials is divorced from the violence of interpretation, as if the act of speaking or writing the words of law could be separated from the inscription of those words on the bodies of citizens.[21] This absence and this divorce have serious consequences. By equating the conditions of legal legitimacy with that separation, much of jurisprudence promotes righteous indifference and allows us to assume that law can comprehend and control violence, death, and disaster, that law can rationalize violence and turn it to productive purposes.

Felman's work unsettles such assumptions by showing that law always misses something in its encounters with death and disaster and in its efforts to reorder what the catastrophic has disordered. Yet it also opens up a way of speaking about law's relationship to violence that does not sit easily with her own confident separation of art and law and her description of the legal trial as "grounded in the sanctioned legal violence it has the power . . . to enact." Could it be that law's relationship to violence is more troubling and troubled than this description acknowledges? Could it be that violence, like death and disaster, is a dimension of reality that "law has to confront, but is structurally bound to miss" and that the encounter between law and violence is always, at least in part a "missed encounter" that is constitutive of law? Reading "The Ghost in the House of Law: Death and the Language of Law" suggests that the answer to these questions is yes.

Felman invites legal scholars to examine the fissures, the silences, the gaps, the moments when language fails. As she puts it, "Great trials are perhaps specifically those trials whose very failures have their own necessity and their own literary, cultural, and jurisprudential *speaking power*."[22] By attending to law's failures and "missed encounters," Felman helps reorient the study of law, asking us to consider madness as well as reason, senselessness as well as sense making, the unspeakable as well as the spoken. She shakes us from any trace of righteous indifference and points toward the recognition that violence, death, and disaster always exceed law's capacity for comprehension and control.

Trauma, Justice, and the Political Unconscious: Arendt and Felman's Journey to Jerusalem

The seminal work on trauma and testimony by the psychoanalytic and literary critic Shoshana Felman centers on two fundamental insights: the historical shape of traumatic experience, on the one hand, and, on the other hand, the urgency and difficulty of bearing witness in an era that is nonetheless imperatively, ethically, and by historical necessity an "age of testimony." In her book (coauthored with Dori Laub) entitled *Testimony: Crises of Witnessing in Literature, Psychoanalysis, and History* (1992), Felman argues that there exists a profound relation between the urgent need for testimony after the Holocaust and the "crisis of witnessing" at the heart of this history and of this critical testimonial demand.[1] What would it mean, Felman asks, to rethink the event of the Holocaust itself—and not only its later remembering—around this crisis of witnessing, this inherent difficulty of bearing witness to it, this impossible narration? And conversely, how do the forms of testimony that occur after the Holocaust (in art, film, and videotaped testimonies) reenact this crisis of witnessing, and in their turn participate in—and transmit—the actual occurrence of the event?

In the book that follows *Testimony* (1992) and rethinks its issues ten years later, under the title *The Juridical Unconscious: Trials and Traumas in the Twentieth Century* (2002), these questions, originally understood through the realms of psychoanalysis and art, are reformulated around a surprising, new

393

conceptual conjunction between trauma and the law. The traumatic history of two World Wars, Felman argues, which resolved itself in a series of unprecedented international and national postwar trials inaugurated by the Nuremberg Trials, has brought to light something that always existed but that the twentieth century for the first time brings into dramatic focus, in making more explicit and more visible what Felman calls, in a pathbreaking analysis, "the hidden link between trials and traumas." [2] In the two chapters of *The Juridical Unconscious* devoted to the 1961 trial of Nazi perpetrator Adolf Eichmann in Jerusalem, Felman suggests that the trial not only provides a legal framework for the judgment of Eichmann's crimes but also becomes, itself, a "theater of justice," the legal stage becoming the actual site of visibility of a traumatic historical occurrence, which inadvertently is reenacted on the site of the law. In this legal reenactment of the trauma—and in the disruptive and novel possibilities of legal testimony that arise from it—history and justice emerge in the disruption and in the reformulation and reinterpretation of legal consciousness as such.

Felman's insight into the relation between law and trauma in the Eichmann trial takes place, however, not simply through a direct analysis of the trial but also through a confrontation and encounter with the text of one of the trial's most prominent reporters, the celebrated German-Jewish, American political philosopher Hannah Arendt, whose controversial and pathbreaking trial reports for the *New Yorker* and the 1963 book that arose out of them under the title *Eichmann in Jerusalem: A Report on the Banality of Evil*, are the point of departure for Felman's own analysis. Coming to Jerusalem with her past expertise as a political thinker (previously crowned by her innovative political analysis of the unprecedented historical phenomenon of totalitarianism), Arendt believes that the trial of the Nazi perpetrator can only acknowledge and do justice to the Nazis' unique crimes by preserving the strict legal focus of the law. She criticizes the Israeli state and the state's prosecution for focusing heavily instead on the victims' testimonial stories, which in her eyes distract from the trial's strict legal purpose of defining and of proving Eichmann's crimes. Moreover, Arendt charges the prosecution with exploiting the victims' "tales of horror" to shore up a particularist version of Jewish justice related to an exhibition of the power and political significance of the Jewish state, a justice that Arendt does not share and passionately fights from her cosmopolitan and universalist perspective. It is Arendt's critique of the use of victims' testimonies as the focus of the trial that is the starting point of Felman's contrary argument that the trial is a transformative legal and testimonial event precisely because it creates a new language and a new legal space in which the victims become witnesses and in which traumatic memory can emerge as history for the first time, that is, come into being as a traumatic history capable of speech. I will argue in my turn that it is in the confrontation and the meeting between the differential modes of understanding of Arendt and Felman—in their insights joined together in the critical encounter between the psychoanalytic-literary and the philosophical-political perspectives on the trial, as well as, I would add, in the unconscious ways in which the two texts (and the two untold life stories) of the two women thinkers unwittingly resonate with and shed light on each other—that we can best understand the emergence of justice, and of history, at the site of the law.

I. Critical Encounters

A BATTLE OVER LEGAL MEANING

Felman's response to Arendt takes place through her discovery that the philosophical core issue behind Arendt's passionate analysis of the trial is the larger question of the significance of law as source of meaning (legal meaning), and as a tool of recovery of the human—after the dehumanization of the Holocaust. Felman analyzes Arendt's famous and controversial claim, her contention that a central lesson of the Eichmann trial was its illustration, in the person of Adolph Eichmann—the man responsible in the Third Reich for coordinating the transportation of the Jews to the death camps—of what Arendt designates as the new totalitarian phenomenon of the "banality of evil."[3] Arendt suggested that Eichmann participated in an unprecedented criminal event not because he was the incarnation of evil motivations, but rather out of his personal ambition to advance in the Nazi regime and because of his inability to think or speak in terms other than those that were ideologically handed to him. This banality of Eichmann was linked, for Arendt, to a larger vision of the unprecedented nature of the Holocaust, which she understood, as Felman emphasizes, both in terms of the lack of the usual psychological causal explanations for the crimes of the perpetrators and as the attempt, within the totalitarian

the man fr. the
p. Korean work camp

system, to eradicate not only individuals and groups but ultimately also "the concept of the human being" as such.[4]

Arendt's notion of the banality of evil was immediately misunderstood, when her report appeared, as a trivialization (banalization) of the Nazi crimes. Felman, in contrast, understands the gist of Arendt's central concept of "banality of evil" as a political (and legal) insight into the crucial role of language in the disaster of the Holocaust. Noting that Arendt's description of Eichmann's banality concerns his apparent lack of personal motivation against the Jews and his empty, clichéd borrowings of Nazi language, his archaic and anachronistic Nazi bureaucratic use of German even during the trial, Felman suggests that Arendt's notion of banality is "not psychological but legal and political" (JU, 107–8). Arendt sees the goal of the trial, Felman argues, as that of redefining legal meaning and restoring linguistic meaning and a capacity of speech to a world that the Holocaust has shattered, dispossessing in it both language and the law of any human meaning:

> If evil is linguistically and legally banal (devoid of human motivations and occurring through clichés that screen reality and actuality), in what ways, Arendt asks, can the law become an anchor and a guarantee, a guardian of humanity? How can the law *fight over language* with this radical banality (the total identification with a borrowed language)? When language itself becomes subsumed by the banality of evil, *how can the law keep meaning to the word "humanity"*? (JU, 108)

Arendt's insight into Eichmann's actions — her sense that he, and other Nazis, were capable of mass annihilation in a manner not understandable through the usual psychological explanations but rather through a radical loss of language and thought that encompassed the totalitarian world — is for Felman a political insight that ties the trial to the struggle to restore and redefine human meaning after the catastrophic event. The banality of evil "designates a gap between event and explanations" (JU, 108), a gap that defines the Holocaust within the entire framework of Arendt's concept of totalitarianism, which undid previous political (and legal) frameworks of human meaning. The power of Arendt's political analysis, Felman would thus suggest, lies in focusing the trial on the problem of meaning and in particular on the problem of the legal meaning of the word "humanity." It is this understanding of the trial as a "fight over language" against its radical banalization and dehumanization—its loss of human and legal meaning during the Holocaust—that in Felman's understanding gives its specificity to Arendt's analysis and to Arendt's insight into the trial, an insight Felman considers as truly pathbreaking. What Felman defines as Arendt's specifically political perspective on the trial thus emerges as a larger question concerning justice and human significance: *What does it mean for the law to restore language and restore meaning after the Holocaust? What is the relevance of justice to a redefinition of the Human?*

TRAUMATIC HISTORY AND JUSTICE AS THE EMERGENCE OF SPEECH

The answer to this question, Felman suggests, first of all concerns the remedial power, after the unprecedented devastation of the Holocaust, of legal speech.

As Felman summarizes Arendt's argument in the first of her two chapters on the Eichmann trial (chapter 3, entitled "Theaters of Justice: Arendt in Jerusalem, the Eichmann Trial, and the Redefinition of Legal Meaning in the Wake of the Holocaust"), the political thinker insists that the unprecedented nature of the historical event of the Holocaust—its radical rupturing of political, legal, and human meaning—requires a strict legal language and a narrow legal focus on the actions of the perpetrator in order to preserve, against the unsettling effects of the totalitarian disruption, the notions of legal judgment and justice. One must step out of the abyss by means of the remedial power of the traditional legal language of the law. This means focusing the trial's legal functions on the actions of Eichmann and passing judgment on their criminality in spite of their unusual lack of ordinary criminal motivation. The problem with the prosecution's focus on witness testimonies is that it places "history at the center of the trial"[5] rather than Eichmann's actions and thus contaminates the law with history. This contamination by the victims' stories undermines the judicial power of legal language to transcend the history that it judges.

But this contamination of the law and history within the legal testimony also hides, for Arendt, the reality of the history it is meant to judge. Because the prosecution uses the witness stories as new versions of the old stories of anti-Semitism—and presents the Holocaust as one more anti-Semitic event among others—the trial and the witnesses

cover over what is new in the event. Felman argues that Arendt's condemnation of the contamination of law and history derives from her
perception of the trial as an effect of trauma:

> The trial perceives Nazism as the monstrous culmination and as
> the traumatic repetition of a monumental history of anti-Semi-
> tism. But for Arendt this victim's perspective, this traumatized
> perception of history as the eternal repetition of a catastrophe is
> numbing. . . . A trial is supposed to be precisely a translation of
> the trauma into consciousness. But here the numbing trauma is
> mixed into the form of the trial itself. In litigating and in arguing
> the charges on the basis of a numbing repetition of catastrophe,
> Jewish historical consciousness — and the trial as a whole —
> submits to the effects of trauma instead of remedying it. History
> becomes the illustration of what is already known. . . . In the Is-
> raeli vision of the trial, the monumental, analogical perception of
> the repetition of the trauma of anti-Semitism *screens the new* —
> hides from view precisely the unprecedented nature of the Nazi
> crime, which is neither a development nor a culmination of what
> went before, but is separated from the history breaching it by an
> abyss. (*JU*, 121–22)

For Arendt, then, in Felman's recounting of her argument, the contamination of law and history — through the victims' repetition of traumatic meaning as return to the old — in reality preserves neither the
law nor history. It replaces a recognition of an adequate legal response
to the Holocaust with the captive, entrapped vision of a return that is
then, furthermore, co-opted by the Israeli state, which uses the anti-
Semitic story as a particular (distorted) version of Zionist claims to
return to the homeland as the central and, in fact, only legitimate
representation of Judaism. Both justice and history can be preserved,
however, only if the law preserves, in its own judging function, their
respective discreteness, the clear-cut demarcation line between the
two domains, the radical separation between the two disciplines and
the two epistemologies.

For Felman, in contrast, the intercontamination of law and history
in the witnesses' testimonies precisely makes possible the remedial
power of the law. This is because the victim's stories, for Felman, are

not returns to the old but rather attempts to translate an event that has not yet been articulated into a new form of speech:

> A victim is by definition not only one who is oppressed but also one who has no language of his own, one who, quite precisely, is robbed of a language with which to articulate his or her victimization. (JU, 125)

> I will argue . . . that, in focusing on repetition and its limits in the Eichmann trial, Arendt fails to see the way in which the trial in effect does not repeat the victim's story, but historically creates it for the first time. I submit, in other words, that the Eichmann trial legally creates a radically original and new event: not a rehearsal of a given story, but a groundbreaking narrative event that is itself historically and legally unprecedented. (JU, 123)

For Felman, in other words, the erasure of the victim, the trauma of the Holocaust, is defined by an erasure of language, an erasure that takes away the victim's story. What is unprecedented in the event can only emerge or be known for the first time *in the trial itself*, which does not repeat an old story but creates a new one that has never existed as consciousness before:

> The trial shows how the unprecedented nature of the injury inflicted on the victims cannot be simply stated in a language that is already at hand. I would argue that the trial struggles to create a new space, a language that is not yet in existence. This new legal language is created here perhaps for the first time in history precisely by the victims' firsthand narrative. (JU, 123)

The trial (through the witnesses' testimonies) testifies to the uniqueness of the Holocaust by creating the story of the event for the first time. Prior to the Eichmann trial, Felman argues, "what we call the Holocaust did not exist as a collective story" (JU, 127).

What Arendt sees as the contamination of the law by history is thus for Felman the only form of translation of this history, whose articulation does not preexist the trial. The victims were erased by history: they could not in real time assume themselves as subjects, they had no language except for the oppressor's language, which dehumanized them and erased their voices and their narrative perspectives. The trial creates this narrative perspective for the first time, in giving voice to their historical voicelessness. The trial is thus in itself also a legal remedy of sorts: it creates what Felman calls "a revolution in the victim":

> It is this revolutionary transformation of the victim that makes the victim's story happen for the first time, and happen as a legal act of authorship of history. (126)

| | | |

If Arendt thus sees the Holocaust, from her political perspective, as a political annihilation and erasure of the human requiring a separate legal remedy, Felman sees the Holocaust as a linguistic erasure of the victims' subjecthood that can only be remedied by repossessing one's own history and one's own subjectivity through the instruments of law and by recreating thus the language of the law as an *original* and *revolutionary* historical testimony.[6] The act of justice emerges in the transmission (and transformation) of the historical event within the language of the trial. We might then suggest that Arendt's question as interpreted by Felman, *What does it mean for the law to restore human meaning from the banality of evil and to recover language after the Holocaust?* becomes, in Felman's own revised perspective, *How can a traumatic history give rise, within the law, to a meaningful story? How can the law transmit a traumatic history (previously untransmittable as such)?* Philosophically: *What is the relation, in legal testimony and, in general, in the proceedings of the law, between trauma and justice?* And, ultimately: *How can justice be (become) a remedy to trauma?*

A GHOST IN THE HOUSE OF JUSTICE

The first chapter devoted to the Eichmann Trial in *The Juridical Unconscious*—"Theaters of Justice: Arendt in Jerusalem, the Eichmann Trial and the Redefinition of Legal Meaning in the Wake of the Holocaust"—thus focuses on the remedial powers of the law through its creation of a new collective story of the Holocaust, and through the revolution in the witnesses that gives them back authority, subjecthood, and speech and thus redeems them from a history of muteness and silent trauma. *The Juridical Unconscious*'s second chapter on the Eichmann trial, "A Ghost in the House of Justice: Death and the Language of the Law," in contrast, focuses on one witness' collapse to silence on the legal stage. The division between the two chapters dealing with the Eichmann trial in *The Juridical Unconscious* can thus be understood as a structural division between, on the one hand, the way in which the law illuminates the witnesses' speech, and, on the other hand, the way in which the law illuminates the witness's silence.

The second chapter starts abruptly, with the narration of a surprising incident of loss of voice and loss of consciousness within the trial:

> A witness faints on the stand during the Eichmann trial. This chapter will explore the meaning of this unexpected legal moment, and will ask: Is the witness's collapse relevant — and if so, in what sense — to the legal framework of the trial? How does this courtroom event affect the trial's definition of legal meaning in the wake of the Holocaust? Under what circumstances and in what ways can the legal default of a witness constitute a legal testimony in its own right? (*JU*, 131)

Felman's analysis here focuses on the memorable moment of the collapse on the witness stand of Yehiel Dinoor, who is rather known under the pseudonym "K-Zetnik," a notorious literary writer of bestselling autobiographical novels on the Holocaust. Dinoor had met Eichmann at Auschwitz and is brought on to testify for the prosecution as one of the central eyewitnesses of Eichmann in his Nazi role. But Dinoor collapses on the stand mid-speech. Seeing Eichmann again causes him to faint. As Felman recounts and interprets the scene, the collapse occurs just after the witness has confirmed his legal name (Dinoor) and is asked to explain his self-imposed name as a writer, "K-Zetnik," a pseudonym that designates "a concentration-camp inmate" in general and is thus meant to symbolize a certain anonymity of shared traumatic fate. "What is your full name?" asked the presiding judge. "Yehiel Dinoor," answered the witness. The prosecutor then proceeded: "What is the reason that you took the pen name K-Zetnik, Mr. Dinoor?" "It is not a pen name," the witness began answering:

> I do not regard myself as a writer who writes literature. This is a chronicle from the planet of Auschwitz. I was there for about two years. Time there was different from what it is here on earth. . . . And the inhabitants of that planet had no names. . . . They did not

live, nor did they die, in accordance with the laws of this world. Their names were the numbers "K-Zetnik so and so." . . . They left me, they kept leaving me, left. . . . For close to two years they kept leaving me and always left me behind. . . . I see them, they are watching me, I see them . . .

At this point the prosecutor gently interrupted, "Mr. Dinoor, could I perhaps put a few questions to you if you will consent?" But Dinoor continues speaking [Felman points out], as a man plunged in hallucination: "I see them, I saw them standing in the line. . . ."

Thereupon the presiding judge matter-of-factly intervened, "Mr. Dinoor, please, please listen to Mr. Hausner; wait a minute, now you listen to me!"

The haggard witness vacantly got up and without a warning collapsed into a faint, slumping to the floor beside the witness stand. (JU, 136)

Taking this scene as a central symbolic moment of the proceedings, Felman argues that this collapse of the witness and this unexpected breakdown of speech and failure of the legal testimony is, nevertheless, highly significant to the unfolding legal meaning of the trial. It is not, paradoxically, the witness' mere speech, but the collapse of this speech into silence, that operates here as the central site of a possible new mode for rethinking legal testimony.

If in Felman's first chapter on the trial and her first confrontation with Arendt, then, the collective testimonies of the witnesses appear to her as new and revolutionary voices, here it is the muteness and the silence of the fainted witness—and the dramatic, speechless, yet telling intervention of his unconscious body on the legal stage—that will create an unexpected testimonial power. The possibility of justice—and of testimony—thus occurs through a point of disruption of the law that explodes the framework of the trial and assumes meaning precisely in exceeding and interrupting the trial's legal frame.

SILENT HISTORY

Arendt narrates the sudden fainting of the witness as a marginal, legally surprising, and hilarious, laughable scene, whose fantastic literary content ("This is a chronicle from the planet of Auschwitz") is irrelevant to the trial testimony except insofar as its sudden drama is symbolic of the errors, misdirection, and legal breakdown of the prosecution in its misguided emphasis on victimhood and in its vain selection of "prominent" witnesses (Arendt is deeply suspicious of writers' testimony as such). Felman's vision of this scene differs radically from that of Arendt, in that she reads the literary pathos of K-Zetnik's speech, punctuated by his fall to silence on the witness stand, as fraught with unintentional embodied and unwittingly enacted legal meaning. Despite the discrepancy between Arendt's and Felman's views, one might argue nonetheless (and Felman herself acknowledges this point) that Felman's insight here also emerges out of her confrontation with Arendt's sarcasm and with her ironic focus on the incongruity of the collapse as an interruption of the legal discourse. For K-Zetnik, Felman notes, Arendt reserves among all witnesses her most caustic, undercutting irony and her funniest, fiercest, and most biting humor, describing the abruptly speechless writer as a witness theatrically and narcissistically involved with his own self-presentation. His dramatic collapse, which blocks the prosecution's ability to move forward with questions, stages for Arendt the general misfire of the prosecution's strategy of using irrelevant witness testimony.

In contrast to Arendt, Felman recasts K-Zetnik's collapse not as a theatrical staging of a "disappointed" witness narcissistically "wounded" by the judge's call to order (as Arendt psychologically depicts him from the distance of her laughter) but rather as a deeply moving moment of traumatic flashback, a courtroom event of actual retraumatization of the witness:

> The witness is not "deeply wounded" but is re-traumatized. The trial reenacts the trauma . . . when the judge admonishes Dinoor from the authoritarian position of the bench, coercing him into a legal mode of discourse and demanding his cooperation as a witness, K-Zetnik undergoes severe traumatic shock in reexperiencing the same terror and panic that dumbfounded him each time when, as an inmate, he was suddenly confronted by the inexorable Nazi authorities of Auschwitz. . . . The call to order by the judge . . . impacts the witness physically as an invasive call to order by an SS officer. Once more, the imposition of a heartless and unbending rule of order violently robs him of his words and, in reducing him to silence, once more threatens to annihilate

him, to erase his essence as a human witness. Panicked, K-Zetnik
loses consciousness. (JU, 146)

The sudden fainting of K-Zetnik on the witness stand, his collapse from
speech to silence, is, for Felman, not a staging of what is known but
rather the reenactment of a moment that cannot be known, the reenactment, on the witness stand and through the legal interrogation, of
the experience of human erasure at Auschwitz. The admonishing,
raised voice of the judge "violently robs him of his words and once
more threatens to annihilate him, to erase his essence as a human
witness." The trial at this moment thus unwittingly repeats the erasure of the witness—the erasure of the human being as a speaking
being and as a conscious witness to the event—an erasure that in Felman's analysis constituted the very ungraspable essence of the Holocaust event. The erasure of the human through the trial as such makes
history erupt into the courtroom not as an individual testimony but
as the trial's own testimonial reenactment of the event.

It is indeed this reenactment of erasure *on the level of the trial*, rather
than simply on the level of the individual human being, that for Felman (I would argue) has important legal and historical significance.
For what repeats the trauma here is not simply K-Zetnik's own intrusive reexperiencing of the past but rather what Felman calls, more
largely, the "missed encounter" between the legal language of the law
(represented by the prosecutor and the judge) and K-Zetnik's traumatized language, a missed encounter that constitutes a break in the
legal framework of the trial. K-Zetnik's fainting interposes both silence
and the sight of his lifeless body on the legal stage of the court, and in
this interruption not only K-Zetnik but the courtroom, and indeed the
law itself, are caught by history:

> The fainting that cuts through the witness's speech and petrifies
> his body interrupts the legal process and creates a moment that is
> legally traumatic not just for the witness, but also chiefly for the
> court and for the audience of the trial. I argue in effect that, in
> the rupture of the witness's lapse into a coma, *it is the law itself that
> for a moment loses consciousness.* But it is through this breakdown of
> the legal framework that history emerges in the courtroom and,
> in the legal body of the witness, exhibits its own inadvertently
> dramatic (non-discursive) rules of evidence. It is precisely through

this break of consciousness of law that history unwittingly and mutely, yet quite resonantly, memorably speaks. (*JU*, 164)

It is the unconsciousness of the law, and not just the unconsciousness of K-Zetnik, that brings history onto the legal stage as a disruption of the legal framework and as a silent (and visible) reenactment in the courtroom.

It is in this legal trauma experienced by the trial, moreover, that the history of the Holocaust emerges in its essential relation to the collapse—and reconstitution—of justice. In the Holocaust, Felman suggests, *justice itself was structured like a trauma*: the collapse of justice that constituted the event is reenacted within the trial in the attempt and failure of the legal testimony to bear witness to Auschwitz. And as such the trial, in its momentary failure, reveals both the essence of the trauma as constituted by this judicial collapse and the essence of this history in the entanglement of trial and trauma.

The collapse into silence of K-Zetnik must be understood therefore as a moment that exceeds the boundaries of the individual and carries with it a larger history—of silence—that testifies to the silence of the groups whose voices have been annihilated. Against Arendt, Felman will suggest that the act of falling into silence is not simply a legal failure but a historical testimony. As such, this silence also reveals the inextricable relation between history (which is silenced) and justice (which occurs as a collapse of the witness and as a returning demand for legal testimony).

It is this traumatic entanglement of law and history that also makes possible, however, the reconstitution of a new language of justice. Because, in the scene of the writer's collapse and in the physical collapse of his testimonial speech, the trial inadvertently enables silence to enter the framework of the law and to explode its containing space, the collapse makes possible the act of witness of those who speak. Because the law (in the form of the trial) bears witness to silence in the breaking of its own frame, the individual witnesses can come to speak, and do justice to history, within the trial.

In response to Arendt, Felman's complex argument, I would suggest, can therefore be summed up by the following four major points: (1) What enters the trial at the moment of collapse is a legal trauma that does not repeat (as Arendt feels) the already known, but rather repeats itself traumatically as *not yet known*: the Holocaust continues to occur on the site of the trial itself. (2) What thus repeats itself is not only an individual trauma but also the trauma of the law itself, the erasure of the law and of the legal human being reenacting itself as a core element of the Holocaust event (in this sense the trial is itself part of the Holocaust event, whose consequences and effects are not yet over). (3) Because the trauma is thus already in some sense legal, the trial can and must be the site of its repetition. (4) Because in this writer's collapse the trial enables silence to enter the framework of the law and to explode the law's containing space, the collapse makes possible the act of witness of those who do speak. Because the law (in the form of the trial) bears witness to silence in the breaking of its own frame, individual witnesses can come to speak within the trial.

DEPARTURE

Looking at K-Zetnik's last words before he faints, Felman locates at the heart of the testimonial moment of this physical collapse on the witness stand no longer simply — as Arendt sees it — the narcissistic exhibitionism of a "disappointed, deeply wounded" witness whose fantastic and slightly delirious discourse has been interrupted by the judge, nor even simply an irrelevant, distracting repetition or intrusion of the traumatic past into the legal present, but, rather, the costly reenactment of a departure into the unknown, into *a future* that has not yet been rehearsed and whose meaning cannot as yet be grasped either by the trial's audience or by the flabbergasted judges:

> Prior to his fainting spell [Felman observes], at the point where the prosecutor interrupts him, K-Zetnik tries to define Auschwitz by re-envisaging the terrifying moment of Selection, of repeated weekly separation between inmates chosen for an imminent extermination and inmates arbitrarily selected for life. This moment is ungraspable, the witness tries to say: "And the inhabitants of that planet had no names. They had neither parents nor children. . . . They did not live, nor did they die, in accordance with the laws of this world. Their names were their numbers. . . . They left me, they kept leaving me, left . . . for close to two years they left me and always left me behind. . . . I see them they are watching me, I see them. . . ."
>
> What K-Zetnik keeps reliving of the death camp [Felman proceeds to analyze] is the moment of departure, the last gaze of the

departed, the exchange of looks between the dying and the living at the very moment in which life and death are separating but are still tied up together and can for the last time see each other eye to eye. (JU, 147–48)

The moment of departure of the survivor separating from those who are about to be exterminated, the uncanny legal moment in which K-Zetnik reenacts his farewell to the departing—his leave-taking from the dead—is also, I would argue, a moment of K-Zetnik's own departure from the concentration camp into the singular moment of the trial. The event of erasure, we might say, repeats itself and, as it were, departs into the trial through the witness and in his very collapse.

| | | |

I would like to pause here and step back a moment, in order to reflect on the whole picture to which the Eichmann trial has given rise, and to create a larger syntax of interrogation, keeping simultaneously in view both Arendt's and Felman's analyses. The emergence of the story of the trial through the trial's fall back into silence leads to several new and urgent questions. How do we understand the translation of silence into speech in this traumatic legal moment? In what ways do Felman's psychoanalytic understanding of the repetition of the trauma of the Holocaust within the Eichmann trial as the return of a traumatizing legal erasure, and Arendt's political understanding of the legal and political erasure experienced by the victims of totalitarianism (an understanding not explicitly articulated in her trial report, but formulated elsewhere and underlying all her political thought) meet around this relation between speech and silence? I argue that despite their differences, Arendt's and Felman's confrontations with the Eichmann trial (with both its discourse and its silence) meet, and can and must be understood, not as contradictory perceptions, but as two insightful, novel visions in effect enhancing one another. I would like to raise, therefore, the larger questions that arise from this encounter: *What are the meeting points and what are, in fact, the unarticulated common grounds between these two women thinkers? What can their encounter tell us about the possibility of rethinking the Holocaust, not through the opposition, but, on the contrary, through the encounter of the political and the traumatic—of trauma theories and of political theories taken together?*

ii. Mute Witness

Felman does not aim at exploring this conceptual combination in her deliberate argument, but she does begin to approach it, I would argue, when she proposes to read a silent subtext in Arendt's book, which will "show how Arendt's legal narrative in *Eichmann in Jerusalem* unwittingly encapsulates not only the reporter's critical account, but also the thinker's own (erased) artistic testimony and the writer's own traumatic narrative" (*JU*, 156). This silent narrative begins to emerge through a different aspect of Arendt's relation to K-Zetnik, not simply her sarcastic dismissal of his self-dramatization and her unsentimental, distant laughter at the legal absurdity of the whole situation, but rather the specific way in which the witness's collapse reenacts a "failure of narration" that, in Arendt's eyes, defeats the logic and the purpose of the trial. Commenting on this scene of unexpected interruption of K-Zetnik's story, Arendt writes: "This, to be sure, was an exception, but if it was an exception that proved the rule of normality, it did not prove the rule of simplicity or of ability to tell a story."[7] Arendt generalizes the collapse of the witness as an allegory of the obstacles to narration the trial comes up against: K-Zetnik's abnormality as a witness is an exception, Arendt concedes, but the exception that proves the rule (of normality): the fact that "normal" testimonies in this trial (witnesses who did not collapse) also lacked "simplicity" or adherence to a strict factual narrative linearity and "did not prove"—fell short of—the "ability to tell," which for Arendt is the basis for a valid testimony. Felman underscores Arendt's analysis of the "failure of narration," in referring it to the general importance Arendt attributes to the act of storytelling, crucial in her eyes for the trial's success. Felman suggests that Arendt inherited this concept of storytelling from her (now dead) friend Walter Benjamin, whose intellectual companionship she had treasured and whose philosophical thought she had listened to and shared during their common exile in France as two fraternal German-Jewish refugees. This shared destiny, this shared loss of and flight from their cherished cultural origins, ended differently, however, for Arendt and for Benjamin: he died, she survived; but for a chance accident, she could have died like him; he should have survived like her. In surviving, she crossed over a line of death, a split in culture, in the world and within herself, which he mutely represents.

During this period of their common French exile, Walter Benjamin authored the famous essay entitled "The Storyteller," which Arendt published posthumously and redeemed from forgetfulness many years later in the United Sates. In Felman's vision, the implicit and perhaps unconscious reference to the storyteller in *Eichmann in Jerusalem* also reenacts unwittingly Benjamin's spiritual legacy and everything that is symbolized, in Arendt and for Arendt, by the mute wound of his loss and of his death. Behind the concept of the storyteller, Felman suggests, the unnamed shadow of Benjamin projects itself over the critically illuminated pages of the book as Arendt's own subterranean and mute testimony, indirectly bearing witness to the wound of her personal loss of her friend (his life, his human warmth, his future insight) to Nazi persecution, this unnamed name embodying the line of death that she has crossed, embodying her own dead self, her own unnamed yet implicitly present silenced personal heartache and trauma. Felman's far-reaching and intuitive analysis grows out of an attempt to unpack the density and the incisiveness of Arendt's comment on K-Zetnik:

> "This [says Arendt], to be sure, was an exception, but if it was an exception that proved the rule of normality, it did not prove the rule of simplicity or of ability to tell a story." (*EiJ*, 224) [Felman proceeds to comment by association, unraveling the subtle threads of a perspective in depth:] As an exception that confirms the rule of normality—that is, as a symbol of the legal abnormality of the trial as a whole—Arendt faults K-Zetnik for his inability to tell a story and thus to testify coherently. "Who says what is . . . always tells a story, and in this story the particular facts lose their contingency and acquire some humanly comprehensible meaning," Arendt will write in "Truth and Politics," doubtless remembering unconsciously the unforgettable essay called "The Storyteller" written by her dead friend Walter Benjamin, whose name she will in 1968—five years after the Eichmann book—redeem from anonymity and namelessness by publishing his work in the United States, but whose lost friendship she will silently mourn all her life as an intimate grievance, a wordless wound, a personal price that she herself has secretly paid to the Holocaust.

I hear [says Felman] a reference to "The Storyteller" in the conclusion of Arendt's account of K-Zetnik's testimony: "It did not prove
the rule of simplicity or of ability to tell a story." (157)

In a totally unexpected manner, Felman taps into a level of sensitivity
of Arendt's text that has been so well concealed and so deeply buried
behind Arendt's irate critique and her sarcastic laughter that it has
previously escaped perception. Ironically enough, Felman points out,
Arendt's ironic insight into K-Zetnik's inability to tell a story also reflects back on Arendt's own mute (unintended, unarticulated) testimony, in linguistically inscribing her own pain, her unhealed grief
over a story she in turn cannot tell, of her loss of her dear friend, the
profound German-Jewish thinker and literary critic Walter Benjamin.
Benjamin committed suicide in 1940 while caught at the border between France and Spain, in his attempt to exit France illegally (like
Arendt) in order to escape the Nazis and emigrate to the United States
(like Arendt). Felman attempts to show how Benjamin's own work on,
and insight into, the silence of the traumatized returning veterans of
World War I (in his article "The Storyteller") is passed on unconsciously into Arendt's reading of the trauma of the Second World War,
and inscribes itself in her own language about the Eichmann trial,
particularly in her comments about the need for storytelling and her
recognition of the failure of narration and this lapse back into silence
in K-Zetnik's case. Arendt's legal critique—her political reading of the
trial—thus contains within it an indirect and unintended personal testimonial element, inscribing at once the trauma of Benjamin's death,
and the survival of his thought, within her book.

"Death," wrote Benjamin precisely in his essay, "is the sanction of
everything that the storyteller has to say. He has borrowed his authority from death" (St., 94n). In the wake of Benjamin's insight into storytelling as a narrative deriving its authority from death, and in the
wake of Benjamin's own death, whose presence Felman reads as the
emotional subtext of Arendt's book, Felman thus asks, offering perhaps her most surprising insight into *Eichmann in Jerusalem*:

Has Arendt in her turn borrowed her authority as a storyteller of
the trial from a legacy of death of which she does not speak and
cannot speak? I would suggest indeed that . . . *Eichmann in Jerusalem*
is also Arendt's book of mourning. It is, in other words, a

book—an unarticulated statement—on the relation between grief and justice, as well as on the counterparts of grief and justice in narrative and storytelling . . . both the Eichmann trial and Arendt's critical rehearsal of it are preoccupied—albeit in different styles—with the translation of grief into justice. Both are therefore mirror images of the translation of grief into grievance. . . . There is, in other words, a crucial story Arendt does not tell and cannot tell that underlies the story of the trial she does tell. (158)

Felman thus suggests that the "testimonial muteness underlying (and exceeding) Arendt's legal story" in fact "reenacts, ironically enough, the literary muteness of K-Zetnik's story" (160).

If we go along with Felman, we might argue, indeed, that in Arendt's own mute testimony (as Felman reads it), the erased victim of the Holocaust—whom Arendt would keep out of the trial—reemerges in the form of Benjamin. Arendt, Felman says, wishes to turn the grief into justice by means of legal speech. Arendt would rather not display grief on the public stage. She faults the prosecutor and his witness for their exhibitionism of grief. She faults the trial for its inadequate translation of grief into strict legal language. Felman has a slightly different take on this central question of the relation between grief and justice:

Arendt

> I would argue differently from Arendt that it was the *inadvertent legal essence* and legal innovation and uniqueness of the Eichmann trial, and not its testimonial accident, to voice the muteness generated by the Holocaust and to *articulate the difficulty of articulation* of the catastrophic story, the difficulty of articulation and the tragic unnarratability of the ungraspable disaster and its immeasurably devastating, unintelligible trauma. The impossibility of telling is not external to this story: it is the story's heart. The trial shows how the inherent inability to tell the story is itself an integral part of the history and of the story of the Holocaust. The function of the trial thus becomes precisely to articulate the impossibility of telling through the legal process and to convert this *narrative impossibility* into *legal meaning*. (159)

Felman poses her argument in opposition to Arendt's argument, but her understanding of the relation between speech and silence in fact grows out of Arendt's reading of the trial, and out of the way in which a testimony arises through and behind Arendt's own muteness. I would further suggest that in her reading—and her conceptual highlighting—of the testimonial "relation between grief and justice" in Arendt's text, Felman implicitly links Arendt's testimony with the untold traumatic story of the erased legal subject that lies somewhere behind (though not explicitly within) Arendt's reading of the trial, and that constitutes the underlying basis for her political understanding of the Holocaust and of its legal remedy. Felman's reading thus begins to point, implicitly, toward an unconscious element of the political theory itself.

BETWEEN TWO LANGUAGES: FELMAN'S MUTE TESTIMONY

I would suggest that Felman's own text, moreover, also has a silent subtext, and in its turn bears mute testimony through Felman's reading and critique of Arendt's text, and that this excess of the argument in the insight and in the layers of sensitivity of Felman's text creates as yet another perspective and another vantage point that compel us to view political theory and trauma theory at the same time and to articulate the two disciplines together. By looking at what resonates behind Felman's text, we can begin to understand why Felman's discussion of the Eichmann trial divides itself into two separate chapters. This duality of chapters—the articulation of the split between the chapters—can itself take place, I will suggest, only through a story, and it is in this new silent story that a possible meeting of the political and the traumatic can perhaps begin to take shape.

Felman's response to the stories of departure and linguistic muteness in Arendt's relation to Benjamin's story in fact echo, I will show, her own responses to Arendt's story. Her most resonant response to Arendt, she has told me in an interview she gave me on this topic, took place when she read Arendt's autobiographical account of the linguistic displacements in her life, entailed by her forced exile and departure from Germany upon the Nazis' rise to power, six years prior to the actual outbreak of the Second World War. Arendt's account is narrated in an interview with Günter Gaus that took place in 1964, shortly after Arendt returned to Germany for the first time since the end of the Second World War.[8] In response to Gaus's question concerning what remains for her now of prewar Europe, Arendt replies:

The Europe of the pre-Hitler period? I do not long for that, I can tell you. What remains? The language remains. . . . I have always consciously refused to lose my mother tongue. I have always maintained a certain distance from French, which I then spoke very well, as well as from English, which I write today. . . . I write in English, but I have never lost a feeling of distance from it. There is a tremendous difference between your mother tongue and another language. . . . The German language is the essential thing that has remained and that I have always consciously preserved. (*Essays in Understanding*, 12–13)

"I have always been moved by this moment of the interview with Gaus," Felman says. "Arendt's fear of losing the mother tongue, her split between her mother tongue and the other languages she speaks and writes so fluently and with such eloquence is also a split in her life, which represents her fractured history as well as a gap among her languages, a gap that embodies an impossible split between the German side of her, which she continues to preserve and secretly treasure through the language that she intimately speaks with her husband and her German friends, and the Jewish side of her, which henceforth defines the remainder of her life and determines her political thinking, her political understanding of herself and of the world subsequent to the Second World War."[9] Felman's response to Arendt's "untold story" of Benjamin's death as an unredeemed, perennially illegal Jew, her resonance with Arendt's muted evocation of Benjamin's aborted departure from Occupied France embodying his failure to escape as a rightless, stateless person from his deadly entrapment in Nazi Europe, the subtext for which is also the untold story of Arendt's own successful illegal departure from Germany and France and her successful emigration to, and citizenship in, the United States, speaks to Felman—testifies for Felman—who can hear and give voice to this muted testimony with the power of insight afforded by her own life. Felman's insight into Arendt's muted pathos inadvertently encapsulates, I would suggest, Felman's own mute testimony and muted story, parallel to Arendt's. Not by coincidence, Felman recognizes Arendt's source of insight in the suppressed pathos and the silent underlying story of a Jewish woman who had left at once her homeland and her native tongue.

Arendt's story of linguistic departure, I would insist, however (adding my own emphasis to Felman's analysis of Arendt's erased trauma)—is also the story of a political refugee of the Holocaust: Arendt's complex geography is a political geography with a political significance, including the significant geographical move of Arendt's journey to Jerusalem to cover the Eichmann trial. Arendt's life itinerary is the story not only of her personal and linguistic experience but also of her political experience. Arendt understood quite early the significance of the Nazis' rise to power. As a German Jew helping the resistance and caught by the Gestapo, Arendt had left Germany in 1933, narrowly escaping incarceration, and crossed the border illegally into France, where for a while she worked for a Zionist organization helping to bring Jewish children to Palestine. It is in Paris during this French exile that she met at once her German-Jewish friend and colleague-thinker and writer Walter Benjamin and her non-Jewish future husband Heinrich Bluecher, another persecuted German who had to flee his native country not by virtue of his race but because of his political communist affiliation. Arendt's Parisian bonding to these two stateless Parisian friends and fellow German refugees must have preserved for her a vital human and linguistic link to her German past and to the high German culture she left behind, during a period in which all three of them daily conversed also in French, the language of the substitute country that took them in and gave them refuge. As mentioned earlier, following this French stay, Arendt emigrates to the United States, where she quite soon acquires, in addition to her fluent French, a new and quite amazing English language fluency, and where, after a few years, she writes and publishes—in English—her seminal book *The Origins of Totalitarianism*, a work that, in proposing an original political analysis of Nazi and Stalinist regimes, also tells the story of the twentieth-century creation of the stateless and the rightless: the key political story of the erasure of the legal subject under totalitarian regimes.

It is by virtue of her growing reputation as a published author and as a noted political and cultural journalist, thinker, and critic in the United States that Arendt is engaged by the *New Yorker* to travel on behalf of the magazine from America to Israel, so as to cover the Eichmann trial held in Jerusalem, and to report back from Jerusalem on this high-profile trial to the civilized world—and to an audience of intellectual Americans. However, Arendt's journey to Jerusalem from the United States in the public mission of an American reporter must have also signified for her a private attempt to account for the Nazi crimes and account for what happened to her as a Jew and as a German. But she is deeply ambivalent about the Jewish state, which in her eyes is overly nationalistic and fails to restrain its power (creating more stateless people in the Palestinians). She is contemptuous of the Jewish prosecution, headed by an Eastern European (Ostjuden) Polish Jew, so complacent in his Eastern European pathos, which for Arendt equals false sentimentality, so unlike the high German culture and the elegant restraint of the German-Jewish judges who remind her of her homeland. Indeed, Arendt's privileging of the judges' strict adherence to the law over the prosecution's criticized contamination of the law with political motives also takes the form of a sardonic and acerbic criticism of the linguistic follies of the state—which cannot even properly translate the testimonies into unmutilated German—and the linguistic prowess of the judges who don't deign to "pretend to need the Hebrew" to pose questions to Eichmann but speak to him directly in a fluent native German, thus bypassing the translator and the earphones. Eichmann's banality, as well, is characterized by Arendt by his clichéd and empty use of the German language and by his vacuous adoption of bureaucratic Nazi jargon in the place of any language of expression or responsibility or any message of his own.

In a sense, then, Arendt, as an expatriated German Jew, goes to Jerusalem to seek, among the state of the Jews, both justice and a reckoning that would enable her to account for her own departure, but finds herself instead angry at the Jewish state and inadvertently valorizing the German language and the culture she had left behind. In Jerusalem, she seeks Israeli justice in an unconscious hope to repair and to redeem not just the trauma of her Jewish origin but the trauma of her lost German origin as well: an impossible conjunction whose contradictions are experienced by her in the split between her approval of the law as a higher universal language and principle of justice and her disapproval of the particularist style of the justice machine of the Jewish state, a disapproval aggravated by the disdain she feels for the prosecution's rhetoric of immersing its universal legal agenda in the particularist political agenda of the judging state. The rupture of the Holocaust, which for Arendt is a tragic rupture of the political as such, is inadvertently enacted—reenacted—throughout her visit to Jerusalem and throughout her act of witness to the trial in what she experiences frustratingly as an impossible return to Israel, unwittingly dramatized for her in the split within the trial between politics and law and between German and Jewish languages.

The grief that Felman reads in Arendt's personal relation to Benjamin's aborted departure from Nazi Europe is therefore also Arendt's own mute narrative of grief, in her own impossible separation from the Europe (and the native Germany) she had left behind, her own impossible split as both German and Jew. At the site of this split, two ruptured stories come together: Arendt's personal journey and the political catastrophe that shadows, though it does not quite overtake, her life. This is, in other words, not simply (as Felman reads it and conceptualizes it) a story of the relation between grief and justice, but also, I would argue, a story of the complex relation between grief and politics.

THE MEETING OF TWO PERSPECTIVES

While Arendt, the German-Jewish refugee who has become a U.S. citizen and a reputed American author and professor, travels to Jerusalem through the trial, Felman, equally a well-known university professor in the United States and a world-reputed author, goes back to the trial, and hence to Jerusalem, through Arendt. Originally, Felman was confronted with the Eichmann trial in its real-time historical occurrence through the daily broadcasts of the proceedings over Israeli radio. But she was very young then, and not terribly impressed by it. As an adult however—living and teaching many years later in the United States—Felman revisits the trial through Arendt's book (in English) and, having also watched, in parallel, documentary films of the trial and reviewed some of the live videotaped testimonies that this time affect her deeply, feels compelled to respond to Arendt's criticism. While her thematic, theoretical response takes place primarily as a critique of Arendt's argument against the Israeli prosecution—that is, as a defense of the vision of the prosecution and of the judgment of the Israeli court—there is also, as I have suggested, a different kind of motivation—an unconscious existential resonance with Arendt's own unconscious, untold story—that permeates and inadvertently steers Felman's own writing.

Shoshana Felman was born in Israel to a family of European origin for whom departure and return had already taken on a powerful linguistic significance: her maternal grandfather had moved the family at the beginning of the twentieth century (before the First World War), from Russia to Palestine, insisting (having made an oath) that from the point they set foot on Israeli soil they were to speak nothing but Hebrew (Hebrew was then not a living, spoken language, but a language of the scriptures that was mastered only by a few enlightened, educated Jews who could read and write it. The oath to speak with one's own family only Hebrew when the family members naturally knew and spoke only their native tongue was a political action/decision, participating in a then revolutionary effort to revive the Hebrew language, to transform it from a dead language to a living, spoken one, one that would be able to assume its role as the national language of the Jews). But, like Arendt, Felman in her turn leaves her homeland and the language she was raised in, Hebrew, not as a political Jewish refugee but as an Israeli Jew choosing to go to Europe to pursue her education. In geographical parallel to Arendt's itinerary, Felman also lands in France, where she completes her advanced literary degree and is born as a writer and a literary critic, writing with complete French fluency on French authors and thinkers whom her work reveals in a new light, contributing to French periodicals and publishing her first three books in France, versed in the culture and the language she has existentially absorbed and emotionally and intellectually assimilated as a second native tongue. Like Arendt, however, Felman eventually leaves France for the United States, where she joins an academic French Department and continues her reflection and research on French literature, French thought, and French psychoanalysis, although she now begins to write in English. In this shift of languages (and continents), her first book published originally in the United States and written originally in English is a study of the psychoanalytic language of a French theoretician: *Jacques Lacan and the Adventure of Insight: Psychoanalysis in Contemporary Thought* (1987). It is not, however, until her 1992 book, *Testimony: Crises of Witnessing in Literature, Psychoanalysis, and History*—coauthored with an American-Israeli psychoanalyst, Dori Laub, and focusing on the relation between speech and trauma through a study of testimony in literary and cinematic responses to the Holocaust—that Felman will first write on Jewish history. What she finds in Jewish history as she returns to it is a collapse of, and demand for, witness. But it is only ten years later, when she writes on Hannah Arendt and the Eichmann trial, in the last two chapters of her 2002 book *The Juridical Unconscious*, that Felman's writing—for the first time ever—turns back upon her homeland, Israel. Like

Arendt, she writes about her homeland not in her native tongue but in the cultural language of her second country of adoption, the United States; like Arendt, she writes in English and looks back at the Jewish question through the mediation of her American (and European) perspective and her American (and European) identity.

Felman's theoretical work on witness will eventually, then, return her, in writing, though not in her native tongue, to Israel. But at this site—the site of the law—she will discover a collapse of consciousness and a call for justice. It is through this discovery that she articulates the possibility of a mute testimony—a testimony linked essentially to an unspoken and, to a certain extent, unspeakable (traumatic) history.

Felman, the born Israeli whose life and education passed through France and who henceforth lives and writes in the United States, thus returns to her homeland in her thought and in her writing, through her encounter with the German-Jewish refugee who is seeking, in the trial in Jerusalem, an answer to her own past. Where Arendt inadvertently and silently encounters, in the trial, a split in her own story—a mute story of political erasure and of exile and loss, from which her powerful political insight and political thought emerges—Felman will consciously articulate a theory of historical trauma and of its legal remedy through justice, by analyzing the unconscious impact of the trauma on the conscious dealings and proceedings of the law. Felman's insight into trauma, I would argue, as developed in her discussion of the Eichmann trial and in her groundbreaking theoretical highlighting of the relation of traumatic history to justice—could not, itself, emerge in its full conceptual scope outside of her own reading and of her own unconscious resonance with the silent story that lies behind Arendt's critique of the trial. In speaking of Arendt's relation to Benjamin, Felman begins, unconsciously, to tell of her own relation to Arendt, a story that links the displacement and survival of each writer (the successful escape of Arendt from Nazi Germany and her arrival first in France and then in America; the story of the academic success of Felman in arriving in France and in America; the larger success of the Jews in returning to the state of Israel, which is at once Felman's homeland and the place at which each woman thinker symbolically arrives in writing about the trial) with a story of departure that cannot be fully contained by the personal successes or by the theoretical articulations that characterize and crown each writer's life and work. In this encounter between Arendt and Felman, then, not only do two personal stories meet—the story of the German refugee and the story of the Israeli who left Israel, each meeting outside of their homelands and outside of their mother tongues on the site of the trial of a Nazi perpetrator in Jerusalem—but also two bodies of theoretical thought meet one another: the political work of Hannah Arendt, originating in an insight into the political predicament of the stateless and the rightless through the annihilation of the legal person under totalitarian regimes, and the psychoanalytic and literary theory of testimony (and of the possibility of an unconscious, speechless testimony) of Shoshana Felman, an insight into trauma and an illumination of the traumatic history of genocide.

I would propose that, while Arendt herself explicitly shunned psychoanalysis and did not focus her work on trauma, and while Felman is not explicitly and not primarily a political thinker but is a literary thinker and critic who focuses on psychoanalysis, trauma, and testimony, the coming together of these two writers around the reading of this trial suggests a coincidence of these two dimensions, which need precisely to be read together. Felman's reading of Arendt permits us to glimpse not only the personal, unconscious testimony to trauma that Arendt carries into her writing, but also, potentially, an unconsciousness within her political theory: Felman permits us to read in Arendt a theory that testifies to (although it does not articulate it as such) a political unconscious at work in the elimination of the political human being at the heart of the totalitarian system. Felman's writing about Arendt's personal trauma, that is, opens up onto what is in fact a political trauma inscribed in Arendt's writing. At the same time, Arendt's work—reread through Felman and through what I have analyzed as the unconscious resonance between their stories—points, potentially, to a political dimension within Felman's own theory that permeates her understanding of the juridical unconscious.

The political erasure of the human as Arendt thinks it through her work on totalitarianism, and the traumatic erasure of witness as Felman thinks it through her work on testimony, thus meet at the point of the law, through their different visions of the trial in Jerusalem, where a key witness dramatically collapses on the witness stand, where the trial inadvertently testifies through its collapse of the witness, and where nevertheless new stories of the Holocaust emerge and are articulated for the first time. While neither woman writer explicitly conceptualizes this coincidence, it is in this meeting of concepts, I would argue, that a certain future of thinking history and memory might take place.[10]

JUSTICE AND WRITING

As a critic of Arendt's position, Felman comes to Arendt's text as a defender of the legal vision of the state of Israel and of the stance of the Israeli prosecution. But in the very process of defending the Israeli positions in the trial, Felman hears in Arendt's text an untold story and reads a subtext, a silenced layer of grief, an indirect testimony through which Arendt's analysis of the trial becomes "a book of mourning." Felman thus receives from Arendt's speech a testimony that others have not heard or received. Felman, as a born Israeli in a certain sense attempting to return to her own lost history and her own lost homeland through her defense of the trial, ends up giving voice to the German-Jewish refugee attempting to find, in the trial, the answer to her own split heritage and to the trauma inscribed in the gap between her languages: a linguistic split and cultural gap that Felman intuitively recognizes and with which, from a different position, she unconsciously identifies. In hearing this mute testimony, and in granting Arendt's dissident thought the status of a creative and important participant in the legacy of the trial, Felman thus speaks for something unspoken, buried, and erased in Arendt's writing, and makes us see and hear Arendt's own erased, restrained pathos and silenced grief, counteracting (in the process of returning to the silent layer of the text its force of speech) also the event of the book's later silencing in the history of its repressive, falsifying, simplifying, and reductive reception. This dimension of external and internal self-imposed silencing related to Arendt's work would have to be understood, I argue, both in terms of Arendt's own understanding of political erasure and annihilation and of Felman's own concept of erasure (the erasure of the witness and the erasure of the human, notions that carry over, as we have seen, from Felman's earlier book, *Testimony*, to *The Juridical Unconscious*). In giving voice to the erased, and in hearing what the text inscribes as muteness, the American-Israeli thinker of trauma and testimony does justice to the American-German refugee and Jewish exile, as well as to the political critic and political thinker's text, in an entirely new and surprising manner that bears witness, I would argue, both to the trauma of Arendt's past and to the experience of erasure at the heart of her political thought.

This justice emerges, however, not only from the transference of the story of erasure from Arendt's political experience (and perspective) to Felman's psychoanalytic experience (and perspective), but also in the groundbreaking insight that occurs at this point of communication in the work of the two women, in the innovative theoretical understanding to which each of them gives rise. Both thinkers create new theoretical concepts out of their parallel (though different) cultural, biographical, historical, and linguistic experiences. Both initiate new thinking at the very site of collective historical and political trauma. For Arendt, this creativity results in a new political theory, and for Felman, in a new type of psychoanalytic or psychoanalytically inspired theory, including the new larger psychoanalytic vision of the relation between law and trauma, and the invention of the concept—the new conceptualization—of the juridical unconscious. Both thinkers are in this sense revolutionary: both bear witness to what is erased (or what remains unheard) in history through the very way in which they revolutionize their fields. Neither theory, however, is completely conscious of the full implications of its insight. Neither is completely articulated as a self-enclosed system of thought. It is precisely in the ways in which the theoretical work of each author carries traces of what within the theory remains unspoken—and in the ways in which the two bodies of work unwittingly illuminate each other—that the truly revolutionary potential of each thinker, I would argue, begins to emerge.[11]

The newness and the power of Felman's work on trauma and testimony is thus recreated, I would suggest—and done justice to in its own way—through its encounter with Arendt's political thought. A certain form of justice takes place between the two writings. It is this form of justice that the present essay tried to underscore and to bring out. Felman hears trauma in Arendt's political thought and helps bring to life an unseen dimension of Arendt's thought. Likewise, I believe, a reading of the notion of traumatic testimony as proposed by Felman, in the light of Arendt's notion of political erasure, could teach us about the as yet ungrasped dimensions of traumatic pasts. The meeting of the two writers—and of the two bodies of thought—thus also, I suggest, does justice in a new way to history itself. In this meeting, and in the testimony that this meeting gives us, I would propose, we might also see a possible pathway toward the study of trauma and

- the experience of trauma might become History

politics together, one in relation to the other. The understanding of such a notion, and of such an opportunity of justice (justice to history), lies, however, in the future, to which the event of this encounter between the paired insights of the two women thinkers will have transmitted its as yet uncharted historical testimony.

PART 7 | Felman as Teacher

Felman as Teacher

Ignorance, argues Barbara Johnson in her essay "Nothing Fails Like Success," should not be taken as an indication of what we have failed to understand or succeed in knowing, but rather as an occasion to question our ways of knowing, or to determine what has impeded the gain of further knowledge.[1] A principal site for such investigations is the classroom. Pedagogy then emerges as the task to alert us to our modes of making sense of the world, and to begin to understand ourselves in the process. Shoshana Felman is first and foremost a teacher. She is a teacher precisely in the sense of activating one's ignorance as a way of opening up what and how one can know. Knowledge itself, then, is not the goal of teaching. Both her writing and her teaching are part of the same project and follow the same logic. It is therefore indispensable to include in *The Claims of Literature* a document of her teaching. What follows are transcripts from two of Shoshana Felman's recent classes. The first of these seminars was part of Felman's last course given at Yale University in the fall of 2001. The second of these seminars is from Felman's first course at Emory University, given in the fall of 2003. These transcripts offer live testimony to Felman's teaching style and method and offer a lesson in pedagogy in a different mode from her essays.

These selections were taken from a range of available recordings and represent the first and last class of the semester, of a class entitled "Art and Acts of Justice (Writers on Trial)." The first class discusses Plato's *Phaedo* and exemplifies Felman's practice of close textual reading. The second transcript is of a class on Jacques Lacan and Baruch Spinoza and presents a look backward from the last session to the whole course, and thus is a synthetic and retrospective overview of the meaning of the whole semester. Each transcript shows the content of a class and how this content is achieved, in Felman's pedagogical practice, through a specific interaction with the students.

13 | Plato's *Phaedo*

September 17, 2001

From class entitled *Literatures of Judgment and Forgiveness: Art and Acts of Justice;* graduate/undergraduate seminar, co-taught with Prof. Sara Suleri-Goodyear

First session of the semester. Reading assignment for the session: Plato's *Phaedo*[1]

Abbreviations: SF = Shoshana Felman; SSG = Sara Suleri-Goodyear; S = students

SF: *Phaedo* is one of the most beautiful texts of Plato. We encounter there a narrative—and a philosophical dialogue—dealing with the issue of death. It is not an *imagined* text, although some of it might be fictionalized. Plato has mostly recorded, and perhaps partly imagined, the last moments of Socrates—but this textual report is based on a true event. The true historical event at stake in this text is the trial and execution of Socrates, whom we have come to view as the father of Western philosophy. So we have to ask ourselves the question: how and why does civilization put on trial such a man, whom posterity will see as the originator of philosophy, the founder of a crucial philosophical tradition? The paradox is even sharper, since what Socrates comes up against is not just any civilization: it is Greek civilization, culture at its highest summit. Greek democracy at that time (Socrates was tried and executed in 399 B.C.) was the most developed, most accomplished form of civilization available. Why would a democracy feel the need to put on trial somebody like that? Within democracy, Socrates embodies controversy as a principle, as a philosophical approach: he in turn becomes controversial because his relentless spirit of inquiry is experienced as a challenge to the faith of the majority and as an iconoclastic threat to the foundations of the state. He seems to shake up the established religious beliefs, in always questioning the grounds of belief as such. He is somebody who constantly questions what others accept and take for granted, and thus constantly shakes up, destabilizes what others feel must be secure, so secure as not to be questioned at all. I invite you to read for next time the *Apology* as well, to see in detail the legal charges against Socrates. The main charge is that he does not believe in the gods of the city. That means that his interrogation injects a thinking process into religion, and thus destabilizes the very grounds of belief as such. The second charge is that he corrupts the youth. That means he was a teacher: an *influential* teacher who *transformed* people. In *Phaedo,* you are seeing him precisely as a teacher. It is not merely a constative text about the execution of a teacher—the putting to death of a philosopher. It is a performative text that powerfully draws us into its performance. Its pedagogical performance takes place both *before* death and *beyond* death. Even today, this text still implicates us as its gripped students, its continued audience. Its acute drama of death and life is at the same time a profound philosophical reflection on the significance of pedagogy—on the very processes of teaching and of learning.

SSG: One of my favorite moments has to be when Socrates is told, "you know if you talk too much the poison's not going to work the first time around," and he says, "well, then tell the poisoner to get three doses ready because I'm going to go on talking right to the end."

SF: Right, this moment in the text is a dramatic moment that encapsulates the passion, the poignancy, of teaching. In other words, the warning is: if you keep talking, you will suffer more. This moment needs to be interpreted. This was the height of technology then, to kill someone by poison. Socrates is warned by the executioner: if you talk, you will lose the technological advantage of a quick death, you will be fighting the poison's effects, delay them, you will have to drink more poison, you will have a slower death, a longer agony, so it is better not to talk. But Socrates disregards this warning, he says, "I'm going to die doing what I've always been doing: teaching to the last breath of my life."

Time, in fact, is very important in this text. As the discourse unfolds, there arise repeatedly issues of time, of deferral, of gaining of time — and, at the same time, there is this dramatic sense that this is the last moment, the last hour. The sense that time is going to be interrupted. Ok, what I want to do with you today is to read with you. Sometimes I'll go about a text by asking first for your general emotional impressions, trying to elucidate your reading experience; but since we have too little time for the *Phaedo* (only this session), I would like to delve right away into the reading: after a very brief general introduction.

This is then a text about death. To some extent, death can always be thought about as an injustice, even when it occurs naturally: we experience death — or even the thought of our future death — as an injustice. All the more so when death is the result of a trial. All the more so when posterity judges the result of this trial to be incorrect. Incorrect in that Western civilization has adopted the values of Socrates and Plato as representatives of the value of truth, and of the search for truth in philosophy. So in this case, someone pays with their life for the intransigence of their search for the truth. It is therefore a text not simply about death but about the relation between truth and death. It is a text, more than anything, about the relation between death and discourse. You know that the text begins when Phaedo is asked, "*What did Socrates say before he died?*" Everybody knows that he was executed — but what did he say in his last hours?

As an introduction to the reading of this text, I want to share with you the thoughts, the words of three different modern thinkers, about this relation between death and discourse. The first of these thinkers is Hannah Arendt. The citation I propose to read to you is from a book by Arendt entitled *Men in Dark Times*[2] — "dark times" meaning Nazi times as well as other dark moments in history. One of the authors Arendt studies is Isak Dinesen, who happens to be a woman, even though she signs under the pseudonym of a man. Arendt analyzes her as a storyteller. She quotes a sentence from Isak Dinesen that seems to me extremely relevant to Plato's account of the trial and death of Socrates. I quote Hannah Arendt quoting Isak Dinesen: "*All sorrows can be borne if you put them into a story or tell a story about them.*" Think how relevant this sentence is to us today, as we are barely emerging from the shock of September 11th. Think how gripped we are by stories, how the media keep telling us the rescue stories, the narratives of the survivors, the stories of the witnesses, repeating the narrative of the disaster. Telling the disaster, listening to these stories, is a way of processing the trauma: it is a way of processing the *unintelligible* in that event. "All sorrows can be borne if you put them into a story or tell a story about them" (104).

Arendt goes on to comment on this quotation: "The story reveals the meaning of what otherwise would remain an unbearable sequence of sheer happenings" (104). So the story takes events that are sheer happenings—an event is something which you don't understand as it occurs—and gives them a meaning. "The story reveals the meaning of what otherwise would remain a sequence of sheer happenings." That is Arendt's understanding of what a story does, in its relation to life—and to death. You can take that as an epigraph to Plato's *Phaedo,* as well as view it as an epigraph for our whole course this semester.

My second epigraph is a citation from Michel Foucault: a French philosopher in the sixties, seventies, and eighties—a political philosopher who still has a momentous impact on political thinkers in Europe and in the United States. Foucault has an essay called "Language to Infinity," published in the collection entitled "Language, Counter-Memory, Praxis."[3] In the beginning of that essay, Foucault reflects on the role of language. He writes the following: "Writing so as not to die, as Blanchot said,"—Blanchot is another twentieth-century philosophical writer and literary critic in France—"Writing so as not to die, as Blanchot said, or perhaps even speaking so as not to die, is a task undoubtedly as old as the word. The most fateful decisions are inevitably suspended during the course of a story. We know that discourse has the power to arrest the flight of an arrow in a recess of time, in the space proper to it. It is quite likely, as Homer has said, that the gods send disasters to men so that they tell of them, and that in that possibility speech finds its infinite resourcefulness." This then is Michel Foucault on the relation between language and death, language as proceeding from death, and language as a sort of remedy for, a way of coping with, death.

The third and last thinker I want to quote before we delve into Plato's text is Walter Benjamin: a German-Jewish cultural thinker and literary critic between the two world wars. In a very famous essay called *"The Storyteller,"*[4] Walter Benjamin analyzes the relation between storytelling and death, as such. He says that the original storyteller was actually a man on his deathbed. He takes this understanding from

medieval paintings which depict a dying man on his deathbed, surrounded by the people who love him, talking to them, telling them a
story, in order to *transmit* something important about the truth of his
life to the next generation. Let me quote the words of Walter Benjamin, in a further point of his essay where he doesn't talk any more
about the deathbed narrator, but about the generalized concept of the
storyteller as such. About the storyteller, Benjamin writes: "It is however characteristic that not only his knowledge or wisdom, but above
all, his real life—and this is the stuff that stories are made of—first
assumes transmissible form at the moment of his death (94). That is,
at the moment of one's death, one's knowledge, one's wisdom, one's
life, becomes *transmissible,* that is, subject to the desire to *transmit* it, to
communicate it to somebody else. Benjamin's essay continues:

> Just as a sequence of images is set in motion inside a man as his
> life comes to an end, unfolding the views of himself under which
> he has encountered himself, suddenly in his expression and looks,
> the unforgettable emerges and imparts to everything that con-
> cerned him that authority which even the poorest wretch in dying
> possesses for the living around him. This authority is at the source
> of the story.
> Death is the sanction of everything that the storyteller has to
> tell. He has borrowed his authority from death. (94)

It goes without saying that Socrates has a tremendous authority for
his students; this authority becomes especially compelling at the moment of his death. According to Walter Benjamin, it is *from death* that
this authority comes.

SSG: I would like to interject and suggest a parallel to these very beautiful quotations Professor Felman has been reading us. Think of Scheherazade, who is able to draw on the authority of death and yet defer
death at the same time: every evening she can come up with a new
story. The linkage between narrative and its authority with death and
dying is one that we have to look at in terms of the question: why
should death lend a greater authenticity to narrative? How does that
occur?

SF: Foucault is actually thinking of Scheherazade when he says, "the
most fateful decisions are inevitably postponed during the course of a

story." Decisions are postponed during a narration, and the decision par excellence is the decision to execute somebody. Scheherazade is able to postpone this decision—to postpone her death—by telling stories. Foucault is definitely alluding to this power of discourse—the power of holding death at bay.

With these epigraphs in mind, let's move back to Plato's text. I want us to look together at the narrative *frame* of the story—not so much the philosophy of Plato, not so much the dialectics and the explanation of what dialectics is, but at the narrative *frame* of this story. Yes?

s: Thinking of these quotes I thought about how in that interregnum between Socrates' trial and his execution, the Athenian boats are gone to Delos for a holy period of purification of the city, during which Socrates' death is postponed. Which is ironic, since Socrates talks about death itself as a purification of the soul. It's just really interesting since he opposes the work of the story to the work of philosophy. He talks about versifying the fables of Aesop and he says, "I always had a dream about wanting to do beauty and I had never interpreted it this way but during this period I did." It's like he's inhabiting this whole other world, becoming a poet instead of a philosopher, and that sort of purification—the purification of the city and of religion as opposed to the purification of the soul by death. I think that's an interesting tension between various kinds of purifications. Because the purification death brings for the philosopher's soul doesn't seem to work for Socrates' students, they seem to prefer the purification of the story.

sf: I'm not sure if what the story is designed to bring is purification exactly. But you're right that it is a moment when Socrates *brings in literature,* not instead of philosophy—he is always a philosopher above all—but *in addition* to being a philosopher he becomes a poet and a writer, and we want to see why at that moment. I suggest we look at that moment in the text.

ssg: The textual message Socrates receives, essentially, is "make and cultivate music." That's what his dream tells him. He says, "first I thought philosophy was the best music of all, so that's what I've been doing all my life," and yet here is where we get into the almost uncanny resort to discourse, whether it be poetic or philosophical.

sf: In the phrase "make music," music includes, in the Greek sense, poetry. So it is really a recourse to poetry, to literature. Socrates is a philosopher and *Phaedo,* by Plato, is also a summary of Plato's own philosophy. But philosophy is *insufficient* at the moment of death. That is what Socrates teaches us. At the moment of death there is another mode: there is the literary mode that has to come in and be included in order for this death to have its significance, to create its significance. So the question is: what is the difference between the literary and the philosophical? Let me sketch an answer very quickly. One of the things that Socrates, and Plato in his wake, did philosophically, is to *define.* Defining things, defining essences—what is beauty, what is justice? So it is defining *concepts,* what we call concepts, the conceptual. The conceptual is something that is of the essence and not of the accident, and is also identical to itself. There is a reflection about what the concept means in *Phaedo* as well as in other dialogues. But the *literary,* the musical, the poetical, is precisely what *cannot be reduced to the concept,* what is in excess of the concept. That other kind of discourse has to be present at the moment of death, for the account to have its meaning. Socrates feels the need of that: Socrates who *is* not just a philosopher, but a philosopher who has *never written anything,* feels the need to write poetry before his death. All we know about Socrates is from his students, from Plato. He never wrote anything, but at the moment of death he is solicited to write poetry. Because he says he has no invention, he is doing variations on the fables by Aesop. So this sudden shift in mode of discourse, as you judiciously pointed out, is one very significant moment of this text.

I want to move on to others. I'm torn between the wish to read with you the beginning of *Phaedo* and the wish to read with you the end of *Phaedo.* Ideally, I would have liked to do both, but time is short. In the middle, there is the philosophy of Plato; the explanation of what dialectics is; the explanation of what the concept is; and of what learning is; and of what knowledge is, according to Socrates and according to Plato; and what the soul is, and why it is immortal.

ssg: I have to interrupt you. Why does Phaedo say, "Plato was sick"?

sf: That's a very good question. Plato, as we know from this dialogue, was not present at the execution. Plato refers to himself in the third person, having somebody say "Plato was not there." Do you think this is important? What comments do you have to make on the fact that Plato was absent? How does Plato's absence mark the dialogue? Yes?

s: He has to distance himself from it, in order to lend credence to what he believes, by saying that Socrates believes what he believes. It has much more clout.

sf: Yes. Any other thoughts?

s: I was thinking about the philosophy of Plato in the context of Socrates' setting things in verse. I had a classical education, and I knew that Plato detested the imitative arts, such as poetry. I hadn't picked up on that.

sf: Not exactly detest, because Plato is a fantastic literary writer. But he thought that in the hierarchy of knowledge, poets didn't really know what they were doing. He wanted to exclude poets from the Republic. But he was himself a poet. Which makes it a little more complex.

s: Which is why he can't be there. At this time. In reading his philosophy, he does seem opposed to imitative art, but to encompass more fully this moment of death, he has to include the truth of this situation to reach these truths, he feels like he should include the imitative arts which he is otherwise opposed to, and in doing so, if he had been there, I don't think he could have fully shown the synergy that creates this big human truth that he would otherwise have disagreed with.

sf: Do you think he thought about all that and then decided not to go to the execution? I believe that he was really not present. I believe that's not an invention.

s: Then we raise questions about whether the dialogue he was writing was truthful as well, which is very questionable.

sf: I don't know if it's important. Probably he had accounts. Some dialogues are supposed to be very accurate, like the *Apology*. Other dialogues like these are the mid-dialogues. They have more of the invention of Plato, but they are based on true accounts. But I don't know if that's important. One thing that is certainly true is that Plato was not present at the execution. There's no reason not to believe him. He didn't make a fiction of his absence. So how can we interpret the significance of this absence?

s: To me it made me think about the relationship between recollection and experience. The question is not so much whether or not what Plato said is true, but rather what this situation means—the fact that Plato is not there in the flesh, that he is not present, but that he testifies to a certain presence, in fact, a transcendent presence, the regeneration of the soul. It's not so much whether we can assess the validity of his truth claims, but rather what are the structures by which we would assess the validity of his truth claims, which always have to do with experience and the experience of death, which is incalculable.

SF: It strikes me that a very simple answer doesn't seem to occur to you, why Plato was absent. Yes?

S: Too painful.

SF: *Too painful.* Maybe he couldn't look at it. Writers have written about having witnessed executions. For instance, there is an account of a witnessed execution by Turgenev, who says: at the moment that the guillotine was just about to cut off the head of that victim, I turned my head away. There is a response to this account by Dostoevsky, who says that the way in which Turgenev testifies to the execution is, in Dostoyevsky's view, unethical. We don't have the right to attend an execution and turn our head away at the moment of death, in order not to see it, not to witness the moment of the horror. In the case of Plato, it could be then that Plato was really sick. Or sick with anxiety— *afraid* that it would be unbearable, excessively painful. Plato is known to have fled Athens after the execution. A number of the students feared forthcoming persecution as students of Socrates, and Plato, who had planned to be a politician, gave up this plan to become an Athenian politician and took refuge in Megara. Twelve years later, he founds the Academy, his school for philosophers. Plato is known to have been entirely writing under the impact of Socrates, and under the impact of this trauma of Socrates' execution. This momentous execution, not just for Socrates' students, was a horrifying trauma. For Plato it could have been too important to be able to be present. That's why he collects the accounts, that's why he represents the other people who were not there but would like to know. He marks, for historical truth, that he was not actually there. But I can't avoid the thought that he *chose* not to be there because it was too much for him. This was an event of the body, and the body was a little bit scary for Plato. He didn't want to be intoxicated by the body.

s: Your idea of choice is interesting. Essentially what Plato is saying is that to desire truth in a strange way is already to choose death, to desire death.

sf: Yes, he says that philosophy as such is a practice of death. Philosophy is learning how to die.

s: That affords a kind of circular justificatory strength to Plato's choice of career—which he may have had some hesitations about, and he does a lot to avoid those hesitations . . .

sf: I think we should start our close reading of the text. We'll take it right away at its climax toward the end, because time is running short. I wanted to look together at both the beginning and the end of the text, which, like you, I found incredibly moving. Some of you remarked in your written notes on how powerfully moving you found it. I want us now to read the end together, and then look at how the end resonates to the beginning. Let's start reading at the top of page 113. Amos, can you please read this page aloud?

s: "When he had done speaking, Crito said: 'And have you any commands, for us, Socrates—anything to say about your children, or any other matter in which we can serve you?'

"'Nothing particular,' he said: 'only, as I have always told you, I would have you look to yourselves'" (113).

sf: Okay, anything that you notice here?

s: Just that none of them gets it. Gets what Socrates is always saying to them. I'm going onto another place. This is only my body, what is about to die is only my shell.

sf: Do you think they don't get it because they are dumb?

s: No, even with his smartest students—Plato's not there—there's a disconnect between the intellectual grasp of the philosophical conception and the human realities of belief and conviction and value. They say, "Alright, fine, your soul is going to be immortal, but we still value you as a person and you're not going to be with us any more."

sf: Right.

other s: I think they're also looking for him to pass on insight from the teacher to the student. He says I don't really need to pass anything on to you, I just need to exemplify the way in which you can get it in yourself. What you think is coming from me is already in yourself.

SF: But see what Crito is asking. "Do you have any instructions about your children?" It's completely personal. Socrates says no, nothing about the children. The students are sort of mixed in with the children. The students are like the children. There is a place previously in the text where Phaedo says that Socrates was a father figure to us, and there is a child in all of us, and the fears were voiced not by us but by this child that is in all of us. So Crito says, and what do you have to say to your children? And Socrates says, "Nothing."

S: Well, I wanted to relate this to the beginning of the dialogue. There is a way in which at the beginning Socrates is also denying contingency. He's saying, "I don't care that through this contingent circumstance my death has been postponed, I would be happy to get it over with now." There is a way in which at the end he is also denying what is particular and contingent about this experience.

SF: Okay, let's try to avoid jargon: I don't know if we need to use bombastic philosophical words. I would rather bring it back to simple words. The word "children" is simple enough for me. Is there something about the children at the beginning?

S: Aren't they sent away?

SF: Precisely. His wife Xanthippe and his children are there and he sends them away so that he can pursue the dialogue with his students. Do you remember what Xanthippe says? Maybe we should look it. Page 57 at the bottom of the page. "On entering, we found Socrates just released from chains and Xanthippe, whom you know, sitting by him and holding his child in her arms." So there is in this picture, in this scene, the children and the wife, both of whom are present twice in the text. Once in the beginning and once at the end. Socrates sends them away but they are there; they add to the meaning of this scene. Xanthippe is known to always have complained to Socrates that, on the one hand, he never provided for the family, and, on the other hand, he was never much with the family, and she has come to be known as the complaining woman. But we can understand her. This is a certain set of values. For the philosopher, women are hierarchically placed in a different, less important place. Women are not doing philosophy, they are taking care of the family. We can dispute those values. I want to dispute those values. But we are just remarking on it. I want to go very quickly over the pathos of Xanthippe. "When she saw us, she uttered a cry and said"—it's Phaedo speaking—"she uttered a cry and said, as women will,"—men do not cry—"oh Socrates, this is the last time that either you will converse with your friends or they with you" (57). She does not even speak about herself, the wife, nor about their common children. But she is lamenting that this is the last time that Socrates is doing what is important to him, which is to converse with his students—

SSG: Isn't it so remarkable that after having banished her—he just sends her away—his first comment (and I know it's because he's just been released from the chains) is to talk precisely about pleasure and about the connection between pleasure and pain.

S: In Socrates, I think there's a very necessary, systematic exclusion of the body. He's trying to divide an intellectual pleasure from what can be termed a physical pleasure.

SF: The woman and children are part of the life of the body. Pleasure and pain are also associated with the life of the body.

S: Though he does take a sort of fraternal pleasure in conversing with his friends.

SF: Right. I wouldn't insist so much on the pleasure here. I'm more sensitive to the fact that there is pain—and a gentleness in the way that Socrates says, "Crito, let someone take her home." Notice the role of Crito, who is the title character of the next dialogue we study. Crito has a special position with Socrates: among all the students, he is the closest one to Socrates. "Some of Crito's men accordingly led her away, crying out and beating herself." This adds to the pathos of this scene. This is a scene charged with pathos by precisely what it eliminates. Mark the elimination of pathos from the scene—which is symbolized by the sending away of the wife and the children. It doesn't mean that Socrates doesn't have any grief or pain, it just means that he's restraining it. It's part of the restraint to send them away so he can go on and pursue philosophy. You see that she's there in the beginning and she's there again at the end of the text.

s: It's just very interesting that Phaedo says about her crying, "as women do"—describing how she cried out and beat herself—but at the very end, they all join in . . .

sf: I want to read that. I want to read the text aloud from this point to the end. You have a very good comment, but save it for a little later, let's read it first. Yes?

OTHER s: I was struck by the fact that Crito is asking if there was anything he wanted to say to his children, but Socrates says, "Nothing." I think a distinction is being made here between children in the literal sense and children in the other, larger, metaphorical sense. That's a purposeful thing, that the message to his children is "nothing."

sf: Yes, the orphans are really the students. This is Plato. Plato's persistent pain in saying, from a lot later, when he wrote this dialogue, "He was like a father of whom we were being bereaved. And we were about to pass the rest of our lives as orphans" (113). Not just he is dead, but we were about to pass the rest of our lives as orphans. So you're not an orphan only at the moment he is executed, but these philosophers-to-be, Plato, is going to be an orphan, a philosopher-orphan, for the rest of his life. Yes?

s: I think it's very consistent with the rest of the dialogue, with Socrates dismissing the children who, while they may biologically carry on his genes, don't carry on any part of him in history, or any of his ideas. He values his soul, his ideas, that's what is important. So in these last minutes, it's not his children or his family that are most important. What he wants is what is happening right now right here, we're sitting around the table here at Yale in 2001, discussing his ideas years and years and years later. For posterity to do that, he needs to focus on his students rather than on his children.

sf: Right. The children are the survival of the body. The philosophy that makes an impact on the future thousands of years later—this is the survival of the soul. This is the process of learning that he transmits to humanity.

ssg: But also the banishing of the children could be a gesture of protection toward them. So that there's a wonderful subtext of compassion coming out.

s: My translation's slightly different, but I think that's also evident in my text, how the children should be handled by Crito, how Crito is concerned about Socrates' welfare, how Socrates wants to greet death and is braving it and looking forward to it, but how he's also holding back and realizes the traumatic effects of it.

sf: Yes, very good. Let's read now to the end, from page 114. Who wants to read aloud for us? Amos?

s: "Soon the jailer, who was the servant of the eleven, entered and stood by him, saying: 'To you, Socrates, whom I know to be the noblest and gentlest and best of all who ever came to this place, I will not impute the angry feelings of other men, who rage and swear at me, when, in obedience to the authorities, I bid them drink the poison — indeed, I am sure that you will not be angry with me; for others, as you are aware, and not I, are the guilty cause. And so fare you well, and try to bear lightly what must needs be; you know my errand.' Then bursting into tears he turned away and went out.

"Socrates looked at him and said: 'I return your good wishes, and will do as you bid.' Then turning to us, he said: 'How charming the man is; since I have been in prison he has always been coming to see me, and now see how generously he sorrows for me. But we must do as he says, Crito; let the cup be brought, if the poison is prepared: if not, let the attendant prepare some.'

"'Yet,' said Crito, 'the sun is still upon the hill-tops, and many a one has taken the draught late, and after the announcement has been made to him, he has eaten and drunk, and indulged in sensual delights; do not hasten then, there is still time.'

"Socrates said, 'Yes, Crito, and they of whom you speak are right in doing thus, for they think that they will gain by the delay; but I am right in not doing thus, for I do not think that I should gain anything by drinking the poison a little later; I should be sparing and saving a life which is already gone; I could only laugh at myself for this. Please then to do as I say, and not refuse me.'

"Crito, when he heard this, made a sign to the servant; and the servant went in, and remained for some time, and then returned with the jailer carrying the cup of poison. Socrates said: 'You, my good friend, who are experienced in these matters, shall give me directions how I am to proceed.'

"The man answered: 'You have only to walk about until your legs are heavy, and then to lie down, and the poison will act.'

"At the same time he handed the cup to Socrates, who in the easiest and gentlest manner, without the least fear or change of color or feature, looking at the man with all his eyes, Echecrates, as his manner was, took the cup and said: 'What do you say about making a libation out of this cup to any god? May I, or not?'

"The man answered: 'We only prepare, Socrates, just so much as we deem enough.' 'I understand,' he said, 'yet I may and must pray to the gods to prosper my journey from this to that other world—may this then, which is my prayer, be granted to me.' Then holding the cup to his lips, quite readily and cheerfully he drank off the poison. And hitherto most of us had been able to control our sorrow; but now when we saw him drinking, and saw too that he had finished the draught, we could no longer forbear, and in spite of myself my own tears were flowing fast; so that I covered my face and wept over myself, for certainly I was not weeping over him, but at the thought of my own calamity in having lost such a companion. Nor was I the first, for Crito, when he found himself unable to restrain his tears, had got up and moved away, and I followed, and at that moment, Apollodorus, who had been weeping all the time, broke out into a loud cry which made cowards of us all. Socrates alone retained his calmness. 'What is this strange outcry?' he said. 'I sent away the women mainly in order that they might not offend in this way, for I have heard that a man should die in peace. Be quiet then, and have patience.' When we heard that, we were ashamed, and refrained our tears, and he walked about until, as he said, his legs began to fail, and then he lay on his back, according to the directions, and the man who gave him the poison now and then looked at his feet and legs; and after a while he pressed his foot hard, and asked him if he could feel; and he said, "No"; and then his leg, and so upwards and upwards, and showed us that he was cold and stiff. And he felt then himself and said: 'When the poison reaches the heart, that will be the end.' He was beginning to grow cold about the groin, when he uncovered his face, for he had covered himself up, and said (they were his last words)—he said: 'Crito, I owe a cock to Asclepius, will you remember to pay the debt?'

"'The debt shall be paid,' said Crito. 'Is there anything else?' There was no answer to this question; but in a minute or two a movement was heard, and the attendants uncovered him; his eyes were set, and

Crito closed his eyes and mouth. Such was the end, Echecrates, of our friend, whom I may truly call the wisest, and justest, and best of all men whom I have ever known" (114–15).

SF: So what strikes you in the end?

S: His last words are quite striking, aren't they? You're waiting for this gem of wisdom to come out and he says, "don't forget to pay Asclepius."

SF: "I owe a cock to Asclepius." Asclepius is . . . ?

S: A healer.

SF: Yes, the god of healing. What does that mean?

S: He has a debt to the god of healing because he's being cured of his body.

SF: Right, that's one way of understanding it. It's enigmatic. Why he feels that he owes a debt to the god of healing. So one way of understanding it is that he's cured—by leaving the body, dying, departing into philosophy—he's cured from the disease or from the insufficiency of the body. I have seen another commentator suggest that—it doesn't convince me—that it's about Plato being sick, and that he owes something to the god of medicine [laughter]. I know, I know. In any case, the most important thing to remember is that there is a debt to the god of healing.

S: By that same token, it's still a debt in the transient realm of the living, and as such, even if it's a debt to cure him of his body, it's pulling in the opposite direction, into all those minute, practical things that should not concern him any more. It's a tie to life.

SF: Right. But there's more to it. The very idea of a debt—what does that concept have in it? A debt declared at the ultimate moment? There is a tension between the ultimateness of the moment—the fact that it's the last moment, the fact that it's the last word, and the content of those words. There is a paradox in the fact that the last words are about a debt—what is the contradiction of this?

S: It's a mundane debt that will live beyond his body.

SF: Right; what is important is the end of your sentence: not necessarily that it's a mundane, incongruous debt, but that it is a debt that would live beyond his body, a debt *for the future.* An unpaid debt implies a future. It's an unfinished business. Somehow, the whole ending here is about something finished and also something unfinished, and the debt is a symbol of that. The debt—and the near-triviality of the debt—in the face of this ultimate moment of death—

s: I'm making a large comparison, thinking of Professor Goodyear's statement that neither judgment nor forgiveness (in our topic this semester, in the title of our course) were a final thing, and Socrates is saying here that death itself is not a final thing. It's a process. Here's the death but then there's one more thread that's not tied up in a little bow.

sf: Yes, there are quite a number of loose ends, of things that are unfinished there. How is the unfinished marked? I said that the debt is a mark of the unfinished, what else?

s: He doesn't know for sure if he can pay it off, so he has to rely on someone else.

sf: Yes, but Crito is the most reliable of persons. So he knows that if Crito says it will be paid, it will be paid. But there is a question that comes after that. "Crito, I owe a cock to Asclepius, will you remember to pay the debt?" And Crito says, "The debt shall be paid, is there anything else?" This further question remains unanswered. That's how we know that Socrates has died. So the dialogue continues, but it is interrupted; it has not ended. Sometime before that, in the core of the philosophical exposition, Socrates says, "I can never prove that my tale about the soul is a true tale because, even if I could, I will not be able to finish my argument." My argument is unfinished. My dialogue is unfinished. My philosophy is unfinished. So there is this tension between the finished and the unfinished. The end and the no-end. The interruption. The silence and the speech. You can study the modes of exchange between the moments of silence and the moments of speech in this text.

ssg: It reminds me somewhat of the very poignant ending of King Lear, when after he's come in with dead Cordelia and made all his grand speeches, he stops and says, "Pray you, undo this button." You think—this man has been in these grandiosities of grief, how can he stop and say, "Pray you, undo this button." Then to end again on a note of complete unfinishment, if there is such a word, when he says, "Look on her, look, her lips, look there, look there." So everything opens up beyond the literature.

SF: Yes. Exactly. Something opens up beyond the literature, precisely through the incommensurable ending. Let's get back to the silence at the end of the text, the silence responding to the question of Crito—is there anything else? What is the other side of this scene of silence at the end? There is discourse, there is silence, what else? In terms of modes of expression?

S: There's the very, very explicit description of the bodily death. It's very powerful.

SF: Yes, the poison reaches the heart.

S: It's that progress of death. You watch the whole thing.

SF: Right. That's the body. That's the end of the body. That's one thing that does have an ending. But in terms of the discourse and the silence, what else is there?

S: There's also the response of the sorrow of the students, which relates to the whole unfinished thing because it breaks the passage of his philosophy and his intellect. They can't receive it in the same kind of calm.

SF: So there are the tears of the students. More than tears, what else is there at this dramatic moment?

S: He calls it weeping and unseemliness. He explicitly compares them to women.

SF: He compares them to women to make them ashamed enough to stop. So they would contain themselves. But what does that echo back to?

S: It echoes back to the realm of the body, the family—

SF: Yes, it echoes back to the beginning. To the wife who is beating herself, who lets out a *cry*. There is a cry. This is a text about discourse, philosophical discourse, but it is paradoxically marked and framed by silence, on the one hand, and, on the other hand, by cries. Socrates never cries. It's as though other people cry for him. Somebody has to issue the cry. In the beginning, it's the wife, and in the end, it's the students. It's Apollodorus who was weeping the whole time, and who "all of a sudden broke out into a loud cry which made cowards of us all," Phaedo narrates. "Socrates alone remained calm." "What is this strange outcry?" he says (115). He hushes it. He forces them back into the silence. But it is a silence that henceforth *contains* the cries, and that contains the tears and that contains also the discourse and the articulated conceptual philosophy. The silence is the ultimate moment, but it is pregnant with speech and with what cannot even have words.

SSG: But you wouldn't say then that the cry belongs to the realm of the inarticulate?

SF: Absolutely. The cry is inarticulate and it is *excessive*. It's the moment of breakdown of expression and of its excess. It relates in my mind to the literary, the poetic moment, because it's the moment of excess over the concept, it's the moment of excess over and beyond the articulateness of words. But the cry has to be there. It's not only that Socrates is trying to calm his students and make them restrain themselves, but it is important that somebody expresses that sense of a cry, of an *outcry*. He expresses it for all the others. There is always one person who cries in the *Phaedo*—Xanthippe in the beginning and Apollodorus at the end. "Apollodorus, who had been weeping all the time, broke out into a loud cry which made cowards of us all," says Phaedo (115). So they all are swept by the cry, identified with the cry. This is the tension of the whole scene which frames the dialogue. In fact, it could be said that the whole dialogue is a cry of Plato. An outcry of Plato. A *philosophical outcry* of Plato. Yes?

S: I wonder if the cry isn't another kind of debt. A kind of debt that is contained within—it's the paradox of an articulated silence. That space, that silence is made possible by a limit. Socrates, by being in debt to Asclepius, passes the debt on to Crito, then Crito in turn is in his debt too. There's a way in which Socrates forces Crito to perform an oath, to continue the responsibility. An oath in the face of Socrates' death. A continuing responsibility for what Socrates was responsible for.

SF: Right. Good. So the debt is what is left, actually, from this whole thing. They are all in a mode of debt. In a mode of debt to Socrates, in a mode of debt to philosophy. Not with respect to the past, but to the future as well. A mode of the debt is what remains.

s: In the *Iliad,* there's a certain prescribed period during which women have to perform lamentations. It's an extremely precise way—an interesting way in which this touch of the real, which is the cry, is contained by the very prescribed system of the debt.

sf: Right. Good.

s: We were talking about the cry as expressing something which cannot be expressed by philosophy. You have to make a human content with this death. It's not sufficient to make contact with it through your soul. That basic insufficiency is repeated over and over. The dialogue itself fits right in there. Socrates, as the wisest and most upright man they have—all his students, including Plato, cannot reach that level, they cannot ignore their body. Indeed, the very death of Socrates is the obstacle—in order for them to achieve the purity of soul he had attained, they would have to forget their mourning for him. So it's a choice: do we value him or do we value his teachings?

sf: Right. What Socrates is talking about throughout this dialogue is the transcendence of himself. He is *about* something that transcends him. To that extent he is a witness to that which transcends him, his person, a witness to that which transcends his person and transcends his end. The students cannot reach this state of transcendence of him, or of themselves. That's why Phaedo says, "we were crying about ourselves, not about Socrates." We were crying about ourselves. So there is this pain that points back toward themselves. A moment that is *unsurpassable,* however much they are trying to surpass it. There is the unintelligibility of death that is inscribed in this text. It can never be reduced to meaning. Not for Plato, no matter how good a philosopher he is. The unintelligibility of death will remain there. It is a text that is marked tremendously by the body. The body is *present* in the text even though the philosophical discourse disparages the body. The body is present—this is the literary quality of Plato. This is not an abstract text in any way. Notice how it is a text full of physicality. You have an exact account of how Socrates is sitting on the couch, rubbing his leg, and where he is exactly, how he is lying, how he is standing, how he is walking, how he is smiling, how he is looking into the eyes of the jailer when he drinks the poison, how he is making eye contact, and Plato says, "as was his habit." He is someone who makes eye contact. So there is the powerful presence of the body in all of these events, and the presence of the unintelligible that cannot be surpassed, that underlies this event as what cannot be grasped, what exceeds the meaning of the text. This is why this text is so profound, and so powerful. I guess we should stop here.

— transcribed by Charles Boardman

14 | Between Spinoza and Lacan and Us

December 6, 2004

Closing session of a semester's graduate seminar entitled *Art and Acts of Justice*

Abbreviations: SF = Shoshana Felman; S = student

Introduction: Pedagogical Remarks

SF: We have a very ambitious session, as you may have realized from reading the texts [laughter]. In a way, it might be too ambitious to close the course with this, but, on the other hand, it might shed light also on the whole course.

Now, before we move on to the task of elucidating Lacan's text, I want to share with you some further thoughts about my pedagogy in general—because, what seems self-evident to us as teachers—the rationale behind our teaching methods—is never really clear to all.

So let me tell you something about my perception of this course and my perception of the seminar as such. For me, a seminar is not a lecture course. Because a lecture course bears on something that is *finished for you,* you have reached the final conclusions about something, and you translate these conclusions into knowledge, and present an interpretation that is *finished.* This is what I do in my books. And in my lectures. Not in my teaching. I don't consider that it's the most interesting thing that can be done with teaching. A seminar, in my conception, is a process of investigation. This is in general the conception of a seminar, though not all professors actually follow that practice. It is a process of investigation, and because we are a group, it's a dynamic *group* process of investigation, in which you are called on to participate, within the structure that the syllabus has given to the course. The seminar is designed to develop a perspective, it definitely has a structure, and that structure is driven by a creative vision behind it, but that creative vision is not entirely finished in my mind. I am following an intuition, a direction, but the intuition is not finished. The vision is not finished. It is not entirely even clear to myself, so it cannot be entirely clear and completely grasped by you, but the confusion, the debating, the struggling with the texts and with what they have in common—reveal in common—is what we are researching. All my classes are trying to communicate above all an emotional and intellectual *experience* of the texts, an experience which I strive to make as primordial and as vital as I can. The experience is what matters. This experience is a fact or an event created through a practice. The class is for me a field of praxis, not a finished concept. If the experience created in the classroom is powerful enough, it will eventually engender its own conceptualization. But this is only at the end of the process, at the horizon. So I have given you here a significant choice of writers, a series of texts *to experience* in their uniqueness but also in their significant (progressive) relation to one another. I have framed the class around the vision, which is basically an intuition that I had, at the cutting edge of my own thought. This is where I'm going, but where I haven't yet arrived. I'm taking you with me, and I'm asking you to share in this process of creation. So you have to acquire the maturity to deal with what you don't understand and to deal with the confusion that it triggers, because that is precisely part of the research: not simply getting chewed-up material that is called knowledge. Knowledge is doubtless imparted in the class, but my purpose is not to pass on knowledge that is finished, but to invite you inside the process of my own investigation. I see my role in a seminar a little bit like that of an orchestra conductor producing music with his orchestra. You are the orchestra. Every musical instrument is very important and every musical instrument has their own interpretation. It is a sort of music which is, in the end, produced from the orchestral ensemble, from the interaction between individuals which it is my role to inspire, to guide, and to moderate. This is my general conception of a seminar.

I will now say a few things about the guiding intuition of this particular seminar. But first of all, I want to clarify the particular pedagogical method I used here. Obviously, all the writers we studied have in common the fact that they were put on trial, with the exception of the fictional trial dramatized in the novel of Forster. In order to understand the real trials which convicted these writers, we had to look at their lives, and not only at their works, and we did so. We looked at the history. We looked at the events surrounding their writings. At least, at some events. I said at a certain point in this course that after teaching it three times—this is the third time (I had taught it twice before at Yale)—I have discovered this year, for the first time, that it is a lot about biography. But I think I have misled you by saying that, because obviously it wouldn't have taken me three years to discover it if it was the simple, conventional sense of biography—a life narrative that is empirically available, ready-made, so to speak, and well known. I mean, this is something else. It's actually displacing the very concept of biography. And it's not exactly biography, because a lot of times it's autobiography—it's the way in which the biography is involved with the text and the way in which those texts are autobiographical, and they are autobiographical before and after the event. Some are prophetic in a way, and some are after, in the impact of the event. So what is important to see is that it is not life and literature as a dichotomy here. But all the cases we have examined dissolve this dichotomy. What is pathbreaking in this emerging understanding of life in relation to the text is that the dichotomy, the opposition of life and literature in the traditional sense—the belief that life is made of a few empirical facts that are given to us and known, and then, we have the literature that becomes a mirror or a symmetrical representation of those empirical facts—this simplistic understanding and this conventional demarcation line were exploded in this class. Biography in this sense is a very reductive concept that the old criticism used to use. And it is definitely not what I am trying to bring into this class in discussing the almost epic saga of these writers, who are faced—through their own public prosecutions—with the unforeseen drama and the unexpected legal crisis of something which they stand for but which is beyond themselves, something that is triggered by their texts, by the *event of literature*. It is rather a process of deconstruction of the opposition between life and text, a deconstruction of the polarities that are so popular in academic departments—polarities such as art and reality, art *versus* reality. I'm trying to look at art as being part of the reality and at reality as being part of the art. So there is no opposition between the two. They go together. I mean, appearance and reality, life and art—all

those polarities are here exploded in the sense that the borderline between them breaks down. They are really working together. They are
inextricably implicated within one another. It is hard to say where life
ends and where literature begins. There is sometimes more of a mystery and a call for interpretation about the life than about the texts.
The texts are sometimes clearer than the life. What is at stake is always
an enigma. It is always about an enigma in the relation of text to life.
And the question, of course, is why all those great people—and that is
my sense of them, I believe that all the writers we studied in this class
are very, very *great* human beings, as well as outstandingly creative
thinkers and brilliant writers. And they had an impact on posterity as
well. I mean, in terms of their genius, their genius had consequences.
So why were they all put on trial? This is my question. I don't have an
answer for it, and I don't think I will ever have a simple answer for it.
But I think it is an interesting question. You know, another way to
put the subject, retrospectively—another way to tackle the intuition
behind the course—would be to say that this was really a course about
greatness. About what makes creators great. And the price paid for the
greatness. Because greatness is not simply given as a gift of God. It is
acquired. It is acquired, in the course of a struggle, through the texts
and through the lives. And, in a way, we have been studying what Hannah Arendt calls somewhere else "anecdotes of destiny." Anecdotes of
destiny. We have been studying *fates.* The fates are inscribed in the
texts. But the texts are part of the events that have given rise to these
fates. They are not simply a reflection of the facts or a representation
or a mimesis. But they are an inscription of the events. To the extent
that literature inscribes life events that remain enigmatic to the end,
literature *participates in the event-ness.* It is not simply that literature is
part of reality and is not merely fiction in a conventional sense, but
that literature itself is an event, an incalculable event. There is something that constitutes a performative literary event—it does something. It acts. And that textual action explains the great influence that
these writers have, the impact that they have left, and also the threat
that they pose. It is because of what they do with what they say, and
not simply because of what they say. So, this intuition was at the core
of this class. Perhaps after we elucidate Lacan, we can start to articulate a sketch, an overview of the perspective, of what is common to all
the writers studied in this course, despite their singularity and despite

the very obvious historical, philosophical, political, and literary differences that separate them and do not permit their assimilation to each other or their reduction to their common denominators.

Presentations; Elucidation and Discussion of Lacan's Text

SF: I would like now to give the floor to the two presenters of Lacan, who, having worked together, are going to present for us the reading assignment for today: Lacan's 1964 lecture entitled "Excommunication."[1] This text is Lacan's public response to his expulsion from the International Psychoanalytic Association. It was delivered as the first session of Lacan's yearly seminar, today published as the opening chapter of Seminar 11, *The Four Fundamental Concepts of Psychoanalysis*.

S (JESSI): Okay. I'm going to begin by backgrounding the facts that contextualize this text. . . . Lacan is trained as an analyst, he becomes a member of the SPP. . . .

SF: The French Institute, let's call it the French Institute.

S (JESSI): Okay. And at this time, he and some others from his group were discontent with the authoritarian turn that was happening in this organization and in other cities, such as New York. There had been breaks with the major organization, and the group that broke away was recognized. So, they thought, "well we'll do the same and have our organization run more in the way that we envision it." So, they leave the French Institute—

SF: What year is this? Let's remember the dates. It's 1963, the year before he gives the lecture. Lacan and some other psychoanalysts leave the organization that they belong to and while leaving, they are asking for the new group they are constituting to be recognized by the International Psychoanalytic Association.

S (JESSI): And they're denied that. They're denied that for a while, even though there had been in New York and in other places precedents for such a group to be recognized, so they felt that in leaving, they could gain recognition. The International Psychoanalytic Association is upset, especially with Lacan, so they say to his group, "well, we'll let you back in if you remove Lacan from your list of trainers of new analysts."

SF: Let us just make sure we understand what a training analyst is. Can you explain it, Jessi?

S (JESSI): What I got from your readings and these little biographies I read is that a training analyst is someone who has students under him, who have to go through a process of being analysands—someone who is analyzed—and, once they go through this breakthrough of being analyzed and knowing what that is, then they can themselves begin to analyze someone else. But they have to be trained in the method of doing that, following Freud.

SF: Right. What we are talking about is the process of education of psychoanalysts, education that brings about their *being licensed to practice as psychoanalysts*. This happens in institutes of psychoanalysis. In order to have what it takes to become an analyst, every candidate should undergo psychoanalysis themselves in order to, in Socrates' terms, learn to know oneself first of all. This is called "didactic psychoanalysis," which has two parts. One is they take courses in psychoanalysis. The institute gives them required courses. At the same time, they have to undergo psychoanalysis. But, if this psychoanalysis is "didactic," it has to take place with what is called a "training analyst." Every institute names the most authoritative psychoanalysts—who they think are the most authoritative, the most experienced—and it is only these named authorities who in an institute of psychoanalysis would have the right to license psychoanalysts-to-be. So every institute has about ten training analysts, while it may have a hundred or two hundred analysts. This is the institutional structure. So, in a way, the training analysts are the most important analysts, to whom the *right to license* belongs exclusively. And Lacan was a training analyst of his society before he left that society. Then, he and a group of his friends, or colleagues, left that institute in France because they didn't like the direction that that institute was taking—they were critical of it. They hoped that they would found another society which consequently would be recognized by the International Psychoanalytic Association, and Lacan would be a training analyst in this new society. Psychoanalysis is full of splits—that is part of its history. The splits happen as a result of a dispute, of different understandings, so then they split and form a new society. So that is what Lacan did, with several others, in 1963.

s (JESSI): And then the International Psychoanalytic Association comes back and says, "we'll grant you all acceptance if you'll take Lacan off your list as a training analyst."

SF: They began by saying that Lacan should give up some of his teaching. They had a specific list of things he was supposed to correct, but he was uncompromising. So, there was, first of all, a process of negotiation about what he could give up or censor from his own theory or from his own practice. Because he did not agree, they came up with the idea that his new association would be recognized *on the condition* that Lacan be *excluded as a training analyst.* That does not mean that he would not continue to be an analyst. It means that his analysands — his patients — would not have the right to become psychoanalysts.

s (JESSI): There are many, many other analysands who want to train with Lacan. So he continues with the seminar he's been doing for ten years. At the beginning of the initial session of his seminar, he starts off with the question, "am I qualified?" Let's discuss whether or not I am qualified.

SF: Right, let me just didactically add some clarification. Before he gives this lecture, a decision is made. For two years before, there has been a negotiation between the representatives of this new society that is going to be called *Société Française de Psychoanalyse* and the representatives of the International Psychoanalytic Association. In the end, they say that Lacan must be ousted as a training analyst. The decision is *made* by his association to accept it. This decision accepting to exclude him is made by his friends, his colleagues, and some of the negotiators *are his disciples:* his students and his analysands. One day, in September 1963, Lacan learns that the decision is made. His group is recognized, but he is no longer a training analyst. This is the background.

s (JESSI): It's at this point that I'd like to go into the text of "Excommunication." Because, as he says on page 4, "I was the object of what is called a deal" — a deal is what was made. For all these other people, he was put on the line. He says, "There was nothing particularly exceptional then about my situation, except that being traded by those whom I referred to just now as colleagues and even pupils is sometimes, seen from the outside, called by a different name" —

SF: What is the name, which he doesn't mention, but we are supposed to understand?

s (JESSI): I had a lot of different names—

SF: Well, suggest a name that somebody from the outside could call it.

s (JESSI): Betrayal.

SF: Betrayal! It goes back to Wilde's sense of betrayal, at the end—you'll remember in *The Judas Kiss,* Wilde talks about his betrayal by a lover, by a disciple, in the same way that Christ was betrayed by Judas! And why was Christ betrayed by Judas? For money. Here we have something of the same order, which Lacan never names explicitly as betrayal—it is interesting that the word remains unspeakable in his text. He says, "somebody from the outside could have called it by a different name."

s (JESSI): And I think the separation is really interesting—how he makes this differentiation between an inside and an outside. And how, in the beginning, he compares it, abstrusely, to a church, and the whole idea of excommunication, as we examined with Spinoza, is the religious ousting from a community.

SF: From a community of faith. From a religious community.

s (JESSI): So we have this inside of the psychoanalytic community, but then he says that this can be appreciated only by a psychoanalyst. He's speaking from the community, but he's also very aware of what an outsider would see, because in a way, he has been put outside of it. He has been in it, and he has been put outside of it.

To go on from there, in terms of "Excommunication," one of my first thoughts, besides the religious implications, is that Lacan was Catholic and he refers to Spinoza and the Jewish excommunication, and there's this sort of sense of being cut off from a discourse—from a former discourse—that he's removed from. But, in giving the seminar, he's continuing a discourse; he's continuing on despite other people's efforts to make him stop teaching. Why the community would want him out—why is Lacan a danger? It all comes back to what we saw with Socrates, what we saw with Wilde—*teaching is a threat to the youth.* These up-and-coming analysands being taught by someone who the International Psychoanalytic Association feels is not going with what they want for the future. So, there's this danger in Lacan—he's working against the set principles, against the conventions.

SF: Yes. Let me just add an informative detail. Lacan was also accused for his practice, which did not follow the rules set up by Freud.

S (JESSI): The short sessions.

SF: Yeah, the short session. One of the rules of the practice set up by Freud is that a session has a limited time—normally Freud was seeing patients for fifty minutes. The modern psychoanalysts cut it short to forty-five. But today it's sacrosanct that forty-five minutes is the time of a session. Lacan had too many analysands and he didn't want to refuse the analysands who wanted to work with him, so he had to play with time. That's my interpretation already [laughter]. What he actually did was to say that he is instituting a session that does not have a fixed time. In other words, the analysand comes but he does not come for forty-five minutes or fifty minutes. He comes for an unknown amount of time and begins analysis. Lacan had a theory about that: when he suddenly ends the session, it's like an intervention or an interpretation. When he thinks something important has happened, he ends it there. And that has an impact on the patient. Also, he claimed that patients, a lot of times, just say blah blah blah without any fruitfulness, and if they know that they can be cut off at any point, they will go to the point quicker [loud laughter]. That was the theory.

S (JESSI): He refers to it, he sped up the analysis.

SF: Yes, he sped up the analysis and he is interpreting by making the end of the session a theoretical point. However, his sessions normally were shorter than forty-five minutes, and he got to having sessions of five minutes and of three minutes. That didn't prevent people from *flocking* to Lacan, as a psychoanalyst, while knowing they were going to have short sessions. There was this desire to have Lacan as an analyst. It had its own reasons. God knows, I admire Lacan and I think he is a genius—but I can understand the Psychoanalytic Association that thought this was extremely dangerous.

S (JESSI): Lacan did base this short session on the whole idea that the unconscious has no time limit.

SF: Yeah, he had a theory that legitimated it by a rationale. The time of the unconscious, in Freud, is *different from the temporality of consciousness,* and thus he wanted to play with the time of the unconscious.

Let's move now to the second presentation.

s (DEVIN): I'm going to focus on the text of "Excommunication." I thought it was a very layered text that I read multiple times. I'm going to try focus on a reading of this text as illustrating what Dr. Felman hit on earlier, which is not simply a text that means something, but a text that *does something*. I think the doing starts with the question that he poses at the beginning ["am I qualified?"], and culminates with his critique of Freud's desire at the end.

SF: Devin, Devin—if I can intercede right away, because later I will forget. I am not sure that it's accurate to say that he's doing a "critique of Freud's desire." I would say that he's *questioning* what is the Freudian desire. And this question is already perceived as sacrilegious—but questioning it and interpreting Freud's desire is not necessarily criticizing it. I wouldn't think that he criticizes Freud's desire. He may be critical of something else, but it's not Freud's desire. But obviously, the concept of desire—and his questioning of Freud's desire—is very much at the core of what Lacan is doing.

s (DEVIN): . . . So, when he says, "Am I qualified to do so?" there's the begging of the question: *who* is qualified to do so? This becomes the heretical discourse. And while he's saying, "I consider this problem deferred for the time being," I don't think he defers it, but rather, he subtly places that question—and his answering, "Am I qualified to do so?" and "What qualifications are those?"—throughout the whole text. I went back and looked into the definition of "excommunication." It's "a censure which is used to deprive or suspend membership within a religious community." Then I found another secondary definition, which literally means *out of communion*. Communion, in a religious context, is "the mutual recognition by members that a person or a church within that religion has the essential elements of that faith."

So, that mutual recognition is the defining element that structures the rest of the text. What happens when you're excommunicated? You're sort of *cut off*. You're denied this form of communication with your community. And it's from that position of silence that it becomes very important for Lacan to articulate this discourse, which is deemed to be problematic or harmful to the normal understandings of psychoanalysis. And he ends this introductory section by saying: "All this concerns the base—in a topographical and even the military sense of the word—the base for my teaching. And I shall now turn to what it is about—the fundamentals of psychoanalysis." When people were tweaking at the details of what psychoanalysis was and still interpreting within the confines of Freud's texts, they were still allowed to practice and teach, but at the point at which he begins to question that base—that's when the major impact starts to occur and that's why they feared him so much.

SF: Yes. You are right. And I want to underscore it right away. He says, "My topic is the fundamentals of psychoanalysis." The sacrilegious act is *questioning the foundations*. Questioning the foundations. The act of questioning, as we have seen in all our writers, beginning with Socrates—introducing the act of questioning as a new method—is what makes it so dangerous. Okay.

S (DEVIN): Which makes it all the more interesting for why he allies himself with Spinoza, who comes from a Jewish faith, and I was wondering if—okay, he comes from the Catholic tradition, but he's referencing back to Spinoza. The unifying element between the two is what becomes an intellectual heresy for both of them.

SF: Just to underscore, again, something you are implying. You are right to say, "Why is he comparing himself to Spinoza, and to a Jewish excommunication, when he is from a Catholic origin?" I want to emphasize the paradoxical fact that he compares himself to Spinoza, who is Jewish, and that paradoxical comparison requires an interpretation, because—I want now to add a fact—because in history there exists a Catholic excommunication: when he says "major excommunication," he is implicitly referring to a Catholic thinker, Luther, who, a century before Spinoza, undergoes what is called "a major excommunication" by the Catholic Church, and founds Protestantism. So, what is at stake implicitly is also an act of foundation. When he says "major excommunication," this term is not exact for Spinoza—what was done to Spinoza was not the "major excommunication" that was what was done to Luther. So, he has implied a reference to Luther as well. "So," says Lacan, "what it amounts to is something strictly comparable to what is elsewhere called major excommunication. . . . The latter exists only in a religious community designated by the significant symbolic term *synagogue*, and it was precisely that which Spinoza was condemned to. On 27 July 1656—a singular bicentenary, since it corresponds to that of Freud—Spinoza was made the object of the *kherem*, an excommunication that corresponds to major excommunication. . . . I am not saying—though it would not be inconceivable—that the psychoanalytic community is a Church. Yet the question indubitably does arise what is it in that community that is so reminiscent of religious practice?" (3–4)

Now, the question I want you to think about and try to answer later—bringing it from your exposé, Devin—is the following: in this whole Lacanian comparison that is very complex—of the psychoanalytic community to a religious community and of psychoanalytic practice even, to a religious practice, and his underlying ironic questioning of that—why does he choose to compare himself to a *Jewish* figure excommunicated from the Jewish community? This choice must have significance. The question is *why not Luther?* Why not compare himself to Luther, when that example is out there? That means he chooses to compare himself to a Jew for a cause.

s: It always strikes me as kind of odd—to me, that move of comparing oneself to a Jew, when he's talking about "the church": it is true the psychoanalytic community was founded by Freud. Even though Freud was a very secular Jew; nevertheless he was a very prominent Jewish figure.

sf: Yes, that is important. So, Lacan is seeing a lineage from Spinoza to Freud. Both of them being Jews, both of them being *universalizing* Jews. What they have created is *not Jewish*. There is more to what Lacan was thinking about. I mean, Freud was an assimilated Jew. His Jewishness did not matter to him *until the Nazis began persecuting him.* And when he was persecuted—when anti-Semitism was in a *fury* in Austria, that is when he said, "Okay, now I am going to define myself as a Jew." You know, it is the same as kind of defiance as that of Socrates and Wilde saying, "We are not going to run away." Freud did flee from Austria in the end, because his disciples pressured him to leave Austria, and he was saved by that departure, when all his sisters who stayed in Austria died in concentration camps. He was saved. But, he was beginning to identify himself as a Jew only then, as a definite *response* to persecution. Then, writing one of his most important final works, which is really a work on trauma, *Moses and Monotheism,* in which he has a very strange theory, strange to the Jews, that Moses was actually an Egyptian. That Moses founded the Hebrew nation by coming from his own nationality as an Egyptian. This was very unorthodox to Jews. But, this was Freud's understanding, emerging as a response to persecution. Now, Lacan in turn is identifying himself with the trauma of persecution, and he *chooses deliberately* to identify himself with the Jewish community, even though he is not Jewish, because he wants to identify with the Other. With the persecuted. And with Freud, whom he admires. And he acknowledges that there is something of a Jewish tradition there, that is in a lineage to Spinoza. So, Freud and Spinoza, two Jews, two heretics, two founders, with whom Lacan identifies.

s: I think that in addition to identifying with the Other, there are also major intersections between Spinoza's philosophy and Lacan's psychoanalytic process.

sf: Absolutely. Lacan sees that process of liberation in Spinoza's *Ethics*. This was not required reading for you, but you are invited to read it after the course. Spinoza is the first person who defines desire as the essence of man. Then, he defines the emotions. Then he defines what he calls "*of human bondage,*" which is the way in which we are slaves to our emotions without even being aware of them, without even being conscious of what drives us. So, you could say that the ethics of Spinoza is all about the unconscious, and in a way, *prefigures psychoanalysis*. This is Spinoza's genius. That, in the seventeenth century— psychoanalysis is an invention of the twentieth century—and Spinoza discovers it already, on his own, in his solitude, you know, three centuries before. But the *Ethics* is also Spinoza's response to the all the traumas that he underwent, including the trauma of his excommunication. He understands human nature as being that nature that can traumatize you, also. It is a very forgiving understanding of humanity. You are right, he also implicitly compares his theory to Spinoza's theory. And let me make a personal confession: I superficially thought, when I at first read Spinoza with Lacan in this course, that Lacan *conveniently compared himself to Spinoza* when he was expelled from the IPA, because that provided a convenient metaphor for himself. But then, I discovered that Lacan's thesis in medicine, which dates from 1932, already starts with an epigraph from Spinoza. So Lacan is thirty-two years old when he writes his thesis in medicine—and when he is doing this lecture, "Excommunication," delivered in 1964, he is sixty-three years old. And already at age thirty-two, doing his thesis in medicine, he starts with an epigraph from Spinoza. What's more, the epigraph is in Latin—in Latin, Spinoza's language, so we normal people cannot understand it [laughter]. But he gives us the reference: "Spinoza, *Ethiques,* III, Proposition 52"—so we can go and read it in English. "Any emotion of a given individual" — it's a very hermetic quotation — "any emotion of a given individual differs from the emotion of another individual only insofar as the essence of the one individual differs from the essence of the other." Later on in the *Ethics,* Spinoza will say that the essence of the individual is desire. So, the emotion differs insofar as the desire differs. But, in any case, you see that Lacan was enthralled with Spinoza very early on. He was reading Spinoza — Lacan was a devouring reader of *bric-à-brac.* He was an encyclopedia of science, poetry, religion, you name it. And Spinoza was one of his youthful readings. And he must have recognized that Spinoza said everything there was to say about psychoanalysis. And, in a way, the whole of Lacan can be understood as putting Freud and Spinoza together. Seeing how they go together. So, you are right, Lauren, it is because of what Spinoza wrote. And the *Ethics* will continue to impact Lacan, who is going to entitle one of his seminars *The Ethics of Psychoanalysis.* So, his preoccupation with ethics he inherits from Spinoza. So Spinoza is important. It doesn't just come when Lacan was excommunicated. There was an influence of Spinoza and perhaps an identification with Spinoza before. I would say right away, even though we are interrupting Devin, that what characterizes Spinoza, besides the psychoanalytic content of the *Ethics,* was the discovery of the unconscious in the *Ethics* in the new concept that Spinoza forged of "human bondage." And all this research in the *Ethics* into the conditions of happiness: what, given this human nature and its human bondage, what can bring a human being who has a human condition that is fundamentally miserable, to happiness, what can bring about happiness in that condition? This is Spinoza's question in the *Ethics,* and this is the question of *a healer.* A healer! Not only a philosopher or an ethicist, but a healer. And Spinoza calls this condition of happiness that can be reached through the *Ethics* "blessedness." He doesn't call it happiness, he calls it blessedness. His own name is "blessed [Baruch]," so in a way, it's his signature also [laughter]. It's what he was trying to give to himself. His identity is connected to the *curse* of the excommunication and then to his translation of the curse into his signature — his name was Bento in Portuguese (meaning blessed) and Baruch in Hebrew, a translation of "blessed," and he calls himself Benedictus, after he is excommunicated, which means "blessed" in Latin. And he goes to the universal language of Latin, the language of the scholars, and of science in that period, a language that Lacan also continues. Okay, I am sorry for having interrupted you —

s (DEVIN): That's fine. I guess—the curse question. Lacan gets into this and it sort of helps him in his later discussion of science and religion. He begins to talk—and Jessi read the paragraph where he's the object of this deal—and then the subsequent paragraphs, where he begins to talk about exchange and the production of truth through the intersubjective rather than the subject-object relation. And that becomes this important element for psychoanalysis: on the one hand, he is in this position of being on the margins, because of this mutually defined, mutually understood idea of what psychoanalysis is, and at the same time, there's the intersubjective. That is what defines psychoanalysis. So, on the one hand, they're using the intersubjective to oust him, but on the other hand, they're not really interrogating what the intersubjective can do and how it can produce new knowledge beyond what Freud can say. In the next section, he begins to define questions of practice and why this becomes important. For him, this becomes important because psychoanalysis is defined by its practice. You can't separate the idea of practicing, being an analyst and being a training analyst—psychoanalysis cannot occur unless you have that practice. For that, the field of psychoanalysis as a science or a religion is always going to be demarcated—always defined—by the fact that it's involved in a practice. In this section, he provides some interesting analogies of the religious term of a *shibboleth*. "Shibboleth" is a Hebrew word, and it's been used in the context of the inner circle, the inside as opposed to the outside. This becomes an analogy of his excommunication.

sf: It is. It is. To make it clearer, it's a kind of conduct or password that is recognizable—coded as defining *belonging*. You say a password and you are defined as being from that camp. Shibboleth. So, he is questioning that. And it's this that he doesn't accept: that saying the password would define a belonging to psychoanalysis.

s (DEVIN): And it's this question of "Can there only be one password?" He then gets to a discussion of: if we're going to take Freud's conclusions and ideas—psychoanalysis is supposed to be a science—how do we define it as a science? He begins this question, borrowing from Saussure, saying that science necessarily is supposed to be defined by an object. But the nature of psychoanalysis being sort of a practice and a practice that's done from the intersubjective, it doesn't have a stable object of inquiry. So, it's not necessarily a science in the traditional sense.

SF: And this, Devin, is again a sacrilegious question, because Freud said that he wanted psychoanalysis to be a new science and so everybody accepts that, but Lacan is coming along and saying "*is psychoanalysis a science?*" And he's seriously asking the question. And by the way, here he does not give an answer, but later on in his life, he will give an answer, and he says that psychoanalysis is *not* a science, it is a practice, but all the same, it is a practice that has consequences.

S (DEVIN): So this distinction he's making about whether or not it can possibly be called a science leads to this concluding statement of the section, which is, "What is the analyst's desire?" So, this is sort of similar to the heresy of the question of what is the desire of god. "Why hast thou forsaken me?" It becomes that ultimate, culminating question that breaks him from this normal Freudian self-contained discourse into a question of the desire of the person who created this. Which then leads us to the last section, which is one of the more difficult sections, in that he wants to say that psychoanalysis up to this point has been sort of ignorant of the manner in which Freud's desire has been implicated within the system. I think this comes from his structuralist background, especially with respect to the question of whether or not he's performing a psychologism or psychoanalysis by asking about Freud's desire. For him, it becomes—

SF: He's answering—he's saying, "When I talk about Freud's desire, I am not psychological." That's very important.

S (DEVIN): Yeah. For him, it becomes a structural desire that's the generating force for psychoanalysis. That analysis must necessarily come from this origin, this code, this structure that can produce these different ideas—but at the base of it, there's this desire that situates the system for him. The Freudians have not actually interrogated—not actually thought about desire in this way—which has particular implications about why they're stuck within that system, why they can't escape the ideas of Freud's text, or develop ideas outside them, or question the basis of them. And it's this questioning of Freud's desire, this heretical question, that becomes the base that causes all the problems, within this sort of drama.

SF: Let me add something right away. Concerning his questioning of Freud's desire—which is very deep and he only gives us the tip of the iceberg on that. I want to add that his vision—because psychoanalysis is about desire—is *not* doing exactly a psychoanalyzing of Freud. That's why it's not psychological. But it is structural, as you said. But, also, to the extent that Freud had that desire and that that desire created psychoanalysis—in going beyond itself—he says that "desire is always unconscious, at least in part"—and so, what that means is that *part of Freud's own discovery* was unconscious to him. That is why there is more to do in this field beyond Freud. Freud did a self-analysis—Freud was the only analyst who was not subjected to his own rule, that every psychoanalyst should be psychoanalyzed, because he was *psychoanalyzed by himself*—by using *The Interpretation of Dreams* as his own analysis. He discovered his own unconscious by writing down his dreams and interpreting them. Lacan said that no matter how much he could discover in a self-analysis, there was still an unconscious there, something unanalyzed. So, when he talks about Freud's desire, he talks about what remains *unthought* in psychoanalytic theory, in Freud's structure. What remains unthought—needs to be thought out, so there is place for continuation. I just wanted to add that to your very accurate elucidation of what he says about Freud's desire.

S (DEVIN): He wants to question the foundations of—and he's not being critical—he's just questioning how we came to the foundations of psychoanalysis. Then, he ends this on page 12 by saying, "So, hysteria places us, I would say, on the back of some kind of original sin in analysis. There has to be one. The truth is perhaps simply one thing, namely, the desire of Freud himself, the fact that something in Freud was never analyzed." So, it becomes this original sin, this original action—the generating action that changes the entire universe. Eating the apple—it's something that becomes the generating force for all the rest of psychoanalysis. But at the same time, it is *because* it's a generating force, because there's something unknown about that, because this origin remains unconscious, that we can continue to talk about things that are not simply limited to the writings of Freud and we *can* investigate the unconscious of Freud and what he overlooked. And, for that reason, I read this text as being that performative action—because this is the major seminar he gave after being excommunicated—that this becomes the constitutive act. Not simply going away but giving this new—

SF:—foundational—

S (DEVIN):—foundational analysis that provides the foundation for a new way to understand Freud, and to move beyond Freud.

s f: Very good. I mean, I thank you so much for those presentations—both of you were really fantastic in coping with the difficulty of this text.

Now we can do one of two things: either engage in a line-by-line close reading of Lacan's text—which is really an incredible text, very complex, very ironic. Or, we can try to compare Lacan to the other writers that we studied. I don't think we'll have the time to do both. So, what do you *choose?*

s: Compare.

s f: Compare. Okay. Let's go back to Spinoza, because we didn't finish with the comparison. The comparison with Spinoza itself is a comparison of geniuses. Yes?

s: Something that seems striking between Lacan and Spinoza is that they both speak *out of* the excommunication. It's almost as though Lacan needs the excommunication in order to move forward and write everything else.

s f: Right. That leads to his reclaiming of his own theory, of his own innovation. Whereas before, as Jacques-Alain Miller testifies, he was doing seminars always taking a text by Freud to understand, and now he still remains very close to Freud's work, but he is *reclaiming his own contribution.* Yes, Jessi?

s (jessi): And almost reclaiming his own voice, because Jacques-Alain Miller talks about how this seminar was announced to be *The Names of the Father,* which obviously has other religious implications. But, you know, there was this dispute—are they ready for this idea?—and him giving this seminar but under a different title: "The Fundamental Concepts of Psychoanalysis."

s f: Yes.

s (jessi): That's more acceptable to the community.

s f: Yeah, this whole mysterious thing—that Lacan wants to give a seminar that . . . then he said he will never give . . . then he gives it under different names . . . and then it remains the enigma of what is *unspeakable in Lacan.* That self-censored title remains Lacan's own reference to something that is unspeakable, even though the censorship against him does not work—he is not silenced. He is actually reclaiming his voice. But he changes his audience. Rather than addressing only professional psychoanalysts, now he is going to address the intellectuals at large. The Parisian intelligentsia as such. The scientists, the philosophers, the artists, the literary writers, and of course the psychiatrists as well, now *everyone* was coming to Lacan's seminars. I had the chance to visit some of them and it was really incredible. This was at the later phase, when six hundred people were coming. He had an auditorium that could contain three hundred and six hundred were coming. He was doing it twice a month from twelve to two. So, if you wanted to be able to enter into that room, you had to go at nine. I went at nine—and for me, I am not a morning person [laughter]. But I wanted to be there. And you had to be there at nine if you wanted to sit. Then, there were people standing. And it was really a torture to be in that room, from nine to twelve. The room was so full of smoke that you couldn't breathe. You really couldn't breathe. I mean, I was really choking there, and I stayed until twelve. Then, Lacan would come and he would speak for two hours. And it would be really unintelligible until about a quarter of an hour before the end, when all of a sudden there would be an illumination—something of a genius will get to you. You didn't go there with the understanding that you would understand every word that would be said. I mean, this was notoriously unintelligible discourse—difficult discourse. There were a few figures like that in history—the more difficult they were, the more they drew students. Mallarmé, the French poet, was giving lectures that were called *Les Causeries du Mardi,* and he would just talk like his poems. And poets would come to listen to him. And it was impossible to understand, but people would be fascinated because they felt there would be *something* extraordinarily significant in that unintelligible language. Another philosopher who was like that is Wittgenstein. People didn't understand, but they *flocked* [laughter]. But, other people attacked that phenomenon from the outside, they called it "obscurantism"—they gave a lot of names to it—as though these people were trying to be deliberately obscure, but there was something mysterious about it nonetheless. My understanding of Lacan was that Lacan *could not speak simply,* first of all, because what he had to say was so complicated; second, because everything that he had to say was *embattled.* So he could only speak in a *tortured* way, his discourse was tortured—it's not that he chose to be difficult. And yet, people were going because they felt that they were in touch with genius. It is—yeah, okay. So that was just an anecdote.

S (LAUREN): When you were telling us how you used to go and listen to Lacan, that makes me think about the connection I see among all the people we've read, it's that they have this pedagogical impulse. I think it's interesting that Lacan wasn't really excommunicated, per se, but he was just restricted from being a training analyst. That exclusion was so important to him—he couldn't be a part of the community anymore, *if he couldn't teach.*

SF: Right, right.

S (LAUREN): I think that's true for the other people we've read, too—

SF: Socrates says, "If you put me to a hundred deaths and you ask me to stop teaching by putting me to a hundred deaths, I will undergo all those deaths, rather than stop teaching what I want to teach." That's very good, Lauren. So, all these people have a vocation for teaching—they are not simply enjoying the provocation. They feel they are *compelled* to teach what they have—to contribute. Yes?

S: Where does Forster fit into this?

SF: The way in which Forster can be connected is the following. There are two real trials behind his novel *A Passage to India.* We did in fact mention one, when we were reading Wilde. Wilde's trial for homosexuality concerned so many others beyond himself; among those, Forster, because Forster was in turn a homosexual, and he, like so many others, was living under the political shadow of the terrifying legal verdict against Wilde. And, after Wilde's trial, homosexuals in England went to the colonies to take refuge there because it was too dangerous to practice their sexuality in England, so they went to India, also for this purpose, as sort of refugees. So, there is this real historical trial of a fellow writer behind Forster, this legal condemnation of the sexuality that he identifies with. Homosexuality is also present—albeit implicitly—in *A Passage to India,* which is underwritten by indirect, elliptical sexual implications (remember how the book revolves around the friendship between Aziz and Fielding, in the same way that *Dorian Gray* is underwritten by the homoerotic friendships between men?). The second trial pertaining to the historical legal reality behind Forster's novel is a political trial concerning colonialism, a trial that was taking place in England at the end of the eighteenth century: its proceedings were held before the House of the Lords and were known as "The Impeachment of Warren Hastings." Warren Hastings was the head of the East India Company, a commercial British company by which England exploited the economic resources of India. The head of this company, who was an important British emissary, was accused of corruption, and Edmund Burke was his accuser and prosecutor. Burke wrote these very beautiful speeches to indict the abuses of power of the British Empire and to protest against its corrupt economic usurpation of its power in India. Burke was politically a conservative, but he saw the tremendous injustice of colonialism through the case of this man against whom he was drawing up the charges. The trial lasted seven years. But at the end of these long and taxing proceedings, Hastings was acquitted: the British could not bring themselves to convict one of their own and delegitimize a man who acted as their representative and as the symbol of the power of their Empire, even though his guilt was proven. So they finally acquitted him in 1795: that is parallel to how the French, conversely, could not bring themselves to acquit Dreyfus, even though they had evidence of his innocence, so they continued to convict him to the end, and then "pardoned" him, to reverse the conviction they knew to be unjust. In Hastings's case, it was well known he was guilty, but there was an acquittal, an official consecration of the injustice of colonialism. So, Forster writes under the shadow of those two trials and the symbolic impact of their two public verdicts: the conviction of Wilde for homosexuality, on the one hand, and, on the other hand, the acquittal of Hastings from charges of colonial abuses of power. Forster's novel confronts the political reality of colonialism—he symbolizes this reality through the fictional drama of a lynch-trial, depicting the British communal prosecution of an Indian, based on a false accusation of his having raped an Englishwoman. As you know, such false charges of rape against a background of racism and racial conflict are not uncommon in history: there are many lynch-trials in actual history—they respond to what is perceived as the threat of interracial erotic attraction, and Forster makes a political symbol of such an archetypal legal drama in his novel A Passage to India. So, this is the case of Forster: he was part of a minority, so to speak, and as such became sympathetic, politically, to the occupied rather than the occupier. Forster went to the colonies as part of *a minority that seeks refuge.*

That brings me back to Lacan. We did not clarify his reference to "his position as a refugee." The concept of refugee is important—this is 1964, roughly two decades after the Second World War. When you think about refugees, you cannot not think about the reality of the Holocaust in the aftermath of the war. In fact, Seminar XI, which is opened by this inaugural lecture, "Excommunication," noteworthily *ends* on an explicit reference of Lacan to the Holocaust, which, as far as I know, is the only explicit reference to the Holocaust that Lacan ever makes. So the Holocaust is in the background, at the horizon, so to speak, of this seminar, inaugurated by the naming of Lacan's position as a refugee of his group and of the International Psychoanalytic Association. Lacan truly deferred to the Judaism of Freud. Lacan is attracted by that otherness. He talks a lot about the other—he is a *liberator* in the sense that he wants us to understand the other, rather than to exclude the other.

Other writers that we have studied here can be equally viewed as liberators—*liberators.* Socrates was a liberator, certainly. Zola was trying to be a liberator. Wilde was a liberator. So the reference of Lacan to Judaism is also very interesting and pregnant with implicit meaning. You know, he was married twice. And his second wife was Jewish. And he married her before the Second World War. So, during the Second World War and the Nazi occupation of France, Lacan was truly *tied up* with that community of Jewishness, experiencing the war from that vantage point. Remember how Freud was defiant. A situation of war in the context of the fanaticism of German anti-Semitism always spells danger for Jews. Yet Lacan called his daughter—born in 1941 from her Jewish mother—during the war, he calls her Judith, which means Jewish. This exchange between Christianity and Judaism is already very interesting.

Now, this can also be seen in Spinoza's existence. The exchange between Christianity and Judaism, which constitutes the ambiguity of Spinoza, is precisely what triggers his censorship, his excommunication by the Jewish community—the expulsion by that community of the threat of that ambiguity. This historically comes from the history of conversion of the previous generation of Jews, among whom Spinoza's parents, born in Portugal and emigrating to the Netherlands from Portugal. There is another interesting issue that emerges in Spinoza being the figure that Lacan identifies with—does anybody see that? What would you say are the two key concepts that Lacan is exploring in this seminar, that are not among "the four fundamental concepts of psychoanalysis," but are rather his tools of interrogation, concepts through which he calls psychoanalysis into question?

s (DEVIN): Desire.

sf: Desire is very important in effect as the essence of man and the essence of Freud, but it's more the disciplines of religion and science! This is an apparent opposition, right? Normally, science is secular, and as secular it is fundamentally nonreligious. That is how science was born, out of the secularization of the seventeenth century, with all of its philosophical and scientific geniuses. Now, Spinoza is precisely a figure that is ambiguous, insofar as the question arises: was he a scientist or was he a religious person? You know, I told you that there is a controversy among scholars in determining whether Spinoza was religious in an unconventional way or was just *hiding behind a religious appearance* and was really, at the core, an atheist. If there was this ambiguity in Spinoza's religion, that was because Spinoza was a devouring reader of all the works of philosophy and science of the seventeenth century—he was a scientist, to a large degree. And he was really moving *between science and religion.*

Spinoza is situated at the precise borderline between religion and science. We have said that the two key terms Lacan uses to question psychoanalysis—are precisely religion, on the one hand (Is psychoanalysis a religion? Why is it behaving like a religion?) and science, on the other hand (Freud strives to give a scientific status to psychoanalysis, and the psychoanalytic establishment takes this status for granted). And Lacan comes and very provocatively says, *"Is it a science?"* And in the end, he says it is not a science, but that does not mean it is not important. He also speaks here about religion—in a most ironic, sarcastic, witty way, yet at the same time he is dead serious in asking: what are the common denominators between psychoanalysis and religion? Obviously, the title "Excommunication" is a tremendously *ironic* title—because inasmuch as we "know" that psychoanalysis is a science, we "know" that it is not a religion. But Lacan suspends these two kinds of knowledge, even wavers between them, despite and perhaps because of their apparent contradiction. "Do we really know what science is? Do we really know what religion is?" That is his real questioning work. He suspends the commonplace answers, the oppositional definitions! Let's not be so sure, so quickly—we do not know if it is really a science, and we do not really know if it is or isn't a religion, because the institution functions as religious institutions function, by expelling and censoring otherness. And Lacan says that this expulsion, this excommunication, has a psychoanalytic logic — it's not *by chance* that it happens. Religion doesn't stay in his text only in terms of the irony — underscoring the fact that psychoanalysis behaves like a church. As his question develops, there is a way in which the ambiguity ceases to be ironic and he is saying *very seriously* that there is something mysterious that remains enigmatic in psychoanalysis, and that something, that mystery, can be likened to the one underlying and driving a religious practice. For instance, "I do not search unless I have already found." This, and some other passages, are actually seriously saying that religion, in its deepest sense, has a meaning that we cannot completely exclude. This is coming from a person whose medical thesis is dedicated to his brother, who is a religious Catholic. So there is also a serious question — Lacan is ambiguous — whether talking about religion is a joke or whether it's serious. And it's both and you can't know. He's really moving in between and he's using *the movement between religion and science* precisely as his movement that is *affiliated with Spinoza*. Spinoza was doing that very seriously, taking science very seriously and taking religion very seriously and doing something in between. The in-between is the *pathbreaking* work.

So, to return to our comparison — all those thinkers are thinkers of ethics, some directly and others indirectly. Socrates, having invented the ethics — but even somebody like Wilde, who says that literature is about aesthetics, not about ethics, it obviously *is* about ethics for him as well, albeit in a provocative way. Wilde's provocative witticisms — statements such as: "There is no such thing as a moral or an immoral book. Books are well written, or badly written. That is all" — cannot be taken at their face value. What he wants to root out of literature is moralizing — moralizing is not ethics. So, all of them are, in a way, interested in the foundation of new religions, whether it's good or bad. All of them, like Spinoza, are lonely figures. There is a solitude in the figure of Lacan — despite the hundreds of people that flocked to Lacan's seminars and came to be analyzed by him and to study with him, *he is alone*. He is alone. And "Excommunication" is the speech of someone *lonely*. And as Devin underscored very accurately, in his definition of the excommunication, part of it is that they are prohibited communication. They do not accept it, but still, this is a wound that they carry.

They are wounded writers. The trials for most of them are traumas. They are all thinkers of desire. Spinoza starts by establishing desire as a central philosophical concept. But Socrates also has implied desire in saying that the philosopher is *a lover of wisdom.*" That is what *philosopher* means, etymologically—a lover. A lover of wisdom. That means that philosophy is motivated by a desire. The desire of a lover of wisdom. They all are trying to be healers. It's striking that even Socrates, who is a philosopher, says that it is the role of the philosopher to "heal from the wound of the argument" and from the uncertainty about the immortality of the soul. So, even Socrates is as a healer—his very last words—"Crito, I owe a cock to Asclepius"—confirm that: this surprising closure of *Phaedo,* which names open-endedly, at the end of Socrates' life, an unfinished debt to Asclepius, the god of healing, and ends with an unfinished business of the philosopher, this choice, at the moment of death, to name the debt to Asclepius, the god of healing, means that philosophy is—in Plato's terms—"a practice of death" only to the extent that it is also about *healing the human condition.* They are all about healing the human condition and they are all about freeing—they are liberators. Spinoza is going to put freedom as a very central concept, as the *aboutissement* of the *Ethics:* the crowning of the *Ethics* is freedom. The attainment of freedom. All of them understanding that freedom is not a given. And the one that is practicing pseudofreedom, in a promiscuous way, Wilde in his rebellious and provocative *libertinage*—he is, in fact, among all these writers, one of the most enslaved to what Spinoza defines as the constitutional "human bondage." So, freedom is not given but is something that is *searched.* All of them are radical thinkers—you will remember Peirce's definition of radicalism, which we read the last time. "Conservatism, in the sense of the dread of consequences, is altogether out of place in science, which has always been forwarded by radicals and radicalism, in the sense of the eagerness to carry consequences to their extremes." Those people are not afraid to face the consequences—they are always taking consequences to their extremes. This is what makes them dangerous. They are objectively dangerous people—to the institutions and the axioms that surround them. So, they trigger censorship—the trials come in order to censor those people, to censor their teaching—and what needs to be censored is precisely their relentless questioning, the endless, interminable questioning that drives them to develop a self-critique of their own discipline and question its foundations. They are all—all of them—tremendous ironists. Lacan has an incredible *esprit*—reading in French, you see the sharpness of this *esprit,* this sense of humor, which is not the *wit,* the British or Irish wit of Wilde, but the French *esprit,* the specifically French sense of humor. They are all ironists. They are all irreverent with conventions. And, with all of them, what is feared is that they are *creative teachers.* Their creativity is translated into their style—I think I end my essay on education with Lacan's wonderful quotation—his enigmatic quotation—that all he has to transmit to his students is a style. "Any return to Freud founding a teaching worthy of the name will occur only on that pathway . . . where truth becomes apparent in the revolutions of culture. That pathway is the only training we can claim to transmit to those who follow us. It is called—a style." All of these thinkers and artists have a style. It is the style which distinguishes them—the style is not opposed to the content of their thought, it is a "pathway to the truth," a truth which they transmit—and perform—through the style. All of them are teachers precisely insofar as they have a signature style.

Well, this is, more or less, the intuition I was offering to you, but I am really, really interested in your response to this intuition, which I expect to read in your final paper. So, I want to thank you all for having taken this class. That's it.

—Transcribed by Charles Boardman

Photo Gallery

Shoshana Felman delivers her first lecture at the Colloque Stendhal International in Parma, Italy, in 1967.

Felman with Paul de Man and Jacques Lacan at Lacan's visit to Yale University in November 1975.

Felman at the time of the 1980 French publication of *The Scandal of the Speaking Body*.

Felman greets a well-wisher at the farewell party on her departure from Yale University, March 26, 2004.

Shoshana Felman's last class at Yale, taught jointly with Sara Suleri, *left*, "Literatures of Judgment and Forgiveness: Art and Acts of Justice."

Shoshana Felman, 2007. Photo by Yanai Yechiel.

Notes on Contributors

JUDITH BUTLER is Maxine Elliot Professor in the Departments of Rhetoric and Comparative Literature at the University of California at Berkeley. Butler is the author of numerous books, including *Gender Trouble: Feminism and the Subversion of Identity* (Routledge, 1990), *Antigone's Claim: Kinship Between Life and Death* (Columbia University Press, 2000), and *Giving an Account of Oneself* (Fordham University Press, 2005).

CATHY CARUTH is Winship Distinguished Professor of Comparative Literature and English at Emory University. She is the author of *Unclaimed Experience: Trauma, Narrative, and History* (Johns Hopkins University Press, 1996) and *Empirical Truths and Critical Fictions: Locke, Wordsworth, Kant, Freud* (Johns Hopkins University Press, 1991), co-editor of *Critical Encounters: Reference and Responsibility in Deconstructive Writing* (Rutgers University Press, 1995), and editor of *Trauma: Explorations in Memory* (Johns Hopkins University Press, 1995).

STANLEY CAVELL is Professor Emeritus of Philosophy at Harvard University. The author of many books, including *The Claim of Reason* (Oxford University Press, 1979), *Pursuits of Happiness* (Harvard University Press, 1981), *Emerson's Transcendental Études* (Stanford University Press, 2003), *Cities of Words* (Harvard University Press, 2004), and *Philosophy the Day After Tomorrow* (Harvard University Press, 2005), Cavell is one of America's foremost philosophers and a major theorist of film, literature, and opera.

JULIA KRISTEVA is a philosopher, psychoanalyst, fiction writer, and literary theorist who teaches at University of Paris VII and has held regular visiting appointments at Columbia University. Among her many books are *Time and Sense: Proust and the Experience of Literature* (Columbia University Press, 1996), *New Maladies of the Soul* (Columbia University Press, 1995), and a trilogy on feminine genius that includes the volume *Hannah Arendt* (Columbia University Press, 2001).

WINFRIED MENNINGHAUS is Professor of Comparative Literature at the Free University of Berlin and Visiting Professor at Yale University. He is the author of many books in German on such figures as Walter Benjamin and Paul Celan as well as, in English, *In Praise of Nonsense: Kant and Bluebeard* (Stanford University Press, 1999) and *Disgust: Theory and History of a Strong Sensation* (SUNY Press, 2003).

JULIET MITCHELL is Professor of Psychoanalysis and Gender Studies at the University of Cambridge and a Fellow of Jesus College, Cambridge. She is a Full Member of the British Psychoanalytical Society and the International Psychoanalytical Society. She is the author of *Psychoanalysis and Feminism* (Penguin, 1974) and *Women: The Longest Revolution* (Virago, 1984). Her most recent books are *Siblings: Sex and Violence* (Polity Press, 2003) and *Mad Men and Medusas: Reclaiming Hysteria and the Sibling Relationship for the Human Condition* (Allen Lane/Penguin Press and Basic Books, 2000).

AUSTIN SARAT is William Nelson Cromwell Professor of Jurisprudence and Political Science at Amherst College. He has authored many articles and coedited numerous books, including *Law on the Screen* (Stanford University Press, 2005), *The Rhetoric of Law* (University of Michigan Press, 1994), and *Law's Violence* (University of Michigan Press, 1992).

Notes

INTRODUCTION
Emily Sun, Eyal Peretz, and Ulrich Baer

1. Shoshana Felman, *The Scandal of the Speaking Body* (Stanford, Calif.: Stanford University Press, 2002), 65.

2. Judith Butler, afterword, in Shoshana Felman, *The Scandal of the Speaking Body*, 123 (reprinted in this volume).

3. Stanley Cavell, foreword, in Shoshana Felman, *The Scandal of the Speaking Body*, xiii (reprinted in this volume).

CHAPTER 1
From "*Henry James: Madness and the Risks of Practice (Turning the Screw of Interpretation)*"
Shoshana Felman

1. This chapter has not been translated; it is the author's original English version.

2. Unless otherwise specified, all quotations from the New York Preface and from *The Turn of the Screw* are taken from the Norton Critical Edition of *The Turn of the Screw*, ed. Robert Kimbrough (New York: Norton, 1966); hereafter abbreviated "*Norton*." As a rule, all italics within the quoted texts throughout this paper are mine; original italics alone will be indicated.

3. "A Note on the Freudian Reading of *The Turn of the Screw*" in: *A Casebook on Henry James's "The Turn of the Screw,"* ed. Gerald Willen, 2d ed. (New York: Thomas Y. Crowell, 1969), 239. This collection of critical essays will hereafter be abbreviated *Casebook*.

4. "Another Reading of *The Turn of the Screw*," in *Casebook*, 154.

5. "The Freudian Reading of *The Turn of the Screw*," in *Modern Language Notes* 62, no. 7 (Nov. 1947): 433. This essay will hereafter be referred to as: FR, *MLN*.

6. "James's Air of Evil: *The Turn of the Screw*," in *Casebook*, 202.

7. "James: *The Turn of the Screw*. A Radio Symposium," in *Casebook*, 167.

8. Robert Heilman, "*The Turn of the Screw* as Poem," in *Casebook*, 175.

9. Mark Spilka, "Turning the Freudian Screw: How Not to Do It," in *Norton*, 249–50.

10. Edmund Wilson, "The Ambiguity of Henry James," in *The Triple Thinkers* (Penguin, 1962), 102. This essay will hereafter be referred to as *Wilson*.

11. Cf., for example, *Wilson*, 126: "Sex *does* appear in his work—even becoming a kind of obsession," but we are always separated from it by "thick screens."

12. Cf., ibid., "The people who surround this observer tend to take on the diabolic values of *The Turn of the Screw*, and these diabolic values are almost invariably connected with sexual relations that are always concealed and at which we are compelled to guess."

13. Cf., ibid., 108: "When one has once got hold of the clue to this meaning of *The Turn of the Screw*, one wonders how one could ever have missed it. There is a very good reason, however, in the fact that nowhere does James unequivocally give the thing away: almost everything from beginning to end can be read equally in either of two senses."

14. "'Wild' Psycho-Analysis," in *The Standard Edition of the Complete Psychological Works of Sigmund Freud*, Vol. XI (1910), 221–22. This edition will hereafter be abbreviated *Standard*.

15. Jacques Lacan, "Discours de clôture des journées sur les psychoses chez l'enfant," in *Recherches*, special issue, "Enfance aliénée" (11 December 1968): 145–46; translation mine. Unless otherwise indicated, all quotations from Lacan's work in this paper are in my translation.

16. And if that adequation does not appear in James's work, it is, in Wilson's view, because James, too, like the governess, missed out on the simplicity of the normal status of normal sex and knew only the lack of satisfaction involved in its pathological manifestations: cf. *Wilson*, 125: "*Problems of sexual passion* . . . were beginning to be subjects of burning interest. But it is probably that James had by this time . . . come to recognize *his unfittedness for dealing with them* and was far too honest to fake."

17. J. Lydenberg, "The Governess Turns the Screws," in *Casebook*, 289.

18. J. Lacan, *Le Séminaire—Livre XX: Encore (1972–1973)* (Paris: Seuil, 1975), 66. This work will henceforth be referred to as *Encore*.

19. These two types of reading thus recall the illusory "two turns" that the mistaken reader in the frame attributes to the screw of the text's effect. (Cf. prologue, p. 1, and, above, note 17.) But we have seen that the "two turns" in fact amount to the same: based on the symmetry implied by the "*two* children," the apparent *difference* between the "two turns" is purely

specular. This is the final irony of the figure of the turn of the screw: while appearing to double and to multiply itself, the turn of the screw only *repeats* itself; while appearing to "turn," to *change* direction, sense, or meaning, the turning sense in fact does not change, since the screw *returns upon itself*. And it is precisely through such a "return upon itself" that the trap set by the text, says James, catches the reader.

20. The formula is Paul Ricoeur's.

21. Jean Starobinski, *La Relation critique* (Paris: Gallimard, 1979), 271; my translation.

22. Cf. chap. 6, p. 28: "... a suspense ... that might well ... have *turned* into *something like madness.* ... It *turned* to *something else altogether* ... from the moment I really *took hold.*" Cf. also chap. 12, p. 48: "I go on, I know, as if I am *crazy*, and it's a wonder I'm not. What I've seen would have made *you* so; but it only made me more lucid, made me *get hold* of still other things ..."

23. To begin with, she claims they are "possessed," that is, *unseizable*, possessed precisely *by the Other*: "Yes, *mad* as it seems! ... They haven't been good—they've only been absent. ... They're simply leading a life of their own. They're not mine—they're not ours. They're his and they're hers!" (chap. 12, pp. 48–49).

24. Cf.: "'It's a game,' I went on—'it's a policy and a fraud!' ... 'Yes, *mad* as it seems!' The very act of bringing it out really helped me to trace it— follow it up and *piece it all together*" (chap. 12, pp. 48–49).

25. Freud, *Three Case Histories*, ed. Philip Rieff (New York: Collier Books, 1963), 182.

26. *Scilicet*, no. 1 (1968): 31 ("La Méprise du sujet supposé savoir").

27. S. Freud, "The Uncanny," trans. Alix Strachey, in *Freud on Creativity and the Unconscious* (New York: Harper Torchbooks, 1958), 137.

28. H. James, *The Sacred Fount* (New York: Charles Scribner's Sons, 1901), 318.

29. Ibid., 319.

30. J. Lacan, "Séminaire sur *La Lettre volée*," *Ecrits*, 17.

31. F. Nietzsche, *The Will to Power*.

32. Cf. "Our noted behaviour at large may show for ragged, because it perpetually *escapes our control*; we have again and again to consent to its appearing in undress—that is, in no state to brook criticism." "It rests altogether with himself [the artist] not to ... 'give away' his importances" (*AN*, 348).

33. "Il faut assi que tu n'ailles point / Choisir tes mots sans quelque méprise / Rien de plus cher que la chanson grise / Où l'Indécis au Précis se joint / ... Et tout le reste est littérature." (P. Verlaine, *Art poétique*.)

CHAPTER 2

Foucault/Derrida: The Madness of the Thinking/Speaking Subject

Shoshana Felman

1. This chapter has not been translated; it is the author's original English version.

2. Author's translation. All passages quoted in this chapter have been translated by the author, either from the French original or from the French edition cited in the endnotes.

3. Hegel, "Philosophie de l'esprit," in *Encyclopédie* (Paris: Germer Baillère, 1867), 383.

4. Nietzsche, *Ainsi parlait Zarathustra* (Paris: Le Livre de Poche, 1968), 193.

5. J.-J. Rousseau, "Le Persifleur," in *Œuvres complètes*, t. I (Paris: Pléiade, 1959), 1110.

6. Cf. Heidegger, *Nietzsche* (Paris: Gallimard, 1971); and Georges Bataille, "Sur Nietzsche" and "La Folie de Nietzsche," in *Œuvres completes*, t. I, III (Paris: Gallimard, 1973).

7. The work has so far appeared in three French editions: Plon, Paris, 1961 (original edition); 10/18 (abridged edition), Paris, 1964; and Gallimard, "Bibliothèque des histoires," Paris, 1972 — a new unabridged edition from which, however, the original Preface has been eliminated, and to which two formerly unpublished Appendices have been added. Unless otherwise indicated, my references to Foucault's work are to the recent Gallimard edition, hereafter cited as *HF* in the text. (Quoted passages are my translation.) The English edition of Foucault's book, entitled *Madness and Civilization* (Vintage), is a translation of the abridged edition of 10/18.

8. A similar conception of the Western world's attitude toward madness is outlined in the works of the American psychiatrist Thomas Szasz. Cf., for instance, this sharp passage from *Ideology and Insanity* (Garden City, New York: Doubleday Anchor, 1969): "Modern psychiatric ideology is an adaptation — to a scientific age — of the traditional ideology of Christian Theology. Instead of being born into sin man is born into sickness. . . . And, as in his journey from the cradle to the grave man was formerly guided by the priest, so now he is guided by the physician. In short, whereas in the Age of Faith the ideology was Christian, the technology clerical, and the expert priestly; in the Age of Madness the ideology is medical, the technology clinical, and the expert psychiatric. . . . Indeed, when the justificatory rhetoric with which the oppressor conceals and misinterprets his true aims and methods is most effective — as had been the case formerly with tyranny justified by theology, and is the case now with tyranny justified by therapy — the oppressor succeeds not only in subduing his victim but also in robbing him of a vocabulary for articulating his victimization, thus making him a captive deprived of all means of escape" (5).

9. *Histoire de la folie*, Preface of the original edition (Plon, 1961).

10. Ibid.

11. Ibid.

12. Ibid.

13. Jacques Derrida, "Cogito et histoire de la folie," in *L'Écriture et la difference* (Paris: Le Seuil, 1967). Hereafter cited at *ED* in the text.

14. *Histoire de la folie* (Paris: Gallimard, 1972), Appendice II: "Mon corps, ce papier, ce feu," 601. Foucault's italics.

15. Ibid., Appendice I: "La Folie, l'absence d'œuvre," 582. My italics.

16. It should be noted that the French word "folie" is both more inclusive and more common than the English word "madness": "folie" covers a vast range of meaning going from slight eccentricity to clinical insanity, including thus the connotations both of "madness" and of "folly," and in addition, appearing as an indication of excess, almost in the role of a superlative, in clichés such as "amoureux fou," "aimer à la folie," etc. It is perhaps not insignificant as well that "folie" in French is feminine: its grammatical gender confers upon it a kind of elusive femininity that is lost, along with its varied connotations, in an English translation.

17. Preface of the original edition (Plon, 1961).

18. Derrida, "Cogito et histoire de la folie," 66. My italics.

CHAPTER 3
Shoshana Felman

Rimbaud with Mallarmé: Modernity, Poetry, Translation (Postface)

1. Stéphane Mallarmé, "Arthur Rimbaud," in "Quelques médaillons et portraits en pied," in *Oeuvres complètes de Stéphane Mallarmé*, ed. Henri Mondor and G. Jean-Aubry (Paris: Pléiade, 1965). Page numbers in subsequent citations from Mallarmé's essay refer to this French edition cited in *Divagations*, by Stephane Mallarmé and Barbara Johnson (Cambridge: Harvard University Press, 2007).

2. "Verlaine héroique," *La Rêvue blanche*, February 15, 1986.

"You were right to leave, Arthur Rimbaud": Poetry and Modernity

1. "Il faut etra absolument moderne," "Adieu," in *Une Saison en Enfer* [*A Season in Hell*], 241. Page numbers of Rimbaud citations refer, unless otherwise indicated, to *Rimbaud, Oeuvres,* the French Classiques Garnier edition (Paris, 1960), edited by Suzanne Bernard. Unless otherwise indicated, all citations from French writers in this essay (including all citations from Rimbaud, and other French poets) are here in Barbara Johnson's original translation from the French. For other English versions of Rimbaud, see Rimbaud, *Complete Works, Selected Letters,* bilingual edition translated by Wallace Fowlie (Chicago and London: The University of Chicago Press, 1966); Arthur

Rimbaud, *Complete Works,* translated by Paul Schmidt (New York: HarperCollins, Perennial Classics, 2000); and Arthur Rimbaud, *Rimbaud Complete,* translated by Wyatt Mason (New York: The Modern Library, 2002).

2. "Être moderne, c'est bricoler dans l'incurable."

3. René Char, *Recherche de la base et du sommet* (Paris: Gallimard, 1965), 102.

4. Cf. René Char: "Tu as bien fait de partir, Arthur Rimbaud! Nous sommes quelques-uns à croire sans preuve le bonheur possible avec toi." ("You were right to leave, Arthur Rimbaud! We are of several who believe, without proof, that happiness is possible with you.") "Tu as bien fait de partir, Arthur Rimbaud," *Fureur et Mystère* (Paris: Poésie/Gallimard, 1967), 212.

5. Thus Mallarmé names "the great Verlaine," in referring to the "greatness" of the (poetic and personal) voice that the patient Rimbaud, having returned from Africa to France to undergo a knee operation, did not answer, but must have heard calling him, upon his unexpected return to his native country, on his hospital bed, just before his death: "Or, between the patient and the voices that called him, especially that of the great Verlaine, he took refuge in the muteness offered by a wall or a hospital curtain." Mallarmé, "Arthur Rimbaud," in "Quelques Médaillons et Portraits en pied," in *Œuvres complètes de Stéphane Mallarmé* (Paris: Bibliothèque de la Pléiade, 1965), 518, English translation by Barbara Johnson.

6. As opposed to poetry focused on the poet's subjectivity (basically, the conception of romantic poetry), Rimbaud aspires to create a so-called objective poetry, by pursuing and exploring visions of "the unknown," located and researched well beyond the conscious self (for the concept of objective poetry, see Letter to Izambard, May 13, 1871, Classiques Garnier, 343.

7. These three opening paragraphs were rewritten in 2005. The remainder of the text is faithful to the historical, original French text of 1973.

8. "Drapeaux d'extase." The expression is Rimbaud's: "Génie" ["Genius"], in *Illuminations,* 308.

9. "L'éclair," in *Une Saison en enfer,* 238. Emphasis Rimbaud's.

10. "Tous les habiles croiraient avoir satisfait à cette demande.—*Ce n'est pas cela,*" Letter to Paul Demeny, May 15, 1871 (the "Lettre du Voyant"), 348. Emphasis added.

11. *Recherche de la Base et du Sommet,* 36. Emphasis Char's.

12. Valéry, *La Crise de l'esprit,* in *Essais quasi politiques, Íuvres* (Paris: Pléiade, 1957), 1:991–92. Emphasis Valéry's.

13. "*Une* vie moderne et plus abstraite," Baudelaire, *Petits poèmes en prose,* Préface: "A Arsène Houssaye" (Paris: Garnier, 1962), 6.

14. Baudelaire, *Le Peintre de la vie moderne:* "Ainsi, il [l'artiste] va, il court, il cherche. . . . Il cherche ce quelque chose qu'on nous permettra d'appeler la *modernité.* . . . Il s'agit pour lui, de dégager de la mode ce qu'elle peut contenir de poétique dans l'historique, de tirer l'éternel du transitoire," in *Íuvres complètes* (Paris: Pléiade, 1961), 1163. Emphasis Baudelaire's. ("Thus the

artist goes, he runs, he seeks. . . . He seeks that something that we will be permitted to call *modernity*. . . . What is at stake for him is to distill from fashion what the historical contains of the poetic, to draw the eternal out of the transitory.")

15. Letter to Izambard (May 13, 1871), 349.

16. "If this consideration is untimely, it is also because I'm trying to understand as an evil, a defect, a lack, something in which our time takes pride. . . . I have felt sentiments so out of keeping with the times . . . although I also feel like a child of the times . . . I don't see what use classical philology would be for our times, and it's by undertaking an untimely action *against our times,* thus also *of our times,* that I hope to benefit times to come." Nietzsche, "On the Use and Abuse of History for Our Times," in *Untimely Meditations [Thoughts Out of Season]*, French translation (Paris, Aubier, 1964), 199, 201.

17. "Génie" ["Genius"], in *Illuminations*, 308–9. Unless otherwise indicated, all emphasis in Rimbaud's texts is added.

18. Breton, *Manifestes du surréalisme [Manifestos of Surrealism]* (Paris: Gallimard/Idées), 62. Emphasis Breton's on the word *modern.*

19. Cf. Roman Jakobson, "Les embrayeurs, les catégories verbales et le verbe russe," in *Essais de linguistique générale* (Paris: Minuit, 1969), French translation by N. Ruwet; and Emile Benveniste, "La nature des pronoms" ["The Nature of Pronouns"], in *Problèmes de linguistique générale [Problems in General Linguistics]* (Paris: NRF, 1966). [Translator's Note: The French translation of Jakobson to which Felman refers here was very influential in France and has no exact equivalent in any other language. The article mentioned was first published in English in 1957 as "Shifters, Verbal Categories, and the Russian Verb."]

20. Letter to Paul Demeny, called "Lettre du Voyant" (May 15, 1871), 345.

21. Letter to Georges Izambard (May 13, 1871), 344.

22. "Je suis en mots, je suis fait des mots, des mots des autres. . . . Je suis tous ces mots, tous ces étrangers, cette poussière de verbe . . ." Beckett, *L'Innommable* (Paris: Minuit, 1953), 204.

23. Letter to P. Demeny (May 15, 1871), 345.

24. Letter to G. Izambard (May 13, 1871), 344.

25. "Nuit de l'enfer" ["A Night in Hell"], in *Une saison en Enfer*, 221.

26. Letter to Paul Demeny (May 15, 1871), 346.

27. Ibid., 345.

28. "Le Cœur volé" ["The Stolen Heart"], 100–101.

29. "La violence du venin tord mes membres," "Nuit de l'enfer," 100–101.

30. "Toutes les monstruosités *violent* les gestes atroces d'Hortense." "H," *Illuminations*, 303.

31. "Chant de guerre parisien" ["Parisian War Song"], 88, enclosed by Rimbaud in a letter to Demeny, where again he outlines the famous "I is another."

32. This term, it is true, is already foreshadowed, linguistically prefigured in the sailor's dream of the "Seven Years Old Poets": "—seul, et couché sur des pieces de toile / Ecrue et préssentant violemment la voile"; *Les Poètes de sept ans*, 97.

33. "Le Bateau ivre" ["The Drunken Boat"], 128–29.

34. "'Saisons!' chateaux," 180.

35. "Le Bateau ivre," 130.

36. Letter to P. Demeny (May 15, 1871), 346. Rimbaud's emphasis.

37. "Aucun des sophismes de la folie—la folie qu'on enferme—n'a été oublié par moi. Je pourrais les redire tous, je tiens le *système*." ["None of the sophisms of madness—the madness they lock up—has been forgotten by me. I could repeat them all; I know the *system*."] "Délires II," in *Une Saison en enfer*, 233.

38. Ibid., 228.

39. Cf. "Je *travaille* à me rendre voyant. . . . Il s'agit d'arriver à l'inconnu par le dérèglement de tous les sens." Letter to G. Izambard (May 13, 1871), 343–44.

40. Translator's Note: An allusion to the title of a famous poem by Mallarmé ("Un Coup de Dés," in *Íuvres completes de Stéphane Mallarmé*, op. cit., 457), at the same time playing with, and underscoring, the way in which Rimbaud's poetic language emphasizes and repeats (both phonetically and semantically) the prefix "dé," a signifier of negativity and deconstruction.

41. "Eclairs de tonnerre—montez et roulez;—Eaux et tristesse, montez et roulez les Dé-luges," "Après le Déluge" ["After the deluge"], in *Illuminations*, 254.

42. "Faim" ["Hungers"], in "Délires II," 231.

43. Letter to P. Demeny (May 15, 1871), 346.

44. "Le Démon!—Cest un Démon, vous savez, *ce n'est pas un homme*." ["The demon! It is a demon, you know, it is not a man."] "Délires I," *Une Saison en enfer*, 224.

45. "Délires II," 230.

46. "Délires I," 223.

47. Cf., in Jean Genet's *The Blacks*, the following very Rimbaldian credo: "Inventez, sinon les mots, des phrases qui coupent au lieu de lier. Inventz, non l'amour, mais la haine, et faites donc de la poésie, puisque c'est le seul domaine qu'il vous soit permis d'exploiter." ["Invent, not words, but sentences that cut instead of linking. Invent not love but hate; and thus write poetry, since poetry is the only domain you are permitted to exploit." (Paris: Marc Barbézat, 1963), 38.

48. "Délires I," 228.

49. Ibid.

50. "Le Bateau ivre":

Où, teignant tout à coup les bleuités, délires
Et rythmes lents sous les rutilements du jour,
Plus fortes que l'alcool, plus vastes que nos lyres,
Fermentent les rousseurs amères de l'amour!

51. Letter to P. Demeny, 347.

52. "Inventer un verbe poétique accessible, un jour ou l'autre, à *tous les sens.*" *"Délires II,"* 228.

53. Ibid.

54. Ibid.

55. "Délires I," 226.

56. "L'impossible" ["The Impossible"], 235.

57. "Délires I," 224.

58. "Départ" ["Departure"], 266.

59. "En poésie, on n'habite que le lieu que l'on quitte." *Recherche de la Base et du Sommet*, ed. cit., 104.

60. The question that obsesses biographers — that is, whether "Adieu" (*Une Saison en enfer*) is, yes or no, Rimbaud's final text, does not have overriding importance, since, in any case, "Adieu" is the text of *the last word*, which means, symbolically, the writing of an (impossible) end.

61. Indeed, far from being the last text chronologically, "Adieu" is the paradigmatic "untimely" text, the text that is always "out of season": "Autumn already! — But why regret an eternal sun, if we are off in quest of divine clarity — *far away from those who die on the seasons*" (240). Cf. "Barbare," *Illuminations*: "After all the days and the *seasons*, the beings and the countries. . . ." (292). Cf. also a letter to Delahaye dated June 1872: "Et merde aux saisons et colrage. Courage" (352), and the draft of "'Saisons, ô chateaux" preceded by the following lines: "It is to say that it's nothing, life; that is what the *Seasons* are about" (448).

62. "Adieu," 241.

63. "Délires II (*Alchimie du verbe*) [*The Alchemy of the Word*]," 230.

64. Baudelaire, "Le Voyage" ["The Voyage"], *Les Fleurs du Mal* [*The Flowers of Evil*], (Paris: Garnier, 1961), 156.

65. "On ne part pas." "Mauvais sang" ["Bad Blood"], *Une Saison en enfer*, 215.

66. "Soir Historique" ["Historical Evening"], *Illuminations*, 301.

67. Baudelaire, "Le Voyage," op. cit., 159.

68. Ibid., 155.

69. "Le Bateau ivre" ["The Drunken Boat"], 131.

70. "A Une Raison" ["To a Reason"], *Illuminations*, 268.

71. "Génie" ["Genius"], *Illuminations*, 308.

72. "Délires I," 224. Cf. "Génie," 308.

73. "Génie," 308.

74. "Adieu," 241.

75. "Conte" ["A Tale"], *Illuminations*, 259.

76. Maurice Blanchot, "Le Sommeil de Rimbaud," in *La Part du Feu* (Paris: Gallimard, 1949), 158.

77. Denis Roche, in *Tel Quel, Théorie d'Ensemble* (Seuil, 1968), 221–27. Cf.: "We claim to say precisely by means of poems that this conception of poetry is not viable, does not exist," 223.

78. Georges Bataille, *L'Orestie* (Paris: Ed. Des Quatre Vents, 1945), 63.

79. "Adieu," 240. Cf. draft of *Alchimie du Verbe*, 338: "Maintenant je puis dire que l'art est une sottise. [Now I can say that art is silliness]."

80. "Mauvais Sang," 218.

81. "Adieu," 241.

82. Ibid.

83. "Adieu," 241.

84. Ibid., 240.

85. Ibid, 241.

86. Gérard de Nerval, "Le Christ aux Oliviers" ["Christ Among the Olive Trees"], in *Les Chimères* (Paris: Garnier, 1965), 242–43.

87. "Le Bateau ivre" ["The Drunken Boat"], 131.

88. Georges Bataille, *L'Orestie*, op. cit., 60.

89. C. G. Jung, "Le problème psychique de l'homme moderne," in *Problemes de l'âme moderne*, French translation by Fr. Yves Le Lay (Paris: Buchegt-Chastel, 1960), 165.

90. "Génie," 308–9.

91. Cf. M. Grevisse, *Le Bon Usage* (Duculot, Gembloux and Hatier, Paris: 1969), 653.

92. "L'Impossible" ["The Impossible"], *Une Saison en enfer*, 236.

93. "Délires I," 226.

94. "Nuit de l'Enfer" ["A Night in Hell"], 220.

95. "Délires I," 224.

CHAPTER 4

From The Scandal of the Speaking Body: Don Juan with J. L. Austin, or Seduction in Two Languages
Shoshana Felman

1. Besides the works of J. L. Austin, which I shall examine in some detail further on, and the work of Searle mentioned in the following note, see also R. M. Hare, "The Promising Game," *Revue internationale de philosophie* 18

(1964): 398–412; Jonathan Harrison, "Knowing and Promising," *Mind* 71 (October 1962); John R. Searle, "How to Derive 'Ought' from 'Is,'" *Philosophical Review* 73 (1964); Jerome B. Schneewind, "A Note on Promising," *Philosophical Studies* 17 (April 1966).

2. John R. Searle, *Speech Acts: An Essay in the Philosophy of Language* (Cambridge: Cambridge University Press, 1969), 54.

3. The two principal references to the Don Juan myth in this book will be, first, Molière's *Don Juan* and, second, the *Don Giovanni* of Mozart and Da Ponte. As a general rule, all quotations followed by roman numerals (indicating act and scene) refer to Molière's play. For the French text, see Molière, *Oeuvres completes* (Paris: Seuil, Coll. "L'Integrale," 1962); for a complete English translation, see Wallace Fowlie, *Don Juan or the Statue at the Banquet* (Great Neck, N.Y.: Barron's Educational Series, 1964). All passages quoted here have been translated directly from the French.

THE REFLECTIONS OF J. L. AUSTIN: BETWEEN TRUTH AND FELICITY

1. *How to Do Things with Words*, 2nd ed., ed. J. O. Urmson and Marina Sbisà (Cambridge: Harvard University Press, 1975), 101–2. This work will be identified henceforth by the abbreviation *HT*.

2. *HT*, Lecture 2. Failures are divided into two major categories: "misfires" and "abuses." Misfires result when the intended outcome of the performative utterance does not occur, *is not carried out*, owing to inappropriate circumstances: for example, because the conventional procedures to which performatives are always attached through their more or less ritual accomplishment were not respected or were not in order. If I say, for example, "I take this woman as my lawful wedded wife" outside of the ritual ceremony, or when I am already married, the marriage is of course null and void, the act is not accomplished; it succumbs to the "infelicity" of failure; the performative utterance misfires. If on the other hand I say "I promise," but *without* the intention of keeping my promise, or in full knowledge that I will be unable to keep it, the performative act of promising is infelicitous because of an "abuse," not because of a misfire—it is not null and void. Indeed, whether or not I am sincere, when I utter the words "I promise" I in fact *carry out* the *act* of promising; the act succeeds, it is executed; but it may be executed in bad faith: by executing the act of promising, in such a case, I deceive my interlocutor. Although the act is "successful," then, it entails a form of failure; it is infelicitous because of my abuse.

3. J. L. Austin, "Performative Utterances," in *Philosophical Papers*, 3rd ed., ed. J. O. Urmson and G. L. Warnock (Oxford and New York: Oxford University

Press, 1979), 249–50. This collection of Austin's articles will be identified hereafter by the abbreviation *PP*.

4. Emile Benveniste, *Problems in General Lingustics*, trans. M. E. Meek (Coral Gables, Fla.: University of Miami Press, 1971), chap. 22: "Analytical Philosophy and Language," 238. All quotations from Benveniste are taken from this study, to which I shall return several times in the course of this book.

5. As a general rule and uless otherwise indicated, passages italicized in quoted material are those I myself have chosen to emphasize. Passages that are emphasized by the authors themselves will be identified parenthetically.

Beyond the Felicity Principle: The Performance of Humor

1. Sigmund Freud, *Jokes and Their Relation to the Unconscious,* trans. James Strachey (New York: Norton, 1960), 147. This work will hereafter be designated *Jokes.*

2. Sigmund Freud, "Humour" (1928), in *Character and Culture* (New York: Collier Books, 1963), 263–64.

3. Baudelaire, "On the Essence of Laughter," in *The Mirror of Art,* trans. Jonathan Mayne (London: Phaidon Press, 1955), 141; hereafter designated "Laughter."

4. This figure of speech is called *zeugma* ("yoking"). Cf. the famous example of it (and of its heroï-comic effect) in Pope, *The Rape of the Lock:* "Here thou, great Anna! whom three realms obey / Dost sometimes counsel take — and sometimes Tea."

5. Cf. the *credo* of the later Wittgenstein (one of the major influences on analytic philosophy), who used to say that philosophy would have no future except to become (like aesthetics, and like ethics) a "synopsis of trivia." See G. E. Moore, "Wittgenstein's Lectures in 1930–1933," in *Classics of Analytic Philosophy,* ed. R. R. Ammerman (New York: McGraw-Hill, 1965), 284.

6. Austin, *Sense and Sensibilia,* 4–5.

7. Søren Kierkegaard, *Either/Or,* trans. D. F. Swenson and L. M. Swenson (Garden City, N.Y.: Doubleday, 1959), 1:35.

8. "I venture out alone to drill myself / In what must seem an eerie fencing-match / Duelling in dark corners for a rhyme / *And stumbling over words like cobblestones* / Where now and then realities collide / With lines I dreamed of writing long ago" (Baudelaire, "The Sun," in *Les Fleurs du Mal,* trans. Richard Howard [Boston: Godine, 1982], 88).

9. "Artists . . . know that such-and-such a being is comic, and that it is so only on condition of its being unaware of its nature" (Baudelaire, "Laughter," 153).

10. Cf. Claude Reichler's highly suggestive book *La Diabolie* (Paris: Minuit, 1979).

11. These latter two popular titles are both by Dale Carnegie (New York: Pocket Books, 1st ed., 1936).

12. "Perhaps we should even carry simplification further still, go back to our oldest memories, and trace in the games that amused the child the first sketch of the combinations which make the grown man laugh. . . . Above all, we too often fail to recognize how much of childishness, so to speak, there still is in most of our joyful emotions" (*Jokes,* 223 n. 1).

13. Mallarmé, "L'Action restreinte," in *Oeuvres complètes,* 370.

14. Cf. Paul de Man, "The Epistemology of Metaphor," *Critical Inquiry* 5 (Fall 1978): 30. "Finally, *our* argument suggests that the relationship and the distinction between literature and philosophy cannot be made in terms of a distinction between aesthetic and epistemological categories. All philosophy is condemned, to the extent that it is depended upon figuration, to be literary and, as the depository of this very problem, all literature is to some extent philosophical. . . . Contrary to common belief, literature is not the place where the unstable epistemology of metaphor is suspended by aesthetic pleasure. . . . It is rather the place where the possible convergence of rigor and pleasure is shown to be a delusion."

15. *Les non-dupes errent* — title of one of Lacan's *Seminars.*

Foreword to The Scandal of the Speaking Body
Stanley Cavell

1. J. L. Austin, *How to Do Things With Words,* 2nd ed., ed. J. O. Urmson and Marina Sbisà (Cambridge: Harvard University Press, 1975), 9–10. This work will be cited hereafter as *HT.*

2. See Jacques Derrida, "Signature Event Context," in *Limited Inc.,* trans. Samuel Weber and Jeffrey Mehlman (Evanston, Ill.: Northwestern University Press, 1988), 1–24; also in *Margins of Philosophy,* trans. Alan Bass (Chicago: University of Chicago Press, 1982), 307–30.

Afterword to The Scandal of the Speaking Body
Judith Butler

1. Jacques Derrida, "Limited Inc. *a b c . . . ,*" trans. Samuel Weber, *Glyph* 2 (1977).

2. Sedgwick uses Felman's reading of Austin to inaugurate a queer reading of Henry James. She writes: "The marriage ceremony is, indeed, so central to the origins of 'performativity' (given the strange, disavowed but unattenuated persistence of *the exemplary* in this work) that a more accurate name for *How to Do Things with Words* might have been "How to say (or write) 'I do' about twenty million times without winding up any more married than you started out." Later on the same page, Sedgwick makes clear that "Felman's work in *The Literary Speech Act* confirms the weird centrality of the marriage example for performativity in general." (Eve Sedgwick, "Queer Performativity: Henry James's *The Art of the Novel,*" *GLQ* 1, no. 1 [1993]: 1–16.)

The failure of the marriage ceremony to do what it says opens up the possibility of understanding marriage as that which harbors queer possibilities. See, as well, Andrew Parker and Eve Sedgwick's Introduction to their co-edited *Performativity and Performance,* English Institute Papers (New York: Routledge, 1995), 1–18; see also Felman, 6 and 20, above, for the salience and vulnerability of the marriage vow in the theorization of the speech act.

CHAPTER 5

Textuality and the Riddle of Bisexuality: Balzac, "The Girl with the Golden Eyes"
Shoshana Felman

1. Sigmund Freud, "Femininity," in *New Introductory Lectures on Psychoanalysis,* trans. James Strachey (New York: Norton, 1965), 112.

2. Freud, Preface to *New Introductory Lectures,* 5.

3. Ibid., emphasis mine.

4. Honoré de Balzac, "La Fille aux yeux d'or," in *Histoire des Treize.* Citations are to "The Girl with the Golden Eyes," in *History of the Thirteen,* trans. Herbert J. Hunt (Baltimore: Penguin, 1974). Where I have modified the English translation, the page reference is followed by the abbreviation TM (translation modified).

5. Unlike Henri, however, Paquita, in time, renounces her model of sexual hierarchization, her rhetorical subordination of the masculine to the feminine pole. In their second sexual encounter,

> "Put my velvet gown on me," said Henri coaxingly.
> "No, no" she impetuously replied. "*Remain what you are,* one of these angels I had been taught to detest and whom I looked upon only as monsters." (380, emphasis mine)

6. Freud, "The Uncanny," in *Sigmund Freud on Creativity and the Unconscious,* ed. and trans. Alix Strachey (New York: Harper Torchbooks, 1958), 148.

7. As the prologue indeed paternalistically affirms: "*quod erat demonstrandum,* if one may be permitted to apply a Euclidean formula to the science of manners" (327). What the "demonstration" consists of, however, is by no means clear.

8. See the remarkable article by Leyla Perrone-Moisès, "Le Récit euphémique," *Poétique* 17 (1974).

CHAPTER 6

From "Competing Pregnancies: The Dream from which Psychoanalysis Proceeds (Freud, The Interpretation of Dreams*)"*
Shoshana Felman

1. Juliet Mitchell, *Psychoanalysis and Feminism: Freud, Reich, Laing, and Women* (New York: Vintage Books, 1975), xiii.

2. Jacques Lacan, "Une pratique de bavardage," *Ornicar* 19 (1979): 5; my translation.

3. Betty Friedan, *The Second Stage* (New York: Summit Books, 1981).

4. See Betty Friedan, *The Feminine Mystique* (New York: Norton, 1974; New York: Dell, Laurel Books, 1982).

5. Sigmund Freud, letter to Marie Bonaparte, quoted in Ernest Jones, *The Life and Work of Sigmund Freud* (New York: Basic Books, 1955), 2:421.

6. Freud, "Femininity," in *New Introductory Lectures on Psycho-Analysis,* the Standard Edition of the Complete Psychological Works of Sigmund Freud, ed. and trans. James Strachey (London: Hogarth Press and the Institute of Psychoanalysis, 1964), 22:114.

7. See Freud's letter to Fliess on June 12, 1900 (Freud, Letter 137): Freud describes a visit to Bellevue, the house where he earlier had this dream. "Do you suppose," he writes, "that some day a marble tablet will be placed on the house, inscribed with these words?—

In this house, on July 24th, 1895

the secret of Dreams was Revealed

to Dr. Sigm. Freud

At the moment there is little prospect of it" (4:121). July 24th, 1895, was the date of the Irma dream.

8. This had invariably been the feminist approach to the Irma dream. See in particular Monique Schneider, *La Parole et l'inceste* (Paris: Aubier-Montaigne, 1980); and Sarah Kofman, *L'Enigme de la femme* (Paris: Galilée, 1980), whose feminist rereadings of the dream I summarize and methodologically discuss in a later section of this essay. See also Mary Jacobus's use of the Irma dream in her perspicacious article, "Is There a Woman in This Text?" *New Literary History* 14 (Autumn 1982): 117–41. The demystifying posture with respect to Freud is by no means particular, however, to the feminist critics of Freud's work: it characterizes many psychoanalytic (or psychiatric) reinterpretations of the dream, such as: Max Schur, "Some Additional 'Day Residues' of 'The Specimen Dream of Psychoanalysis,'" in *Freud and His Self-Analysis,* ed. Mark Kanzer and Jules Glenn (New York: Jason Aronson, 1979), 87–116; R. Greenberg and C. Perlman, "If Freud Only Knew: A Reconsideration of Psychoanalytic Dream Theory," *International Review of Psychoanalysis* 5 (1978): 71–75; Adam Kapur and Alan A. Stone, "The Dream of Irma's Injection: A Structural Analysis," *American Journal of Psychiatry* 139 (October 1982): 1125–34. In the last essay, the demystifying, condescending attitude toward Freud reaches its climactic point: "Freud censored any associations to the dream that would have reflected adversely on Fliess and, in the place of what was censored, offered what we think are less relevant, even misleading, associations. Schur hypothesized that Freud's censorship was unconscious. Greenberg and Perlman accepted this hypothesis. . . . We disagree. . . . We

believe . . . that Freud consciously and deliberately misled his readers in order to conceal Fliess's involvement in the treatment" (1128).

In opposition to this (non-self-analytic) posture of critical condescension and epistemological superiority with respect to Freud ("Freud did not yet know that such protestations and negations stood for their opposite" [Schur, "Some Additional 'Day Residues,'" 1979], 98; "This solution was evident to us and not to Freud, Erikson, Schur and other commentators" [Kuper and Stone, "The Dream of Irma's Injection," 1233]), I would propose a type of textual approach that endorses Jacques Lacan's conception of an "ethics of psychoanalysis" that is also, among other things, an *ethics of interpretation:* an ethics of approach to the interpreted. "Inasmuch as it is out of the question," writes Lacan, "to psychoanalyze deceased authors, it is out of the question to psychoanalyze Freud's dream better than Freud himself. . . . What we can do is not supply an exegesis where Freud himself interrupts himself but rather take together [as an object for a new examination] the whole textual corpus of the dream and Freud's interpretation of the dream. There, we are in a *different position* than that of Freud." Jacques Lacan, "Le Rêve de l'injection d'Irma," in *Le Séminaire.* Bk. 2, *Le Moi dans la theorie de Freud et dans la technique de la psychanalyse* (Paris: Seuil, 1978), 183; my translation.

The interpretive claim of the reading endeavored here is thus not one of superiority (over Freud or any of his commentators) but (self-analytically, I hope) one of difference, of a different position (vantage point) with respect to the insight of Freud's text.

9. Life experience: Freud's as well as mine. For the reader is indeed invited to dream (and to interpret dreams) along with Freud: "And now," writes Freud, "I must ask the reader to make my interests his own for quite a while, and plunge, along with me, into the minutest details of my life; for a *transference* of this kind is peremptorily demanded by our interest in the hidden meaning of the dream." (4:105–6; my emphasis)

10. Pregnant, indeed, with Anna Freud.

11. Strachey's translation modified in accordance with Jane Gallop's correction. Jane Gallop, *The Father's Seduction* (Ithaca, N.Y.: Cornell University Press, 1982), 66.

12. Kate Millet, *Sexual Politics* (Garden City, N.Y.: Doubleday, 1969; New York: Avon Books, 1971). All citations are to the Avon edition.

13. I put "first stage" in quotation marks because it seems obvious to me that a feminist reflection—and a feminist position in concrete existence—cannot simply coincide with a linear chronology, much less with a chronology of progress. The first stage is not simply necessary as a starting point: it can never be simply overcome, simply transcended; it *persists,* in fact, throughout the second (and the third) stage. Rather than a mere chronology,

the metaphor of "stages" is a figure, here, for an increasingly nuanced perception — and account — of complexity. The stages, paradoxically, coexist.

14. Schneider, *La Parole et l'inceste*, 132. Translations of this work from the French are mine.

15. Erik Erikson, "The Dream Specimen of Psychoanalysis," *Journal of the American Psychoanalytic Association* 2 (1954): 5–56. A summarized version of this reading is in E. Erikson, *Identity, Youth, and Crisis* (New York: Norton, 1968). I use "DS" ("Dream Specimen") to refer to the longer essay and "IYC" ("Identity, Youth, Crisis") to refer to the book.

16. "*Trimethylamin.* I saw the chemical formula of this substance in my dream. . . . What was it, then to which my attention was to be directed in this way by trimethylamin? It was to a conversation with another friend who had for many years been familiar with all my writings during the period of their gestation, just as I had been with his. He had at the time confided some ideas to me on the subject of the chemistry of the sexual processes, and had mentioned among other things that he believed that one of the products of sexual metabolism was trimethylamin. Thus this substance led me to sexuality, the factor to which I attributed the greatest importance in the origin of the nervous disorders which it was my aim to cure. . . . I began to guess why the formula for trimethylamin had been so prominent in the dream. So many important substances converged upon that one word. Trimethylamin was an allusion not only to the immensely powerful factory of sexuality, but also to a person whose agreement I recalled with satisfaction whenever I felt isolated in my opinions" (4:116–17).

17. Kofman, *L'Enigme de la femme*, 55. Translations of this work from the French are mine.

18. See Edgar Allan Poe's short story "The Purloined Letter"; J. Lacan's famous analysis of it entitled "Seminar on the Purloined Letter," in *Écrits* (New York: Norton, 1977); and my analysis of Lacan's interpretation in chapter 2 of my *Jacques Lacan and the Adventure of Insight: Psychoanalysis in Contemporary Culture*, 26–51.

Response by Juliet Mitchell
On Asking Again: What Does a Woman Want?

1. Juliet Mitchell, *Psychoanalysis and Feminism: Freud, Reich, Laing, and Women* (New York: Pantheon Books, 1974).

2. All references to Freud are to *The Standard Edition of the Complete Psychological Works of Sigmund Freud*, ed. and trans. James Strachey et al., 24 vols. (London: The Hogarth Press, 1953–74), cited parenthetically in text as *SE* followed by volume and page number.

3. See chapter 1 of Jane Gallop, *The Father's Seduction* (Ithaca, N.Y.: Cornell University Press, 1982), 1–14.

4. Simon Baron-Cohen, *The Essential Difference: Male and Female Brains and the Truth About Autism* (New York: Basic Books, 2004).

5. See also Gregorio Kohon as well as many others.

6. See the works of Judith Butler.

CHAPTER 8
From "Beyond Oedipus: The Specimen Text of Psychoanalysis"
Shoshana Felman

1. Melanie Klein, "The Importance of Symbol-Formation in the Development of the Ego" (1930), in her *Contributions to Psycho-Analysis, 1921–1945* (New York: Hillary House, 1948), 236–50.

2. See "The Mirror-Stage as Formative of the Function of the I as Revealed in Psychoanalytic Experience" (E 93–100, N 1–7).

3. See E 277–78, N 66–67: "Even when in fact it is represented by a single person, the paternal function concentrates in itself both imaginary and real relations, always more or less inadequate to the symbolic relation which constitutes it. It is in the name of the father that we must recognize the support of the symbolic function, which, from the dawn of history, has identified his person with the figure of the law."

4. I am using the term "performative" as established by J. L. Austin in *Philosophical Papers* (New York: Oxford University Press, 1970) and *How to Do Things with Words* (Cambridge: Harvard University Press, 1975). For a different, complementary perspective on the relation between speech acts and psychoanalysis (as well as on the theoretical relation between Austin and Lacan), see my *The Literary Speech-Act: Don Juan with J. L. Austin, or Seduction in Two Languages,* trans. Catherine Porter (Ithaca, N.Y.: Cornell University Press, 1983); original edition in French, *Le Scandale du corps parlant: Don Juan avec Austin, ou La Séduction en deux langues* (Paris: Seuil, 1980).

5. Schafer, 218. Even though Schafer's account of "Narration in the 'Psychoanalytic Dialogue'" is very different from Lacan's, it is remarkable in its own right, reaching the complexity and subtlety of psychoanalytic insight by a different pathway. It is only at the opening of his inquiry that Schafer seems to hold the commonsensical view of psychoanalytic dialogue, of which Lacan's more paradoxical, radical approach challenges precisely the common sense. But Schafer's own study in effect unsettles, through infinite refinement and subtle complications, the commonsensical description that is its starting point. As Schafer himself puts it, "psychoanalysis does not take common sense plain but rather transforms it into a comprehensive distillate"; and "more than one such distillation of common sense has been

offered in the name of psychoanalysis" (214). No more than Lacan's, Schafer's own creative psychoanalytic thinking does not take common sense plain.

CHAPTER 9
Flaubert's Signature: The Legend of Saint Julian the Hospitable
Shoshana Felman

Translated by Brian Massumi, Rachel Bowlby, Richard Russell, and Nancy Jones, with the collaboration of the author.

1. Flaubert, *La Légende de saint Julien l'hospitalier*, 178, in vol. 2 of the *Œuvres complètes*, 2 vols. (Paris: Seuil, 1964). All passages quoted from the French, here as elsewhere in this essay, are from this edition and have been rendered into English by the essay's general translators. In the texts quoted, emphasis is mine, unless otherwise indicated.

2. Only the oracle communicated to Julian appears in the form of the curse: "Accursed! Accursed! Accursed! One day, cruel heart, you will assassinate your father and your mother!" (181). Thus the filial curse (Julian's oracle) is the obverse of the parental blessing (the parents' oracle).

3. For a different analysis of the significance of the opposition between Julian's parents—an analysis to which the present one is indebted—see Frank Yeomans, "*La Légende de saint Julien l'hospitalier*: This Side of Parricide," in "Flaubert's Trinity: A Psychoanalytic/Semiotic Reading of the *Trois Contes*" (Phd. D. diss., Yale University, 1979), 56–132.

4. Stéphane Mallarmé, "L'Action restreinte," in *Œuvres complétes* (Paris: Pléiade, 1945), 370.

5. Flaubert to Louise Colet, end of October 1851, *Extraits de la correspondance; ou, Préface à la vie d'écrivain*, ed. Geneviève Bollème (Paris: Seuil 1963), 59. Unless otherwise indicated, references to the letters refer to this edition.

6. We know, by Flaubert's own account in his letter to his niece Caroline, dated September 25, 1875 (mailed from Concarneau), that it was while looking at the reproduction of the Rouen cathedral window in E. H. Langlois's *Essai historique et descriptif sur la peinture en verre* (Rouen, 1832) that Flaubert began to write the tale (cf. *Préface*, 266–67).

7. Flaubert, *Correspondance*, 9 vols. (Paris: Louis Conard, 1926–33), 2:6–7.

8. For Narcissus, compare the scene where Julian contemplates, with suicidal desire, his own reflection in the fountain (186).

Like Ajax, Julian massacres animals that, here as well, are in reality substitutes for humans. In his letters, Flaubert mentions Sophocles' *Ajax*, which he read repeatedly.

Compare the crossing of the river, which recalls Charon welcoming passengers and taking them across the river (Acheron or Styx) to the shore of Hell.

For Adam and Noah, see my analysis below. Cain, like Julian, bears a mark on his skin—a sign imprinted by God to mark him as a murderer. Julian's parents, on the other hand, after the predictions about their son's future, think he has "been marked by God" (179).

9. "He resembles a little Jesus. His teeth came in without his crying a single time" (179).

10. "At the edge, two wild goats were looking into the abyss. . . . He finally got to the first goat and plunged a dagger through his ribs. The second, terror-struck, jumped into the void. Julian leapt to strike it, and, his right foot slipping, he *fell onto the other's corpse*, his face above the abyss and *his arms stretched out*" (180–81). Compare, during the parents' burial: "During the mass he stayed *prone* in the middle of the doorway, *his arms outstretched in the form of a cross*" (185).

11. *Moses and Monotheism*, in *The Standard Edition of the Complete Psychological Works of Sigmund Freud*, ed. and trans. James Strachey, vol. 23 (London: Hogarth Press, 1964), 43 (translation modified).

12. Cf. Gérard de Nerval's retort when reproached for having no religion: "I, no religion? I have seventeen of them . . . at least!"

13. In an earlier version of this sentence, Flaubert actually wrote "my native town" instead of "my country."

14. "A small table, a stool, a bed of dead leaves and three clay cups, that was all his furniture. Two holes in the walls served as windows" (186).

15. *Le Petit-Robert's* definition of *légende*.

16. "I am a pen-man. I feel through it, because of it, in relation to it and much more with it" (Flaubert to Louise Colet, Le Croisset, February 1, 1852, *Préface*, 64).

17. To Louise Colet, January 16, 1852, ibid., 63.

18. Friederich Nietzsche, *Thus Spoke Zarathustra*, trans. Walter Kaufmann, in *The Portable Nietzsche* (New York: The Viking Press, 1968), 152 (translation modified).

19. Flaubert, *Préface*, 285.

20. Flaubert to George Sand, April 3, 1876, ibid., 272.

21. Flaubert to Louise Colet, August 14–15, 1846, ibid., 39.

22. Flaubert to George Sand, March 27, 1875, ibid., 264.

23. Flaubert to Madame Roger des Genettes, October 3, 1875, ibid., 267.

24. Flaubert to Louise Colet, Rouen, December 11–12, 1847, ibid., 48.

Response by Winfried Menninghaus
Hölderlin's Sapphic Mode: Revising the Myth of the Male Pindaric Seer

1. Cf. Thomas Schmitz, *Pindar in der französischen Renaissance: Studien zu seiner Rezeption in Philologie, Dichtungstheorie und Dichtung* (Göttingen: Vandenhoeck & Ruprecht, 1993) (= Hypomnemata 101).

2. Cf. Penelope Wilson, "The Knowledge and Appreciation of Pindar in the Seventeenth and Eighteenth Centuries," PhD diss., Oxford, 1974; Rudolf Sühnel, "Pindars Musen-Anruf und die Englische Musik-Ode," in *Geschichte des Textverständnisses am Beispiel von Pindar und Horaz*, ed. Walther Killy (Munich: Kraus, 1981), 219–42.

3. Martin Opitz, *Buch von der deutschen Poeterey*, ed. Cornelius Sommer (Stuttgart: Reclam, 1970), 60.

4. Sappho Fr. 168 (Voigt). Cf. fr. 117 B (Voigt).

5. Cf. Marius Plotius Sacerdos, *Artes* grammaticae, in: *Grammatici latini*, ed. Heinrich Keil (Leipzig: Teubner, 1874), 6: 516, and *Hesychii Alexandrini Lexicon*, s.v. *adonion*. In the context under consideration, I can disregard the fact that in 20th century scholarship the very notion of an Adonic clausula of the Sapphic strophe has become highly disputed. For Hölderlin, the Adonic verse was undoubtedly as much a determining feature of the Sapphic strophe as it was for virtually every scholar up to Wilamowitz-Moellendorf. I have discussed this issue in more detail in Winfried Menninghaus, *Hälfte des Lebens: Versuch über Hölderlins Poetik* (Frankfurt am Main: Suhrkamp, 2005), 20–22.

6. Sappho fr. 140 (Voigt). Cf. Also fr. 168 (Voigt).

7. Ferdinand de Saussure, who introduced the term to literary analysis, thinks of the "hypogram" as a *thematic* word, typically a latent proper name, which is recovered from the text, and he even expressly excludes the meaning of signature (cf. Jean Starobinski, *Wörter unter Wörtern: Die Anagramme von Ferdinand de Saussure* [Frankfurt am Main; Berlin; Wien: Ullstein, 1980], esp. 23–25). Nevertheless the concept of a metrical hypogram used here is an analogy to Saussure's theory of a "*verbal latency* under the words." See also Michael Riffaterre, *La production du texte* (Paris: Seuil, 1979), 75–88, and Paul de Man, "Hypogram and inscription," in de Man, *Resistance to Theory* (Minneapolis: University of Minnesota Press, 1986), 27–53.

8. Cf. Wolfgang Binder, "Hölderlins Odenstrophe," in Binder, *Hölderlin-Aufsätze*, (Frankfurt am Main: Insel, 1970), 47–75.

9. Hölderlin quotations in the text are taken from *Sämtliche Werke*, ed. Friedrich Beissner (Stuttgart: Cotta/Kohlhammer, 1948–85). A roman numeral indicates the volume; an arabic numeral, the page.

10. Friedrich Gottlieb Klopstock, *Sämmtliche Werke* (Leipzig: Göschen, 1854), 4:96. The two other Sapphic odes are "Die todte Clarissa" (1750; 68–69) and "Mein Wäldchen" (1778; 244–45).

11. See Friedrich Schlegel, *Lucinde*, in: *Kritische Friedrich-Schlegel-Ausgabe*, ed. Ernst Behler in cooperation with Jean-Jacques Anstett and Hans Eichner (Paderborn; München; Wien; Zürich: Schöningh, 1958), 5:25 (henceforth all quotations from this edition are referred to as "KSA"); Friedrich Schlegel,

"Über die Diotima," KSA 1:115, Johann Gottfried Herder, "Alcäus und Sappho. Von zwey Hauptgattungen der lyrischen Dichtkunst," in Herder, *Sämtliche Werke*, ed. Bernhard Suphan (Berlin: Weidmannsche Buchhandlung, 1881), 27:182–98.

12. Rainer Maria Rilke, *Die Aufzeichnungen des Malte Laurids Brigge*, in Rilke, *Sämtliche Werke* (Frankfurt am Main: Insel, 1966), 6:929. Cf. also Martin L. West, *Die griechische Dichterin. Bild und Rolle* (Stuttgart; Leipzig: Teubner, 1996, esp. 9, 12–15.

13. Cf. Glenn Most, "Reflecting Sappho," in *Bulletin of the Institute of Classical Studies* 40 (1995): 21, 22, 25.

14. Aelianus, *Varia historia* 12, 19. Cf. Plato, *Symposium* 235c.

15. Schlegel, *Philosophische Lehrjahre*, KSA 18:207.

16. Cf. Julia Kristeva, *Pouvoirs de l'horreur: Essai sur l'abjection* (Paris: Seuil, 1980).

17. According to Panyassis the time spent with Aphrodite was twice as long as that spent with Persephone (Apollodorus, *Bibl.* III 14.4). Other versions of the myth, however, divide the year into two halves (cf. Hyginus, *Astronomica* II 7).

18. Macrobius, *Saturnalia* I 21, 1–6.

19. Sappho fr. 168 (Voigt).

20. Aristophanes, *Lysistrata*, 387–402.

21. Plato, *Phaidros*, 276 b.

22. Cf. Eva C. Keuls, *The Reign of the Phallus: Sexual Politics in Ancient Athens* (New York: Harper and Row, 1985), and Eva Stehle, "Sappho's Gaze: Fantasies of a Goddess and Young Man," in: *Reading Sappho: Contemporary Approaches*, ed. Ellen Greene (Berkeley; Los Angeles, 1996), 193–225. For a critical review see Winfried Menninghaus, *Das Versprechen der Schönheit* (Frankfurt am Main: Suhrkamp, 2003), 302–9.

23. James Frazer, *The Golden Bough: A Study in Magic and Religion* (London: Macmillan, 1955), 77–100, esp. 92–94.

24. Ovid, *Metamorphoses* III, 474–96.

25. Walter Benjamin, "Goethes Wahlverwandtschaften," in Benjamin, *Gesammelte Schriften*, ed. Rolf Tiedemann und Hermann Schweppenhäuser (Frankfurt am Main: Suhrkamp, 1974), 1:123–201, here 181–82.

26. *Ewiger Vorrat deutscher Poesie*, ed. Rudolf Borchardt (München: Verlag der Bremer Presse, 1926), 354:

SKIZZE ZU EINER ODE

Hälfte des Lebens.
MIT gelben Birnen hänget und (– –) voll
Mit wilden Rosen–– – das–– –

Land in den See: Ihr holden Schwäne

————————— —

————————— —

Und trunken—von Küssen—tunkt ihr das
—————Haupt ins heilig
Nüchterne Wasser ———— —
Weh mir wo nehm ich,—wenn es Winter ist
Die Blumen—und wo—den Sonnenschein
Und Schatten der————Erde

————————— —

————————— —

————————— die Mauern stehn
Sprachlos und kalt; im——Winde
Klirren die Fahnen————

27. Rudolf Borchardt, "Hölderlin und endlich ein Ende," in: Borchardt, *Gesammelte Werke,* vol. 4 (*Prosa I*), ed. Marie Luise Borchardt (Stuttgart: Klett, 1957), 469–70.

28. Cf. Michael Knaupp, *"Hölderlin und endlich ein Ende,"* in *"Le pauvre Holterling"—Blätter zur Frankfurter Ausgabe,* no. 8 (Frankfurt am Main: Roter Stern, 1988), 98–194, and Gerhard Neumann, "Rudolf Borchardt: Der unwürdige Liebhaber," in *Zeit der Moderne—Zur deutschen Literatur von der Jahrhundertwende bis zur Gegenwart,* ed. Hans-Henrik Krummacher and Bernhard Zeller (Stuttgart: Kröner), 90–91.

29. Eduard Lachmann, *Hölderlins Hymnen in freien Strophen: Eine metrische Untersuchung* (Frankfurt am Main: Klostermann, 1937), 16–17, 314–18.

30. Karl Viëtor, *Die Lyrik Hölderlins: Eine analytische* Untersuchung (Darmstadt: Wissenschaftliche Buchgesellschaft, 1967), 116–17.

31. Cf. Rudolf Krieger, "Sprache und Rhythmus der späten Hymnen Hölderlins," in *Zeitschrift für Ästhetik und allgemeine Kunstwissenschaft* 22 (1928): 256–91; Dietrich Seckel, *Hölderlins Sprachrhythmus* (= Palästra 7) (Leipzig: Mayer & Müller, 1937); Hannes Maeder, "Hölderlin und das Wort: Zum Problem der freien Rhythmen in Hölderlins Dichtung," in *Trivium* 2 (1944), 42–59.

32. Herder, *Alcäus und Sappho,* 183.

33. Schlegel, *Geschichte der lyrischen Dichtkunst unter den Griechen,* KSA 11:201.

34. Schlegel, *Geschichte der europäischen Literatur,* KSA 11:61–62.

35. Georg Wilhelm Friedrich Hegel, *Vorlesungen über die Ästhetik,* in: G. W. F. Hegel, *Werke* (Theorie Werkausgabe) (Frankfurt am Main: Suhrkamp, 1970), Bde. 13–15, here 15:466.

36. Friedrich Gottlieb Klopstock, *Vom deutschen Hexameter,* in F. G. Klopstock, *Gedanken über die Natur der Poesie,* ed. Winfried Menninghaus (Frankfurt am Main: Insel, 1989), 127, 136.

37. Ibid., S. 148.

38. Klopstock, "Von der Darstellung," in: Klopstock, *Gedanken über die Natur der Poesie*, 172.

39. Vgl. Michael Jakob, *"Schwanengefahr": Das lyrische Ich im Zeichen des Schwans*. (München: Hanser, 2000), 240–68.

40. The concept of "Umkehr" (inversion, turning, turnabout) is used by Hölderlin — superimposing the theoretical concept of *peripeteia* in tragedy with the rhetorical concept of inversion and the spiritual notion of an inner turnabout — in the *Anmerkungen zum Ödipus* (V 202) and the *Anmerkungen zur Antigonä* (V 271).

41. Cf. Walter Hof, *Hölderlins Stil als Ausdruck seiner geistigen Welt* (Meisenheim am Glan: Hain, 1954), 90–91, and Manfred Frank and Gerhard Kurz, " 'Ordo inversus': Zu einer Reflexionsfigur bei Novalis, Hölderlin, Kleist und Kafka," in *Geist und Zeichen: Festschrift für Arthur Henkel*, ed. Herbert Anton, Bernhard Gajek, and Peter Pfaff, (Heidelberg: 1977).

42. Friedrich Nietzsche, *Die Geburt der Tragödie*, in Nietzsche, *Sämtliche Werke. Kritische Studienausgabe*, ed. Giorgio Colli and Mazzino Montinari (München: de Gruyter, 1980), 1:47, 57, 64–65.

43. To give just a few other examples of Adoneic strophe endings in Hölderlin's Pindaric odes: "Wie wenn am Feiertage" ("Bäume des Haines," "Kräfte der Götter," "Seele des Dichters," "heiligen Bacchus," II 118–20), "Der Mutter Erde" ("Wolke des Wohllauts," "Herz die Gemeinde," "Laute gegründet," II 123–25), "Die Wanderung" ("besser zu wohnen," "Ahnen gedenken" "Milde gerühret," "Wolken des Ida," "kommet, ihr Holden," II 138–41), "Der Rhein" ("Küsten Moreas," "Rasen des Halbgotts," "Seele gegeben," "die er gegründet," "werden getrachtet," "nenn ich den Fremden," "alte Verwirrung," II 142–48), "Mnemosyne" ("áber was íst diß," "féhlet die Traúer," II 194). Lachmann (*Hölderlins Hymnen in freien Strophen*, p. 99) and Gaier (*Hölderlin: Eine Einführung* [Tübingen and Basel, Francke, 1993], 228) mention the frequency of this group as a clausula in the hymns, without recognizing them as instances of adoneus.

44. Martin L. West, *Greek Metre* (Oxford: Clarendon, 1982), 65.

45. Cf. Bruno Snell, *Griechische Metrik* (Göttingen: Vandenhoeck & Ruprecht, 1982), 44–57, for the significance of eolic lyric poetry for this development, esp. 48–50.

46. Cf. Alcaeus fr. 34, 41, 42, 45, 66, 68, 69, 150, 283, 308, 362 (Voigt) and Sappho fr. 137 and 168 C (Voigt).

47. Cf. Snell, *Griechische Metrik*, 44–57, for the significance of eolic lyric poetry for this development, esp. 48–50.

48. See, for instance, VII, 4, pp. 124, 130–31, 214–17, 272, 298, 304.

49. Ibid., ix (preface).

50. Demetrius, *De elocutione* 127, 140–41, 166; Dionysius, *De compositione verborum* 23.

51. (Pseudo-)Longinus, *De sublimitate* 10, 3.

CHAPTER 10

From "The Return of the Voice: Claude Lanzmann's Shoah"

Shoshana Felman

1. "The Loneliness of God," published in the journal *Dvar Hashavu'a* (magazine of the newspaper Davar), Tel-Aviv, 1984. My translation from the Hebrew.

2. "To tell the truth, the whole truth, and nothing but the truth"; an oath, however, which is always, by its very nature, susceptible to perjury.

3. *The Record*, October 25, 1985; an interview with Deborah Jerome ("Resurrecting Horror: The Man Behind *Shoah*").

4. *Shoah,* the complete text of the film by Claude Lanzmann (New York: Pantheon Books, 1985). Quotations from the text of the film will refer to this edition, and will be indicated henceforth only by page number (in parenthesis following the citation).

5. John Kaplan, foreword to Elizabeth F. Lotus, *Eyewitness Testimony* (Cambridge, Mass.: Harvard University Press, 1979), vii.

6. Categories that Lanzmann borrows from Hilberg's historical analysis, but which the film strikingly *embodies* and rethinks. Cf. Raul Hilberg, *The Destruction of the European Jews* (New York: Holmes and Meier, 1985).

7. See chapter 3, II, "An Event Without a Witness."

8. Interview given by Lanzmann on the occasion of his visit to Yale University, and filmed at the Fortunoff Video Archive for Holocaust Testimonies at Yale (interviewers: Dr. Dori Laub and Laurel Vlock) on May 5, 1986. Hereafter, citations from this videotape will be referred to by the abbreviation *Interview.*

9. See Walter Benjamin, "The Task of the Translator," in *Illuminations,* trans. Harry Zohn, ed. Hannah Arendt (New York: Schocken Books, 1969), 69–82.

10. "An Evening with Claude Lanzmann," May 4, 1986; first part of Lanzmann's visit to Yale, videotaped and copyrighted by Yale University. Transcript of the first videotape (hereafter referred to as Evening), 2.

11. For instance, the Frenchman Robert Faurisson wrote: "I have analyzed thousands of documents. I have tirelessly pursued specialists and historians with my questions. I have tried in vain to find a single former deportee capable of proving to me that he had really seen, with his own eyes, a gas chamber" (*Le Monde*, January 16, 1979). We have a "selective view of history,"

comments Bill Moyers, "We live within a mythology of benign and benevolent experience. . . . It is hard to believe that there exists about a hundred books all devoted to teach the idea that the Holocaust was a fiction, that it did not happen, that it had been made up by Jews for a lot of diverse reasons." Interview with Margot Strom, in *Facing History and Ourselves* (Fall 1986): 6–7.

12. Statement made in a private conversation in Paris, January 18, 1987: *"J'ai pris un historian pour qu'il incarne un mort, alors que j'avais un vivant qui était directeur du ghetto."*

13. In this respect, the filmmaker shares the approach of the historian Hilberg: "In all my work," says Hilberg, "I have never begun asking the big questions, because I was always afraid that I would come up with small answers; and I have preferred to address these things which are minutiae or details in order that I might then be able to put together in a gestalt a picture which, if not an explanation, is at least a description, a more full description, of what transpired" (70).

Response by Julia Kristeva
For Shoshana Felman: Truth and Art

1. Shoshana Felman, "À l'âge du témoignage: Shoah de Claude Lanzmann," in *Au sujet de Shoah* (Paris: Édition Belin, 1990). Translation of chapter in *Testimony: Crises of Witnessing in Literature, Psychoanalysis, and History.*

2. *Ibid.,* 55.

3. *Ibid.,* 79.

4. *Ibid.,* 61–64.

5. *Ibid.,* 63.

6. *Ibid.,* 60.

7. *Ibid.,* 79.

8. *Ibid.,* 93.

9. *Ibid.,* 96.

10. *Ibid.,* 97.

11. *Ibid.,* 57.

12. *Ibid.,* 73.

13. *Ibid.,* 77.

14. *Ibid.,* 65.

15. *Ibid.,* 68.

16. *Ibid.,* 101–2.

17. *Ibid.,* 98.

18. *Ibid.*

19. *Ibid.*

20. *Ibid.,* 66.

21. *Ibid.*, 102.

22. *Ibid.*

CHAPTER 11

From "The Storyteller's Silence: Walter Benjamin's Dilemma of Justice"

Shoshana Felman

1. Compare Franz Kafka, *The Trial,* trans. Willa and Edwin Muir; rev., with additional material trans. E. M. Butler (New York: Schocken Books, 1992), 213–15.

2. Walter Benjamin, "Franz Kafka: On the Tenth Anniversary of his Death" (hereinafter abbreviated "Kafka"), in Walter Benjamin, *Illuminations,* ed. with an introduction by Hannah Arendt (New York: Schocken Books, 1969), 139. This collection will be referred to by the abbreviation *Ill.*

3. Walter Benjamin, "The Storyteller," in *Ill.,* 108. The essay "The Storyteller" will be indicated by the abbreviation "St."

4. At Nuremberg, history was asked in an unprecedented manner to account in court for historical injustices that were submitted for the first time to the legal definition of a crime. The prosecution and the judgment conceptualized as crimes atrocities and abuses of power that until then had not been justiciable: "crimes against humanity," crimes committed at the time of war against civilians, injustices that a totalitarian regime inflicts on its own subjects as well as on outsiders and opponents. On the pathbreaking concept of crimes against humanity and generally on the historical significance and vision of the Nuremberg trials, see "Introduction"; chapter 3, section V; and chapter 4, part 1, subsection entitled "Two Visions of Historic Trial."

5. Compare Robert Cover, "Nuremberg and the Creation of a Modern Myth," in "The Folktales of Justice," in *Narrative, Violence, and the Law: The Essays of Robert Cover,* ed. Martha Minow, Michael Ryan, and Austin Sarat (Ann Arbor: University of Michigan Press, 1995), 195–201; Jonathan Turley, "Symposium on Trials of the Century: Transformative Justice and the Ethos of Nuremberg," in *Loyola of Los Angeles Law Review* 33 (2000): 655; Gerry J. Simpson, "Conceptualizing Violence: Present and Future Developments in International Law and Policy on War Crimes and Crimes against Humanity: Didactic and Dissident Histories in War Crime Trials," in *Albany Law Review* 60 (1997): 801; Lawrence Douglas, "Film as Witness: Screening Nazi Concentration Camps Before the Nuremberg Tribunal," *Yale Law Journal* 105 (1995): 449.

6. This change (which is related to the new tie between law and history) also entails and represents a basic reconfiguration of the relationship between "the private" and "the public" in criminal justice. Previously, criminal

trials were "private" in the sense that they judged individual perpetrators (and their individual or private criminality) in the name of society and of its public interest. The new kind of trial puts on trial not only the private but also (through the private) the very realm of "the public." In the name of the public and of the collective interest, what is judged as criminal is henceforth both the private and the public.

7. Hannah Arendt precisely disputed the Eichmann trial's project to put history on trial in the name of the conservative jurisprudential necessity (requirement) to judge the private, to focus on the individual (the criminal), to target strictly the literal and not the representative responsibility of the accused. For a discussion of Arendt's objections to a prosecution of history, see chapter 3, section III.

8. Walter Benjamin, "Theses on the Philosophy of History," in *Ill.*, 257. The essay will hereinafter be abbreviated "Theses." The "tradition of the oppressed" is the tradition of their silenced narratives and of their silenced trauma. For an analysis of this proposition through a close reading of Benjamin's "Theses," see here part 2, the subsections entitled "A Philosophy of History" and "History and Speechlessness."

9. Compare Benjamin, "Goethe's *Elective Affinities*," trans. Corngold, in Walter Benjamin, *Selected Writings, Volume I: 1913–1926*, ed. Marcus Bullock and Michael W. Jennings (Cambridge, Mass.: Harvard University Press, 1996), 340–41. The essay will hereinafter be abbreviated "GEA"; the volume will be abbreviated *SWI*.

10. In the expressionless, "every expression simultaneously comes to a standstill" ("GEA," 340).

11. Twentieth-century critiques of history include (but are not exhausted by) the postcolonial critiques of colonialism as well as more generally the antinationalist, antimilitarist, feminist, gay, antiracist critiques, including the economically oriented Marxist critiques, the critique of capitalism, and, more recently, the critique of globalization.

12. The expressionless, I argue, is a term that implicitly *conceptualizes trauma* and conceptualizes the inherent relation between trauma and literature. If trauma has in Benjamin a *literary* power of expression (the "shattering" power of its muteness), it is because, like literature, trauma in its turn is *an utterance that signifies although and because it has no possibility of statement.*

13. See the discussion of this concept later in this chapter (in part 2, section 7, the subsection entitled "Prosopopeia"), and the substantial discussion in chapter 4, part 3, section 9, the subsection entitled "The Caesura of the Trial: The Expressionless."

14. Levinas in turn speaks of "the stripping away of expression as such." Emmanuel Levinas, "Philosophy, Justice, and Love," in Levinas, *Entre Nous:*

Thinking-of-the-Other, trans. Michael B. Smith and Barbara Harshav, European Perspectives (New York: Columbia University Press, 1998), 145. (This collection of essays will be hereinafter abbreviated *EN.*) Although Levinas does not use the term *expressionless,* he situates in the expressionless face of the other (in the face stripped of expression) "the original locus of the meaningful" (EN, 145). For Benjamin, in turn, the expressionless is the original locus of the meaningful. Levinas's thought profoundly resonates with the thought of Benjamin, although it does not overlap with it on all points. The origin of meaning is for Levinas (as for Benjamin) "pure otherness." Pure otherness is signified in Levinas precisely by the image of the *expressionless* face of the other: the other's face is a naked, vulnerable, exposed human face, a face "before all particular expression . . . a nakedness and stripping away of expression as such; that extreme exposure, defenselessness, vulnerability itself" (*EN,* 145). This exposure, this vulnerability of the other is (for Benjamin as well as for Levinas) the original locus of the meaningful. I thus include in Benjamin's concept of the expressionless the resonance of Levinas's concept of the face (and of the always present possibility of the erasure of the face by violence).

15. What follows is a definition of the synthetic, enlarged sense in which I use the Benjaminian concept, in applying it specifically to the context of the law and of the new relationship between law and history.

16. I borrow here the emphasis on the face from Levinas, for whom "the vision of the face" is a correlative of the emergence of ethics and of justice, and who rigorously defines violence (conceptualizes violence) as the effacement of the human face. This violent effacement of the living (human) face is also crucial, I propose, to Benjamin's concept of the expressionless. "What is there in a face?" asks Levinas. "The relation to the Face is both the relation to the absolutely weak—to what is absolutely exposed, what is bare and destitute . . . what is alone and can undergo the supreme isolation we call death and thus, in some way, an incitement to murder . . . and at the same time . . . the Face is also the 'Thou shall not kill' . . . ; it is the fact that I cannot let the other die alone, it is like a calling out to me" (*EN,* 146). Violence is what precisely effaces the face in obliterating both its vision and its mute call or its human appeal, the "Thou shall not kill." Struck by violence, a face that (through trauma or through its erasure by the other) loses the capacity to express life and to express itself becomes expressionless, expressing only the rigidity of death.

So far as Benjamin's linguistically precise use of the term *expressionless* is concerned (as distinguished from the added resonance of Levinas that I include in my enlarged use of the term), it should be noted, however: (1) that Benjamin deliberately never said that some person is expressionless (which in German would be the traditional use of the term as implying a lack of expression in a face or in a person), but only that specific acts (including speech acts), both moral and artistic, are expressionless in his sense; (2) that the expressionless paradoxically is the only form in which specific acts and phenomena can possibly find expression (rather than being excluded from it and first having to find a way to express themselves). For a detailed philological analysis of the concept of the expressionless in Benjamin, see Winfried Menninghaus, "Walter Benjamin's Variations of Imagelessness," in *Jewish Writers, German Literature: The Uneasy Examples of Nelly Sachs and Walter Benjamin,* ed. Timothy Bahti and Marilyn Sibley Fries (Ann Arbor: University of Michigan Press, 1995), 155–73.

17. "There is no document of civilization," Benjamin writes, "that is not at the same time a document of barbarism." The "cultural treasures," therefore, have an origin that a historical materialist "cannot contemplate without horror" ("Theses," 256).

18. "Not man or men, but the struggling, oppressed class itself is the depository of historical knowledge" ("Theses," 260).

19. The political unconscious consists in the structure of oppressions and repressions specific to a given historical moment. Compare Fredric Jameson, *The Political Unconscious: Narrative as a Socially Symbolic Act* (Ithaca, N.Y.: Cornell University Press, 1982).

20. In this apparently Messianic theme, Benjamin again predicts the new relationship between trials and the dead, a relationship that will predominate some of the later "trials of the century" and that this book will in its turn study and attempt to think through and concretely meditate about. See chapters 3 and 4.

21. Mariana Varverde, "Derrida's Justice and Foucault's Freedom: Ethics, History, and Social Movements," *Law and Social Inquiry* 24 (1999): 657. Compare Jacques Derrida, *Specters of Marx: The State of Debt, the Work of Mourning, and the New International,* trans. Peggy Kamuf (New York: Routledge, 1994).

22. Benjamin, "Critique of Violence" (hereinafter abbreviated "Critique"), in Walter Benjamin, *Reflections: Essays, Aphorisms, Autobiographical Writings,* trans. Edmund Jephcott, ed. with an introduction by Peter Demetz (New York: Schocken Books, 1986), 277. This collection is hereinafter abbreviated *R (Reflections).*

23. It was to some extent this critique of legal violence, this awareness of the problematic nature of the law and of the limits and flaws of prosecutorial trials that (among other reasons) was at the origin of the contemporary institution (in South Africa and elsewhere) of an alternative mode of dealing with the crimes of history: the Truth and Reconciliation Commissions.

24. For a synthetic summary of this well-known critique of the Nuremberg trial as "victor's justice," compare for instance Gerry Simpson, "Conceptualizing Violence: Present and Future Developments in International Law and Policy on War Crimes and Crimes against Humanity: Didactic and Dissident Histories in War Crime Trials," *Albany Law Review* 60 (1997): 805–6: "In the absence of a uniform and global approach, the trials of war criminals generally occurred only where defeat and criminality coincide. This was undoubtedly the case at Nuremberg and Tokyo. The phrase 'victor's justice' is by now a truism. The victorious allied powers tried their German and Japanese adversaries without considering the possibility of applying these same laws to their own war-time behavior." See also Cover, "Nuremberg and the Creation of a Modern Myth," in "The Folktales of Justice," in *Narrative, Violence, and the Law,* 195–201; Lawrence Douglas, "Film as Witness: Screening Nazi Concentration Camps Before the Nuremberg Tribunal," *Yale Law Journal* 105 (1995): 449; Ruti Teitel, "The Universal and the Particular and International Criminal Justice: Symposium in Celebration of the Fiftieth Anniversary of the Universal Declaration of Human Rights," *Columbia Human Rights Law Review* 30 (1999): 285.

25. Compare Robert Cover, "Bringing the Messiah" and "Nuremberg and the Creation of a Modern Myth," in "The Folktales of Justice," in *Narrative, Violence, and the Law,* 185–87 and 201: "Integrity [in judges] . . . is the act of maintaining the vision that it is only that which redeems that is law. "

26. The dead can have an afterlife, but they cannot come back to life, and if they do, they do so *as precisely dead.* Benjamin is well aware of this reality, and of the fact that the historical *resuscitation* of the dead *does not entail their resurrection.* "The angel [of history] would like to stay, awaken the dead and make whole what has been smashed," but he cannot make whole what has been broken: his wings are impotently caught in the wind (the storm) of "progress" ("Theses," 257–58).

27. Emmanuel Levinas, "Uniqueness," in *EN,* 196.

28. Hannah Arendt, "Introduction," *Ill.,* 5–18.

29. Compare Franz Kafka, *The Trial,* 213–15.

30. Benjamin, "Kafka," 131. Indeed, as Benjamin notes after Brecht, "Kafka perceived what was to come without perceiving what exists in the present" ("Some Reflections on Kafka" [*Ill.,* 143], hereinafter abbreviated "SRK"). And Benjamin adds: "He perceived it essentially as an *individual* affected by it" (ibid.). Like Kafka's, Benjamin's perception of the future proceeds, I argue, from his position as affected individual, from his insight, that is, into his historical position as a persecuted subject.

31. Kafka, *The Trial,* 227–29, italics mine.

32. Hannah Arendt, *Eichmann in Jerusalem: A Report on the Banality of Evil* (New York: Penguin Books, 1963), 125–26; hereinafter abbreviated *EiJ*. Arendt is commenting on the collaboration of the *Judenrat*: "Wherever Jews lived, there were recognized Jewish leaders, and this leadership, almost without exception, cooperated in one way or another, for one reason or another, with the Nazis" (*EiJ*, 125). But this cooperation between victim and executioner (the essence of the moral calamity triggered by the Nazis) was not specific to Jews, Arendt insists. "David Rousset, a former inmate of Buchenwald, described what we know happened in all concentration camps: 'The triumph of the S.S. demands that the tortured victim allow himself to be led to the noose without protesting, that he renounce and abandon himself to the point of ceasing to affirm his identity. And it is not for nothing. It is not gratuitously, out of sheer sadism, that the S.S. men desire his defeat. They know that the system which succeeds in destroying its victim before he mounts the scaffold . . . is incomparably the best for keeping a whole people in slavery. In submission. Nothing is more terrible than these processions of human beings going like dummies to their deaths' (*Les Jours de notre mort*, 1947)" (Arendt, *EiJ*, 11–12).

33. See Kafka, *The Trial*, 227–28 (emphasis mine): "The two of them laid K. down on the ground, propped him against the boulder, and settled his head upon it. But *in spite of the pains they took and all the willingness K. showed, his posture remained contorted* and unnatural-looking." Compare Benjamin, "Kafka," 135 (emphasis mine): "This story takes us right into the milieu of Kafka's world. No one says that *the distortions which it will be the Messiah's mission to set right someday* affect only our space; surely they are *distortions of our time* as well. Kafka must have had this in mind."

34. *EN*, 187.

35. Walter Benjamin, "The Metaphysics of Youth" (hereinafter abbreviated "MY"), in Benjamin, *SWI*, 6.

36. "The Task of the Translator," *SWI*, 261.

37. Ibid., 259.

38. Ibid., 257.

39. Hannah Arendt, *On Revolution* (London: Penguin, 1990), 11.

40. Ibid., 11–18.

41. Ibid., 11.

42. This textual juxtaposition of the theory and the autobiography will be illuminated, in its turn, by Benjamin's work as a literary critic, especially in the early literary essays on Hölderlin, on Dostoevsky, and on Goethe's *Elective Affinities*. I will thus borrow metaphors from Benjamin's own literary criticism and will in turn use them as interpretive tools and as evocative

stylistic echoes. My methodology will be attentive, therefore, to three distinct levels of the text that the analysis will bring together: the conceptual level of the theory, the narrative level of the autobiography, and the figurative level of the literary criticism.

43. *SWI,* 18–36.

44. Ibid., 33.

45. "St.," 83.

46. "Karl Kraus," *R,* 242. Compare "St.," 88–91. Information and narration are not simply two competing modes of discourse (two functions of language). They are in fact two strategies of living and communicating, two levels of existence within culture. Narration seeks a listener; information, a consumer. Narration is addressed to a community, information is directed toward a market. Insofar as listening is an integral part of narration, while marketing is always part of information, narration is attentive and imaginatively productive (in its concern for the singularity, the unintelligibility of the event), while information is mechanical and reproductive (in its concern for the event's exchangeability, explainability, and reproducibility).

Benjamin was concerned not only with communication but (implicitly, essentially) with education. Educationally, these two modes conflict not only as two separate roles or institutions. They wage a battle *within* every institution and *within* every discipline of knowledge. They are in conflict, in effect, *within* every pedagogy. They struggle (to this day) within every university.

47. "Today people live in rooms that have never been touched by death and . . . when their end approaches they are stowed away in sanatoria or hospitals by their heirs" ("St.," 94).

48. "Death is the sanction of everything the storyteller has to tell. He has borrowed his authority from death" ("St.," 94).

49. Since the storyteller (in Leskov and his tradition) is "a righteous man," a "teacher," and a "sage" ("St.," 108), what now falls to muteness is the very possibility of righteousness. Similarly, literature as teacher of humanity (in the manner of Leskov) has lost its voice. In the collapse of narrative as a generic, literary mode of discourse, literature as ethics— "counsel," education—is thus inherently, historically, and philosophically reduced to silence.

50. Among the theories of history that Benjamin critiques and "deconstructs" are pure theology (religion), pure historicism (positivism), pure liberalism (idealism), and pure Marxism (uncritical historical materialism).

51. Compare Hitler's harangue to his top civilians and military officials in 1939, on the occasion of the invasion of Poland: "Destruction of Poland is in the background. The aim is elimination of living forces, not the arrival at a certain line. . . . I shall give a propagandistic cause for starting the war—

never mind whether it be plausible or not. The victor shall not be asked later on whether he told the truth or not. In starting and making a war, not the right is what matters but victory." Quoted by Robert Jackson in his introduction to Whitney Harris, *Tyranny on Trial: The Evidence at Nuremberg* (New York: Barnes and Noble, 1954, 1995), xxxi.

52. In this conception, Benjamin is the interpreter—the synthesizer—of the diverse legacies of Nietzsche, Marx, and Freud.

53. Walter Benjamin, "Paralipomènes et variantes des *Thèses 'Sur le concept de l'histoire,'"* *Écrits français*, ed. Jean-Maurice Monnoyer (Paris, 1991), 352; my translation.

54. The reality of history is grasped (articulated) when the historian *recognizes* a historical *state of emergency* that is, precisely, *not* the one the ruler has declared or that (in Hobbes's tradition, in Carl Schmitt's words) is "decided by the sovereign." Compare Carl Schmitt, *Politische Theologie* (Munich and Leipzig, 1922), a work cited and discussed by Benjamin in *The Origin of German Tragic Drama* (1928; London: NLB, 1977), 65, 74, 239, nn. 14–17.

55. *A Berlin Chronicle* (hereinafter abbreviated *Be*), in *R*, 56–57.

56. "GEA," 355. Redemption seems, therefore, to be linked to the moment of illumination that suddenly and unexpectedly gives us the capacity to *hear the silence to tune into* the unarticulated and to *hear* what is in history deprived of words. Redemption starts by redeeming history from deafness.

57. For a historiography free of complicity, we must disassociate ourselves from our accustomed thinking: "Thinking involves not only the flow of thoughts, but their arrest as well. Where thinking suddenly stops in a configuration pregnant with tensions, it gives that configuration a shock, by which it crystallizes into a monad. A historical materialist approaches a historical subject only where he encounters it as a monad. In this structure he recognizes a sign for a Messianic cessation of happening, or, put differently, *a revolutionary chance* in the fight for the oppressed past" (XVII, *Ill.*, 262, emphasis mine).

58. The original and current German title of the essay is, precisely, "On the Concept of History."

CHAPTER 12
A Ghost in the House of Justice: Death and the Language of the Law
Shoshana Felman

1. Friedrich Nietzsche, *The Use and Abuse of History for Life*, trans. Adrian Collins, introduction by Julius Kraft (New York: Liberal Arts Press, 1949, 1957), 12–17. See chapter 3, section II, subsection entitled "History for Life."

2. Robert Jackson, "Introduction," in Whitney Harris, *Tyranny on Trial: The Evidence at Nuremberg* (New York: Barnes and Noble, 1954, 1995), xxxv–xxxvi.

3. "Novelist Rebecca West, covering the first 'historic' Nuremberg trial for the *New Yorker,* found it insufferably tedious," writes Mark Osiel (Rebecca West, "Extraordinary Exile," *New Yorker,* Sept. 7, 1946). "This reaction was not uncommon. As one reporter notes (Alex Ross, "Watching for a Judgment of Real Evil," *New York Times,* Nov. 12, 1995): "It was the largest crime in history and it promised the greatest courtroom spectacle. [But] . . . what ensued was an excruciatingly long and complex trial that failed to mesmerize a distracted world. Its mass of evidence created boredom, mixed occasionally with an abject horror before which ordinary justice seemed helpless." Quoted in Mark Osiel, *Mass Atrocity, Collective Memory, and the Law* (New Brunswick, N.J.: Transaction Publishers, 2000), 91.

4. Gideon Hausner, *Justice in Jerusalem* (New York: Harper and Row, 1968; orig. pub. 1966), 291–92.

5. In a short text called "The Witness," Jorge Luis Borges writes: "Deeds which populate the dimensions of space and which reach their end when someone dies may cause us wonderment, but one thing, or an infinite number of things, dies in every final agony, unless there is a universal memory. . . . What will die with me when I die, what pathetic and agile form will the world lose?" (Jorge Luis Borges, *Labyrinths: Selected Stories and Other Writings* [New York: New Directions, 1962], 243). It is because humans, unlike documents, do not endure that the Eichmann trial calls upon each witness to narrate the singular story that will die when he or she dies. Transience is inscribed within this legal process as the witness's death is, from the start, implicitly inscribed within each testimony.

While documents — unlike the living witnesses — exclude death as a possibility inherent in the evidence, and while the Nuremberg trials claim authority precisely in the act of sheltering the courtroom from the death it talks about, in the Eichmann trial, on the contrary (to use Walter Benjamin's expression), "Death is the sanction of everything the storyteller has to tell. He has borrowed his authority from death" (Benjamin, "St.," 94).

6. Attested to by the chief prosecutor's widow in *The Trial of Adolf Eichmann,* a PBS documentary Home Video (B3470), a coproduction of ABC News Productions and Great Projects Film Company, 1997.

7. The Eichmann trial was the first trial televised in its entirety. The complete trial footage is kept in the archives of the State of Israel.

8. "Our memory," writes Paul Valéry, "repeats to us the discourse that we have not understood. Repetition is responding to incomprehension. It signifies to us that the act of language has not been accomplished." Paul Valéry, "Commentaires de *Charmes,*" in Valéry, *Oeuvres* (Paris: Gallimard, Bibliothèque de la Pleiade, 1957), 1:1510; my translation.

9. The writer published the English translation of his works under the pseudonym Ka-Tzetnik 135633. An alternative orthography of the author's name, the one used in the trial's English transcripts and in Arendt's *Eichmann in Jerusalem*, is K-Zetnik (since the name is modeled on the German letters KZ, pronounced Ka-tzet, from *Konzentrationslager*, "concentration camp"). This latter orthography is the one I will use.

10. See Criminal Case 40/61 (Jerusalem), *Attorney General v. Eichmann* (1961). English translation of the trial transcripts in *The Trial of Adolf Eichmann: Record of Proceedings in the District Court of Jerusalem*, vol. 3, Session 68 (June 7, 1961), Jerusalem (1963), 1237. I use here the modified English version quoted by Hannah Arendt in *Eichmann in Jerusalem (EiJ*, 224).

11. K-Zetnik, *Tzofan: Edma* (Tel Aviv: Hakibbutz Hameuchad Publishing House, 1987), 32; in English: Ka-Tzetnik 135633, *Shivitti: A Vision*, trans. Eliyah Nike De-Nur and Lisa Hermann (San Francisco: Harper and Row, 1989), 16. I will hereafter refer to this text by the abbreviation *Shivitti*. The letter H (Hebrew) will designate the original Hebrew edition; the letter E (English) will refer to this American edition. The abbreviation "tm" (translation modified) will mark my occasional modifications of the English translation according to the Hebrew original.

12. The narrative that follows is a literal transcription of the trial footage (session of K-Zetnik's testimony), as seen in the PBS documentary *The Trial of Adolf Eichmann*. See also Criminal Case 40/61 (Jerusalem), *Attorney General v. Eichmann* (1961), in *The Trial of Adolf Eichmann: Record of Proceedings in the District Court of Jerusalem*, vol. 3, Session 68 (June 7, 1961), Jerusalem (1963), 1237. Hereinafter abbreviated *Proceedings*.

13. Yehiel Dinoor was forty-five years old at the time of the trial. He passed away in his house in Tel Aviv in July 2000, at the age of eighty-four. Born in Poland as Yehiel Feiner (Segev, *The Seventh Million*, 4), he had changed his legal name to the Hebrew name Dinoor, meaning "a residue from the fire." The name Dinoor is spelled alternatively as Dinur (in the trial's English transcripts, see *Proceedings*, 3:1237), as De-nur (in *Shivitti* and, consequently, in Segev), and as Dinoor (in Arendt, *Eichmann in Jerusalem*). I am following Arendt's orthography because it best corresponds to the Hebrew pronunciation of the name.

14. "All Israel held its breath," Tom Segev will remember thirty years later. "It was the most dramatic moment of the trial, one of the most dramatic moments in the country's history" (Segev, 4).

15. Haim Gouri, *Facing the Glass Cage: The Jerusalem Trial* (Tel Aviv: Hakibbutz Hameuchad Publishing House, 1962), 124; my translation from the Hebrew.

16. Nietzsche, *The Use and Abuse of History for Life,* 12–17. On the difference between the monumental and the critical versions of the Eichmann trial, see chapter 3, section II, subsection "History for Life."

17. Compare Karl Jaspers, *The Question of German Guilt,* trans. E. B. Ashton (New York: Fordham University Press, 2001; orig. pub. 1947).

18. Hannah Arendt, letter to Karl Jaspers of August 18, 1946 (letter 43), in Arendt and Jaspers, *Correspondence: 1926–1969 (AJ Corr.),* 54; emphasis mine. In cited passages the emphasis is mine unless otherwise indicated.

19. Letter 46 (October 19, 1946), *AJ Corr.,* 62.

20. Letter 50 (December 17, 1946), ibid., 68.

21. Letter 173 (December 16, 1960), ibid., 413.

22. Letter 274 (December 23, 1960), ibid., 417.

23. Arendt refers to the common sense of the situation. But, as Robert Ferguson notes, "common sense, as anthropologists have begun to show, is basically *a culturally constructed use of experience to claim self-evidence;* it is neither more nor less than 'an authoritative story' made out of the familiar." Robert Ferguson, "Untold Stories in the Law," in *Law's Stories: Narrative and Rhetoric in the Law,* ed. Peter Brooks and Paul Gewirtz (New Haven, Conn.: Yale University Press, 1996), 87, referring to Clifford Geertz, "Commonsense as a Cultural System," in Geertz, *Local Knowledge: Further Essays in Interpretive Anthropology* (New York: Basic Books, 1983), 73–93.

24. In the PBS and ABC News documentary *The Trial of Adolph Eichmann,* Hausner's wife corroborates this fact, explaining why her husband chose to call K-Zetnik despite the reluctance of the writer.

25. I analyze this *missed encounter* and this *professional misunderstanding* for different purposes than simply to contrast (as does, for instance, Mark Osiel) *disciplinary differences.* "It is this confessedly subjective experience — irrelevant to criminal law," writes Osiel, "that oral historians have only recently sought to explore. In this respect, scholars have perceived the need to overcome what they perceive as a 'legal' concern with the factual accuracy of personal testimony in order to apprehend its historical significance. That is, these scholars try to grasp the meaning of the period's most traumatic events through the continuing memory of those who lived through its trauma. One such scholar writes: 'Testimonies are often labeled as "subjective" or "biased" in the legal proceedings concerning war crimes. The lawyers of war criminals have asked the most impertinent questions of people trying to find words for a shattered memory that did not fit into any language. . . . They demand precise statements of facts. . . . A lawyer's case is after all merely another kind of story. . . . It is not the task of oral historians to give the kind of evidence required in a court of law. . . . [Some historians

attempt to uncover] the ways in which suffering is remembered and influences all other memory. . . . One is dealing with an effort to create a new kind of history that cannot be used as legal evidence since it explicitly records subjective experience." (Selma Leydersdorff, "A Shattered Silence: The Life Stories of Survivors of the Jewish Proletariat at Amsterdam," in *Memory and Totalitarianism,* ed. Luisa Passerini [New York: Oxford University Press, 1992], 145, 147–48. Quoted and surveyed in Mark Osiel, *Mass Atrocity, Collective Memory, and the Law* [New Brunswick, N.J.: Transaction Publishers, 2000], 103–4.)

My own interest is not in contrasting the historical recording of trauma with that of the law, but in exploring and in analyzing, on the contrary, ways in which collective trauma is apprehended (and misapprehended) by the law, and ways in which the very *limits of the law* in its encounter (or its *missed encounter*) with the phenomenon of trauma *repeal* precisely cultural aspects of its traumatic meaning.

26. *Shivitti,* H 50, E 32, tm.

27. For an elaborate analysis of my own "jurisprudential trauma theory," see chapter 2, in particular sections I, IV, V. For the philosophical and psychoanalytic insights of trauma theory in general, see, in particular, *Trauma: Explorations in Memory,* ed. Cathy Caruth (Baltimore: Johns Hopkins University Press, 1995); and Cathy Caruth, *Unclaimed Experience: Trauma, Narrative, and History* (Baltimore: Johns Hopkins University Press, 1996).

28. On the phenomenon of intrusive memory and of traumatic repetition prevalent in the aftermath of trauma, see, for instance, Bessel A. van der Kolk and Onno van der Hart, "The Intrusive Past: The Flexibility of Memory and the Engraving of Trauma," in *TEM,* ed. Caruth, 158–82.

29. This terrified collapse is at the same time an improbable act of resistance, a gesture of defiance of the court and of its ruling.

30. *Shivitti,* H 24, E 9, tm. I will use this literary, autobiographical narrative, written subsequently by K-Zetnik to describe his psychiatric therapy for his recurrent Auschwitz nightmares, to retrospectively illuminate the drama of the courtroom scene.

31. Ibid., H 107, E 95.

32. Ibid., H 57, E 40, tm. Compare: "But I have no choice. I am unable to answer questions. In general I cannot sustain interrogation. This is a trauma whose origin is in the torture cellar of the Gestapo in Katowice." *Shivitti,* H 37, E 20, tm.

33. *Shivitti,* H 8–9, E x–xi.

34. Ibid., H 32, E 16, tm.

35. Ibid., H 33, E x–xi, tm.

36. Ibid., H 34, E 18, tm.

37. *Proceedings,* vol. 1, Session 6 (April 17, 1961), Jerusalem (1962), 62. Quoted in Hausner, *Justice in Jerusalem,* 323–24; Arendt, *EiJ,* 260.

38. Under this name with which he signs his literary work and that materializes his oath to the dead, Dinoor continues not just to remember those who left him, but also, as a writer, to give literary voice to their last look and to their final silence.

39. "It now appeared," writes Arendt, "that the era of the Hitler regime, with its gigantic, unprecedented crimes, *constituted an unmastered past* not only for the German people or the Jews all over the world, but for the rest of the world, which had not forgotten this great catastrophe in the heart of Europe either, and had also been unable to come to terms with it. Moreover—and this was perhaps less expected—general moral questions, with all their intricacies and modern complexities, which I would never have suspected would haunt men's minds today and weigh heavily on their hearts, stood suddenly in the foreground of public concern" (*EiJ,* 283, emphasis mine).

40. On the relation between trials and historical and cultural abysses, see chapter 2, section V.

41. This abyss, this epistemological rupture, is what the Eichmann trial and its monumental history (at once the prosecution's case and the text of the judgment) precisely fails to perceive, in Arendt's eyes. "I have insisted," Arendt writes, "on . . . how little Israel, and the Jewish people in general, was prepared to recognize, in the crimes that Eichmann was accused of, an unprecedented crime. . . . In the eyes of the Jews, thinking exclusively in terms of their own history, the catastrophe that had befallen them under Hitler, in which a third of the people perished, appeared not as the most recent of crimes, the unprecedented crime of genocide, but on the contrary, as the oldest crime they knew and remembered. This misunderstanding . . . is actually at the root of all the failures and the shortcomings of the Jerusalem trial. *None of the participants were arrived at a clear understanding of the actual horror of Auschwitz, which is of a different nature from all the atrocities of the past.* . . . Politically and legally, . . . these were 'crimes' different not only in degree of seriousness but in essence" (*EiJ,* 267; emphasis added).

Compare Arendt's insistence in her 1946 letter to Jaspers on the abyss that, henceforth inhabiting both guilt and innocence, explodes the tool of law in bursting open all legal frameworks: "The Nazi crimes, it seems to me, *explode the limits of the law* . . . this guilt, in contrast to all criminal guilt, oversteps and *shatters any and all legal systems.* That is the reason why the Nazis in Nuremberg are so smug. . . . And just as inhuman as their guilt is the innocence of the victims. . . . *This is the abyss that opened up* before us as early as 1933 . . . and into which we have finally stumbled. I don't know how we will ever get out of it" (letter 43 [August 18, 1946], *AJ Corr.*, 54; italics mine).

42. Hannah Arendt, "'What Remains? The Language Remains': A Conversation with Günter Gaus," in Hannah Arendt, *Essays in Understanding, 1930–1954,* ed. Jerome Kahn (New York: Harcourt Brace, 1994), 13–14.

43. Ibid., 14.

44. Susan Sontag, "Reflections on *The Deputy*," in *The Storm over* The Deputy, ed. Eric Bentley (New York: Grove Press, 1964), 118. This comment was, of course, an utterly astonishing remark whose value lay in the surprise that it reserved, in its unsettling power with respect to any simple-minded or reductive legalistic understanding of the trial.

Provocatively, Sontag argued that there was a dimension in the trial that was excessive to its legal definition. She called this dimension "art," because she felt the trial left an impact on the audience that was, in its strength and depth, comparable to the expressive power of a work of art. The trial moved her and existentially and philosophically engaged her. Sontag insisted, therefore, that the trial had a *literary meaning* in addition to its *legal meaning,* and that this extralegal meaning was somehow utterly important for a full grasp of what was at stake in this event of law. The value of Sontag's interpretation lies, in my eyes, not in its axiomatic categorization of the trial as a work of art (a categorization I cannot accept), but in the power of this unexpected categorization to destabilize the category of the legal and to open it for further thought and for a larger cultural interrogation.

45. Ibid., 118–19. Art, says Sontag, no longer stands in opposition to reality: while twentieth-century reality becomes more and more hallucinated, more and more divorced from what we used to call reality, art moves closer to reality than it ever was before, and mixes in with its jurisprudential gestures. Art no longer is a statement: it is an intervention in a conflict, an action, a commitment, an engagement. It is *politicized* and *de-aestheticized.* A "work of art" no longer is aesthetics, it is politics.

46. Compare Robert Cover, "Violence and the Word," in *Narrative, Violence, and the Law: The Essays of Robert Cover,* ed. Martha Minow, Michael Ryan, and Austin Sarat (Ann Arbor: University of Michigan Press, 1995), 203–38.

47. *Shoah* borrows some of its main witnesses from the Eichmann trial. The most striking example is that of Simon Srebnik, whose extraordinary testimony was first heard during the proceedings of the Eichmann trial. See *Proceedings,* vol. 3, Session 66, 1197–1201, and *Shoah's* extraordinarily moving opening scene, in *Shoah: The Complete Text of the Film by Claude Lanzmann* (New York: Pantheon Books, 1985).

48. Like the Eichmann trial, Lanzmann's film puts in evidence before the audience a fact-finding process whose goal is—like that of the legal process—to elicit truth and to prohibit its evasion. Lanzmann borrows his procedures—his techniques of cross-examination and of detailed, concrete

interrogation—from the legal model of a trial. Like the Eichmann trial, *Shoah* hears testimonies in a multiplicity of languages and uses an interpreter to simultaneously translate them into the language of its legal process. And like the Eichmann trial, the film wishes not only to *prove* but to *transmit*. "My problem," Lanzmann says, "was to transmit. To do that one cannot allow oneself to be overwhelmed with emotion. You must remain detached. . . . I tried rather to reach people through their intelligence" (Claude Lanzmann, interview in *L'Express,* quoted in Shoshana Felman and Dori Laub, *Testimony: Crises of Witnessing in History, Psychoanalysis, and Literature* [New York: Routledge, 1992], 239). For a more elaborate study of the film *Shoah,* see Felman, "The Return of the Voice," in Felman and Laub, *Testimony,* 204–83.

49. Arendt, "Truth and Politics," in *Between Past and Future* (New York: Penguin, 1993; orig. pub. 1961), 261.

50. Claude Lanzmann, interview with Deborah Jerome ("Resurrecting Horror: The Man Behind *Shoah*"), *The Record,* October 25, 1985.

51. Claude Lanzmann, "From the Holocaust to 'Holocaust,'" *Dissent* (Spring 1981): 194, my emphasis; French original in *Les Temps modernes 395* (June 1979), reprinted in *Au Sujet de* Shoah: *Le film de Claude Lanzmann,* ed. Michel Deguy (Paris: Belin, 1990), 306–16.

52. On the historicizing role of the judges and more generally on the relation between law and history, compare the remarkable analysis of Michal Shaked, "History in Court and the Court in History: The Opinions in the Kastner Trial and the Narratives of Memory," *Alpayim* 20 (2000): 36–80 (Tel Aviv: Am Oved), in Hebrew.

53. *Shivitti,* H 49, E 31–32.

54. Compare Arendt, *EiJ,* 231: "During the few minutes it took Kovner to tell of the help that had come from a German sergeant, a hush settled over the courtroom; it was as though the crowd had spontaneously decided to observe the usual two minutes of silence in honor of the man named Anton Schmidt." There were moments in which even the prosecutors were overcome by silence and, for a minute, could not go on. On these inadvertent moments of silence, compare the retrospective testimony of Justice Gabriel Bach, at the time assistant prosecutor in the Eichmann trial, in the documentary film *The Trial of Adolf Eichmann,* and Hausner, *Justice in Jerusalem,* 324–25: "The story of the extermination in Poland followed, and the wholesale killings by the *Einsatzgruppen.* . . . There, I knew, words could not describe the mass shooting of close to a million and four hundred thousand people before open pits. I cut short the address and read, instead, a lullaby composed at the time in the Wilno ghetto. . . . When I finished reading there was silence for a moment. I simply could not go on. Fortunately it was almost 6 P.M., about time for the adjournment of the session. The presiding judge

must have realized my predicament; he asked whether this was a convenient place to stop. I nodded thankfully."

55. Gouri, *Facing the Glass Cage,* 244; my translation from the Hebrew.

56. "Reading of the Judgment of the District Court," *Proceedings,* vol. 5, Session 121 (December 15, 1961), Jerusalem (1994), 2218.

57. "Hence," Arendt concludes, "to the question most commonly asked about the Eichmann trial: What good does it do?, there is but one possible answer: It will do justice" (*EiJ,* 254).

58. "Reading of the Judgment of the District Court," *Proceedings,* vol. 5, Jerusalem (1994), 2146; emphasis mine.

59. In her own turn, Arendt narrates not only the totality of facts, but also what is different from, and more than, that totality. Arendt's encounter with the Eichmann trial in turn partakes not only of law's story but also (mutely, indirectly) of art's story, or, more precisely, of the way in which law's story in the trial is transpierced, pervaded by the writer's testimony.

60. "Perhaps it is symbolic," said the judges, "that even the author who himself went through the hell named Auschwitz, could not stand the ordeal in the witness box and collapsed."

61. "The telling of factual truth comprehends much more than the daily information supplied by journalists. . . . Reality is different from, and more than, the totality of facts and events which, anyhow, is unascertainable. Who says what is . . . always tells a story, and in this story the particular facts lose their contingency and acquire some humanly comprehensible meaning." Hannah Arendt, "Truth and Politics," in *Between Past and Future* (New York: Penguin, 1993; orig. pub. 1961), 261.

62. Walter Benjamin was a friend of Arendt's during their exile years in Paris. She admired his works and wanted to help him emigrate to the United States, but she learnt soon after her own arrival in America that he had committed suicide during his illegal and aborted escape from France (see chapter 1). In 1942, when Arendt first learnt about the existence of the Nazi death camps, she wrote "a poem for her dead friend, a farewell and a greeting," entitled simply "W. B.": "Distant voices, sadnesses nearby / Those are the voices and these the dead / whom we have sent as messengers ahead, to lead us into slumber." Quoted in Elisabeth Young-Bruehl, *Hannah Arendt: For Love of the World* (New Haven, Conn.: Yale University Press, 1982), 162–63. The last time Walter Benjamin saw Hannah Arendt, in Marseilles, he entrusted to her care a collection of manuscripts he hoped she could deliver to the United States. After his death, Arendt traveled to the cemetery of Port Bou on the Franco-Spanish border only to discover that her dead friend, who was buried there, does not even have an individual, *named* grave. In a letter to Scholem written on October 21, 1940 (less than a month after Benjamin's

death), Arendt describes the shock of her realization that in this cemetery, "the most fantastic . . . and beautiful spot" she has ever "seen in [her] life," there is nothing left to bear witness to Benjamin's life and death: "[His grave] was not to be found, his name was not written anywhere." Quoted in Gershom Scholem, *Walter Benjamin: The Story of a Friendship,* trans. Harry Zohn (Philadelphia: Jewish Publication Society of America, 1981), 226.

In 1968, Arendt redeems Benjamin from namelessness by publishing his manuscripts in the United States. In her introduction to Benjamin's *Illuminations* Arendt narrates (and mourns) her friend's absurd, untimely, and tragically ironic (needless) suicide (*Ill.,* 5–18). She recapitulates this narrative and briefly mentions her own mourning in her letter of May 30, 1946, to Gertrude Jaspers, the Jewish wife of the German philosopher (the letter is discussing another dead mutual acquaintance and the two correspondents' common personal relation to the Jewish problem): "Or perhaps he was just tired and didn't want to move on again, didn't want to face a totally alien world, a totally alien language, and the inevitable poverty, which so often, particularly at first, comes close to total destitution. *This exhaustion,* which often went along with *the reluctance to make a big fuss, to summon so much concentration for the sake of this little bit of life,* that was surely *the biggest danger we all faced.* And it was *the death of our best friend in Paris, Walter Benjamin,* who committed suicide in October 1940 on the Spanish border with an American visa in his pocket. This atmosphere of *sauve qui peut* at the time was dreadful, and suicide was the only noble gesture, if you even cared enough to want to perish nobly. . . . What you wrote about *'our' problem* moved me very much . . . and today that means *our dead*" (letter 36, *AJ Corr.,* 40–4:1; emphasis mine).

63. There is another witness who, in contrast to K-Zetnik, did prove the ability to tell a story. His name is Zyndel Grynszpan, and the story he narrates is that of his forced deportation, at the beginning of the war, from Germany to Poland. He is, in Arendt's eyes, the ideal storyteller—the ideal witness—although no other witness in the trial can live up to his example. His plainly factual and chronologically coherent narrative stands in contrast to the disjointed account of K-Zetnik. "*Now he had come to tell his story,*" Arendt writes, "carefully answering questions put to him by the prosecutor; *he spoke clearly and firmly, without embroidery, using a minimum of words*" (*EiJ,* 228; italics mine). Compare Benjamin's similar stylistic preference in "The Storyteller": "There is nothing [writes Benjamin] that commends a story to memory more effectively than the *chaste compactness* that precludes psychological analysis. And the more natural the process by which the storyteller forgoes psychological shading, the greater becomes the story's claim to a place in the memory of the listener, the more completely is it integrated into his own experience,

the greater will be his inclination to repeat it to someone else" ("The Story-teller," in *Illuminations,* ed. and with introduction by Hannah Arendt (New York: Schocken Books, 1969), 91. Afterwards refered to as "St."). Arendt in-deed repeats verbatim Grynszpan's testimony and does not paraphrase or summarize it, as she does with K-Zetnik's discourse. Arendt is so remarkably and deeply moved by Grynszpan's testimony that she steps out of her bound-aries and (for a moment) pleads against her own legal objection to the vic-tim's story and against her own puristic, legalistic emphasis on strict legal relevance: "This story took no more than perhaps ten minutes to tell, and when it was over—the senseless, needless destruction of twenty-seven years in less than twenty-four hours—one thought foolishly: *Everyone, everyone should have his day in court.* Only to find out, in the endless sessions that followed, *how difficult it was to tell the story,* that—at least outside the trans-forming realm of poetry—it needed a purity of soul, an unmirrored, unre-flected innocence of heart and mind that *only the righteous* possess. No one either before or after was to equal the shining honesty of Zindel Grynszpan" (*EiJ,* 229–30; emphasis mine).

The reason Arendt is so overwhelmed with emotion, I would suggest, is that her own traumatic story of *the loss of Germany* is unwittingly, uncon-sciously effected back to her from Grynszpan's modest story. This narrative of a forceful removal across national borders is also Benjamin's story (and the cause of his death).

What is significant for my point here, however, is that Arendt describes Grynszpan *in Benjamin's literal words.* The apotheosis of Arendt's uncharacter-istic pathos in this passage is a literal stylistic echo, a literal rhetorical and verbal reminiscence of Benjamin's concluding sentence in "The Storyteller." Benjamin writes, in his signature phrase: "The storyteller is the figure in which *the righteous man* encounters himself" ("St.," 109). Similarly, reso-nantly, Grynszpan is described by Arendt as having "a purity of soul" that *"only the righteous possess"* (*EiJ,* 229).

Another reference to "The Storyteller" makes itself evident at the begin-ning of the book. In the first chapter, in one of her rare moments of self-inclusion, Arendt situates herself as part of the audience of the trial whose task it is *"to face the storyteller."* "[The audience] was filled with *survivors,* with middle-aged and elderly people, immigrants from Europe, like myself, *who knew by heart all there was to know,* and who were in no mood to learn any lessons. . . . As witness followed witness and horror was piled on horror, *they sat there and listened in public to stories* they would hardly have been able to endure in private, when they would have had *to face the storyteller"* (*EiJ,* 8; my emphasis). Arendt here places herself significantly among the *survivors,* those who inadvertently *share with those who took the stand the knowledge* of how difficult it is to tell the story of survival (to testify at once to life and to the death—the dying—the survival has entailed). (The expression "to face the storyteller" [in which Arendt as a listener and as a survivor also faces herself] is reminiscent again of Benjamin's "Storyteller," in which *the listener becomes a storyteller* in her turn.) "For storytelling is always the art of repeating stories," writes Benjamin: "The more self-forgetful a listener is, he more deeply is what he listens to impressed upon his memory.... [The listener] listens to the tales in such a way that the gift of retelling them comes to him all by itself" ("St.," 91). It is as though Arendt, facing Eichmann in Jerusalem and judging the trial at the level of her statement, were also at the same time, at the level of her utterance, listening to the whisper of Benjamin's voice reciting, as it were, "The Storyteller" from his deathbed (like the original narrator in his essay): "It is ... characteristic that *not only a man's knowledge or wisdom,* but *above all his real life*—and this is the stuff that stories are made of—*first assumes transmissible form at the moment of his death.* Just as a sequence of images is set in motion inside a man as his life comes to an end, unfolding the views of himself under which he has encountered himself without being aware of it—suddenly in its expressions and looks the unforgettable emerges and imparts to everything that concerned him that authority which even the poorest wretch in dying possesses for the living around him. This authority is at the very source of the story" ("St.," 94).

64. Compare Arendt, *EiJ,* 6: "Justice ... demands seclusion, it permits sorrow rather than anger."

65. Arendt borrows this sentence from Isak Dinesen, "who not only was one of the great storytellers of all times but also—and she was almost unique in this respect—knew what she was doing." Arendt, "Truth and Politics," 262.

66. Compare the prosecutor's opening statement (see above and note 37).

67. I am arguing that Benjamin and Heidegger are the two *absent addressees* of *Eichmann in Jerusalem* (symbolically, the German-Jewish casualty and the compromised German philosopher: a lost friendship and a lost love).

68. "Even where there is only a rustling of plants," Benjamin writes lyrically, "there is always a lament. Because she is mute, nature mourns ... [and] the sadness of nature makes her mute." Walter Benjamin, "On Language as Such and on the Language of Man," *Selected Writings I,* edited by Marcus Bullock and Michael W. Jennings (Cambridge: Harvard University Press, 1996), 73.

69. Ibid.

70. This speechless story is a story of mourning and of the inability to mourn: the story of a trauma and of the trauma's silencing and willful disavowal.

In the middle of the writing of *Eichmann in Jerusalem,* Arendt also was in a violent car accident in which she almost died: another brutal inner rupture, another intimate relation to death that similarly, equally, was silenced and has left no visible mark on the tight argument of the book. Arendt tells Jaspers about this nearly fatal accident: "It seemed to me that for a moment I had my life in my hands. I was quite calm: death seemed to me natural, in no way a tragedy or, somehow, out of the order of things. But, at the same time, I said to myself: if it is possible to do so *decently,* I would really like, still, to stay in this world." Quoted in Young-Bruehl, *Hannah Arendt: For Love of the World,* 335; emphasis mine.

71. "It is only for convenience that we speak of . . . *traumatic memory,*" writes the psychiatrist Pierre Janet. "*The subject is often incapable of making the necessary narrative which we call memory regarding the event;* and yet he remains confronted by a difficult situation in which he has not been able to play a satisfactory part." Quoted in van der Kolk and van der Hart, "The Intrusive Past," in *TEM,* ed. Caruth, 160; emphasis mine.

72. On Benjamin's relation to the First World War and on the role of silence and of trauma in his work, compare chapter 1, part 2, "Benjamin's Silence."

73. *Shivitti,* H 34, E 18, tm.

74. The importance of the story element in trials is by now a common-place in legal scholarship. What is less well known is that, to the extent that trauma is what cannot be narrated (Benjamin, Janet), it also incorporates the paradoxical story of an inherent resistance to storytelling. Every trauma thus includes not only a traumatic story but a *negative story element,* an *anti-story.* I argue that the Eichmann trial is an unprecedented legal event that articulates at once a monumental *legal story* and a collective, monumental *anti-story,* the unanticipated story of the impossibility of telling.

On trauma theory as incapacity for narration, see, among others, van der Kolk and van der Hart, "The Intrusive Past," 158–82, and Caruth, *Unclaimed Experience.*

For general discussions of the relation between law and narrative, see, among others: James R. Elkins, "On the Emergence of Narrative Jurispru-dence: The Humanistic Perspective Finds a New Path," *Legal Studies Forum* 9 (1985): 123–56; Derrick Bell, *And We Are Not Saved: The Elusive Quest for Racial Justice* (New York: Basic Books, 1987); Mari Matsuda, "Looking to the Bottom: Critical Legal Studies and Reparations," *Harvard Civil Rights–Civil Liberties Law Review* 22 (1987): 323–99; James R. Elkins, "The Quest for Meaning: Narrative Accounts of Legal Education," *Journal of Legal Education* 38 (1988): 577–98; Richard Delgado, "Storytelling for Oppositionists and Others: A Plea for Nar-rative," *Michigan Law Review* 87 (1989): 2411–41; Kathryn Abrams, "Hearing the Call of Stories," *California Law Review* 79 (1991): 971–1052; *Narrative and the Legal Discourse: A Reader in Storytelling and the Law*, ed. David Ray Papke (Liverpool: Deborah Charles, 1991); Patricia Williams, *The Alchemy of Race and Rights: Diary of a Law Professor* (Cambridge, Mass.: Harvard University Press, 1991); Robin West, *Narrative, Authority, and Law* (Ann Arbor: University of Michigan Press, 1993); Daniel A. Farber and Suzanna Sherry, "Telling Stories Out of School: An Essay on Legal Narratives," *Stanford Law Review* 45 (1993): 807–55; Richard Sherwin, "Law Frames: Historical Truth and Narrative Necessity in a Criminal Case," *Stanford Law Review* 47 (1994): 39–83; *Narrative, Violence, and the Law: The Essays of Robert Cover*, ed. Martha Minow, Michael Ryan, and Austin Sarat (Ann Arbor: University of Michigan Press, 1995); *Critical Race Theory: The Cutting Edge*, ed. Richard Delgado (Philadelphia: Temple University Press, 1995); *Critical Race Theory: The Key Writings That Formed the Movement*, ed. Kimberlé Crenshaw et al. (New York: New Press, 1995); Austin Sarat, "Narrative Strategy and Death Penalty Advocacy," *Harvard Civil Rights–Civil Liberties Law Review* 31 (1996): 353–81; *Law's Stories: Narrative and Rhetoric in the Law*, ed. Peter Brooks and Paul Gewirtz (New Haven, Conn.: Yale University Press, 1996); *History, Memory, and the Law*, ed. Austin Sarat and Thomas Kearns (Ann Arbor: University of Michigan Press, 1999).

75. Because the unanticipated force of the event of the impossibility of telling caught everyone off guard and must have been surprising even to the trial's architects and to its legal actors, Arendt treats it as a symptom of their oversight and of their failure. I see it as a proof of the success of their conception beyond their grasp.

In the same way that K-Zetnik's fainting could not be foreseen and was not planned, the legal narrative of the impossibility of telling could not be planned. It had to happen. It was the human and the legal meaning of what happened. *But no one could articulate this meaning at the time.* It was the unanticipated essence of the event, not part of the trial's stated ideology. It is only now in retrospect that this significance comes into view and can be recognized and formulated.

76. Segev, 4, my emphasis.

77. I now return from the "subtext" of *Eichmann in Jerusalem* to Arendt's conscious and explicit *text*: her conscious critical report as a legal historian of the trial.

78. Oliver Wendell Holmes, "The Path of the Law," *Harvard Law Review* 110, no. 2 (1997): 991.

79. Ibid., 1006. "When we study law," Holmes asserts, "we are not studying a mystery" (ibid., 991). Eichmann's banality, Arendt insists, and the banality of Nazism as a whole, is not a mystery. Its essence is its shallowness, its hollow lack of depth. And this, says Arendt, is why "it is in the nature of

this case that we have no tools to hand except legal ones, with which we have to pass sentence on something that cannot even be adequately represented either in legal terms or in political terms" (Arendt to Jaspers, letter 274 (December 23, 1960), *AJ Corr.*, 417). The tool is purposely, revealingly reductive: "When we study law, we are not studying a mystery."

80. Sontag, "Reflections on *The Deputy*," 118–19; emphasis mine.

81. In this sense, the Eichmann trial did fulfill its function, even in Arendt's critical eyes. "Those who are convinced that justice, and nothing else, is the end of law will be inclined to condone the kidnapping act, though not because of precedents. . . . This last of the Successor trials will no more, and perhaps even less than its predecessors, serve as a valid precedent for future trials of such crimes. This might be of little import in view of the fact that its main purpose—to prosecute and to defend, to judge and to punish Adolph Eichmann—was achieved" (*EiJ*, 264–65, 272–73).

82. Benjamin, "GEA," *SWI*, 355; emphasis mine.

83. Compare Pierre Nora, "Between Memory and History: *Les Lieux de mémoire*," trans. Mark Roudebush, *Representations* 26 (Spring 1989): 7–25.

84. Benjamin, "GEA," 340.

85. Benjamin (using Hölderlin's terms) speaks of "the caesura of the work" (ibid., 354 and 340–41).

86. "Thereby, in the rhythmic sequence of the representations . . . there becomes necessary what in poetic meter is called the caesura . . . the counter-rhythmic rupture . . . that caesura in which, along with harmony, every expression simultaneously comes to a standstill, in order to give free reign to an expressionless power" (ibid., 340, 341).

87. It is as though, summoned to court, history acquired power of speech in amplifying and in making audible K-Zetnik's own repeated yet repeatedly mute cry: "That mute cry" [K-Zetnik writes] "was again trying to break loose, as it had every time death confronted me at Auschwitz; and as always when I looked death in the eye, so now too the mute scream got no further than my clenched teeth that closed upon it and locked it inside me. Indeed that was the essence of that cry: it was never realized, never exposed to the outside air. It remained a strangled flame inside me" (*Shivitti*, H 18, E 1–2, tm).

88. Compare the strikingly resonant statements of the French philosopher Emmanuel Levinas: "The relation to the face is all at once the relation to the absolutely weak—what is absolutely exposed, what is naked and what is deprived . . . and at the same time . . . the face is also the 'Thou shall not kill.' . . . It is the fact that I cannot let the other die alone, it is as though there were [from the face] an appeal to me. . . . For me, he is above all the one for which I am responsible." *It is always from the face, from my responsibility for the other, that justice emerges.*" Emmanuel Levinas, "Philosophie, Justice,

Amour," *Entre Nous: Thinking-of-the-Other,* trans. Michael B. Smith and Barbara Harshav, European Perspectives (New York: Columbia University Press, 1998), 114–115; my translation and emphasis.

89. Walter Benjamin, *The Origin of German Tragic Drama* (1928; London: NLB, 1977), 166.

Response by Austin Sarat
On "Missed Encounters": Law's Relationship to Violence, Death, and Disaster

1. See Shoshana Felman, *The Juridical Unconscious: Trials and Traumas in the Twentieth Century* (Cambridge, Mass.: Harvard University Press, 2002), chapter 4.

2. Ibid., 144.

3. Ibid., 165.

4. The next three paragraphs are taken from Lawrence Douglas, Austin Sarat, and Martha Umphrey, "At the Limits of Law: An Introduction," in *The Limits of Law*, ed. Austin Sarat, Lawrence Douglas, and Martha Umphrey (Stanford, Calif.: Stanford University Press, 2005).

5. Hannah Arendt–Karl Jaspers: Correspondence, 1926–1969, ed. Lotte Kohler and Hans Saner, trans. Robert Kimber and Rita Kimber (New York: Harcourt Brace and Jovanovich, 1992), 54.

6. Trial of the Major War Criminals Before the International Military Tribunal (Nuremberg: International Military Tribunal, 1947), 1:98.

7. See Opening Statement for the Prosecution, International Military Tribunal, Nuremberg, November 21, 1945: http://www.law.umkc.edu/faculty/projects/ftrials/nuremberg/Jackson.html.

8. Linda Meyer, "At the Edge of Reason: Law and Catastrophe," in *Law and Catastrophe*, ed. Austin Sarat, Lawrence Douglas, and Martha Umphrey (Stanford, Calif.: Stanford University Press, 2006), 3.

9. Ibid., 4.

10. Peter Fitzpatrick, "Life, Death, and the Law—And Why Capital Punishment Is Legally Insupportable," *Cleveland State Law Review* 47 (1999): 483, 486, 487.

11. Ibid., 484.

12. Felman, *The Juridical Unconscious: Trials and Traumas in the Twentieth Century*, 152. Emphasis added.

13. As Martha Minow puts it, "Law is itself violent in its forms and methods. Official power effectuates itself in physical force." See "Words and the Door to the Land of Change: Law, Language, and Family Violence," unpublished paper (1990), 14.

14. Self-defense provides perhaps the best example of such after-the-fact authorization of violence. See *People v. La Voire, 155 Colo.* 551 (1964); *State v. Gough*, 187 Iowa 363 (1919); and *People v. McGrandy*, 9 Mich. App. 187 (1967).

16. Michel Foucault, *The History of Sexuality: An Introduction*, trans. Robert Hurley (New York: Viking, 1990), 135.

17. See, for example, Austin Sarat, *When the State Kills: Capital Punishment and the American Condition* (Princeton, N.J.: Princeton University Press, 2001).

18. Robert Cover, "Violence and the Word," *Yale Law Journal* 95 (1986): 1601. See also, Austin Sarat, ed., *Pain, Death, and the Law* (Ann Arbor: University of Michigan Press, 2001).

20. Walter Benjamin, "Critique of Violence," in *Reflections*, trans. Edmund Jepchott (New York: Harcourt, 1978), 286.

21. Robert Cover, "Violence and the Word," *Yale Law Journal* 95 (1986): 1601.

22. Cover himself divorces interpretation from violence as if the latter were merely a matter of implementation or a defect of administration.

Response by Cathy Caruth
Trauma, Justice, and the Political Unconscious:
Arendt and Felman's Journey to Jerusalem

1. Shoshana Felman and Dori Laub, *Testimony: Crises of Witnessing in Literature, Psychoanalysis, and History* (New York: Routledge, 1992). For explicit discussion of the "crisis of witnessing," see for example 200–1 and 206.

2. See Shoshana Felman, *The Juridical Unconscious: Trials and Traumas in the Twentieth Century* (Cambridge, Mass.: Harvard University Press, 2002), 1, and more generally 1–9 and their relative explanatory notes, 171–82. Citations from this text will be hereafter indicated by the abbreviation *JU*, followed by page number.

3. See Hannah Arendt, *Eichmann in Jerusalem: A Report on the Banality of Evil* (New York: Penguin Books, 1963), especially 252. Citations from this text will be hereafter indicated by the abbreviation *EiJ*, followed by page number. The topic of the banality of evil is discussed in Felman, *The Juridical Unconscious*, chap. 3, "Theaters of Justice: Arendt in Jerusalem, the Eichmann Trial, and the Redefinition of Legal Meaning in the Wake of the Holocaust," especially 107–110.

4. On the erasure of the concept of the human being, see Arendt to Jaspers in *Hannah Arendt and Karl Jaspers, Correspondence: 1926–1969*, ed. Lotte Kohler and Hans Saner, trans. Robert and Rita Kimber (New York: Harcourt Brace, 1992), quoted in *The Juridical Unconscious*, 108. With regard to the annihilation and eradication of political groups and individuals, see Hannah Arendt, *The Origins of Totalitarianism* (New York: Harcourt, 1951), especially chap. 9 and the chapters that follow. Arendt suggests that in totalitarian states there is first the killing of the juridical person in man, then the murder of the moral person, then the killing of man's individuality (447, 451,

and 454, respectively), terminologically defined as the murder of the moral person, the annihilation of the juridical person, and the destruction of the individuality (455). The groups upon whom this is perpetrated tend originally to be the groups of those who (after the First World War) have become stateless and rightless, although in the world of terror, other groups or persons become included.

5. See Felman, *JU*, 112, discussing Arendt, *EiJ*, 19.

6. Felman uses the notion of "erasure" in her book *Testimony* (1992) as well as in *The Juridical Unconscious* (2002) to describe what happens to the witness during the Holocaust. This is juxtaposed, I will argue, in Felman's reading of Arendt, with Arendt's notion of the killing, murder, or annihilation of the individual (or group) as a political, legal, and individual subject in totalitarian regimes. One of the interesting questions raised by the encounter of the two writers is the way in which Felman's notion of erasure can shed light on Arendt's notion of annihilation and vice versa.

7. *EiJ*, 224; quoted and discussed in *JU*, 158ff.

8. "'What Remains? The Language Remains': A Conversation with Günter Gaus," in *The Portable Hannah Arendt*, ed. Peter Baehr, 3–24 (New York: Penguin Books, 2000).

9. Interview of Shoshana Felman by Cathy Caruth. Forthcoming.

10. Felman and Arendt meet in another way as well, I would suggest, although this story must be taken slightly beyond the narration provided by Felman, in what remains unaddressed in her text on the trial and on Arendt, the post-trial history of the reception of Arendt's *Eichmann in Jerusalem*. When Arendt's trial reports came out (first in the *New Yorker* and then in book form in 1963), Arendt was vehemently attacked, in particular by the American Jewish community, as well as by Israeli circles and by Jewish friends around the world. On the controversy triggered by *Eichmann in Jerusalem* see, for example, Elisabeth Young-Bruehl, *Hannah Arendt: For Love of the World* (New Haven, Conn.: Yale University Press, 1983); and Hannah Arendt, *The Jew as Pariah*, ed. Ron H. Feldman (New York: Grove Press, 1978). Indeed, the essay that Felman quotes to demonstrate Arendt's emphasis on the importance of storytelling, "Truth and Politics," was originally written, as Arendt noted, as a response to the controversy surrounding her book. See "Truth and Politics," in Hannah Arendt, *Between Past and Future: Eight Exercises in Political Thought* (New York: Penguin, 1954), 227, author's note. The essay is, in fact, primarily about what Arendt calls the "modern lie" and its manipulation and distortion of truth in the political world, both in totalitarianism and, somewhat differently, in democratic societies—the lie aiming at eliminating without any trace the factual reality it claims to represent but in effect wishes to deny or to erase. Arendt seems spurred to write this essay, in part,

because of the way in which her own Eichmann book was systematically falsified throughout the controversy. It was, for example, summarized incorrectly in a special issue of the journal of the Anti-Defamation League, ironically entitled *Facts* and circulated among Jewish intellectuals, who then attacked her on the basis of the falsified summary. See "A Report on the Evil of Banality: The Arendt Book," *Facts* 15, no. 1 (July–August 1963), published by the Anti-Defamation League of B'Nai B'rith. This piece appears to have been the basis, along with a later book by Jacob Robinson, *And the Crooked Shall Be Made Straight: The Eichmann Trial, the Jewish Catastrophe, and Hannah Arendt's Narrative* (New York: Macmillan, 1965), of many refutations of—and attacks on—Arendt's book. See also Hannah Arendt, "The Formidable Dr. Robinson: A Reply," in *The Jew as Pariah*. Arendt was said to be anti-Zionist and anti-Israeli (which she was not) and to blame the Jews for not resisting their annihilation (which she did not); she was consequently shunned by the Jewish community and her book, influential and translated into many languages, was not translated into Hebrew by any Israeli press for about forty years (until 2000). Arendt must have thus experienced again, in the United States, through the Eichmann controversy, a potential erasure of her thought, if not of her person, a threat she believed she had overcome in leaving Germany. This experience of attempted erasure of her thought within Jewish and Israeli circles must also, I would suggest, be added to the event that Felman names as the event created by the Eichmann trial and Arendt's book together.

It is true that Arendt's vision and critique of the Eichmann trial nowadays prevails, beyond the attempts at its censorship and its erasure. Nevertheless, I would suggest that Felman's passionate, complex response to Arendt, her critique of Arendt's argument but also her intuitive, empathic understanding of the layers of silence within Arendt's text, are also, in their own way, an enactment of justice, a (not fully conscious) attempt to do justice to what remains half-erased (silenced both from within and from without) in Arendt's writing and thought.

11. It is perhaps not an accident that the word "revolutionary" plays a significant role in Felman's vocabulary in the first of her two chapters on the trial, when she describes both Arendt's insight into the Holocaust and the pathbreaking status of the Eichmann trial: "I will argue in what follows [Felman writes] that the Eichmann trial is, at the antipodes of Arendt, historiographically conservative but jurisprudentially revolutionary. Arendt, on the contrary, is historiographically revolutionary but jurisprudentially conservative" (*JU*, 122). The notion of the trial as jurisprudentially revolutionary is repeated later when Felman describes the transformative effect of the trial on the victim: "In this sense, the Eichmann trial is, I would submit, a

revolutionary trial. It is this revolutionary transformation of the victim that makes the victim's story *happen* for the first time, and happen as a legal act of *authorship of history*. This historically unprecedented revolution in the victim that was operated in and by the Eichmann trial is, I would suggest, the trial's major contribution not only to Jews but to history, to law, to culture—to humanity at large" (126).

The notion of revolution is, in fact, central to Arendt's own work—it represents the political enactment of man's essential and unique capacity to begin something new—and Felman remarks in a footnote that Arendt will publish her book *On Revolution* right after her book on the Eichmann trial, suggesting that the trial's innovative power may have subtly inspired some of Arendt's thinking about revolution.

But Arendt's work on revolution also stands in a complex and perhaps even paradoxical relation to her previous work on totalitarianism, which traces the ways in which political systems can come to eliminate the capacity of origination that is essential to the political (and the human). The notion of the revolutionary for Arendt (as the political site of creation of the new) is thus inseparable from the notion of totalitarianism (as a radically new political system that eliminates the new). I would argue that Felman's use of the notion of the revolutionary has at least two functions in her first chapter on the trial: first, it is a reflection of the peculiar innovative capacity of each writer and the resonant conceptual and personal stories of innovation that link the (political and psychoanalytic) insights of each, and, second, it binds the innovative force of each writer's theoretical work with the theorized and untheorized traces of erasure and trauma that lie behind their writing and thought.

Felman as Teacher

1. Barbara Johnson, *A World of Difference* (Baltimore: Johns Hopkins University Press, 1987), 11–16.

Chapter 13

Plato's Phaedo

1. Edition used in class, to which page numbers of citations will refer: Plato, *The Trial and Death of Socrates: Four Dialogues,* trans. Benjamin Jowett, ed. Shane Weller (New York: Dover Thrift Editions, 1992).

2. Hannah Arendt, *Men in Dark Times* (1968; New York: Harcourt Brace, 1983).

3. Michel Foucault, *Language, Counter-Memory, Practice,* ed. Donald Bouchard (Ithaca, N.Y.: Cornell University Press, 1977).

4. Walter Benjamin, "The Storyteller," in *Illuminations,* ed. Hannah Arendt (New York: Schocken Books, 1968).

CHAPTER 14
Between Spinoza and Lacan and Us

1. "Excommunication," in *The Seminar of Jacques Lacan,* Book XI, *The Four Fundamental Concepts of Psychoanalysis,* ed. Jacques-Alain Miller, trans. Alan Sheridan, 1–13.